Recited and imparted, a journey through li Lambert.

Written by Justin Dabrow and Steven Lambert

(My writing partner and I at the iconic tv show MASH site.)

Copyright 2019 by Steven Lambert and Justin Dabrow

"I've spent my whole career with Steve, and, boy oh boy, this is one unique individual. Steve saved my life a hundred times. He performed stunts that were unthinkable. Though one of the sweetest guys you could ever meet, I wouldn't want to get into a fight with him. His martial arts skills are so scary, they are the stuff of nightmares. For all his skills and charms, his greatest gift is that he is one of the noblest people I've ever met."

(Friends and Brothers. James Woods and his favorite Jewish Stuntman.)

It started in 1950´s Brooklyn...
some say the best decade ever.

Join a punk kid as he is taken away from the streets to the strange land of California where he redescovers himself in martial arts, ultimately leading to a life as a Hollywood stuntman

Explore the true stories of Hollywood, from the funniest, never told tales of the biggest stars to the darkest depths of humankind in show business.

This work of art and book cover designed by Alan Pirie.

Hold on to your life and listen to mine from the Streets of Brooklyn. This book takes you on a journey like no other as I paint you visions about coming of age in early 1950s Brooklyn. Kid Gangs, the Mafia and a few games of skelly and stickball, but hey I was just a kid. Then I'll reveal the world of Martial Arts to you and how I stumbled into it without knowing the life lessons and skills I would learn from my master and the art itself, before leading you into the Halls of Hollywood where I will talk to you about many famous Actors, Producers and Directors. I will show you life as an action actor and stuntman where you will go through many emotions. Shock, surprise, laugh and joy as the lines between black and white fade to gray. You will gain knowledge from my experiences and find surprises, secrets and stories on every page. Everything you never knew and nobody would ever tell you revealed before your eyes. Here is the truth as experienced through the life of a punk kid from Brooklyn. Buckle up.

TABLE OF CONTENTS

I ran through the forest as fast as I could, but it was too late. They had found me. Someone in a control room far away pushed a button. I heard the tank fire in the distance and increased my speed. The ground started to shake as I peered behind me. That's when the first explosion hit. An orange cloud birthed from the fires of hell racing to meet me. The second and third shells exploded just seconds after. I pushed myself to run faster, I could feel the heat of the explosions start to surround me in its deadly embrace. The explosions were getting closer together. I looked ahead and saw the edge of the cliff. It was a hundred and ten-foot drop below. For a second, I cleared my mind and prepared for what I was about to do. Wondering what would be nobler; to fall and die in a fiery explosion or to fall off a jagged cliff into the depths below. But that decision was long made. I had to jump and I had to fall perfectly, everything was depending on it. Another explosion blew the trees apart to my right. I shielded my eyes from the bark and the dirt flying into and past my face like shrapnel. I turned to the right towards the cliff as another fireball erupted, mere feet from my body.

I took one last look at the approaching cliff and remembered in my head that I was prepared for this. All those years of learning to outrun the older kids during our childhood games were about to come in handy in about two seconds. As I reached the edge of the cliff, one last explosion tore through the ground that shook beneath my feet, closer than ever. Then I jumped over a ravine as one last explosion blew apart the ground my feet had just been touching. With arms outstretched I leaped out. Down I went, gracefully like a ninja flying quietly in the night. I felt the adrenaline, every second seemed like a minute as I went over everything in my head. Did I jump far enough? Am I dropping too fast? And then I fell through the oncoming branches…..and into fifteen layers high of boxes. Down I went, through layer after layer until I finally stopped. I looked down below me and saw just two layers of boxes left. A sigh escaped my lips as the adrenaline left my body, glad to be still alive. Boy, that was close. I looked up as a hand appeared to assist me. I took it and was lifted back into reality. Bright lights surrounded me as bodies moved into my field of vision. The layers of boxes had cushioned my fall as I had expected. I just hoped the camera captured it all. Like always, I made my way over to the Director of Photography first. He had a look of joy on his face. "You got that? Did you get it?"

The D.P. nodded. "That was great Steven."

"Thank you," I replied.

"You betcha pal," he said.

` I watched the playback on the screen, seeing if my movement was what I wanted it to be, making sure I got close enough to the explosions, checking my body language and the gracefulness of my fall. Satisfied, I looked up to see the Director, Guy Hamilton coming over to me. This man was a legend. The Director of a handful of Bond films such as *Diamonds are Forever* and *Live and Let Die.* Not to mention a trophy case full of awards including the Evening Standard British Film Award. My heart skipped a beat as to what he was going to say. His mouth was taut and his eyes were busy looking me up and down. I waited for the next words that would be spoken. I knew they would be his. He glanced at the playback screen, then back to me. I tried reading his thoughts but it was hard to tell what this great man was thinking. You see, him being from England, he had very little expression but a lot of humor. Slowly, a smile broke on his lips and he opened his hand to embrace mine. "That was wonderful Steven."

I let out a sigh of relief and shook his hand. It was even better when the Director loved it as much as you did.

"Thank you Mister Hamilton," I responded. Before I could say another word, his face grew serious again. He turned and I was completely ignored.

"Moving on to shot twenty seven," the Director screamed. "Fifteen minutes until the next setup." He looked at a P.A and shouted. "And would someone get me a god damn coffee." The P.A. smiled sheepishly.

"I did sir, five minutes ago, on your chair," he stammered.

"Bullox!" Guy responded. "Get me a hot one." Just like that, the crew went back to work. There went my one minute of fame. That's the movie business. I turned to my boss. Yes, my boss, the Stunt Coordinator Glen Randall. Let me say something about him. He and his family are legends in the film industry. It's great when you complete a full piece of action like that and you feel good about it, you see usually a sequence like this is done in pieces but that's what makes me different than most. I like to do one complete sequence at once and that's why people noticed me. I walked over to the guys working the special effects and the explosions. They were happy to see me unharmed, meaning they did their job well. "Great work guys, that went perfect. The timing of the explosions, the number of explosives, I couldn't see it be done better." The guys thanked me on my performance in return, genuinely touched that I would consider them such an integral part of the scene. As a stuntman, you have a much greater appreciation of certain people that you work with, especially when they have the detonator in their hands. Before the scene, we walked through the forest and I told them the best places to plant the explosives and where I thought the best places to run were. "Put one here, I can turn at the last second as it explodes. And put another one here, I'll run to my left as it goes off." I had it laid out perfectly in my head. The pyrotechnic guys nodded and took down notes, probably thinking I was crazy. But I knew what I was doing. I never ran from exploding bombs when I was a kid, but I did have my fair share of firecracker explosions. To me, this was no different. These were just bigger firecrackers. It was my idea to land in boxes after the fall. Now these days, stuntmen would look at you like you are crazy if you mention boxes. They would be too afraid to do it. Using boxes are a thing of the past. I learned from the old timers, that before there were airbags, they used cardboard boxes and mattresses. But today, all the new stuntmen don't know anything about old style equipment for stunts. And in my view, that's a mistake. You should always keep the old with the new, it makes you a better action coordinator. But I knew boxes would work if you prepared them and layered them correctly.

The Director trusted me on this. Everyone did. "Boxes?" He would say. "Are you sure you don't want an airbag?" I would assure him boxes would work fine.

"This way the camera has time to follow me all the way down since I'm going feet first," I said. I had the trust of the crew and the Director, and every stunt I did successfully would cement that trust. Just like the childhood adventures and games had shaped me for this. But perhaps I'm getting ahead of myself. I wasn't born into the stunt world, or perhaps in a way, I was. It all started many years ago in a city thousands of miles away, where Hollywood was a mythical place, but one, that no one ever expected to wind up in. Certainly not me. But life has a way of bringing you to the strangest of places.

(The Lambo Leap)

CHAPTER 1
(A Punk Kid Growing Up In Brooklyn.)

At this point, some of you might be wondering how I became so good at being a Hollywood Stuntman. I think it had something to do with being a punk kid growing up in Brooklyn in the fifties and sixties. Raised on the corner of Avenue B and 96th, on the outskirts of Canarsie, in a time where life for a kid was vastly different than today. We practically lived outside, our neighbors were like family, and we were always looking for innocent mischief. Instead of shooting people in video games, we were shooting people (and each other) outside with roman candles. At night we wore all black with ski masks and we had 10 roman candles apiece. It was like little ninjas running around Brooklyn, shooting each other with our Roman Candles. If we got hit in the head it wouldn't hurt much because we were wearing ski masks, gloves and a thick coat. It was a familiar sight to see kids running around with dangerous things in those days, but it was normal. A different time. We had our plastic guns and rifles, pretending we were cowboys or lawmen. Similar to the cowboy gun that Steve McQueen used in *Wanted Dead or Alive.* When we played Army with machine guns and helmets, it was like the television show *Combat,* with Vic Morrow. (Can you say helicopter propeller? Research my friend, it was a sad thing). When we played secret agent, it was similar to *The Man From U.N.C.L.E.* We would play stoopball and stickball, always challenging each other to a game.

(Playing stoopball with my friend Eugene)

When it got too hot, we would find a wrench and yank open the top and sides of a fire hydrant. This created a stream of water we could control with a vegetable can that was cut out on both ends. When we got tired of playing in the water, we would find another way to have some fun. Being on the street, we waited as unsuspecting drivers rode past us. We would smile and wave politely. Nobody knew the mischief we were planning. "Wait for it," I would say to the one in charge of the can. When we saw a nice car drive by, or an unhappy driver would frown at the bunch of soaked kids gathered next to a fire hydrant, I would give the signal. I would yell, "hose 'em," to the one by the nozzle.

The can was put on the stream of water coming out of the hydrant and a spray of water would go right into the open window and soak the driver. It was a normal everyday thing to do in the fifties and sixties in Brooklyn. That was almost as good as watching a funny movie. When it got too cold, we found other ways to entertain ourselves. Brooklyn got tons of snow, piled high on top of the cars. We would take the snow and construct a fort of a massive web of tunnels that would make an ant colony look simple. We would jump off a balcony down one tunnel, shoot between two snow covered cars and come rolling out the other end, fifty feet away. Even though we didn't have video games, we did have games. We would take the soda caps off the bottles my mother bought and put them in a pile. Next, I would take a box of crayons and light a match to melt the crayon. The melted crayon would drip down into the cap to make it heavier. We would use different kinds of colors, don't forget it was the sixties, man. Peace love and war. After ten minutes, the melted crayon would harden and the bottle cap would be the perfect weight for a game called skelly. Then would come the time to play. The objective was to get your bottle cap into the center of the square where the most points would be given. Of course, you could knock other player's caps out to prevent them from getting the high points. Remember the 1964- 65 World's Fair? Most of you don't, but yes, I went to it.

For entertainment, we had Coney Island. I would hop on my bike and head down to where we had drawn the skelly court. Everyone would hear me coming by the clankity-clank of my baseball cards. What's that you say? Baseball cards don't make noise? They do if you stick them to your spokes in your wheels with clothes pins. Why did we do that you may ask, and the answer is simple. To annoy everyone. I would arrive at the skelly court to find my gang there waiting. That's right, I had a gang. I told you I was a punk kid. My gang was like the *East Side Comedies*, the Bowery Boys. Think Muggs, Satch and Whitey. Innocent mischief was what we were good at. Each one of us had our own character, our own personality. As I arrived on my bike, the first person that got up to meet me was Jeffrey Elkins. His rippling muscles looked strange on a twelve year old. He lived directly across the street from me. He was the super kid of our gang. The King Kong, the Arnold

Schwarzenegger. Can you believe it? He started lifting weights when he was nine, ten years old. He was the muscle, and whatever he said to do, we did it. Whenever we had a plan, we always wanted to do it without him, because we would always have to follow his orders. It was his way or the highway. If he decided to punish us by keeping us on our stoop, he'd make sure he had eyes on us. Unfortunately, his bedroom window was across from my stoop. When he told me to stay on my stoop, I'd see him lifting weights in his bedroom. He was King Kong and I was his nut to be crushed. At times I escaped. Or tried to. He was our head honcho. He was at least as fast as I was so I really had to worry because if he caught me, I'd be crushed like a knish. That's an old Brooklyn saying. Yeah.

In the corner of the skelly court was a boy drawing in his sketchbook. He had a big Jewish nose like a crow. That was Eugene Fisch. He was a great friend and he lived one brownstone over from me across the street. Eugene loved to draw superheroes and boy was he good at it! We always thought he was going to work for Marvel Comics one day and draw all the superheroes. Any superhero you asked he would draw beautifully. You see, he was that good. "Draw Superman, Batman, Spiderman, the Sub-Mariner," we would say. And draw them he did. Beautiful drawings that one would swear was from the Marvel Studios. If anyone was going to make it in life, we were banking on Eugene. I loved to draw with him as well. He taught us how to draw and it kept us out of trouble. I remember those times well. The whole gang. Even Elkins would draw, which made us happy as it would shut him up for five minutes. We used to be good drawers when we were younger, and we would sit out on Eugene's porch and draw.

This would upset Eugene's neighbor who they shared the stoop with, Mister Wolfson. An old grumpy German man who owned the brownstone. Mister Wolfson reminded us of a German soldier. When he caught us drawing on his side of the stoop, he would boil water and try to dump it on us from the second story window. Always had to keep one eye out for that. Can you imagine that? Eugene would sing the Batman theme song over and over again until it was loud enough to bother Mister Wolfson. Then we would wait for the water. Once it was raining down towards us, we would sprint away at the last second. Strange as it sounds, we would enjoy it, because it tested our speed. Something I would be grateful for in the years to come.

Back on the skelly court, watching Eugene draw was Arthur. We took care of him and even though we made fun of him in a playful way, we made sure no one else did. Unfortunately, he was a little slow, but that didn't matter to us. He was a great friend and part of our gang. Arthur was able to do many things on his own, he just had more trouble than most at some other things. We loved him and only teased him because he knew it was in good fun. He was always willing to do anything we said because he loved being with us. We were his only friends. Watching me from behind Jeffrey was Neil. Neil was like Jerry Lewis in *The Nutty Professor*. He was the quiet one, never really smiled unless something was very funny to him. He was the most intelligent out of all of us. Which please let me tell you, doesn't say much. He wasn't very athletic, and always got caught first when we got into trouble. He always tried to tell us our innocent mischief wasn't a good idea. But we knew that, so we gave him a noogie and told him to shut up. His father was a professor at a college, so he was the one of us that always did his homework. He had a coin and stamp collection. We all collected something. I had a big comic book collection, as did Eugene. Neil was the one that taught us how to dance. Now can you imagine a big nerd teaching smaller nerds, as we thought of ourselves, how to dance? Our school always had a dance, but we never went, being the nerds that we were. Everyone in our gang except for Jeffrey Elkins was considered to be the nerdy type. The only reason why Elkins was exempt, is because people were afraid of him. He was known for miles and that's how far people stayed away from him. Just like Benny Urquidez was, when he was a kid. The tough guys of the neighborhood.

One day, Neil decided that we should go to one of the school dances. I said, "no way. Neil, we can't dance, are you nuts!? Jewish athletic nerds don't dance." So, he taught us how to dance. He would put on an album in his room and he would try to teach us. You know those dances. The swim, the jerk, the twist. For hours we would monkey around, (that was a dance too) until Neil was satisfied. Finally, a school dance was not as frightening to us in our nerdy heads. Playing leapfrog in the middle of the skelly court, much to the annoyance of players, were the Twerp Twins, Jim and Steve. They were silly twins, goofballs, so we called them twerps. They did silly stuff. They would steal candy from the store and walk back in eating the candy to see if anyone would notice. They were the comics in our gang, always making us shake our heads or laugh. Coming over to greet me, was Steve Lees. We called him Lees. We had three people named Steve in our gang, so it made it easier to remember. He was a tough, anxious, clean cut kid and had a lot of street smarts. He preferred to stay innocent, but that never happened with us. Before I could nod to him, I saw another kid, tall and chubby and with a smile full of rotten teeth. That was Steven Ellis. He reminded me of one of those inflatable pop bags that you would punch and it would come right back at you. You know the inflatable clown bag. Steven was a dedicated friend and very goofy. His mannerisms and looks would make you burst out laughing.

For example, Steve Lees, Steven Ellis, and I had newspaper routes. We would take newspapers and go off early in the morning and deliver them to houses and brownstones. Even though we each had individual routes, we came up with an idea. "Let's deliver to each other's jurisdictions," I said. "That way we can deliver more papers and get paid more." The other Stevens liked my idea.

"That's not bad. We'll get a promotion in no time," Steven Ellis commented. It was foolproof. Or so I thought. Steven Ellis had a bad habit of not wrapping the papers with a rubber band. When he went to throw the paper, the paper would go flying all over Mr. Johnson's flower bed. If he was lucky, the sports section would fail to blow away, and the homeowner could find it tucked safely in between the cracks on the roof of their brownstone. It only took three times of him getting caught before it got so bad that we were all fired. Then we went onto another misadventure. Next, there was Mordechai. He was an Orthodox Jew, always wore a yarmulke. His parents didn't like him hanging around with us, they thought we were too mischievous and I can't say we weren't. They were very religious, the yarmulkes of the neighborhood we would say. It wasn't long before we convinced him to eat ham and he started becoming one of us. What we would call a Goy Jew. For all you Goyim out there, he's been a bad boy.

I remember a frightening moment, but now when I think of it, it is hysterical. We went to King's plaza. There was a record store, Sam Goodies, where we would buy albums. The Beatles, Black Sabbath, Elvis, we loved it all. Mordechai wasn't allowed to work because he was Orthodox, and wasn't allowed to take normal jobs like we had. So he never had a lot of money. I remember this well. I was looking at a new Beatles album. In fact I remember it was "Sargent Pepper's Lonely Hearts Club Band," when we heard yelling from behind me from a few rows back. I turned and there was Mordechai with a security guard yelling at him. He was making poor yarmulke boy lift up his shirt revealing about eleven albums. Walking over we hear Mordechai screaming "My Ima is going to kill me, my Ima is going to kill me." Ima means mother in Hebrew. At first, we felt bad for him, but we couldn't help but find some humor in the whole situation. His parents came and got him and the next time we went by his house, there he was, looking down at us sadly in the second story window. His parents didn't let him open the window when he was punished so he would peek out and do hand signals, shaking his finger through the crack in the window to let us know that he couldn't come with us. Poor Mordi. Every few seconds he would yell at his mother who was screaming for him to get away from the window and we would call him out more to get his parents more farmisht. That's a Yiddish word for confused and befuddled.

The last person in our gang was Harry Malinofski. He was the youngest of us, sweet, innocent and helpless. He was from Minnesota. He wasn't much of a thinker or a doer. He couldn't even climb a fence and was scared of everything. He just followed whatever we were doing. We let Harry hang around with us for a couple of reasons. One was because his father owned a bagel place. At the end of the day, we would go to his father's store and get free bagels and take it home to our family. We would have a knosh with bagels and cream cheese, I hated lox. That was our hierarchy. I got off my bike and headed over. "Hey lambchops, you made it," Jeffrey Elkins smiled down at me.

"Hey, guys. I had to make a new bottle cap." I took out my new bottle cap and showed it to the gang.

Jeffrey Elkins turned and cupped his hands over his mouth. "Lambchops is here, let's skelly!" One by one the gang came over. Arthur was the last one. I think he was still a little bit shaken from what happened a few days ago. You see, we were bored that night. When we get bored we get into innocent mischief. Me, Neil, the Twerp Twins, Mordechai, Harry, Steve Lees and Steve Ellis were all together. I was in the middle of playing chess with Neil, a game he had taught all of us. This was a feat on its own. Do you have any idea how hard it is to get six kids from Brooklyn to sit down longer than five minutes and concentrate on a game like chess? You would have better luck teaching a dog to play piano. Yet, I did learn how to play, and to be patient. This would serve me well in my future when I had to put together a complicated stunt and think things through. He checkmated me as usual and stood up, ready to do something else. For the record, I never checkmated anybody in my whole life. I could never win that game. Then an idea came to us. Down the block around the corner, we knew of an old abandoned two story house that everyone knew as the "haunted house." It was called the Kravitz house. You see the story goes that there was an old couple that lived there, and the rumor was around the neighborhood that the old man killed his wife and plastered her inside the walls. Who knows if it was true or not, although we did take apart some of the walls over the years, as did many other kids in the neighborhood. It used to be boarded up until other kids broke into it and we followed suit and found stuff. Eventually, it became empty and we used it for forts and to play hide and go seek. "Let's take Arthur to that old abandoned house, pretend we are going to go up into space and we have our rocket ship hidden inside."

The Twerp Twins stopped gluing their hands together and stood up. "Yea, that would be fun." Steve Lees shook his head. "Naw, guys. That's a bad idea. You know how scared Arthur can get." A quick punch in the arm from Steve Ellis made him reconsider. And here comes Neil, the brainiac opening his big mouth, explaining why we shouldn't do it. So we just gave him all noogies and told him to shut up. "Fine," he would say. "But you know it's a bad idea." We went down to Arthur's house and as soon as he saw us, he began jumping excitedly. When we would gather the gang, I would go across the street and get Jeffrey, (no not him, he would ruin everything) then Eugene who lived next to him, back on my side we'd get Mordechai, then Harry who lived two brownstones from Eugene. Then back on my side, we would get the Twerp Twins and Steve Lees and Steve Ellis. Nobody would ever knock on doors, we would just yell. Arthur Schneider lived at the end of the block so he was always the last one. His parents didn't want him going out with us, I mean they trusted us, but they didn't like the mischief we got into. They always said no, but he didn't listen. Before we even got to Arthur's house, he would run outside over to us, happier than could be. Today was no different. I put my hand around his shoulder and beamed excitement at him. "Hey Arthur, we found a spaceship. A real spaceship and we want you to fly it!" Arthur shook his head. "Oh, no I can't fly a spaceship. My mom won't let me go."

"Sure ya can, we'll protect you and we'll go with you, don't worry," the rest of the gang cheered. Arthur never wanted to let his friends down. "Ooook." I took a blindfold from the Twerp Twins and held it up to Arthur. "First we gotta blindfold you. We can't let you see where we found the rocket. It's a secret." Arthur didn't want to be blindfolded, but after some convincing he let us cover his eyes. "All right, if it's the only way." We led him to the old abandoned house and opened the door.

"Here we go up the stairs to the rocket," we'd say. And we climbed up to the second floor. Every now and then he'd want to chicken out, but we kept him going. We put a chair in the center of the room and sat Arthur on it. It got colder up there. "It's colder in here because we are inside the rocket now," I said. I covered my mouth and pretended to be the announcer. "We will be launching in ten seconds. Five. Four. Three. Two. One." Steve Lee's would be vibrating the chair.

Mordechai would say, "We are launching!"

Harry would yell, "I have no seat belt!"

Arthur screamed, "I don't have one either." Well, that did it. Harry should have shut up. Throughout the simulated ride, Arthur would yell out, "no seatbelt, no seatbelt, no seat belt." (can you picture this?) The Twerp Twins would start whistling the Star Trek Theme.

I would yell "hang onto your heads, here we go!"

Steve Ellis would shout, "Ready to drop the booster rocket." Arthur squeezed tightly onto the chair, his knuckles white. Arthur screamed and held tight and we would be trying to constantly calm him down as we were laughing and chuckling. We would be yelling at the same time. "Hold on!" Steve Lees smiled and patted Arthur on the shoulder. "Wow, you're doing it, Arthur! I can see the Earth, it's so tiny now. Here comes the moon, we are passing by it."

"NO SEAT BELT," Arthur would yell. He tried to take off the blindfold but we wouldn't let him.

"It will burn your eyes Arthur, you're the driver, you gotta keep it on." What we said didn't make any sense but we would say it, and he'd believe it. Eventually, we decided to have more fun with Arthur. I cleared my throat and declared, "Arthur, we just hit a small asteroid, our booster rocket is damaged!" The Twerp twins would provide more shaking as Arthur began to panic. "Help, I can't do this, I can't control it! I need to go home! My mom's gonna be mad! Save me!" We had to hide our laughter over Arthur's screaming as he tore off the blindfold and bolted out of the chair. He could clearly see he wasn't in a spaceship, but that didn't stop him. He almost killed himself running out of the house, and continued onto the street running home, yelling "NO SEAT BELT NO SEAT BELT!" We tried to catch him before he ran off, but he had turned into the roadrunner. Besides, we were busy laughing. We managed to get downstairs and in the distance we see Arthur screaming towards his house. We knew not to go near his house for the rest of the day because his parents wouldn't be too happy. Now a day later, I smiled at Arthur who to my surprise, smiled back. Half the time he would smile at us, the other half he would get mad. I knew his parents were mad at us, but he couldn't stay that way. We were his friends after all. What happened to that abandoned house you ask? Nothing much, about a year later we accidentally set the place on fire, building a campfire inside. Then like the geniuses we were, we went back to watch the firemen put it out. That's when one of the neighbors identified us as the culprits and we sprinted out of there. Never got caught. Just like the Bowery boys. How stupid we were. Yep, that was our gang. It wasn't long before two big guys appeared behind us. These guys were the teenage gang, the bigger guys. Four to five years older than us. Whenever we played a game, they would want to join. I knew what they wanted. They wanted to kick our ass. At times we would begin a game you may be familiar with. Freeze tag, or Ring-o-levio. The rules of the game were simple. Grab onto someone and say "Ringo-o-levio" three times before the person pulled away. You'd try not to get caught. If the big guys caught you, they would beat you up and take you to the "jail." If you escaped you would upset them even more and get a beating anyway. Talk about stuck between a rock and a hard place. Of course, I would often outrun them and climb up a fence or a wall. I'd turn around and throw pebbles and rocks that were on the roof of the nearest garage. Sometimes I would get lucky and find a tin can. Those would make for good deterrents. Arthur was the one that never got caught. The big guys would pretend not to catch him. "You're too fast Arthur," they would yell after him. Arthur would be very pleased with this and use his abilities to help us out. One time I was being chased down by three big guys in an alleyway. I was losing ground quickly, and I knew I was going to be caught. I turned and saw Arthur at the entrance of the alleyway, a big goofy smile on his face.

"I'll save you, Steven! Hey, over here, get me!" he yelled. I watched as the big guy chasing me turned and headed towards Arthur. I stopped to catch my breath, lucky that Arthur showed up on time. This would be the only thing we would get any relief from when it came to the bigger guys. God bless Arthur. You see, I was small, wiry framed and didn't know how to fight, but sure as hell wouldn't back away from one. I'd get punched, fall down and get right back up and come at you. After three or four times of this, either you'd get tired or you gave up before I got a lucky punch in. It was in these situations that I learned how to take a beating and toughen up my body. Something that I didn't know would be crucial for my future in Martial Arts and stunts. How about that. Luckily Jeffrey Elkins convinced the big guys to leave us alone for once. Unfortunately, Jeffrey had other plans. "There's a gang I saw, full of kids from another neighborhood. I think we need to go teach them a lesson."

My jaw dropped. "We don't know how to fight," I said.

Jeffrey shrugged. "It's simple you just kick and punch. Now come on." I looked at Eugene who had a look of horror on his face. Mordechai was mumbling something in Hebrew, and the Twerp twins were pretending to warm up by punching and kicking Harry playfully. Neil shook his head and Steve Lee's and Steve Ellis just shrugged. Jeffrey was the boss, so it was either we get beat up by him or by someone else, so off we went. When we arrived at the park, we spotted a group of about thirty five kids. I shook my head. "No way, we're outnumbered ten to one."

Elkins smiled. "Nah, just watch," Jeffrey said. He called out to the gang, taunting them. In less than five seconds they were on us. They swarmed us like bees at a hive. It was a slaughter. Luckily I had my trusty stingray bicycle and managed to avoid the brunt of the beatings for the first few minutes, swinging my bike all around and trying to protect myself. Neil got it the worst. A black eye, a broken nose, blood all over. It wasn't long before they caught me on my stingray and let me have it. They stole my stingray and I was lucky to walk away on my own two feet. Jeffrey was the one that got hit the least, the irony kills me to this day. Needless to say, we never fought a gang again. Back then there were no knives or guns, we fought with garbage can lids or sticks. When we weren't outside hanging out or sleeping, we were in school. If you saw my report card you would find tons of C's, D's and F's, except for one subject where there would always be an A. Guess what that was. Good old gym. For some reason, I could never do anything wrong in that class. Does it sound familiar? English, Math, History, my heart wasn't in, but gym class was the one place where I flourished because I was an athlete first and foremost. "Of course you'd get an A in gym," my parents would say, and they were right. As I mentioned, I was a very thin framed and skinny kid who was very active. In sixth grade, I found out about the John F. Kennedy award for Physical Fitness. I didn't know exactly what it was, but I knew I wanted to compete for it. That day at gym class, the teachers laid out the obstacle course for us. Climbing pegboards, climbing rope, track, push ups, sit ups, jumping rope, etc. As other students moaned, a smile spread across my face. I knew what I had to do. This was the kind of physical challenge I lived for. Little did I know it would be these challenges that I would be making a living out of. I pulled up, sat up, pushed up, sprinted and climbed my way to the best in the class. It wasn't long before the award was presented to me and I got a shiny new dictionary as my prize. Maybe they wanted me to enter a spelling bee next, yeah right. I was proud of myself, yet I had no idea just how that athleticism would benefit me in the future.

Sometimes we would get the opportunity to take special classes like woodshop. I remember making a shoeshine box once to take out and shine people's shoes and make some money. I think I was one of the youngest shoe shiners in the neighborhood. I started really working when I was seven in the back of my father's bakery truck. He inherited a bakery business called Fox Bakers where he would pick up manufactured cakes, donuts, and pies to deliver them to the delis, restaurants and luncheonettes around town. He worked from ten at night to six in the morning the next day. While most of my school mates were going to bed, I was just getting up to work with my father.

"Let's go, Steven," my father would say, rousing me from sleep. I made my way, half asleep to the small bakery truck where the aroma of fresh baked pies and cakes tickling my nose and woke up my stomach. We would drive to the factories and load the truck up with shelves of pastries. Then we would go to the delis and the luncheonettes and fill up their displays with cakes and pies. I'd get tired half way through. Luckily there was a flat surface by the motor and I would sleep on there when I was tired. One time we brought our dog Duke, a beautiful German Shepherd pedigree. Very smart, loved him like crazy. One night, a man with a gun tried to rob us. Duke snarled and growled at him, and my father told Duke to stay. Duke didn't listen and ran after the thief. A shot rang out and my heart dropped. I peered out and saw Duke lying dead on the ground, the man sprinting away into the night. We buried him in a plot of land owned by an electric company and dug a ditch with a stick and placed him inside. It took an hour to bury him. We were devastated. It was one of the first times I saw my father feel bad for something. My father was a quiet man, kept his emotions to himself. He loved to gamble and always lost a lot of money. Thank god I was a working kid because we were constantly poor, and I really think if he hadn't gambled we would have had a lot more money. Poker was his favorite card game, and horse betting his favorite past time.

I remember when he took me to the Aqueduct racetrack. He wanted to bet but he also had to watch me. Children weren't allowed in there, so I had to climb up the fence to the top, in a nine year old kid's eyes it had to be a hundred feet tall. With every inch of the climb, I would look down but knew I had to go up because my father was waiting. When I reached the top, I would be so proud. One time wouldn't you know it, a cop saw me and grabbed me. He dragged me down while my father saw what was happening from above. He watched the whole thing from ten feet away, and can you believe it, he never moved a muscle. After proclaiming that I didn't know where my parents were, the cop let me go. I walked back to the car and I found my father waiting for me like nothing happened. Don't get me wrong, he wasn't a bad father, but he just didn't give me any direction in life. He mostly kept to himself. One time I tried to run away and my father was out all night looking for me. He found me the next day playing baseball with some of my friends. I always wanted to be a baseball player in the professional league. My father watched me go up to bat many times and get on base. All while not saying a word. Eventually, one of the players saw him and pointed him out to me. I knew I was busted. I dropped the bat and saw the look on his face. I had hit a triple and he said he was proud of me, "but wait until you get home with to your mother." I thought to myself, that was going to be a piece of cake. No trouble there. Boy was I wrong. My mother was the one who gave the beatings with the belt. My father stopped a long time ago. Whenever he tried to punch me, I would be so skinny that he would hurt his hand. Then he went to a belt and got tired of trying to catch me. So when I got home, I got a big beating from my mother. You did not want to mess with that woman. My rear end was redder than a tomato from the Garden State. Just as important as my mother, were my grandparents. My grandparents on my father's side I always thought were prudish. My grandfather was a scrapper, reminded me of a James Cagney type. It was my grandparents on my mother's side, Rita and Nathan that really took care of us. When I was born, I needed an operation on my behind. Yes, my behind. There was a piece of skin covering my rectum and I couldn't go poo poo. My grandparents stayed for that. My father wasn't there, they said he was out gambling. Nathan was a very quiet man, only spoke when he needed to. We thought he became quiet after seeing atrocities while being involved with Hitler and the Holocaust in World War 2. My grandmother Rita gave me morals, compassions, values. She was a very sweet lady and loved me no matter what mischief I got in.

By nine I was working in a luncheonette owned by an Italian named Tony Albenese. He was very well known around the neighborhood since he grew up there. At the same time, he was a tough guy. He came from a tough family, as one of his brothers went to prison for robbery. The funny thing was he would always stand at the end counter. You see, he had hemorrhoids and couldn't sit down. I did a good job working for Tony to stay on his good side. I cooked, cleaned, worked the register. I used to also work at a pizza place across the street at the same time. I used to mix the dough with the water and yeast, spin the dough, make it a circle, and add cheese and tomato. It was great. We sold it with a coke for fifteen cents. We also sold "Icees" in a cup. A Brooklyn delicacy. You non-New Yorkers wouldn't understand, but I'll forgive you. The luncheonette place was half way to our school and me and my gang would always meet there for lunch. My favorite sandwich to this day that I had there was a cold meatloaf sandwich on a Kaiser roll with ketchup. Again, I hated mayonnaise. Every day there was a different special, but the meatloaf was the best. I was paid well and never had to worry about where my next dollar was coming from, as work was part of life back then. Kids these days look to their parents for money, but back then we had to earn it. If you wanted to go to the movies, or buy a new pair of Keds or Converse tennis shoes, you had to work for it. You shoveled snow, collected coke bottles or coupons. You would get five, ten, fifteen cent coupons where you could bring them to a grocery store and get the equivalent money for it. There were always ways for kids to make money. Since we did such a good job at the luncheonette and pizza place, Tony would hire us for "other" work. One day I walked into the luncheonette and saw Tony smiling at me. That meant work. "Hey kid, you want some extra dough?" Of course, I wanted more money, so I told him yes. He nodded and waved to the back of the luncheonette.

"I have some stuff to show you in the back." I followed him back there and soon found out what he wanted me to do. Tony worked for the Mafia, and it was pretty normal for kids to sell stuff for the Mafia at that time. We would sell old lady pocketbooks and mumus, which were old lady baggy dresses with different colors and designs. I would take an old ladies shopping cart, the ones with the two wheels, and load it with pocketbooks and mumus that Tony had given us. They were all different shapes and sizes.

"The old broads clamor over these," he'd say. Some we sold for two dollars, others we sold for as much as ten to fifteen dollars. I made damn good money doing that. I would make a hundred dollars a week, which is pretty good for a kid back then. Thank God for old ladies. Nothing personal about old ladies, but they made me a lot of money when I was a kid. My favorite part was selling fireworks. Tony would get them in and give them to us kids to sell around the neighborhood and we'd get a percentage of the sales. Instead of continuing to be a paperboy, I became a fireworks boy. I'd ride my new stingray that I put together from junkyard parts and sell fireworks. You see, that's how most of us got our bikes. It's not that I didn't have the money to buy one, but it was the thing to do. I remember my grandfather Nathan, who worked construction bought me a red and white toolbox. I remember that vividly and loved to build things with him. Whenever I had to change my tire or fix something on my bike, I would take out that toolbox. Now, of course people would try and steal the fireworks from me. I would get lured to a park under the pretense some boys wanted to buy fireworks and they would surround me and I'd have to try to fight off twelve guys. I'd get the shit beaten out of me, but I never gave up. If they wanted the fireworks, I was going to make them work for it. You never backed down from a fight, a lesson that would serve me well later on. It was rough, having my fireworks stolen and walking home crying, having to explain to Tony what happened. Having to look into his eyes as he shook his head. He'd understand but he would give me shit anyway. "That's all right you punk," he'd say. Then he would slap me on the head. Not all of the people in our area were up to this kind of Eastside gang innocent mischief. We had a guy who was a beatnik, a homeless man. We would see him at the park and he would see we had candy money. So he would play us in handball. We talked amongst ourselves and decided why not? How good could a homeless man be at handball? That was our game.

So we played him and he beat our butts. We couldn't believe it. So we lost our candy money to a game of handball. We had other people that would sell candy in baby carriages, walk right down the sidewalks selling it to kids. We had ice cream trucks, good humor man, the Bungalow Bar. We had a produce truck that came down the street. The driver would sing, "strawberries, blueberries, cherries, and we also have vegetables." All the grandmothers and kids would come running out with a couple of cents, ready to buy food. A lot of those venders were immigrants, this is how they made a living.

By now you're probably wondering if I had any girls I liked in the neighborhood, and indeed there was one. Her name was Donna D'Oreo and all the neighborhood boys would clamor over her. She was Italian and had the biggest bochonkas (you know what that is, don't you) a young boy like me ever saw. One day I was passing her house on my way to Hebrew school, my yarmulke perched flawlessly on top of my head, my books in my hand. I jumped up on top of the U.S. mailbox as I normally did when waiting to catch a glimpse of Donna. I would love to have asked her out, but I couldn't.

You see, for all my athleticism and street smarts, I was one big chicken when it came to asking girls out. I just wanted to see Donna, to say hi, that was enough for me. You've been there before, haven't you? I waited for five minutes, then ten more. I didn't want to be late for my class so I started to get down from the mailbox. That's when Donna came out. Her dark hair flowing in the wind, her gorgeous self. I was in love. "Hi Donna," I stammered, almost falling off the mailbox onto my head. Donna looked at me and smiled back. "Hey," she would giggle and head off to wherever she was going.

I would watch her walk down the street in a daze. That's the way it was each time we met. What a goofball I was. Once she was gone, I walked the rest of the way to Hebrew school.

My Hebrew school was quite an interesting place. Steve Ellis and Steve Lees were the only ones from my gang that had a class with me, but that was enough of us to still engage in some innocent mischief. We had the same rabbi for years so we knew how to push his buttons. Steve Ellis and I would get to class early and find some prayer books lying around. We decided to glue the pages together so our rabbi would have some trouble reciting the prayer we were supposed to memorize. When that got old, we turned to other tricks. The rabbi always put his fedora and overcoat in a closet in the back of the room.

One day we decided to nail it shut and had a fun time watching him getting it open. We would play tricks like that and this time was no different. Steve Lees came in early with us, but we saw he had brought an apple for the rabbi. Maybe he was trying to score brownie points. What a suck up, we thought. He smirked at us as he placed it on the rabbi's desk. I looked at Steve Ellis and smiled. We waited until Steve Lees turned his head and took a bunch of pencils we had sharpened. One by one we put them into the apple, laughing as each one slid in. Steve Lees turned back at the same time as the Rabbi.

Luckily for us, the rabbi saw the apple first. He marched over to it and picked it up. "What kind of a joke is this? Who put this apple here!?" We both turned around and pointed at Steve Lees whose face went pale. We had a lot of fun in that class, let me tell you. Of course, as it was normal at that time, we would get hit with rulers when we misbehaved. I think I could give you an accurate measure of my palm, that ruler was on me so much. That's the way it was in those days. If you tried to tell your parents that the teacher hit you for misbehaving, they would hit you more for getting into trouble.

Believe it or not, I was a good student in Hebrew school. For my Bar mitzvah, as all boys are required to do, I had to memorize a long passage in Hebrew called the Haftarah. This was to be recited at my Bar-mitzvah by memory. The Haftarah for my bar- mitzvah happened to be in October. Lucky for me, it was the longest Haftarah of the year. I studied it long and hard and when the day came to read it, I recited it perfectly. This was a big deal because very few people could recite a normal length Haftarah without making a mistake, but I recited the longest of the year flawlessly. My parents were happy and proud of me and the rabbi was shocked and we all celebrated that day.

At my Bar-mitzvah, my parents introduced me to an old lady in a wheelchair. I had never seen her before and was told her name was Sylvia Sidney. I had never heard of her, nor really cared at the age of thirteen, since it was the first and only time we had met. All I was interested in was the envelope with my name on it sitting on her lap.

Years later to my surprise, I found out exactly who she was. She starred in classic movies such as *Dead End* with Humphrey Bogart and the Dead End Kids, *City Streets* with Gary Cooper and *The Trail Of The Lonesome Pine* with Harry Fonda. How about hem apples. A cousin that was somebody. During the filming of Alfred Hitchcock's *Sabotage,* she was the highest paid actress in the industry. She had a long career even well into the nineties with films like *Beetlejuice* and *Mars Attacks!* Years later, I always kept an eye open in the hopes that someday I might see her on the set, but whenever I discovered she was working, it was always too late.

She was a legend and a cool cousin. Especially when I opened her envelope and there were two crisp one hundred dollar bills in it. I love old time actors and actresses. Here, she was just another family member at my Bar Mitzvah. The only difference was that she was a movie star. Who knew? I was more focused on the gifts than dancing the upcoming Hora or Hollywood Sylvia Sidney. I had a lot of fun at my bar-mitzvah and got a lot of gifts.

(One of my gifts at my Bar Mitzvah. Maracas. Go figure.)

Too bad none of them were whistle chasers. Out of all the kinds of fireworks, whistle chasers were one of my favorites. Not just because they were fun to watch and fly around, but because you never knew where they were going to go. Plus they were good to make trouble with and they blew up at the end. For instance, I decided to play hooky from a school assembly. I grabbed a few whistle chasers and headed back to the auditorium where dozens of kids and teachers would be gathered. Eugene was with me that day, and we had an ingenious plan. No real reason why, just ingenious (but stupid). When the assembly had started, we got five whistle chasers together and had to somehow get to the auditorium. We had to be like ninjas, quiet, quick, and with good timing. Pretty average stuff for a thirteen year old, yeah right. Imagine that. These abilities helped me become the ninja I am today. We quickly lit and threw them into the auditorium. I couldn't tell you what was happening inside the auditorium as the whistle chasers whizzed around, but I could certainly figure it out by the screams and yells from within. I started to run away, but I didn't want to get too far. So like a dummy, I headed back to see the faces of those inside, hiding behind a fence. Man, I thought I was so smart. The whole point was to hear the chaos that ensued as those two hundred kids and teachers went berserk. This was probably a bad idea because guess what, I got caught. One of the teachers who were part of the mass exodus from the school saw me and took me to the principle. I was expelled from school for three days. Of course, Eugene got away, lucky crow. Oh yeah, I forgot to tell you that was his nickname. Why? Because only the nose knows. It was big and pointy. You would think that would end my fun with whistle chasers, but it didn't. We had heard of a Chinese restaurant that had opened up not too far away. We went to check it out, and you know, goof around. In those days, it was unusual for Caucasians such as ourselves to frequent Chinese restaurants. Not that we were prejudice, it was just a rarity in Brooklyn.

When we did, we were always up to innocent mischief. As we sat down we began to play around. On the table were jars of soy sauce, mustard and hot sauce. You know all the condiments. Steve Ellis and Steve Lees started to mix some of the condiments together, Henry joined in too, as did Eugene. I just shook my head and told them not to do it. When the waiter came over and saw what we had done, wouldn't you know it, his eyes went right to me. But I hadn't done anything! I got yelled at and he physically escorted me to the door. So we were all kicked out of the restaurant. I tried to explain to him, but he wouldn't listen. Well, there was no way I was going to let them get away with this. They thought I was the trouble maker. So I decided to live up to my name. I went home and got a few of my whistle chasers I was selling for Tony and the Mafia. I gave a few whistle chasers to Eugene and the other members of the gang. We tied a few of them together and went to the back of the restaurant. At the back of the restaurant was a fan in the window that was off. We could see through the fan into the restaurant. The cooks were washing dishes and cutting food with meat cleavers. The servers were going about their business delivering food to tables. We lit the whistle chasers, all tied together and guess what we did? Stuffed them into the hole in the unplugged fan.

We threw them in and we ran about ten feet, because like a bunch of idiots, we wanted them to see us. We knew they couldn't catch us. Or so we thought. We were waiting with anticipation like a bunch of laughing hyenas in an alleyway, not knowing - Boom! The whistle chasers exploded and flew around the kitchen. Then there was silence. We were waiting and waiting. Then we relaxed. All of a sudden, the back door burst open and out came two china men wielding meat cleavers. Our smiles went away and our eyes bulged out in horror. Scared shitless, we turned and ran. They began to charge at us, steamed rice practically coming out of their ears. We turned tail and began to run down the alleyway behind us. All of a sudden this slow Chinese cook that was supposed to be way behind us was right on my heels! He was swinging the meat cleaver inches away from my back. The sounds that came out of my mouth were part animal and part human, but let's face it, I sounded like a girl. Finally, we reached the end of the street. I could either go left down the sidewalk or run across the street. I figured if I went left down the sidewalk, he would still continue the chase and turn me into chop suey. So I decided to run into the street because who in their right mind would follow me into the road filled with busy cars? Well, the Chinese cook was apparently not in his right mind, because he sprinted right after me into the middle of a busy Brooklyn intersection. Sure enough, a car was there to greet me as it whizzed by. Screech... Smack! My body collided like a pancake with the middle of the car so hard I bounced off like a rubber ball. Right on top of Mister meat cleaver. We both fell to the ground in a heap. Unharmed, but fearing I may not be that way for long, I jumped up and continued running. Luckily, no one followed me. It was a long time before we ever had Chinese again. That was another lesson that would benefit me in the future. Speed and focus to get the hell out of there. Of course, screaming like a girl helped.

When I was growing up, I loved various television shows and movies. I would sit in front of the television and watch *The Dead End Kids, The Three Stooges, The Riflemen, Abbott and Costello, and Wanted Dead or Alive*, with Steve McQueen. Being from Brooklyn, Hollywood was a world away, and we would always imagine the cowboy, the desperado, out on the range. It was a world that seemed in our imagination. I would be enthralled by John Wayne, Gene Kelly, Betty Hutton, Humphrey Bogart, Douglas Fairbanks Senior and Junior, The Marks Brothers, and Buster Keaton. Didn't know why, but I was. I enjoyed living in Brooklyn, it was all I knew. Places like Coney Island, the World's Fair, Canarsie Pier. But all that was about to come to an abrupt end.

My grandfather Nathan was a construction worker. One day he was walking from a wooden beam to another beam five stories up when the beam broke beneath his feet. There were five guys on that beam. Two of them died, two survived and my grandfather was crippled from the waist down. He sued the company and was awarded a five hundred thousand dollar settlement. You have to understand, in those days that was equivalent to four to five million dollars or more. My parents received a portion of that money and had a great idea. No, it wasn't using it to gamble, although I'm sure my father ran that thought through his head plenty of times. They decided we were going to take a vacation.

Not to the beaches of Hawaii, or the enchanting streets of Paris, but Los Angeles, California. I was thrilled! I had never been outside of the state and a vacation sounded fun. Little did I know, that my father's gambling had taken its toll. His bakery and luncheonette went bankrupt. So off we were going for the summer, to a wonderful vacation they said will be fun. I didn't want to leave my friends, but I knew I would be back soon and would tell them all about it. Boy, was I wrong.

CHAPTER 2
(Tricked And Trapped In A Strange New World Called California.)

We went to stay with my grandparents on my father's side, who had moved out there by using the money from the lawsuit. They owned an apartment complex, so we could stay there for free. California was a whole new world for me. I had never seen so many strange trees and plants, and boy was it hot! There were strange things called Mexican restaurants (in Brooklyn there weren't any so I didn't even know what a taco was back then if you can believe it.)

Film Studios, backyard pools, things I had never seen before. The thing I noticed most was that the people were not very friendly. In Brooklyn, everyone talked to each other, neighborhoods were like family. People in California preferred to keep to themselves, which shocked me. I loved to Kibitz (Yiddish for talk), but out here it was hard to find anyone to talk to, people's personalities were so different, things were so spread out. Soon our vacation was coming to an end, and I was excited to start school again.

Getting out of California and back to my gang, to the streets of Brooklyn was all I cared about. That's when my parents told me the truth. They were going back to Brooklyn. They were taking their suitcases, my siblings, the car, but they forgot one thing. Me! Of all people.

My parents explained they were going back with my siblings to pack up and then they were going to move out here to stay permanently. I was going to go to a wonderful school out here and have tons of fun with my new friends and be happy in my new environment. Are you kidding me!? No, I wasn't! My head was exploding with thoughts. Eugene, Jeffrey, The Twerp Twins and the rest of the gang. Never going to see them again? The hot Brooklyn days, playing with the fire hydrant. Over? No more Donna D'Oreo or Tony Albanese? Never having to run from the hot water of Mister Wolfson or shoot each other with whistle chasers? Were the days of my innocent mischief over? I wanted to cry, to scream, to stop my parents from making the worst decision of my life. In the end, I had no choice but to stay.

I was screwed. Stuck in my grandparent's apartment building, with nothing to do and no one to talk to. The people out here were different. They weren't like people from Brooklyn. They tended to keep to themselves and I just couldn't for the life of me, understand them. I would go down at night, lonely and bitter, thinking my life was over, to the recreation room. The residents would come down there and do various activities for entertainment. One of those things was ping pong. Whoopee. Instead of lighting firecrackers or selling mumus, I was watching ping pong. Soon I began to play it. Every afternoon I was down there, playing ping pong. I got good, really good. Amateur Professional ping pong player Steven Lambert. That was me. Whoopee. When my parents came back to California, I still resented them. They told me they were going to stay in Brooklyn for another year before moving out and I wasn't going back with them. Instead, they were taking my dumb ass of an older sister. I was furious inside. Why did they choose to leave me in this place, where the buildings were so different and spread out, where brownstone neighborhoods didn't exist and where the most fun I could get out of life was ping pong. It wasn't long before I was sent to a Junior High in the area. This place was so different than my old school in Brooklyn, I didn't know what to do.

Imagine living for thirteen years in one place and all of a sudden living in a whole new world. My grandparents wanted me to make new friends in school, get a social life. I didn't know how to make friends, I had grown up with the people in my gang my whole life. I joined a Tae Kwon Do class to try and get my mind off of things and get my aggression out. I had taken a class like this in Brooklyn before it closed down. This one must have been owned by some of the same people because after six months it shut its doors too. In Brooklyn, you could find me playing stickball with my friends, or climbing up trees to get away from the big guys. In California, I did none of that.

There were no friends to play stickball with, no big guys to run after me. Did I mention I hated it? I did? Okay, we'll I'll say it again. I absolutely despised it. I needed to find work to get my mind focused on something to do. Without the opportunities in Brooklyn, I turned to my grandparents for ideas.

They told me I could paint the walls in apartment units. It wasn't as fun as convincing old ladies to buy the newest style of mumus, but it was work so I took it. I worked hard and I worked fast and made good money from it. One day I was starting on a unit whose occupants were away for a few days. I had just dipped my roller in the paint when I heard strange noises coming from the bedroom. I looked over and saw the door was shut. Then I heard the noises again. That was odd, there shouldn't be anyone in the bedroom.

Maybe it was a dog or a cat, I thought. Pets were not allowed in the building, so I knew if I found one, my grandfather would hear about it right away. More noises came out of the bedroom. The more I listened, I started to realize that it didn't sound like a cat or dog. I wanted to keep painting, but curiosity got the best of me. I got up and headed to the door. The noises stopped. I turned the doorknob and walked in like you would walk into any room. I went I looked around trying to find the cat or dog that had been left in the room. A head popped up on the other side of a cabinet. My mouth dropped open. It wasn't a dog or a cat as I was expecting.

It was a monkey. It jumped up onto the bed and screamed. The athletic and fearless Steven Lambert disappeared and I became a scared little baby. I bolted back the way I came and tried to shut the door, but this thing was quick. It came screaming at me, preventing me from closing the door fully. I scrambled across the living room and straight for the front door. I opened it and slammed it shut, inches away from my pursuer. It almost got its fingers caught it was that close. I stood outside the door, breathing heavily and trying to make sense of everything.

I could hear the monkey on the other side of the door screaming. I remembered I left the roller of paint in the room and I started thinking about what that thing will do if he got a hold of it. I was too scared to go in there and do anything about it. I'm a kid from Brooklyn, the only monkey I've ever seen was in the zoo. I was not prepared for this. I went to tell my grandparents. "Grandpa, there is a monkey. A monkey in the apartment I was painting," I blurted out. My grandfather turned his head. "Steven, I need that room done, now stop this funny business and finish up."

I shook my head. "No, no funny, there is a monkey, a big monkey. You gotta call the police, it chased me. Come look, I'll show you." My heart was beating out of my chest. They had to believe me. I knew I was always getting into innocent mischief, but this wasn't it. My grandfather shook his head and turned off the television. Before he could open his mouth, I was ready. "Come on, just follow me." I led my grandfather back to the room with the monkey as he continued to yell at me, "this better not be your imagination." The screaming had stopped, and I figured the monkey had gone back into the bedroom. My grandfather peeked through the window and saw nothing as the blinds were closed. He looked back at me and I could tell he wasn't happy. "Don't go in there, there is a crazy monkey, he came after me like King Kong," I warned him.

My grandfather blurted out, "you've been watching too many movies. I hope you are not smoking that marijuana." Still not convinced, my grandfather opened the door and peered inside. He saw my roller and paint, but no monkey. He looks back at me and I shake my head. "Don't go in." He steps inside and looks around. Silence.

"Hey!" My grandfather's yell bounced around the room. Hearing nothing, he took a step inside. Suddenly, a scream comes from the bedroom. My grandfather takes a step back in surprise as the monkey comes running out of the bedroom. Stepping back faster than his age would allow him, my grandfather closed the door just as the monkey flew towards him. He looked down at me and saw a big grin covering my face. "Told you."

He looked back at the door. "We need to call the police, the animal control, everyone." An hour later, I watched them take the monkey out of the apartment, it's screams of defiance stays with me to this day.

The apartment it stayed in was a mess. I don't know how or why the owners had a chimp in their room and why they left it in there when they knew I was painting. The owners were evicted and I continued my painting job without further incident. In school, I did manage to make a few friends. We didn't have the kind of friendship I had with my gang of course, that could never be replaced.

CHAPTER 3
(Kung Fu. A Way Out.)

One day I was wandering down Van Nuys Boulevard to hang out with some friends when I came across a storefront. Looking through the glass window, my eyes came upon some unusual activities by three individuals that I would soon come to learn were extraordinary Martial Artists and friends.

(The original Sil-Lum Kung Fu school.)

They were wearing unusual black uniforms, with no belts and black shoes that looked like slippers. Mind you, I could have made this easy and simply said black pajamas. I watched them go through motions that were so graceful, they looked like tigers, snakes, cranes, praying mantis doing ballet. Up on the walls, they had weapons I had never seen before, not even in the movies I saw when I was a kid. I was so enthralled that I couldn't turn away. One was reeling a golden sword, single it was. A beautiful sword with poise and power. Golden in color. This man moved like Mikhail Baryshnikov, the ballet dancer and had the flexibility of Gumby as I watched him jump six feet in the air, spreading his legs and coming back down to Earth in the splits. I rubbed my eyes.

His name was JAMES LEW. Then I looked over and I saw another man. He was twirling a staff and they were in three pieces. In the middle there were chains. A three section staff. He was whirling and twirling it with lightning speed all around his body like the Tasmanian Devil with precision. A wildness was coming out of his body like all Hell broke loose. And when he stopped, it was like time froze. I rubbed my eyes.

His name was ALBERT LEONG. Then a third walked out to the middle of the floor. He had a long staff with a huge three sided spearhead on the end and on top there was a long flat, snake like spear with two huge hatchet like half moons on each side. What a magnificent object it was. This man moved like a matador, with strength and elegance emanating out of his body. He moved his weapon so swiftly, I could almost hear it cutting the air itself. When he stopped, he did a very strange thing with his leg. He threw it up so high and it looked like it came out of the socket. A very strange kick it was. I was soon to find out. Inverted. Crane like.

His name was DOUG WONG. I rubbed my eyes in disbelief at all three of them. After thirty minutes of watching these strange movements, I was hooked. Eventually, a man came outside and said his name was Sifu Doug Wong. He asked me if I wanted to come inside and watch. I nodded excitedly. He led me into the building and I sat down and watched the rest of the class. He explained to me this was Sil-Lum Kung Fu, five animal style and it was different than any other style of Martial Arts I had ever seen in my life. I was even more enthralled by what I saw and the desire inside of me grew to learn more. I knew I had money in my bank account from work and this was exactly what I wanted to spend it on. When I got home, I eagerly asked my grandparents if I could take Kung Fu lessons. My grandmother was busy in the kitchen making dinner and my grandfather was as usual, in front of the television. My grandfather shook his head when I asked them for permission to enroll in the Kung Fu School. "Kung what?"

My grandmother laughed, thinking she understood. "I think he wants to work for a Chinese restaurant."

I tried to explain. "No, not a restaurant. A Kung Fu school. Martial Arts. Fighting." I tried to explain to them some of the moves I saw in the class. Slowly they began to understand. My grandfather thought about it and shook his head.

"I think there are better things to spend your money on. I'm afraid it is going to have to be a no this time."

My heart sank. The one thing I wanted, the one activity that would make living out in this miserable place worth something, and I had just gotten denied. I went up to my room and broke down. What was I going to do now? I ignored them. The next day I went back to the Kung Fu School and signed up. Over the next days, weeks and months, I learned the basic punches, kicks, and forms (animals and insects, techniques, major exercise) of the art. Today, now we call it old school which unfortunately most of the schools of today, don't work that way anymore. They are afraid people are going to leave or sue them. Never before had doing something felt so right, so good. I felt free and I felt like I had a family. I had barely met these people and already I felt at home. It cost me twenty five dollars a month for three beginner classes a week which were on Monday, Wednesday and Friday. It was for an hour and a half and I loved every minute of it. We had to learn something called forms, which was brand new to me. These were types of movements all put together. Each movement would be used for fighting and you would be tested on how you would use each move in a combat situation. I was used to Karate, where they maybe had only three forms. In Kung Fu, it seemed endless. They were based on animals and insects such as the crane, the tiger, the snake, the leopard and the dragon. I would go three times a week which became seven days a week. Soon I trained month after month.

Our master Doug Wong would see certain things in people when he taught the classes. One day he pulled me and a few others aside after class and asked me to come on Saturday. Saturday was the intermediate class. Excitement pulsated through my body. Was this really happening? He saw something in me, and this made me feel special. Before I was a part of the crowd, no one paid attention to me. Here, I was given special attention and loved it. Every Saturday from nine in the morning to one in the afternoon, I would be taught all of these forms, weapons and fighting. There would be a group of guys that would teach with Douglas Wong. James, Albert, Tommy, Robin, the Louie brothers, Wilson, Todd, Goodwin. Now let's discuss Albert Leong and James Lew. They were a few years older than me. They started before me. They were already black belts and had teamed with Douglas Wong. I was the first wave of students there, so James and Albert were my superiors, which meant they were higher than me. These and the others are the people I became great friends with, they really took me under their wing. I hadn't had any friends like that since the Brooklyn days. Watching them meant so much to me, how they performed taught me a lot, as well as our hand forms and the way they worked out. We really became like family. We lived like a family. Every punch and kick and weapon we threw was under the supervision of each other. To me, I looked up to them, and I wasn't just happy growing up with them as kids in the Martial Arts world, but to find them a bunch of years later looking to do the same thing I was trying to do was totally unbelievable. You see we grow up and move on, sometimes not expecting to see each other again. (It's a wonderful life.) I was filled with happiness that I found my Martial Art family at my job. Can you believe that? More on that later. They were semi students of Doug Wong's and they were also his friends, equally respected as black belts.

Doug Wong's Kung Fu school was probably one of the first one in the valley. Now we see them all over the place, but back then when I was a very young teen,

Kung Fu schools just weren't around. Let's not forget, this was in the early seventies. Most were private schools only found in Chinatown, so this was a real honor. We had advanced black belts come in to teach the intermediate class, something we never had in the beginner class. People like Carl Totten and Sher Lew, but most of all being taught advanced Kung Fu by Master Douglas Wong. I'm talking about four, five, seven, eight hours a day. It wasn't that it was hard work, it was that Douglas Wong made it fun and at the same time you were working your ass off. That's the sign of a very special teacher and friend. I owe a lot to this man. Not only physically, but spiritually. Because of Kung Fu, it always gave me an understanding of how I should conduct my life. In a good way. Thank you, my friend. Douglas Wong. Let's give a mention to Carl Totten. Now there is a man that everybody wanted to stay away from in a physical way. When he came to the school, it seemed like everyone had something else to do. No one wanted to get smacked. He was long and lanky, his kicks and punches snapped out like a King cobra. When we left practice with him, we were sore. We did dynamic tension where you would go into a stance and do certain moves with your hands. Doug Wong would come around and kick and punch us all over the place. You would have to take the pain and continue the exercise. It was very helpful. It taught me not only how much to give, but sometimes how much you need to take. Everything was taught very thorough but quickly, in the intermediate and advanced classes, and I would gain many years of information in a short period of time. It wasn't long before I was able to teach the beginner class, which of course made me even better. As time went by, I gained knowledge of a black belt.

I lived and breathed Kung Fu and it became my life. I was given a key to the academy to go and train. I would go there after school. I would even cut school to go get in a few hours of practice. There were times when we slept over there, it became my new home. It was heaven as it was to many others. My parents moved back to Los Angeles and I moved in with them. I had to pay for my Kung Fu classes, so I continued my painting job and worked for Mike's Pizza. I could make five hundred dollars a week painting apartments. One bedroom would be thirty five bucks, two bedrooms would be fifty bucks and three bedrooms would be sixty five. To a kid around my age, that was good money. After a while, getting massive amounts of knowledge, where most schools would take around ten years, I was very thankful to be taught by Doug Wong. Being one of his special students and being able to learn so much in such a short time was a blessing. Eventually, Doug Wong invited me to come to tournaments with him. I had seen him compete three times and demonstrate and all three times he had gotten first place, so I was very excited and amazed. You see, Doug Wong had hands graceful as a gazelle and just as powerful. He had a kick called an inverted crane kick. To this day I've never seen anybody perform this kick as good as Doug Wong. Doug also wore a beautiful black uniform with white emblems along the sleeves and the legs. I always admired this uniform. When James Lew started to win, Douglas Wong passed his uniform down to him. I always dreamed of having one like it but I felt like I didn't rate at that time. So I did the only thing I could think of. I went to my grandmother. My grandmother was very good with a sewing machine. She had an old Hoover. Jackets, sweaters, pants, shirts. Whatever you needed, she could make it. I showed her a picture of the uniform and asked if she could copy it. My heart was pounding that her answer would be a yes. To my delight, it was. So she toiled for a few weeks and when she was finished, she presented me with a beautiful uniform almost exactly like Doug's. Well, guess what I did with it? I put it right into my closet and for years, that is where it stayed. Didn't wear it, didn't show it to Doug or anyone in Sil-Lum Kung Fu. I was shy about it, but immensely proud to have it.

It wasn't until my first stunt coordinating job that the uniform would come out of hiding. We were doing an episode of Fantasy Island and we had a scene that had Chinese weapons. Wardrobe provided us with white Karate uniforms, not knowing the difference. I decided to speak up and as shy about it as I was, (believe me I was very shy about it at that time) I wanted to make a point. I told the set designers, Wardrobe, Producers and Director that the set didn't look Chinese and I told Wardrobe that the uniforms were not accurate. They all looked at me in surprise. I was hoping I still had my job. Then all broke out with questions for me. What should the set look like, what should we get for the props? The wardrobe ladies asked me if I had a uniform that would fit with the scene. I told them I did, back in my closet. So the next day I went and got the uniform my grandmother made for me and brought it on the set. I showed them the uniform and suggested to them that they could make a white one for James McArthur and a black one for Mako. They loved the idea and proceeded to do just that. Then I went to sets and straightened them out. Take all this Japanese stuff and replace it with Chinese. A funny story, but one that really meant a lot to me. So if you ever see this episode of Fantasy Island with Mako and James McArthur (remember him? Book 'em Dano. Hawaii Five-O), just know that this show for me, paid homage to Douglas Wong and Sil-Lum Kung Fu. That was the kind of respect I had for Doug. No matter what I've learned before from family or friends, Doug Wong and Sil- Lum Kung Fu taught me the essentials of childhood. The difference between right and wrong, how to deal with people, communication, and how to learn and teach somebody mentally, physically, and spiritually. All this was communicated to me while we were going through hand forms, weapons and fighting. He would teach us how to go to through life and interact with people, never really knowing what use this was going to be to me. Remember, I was just a punk kid with no direction. When he did teach us Kung Fu, he would not only teach us the forms and their names, based on different animals and insects, but he would teach us why these forms exist. In Karate back in Brooklyn, they just showed us what to do without any explanation why. Doug Wong explained to us that each movement has a purpose, and when combined with other movements creates an understanding. Exactly where you are going with each move and what its purpose is. This is what allows you to be successful with the knowledge you are receiving. Not until much later on did I realize how beneficial this would be in the movie land of Hollywood. He taught me how to teach and instruct others which is a very special gift. He became someone that never really existed in my life, a teacher in many different ways. Someone that was strict with me, but believed unconditionally in my potential. He gave me direction, support, and focus. These are the things I brought to my work, that later on, I will show how much this stuff meant when I needed it.

In those days, a lot of tournaments were held in school gyms, I can tell you many wonderful stories, like seeing Chuck Norris, Joe Lewis, Steve Sanders, Benny Urquidez, Eric Lee, Ted Debaro, Howard Jackson. But we will tell you a story about Tadashii Yamashita. In between fighting, the Martial Artists would show off their skills to the crowd. They were called demonstrations. Imagine this, Yamashita would put on a blindfold and cut watermelons and cucumbers with his sword. One time there were a few people who were calling him names in the stands, making fun of him and creating disturbances. Imagine seeing one of the craziest men, and I better (right?) say that with great respect and love, in the world being heckled, and the announcer repeatedly asking them to be quiet. You have to understand, Tadash (that's my nickname for him) was not one to have much sympathy. You don't play with fire without getting burned. The announcer kept telling them again and again, to no avail. He had cut one by one through the cucumbers until he got to the watermelons. As the heckling continued, the watermelon display because more and more violent. Finally, after three or four times, I'll never forget, Yamashita stopped. He "keyade." For all you reading this, that is a scream. He ripped off his blindfold, took his sword, turned toward the crowd, and like a wild banshee, starting running up the stands. I was mystified, as was everybody else. You should have seen the people. It was like Moses parting the red sea. People were falling all over the place to get out of the way of the sword. Halfway up, the three kids started getting real nervous. Never could figure out why they didn't run at first, but I guess they were frozen in fear. He slashed his sword at the students whose throats had closed up and faces turned stone white. The announcer tried to calm everyone down as their screams filled the room. At the last second, he would bring down the weapon going at fifty miles per hour, and miss by inches as they were pleading. "I'm sorry, I'm sorry," they whimpered. The whole gym was roaring with laughter and applause. Yamashita walked back down like a victorious Japanese Samurai. He was never heckled again. From then on, I always knew who Tadashii Yamashita was. A badass that you don't eff with.

It wasn't long before I started to compete with Albert and James. They would compete in black belt and I would compete in brown belt. As time went by, Doug Wong permitted a few of us to begin competing in black belt tournaments. After many times of competing in black belt, Doug finally gave me a chance to compete with Albert and James doing a two man set with Robert Tolzer. I never thought we had a chance against them. James did single sword and Albert did Kwan Do and Robert and I did sword versus spear. I had the spear, and can you believe it? We beat them and won first place! It was about the third time we competed against them and the first time we won against them. Do they remember that day? Who knows. I know I remember that day, and hopefully, Douglas Wong remembers it too. Felt like I was on top of the world. I went on to win thirty to thirty five trophies in tournaments. Some of them were in that famous display case at Douglas Wong's studio along with Albert, James, the Louie brothers, Robin Kane, Todd Takeuchi and many more. Albert Leong and James Lew had hundreds. They never had a trophy in fighting like I did, just forms and weapons. I was one of the few fighters in the school along with Bill Henderson, Robert Tolzer and Alonzo Young, aka Lumpy. The first time Alonzo joined, Doug Wong put him against me and he pinned me to the wall as we were fighting. He grabbed my ribs and started squeezing my skinny ass. After a few seconds, I down blocked his arm like a sledgehammer, Wing-Chun, and the release was quick. There was one student named Bill Henderson, who was one of my classmates. He would compete in tournaments too. He was a great heavyweight fighter, beat everybody he came up against. Then he fought Benny Urquidez. Bill made me and Doug his cornermen. You could see us together in the video, the beginning of the third round. In the first round, they said it was tied. But if you ask me personally, I'd say Bill won. Bill beat Benny up badly. Benny was a world champion, a tough man. Lots of people couldn't believe it. The second round Benny got smart and started to really attack Bill. Cramp him, staying close. Bill had a long reach. He should have used it by separating and keeping arms distance. That is exactly what I was yelling, being one of his cornermen. It was about equal until Benny landed a great shot, right to the jaw. It stunned Bill. That's what happens when you are fighting a shorter man with a shorter arm span. Benny was able to fully extend, Bill wasn't able to. That was Bill's mistake. Benny pulled himself together and started coming at Bill hard. Bill spit his mouthpiece out so they called time out. When Bill came over, he was a little out of it and Doug suggested out of caring and concern that, "maybe we should throw in the towel."

You see we must understand here, Doug knew Benny as he was once a student of Doug's and a great friend. He knew Benny thrived knowing somebody was hurt and would come at them even stronger. Bill was crushed. I was confused. There was a heavy discussion. The towel was kept and Bill went out to fight. For some reason, I felt like something let all the air out of him. He had no more fight in him, Benny was beating him all over the place. The third round started and they were coming at each other like two sumo wrestlers. Whack, whack, whack, Muhammad Ali style. It didn't last long. Benny came back, hitting harder and faster than ever. Doug threw the towel in before the fight ended. Bill was upset. He didn't speak to Doug for a long time after that. Who knows, maybe he could have won, gotten in a lucky punch or something. Doug really cared for him. Benny was world champ so the chances of him being beaten were slim. It was one of the wildest Martial Art full contact fights I have ever seen. Going back to my childhood, remembering getting punched and falling down but getting right back up, these circumstances helped me greatly in my tournaments. There was this one guy, we called "Wild Man." He was a good fight man but didn't know weapons or forms. Anybody out there remember him? Wild man. He would take a weapon, usually borrow it from someone else and make up shit. It was hysterical. You can only imagine it was like watching a cartoon. Everyone always looked forward to Wild Man and his unscheduled performances. He would get a two or a three from the judges, but the audience loved him. At this time, I wasn't thinking about the movies or what I wanted to do with my life. I just enjoyed being where I was day by day, learning from Doug and seeing these great men compete. I had no other guidance. I wanted to be a baseball player since I was young, but had no one to direct me on how to do that. I was in a cheap Martial Arts paper called "Karate-ka" a few times. Pretty hard to get into.

When I competed with James and Albert in black belt weapons and won, there was a front page article about it that I had for many years. Sorry to say it disappeared. That means I have no proof. I wonder if they remember? Doug Wong's brother, Curtis, owned a magazine called "Inside Kung Fu." I remember the fun times we had when Doug would take all the advanced class up to the magazine's headquarters and starting with the very first issue that came out, we would spend hours putting the magazine pages together. We would be busy stapling them and sending them out. I guess you could call that part of our training. Pretty funny, but I wouldn't have traded it for anything. The bond grew tighter. I never knew where I was going with this, but I loved it and it gave me something physical to do to fulfill the void after leaving Brooklyn.

(My first black belt trophy. 17 years old.)

On a side note, I tried other sports as well, don't get me wrong. In high school, I tried out for the football team and got in as a wide receiver. I was small, but I was fast. Nobody could catch me. I was five foot nine, a hundred and fifty pounds. I would be amused at the other players as they tried to catch me. Then the times they did catch me, they would tackle me. They made sure I would remember when they did. Once one person tackled me, several others would come in with an arm or knee, and at times when we were playing the Pirates, a cannonball. Yo ho ho. My coach would yell at me to get up and I couldn't. I didn't like the idea of being elbowed or kneed and not be able to fight back. I tried that a few times with my Kung Fu and got in trouble. So I just said to hell with this and quit. That was my first game and my last game. Pretty funny. I got to meet many greats in the tournament circuit. I'm the last generation who got to see Chuck Norris compete, who got to see Joe Lewis compete. I remember Chuck Norris and many other people I have mentioned, judging me multiple times. Those are the kinds of great memories no one has except me or guys during or before my time. A lot of those fighters, their sons are big stars now. I remember watching Ernie Reyes compete, and his son who was seven to eight years old train with him. Others like Al Decostco and his young son Mark Decostco. Two successful Martial Art actors today.

My last tournament was a BKF, Black Karate Federation tournament. I decided this would be my last because I was getting older and had to get a job. The age of responsibility was kicking in. Again, I had no direction. There were maybe twenty Caucasians that showed up and about four hundred African American guys. You had to have a lot of nerve to take your school there and compete with them. No one was prejudice, but it was hard to win in an all minority tournament like that. By then we were very well known.

There was a six to seven year period where every tournament our school entered, we would win trophies, special thanks to James Lew, Robin Kane and Albert Leong and of course Jimmy Brown and let's not forget Clifford. There were other schools and people who didn't even compete because they knew they weren't going to win. Let me tell you it was amazing to watch and hear top black belts say, "oh the Sil-Lum Kung Fu school was here." We were legendary. We would take home five to ten trophies every tournament.

If I mentioned names you would be shocked who decided not to compete. Sil-Lum Kung Fu was legendary thanks to Douglas Wong, for he was the one that cultivated the soil. I got lucky and got second in weapons, forms and fighting. Three divisions in this BKF tournament which was my last. All of a sudden, I reached the yellow brick road and I didn't know it.

CHAPTER 4
(Hello, Hollywood.)

When I had won my three second place trophies at the BKF tournament, Chuck Norris's casting people came up to me and explained they were doing a Chuck Norris picture. They wanted to know if I would be interested in doing a fight with him. I looked at them funny, not realizing what they were talking about. They explained I simply had to fight and get beat up by Chuck Norris in a movie called *Good Guys Wear Black*. Then I would get five hundred dollars. My eyes lit up.

Five hundred dollars in cash for one night was a lot of money. I went over it in my head. Paint a week full of rooms and chance meeting another crazy monkey, or get beat up and paid all in one night? The answer was obvious. Sure, I said. A few nights later I got a call and they told me to come down to LAX, the airport. I went down there and here I see thirty to forty stunt guys fighting each other. I blinked my eyes and shook my head. Where was I? These were stuntmen? In the back of my mind I had figured that actors had other people to do dangerous actions for them, but only now upon seeing these men, did it click.

Furthermore, this was all stuff I had been doing all my life. Images of climbing up trees in Brooklyn came back to me. Hopping fences to get away from the big guys. Getting hit by the car and falling back onto the Chinese guy. All of this was a part of my life and here these people were getting paid lots of money to do those things. I was called on the set, not knowing what I was doing. All the casting people knew about me was that I could fight. They explained the scene and choreography and before long, we began. Chuck Norris comes out and I swing at him, he blocks and kicks me in the chest. I go flying into the luggage on the baggage claim belt.

I got up and smiled. That was fun. Do people actually get paid for this? I had done these things my whole life and got away with it, I'm an athlete and this would be a dream job for me. Timing, coordination, distance, focus and power of the mind. These were the things most important to me to become a great athlete, fighter and stunt man for the movies.

CHAPTER 5
(The Kahana Experience. One Of A Kind.)

At this time, I was over eighteen and needed a day job. Something more than just painting apartments. I was addicted to this stunt career but didn't know how to get into it. I got a job at a pizza place for a while called Chi Chi's pizza and then remembered I met this guy named Rick Kahana at one of the tournaments. His father, Kim Kahana did a television show with Jane Michael Vincent called *Danger Island*. He was the "stunt monkey." He did silly physical stuff and got thrown around. Well, he would bring his son to the tournaments and that's how we met. Rick would invite me over to his father's motorhome and we would have chicken teriyaki and rice. Rick told me one day that his father had a stunt school in Chatsworth Park, and that he was a stuntman. He had everything there. High falls, motorcycles, horses, airbags, pads, repelling, fire burn equipment, etc. Everything you could possibly need. It was like being in F.A.O Schwartz, you know that famous toy store in New York. Then it hit me. That's where I wanted to go! He asked me if I wanted to teach at the school since I was a black belt.

I said yes. I knew of Chatsworth park because my grandparents on my mother's side had lived four blocks from there. The class I taught were stunt kids that wanted to be stuntmen. I really didn't know much at this time about the things I just mentioned except what I did in good ole Brooklyn as a kid. But what I did know a lot of, was Kung Fu.

Tim Kahana used to bring one of his son's friends, Tom Elliot to the tournaments. He was a real good fighter and became a good friend and a stuntman. He was also a cowboy. He hung around rodeo people, a fighting cowboy is what he was. Kahana let us use his facilities where we trained. If I wanted to learn something, I would teach myself using his equipment or learn from others who trained or worked out there. Using my common sense and having the physical ability that I had, I always seem to get it. But don't get me wrong.

I owe a lot to that man, Kim Kahana and so do a lot of others but for some reason, all the others seem to hide that fact which I was never able to figure out. It seemed like I was one of the few that was proud of it. Two well known stuntmen that I learned from over at Kahana's were Mike Adams and George Wilbur.
They were both boxers and Kahana had a boxing ring. I always saw them at least once a week there and constantly absorbed the physical and mental knowledge of stunts from them. You see, going to Kahana's stunt school, you had to keep on the down low. Why? I never really figured that out.

You couldn't tell professional stuntmen you went to a stunt school at that time.

(Steven Lambert, Tom Elliott and Rick Kahana.)

It was forbidden, can you believe it? You seemed to only be allowed to learn from one person or a special group. Stunt schools and whoever ran them were disliked, even though there really weren't any. I always assumed through my common sense I talk about now and then, that some of it had to do with jealousy and insecurity. Simply put, competition. Stupid at that. Which is a major fault in this business. They didn't want it. So Kahana wasn't really well liked either back then, which in my view was so strange. It was a great time with strange ways. I remember stuntmen that were starting with me like Carl Ciarfalio and John Casino, two excellent stuntmen. When I befriended them, I found out they did live shows. Knott's Berry Farm, Disneyland, and they asked me never to mention it to anybody. I asked them why. They explained to me that famous well known stuntmen didn't like it.

I knew for a fact doing live shows can get you better experience. I used to do live shows in Kung Fu demonstrations. So where do these stuntmen that are constantly working now come off not happy with somebody who is working at places like Knotts Berry Farm or running a stunt school?

My friends, that was mind boggling! They actually resented it and would not hire you in most cases if they knew you were doing live shows or going to a stunt school. Totally ridiculous. But as we know today it is so much different. I guess they tried to keep it to themselves. You can say they were like a bunch of politicians in the Government.

You know what I'm talking about, doncha? It's everyone for themselves. Some things never change. Yes, you know where I stand. I owe a tremendous amount of debt and gratitude for Kahana. Without him, I wouldn't have had the facilities to gain the abilities I have now. Much thanks to Kahana.

(This was one wild jerk off. Full blast.)

Remembering all the good times with Kim Kahana, his son Rick, his daughter Debbie and his son Kim Jr., who I called little ninja. One last thing I have to say about the wonderful times I had with the Kahanas. You can take this story thinking it is pretty funny, downright serious, or absolutely horrible. I take it all the above. I remember being invited to a Christmas dinner at Kim's house. You see, three or four years before, Kim Kahana senior bought Kim Kahana Jr. a baby calf. Little ninja loved that calf to death. He named it Archie and they became inseparable. It was like his pet dog they were so close. He would go out and feed it hay in the morning, play with it in the afternoon and made sure it was happy at night. Now you have to understand what I'm about to say. Kim was a great guy but he did a lot of strange things he thought were funny. I guess I can say it wasn't really meant to be hurtful but you can take it that way. Tom Elliot, Will Quaison, me, Rick and everyone else in the family sat down at the table, while his mother put the food out. We said a prayer, his mother was a woman of faith, and commenced eating. About five minutes into the food which included I hate to say, beef, Kim Kahana Sr. looks up and says to little ninja, "how do you like that meat?"

Little ninja who was busy stuffing the beef into his little cheeks, swallowed and wiped the juice from his lips.

"What do you mean?" He asked.

Kim Kahana leaned over and forked another large piece, this time with a bone in it, and put it on little ninja's plate.

"That's Archie," he said with a smile.

Little Ninja shook his head. He didn't find his father's jokes funny. Then he saw the rest of the table's expressions. We were stunned. His father wasn't joking. Can you imagine what happened next?

Little ninja dropped his fork and had a face on him like I had never seen before. You could call it horror, surprise, anger, fear. I call it sadness. He jumped up, started screaming and ran out of the room. We all looked at each other in disbelief. Of course, Christmas dinner ended right there but Kahana kept on eating, his roaring laugh spread over the dinner table. Just like the laugh he used in the television show *Danger Island*.

We all knew Archie, and we all loved him. Now the reason why I tell you this story is that only the people who knew Kahana would understand. A moment in my life that I will never forget.

Last but not least, I would like to pay tribute to Rick Kahana who is one of the finest movie Martial Artists I have ever met. He could make those fire knives fly Hawaiian Style and his talents and presence will be sorely missed.

(Rick Kahana. One of the best Martial Artists I've ever met. Miss you, pal.)

Around this time, I met a girl. She was a nice Italian girl named Debbie from Hoboken, New Jersey. Her sister lived in the apartment building my grandparents (and now parents) managed. She looked just like Meg Ryan. When she came to visit, I would talk to her. It wasn't long before we started dating. I know what you're thinking. First Donna and now Debbie. What can I say, I like Italian girls whose names start with the letter D. Debbie moved out here and got a job at Kirker Pipes, which was a well known motorcycle shop, not only to outsiders but to movie stunt people. As you can guess, it was full of motorcycle enthusiasts. It was also full of stuntmen. Mike Jenkins, who was the manager, loved hanging around members from the stunt community. He would give them good deals on the motorcycles in return for their camaraderie. Debbie knew I wanted to be in the stunt business and she saw a great opportunity. She would tell the stuntmen who came in. People like Ronnie

Rondell, Roy Harrison and Tommy Huff, that her boyfriend wanted to join the stunt business. You have to understand, they hear this all the time from girlfriends, fathers, mothers, friends and the like. So hearing it from my girlfriend Debbie was nothing new. To them, I was just another excited beginner that wanted to join the stunt world. They probably thought I saw some action in a movie and wanted to dedicate my life to joining them. It happened all the time. So they pretty much ignored her requests to meet with me time after time. That's when Tom Elliot and I decided to become an extra.

We learned at Kahanas that being an extra was a great way to learn more about the movie business and you got paid at the same time. At first, it was slow. But after a month or so it began to pick up and we were working almost every day. I made over a thousand dollars a week, and that's after taxes. Talk about good money. You see I considered myself very lucky. I was twenty one but looked sixteen so I worked that range. Junior High School, High School, even College. I was very lucky. I lived in good health. Never smoked, never drank and looking back at it now, Kung Fu kept me young. I never had any lines but you could always catch me eating, or walking by, always finding a way to get on camera. After a year of doing extra work and constantly working, I had enough money to stop and pursue stunts full time. Always looking for an angle to meet these people that would give me a chance and hire me. As they say, a man who has a good woman can go a long way. In this case, it was the woman's pestering that finally broke the camel's back and Roy Harrison aka Snuffy, and Ronnie Rondell finally cried Uncle and said they would meet me. Debbie left with a telephone number arranged neatly in her pocket. I had heard that Roy Harrison was stunt coordinating on *Fantasy Island* and Ronnie Rondell was doing *Hart To Hart*. At that time, they were two of the top stunt coordinators in the business. Well deserved. So I called Roy Harrison, who you have to understand is a bit of a puppy dog hard ass in a good way, and told him about myself and Kung Fu on the phone. "What the hell is that?" I remember him saying. I told him it was a Martial Art style and I could show him in person if he'd like and he said he would consider it. He replied, "yea, but I know gun." I laughed. A few more phone conversations later, he agreed to have me come by his house and perform for him and Ronnie Rondell.

Now Roy Harrison and Ronnie Rondell were part of a famous motorcycle group called the Viewfinders which many a famous stunt man and movie star were in. They also went to High School together and they were both on the gymnastics team. I went to Roy's house and he led me into his backyard. Ronnie was there waiting for me. Here I was, a skinny young punk from Brooklyn, not knowing his ass from his elbow except for Kung Fu and being a physical monkey, who was going to perform for two hulking guys with scowls on their faces. I knew this was my one shot at impressing them, to show them I was different from every other guy out there wanting to be a stuntman. You have to understand that Kung Fu was something not done by stuntmen in American films at that time. There was Judo, Karate, basic punches and kicks, but no one had seen the things people like Douglas Wong had taught me. Especially no stuntmen that did the things I was able to do physically. I started off with animal forms. Tiger, leopard, crane, snake and dragon. Then I went to the mantis throwing kicks and punches. I looked over and saw looks of confusion mixed with amazement from these guys. I brought a staff and sword with me and did a few routines with them. I did some flying kicks, jumped six feet in the air and landed on my feet. Ronnie would occasionally get up and throw some punches. He asked me what punches he should throw and I replied, "whatever you want."

He looked at Roy and that was the first time I saw the famous Roy Harrison look. He would look over his glasses, not saying a word. It was a very scary look. As the years went by, I grew to understand that look in many ways. You see, for those who knew Roy, that look had many meanings. Ultimately for me, I learned that for myself and a few others, that became a very loving and caring look for few and far between. Anyway, getting back to Ronnie, he started throwing punches like a boxer and through a Martial Arts style I learned from Doug, called Chai-Sau (sticky hands) and Wing Chung, I simply blocked and parried the majority of whatever he threw. I could tell at the end that they both were very impressed with everything I did. I went to the roof of the house and told them I was going to jump down with a front flip onto solid cement. They laughed, no one would dare jump down one story without pads back then. But I did and I sprung back up and posed. Their scowls quickly became open mouths in amazement. I then climbed up his tree which was two stories high and jumped down from it again on solid cement. Again, I feel I owe this to Kung Fu. Horse stances. He would later tell me I looked like some sort of spider monkey jumping all over the place like I had lost my mind. I would jump up and kick a basketball net and do a back or side fall. Needless to say, they were hooked and instantly I became one of their guys. They also liked me too because I was twenty one, but I looked sixteen. This is where I started meeting other stunt guys such as Joel Kramer, John Meier, Danny Weselis, Freddy Heist and Reid Rondell among many others.

I would continue to practice using the equipment at Kahana's and learn from Roy and Ronnie at the same time, teaching me how to change over my fighting abilities to the movie way. I gained much valuable information during the years I spent with them. Learning the old way and the new way of how to do things in the stunt world. You see there is a difference and they are both equally as important.

During this first year of going all SAG, I was living in an apartment building in Northridge, California on Reseda Blvd. Back then there was an awful lot of filming going on throughout the streets of Los Angeles. I would make the rounds, spending hours upon hours trying to meet people from different productions such *as The Hulk, BJ And The Bear, Fantasy Island, Emergency,* and *Rockford Files.* Let alone all the movies that were filmed locally. Just to tell you how different things were then as of now, I remember a group of us used to go to Universal Studios and there was an Irish security guard named Scotty.

He was a wonderful man, always smiling and laughing. One of the reasons he let us in is because we would always talk to him and get to know him. Sorry to say, many years later I heard through the grapevine of the stunt community that somebody tried to break into the studio through the front gate and shot and killed him. It broke my heart when I heard that. He was such an important part of my beginnings and I could say as irrelevant as he was, he was a very important piece of my career.

If he hadn't been there, I wouldn't have gotten into Universal Studios for many years and found the jobs and met the people that would help me move along the way. So here is to you, Scotty. God Bless You. There was a group of us, Dennis Madalone, Kenny Lesko, Tom Morga, Peter Antuigo, Johnny Casino and a couple more I'm probably missing.

They called us the commissary kids.

(From left to right, three of the commissary kids. Chris Doyle, Steven Lambert and Dennis Madalone.)

He would literally let us in the front gate so we could go from stage to stage, but instead, we would go first to a Production Office. It was unbelievable. All the call sheets of all the shows were stapled for that day and anyone who needed a call sheet would go inside and grab one. It was handed to us on a silver platter. That does not happen never more. We would take them and if they were working on the stage we would go to the stage and see if there was any action or Stunt Coordinator on it. Or we would go to the location. That is an incredible thing that does not happen today. How lucky we were. As of the other studios, MGM, Warner Brothers, Paramount, Fox, it was so easy to either walk in the front gate, tell a fib, or we would climb over the fence in the back. There were no eyes upon us or cameras, no security walking around per se. If you got caught, they would simply spank your hand and escort you out. It was an innocent time, and the last time things such as this would occur. It was a time that would be never more in the history of the studios as we can see now. I started to meet many different people who had the same aspirations as I did, who later on in life would become some of the greats of today.

Here is a funny story about one of these men. One day living in Northridge, I got a knock on my door and opened it to find two police officers staring me down. They asked me who I was and if I lived there, so I told them. They wrote down the information while I'm racking my brain trying to figure out why the hell they are bothering me for. I'm just a punk kid from Brooklyn who likes to get into innocent mischief, that's all. One of the Officers takes off his sunglasses and stares me in the eye. "We understand you have been jumping off the roof of your apartment building last week," the Officer stated in a monotone voice. Now before you say anything, I have to say he wasn't wrong. I had jumped off the roof of my building, but that was a year ago. I was practicing high falls into the pool. I would invite guys over from Kahanas and we would practice. No big deal. I told the Officer that no, I hadn't been jumping off my roof last week. They asked me if I was across the street at so and so time last week and I said, "no, why? I live here, why should I be across the street?" The Officer with the sunglasses nodded and wrote something down.

"I hear there is a stuntman around here. We figure he could be the culprit. Are you a stunt man?" I shook my head no as my street sense from Brooklyn kicked in. Inside my head, I'm saying, of course I'm not a stuntman and if I told them I didn't do it, they wouldn't believe me. I'm not going to tell the coppers anything.

"No, I'm not a stunt man," I replied. In my head, I was screaming at myself that I was a stuntman! But the police wouldn't believe that I wasn't the one jumping off the roof, so I kept my trap shut. The Officer nodded, thanked me for my time and excused himself from my door. I went back inside, thoughts swirling through my head. Another stunt man around here? Across the street? Who could it be? Well, I didn't have to wait too long to find out. A week later I got another knock at my door.

Instead of the police, it was a young kid like me, his blonde hair slicked back like Elvis. He had an accent that reminded me of someone from Wyoming or Texas. "Howdy there," he introduced himself. "I understand you're looking to be a stuntman. Whatcha name?"

"My name is Steven Lambert," I replied.

The young man with Elvis hair put out his hand. "Name's Jack Gill. I live across the street." (Yes, can you believe it, Jack Gill.) He pointed across the street to the same house the police pointed at a week before. Then it clicked. "Oh, you're the guy that almost got me in trouble," I laughed. He turned his head to the side and looked at me. I smiled. "You've been jumping off of roofs haven't you?"

He nodded. "Yeah, that was me." He went on to tell me that he heard about me from people in his building, so he decided to come over, find me and introduce himself. He told me he was working at a restaurant as a waiter and a busboy. Can you believe it? You see, we all start off somewhere. Heck, I was making pizza and selling old lady's mumus. We became good friends. He also told me he lived with a roommate and didn't have much money. I also found out he was a top notch motorcyclist. I didn't realize how lucky I was. I had made a thousand dollars clear a week doing extra work and was living in a nice apartment, and poor Jack was a starving waiter. For a period of six to eight months, I would invite him over two to three times a week and I would cook for him what I like to call poor man's food. This delicious menu included things like a whole pot of spaghetti, or chicken and rice, things like that. Cheap and easy. A couple of years went by, we would see each other now and then. Jack was becoming very successful working on shows like *Dukes of Hazard, The A Team.* A couple more years went by and we had a SAG strike. I'll get to how I got into SAG later. I went down to picket along with many other stunt people and actors. Low and behold, I see my good friend Jack Gill there with a few very high profile stuntmen. I walked over and introduced myself and said hello to Jack, and to my surprise, he's pretending like he doesn't even know me. You see, this is very hard to explain. I found out later that stuntmen are like having a girlfriend. You don't want to share and Jack, well he just didn't want to share. I said, "Jack, it's me, Steven Lambert." He just turned around and proceeded to talk to the other high profile stuntmen. I couldn't believe it. That was my first taste of Hollywood if you know what I mean. I call that chicken shit, what do you call it? In my head I'm saying, I just fed this guy for over a year, and he's ignoring me!? When you're a friend with somebody, you're a friend for life. Unless you become friends with someone more famous. That's Hollywood, it never ends. Nevertheless, ancient Chinese proverb, me don't hold no grudges. I laughed it off. I wasn't upset at him, just wiser and more cautious of how some of the stunt community worked. I still see him now and then. Funny story, I hope you are amused, for that was his M.O. From then on there. Unfortunately, we have run into hard lessons learned, it's part of life.

Let's move on, shall we? I mentioned I worked as an extra for a little over a year. Shows *like M.A.S.H., Hardy Boys, James at Fifteen*. You remember those shows, don't you? Speaking of *M.A.S.H.*, I probably did five to six of those shows. Wonderful show to work extra on. Back when I worked extra in the seventies, it was like working extra in the forties fifties and sixties. The things that went on. The only difference was, it was the tail end of an era which I will explain now. Extras were treated like a dime a dozen. You didn't get much respect, money, or lunch. We were outcasts. Not like today where if they tried to do that, they would call the union and put a stop to it. *M.A.S.H.* might have been the only show where they treated extras like the actors. We got to eat with the actors instead of in a separate space. Anywhere else, you wouldn't get hot food. You would get a brown bag with a sandwich, apple, and a drink in most other shows. Here on *M.A.S.H.*, it was amazing. They gave you the same food. You got to sit with the actors. You may think it was nothing, but it was a big deal. It was the first sign of being treated like somebody and it really was an amazing thing to see that on a T.V. show. Many people don't realize that about *M.A.S.H.* Every extra looked forward to work on *M.A.S.H.* Let me tell you something, it was unbelievable what this show did. Every episode, they would pick an extra and give them a line or two so they could get their SAG card, but you had to work enough times for them to get to know you and know your work ethics. Every time I was there, I saw someone get picked to get their SAG card. It was the actors who picked. Wayne Rogers and Allen Alda would pick an extra and give a contract to them if they thought they were good workers. Since I was only working on it five or six times, I never got a chance. But the fact that they did that was amazing, how many shows did that? None as far as I knew.

Now let's talk about *James at Fifteen*, the last time I worked extra. I was a stand in for Lance Kerwin, the star of *James at Fifteen*, now Sixteen. I was told to go to point B from point A and apparently, I didn't move fast enough. The First AD had an attitude and got physical with me because I didn't move quick enough for him. So he pushed me in my chest so hard that I flew back ten feet, over the camera legs right on my backside. I was humiliated. Everybody saw. Right away the five animal styles kicked in. Tiger, Leopard, Crane, Snake and Dragon. I got up as fast as I fell and went right at him. Guess what I did? Yes, right in the chest, a Sun Fist. And guess what, he fell right on his backside too. Holding his chest, guess what the first words that came out of his mouth were? "You're fired!" I turned around, grabbed my bag and walked out of Twentieth Century Fox. As I was walking, I said to myself that this is it. I'm tired of this. No more extra work, I've made enough money over the year. I never felt I was in the wrong, though some might say it was wrong, but you live and learn. That was the Martial Artist in me. Why me? That was my first taste of confrontation in the movie business and to this day I always wonder, why me? I only say this because it happened more than once, twice, three times. Well, I can go on but let's continue with the story. I was brought up with morals, values and ethics. My mother and my grandparents molded me in what was right and what was wrong. In life I was playing the superhero, doing things the way I had been brought up. No lying, cheating, or stealing. Help thy neighbor. In a business that was full of secret villains, that was hard. You needed to be cut throat in this industry, but I wasn't going to cut anything but flowers. What I say to you about the movie business, was, is and will always be. Unfortunately.

Stunts, here I come. I also had to explain this to Central Casting. For those who come from my era and before, you are familiar with Central Casting and the man Carl Joy who was one of the heads. He knew me very well over the year. I explained to him what happened and he was on my side. Thank God. He was my friend and knew how hard I worked. A few months went by looking for stunt work with no avail and then I got a call from Carl Joy asking me if I wanted to work. It was on a religious television movie. They wanted me to play a character at the beach as an extra. I don't know why, but for some reason, I said yes. You always want to be in the movie business to progress your career. After a few months meeting a lot of people but not getting anywhere, I felt kind of lonely and out of sync and you want to be in sync. Not the boy band, hahaha. When I got there, an assistant came over and explained that one of the actors didn't show up. He wanted to know which one of us had a SAG card. Well, I knew I didn't have a Screen Actors Guild card yet. I did, however, have a Screen Extras Guild card. But I decided to play dumb so to speak and raised my hand along with five or six others that actually had their SAG card. They brought the ones who had raised their hands over to the Director who would decide which actor he wanted. I smiled a big smile, cool, calm and collective. Inside I'm sweating bullets! I knew I lied, (don't tell my grandmother) that I could get into big trouble, but hey, I'm a punk kid from Brooklyn with a chance to play a SAG role, so I'm winging it. I mean how did actors like Humphrey Bogart and James Cagney get it? They probably did the same thing. Please, don't hold it against me. The Director walks up and down, spots me and asks if I can do dialogue. Of course, I can do dialogue. I said to myself, what are you kidding Steven? I've never done dialogue in my life, holy shit, I'm digging myself into a deeper hole here. So I tell him yes and he asks my name. I tell him it's Steven. Steven Lambert. He nods at me and then turns to his assistant. He says something and the assistant calls for me to step forward. I couldn't believe it! I try to compose myself. I know I lied, I know I've never done dialogue before and have no idea how much they are going to give me. The assistant tells me to wait for a moment, and I'm shaking, thinking I'm going to get caught in my lie. He comes back and tells me I got the job. He says, "come with me," and I follow him to the Production Office. I wait outside and he comes back with a piece of paper and I look at it and see my dialogue. I'll never forget it. The line was, "she had everything she needed in all the right places." I had no idea what it meant or what it tied into.

So he took me to Wardrobe and gave me a bathing suit and then told me to come to the beach. The story was about a girl who jumped off a pier into shallow water and became a paraplegic and became a famous artist who drew with the paintbrush in her mouth. The scene is that she is drowning and I see her and run to the pier. I jump feet first and rescue her. The jump was about six feet into two feet of water. I did my ninja Martial Arts, jumped, came crashing into the water and landed perfectly. The Director liked it and they moved on. I was in about twenty five shots. Running down the pier, getting up on the sand, rescuing her, wide shots, close ups, different angles. I was now the hero of the movie. The more they did, the more I'm getting nervous. No one is saying anything. Lunch goes by, dinner goes by, I'm still working and I still hadn't done my dialogue. At the end of the day, they told me they want me back for another day to do my line. The next day, the P.A. takes me to a room. "Whose room is this?" I asked.

"It's yours," he tells me. My mouth dropped open. I get a room? It wasn't only a room. It was a huge trailer with a bed, TV, toilet all in one. I'm an actor on a show, I got my SAG card. How about that? I'm on top of the world Mom. "Yes, Cagney." Oh shit, I hope they don't catch me. Actor Steven Lambert swirled around in my head. He hands me a SAG contract and I can't believe what is happening. Too late to turn back, I filled it out and when I came to the section where I had to put in my SAG card number, I put in my SEG number. I'm thinking maybe I got away with not having my SAG card. Boy, was I wrong. I go out and I'm eating breakfast and the Second Assistant comes over and says the First Assistant wants to talk to me. I felt a chill down my spine. You can call it Spidey sense, but Spidey wasn't really around, except for Freddy Waugh. Inside joke for those who know. Well, when I got there, I could tell they had fire in their eyes from twenty feet away. I could tell they were pissed. "Lambert," the Producer yelled.

"Yes sir," I smiled back, hoping I wouldn't be dragged off the set.

"I just talked to the Screen Actors Guild," he said through gritted teeth. "You ain't one of them!" Now before you think you know what happened next, I got very lucky here. You see, they had sent the paperwork in late and they had already filmed a full day of me. They had a lot of footage and they couldn't just redo it.

"You lied to us," the First Assistant Director steamed. I shook my head very innocently, and in my head was trying to get myself out of this situation.

"Huh? No, I didn't. I am SAG," I replied very gingerly. The Producer looked like he was ready to have a stroke.

"The Guild said you aren't! Let's see your card then," he snapped. I knew I didn't have a SAG card, but if I played dumb, they just might buy it. I can't believe how quickly I was thinking, that's the Brooklyn in me, the streets. I reached for my wallet and pull out my SEG, Screen Extras Guild card. He takes it, looks at it and throws it on the ground. "That's not your SAG card you dummy. That's your SEG card."

I pretended to look as innocent as I could and shook my head. "Oh, I didn't know. I thought it was the same thing." He goes on to tell me that they are two different things, and I should know the difference. I tell them I am new to this thing and didn't know there was a difference. The Producer looked at the First Assistant Director and they conferred. "We would love to fire your ass, kid. But because we shot the whole day with you, we will give you a SAG card." I couldn't believe it. That's the ingenuity of the Brooklyn Kid.

CHAPTER 6
(Bette Midler, She Was As High As The Sky.)

Not too long after that, I got another call from Carl Joy asking me if I wanted to work on a movie called *The Rose* starring Bette Midler. I told him that I wasn't doing extra work anymore and he said it wasn't extra work, it was a bodyguard position. Bodyguard? That was the last thing I thought Central Casting would ask me to do. I asked who I was body guarding. Carl said, "Bette Midler." I couldn't believe it. She was the star of the show. Carl went on to tell me that they were going to be doing a concert scene, but instead of extras as concert patrons, they were going to use real people attending a real concert. Now you have to understand this was something that was just not done in Hollywood. Not only would there be real people in the scene, but they were allowing them to drink as well. It's pretty unbelievable. They wanted me and a couple of others to protect Mrs. Midler in case things got out of hand and they were going to pay me five hundred dollars. Carl said he asked Stuntmen Tom Elliot and Rick Kahana and they agreed to do it as well. So I said yes and the next thing I know, I'm on the set watching all these wild party animals, who weren't professional extras. The Assistant Director is explaining where we stand, where Mrs. Midler enters, where the fans are going to be and I'm thinking in my head, this is going to be crazy. You see real fans are not like extras, they don't behave and Bette Midler at that time was a wild child if you know what I mean. She was just as eager to drink as her fans. Yes, she was a wild woman, but a great one. Very heavy on the alcohol and drugs, as everybody knew. We get introduced to the other bodyguards and these guys were five times the size of us. My mind shot back to memories of Jeffrey Elkins, you know young King Kong. These guys were King Kong all grown up. I was the tallest, followed by Rick and Tom. These were muscle men and they stared at the three of us who looked like we were eighteen years old. One of them grunted and another one laughed. Suddenly, the five animal styles kicked in again and I- just kidding. We greeted them and went to our positions below the stage. Some of them were nice sober people that just wanted to have a good time. Others were doing cocaine, smoking pot or drinking booze. I look at Rick Kahana, I'm pushing people back and he is kicking people back. It reminded me of the times I was invited to work at the Tennessee Gin and Cotton restaurant.

An awful lot of stuntmen worked there as bodyguards. Tough guys who wanted to be stuntmen. Billy Lucas, Bobby Mclaughlin, Rick Kahana, Big Black and many more. When somebody did something in the restaurant that was deserving of an expulsion, if they didn't get out, they would have to suffer the wrath of these guys and simply get punched out. They would wait for that to happen and enjoy it and they got paid for punching. It was an unbelievable time. The concert was supposed to be about Janis Joplin, but instead of calling it Janis Joplin they called *it The Rose*. People knew it was a movie so they were trying desperately to get on stage. They didn't care, they were all a bunch of wild maniacs. AsI said, they weren't professional extras. There is a big difference. Bette Midler arrives in a helicopter and is lowered down onto the stage. We start pushing people back and trying to keep them off of the stage. Then they yell, "cut." Extras would stop and listen for their next set of directions. Drunk, riled up, high on cocaine fans could care less. It was like playing Whack-A-Mole. Every time someone popped up, you would have to push them back down before another head popped up. Bette Midler made it worse by provoking everybody by cursing and drinking. Now, this is funny. Eventually, Bette Midler had to take a break and use the telephone which was around the corner of the set. They approached me and asked if I could follow her down because she has to use the phone. I found it funny it was a payphone. So I say okay and follow her along with a sea of Production Assistants in tow. Well as we arrive, she turns around and looks at me up and down as she is smiling with that sweet wonderful face. Wildly, she asks me, "Who are you?"

"I'm your bodyguard," I explain.

She smiled. "You, bodyguard me?"

I nodded. "I'm a Martial Artist."

She reached out and touched my cheek. "You're such a sweet boy."

I blushed and pushed the crazy concert patrons away from the phone booth.

(Right after the collect call. Wanting to know if she needed more alcohol.)

It's not every day Bette Midler calls someone sweet. So if you ever see this movie, *The Rose*, just remember this story. It was wild. I'll never forget that.

CHAPTER 7

(Imagine Meeting Fred Williamson, Jim Brown And Jim Kelly.)

Around this time, the Hollywood Reporter and Variety had breakdowns of films that were going into Production. I called the Production Manager on one of the films and asked if I could come in and see if I could coordinate the show. They said okay, so I went in not knowing anything about the show except it was starring Fred Williamson, Jim Brown and Jim Kelly. Three badass guys in the movies. It was called *One Down, Two To Go*. I entered and the Production Manager told me to wait there for a moment. Now mind you, I look like a fifteen year old kid, even though I was around twenty two. I wonder what she was thinking as she came back out and told me that Fred Williamson would see me now. My eyes bulged out of their sockets. Fred Williamson? He was a huge NFL player back in the day. The Muhammad Ali of Football. Maybe not of talent, but of mouth. They called him "The Hammer." I walked into the office and there he was, big as life. There was Fred Williamson, with his feet on the desk, cigar in his mouth. Out of the corner of my eye, I notice another person sitting in a big leather chair. I'm not sure who he is. I catch a glimpse of another person sitting in a wooden chair to his left. I think to myself, that looks like Jim Kelly from *Enter The Dragon*. One of the luckiest Martial Artists who got to work with Bruce Lee. I introduce myself to Fred politely. "Hello. Fred. My name is Steven."

Fred takes a puff of his cigar and puts an oven mitt of a hand out. "Hello, Steve-o."
I told him how wonderful it was to meet him. He then points over to the leather chair, almost like a fancy couch and explains he wants me to meet the man sitting there. Jim Brown. I couldn't believe it. He was a player for the Cleveland Browns. "Hello Mister Brown," I said. Then he points to the man in the chair and says this is Jim Kelly.

(This movie was originally called Three The Hard Way and boy, were they cool.)

"I know you," I replied. He smiles. I didn't know why I had called them by their last names, maybe it was out of sheer respect. That was something my Mom and Grandmother taught me.

Here I was, a punk kid from Brooklyn, surrounded by two famous NFL players and a legendary Martial Artist. Fred Williamson asks me to sit down so I do, and I tell them about my interest in running the show, getting the script, reading it and breaking it down. I would then tell them how much the action would cost. Fred Williamson smiled and asked me to tell a bit about myself. "I'm a punk kid from Brooklyn."

He stops me and says, "I know, that's a little obvious."
Brown and Kelly laugh. I continue. "I'm a stuntman, I have a few years in the business. A lot of big names are working me, they see something in me. I'm an athlete, I won some awards in athleticism as well as some Martial Arts awards." It was all spur of the moment, I told them the truth. Fred nods and asks me what style I study. I told him Kung Fu. He then asked me who my teacher was and I told him Douglas Wong from Sil-Lum Kung Fu.

(Fred Williamson said he took Tae Kwan Do. Kung Fu was for sissys. I said, we can have fun and fight.)

Fred Williamson shook his head and pursed his lips. "No, I don't know him," he stated. He then looked over at Jim Brown and asked if he knew him. He shook his head and said he had never heard of him. Well, shoot. Here I was trying to impress these superstars and I've already struck out twice. I turned to Jim Kelly and asked him if he knew who Curtis Wong was from "Inside Kung Fu" magazine. Jim slowly began to shake his head and then his eyes lit up. "Oh yeah!" He exclaimed. Jim went on to tell how he knew Curtis through the magazine and that Sil-Lum Kung Fu was the real deal. He realized who Douglas Wong was. Fred, Jim Kelly and I started talking about different fights and then we got into stunt doubles. We talked about who we doubled individually and I told Fred that I had been thinking about who could double in the film for him. I mentioned names such as Bob Minor, Tony Brubaker and Alan Oliney. These were all great stuntmen, which I knew they all were familiar with. Now Bob Minor had doubled for Jim Brown and Tony Brubaker had doubled Fred Williamson in the past. I was going to use Alan Oliney to double Jim Kelly. That was my plan. He had heard of Alan Oliney but had never worked with him. Jim Brown thought the names over in his head and looked right at me. "Bob Minor, you said?" I nodded with confidence, thinking that would give me brownie points. Jim frowned.

"Yeah, he used to double for me but he thinks he is an actor now, so why don't you find somebody else." I was shocked at this announcement. The smile faded fast, but I quickly regained my composure. "Sure. Whatever happens, there will be no problem," I replied. My mind was quickly trying to catch up to what was just said and the gravity of this amazing situation I found myself in. "What about Tony Brubaker?" I asked. Fred said that he was all right. I let out a breath of fresh air. Fred then asked me if I did a lot of Martial Arts. I told him I had a lot of trophies from tournaments and was hired by many stuntmen. Fred nods and asks if I could throw a few kicks. In my mind, I couldn't believe what I was hearing. I get to show off to Fred Williamson? This was unreal. I get up to do as he says when from my left, I hear another voice. "Throw a few kicks at me, throw a few at my hand." I turn and Jim Kelly is standing there in a defensive position. I froze for a moment. Is this really happening? A Martial Arts legend wants me to demonstrate on him? "Come on, throw three kicks," Jim Kelly urged. I nodded and I threw three kicks. A step up side kick, an outside crescent and a whip kick. Each kick I hit his hand with precision. Fred sat back down and considered what he had just seen. I waited with excitement for his reply. Finally, with his cigar in his mouth, he spoke. He told me, "Not bad. We'll get back to you." And then the next sentence I didn't quite understand. He said, "if we give you this show, I'm the Stunt Coordinator and you're my assistant."

"Sure!" I said not really listening. Now an established stuntman would have said, "hell no, I'm the Stunt Coordinator." But I was just a punk kid from Brooklyn. I wasn't smart enough to realize the opportunity I had. Another lesson. I figured I would deal with that when the time came. I walked out of the office with the biggest smile on my face. I thought to myself, I can say I threw kicks at Jim Kelly, ya know. A kid like me. Who would have thought? That night I got a call saying I was on the show as Fred's Assistant. I felt wonderful and knew this was a huge opportunity to show off my knowledge. I called my good friend Bob Minor up, laughing. "Bob, wait until you hear this." I told him that I had just had a conversation with Jim Brown and wasn't sure how to say this. Before I could even continue, Bob Minor said he knew Jim didn't want to use him as his stunt double anymore. He had gotten a few roles and Jim, believe it or not, became jealous. Bob told me I didn't have to use him, and I thanked him for that, being we were very close friends. I called Tony Brubaker and asked if he would be a stunt double and he said of course. So that is how it went down.

CHAPTER 8
(My First Movie Mentor And Fantasy Island.)

After *One Down, Two To Go,* as luck was with me, I got a call from the man himself who ran stunts for *Fantasy Island*. Roy Harrison aka Snuffy. I was overjoyed. Finally, I get a chance. He explained to me that I would be replacing Buddy Joe Hooker, a very famous stuntman from an organization called Stunts Unlimited. He had to go on another job, leaving the opportunity open for me. Little did I realize, it just might have been that he wasn't as crazy as I was if you can believe that. I would be doubling Ken Berry. It was my first big opportunity with Roy Harrison. The scene was in Medieval Times and Ken Barry was a knight looking for his woman in a castle. They had a giant spiral staircase and the bottom floor was cement. On the bottom floor, there was a coat rack with a coat and a fedora hat with shoes on the floor. I didn't ask why they had a coat rack in Medieval times, but this was *Fantasy Island* after all. They explained to me that the coat rack was supposed to be mistaken for the bad guy. They needed someone to jump two stories as Ken Barry, do a head first dive roll, land on the breakaway coat rack, roll forward and come up struggling with the coat on top of them. They would then struggle with the coat thinking it was a person and they were fighting them. (Me personally, this is why Buddy Joe hooker turned it down. Two stories, head first on solid cement just ain't done. But I am going to do it. Successfully, I thought to myself.) I was used to diving twelve feet without a pad and dive roll to the ground and come up like it was nothing. I had no problem with this stunt. Roy Harrison thought I was nuts and the rest of the crew thought I was going to kill myself. But I knew I could do it. I learned five things in my life that all athletes should know. Timing, coordination, distance, focus and power of the mind. "This kid is going to split his head open," I heard one of the crew members saying. I shook my head and knew I might get banged up, but I would come out of this alive. I could try and tell them that, but these guys wouldn't believe me. I had to show them. I went over it again and again in my mind and finally was ready to do it. I only had one take and that's what I intended to do.

They yelled, "action" and I jumped. I hit the coat rack perfectly. When I did the dive roll, my hands and arms took most of the abuse. My head side scraped the cement floor rolling out of it so hard, it bounced off of it and literally knocked me out for a split second. But I had practiced the gag so much in my head that even while I was knocked out, I was still moving my arms with the coat over me until the Director yelled, "cut." That's called muscle memory. It works even when you are out. That's when I came to. I knew I had been knocked out but no one else on the crew could tell because I had the coat over me. They all stood there with their mouths open in disbelief. I was happy, I fooled them all. Nobody knew I was out for a split second. Roy Harrison came over to me and looked at me over his glasses and said that he knew I got knocked out. "You were out."

I shook my head. "No, I wasn't."

He continued his look. "Yes, you were."

I tried to deny it but he just knew. Again, for those who knew Snuffy, the eyeglasses move came. He tilted his head down and looked over his glasses. I had to tell him the truth. I said, "How the hell did you know?" He simply said to me, "I know everything." A quick grin.

I smiled and realized that the gag was a success. Everyone was applauding as I was getting up. The word spread like wildfire in the coming days. Every top stuntman I hustled at Warner Brothers and Universal, told me they had heard what I did and I felt I was on my way. So that really put me on the map with Ronnie Rondell, Tommy Huff, Roy Harrison and Stunts Unlimited. They were all there and saw me. What I believe happened in a fun way just to let you know, my thoughts have always been that Snuffy called Buddy Joe Hooker and said I got this crazy kid who would do a dive roll from two stories on cement. And knowing a little bit about Buddy Joe Hooker, he simply said, "let the stupid f*** do it."

I began to work a lot for Stunts Unlimited, Ronnie Rondell and Roy Harrison. In my second year with Stunts Unlimited, I had worked non- stop for them. I did dozens of episodes of *Fantasy Island*. I met and worked with many different stuntmen from Stunts Unlimited, Stuntmen's Association, as well as Independent stuntmen. So that's how I started my career on *Fantasy Island*. I worked many times with Ricardo Montalban on the set, who was a real class act. He was just like you saw him in every movie. Even when the camera was off, he was very respectful and elegant. Whenever you talked to him, he would listen intently. I remember I talked to him once about physical abilities. Now growing up in Brooklyn, I would always see him in his movies, watching with my grandfather and father. He was always doing big physical stuff. Playing a Matador or a tough guy, doing fight scenes, dancing, etc. When someone is an athlete and a Martial Artist, you can tell by the way they carry themselves. That's what I thought about him when I saw the movies that he had worked in. When we talked, he told me he was a boxer and took Judo when he was a kid in his country. That really helped establish a connection between us, in that we each had our own Martial Art. Every time he saw me, he would rise to the occasion and say hello to me with his fists up like a fighter. You see the way you walk and present yourself, it could be a way you make a simple gesture with your hand, a true Martial Artist is able to tell a person's physical ability. You athletes and Martial Artists out there know what I am trying to say. It gave me satisfaction that I was right in suspecting he did some sort of fighting in his life. We talked about Brooklyn, he in his matador like elegance since he lived in New York when he was trying to make it as a movie star. We were able to relate to each other. Whenever he saw me on set, he would come over and say hello in his own unique and gentleman like way. I felt like I was in a movie whenever I spoke with him, it was like being in a Shakespeare movie, but everything out of his mouth felt sincere. Bigger than life. I always had a smile on my face. I would like to take a moment and acknowledge Roy Harrison and Ronnie Rondell. These are two stuntmen, old school is the best school, two of the people who took me under their wing. They taught me a lot that would come into play for *Fantasy Island.*

For Instance, I was working on a show called *Hart To Hart* and Ronnie would ask me to do a stunt and I would tell him I don't need that pad or this mat because I knew what I could do safely. For example, I knew if you ran through glass you wouldn't get cut unless you stopped. Another time I was doubling these army men with many other stuntmen there for a *Fantasy Island* shoot. They had a rope like a tightrope I was supposed to walk across, and I had never tightrope walked in my life. However, I did have my Kung Fu skills and awareness of balance, so I did it successfully where all the others weren't. They were all amazed, so I wound up playing multiple characters doing it. I began working with Stunts Unlimited and doing all these things I come to find that stuntmen would never do, physically and performance wise, in the way I was performing it. And then I came to realize it was all because of my Martial Arts. Few stuntmen at this time had the training that I had. I would do a bullet hit on *Fantasy Island*, all the other stuntmen would seem to take it on their feet and fall backward. Me? I would do a jumping double kick reaching six feet high in midair and when I got to my max height, I would simply lean back and fall six feet to the floor, right on my back. All the stunt people couldn't believe it. I called that the "Lambo Leap." To me, it was a simple double kick and before I reached my peak, I would turn in the air and land on my back and do a back fall. These stuntmen had never seen anything like that. No pads except elbows and knees. Sometimes, not even that. I'm giving you these little examples you learn in Martial Arts. How to fall.

One time I fought Hulk on the TV show. He pushes me and I do a kick and I get really high. Most people would use a ratchet and fall back on a pad, but not me. My back was used to it from Martial Arts, in a good way already, so I landed right on the ground. Other Stunt Coordinators always loved that move. Going back to

Fantasy Island, it was a joy working with Ricardo Montalban and Herve Villechaize. Herve was one funny little guy and very mischievous. Here is a funny fact for you. For those of you who remember *Fantasy Island* and the beautiful Hawaiian girls that came out, Herve would always be there to look at the girls and may I say, pinch their behinds and other places I can't even tell you. Use your own imagination. Yes, those rumors are true. They practically had to put a fence around him. For some people, they may not find that too funny, but I always thought it was hilariously inappropriate. Listen to this. To keep him out of trouble, production would buy him all sorts of toys. Like bows and arrows, mini bikes, even ponies. Instead of pacifying Herve, he would only become more of a trickster. He would shoot the arrows at some of the guest stars, vehicles and even us stunt people. But never Ricardo Montalban. There was a big time respect there. He would always behave himself in front of that man. He didn't understand you could hurt somebody. He would try to run people over with the mini bikes and the crew would go crazy because they couldn't catch him. With his ponies, he would go off for an unscheduled ride and production would never be able to find him. He loved hanging around stunt people, we fascinated him.

Well, it just so happened I started dating one of the girls on the show who was a regular Hawaiian girl extra. We started going out for a few months and I really enjoyed her company. She was wild and crazy but we won't talk about that either. Little did I know, Herve had asked her out and was dating her on the side. She was playing me. Stuntman against TV star. A little one at that, haha.

(Stuntman versus TV star. Herve Villechaize stole my girlfriend to the left.)

Well when I found out, I couldn't believe it. The little guy got my girl. I said to myself, what the hell is this all about? Well, in this case, I won't go into detail but let me say I broke up with her. Just in time too, as Herve married the girl soon after. Let me tell you, the smallest things come with the biggest surprises. Laugh if you like. Many years later, they got a divorce and she got all his money. Glad it wasn't me. I remember one episode I was working on *Matt Houston*, doubling Sonny Bonno. Remember him from Sonny and Cher? Yes, the same one. I doubled him many times. I was supposed to rescue Zsa Zsa Gabor from a swimming pool. Remember her? The TV show *Green Acres*? We rehearsed it a few times without Zsa Zsa. I have to run over several obstacles to get to the pool and rescue her. When we did the actual shot, she begins to drift into the deep end without anyone realizing it, away from the shallow side of the pool. All of a sudden, she starts yelling that she can't swim! The scene was that I come out of the house, jumping over many obstacles to rescue her. As I was doing that, she was drifting more to the deep end screaming she couldn't swim. Cameras were still rolling. Nobody knew and she didn't tell anybody. I finally got to the pool and jumped in with about an eight foot leap before I splashed down two feet away from her. I'm underwater taking a couple of strokes towards her. I reach her and I grab her. We are in the middle of the deep end. All of a sudden like an octopus, her hands wrap around my head still underwater. I'm trying to get up to get a breath but I can't. Her legs are kicking me, her fingernails are scratching my face, bubbles are coming out of my mouth. I finally reach the edge of the pool with her fingers across my eyes, reaching out of the water to grab the edge of the pool. Pulling myself up and gasping for breath as her screams were still going, I couldn't believe what just happened. Some of the company grabbed her and pulled her out, flopping her on the floor like a beached whale. She looked me in the eye as I spit up a half a pint of water. Still on her back on the floor, she was thanking me for rescuing her. I had no idea it was for real. Pretty funny experience. I'm huffing and puffing, scratches all over me and Snuffy walks over. He looks me up and down. "You just rescued her," he said with a smirk. I pull myself out of the pool, dripping wet. "I know, she almost drowned me," I sputtered.

Snuffy shrugs, looking over his glasses, never batting an eye. "Well I could have just gotten another stuntman if that were the case," he added before walking away. Yep, that was the way Snuffy cracked jokes. Another time, they were shooting an episode in the middle of winter in the San Francisco Bay. Snuffy called me up and said they were taking me to San Francisco. It was my first on location shoot. Free food, free travel. It is a night shot in the middle of winter right under the golden gate bridge. I mean literally under, like in the water. The freeze your ass off before the rest of your body touches it kind of water. Luckily, I brought a wetsuit. Now I had no idea what I was going to be doing. Snuffy likes to keep people he liked a lot in the dark, it was his way of having fun. He would never put you in any danger, but he would enjoy seeing you sweat trying to figure it out. That was Snuffy, he's the best. So we get there and Wardrobe comes out and I'm expecting to get clothes. All I get is a pair of underwater! I walk over to Snuffy and I mention it to him. "Snuffy, I can't wear my wetsuit, the water is freezing it's just underwear!" He looks above his glasses, with that one special look only he has and uttered those famous words, "no Shit Sherlock!" Then Snuffy tells me I am playing a dead body in the water. Believe it or not, I hate cold water. If I have clothes on and I am warm no big deal. But just underwear!? I have thin blood and I'm skinny. No body fat to keep me warm and I'm supposed to play a dead body staying perfectly still. I thought to myself, of all the stunts why did they have to pick this one? So production asks if we want to rehearse and Snuffy laughed. "Rehearse? He's playing a dead body. What's so hard about that? Shoot it," Snuffy said.

So I go to this little ladder at the back of the boat and the character is wearing boxers but they gave me something else to wear underneath it so nothing else was exposed. Snuffy is towards the back on the boat and I put my toes in and thought, "oh, this is miserable!" You out there, you know the worst part is getting past your crouch. It takes me forever if you know what I mean, at least it seems like that, to get that far. Mind you, everyone is waiting on me and here I am putting my dainty little toes in the water. You tell me to get hit by a car. No hesitation. Boom! It's done. Tell me to break through glass. Smash! Finished. But tell me to get into freezing cold water in my underwear? Give me a moment, or never. Snuffy gets impatient and decides it would just be faster to push me in. So that's exactly what he does. He walks over, I look up and what do you think he does? He puts his foot on my chest and pushes. Splash! I'm in and trying hard not to go into shock, making funny girl sounds. Nothing against girls, please. I had to swim away from the boat so the camera wouldn't pick up any waves or anything from the boat's wake. I get about twenty feet and they tell me to lay on my back. They call, "action" and I can't stay still. I'm doing the San Francisco shake, moving more than Elvis Presley, which is a no-no if you're supposed to be a dead body. Finally the Director cuts. He takes his bullhorn and yells out. "You are supposed to be dead Steven. What is with all the flopping around?" He turns to Snuffy and asks, "what's wrong with your stunt guy, he is moving." I tried to apologize but they just rolled again. They were quite resilient. I had to try something to make this scene work. I yelled back at the Director and asked what if we pretended it was the ocean and there were waves. That would be an excuse for my movements. The Director furrowed his brow and looked down and says to everybody, "the damn kid can't even play dead underwater and now he is telling me how to direct!?" I felt so helpless at that moment. I looked at Snuffy and he made me feel smaller by giving me the eyeglass routine again. He just nodded his head. He understood but you bet he wasn't going to speak up in my defense. Never got a good shot out of that, but thankfully Snuffy let me continue to work for him.

(Twenty two years old, playing an eighty year old with Roy "Snuffy" Harrison.)

Everyone thought it was funny and word got out quick. It took them nineteen more takes before they finally gave up and decided to use what they have. I thought my career was over. They got a wuss when it came to cold water, what was I going to do? Whenever I saw someone that knew what happened they would do the Freezin' Steven. They would shake rattle and roll and what could I do? I would just shake my head and smile. One of my few embarrassing moments. Stuntman Greg Barnett (which at that time doubled Robert Wagner *on Hart to Hart*) saw me and would wiggle around saying, "hey brother, I he heard you wo worked in the wa water." Yeah, they all thought it was a good joke. Luckily, they knew it was a humorous thing and could happen to anybody. It was never the kind of thing that affected my career. Everybody has their Achilles heel, in this case, keep my skinny ass the hell away from cold water and I'll be fine.

Let's put a movie in between this TV talk. *Curse Of The Dragon Lady*. I am doubling a freaking icon. Roddy McDowall. *Lassie Comes Home, My Friend Flicka,* and *Planet of The Apes*. I am just tickled to death. The First day on set, Stunt Coordinator Richard Washington showed me a wheelchair.

It was a motorized wheelchair. He asked if I knew how to drive a motorcycle and I told him, "sure I can." He explained I would be doing a chase on the wheelchair and I said, "oh, that sounds like a lot of fun." He then introduced me to the icon. I introduce myself and said, "man, I can't tell you what it means working with an actor like you. How Green Is My Valley, what a great film!"

We shake hands and that was it. The day comes when I am doing this wheelchair chase and we shoot it on this long driveway. I am chasing this nineteen thirties car down the driveway. I got the wheelchair to about thirty five miles per hour.

It was real dangerous and sometimes I was only on two wheels. After the scene was over, I was eating lunch with Richard Washington when Roddy came by with his food and asked if he could sit with us. Of course we told him he could!

He told me how scary it looked as I was going down that driveway and saw that I was tipping on two wheels at certain times. He asked if it was planned and I told him, "no, you don't plan things like that it just happens. You have to know and feel what you are doing and just go with it and hope you don't kill yourself." He laughed.

(Stunt doubling the legend, Roddy McDowell.)

I told him my Martial Arts background and he was instantly hooked. He told me that he had taken Judo as a kid. "Just like James Cagney," I laughed.

His eyes got real wide. "Oh, you know Mister Cagney?" he asked. Here is an old guy calling Cagney, "Mister." I thought it was different. We got along great as the days went by. One day, Roddy and I happened to be sitting together. "May I ask you a few questions about some of the movies you worked in?" I inquired.

"Ask away Steven," he assured me.

I took a deep breath and asked, "What was it like working with Lassie?"

He looked at me and smiled. "I'll tell you something I never told anybody. I don't think there were ever as many cuts as there was in that film."

I looked at him and said, "what do you mean?"

He said, "that damn dog spoiled so many great scenes because he shit and pissed every five minutes."

I laughed and laughed. "The movie My Friend Flicka, what was the hardest thing working on that film?"

He looked at me and said, "that God damn horse spoiled every scene in the movie."

Again, I asked him why.

"He would shit and piss in every great scene, they had to cut all the time," he said.

Well, we both laughed again. He said it so matter of fact, it was hilarious.

"Okay, what about working on Planet Of The Apes? What was that like?"

Roddy nodded. "That God damn costume. I spoiled some good scenes. I had to have them cut all the time so I could get my costume off to go shit and piss."

I nearly fell to the floor with laughter and so did he. What a great and funny story from the legendary Roddy McDowall. I must tell you actors like Roddy McDowall from the forties and fifties have a way about them. A different way, unlike the actors of today. Class, humor, an aura of a time long gone. Moving on.

CHAPTER 9
(Mister Pink Gi, Gene Lebell And Brandon)

Another time, Ronnie Rondell called me on a TV show called *Hart To Hart* and asked me if I knew who Gene Lebell was. Of course I did! He said you are going to be playing an American spy and he will be playing a Russian spy on *Hart to Hart*. You out there, remember that show with Robert Wagner? Speaking of him, the first day we worked, I walked over to him and introduced myself. During the conversation I said may I ask you one personal question? He said sure. I said what was it like working with Fred Astaire on *It Takes A Thief*, the T.V. show? He said four simple words with a smile. "It was cool, baby." Now that's style. Wagner is one of the kings of cool, wouldn't you say? Moving on, there is this huge action sequence in this giant mansion. I told him, of course, I would do it. The scene was that the Russian spy was going to defeat the American spy, in other words, Gene Lebell was going to kick my ass. So I arrive on set and Ronnie is going over the fight scene. They have three vases in this fight sequence. One three foot vase, one five foot vase and one six foot vase. Now I thought Gene was going to throw me into the vases. Okay, no problem I thought. Then we move onto a breakaway table. We would fight, fight, fight and then he would throw me head first into the table. After that, I would get back up and we would fight some more and then he would pick me up and throw me ten feet into a large breakaway display case full of breakaway shelves and trophies. So my boss tells us to work out the fight in between and we start practicing it. Gene loves to throw punches, he don't like kicks.

All he wants to do is choke you out. You have to constantly tell him it's not in the script. He is a grappler first and foremost. So we get to the vases and we go over it and I am getting ready to go head first and Ronnie says that Gene isn't going to throw me into the vase, he is going to pick me up and stuff me into the vase headfirst. I look at the hole which isn't that wide and I ask if he means if he is going to stuff me head first, pile drive me into the air? Ronnie smiles. Oh great, I thought. The three foot one isn't so bad, the five foot vase is okay, but the six foot one, that one left me scratching my head. How am I going to get up there without being airborne? We roll camera and Gene picks me up and stuffs me into the first vase. When I say stuff, anybody who knows Gene Lebell knows what I am talking about. It shatters and I am on the ground all contorted. I get back up and we start fighting again. More punches, more kicks. Then he grabs me, lifts me a little higher and body slams me into the five footer, headfirst into the hole. He put my head in there perfectly, my feet were in the air above me. I'm disoriented and trying to keep it together. Fighting with Gene is like fighting a freaking bear and gorilla at the same time and I'm the lamb-ert of course. So I get back up again and fight some more and Gene grabs me to throw me above the six footer and I'm telling you I was airborne like he was doing a layup in basketball. He released me and with one hand guided me, I swear I was seven feet tall and flew above that six foot vase and right into the open hole. Bullseye. I came down like a sack of potatoes, just eating it onto the floor. I barely get back up again with the help of my nemesis, the red haired maniac and we punch and kick over to the breakaway table. He grabs me and body slams me into the table.

Now, he could have let go and I would have fallen through, but Gene wanted to continue with me on my trip through the shattering glass, so he didn't let go until I was on the ground, oof! The wind knocked out of me. I'm on the floor, getting beat up pretty badly and I pick myself back up and fight Gene some more. We get ready for the last "hoorah," the breakaway display case. I'm delirious. He picks me up and lifts me over his head, full extension. I found myself dangling sideways in the air, right underneath him. So he takes one step and launches me. Like a monkey in a catapult, oy vey! I'm off, flying towards the breakaway display case. I didn't realize how hard he threw me and I start sailing through the air like a rubber ball, sideways, full spread about seven feet high. I'm supposed to hit the display case and fall to the floor. Instead, he threw me so hard that I got stuck! Literally, stuck. Wiggling and squirming, trying to get out and fall with the cameras rolling, I realize that I can't. The more I try, the more seconds go by that I realize I'm stuck like a nail in a wall. Five seconds go by and then ten seconds go by. I start to hear people behind the cameras yelling to "get out." I speak out trying to cover up my words, saying I can't! Then everybody starts laughing. Then the Director yelled, "cut!" I still couldn't get down, they had to come over and pry me out. All this time, that gorilla Gene is having the time of his life watching the monkey get stuck. Since we are on that red headed old man that wears a pink gi, yes for those of you who don't know Gene - YES a pink gi, who in their right mind would wear something like that? Who in their right mind would point that out to him? Me. Next time you see Gene, ask him who is the only one that is allowed on his mats with shoes? You heard it. ME. Let's have fun and tell a few more stories about Gene. These are the ones that stand out and are exceptional.

One day my good friend Mike Vendrell called me and said he wanted Brandon Lee to meet Gene Lebell. I had yet to meet Brandon and was excited to meet him as well. He also told me Bernie Pock was going to be there, who was a good friend of ours too. Mind you, Bernie was a great stuntman and Martial Artist. Bernie's mother was a big star named Nancy Kwan, she did *the Flower Drum Song,* a very famous movie. He was Michael J. Fox's original stunt double in *Teen Wolf.* So, of course, I said absolutely. I get to the LA city college's gymnasium early and Brandon Lee walks in. Now everyone knows Brandon, he is the son of Bruce Lee. Mike, Bernie Pock and Brandon all arrive and Mike introduces me to Brandon. Then Gene arrives a few minutes later to teach his class. The mood changes. He starts to teach his class, which we do every Monday night. Stuntmen, athletes and Martial Artists all came to this class. Mike, Bernie and I are Gene Lebell's assistants. We walk over to where Gene is and I'm watching Mike introduce Brandon Lee, Bruce Lee's son to Gene. Being the people watcher that I am, I sit back to watch and enjoy. It was an amazing moment. Gene starts talking about Bruce and reassures Brandon to make him feel comfortable by saying, "your pop and I were very good friends. He was a skinny toothpick like this guy over here." He points to me and we all laugh, including Brandon to my surprise. Much, much respect. As we walk over to where all the students are on the other side of the gym, I'm thinking this is very cool. Gene continues the class and all the students sit down including Brandon which I thought was very interesting simply being he was Bruce Lee's son. Mike, Bernie and I are standing next to Gene as black belts would do. Usually, Gene would have me and Mike and Bernie go through some techniques and exercises. We would pick people to stand up and work on techniques with them. I couldn't believe a punk kid from Brooklyn was teaching Bruce Lee's son. Let me say that later on, I found out at this time, believe it or not, Brandon wasn't that fully knowledgeable in Martial Arts. This caught me off guard as we all have seen pictures of him training with his father. Before we started the class, Mike quietly imparted to me that Brandon wasn't really knowledgeable and skilled in Martial Arts. Believe me, at this time, very few people knew this about Brandon. I looked back at him confused. The son of Bruce Lee? Are you kidding me? He also told me that he was a pretty shy guy.

After our techniques and exercises, Gene would take over the class and start picking students one by one to grapple with him for two to three minutes. Let me say and all you Martial Artists know this that have worked with Gene, he would only go as hard as you would go. He maintained the status quo. If you were going easy, he would go easy. If you went a little harder, he would go a little harder. If you went hard, then he would stretch your ass out and show you who was boss. It was all up to you. Right?

If you went easy, you would get an easy Gene. If you went a little harder, Gene would begin to make you sweat. If you went all out, may the force be with you. So he picked one student, they did their thing and mate. He picked another student, they did their business and then they mate. A few more went by and they all ended in quick mate, always making students look foolish. Gene loves a happy ending. Then, to my fascination, he picked Brandon. Son of Bruce. Bruce almighty. Not Jim Carey. Gene asks Brandon if he would like to come up and kumite a little bit, which means to freestyle fight for all you novices out there. Brandon says yes and he goes up there and they bow and salute each other.

Now let me say what I'm about to tell you is truly an unbelievable story, but it happened. It really happened. Imagine this. Ten seconds go by and it's easy and they are playing, having fun on their feet. Thirty seconds go by and it's getting a little more intense.

Then a minute goes by and they each start to go a little harder. Brandon is trying to trap Gene and Gene is having no part of it, using his weight and knowledge to keep control. Brandon was a kid at that time, in his early twenties. I was watching Brandon's face after another thirty seconds and it began to change. It seemed like he was possibly getting upset that he was being thrown around and giggled at by the watching students.

Let me say, this wasn't me or Mike or Bernie wrestling with Gene Lebell, this was Brandon, Bruce Lee's son. It seemed to frustrate Brandon and get under his skin. Gene loved to play on that. In return, this seemed to reflect in his attacks. He started going harder in his moves and Gene would answer back equally as strong. In my head I'm going, careful Brandon, don't do that. I looked at Vendrell, worried. He smiled.

(Branden Lee, Gene Lebell, Bernie Pock, Mike Vendrell and Steven Lambert.)

After two minutes it started to get a little more serious. All of a sudden, they were going at each other pretty hard. Back and forth, grappling hard, the fun fight turned into a battle. It seemed like it was real as far as Brandon was concerned. I looked at Mike and Bernie who also had "oh shit" faces on them. Brandon wasn't going to come close to defeating Gene, but that didn't stop him from trying. I hear Mike saying for Brandon to calm down and take it easy, but at this point, he wasn't listening. He was pissed. (That means drunk in Australia. I would say he was drunk on furious frustration.) Gene just had no choice but to pick him up and slam him down onto the mat on the floor. And I mean slam. He got on top of him and wouldn't let him up. You out there who have worked with Gene, you know how it works. He just lays on top of you. It feels like a dead thousand pound gorilla. Brandon's face got red and he started screaming. He was visually and mentally upset! The harder he went, the harder Gene went. I couldn't believe it, I thought I was watching something that was going to end badly. To me and everyone else, it was on. One of the things Gene loves to do was rub his stubbly beard across his opponent's face, and that's painfully embarrassing. Yes, both. That is exactly what he did with Brandon and boy was he screaming. We all know what it feels like when someone with stubble rubs it on your body, especially your face. It doesn't feel good and it could be humiliating. At the same time, Gene was telling Brandon to give up. All Brandon had to do was mate, which means let go, and you tap your hand on the mat. The more Gene told Brandon to mate, the more we yelled out mate, the harder Brandon went. The kid just wouldn't give up. One minute went by, two minutes, three minutes. Mike, Bernie and I, our eyes were popping out. Brandon was screaming in pain and Gene kept yelling at him to give up. But he wouldn't. Finally, Gene realized it and slowly got up off of a furious Brandon Lee. The first words out of Gene's mouth were, "you are just like your dad. You're so freaking hard headed. You didn't mate."

Brandon looked at him with tears literally running down his cheeks and his rage slowly began to fade into calmness. Brandon let his anger go and nodded. "Thank you," he said. Only four people know of this story. Me, Gene Lebell and God bless, the other two are gone from us. Mike Vendrell and Bernie Pock. That's something I will never forget.

Not too long after this moment in time, Mike Vendrell calls me. He says, "hey, Lambo. I'm doing a tv series called Kung Fu The Next Generation. You are doubling one of my leads. Are you available?" I said, "yes I am."

Vendrell says, "I got a surprise for you. When you get on the set, I'll tell ya. It's a biggie."

And boy, was it. I arrive and he tells me I am fight doubling Brandon Lee. I said, "Brandon Lee, Bruce Lee's son?"

He replied, "yeah, but I have to give you this letter." I looked at the letter and it simply said that everyone on set should not mention Bruce Lee to Brandon. If you do, you will automatically be asked to leave the set. I asked Mike why they were giving everyone this letter. Mike said, "because he still doesn't like anyone mentioning his father." Who would have believed it? To me, this was one of the biggest honors and thrills that I've ever experienced. Fight doubling Brandon Lee. Past present and future, since it hasn't arrived yet.

Brandon's first television show. One of the many discussions I had with Mike was still being so surprised that Brandon Lee really didn't know how to fight. I saw it for myself. I trained him, I taught him the moves. Most of them which I did when it came to putting it on film. Brandon did the close ups and I did all the action. His career was just beginning then, but still, I thought all the years with his father should have taught him something.

I can tell you one thing. Whatever he did after this tv series to get himself up to the caliber of excellence in his first movie, whoever trained him, my hats off to you because it was like night and day. Magnificent. He takes after his father. His movie, *The Crow.* Unforgettable in many ways.

(Mike Vendrell, Brandon Lee and me.)

Here is the story that many of you have been waiting for. A lot of you people over the years have tried or got in contact with me, or some of you have made up your own stories about what really happened. You ask, what really happened about what

CHAPTER 10
(The True Gene Lebell And Steven Segal Story.)

(Hey, let's talk about this. Lebell and Segal. What really happened.)

Well, I am the one to set the record straight. Once and for all through the eyes of the beholder, I will tell you one of Hollywood's true stories. There are hundreds and thousands of people that have heard the story, but the only thing is, they haven't heard the truth. I was there, I know the truth. We were working on a film with Gene Lebell and Steven Segal. At the beginning of the day, another stuntman named Lincoln Simon and I, went to our trailer to get dressed for wardrobe. As we were in our honey wagon, I happened to open the door and as I looked to my left, I saw Gene Lebell just walking over to Steven Segal and his two bodyguards. Gene went over to introduce himself and say hello since they had never met. I watched this about thirty feet away and I looked back at Lincoln Simon and said for him to hurry up. I wanted to see what was going on with Gene and Steven, these two great Martial Artists coming together for the first time. So I hopped out of my honey wagon and Lincoln followed. We strolled on over and arrived just in time to hear Gene say to Steven that it was an honor to work with him. Segal answered back in kind, exclaiming how it was a pleasure to meet Gene who he had heard a lot about. They proceeded to talk, while we stood in the back of Gene, as Segal's bodyguards were behind Segal. They were two biggons (big ones) never speaking a word. I was on Gene's left and Lincoln was on his right. The two bodyguards were standing the same way with Segal. It was almost the set up for the O.K. Corral which was only seconds away, but none of us had any idea.

One simple conversation led to another and Gene and Steven started talking about techniques. Gene brought up a technique that he liked to use and Segal disagreed with the effectiveness of it. He said he had a sixth sense that allowed him to escape any hold. Segal then kindly asked Gene if he could show him a hold, to demonstrate how to get out of it and Gene agreed. Now for all you black belts out there, you know when you're showing a technique you don't go hard, you just go slowly and carefully demonstrate and explain. That is what Gene was proceeding to do. Black belt to black belt. Gene casually walked around Segal and stood in the back of him, putting his arms around his neck almost like a sleeper's hold. He did it very slowly and calmly, as two professionals would normally do, and in conversation, describing to Segal what he was doing.

As he got his hands in position on Segal's neck, to all of our surprise, Steven sidestepped at full speed. Gene had his arms around Steven's neck but very loose. As Steven sidestepped, full blast, he drew his left arm up to the sky and brought it down right between Gene's legs. Right into his crotch. My eyes damn near popped out of my sockets. Gene flew into the air, either in pain or because he was trying to dodge the attack which hit him nevertheless. I was astounded and my mouth hung open in horror. In my mind I'm thinking, Steven I wouldn't do that. And why did you just go full force on Gene who is trying to show you something nicely? I didn't understand. All of a sudden, this simple conversation turned into Segal going full blast into Gene's crotch. The minute Gene touched down from being airborne, his hands still around Segal's neck, he sidestepped himself and brought his leg behind Steven. I couldn't believe it, and my mind didn't register until after it was over, that Gene showed no pain from that forearm strike! If it were me, I would be on the floor, screaming with my balls through my mouth. Excuse me for explaining it this way, but I want you to fully absorb the moment. Anyway, let's move on. That brought Gene's arms in front of Segal with his legs in back of him. He pulled straight back with his arm and forward with his leg, sending Segal flying up in the air at least five feet, landing him on his back.

Whamo! The earth shook! He went down like a sack of potatoes. Full force. No pads, no mats, just hard ground. I looked at the bodyguards who had the same face I had. The "Oh My God" face. What just happened. It's contagious when you're around Gene. Now mind you, I looked at Steven on the ground eye to eye, and then back at Gene and then back at Steven who was looking at his bodyguards. One of the bodyguards looked at him. Segal shook his head as if to say, "don't do it." To me, that meant that Segal was telling his guard not to attack Gene because if they did, they would get hurt. Thank God he did, because you need to also factor in that

Lincoln Simon and I would have to fight his bodyguards if they tried to attack Gene. Like I said, the O.K. Corral. Death and destruction. Can you imagine bodyguards attacking Gene? Lincoln and I attacking the bodyguards and oh, can you wonder what Segal would do at this moment and time? Probably just stand back and say nothing, but that's strictly my opinion. But luckily, thank God, the bodyguards never attacked. They were just as stunned and as frozen as Lincoln and I were. At that moment when Segal shook his head at his bodyguards as if to say, "no. Don't." Gene came over and put out his hand to Steven. Segal grasped his hand back and let Gene help him up. Without missing a beat, Gene continued his demonstration saying, "now if I did that to you, let me show you what you could do." I stood there astounded, there was absolutely no reaction with anybody. It was like it never happened. Segal pretended like he wasn't upset, just stunned and shaken. Gene pretended like it was part of Segal's uncalled for petty game. The bodyguards were frozen and I'm standing there scratching my head. Gene had no idea Segal was going to attack him like that, but he went with it naturally like it never even happened. Gene is good like that. He can go from explanation to war in a matter of a second. A real Martial Artist. No movie shit.

Needless to say, that was the end of that, but it wasn't. Now Conrad Palmisano was our boss for this movie, and I'm thinking, I better go tell Conrad that Gene and Segal got into a fight and someone better break it up quickly. Gene continues like nothing ever happened, but you have to understand, I don't know if Segal is going to strike out again at Gene. I don't know if Gene is going to retaliate back at Segal, it was all very spur of the moment. A matter of seconds and my mind was going a million miles an hour. So with not a moment's hesitation, I sprint off and chase down Conrad. I find Conrad, who is busy trying to get a camera on an ATV with the Director. I stopped because we all know you shouldn't interrupt the Director and Stunt Coordinator while they are talking. Meanwhile, seconds go by and I have no idea what is going on outside. Segal could have challenged Gene to a fight to the death and no one would know it. So I decided to take my chances and walk over behind him and I whisper, "Connie, Connie, you got to get to Gene Lebell. He and Segal are having a physical confrontation and it could be leading into a fight." Conrad was still in conversation with the Director and he said nothing. So I try one more time. "Connie, Segal and Lebell are fighting, you gotta call them and separate them." Again, he says nothing. I'm in such a rush and it's not registering with Conrad what the hell I'm saying. I have to get back there! I turn around and take five steps when I hear a voice behind me. It's Conrad. "Steve! Tell Gene to come here right now, tell him I need him! Right now!" I realized it finally clicked into his mind. So

I ran back and Gene and Segal are in heavy conversation. The bodyguards are looking like they are about to attack Gene any second. There's no time for me to finish running over. I yell to them, "Gene! Conrad needs you immediately. It's about what you need to do, he said come now."

Gene walks away from Segal and the bodyguards. Lincoln and Gene start walking over. I stood there and let them go past me and I'm watching Segal and the bodyguards. Segal is not happy and I could tell by his face. I could see Segal standing and talking to his bodyguards with a scowl, wiping himself off. Being a punk kid from Brooklyn, I can feel and sense when there is tension. And you needed a meat cleaver to cut this. I head back over and Conrad tells Gene to go to his trailer and put on his wardrobe and don't come out until he is called. Now, it's over. Gene goes to his trailer and Segal goes to his motor home. The bodyguards still are talking. I feel it is about what just happened. As the minutes and hours go by and we are working, nothing is happening. Everything between them is fine. They worked in the same scene together, everything is cool. It's like it never happened. Day is over, everything is fine. No big deal. To me, the situation was really nothing, it just happened, it worked itself out. Little did I know to Hollywood, it would become a bombshell.

A couple of days later I take a trip to the Stuntmen's Association and I overhear about a dozen guys talking about a Gene Lebell story. I walk over and they are talking about the story with Gene and Segal that I just witnessed mere days ago. All of a sudden, I hear, "Segal pissed in his pants, got put to sleep, went into convulsions." Everybody had Segal going down a different way. I start laughing at everybody. Well, I knew that is not what happened, so I interrupt them and tell them they are mistaken and that Segal never did any of that. I was there. Where did you hear this from? Nobody would tell me and I couldn't get a straight answer. A fifteen minute discussion ensued while I tried to convince all of them what really happened. They thought the world of Gene and weren't going to be swayed otherwise. They shook their heads and told me I didn't know what I was talking about. I said, "you idiots, I was there! Listen to my mouth, it never happened. He never went into convulsions, pissed his pants or was put to sleep." Well, nobody was listening and didn't believe a word I said if they did. I did my best to tell them the truth about Segal, Lebell, Conrad, but it was like talking to kids who just wouldn't listen. They wanted the candy in the empty cupboard and when the cupboard was open and no candy was to be seen, they still thought it was there. A week goes by, two weeks go by, it's all over town. The whole stunt industry and Martial Art industry, (and let me tell you that's BIG), was talking about it. Everybody was talking about the Lebell and Segal story.

Everywhere I went, every job I got, they were talking about it. He made Segal have convulsions, pee his pants or be put to sleep. Or all of the above nonsense. I tried to tell the truth, but nobody was listening. If they were, they didn't care. They got a great story about Gene Lebell. You Martial Artists and stunt people, and yes even a lot of famous actors, know the wonderful great stories with Gene Lebell, and there are a lot that are true. In this case, it's not true. Somebody out there is not telling the truth. Let's see, could it be Lincoln Simon? I don't think so. Could it be Conrad Palmisano? Nah. Could it be the bodyguards? Possibly, but doubtful as they are working for Segal. Could it be Steven Segal? Hell, no. Could it be Gene? I don't know, but I know it wasn't little 'ole me. So days go by, weeks go by, months go by and then I couldn't believe it! In one of the karate magazines, there were about twenty of the world's best Martial Artists pictured on the cover. I couldn't believe it. From Chuck Norris to an eighteen year old full contact world champion, to an eighty four year old master. All well known fighters, with different styles and levels all on the cover. Mind you, during this time, Segal is trying to deny this story which has now become a fact in the stunt and Martial Art and movie industry. This magazine has all these people challenging Segal, putting up something like a hundred thousand dollars. He could pick any of these guys from eighteen years old to eighty four years old and fight them and if he won he would get the money.

Even today it has been talked about by many people, even people like Joe Rogan and Rhonda Rousey. One of the many mistakes I think Ronda Rousey made was bad mouthing someone and their art by saying on film, that Aikido is a bad Martial Art, which is what Segal practices. I'm sitting there thinking, what are you talking about!? You use techniques from the art of Akido in your fighting. Ever since I was a kid, I have learned that out of respect, one black belt or one style should never put down another. That's a golden rule. Shame on her for bad mouthing Segal and saying things that she knows absolutely nothing about. I call that immaturity and disrespect. I mean to watch her on film, she actually enjoyed putting down Steven Segal. Now for Joe Rogan. Joe Rogan tells the story all over the airwaves, which influences other people to believe it. It is ridiculous. Again, I was brought up to have good morals, ethics, to give people their due and tell the truth, whether you like the person or not. It's like that old adage. If you have nothing nice to say, don't say anything at all. It seems to me that people would rather perpetuate an unbelievable lie, than a boring truth, any day of the week. I think we call it P.R. and publicity. They want people to pay attention. Whether or not it's a tall tale or the truth, doesn't matter to them. They want to be noticed. But go ahead, sit down with Gene Lebell and ask him what happened. Oh, with respect don't forget to make sure I am there too. I guarantee you, he'll tell you the truth. The only place Segal pissed was in the toilet. The only time he fell asleep was when he went to bed that night. The only time he had convulsions is probably when he sneezed. Weeks and months went by, close to a year. All kinds of rumors spread about the showdown at the OK Corral with Segal and Lebell.

It was at this time that Segal did a movie called *On Deadly Ground*, with Coordinator Glenn Randall. Glenn calls me up and asks if I could come down to the stage at Warner Brothers and give him a hand gathering up resumes and helping him pick loads of fight guys as he is going to have around seventy five stuntmen lined up for Segal to choose from. Whoever he picked would be working with him. I say of course and I go to the stage and meet Glenn who tells me that Segal wants to go down the line and meet each one of them. He would ask their names and continue the questions. Where were you born, what is your favorite physical sport. What kind of stunt man are you and what is your fight background. One by one they came in and talked to Segal, answering his questions as best they could. **J** Sorry, I caught myself laughing thinking about this story. Don't worry, you will take time to laugh yourself and fill in that space. (Poor Hal.) Now everyone knew not to say a word about the Lebell and Segal incident that had just recently happened, it was common sense. That and Glenn had mentioned to these guys on the phone that the topic was not to be discussed. So one by one they come in and talk and leave. This continues without much excitement until a cowboy comes in to be questioned by Segal. Not just any cowboy, but a cowboy who was clueless, Mister Hal Burton. His past credits included such shows as *Gunsmoke, Little House On The Prairie* and *Bonanza*.

He wasn't a practiced Martial Artist, which made me think this interview would be short. Now Hal was a,a,a,a stutterer when he was n,n,n, nervous and it seemed to me he was always nervous as he always stuttered. I watched intently as he stuck out a hand to Segal. "Mister Segal, my name is Hal Burton, b,b,b,but most of my friends call me Bubba." Segal nodded and became more curious over the stuttering Bubba.

He asked him, "you are a cowboy, huh?"

Hal's face lit up like a Christmas tree on fire. "Ye, ye, ye, yes sir. Bull rider I am."

Segal squinted at Hal, his mouth cracked open. "So you do cowboy fights?" Segal asked him. "Cowboy fights, you betcha. But I know street fights too and some Judo as well. In fact, one of the greatest in the world, Gene Lebell taught me!"

Well, let me tell you what happened next. All the noise in the background of the people in line waiting their turn, turned off. It went silent as Hal Burton said the name that would open up the gates of wrath, the cursed name of the redhead in the pink gi. He he, I'm laughing while you are reading this. You readers, I wish you were there watching this with me. A unified gasp just sucked the air out of the room as time seemed to stop and back up a little. All eyes fixated on Segal as his face became a rice cooker and steam poured out of every orifice he had. Hal didn't know what the hell was going on, still smiling with an innocent look on his face. Segal thought for a moment before turning to Randall. "Bubba. I want you to make sure you hire him and put him a good spot. I'm going to fight him since he was trained by one of the best." Segal said this in such a caustic, yet devious way. "You got that Randall?"

Glenn nodded with a concerned look. "Yea, I got that."
Me, Steven Lambert? Standing right next to Glenn, I managed to have a straight face but boy, inside was I having a party with laughter. I got the pad checking off everybody and I circled Bubba's name. Double circled. When Hal was walking out of the stage, he was looking at the all the stuntmen, wondering why all his stunt compadres are looking away. In fact, he yelled out, "what's the matter with you guys?" They ignored him even more as Segal watched. They would try to whisper, not to be noticed, in his ear as he made his way towards the back of the line out the door. As the whispers flew back and forth from stuntmen to Hal back to them, they eventually found their way to Glenn's ear. As I was a few feet away, they also caught mine. Only this whisper was a bit different.

"Hey Glenn, Hal wants to see you outside. He doesn't want the job anymore," they say. I watched Glenn smile and give a rare giggle.

I start laughing and comment, "there is a coward cowboy amongst us, he's sweating bullets. He wants to go back home, home on his range."

"Bubba came here for a job and he took it, so he's doing it," Glenn replied back to them. This went on two or three times. After the last stuntman met with Segal it was all over. Segal and his entourage started walking to the stage door, when he turned around and yelled out, "hey Randall. Don't forget. Bubba." I started laughing. Segal saw me and laughed with me. We went out the opposite door and who do you think we see? Bubba, coming right at us. He is begging us to take him off the show. He had no idea about what happened with Segal and Lebell and he would never have said his name if he did. "I don't wanna to do it guys, I've heard how Segal likes to hurt people. You gotta find someone else." Randall tries to calm him down and assures Hal that Segal won't hurt him. To make a long story short, I begged Glenn to make sure I was there on that day. Well, the day came and there I was, as Glenn promised. Did Hal get a beating? Yes, he did. A good one. He got smacked in the face, picked up and thrown on a table. Segal somehow missed the table and threw him on the floor. It took Hal five minutes to get up. You have to know this guy Hal Burton, to understand how funny this was watching it. All the stunt people out there that know him understand why it put such a smile on my face. Another great memory that will always be with me.

Now it was around this time I ran into an old friend, most unexpectedly. I was working at Warner Brothers on a show when I saw an eighteen wheeler truck on the lot. This was nothing out of the ordinary as these kinds of trucks were everywhere on studio backlots. As I passed the open end of the truck, I caught a quick glimpse of who was inside getting equipment. I blinked, not believing my eyes! My good pal Albert Leong! I spoke up. "Hey Albert, I didn't expect to see you here."

He looked up at me and a smile formed above his Fu Manchu. "Steven Lambert? Is that you?" He walked over and shook my hand, man it was good seeing him again. "I am here doing grip on a production, trying to get some extra money. I want to become a stuntman, Steven," he told me.

I said, "Al, with your talents and expertise, I'm sure you could become one quite easily." This man meant a lot to me in my formative Kung Fu years and to see him trying to break into the same profession as me, was a great surprise and truth be told, heartwarming and quite touching. You see, there was a two year separation where we hadn't seen each other and now to know that not only a great talent and also an old friend is trying to achieve the same thing, I am grateful that I would be able to see him again in our endeavors.

INCOMING STORY FROM THE FUTURE. TIME MACHINE ACTIVATED! YEAR: 2016 CITY: LOS ANGELES BRRRIIIINNNNNGGGG!!! Hello from 2016. Yes, we jumped ahead but there is a good reason why. Let me explain. It was around this time I got a phone call and a message on my answering machine. The message was from some guy saying that he is connected to Segal and wanted to do a video on what really happened with Segal and Lebell, a story that you THINK, you all now know very well. He goes on to say that he knew I was there and wanted to interview me to find out what really happened. Now, this isn't the first phone call or message I have gotten about people trying to find out the truth. Many people claim to be in contact with Segal, but just want to find out how it all went down on that fateful day. So I ignore the message and go on with my life.

A few days later, Conrad tells me we are shooting at Stuntman Gary Morgan's house in the Hollywood Hills. Gary is a great friend and ex-circus performer. An amazing acrobat, as is the rest of his family. I agreed to meet there. I went up to Gary Morgan's house and as I saw it, I wasn't going to say Segal threw the first punch, all I was going to say was that Segal didn't get choked out and go into convulsions. I made that very clear to Conrad and to the person who was interviewing us. When I got there, I found that Segal wasn't there. I found this surprising as one would think he would be there to oversee everything. So we are at Gary Morgan's house. He has Director chairs for us, right in front of the Hollywood sign and I thought that was pretty funny. A big dramatic opening. Before we start, I turn to the camera guy and say I want to make something clear. I told him I am here to simply tell him and the audience that Segal didn't piss his pants and go into convulsions and he says okay. I also asked where Segal was and they responded he couldn't make it, so that was a surprise. Conrad goes first and boy he is a wonderful talker. He could talk the socks off of you. He proceeds to tell his background and what shows he has done and I am enjoying remembering the good times when we worked together. He is very carefree on camera and I am just the opposite, very serious, direct and to the point.

When they get to me, I state my background and name a few movies I worked on and tell a few stories, before getting into what happened with Segal. I started with me and Lincoln Simon getting dressed in the honey wagon. I STOPPED when it got to the part where Gene Lebell said, "let me show you what I mean," to Segal. I just made it clear that Gene and Segal never got into a confrontation where Segal peed his pants and went into convulsions. I purposely left the physical confrontation part out because, let me remind you, that was not what I was told they wanted. If it was for anybody else, other than Segal, I wouldn't have done this in the first place. But mind you, I just got tired of all the hurtful tall tales. So I left it out. Knight takes pawn. Hope you understand what I'm trying to do here. I went on to talk about Segal in his other films and told some funny stories. I walked out of there having said exactly what I wanted to say and do what I wanted to do. I felt everything went well and emphasized what people like Joe Rogan and Ronda Rousey said was not true of Segal, and I thought it was a mistake to say those things. I realized they were doing it to score brownie points and get five minutes of fame. Mind you, if I would ever meet them, I would always stick out my hand to shake theirs and give them the utmost respect as any proper and decent person should do. I was very happy with the whole session and when it was over, we said goodbye. End of that story. Or so I thought.

About two weeks later, I get a call from Conrad. We talk a little bit and then he asks me for a favor. I asked him what it was, and he explained that the video the guy took was grainy and they wanted us to do it again. My mouth dropped open. What?? He said it didn't come out in certain parts and was bad quality. I couldn't believe this was happening and I got a little upset at Conrad. Everything went perfectly and now I have to do it all over!? Believe it or not, it is a difficult thing to do, because of the way I had to do it and the people that were involved in it. That is why I was so frustrated. He then said Segal wanted to meet us at a restaurant and suggest some other stuff. I said, "wait, let me get this straight. You want me to do it all over again, and before that, Segal wants to meet with us and go over some other things to discuss and then shoot it?" He said yes. So, the chess game goes on. Conrad assures me that Segal just wants to meet me and have a quick discussion. I ask Conrad why don't we just go back to Gary's house and shoot there. Conrad thinks that it is a great idea, only to give me a call back a few minutes later to tell me Segal doesn't want to meet at Gary Morgan's place. So I give in and agree to meet at the restaurant. I'm thinking that at least I'll get free food out of it. We meet at the restaurant and instead of some fancy place, it turns out to be Norm's Diner, can you believe it? Segal is there, surrounded by fans wanting his autograph. It was strange and exciting sitting down with Segal again after all these years. Let me tell you a bit more about Steven Segal. I've worked with Segal many times and it pains me to tell you, I have seen him hurt many people. For instance, I had a huge fight with him in a movie called *Marked For Death,* and at the beginning, he had a shotgun and I disarm him before he gets the gun back and beats the hell out of me. When Segal saw the choreography, he refused to be disarmed. We all tried to explain including his Stunt Coordinator, his stunt double at this time, Jeff Dashnaw, all of us, that it makes you macho. It makes you more human if someone disarms you. He didn't care and they took that part out. With Segal, it's his way or the highway. We cut that part out, which made me depressed as I had a good move there and we go into the fight. In the middle, he has me in an armbar and he is supposed to go with me and let me fly through the air and forward roll to the ground. When we shoot this, as he has my arm, he decides now would be a good time to put in another move. Do you think he told me? No. Do you think he cared if I knew or not? No. So he starts to go the other way, reversed it, knowing full well that could and would rip my arm out of its socket. He didn't want me to disarm him, but he had every intention of disarming me. Literally. Luckily, thanks to Sil-Lum Kung Fu, Doug Wong and my five animal style, I caught what he was trying to do in a fraction of a fraction. Before his mind even moved his muscles. I moved out of it, Segal was certain he had me. When they yelled, "cut", I looked at him knowing full well he had tried to break my arm like many others that worked with him before.

Let me give you another one. This is a good one, as Sven would say. Segal was working with Sven Thorson. Six foot three, he looked like a Swedish Hercules. He was the last person you wanted to mess with. A long time friend of Arnold Schwarzenegger, Arnold brought him here from his home country and he started out as his bodyguard before becoming an action actor. A good friend of mine he will always be. Segal had to show that he was the dominant one though, and proceeded to do just that. They had to do a fight in a pool room and props had put six pool sticks on the wall. The two to the right were breakaway. The four to the left, were real. Everybody made that perfectly clear a number of times. It was so clear, that when it came time for Segal to take the pool sticks, he made sure to take the real ones and hit Sven once, twice, right on the head. Sven went down like a beached whale. The sticks shattered as if they were breakaway, but they weren't. As the blood began to ooze from the gash on Sven's head, Sven just looked at Segal. He got up slowly like an awakened bear, and said nonchalantly, "oh, you low forehead. You took the wrong sticks." I must tell you, anytime anybody did something stupid, those were the words that came out of his mouth. It was gold. Segal's eyes were out of his head. He didn't know Sven was no ordinary man. For all of you out there, a low forehead means in his words, "a retard," but Segal didn't know that. Only friends of Arnold and Sven knew what that meant. Segal was shocked that he even got up. There was silence before we all started laughing and ran over to stop the bleeding. That was my good friend Sven.

Anyway, we sat down at Norms and I reiterated that I was going to say the same thing I did in the first tape. Segal said that was fine and we had our lunch. Of course, I had to listen to Segal bad mouth Gene, but I took it with a grain of salt knowing how much all the rumors and lies did hurt Segal both personally and professionally. As unfavorable as I thought Segal was, it was still wrong for the lies to come out. Again, one of the main reasons I did this was to be a champion of truth and justice, for things very similar have happened to me and even to you people who are reading this. That is why I take it so seriously. I didn't understand how it could get this far. Even though Segal did do mean things and hurt people, so have a lot of other actors. It doesn't justify it, unfortunately, it is part of our job, but that is the last thing you want to happen. Somebody getting hurt by accident, or on purpose is not a good thing. However, two wrongs don't make a right. At the end of lunch, I agreed to meet with him again sometime in the near future. Some time goes by and I get a call from Ron Balicki. This was a surprise. His wife is Diana Inosanto and her father is Danny Inosanto. I let it ring and he leaves a message. I listen to it later and he now says that Conrad Palmisano was going to be at the Beverly Hills Hotel. Now I am curious. Well, instead of taking his word, as we know that people can simply mislead you, I called the guy up and talk to him. Now I want to know what really is going on. I know Ron, he is a cool dude. I said, "Ron, you said on the message that Conrad was going to be there. Is that true?" Ron says it was. He proceeded to explain that all these years of people not saying the truth has caused a lot of unfair rumors and problems for Segal, and he wanted me to come on video and explain what really happened with him there. I made sure that during the conversation with him, that all he wanted me to say was that Segal didn't pee his pants and go into convulsions. Between you and me, I didn't want to tell them the truth, that Segal got knocked on his ass because it would be embarrassing to one and all. So I was more than happy again to simply state that Segal didn't piss himself or go into convulsions. I made it specifically sure to Ron, three to four times that that was all I had to say. I'm thinking in my head, I was in the honey wagon, we went out to see Segal and Lebell, and they started demonstrating moves on each other. I was going to leave what happened next out because I'm quite sure he would have changed his mind if I told him, and besides, that is not what they were asking me to say on video. He agreed that it was OKAY to say just that. My Brooklyn sense told me I had to be careful that they wouldn't fool me into saying things about Gene Lebell that I simply would never say or isn't true.

Again, itt was like a chess game and every move they made, I would counter it. This was the Brooklyn streets smarts, but let me make one thing clear, I was prepared in my head already for any surprises. So he agreed that was all I had to say and I then told him if Conrad was going to do this, as he had stated, then have him call me. He asked me what I meant. I directly told him that I didn't know how serious this was going to be and if Conrad calls me, I would consider it. I said, "listen, I really want to make it clear to you Ron, since you are representing Segal and you are in control of this and are the boss man, that all you want me to say in your video is that Segal didn't piss his pants and go into convulsions. Right?" He said yes and I said "okay, so make sure Segal knows that. Then I'll consider it once I talk to Conrad." The next day, Conrad leaves me a voice message wanting me to call him back. I do a few hours later and he wants me to come in and explain what happened, reiterating what Ron said. The fact was that Segal was tired of people saying he peed his pants and went into convulsions and wanted us to set the record straight. I told him after a long pause, that I would do it for him, but I made sure he knew that I did not want to be put in any position where I had to bad mouth Gene Lebell and I didn't have to say anything after Segal and Gene started demonstrating moves. "Do you understand that Conrad? Don't put me in a position I don't want to be in." He assured me that would not happen and I reiterated the thought again saying that, "I did not want any problems since Segal was going to be there."

He agreed and said that was all I had to say. Everything was going perfectly. There was a part of me that really got frustrated at people like Joe Rogan, Rhonda Rousey and others who kept telling untruths about Segal, and I felt I had a moral obligation to set things straight. Since I was there and witnessed it for myself, I was honor bound to share what I saw with the world, instead of the world hearing lies. I hate lies. About myself or anyone else. We set a date to meet and hung up. I called Ron back and told him, "I'm in." WAIT. STAND STILL. WE ARE MOVING INTO THE FUTURE, GOING FASTER AND FASTER. September 19th, 2019. This is where we have arrived. Let me make one thing clear. Ron Balicki called me. He set this up. He's the boss man. He set the lights, the cameras, he wrote the questions and he was the Director and as far as I was concerned, the interviewer. Anything that went on there, was Ron's creation. That's why I call him the boss man. I was guiding everything towards him. It didn't matter who said what to me, all I knew was anything that happened or was spoken was coming through him. This was his production and the crew was at his command. STOP! WOW CAN YOU BELIEVE IT? WE ARE GOING BACK IN TIME. HOLD ON, OKAY? WE ARE BACK WHERE WE BELONG, LET'S MOVE ON. I'm hoping that this time I have to be getting steak and lobster at this fancy place. The day comes and I meet with Conrad and I follow him to the hotel. We go to Segal's room and boy what a beautiful bungalow it is. We talk and have coffee and I realize there is a familiar face in the room. It was Ron Balicki. We talk about old times until Segal is ready for us to begin. We have a new commentator and Ron is he. So right off the bat again, I go through the motions. I state my name and some of the shows I have worked on and some of the wonderful things I have done and achieved at my job. Then Ron starts with the first question. Right away he asks me a derogatory question about Gene Lebell and I "cut", with my blood boiling, instantly feeling betrayed. Segal is behind camera and I can see once again, he is shocked. I say, "what are you doing? I said from the beginning, I was not here to badmouth anyone, especially Gene Lebell. My dear friend who means the world to me." You out there reading this, please understand that sometimes I have no middle so to say. There is a beginning and an end. I'm usually cool and calm or I go through the roof. They all knew what I was going to say and what I wasn't going to say about Gene. I told them flatly, not to ask me things like that and they apologized. Segal said, "listen to Steven." With everybody watching, I asked for fifteen seconds and composed myself again. They thought that was strange and it was, but remember, my cork was popped. We started rolling a second time, then the commentator asked me what happened and I repeated the story from the beginning. Ron asked me what I was doing on the show and I told him I was doing a fight. He asked me what I thought of Steven and I told them I was excited to work with such a renowned Martial Arts star. The chess game continues. Everything is going well then low and behold, the interviewer starts bad mouthing Gene again with me on camera! Hold on, are you freaking kidding me!? What did I just yell at everyone for doing literally ten minutes ago? Ron "cut." He blinked and said, "oh, I thought you meant only you couldn't speak that way about Gene." I just lost it, stood up and erupted like a volcano. Conrad is looking at me and Segal is looking at me, and I look over at Ron who is just surprised. Ron is the nicest guy in the world, but a pure badass, a straight shooter. He knows me from the past and knows my personality and so does Conrad. Big time. At the same time that I blew my fuse, I was also laughing at the sheer stupidity of them thinking that they were going to take the lead in this chess game. You see, my thought was that they were going to bad mouth Gene on film, so it looked like I agree. That is why I immediately "cut." My queen just got their knight.

They were apologizing left and right to me. I looked at Segal and I said, "I'm sorry Steven, I don't want you to see me like this, but this commentator keeps asking questions I told him not to." I can feel eyes on my back at this point and I'm not just imagining it. Guess what. Behind me are Segal's bodyguards, hulking giants watching me like a hawk, looking like they are going to pounce. Conrad and Ron are trying to calm me down as Segal has a look on his face of clear astonishment. Oh yea, I forgot. He has his sunglasses on as always. I would imagine, nobody has ever acted this way in front of him. I was there to try to make things right, not badmouth Gene! So we do it a third time and I managed to get through it without incident, so relieved. Checkmate, game over. I go in the back of the room as Conrad takes his seat to be interviewed next. I shake Segal's hand and apologize for the outbursts again. He tells me not to worry about it and the interview went great. I walk to the back of the room. I happen to stop in between both of the bodyguards. I look up and smile and ask, "you want to try to beat me up?" They both look down on me and shrug their shoulders. We call that, Brooklyn street smarts. My chest is out trying to counter their intimidation. I stick out my hand to shake one of their hands, and they grab my hand and shake it hard. I can feel Gigantor trying to squeeze my hand, mind you this guy is six foot seven and over three hundred pounds, he has a handshake like the Hulk. He is trying to exert his dominance over me. I looked up at him and put my left hand completely on his forearm and extend my finger and put pressure on his arm. He looks down at his arm and then he looks up at me. I press harder and I turn my hand. He looks back down at his hand and then back up at me. Down to the hand, and then back at me. Hand, me, hand, me. I give a little smile, causing him to completely be thrown off and he realizes I'm not one to give in. So he releases his grip. Boy, sheesh, I am glad that's over.

Now it was Conrad's turn to be interviewed. It started off well and Conrad talked about his background and old times. Then before you know it, things started to take a wrong turn. It was no longer jolly and light, but he started saying things that confused me. He was no longer talking about the fight with Gene and Segal, but he went off on a tangent in an alternate world about his relationship with Gene, which really bewildered me. Another minute went by and it really started to get out of hand. Things were said that didn't have anything to do with anything we were talking about. Things were said that should have never been said, that is all I have to say. Conrad simply blew my mind. He was on an insane crazed rant. He went from calm and cool to something I had never seen before. I didn't know if I should say, "good job" or "what the hell was that about?" So I decided to say, "that was different. If you are happy, I'm happy." I couldn't say any more. There were no more words to say on what just took place in this moment and time, only thinking to myself, self, they are NEVER going to show this. So let's put the chess pieces away and move on. Oh, by the way, Segal told me he would see me again for sure on another movie that he would be doing, coming up. A few months later I heard he had done two movies and none of us worked on it. The video we did in the hotel, still hasn't come out yet. I don't think I will see Segal again and I don't think that video will ever come out. I have to say to Joe Rogan and Ronda Rousey and everyone else that perpetuates the untruth about Segal or anybody else, "before you attempt to bring false information and put a splinter in anybody's eye, please, why don't you look and take out the splinter out of your own eye." As Robert Blake once said on *Baretta,* "that's the name of that tune." Okay. let's go back to where we were. TIME MACHINE ACTIVATED!!!! YEAR: 1982 CITY: LOS ANGELES BIIIIIINNGGGGG!!!!

Oh hey there, did you enjoy that story? I just finished getting gas, can you believe it went up over a dollar? That's the eighties for you. Where was I? Oh yes, I remember. Now let's move on. I have one last Gene Lebell story for you. This one is very precious to me. You see, I have a special bond with Gene. I was always able to do certain things without Gene Lebell retaliating at me. A little smack in the head, a little kick in the butt, slap on the face. I was always able to play with him while most people would never even think of it. I was always his favorite dummy to demonstrate things, he called me his tool, but the real word is dummy. Get ready for a good laugh. A friend of mine, a stuntman named John Moio called me up and said he needed me to double one of his actors and wanted me to come down to the Stuntmen's Association and said Gene would be there too as he was doubling the other actor. Moio, he's one of my favorites. A man with a great heart and a caring soul. The guy has helped many kids getting into the movie business. But I must say he's got a little bit of a Doctor Jekyll and Mr. Hyde in him. But I'll always be fond of him anyway as irritating as he sometimes can be. Just like I could be, or maybe even you. Okay, back to the laughs. So we go into the Board of Director's room in the stunt office. Moio started explaining what he needed in the fight and one thing led to another. The old man in the pink gi, Gene Lebell (mind you I say this with love and he knows it) would think of something. I would think of something and Moio would say, "yea, I like it" or "no, I don't." Finally, we got something together and decided to practice it in slow motion. So Gene asks Moio where he would like him to start. Moio tells Gene his character starts on the floor. Gene looked at him like he was crazy. Telling Lebell to go on the floor, that just seemed odd to me. Then Moio told him he needed him on all fours like a dog and he would get punched looking up. Well, Gene was not happy about that. He was used to putting people on the ground, not being on the ground himself. He looked at Moio and questioned if he really had to get on the ground on all fours and Moio tells him to just get down there and stop trying to direct. See, they were great friends also. He finally gets Gene to go down on all fours like an eighty year old bear.

Now I want you to visualize this. Just as he gets down, I come over and get ready to do the first punch when Moio stops me and asks me a question. I'm standing there explaining to him why what I'm doing is this way, to get him to understand and I'm looking out of the corner of my eye at Gene on all fours who is looking like a dog who wants a bone. His head is turned looking up at me. It seemed very odd and a bit funny. Fifteen seconds go by, twenty seconds go by and Moio and I are still in conversation. Suddenly, I hear Gene yell, "would ya hurry up?" We continued talking and suddenly, like the exorcist, this devilishness comes over me and I look back at Gene and couldn't resist as we are always playful when we are together. I raise my leg and put it on the side of his hip and gut and guess what I did? I pushed him over. I bet you are thinking I'm either gusty or stupid. Well, you can say I was both. Gene fell and Moio was still talking. He kind of glances over and Gene is lying there like a hurt puppy dog. He's on his back looking up at me like, "what the hell did you just do?" I stepped back and said I was only kidding, sorry about that. There was no fire in his eyes, he just stopped. So I bent down and gave him my hand to lift him back up and Moio says, "no, no, no! You gotta stop it, stop screwing around, you gotta start on the ground Gene." Gene gets back down on all fours reluctantly and Moio decides to ask me another question. He starts talking to me again and I feel Gene, he starts looking up at us. Moio's back is to Gene and he can't see John Moio's face. I see Moio's eyes going back and forth to Gene Lebell. I realize that Moio wants me to kick him again. Like a dummy, I don't realize that Moio is setting me up. His eyes are rolling back and forth and okay, he is telling me to do it again.

So I lift my leg, but this time I go a little faster and a little harder. Gene falls and does a three sixty this time onto his stomach. He looks up and I can tell there is a little more fire in his eyes. He starts to get up and now instead of one foot stepping back, I take four. Every word out of my mouth was pleading with Gene. "I'm sorry, I won't do it again, I'm sorry."

Moio cuts in and says, "God damn it, stop fooling around!" Moio, of course, is trying to act like he never had a part in it, he's quick like that. Gene gets back down and what do you think John did? He started giving me the eyes again. What do you think this stupid punk kid from Brooklyn did again? Call me a sucker. I decided to do it one more time. I lifted my leg but I didn't even have time to thrust my leg forward. I never saw Gene Lebell move so fast in my life. For sure, that was no eighty year old bear coming at me. He was up and inches away from me. Grabbing at me with double volcanoes in his eyes. He had enough and I knew it was on. I turned and ran for my life. The more I ran, the more I begged him to stop, but he wouldn't have it. He gave me my chances and now the bear was going to teach the monkey a lesson. I'm throwing tables and chairs in the way as I am hauling ass. John Moio and stuntman Tom Morga are hysterical with laughter and I don't find it amusing as I am running for my life. Oh, I forgot stunt man Tom Morga was there laughing hysterically seeming to know what was about to happen as Moio is screaming at us to stop. There are four rooms all caddy corner to each other on this floor. The only way out of this room is through the door, which the bear was standing in front of and the small sliding window of the secretary's office. Now, who in their right mind would choose to exit the room through the eighteen inch by fourteen inch, about five foot seven inches high, sliding window? I had no choice. I ran and did a Superman dive through the window and somehow got through. The secretary was busy doing work when her window practically exploded and I'm sticking through it with Gene grabbing at my feet. To this day I don't know how I made it through that small space. I plop down on the desk and look up. The door to the room is three feet away. Beyond that are stairs to the left that lead to freedom outside. Now the door is about three feet away from me. Gene has to run 15 feet, then turn the corner and run another fifteen feet. There is no way that fat old man is going to catch me. As stuntman Glen Randall once said," I'm a gazelle." I flopped down face first onto the desk, battered like a floundering fish. I roll off and in a flash, get up. I take a step and to my disbelief guess who is standing in the doorway?

Well, shit. I don't know how Gene got there that fast but there he was, smoke blowing out his nose and ears but I know I'm the one who started the fire and there was only one way to put it out. I'm going to be stretched with love. But he'd have to catch me first. I turn and dive back the way I came, that big red headed Neanderthal grabbing at my feet. The secretary is in tears yelling at us to stop. We've caused so much damage, destroying vases, tables, chairs, a bookcase. As I'm screaming at Gene with the secretary's desk in between us, I'm trying to tell her it's all Gene's fault, he is the one that is chasing me. I know if he gets a hold of me, I'm going to be a stretched Matzah Ball. I'm on one side of this desk and Gene is on the other. I'm pleading and asking for forgiveness but he won't have it. Tom Morga is in the background still cracking up outside the door, as Moio is screaming to stop messing around, as the secretary continues to scream for us to stop. I'm screaming at Moio, "TELL HIM TO STOP." I'm only running for my life here guys. So here goes the stupidity again. I don't know what overcame me but I became foolish enough to reach out and slap Gene Lebell right in the face again and again and go, "haha you can't catch me." You know, love taps on that beautiful face of his. Talk about hell in the beginning, well now his face became as red as his hair. Yes, this story goes on. Gene leans over and tries to grab me with his giant bear paws of his. He reaches over and I slap a few away. Until one of the bear paws latches onto my arm. I pull away but there ain't no way, he's got me! He grabs me with his other arm and now he has a good hold of me. He pulls me over across the desk, and mind you, I'm still begging for mercy but it is falling on deaf ears as they say. Gene is having a good time. With a big smile on that "hambo" face, he lifts me up in the air and body slams me over his shoulder right onto the secretary's desk which has an inch of glass on the top. It shatters into bits. KAKRASSSHH! I could say I was lucky because he released me. I managed to roll over off the desk with the secretary screaming at the top of her lungs and John Moio and Tom Morga having the time of their lives with this greatest show on earth. I run through them as they block the doorway. Now I could have went left to the stairs to freedom but I was so delirious, like an idiot I went into the pool room straight ahead. Don't ask me why I did that, but boy, that was the wrong way to go. That's what being scared shitless does to you, it sometimes puts you on the wrong path. It was like I was a kid again. The big guys were chasing me and I had no fence to climb, but plenty of things to throw. Only this time, the big guys were one guy who made everyone else look not so big. This room had a giant pool table in it. I hop over one side of the pool table like a gazelle and Gene comes into the doorway roaring like a freaking ferocious bear. I can't believe he hasn't been satisfied yet. I'm just standing there looking at him with his hands in the air knowing he can't grab me. I'm on one side of the pool table and Gene is on the other. I know that there is no way he going to be able to get me now. He can't reach across. The distance is too spread, I'm too fast.

So what do you think I do? Deja vu. I reach out and slap him again. I reach over and slap him one more time. Then again. Then again and again. I think, wow, this is easy. Then again, when WHAP! All of a sudden one hand slaps down on the one side of the pool table and the other hand slaps down on the other side. He starts to push the pool table. You would think it would take four or five guys to push a pool table that fast but it only took one. Gorilla Gene Lebell. He pushes the pool table so fast that there was no way in hell I could get around it in time. He pushes it right into me and suddenly I'm trapped between the table and wall. Yes, it was done that fast. Gene proceeds to climb on the pool table and he pries me out. Mind you, I'm still begging for mercy here and mind you, yes, the two clowns are in the room laughing so hard they are practically peeing in their pants. (Which Segal never did, nor me, let me make that perfectly clear.) Gene wraps his arms around my waist and I know it's over. He spent the next ten to fifteen minutes stretching me out like a piece of Gefilte fish while Moio and Morga are laughing like crazy. By this time Jill, our secretary, had stopped screaming and has now joined in with Moio and Morga laughing and having a great time at my expense. Me? I'm being flattened by Gene's forearm, knee, shin and arm, squishing me all over my body. All the while, they are telling Gene Lebell to "give 'em hell Harry."

Finally, it ended. Gene got off the table and what do you think I did? I think I laid there for another fifteen minutes basking in the pain of defeat. It wasn't long after that I get a letter from the Stuntmen's Association asking me to come up to a board meeting with Gene Lebell, explaining what had happened the week prior. Also, it had an explanation in it that the damage was thirty seven hundred dollars and change. You heard me, thirty seven hundred dollars in damage. I called up Gene and asked if he got a letter too. He said he got one. I asked if he was going to pay it and he said, "no, I'm not going to pay it, it's all your fault!"

I said, "my fault? You were the one chasing after me! I was just running for my life." The humor and the playfulness even proceeded on the phone. That was how close we were and still are. So we are called into a meeting with the Board of

Directors a few days later and let me say it consisted of a long table with approximately twelve board members and also about fifteen other members that just wanted to see the humor of what was happening and the outcome. Gene was sitting on one side and I was sitting on the other side of the long table. They wanted us separated. The Board asked us for an explanation for our behavior and requested me to stand up and give them my side of the story.

I say, "let Gene go first."

Gene yelled out, "you're the ugly one, you go first." As everyone is smiling, but at the same time trying to look serious, I proceed. In my defense, I was making it seem like it was Gene's fault, but we all know I was the guy that couldn't resist seeing him on his back. Like I might have mentioned before, I got away with doing things that would cause other people to be put to sleep by Gene. Luckily, Gene loved me and I was doing it out of love too. Therefore, I knew there would never be a serious retaliation. In the middle of my explanation, Gene would pop up and scream I was out of order. "No that's not what happened. Steven, you don't know what you're talking about!" He would yell. Moio began instigating. He would pop up and tell Gene to sit down and shut up and let me explain.

"Leave him alone Gene, let him tell the story," Moio cut in. "

Sit down Moio, or I'll stretch you out next!" Gene retorted.

I would yell back at Gene, "leave Moio alone, God Damn it."

Gene would yell back at me, "shut up, you anorexic pencil, before I break you."

Eventually, I told Gene, "you're paying and that is it! I'm not paying a dime." Well, the whole room was on pins and needles. Mind you I had no intention of not paying, I was just acting out and having a fun time. Now we reach the climax. The head of the Board is banging his gravel yelling that everyone is out of order. Gene and I are going at it verbally. When that failed, Gene erupted and jumped out of his chair. At this moment, I looked into his eyes and I knew the lava and the fire is coming. Uh oh. I went too far.

Half of the room quickly got up and headed towards the corner, no way were they going to be in the way of a charging Gene Lebell. I ran around the table and found Gene on the other side. So what did I do? I reached out my hand towards Gene's face - and stopped. His last words out of his mouth were, "I love you, Steven." I crawled over the table and gave him a loving bear hug and at the same time whispering to him, "be nice Gene. Be nice, be nice. No tricks."

It was a fun time, great memory and was talked about for years to come. I'm tired of talking about that red headed Pink Ki man who is one of my heroes.

CHAPTER 11
(A Shit In A Glass)

Let's move on to *Matt Houston*, a show I worked many times on. Again, I get a call to double Sonny Bonno. He moved from *Fantasy Island* to *Matt Houston* and recommended me. It means a lot to get a call back when you are requested by an actor. That is what a stuntman looks for, consistency. It is a very special thing. So I get the call and I'm doubling Sonny who is playing a Hollywood Movie star. He is in a scene as a Roman Gladiator wearing the white toga that Romans usually wear. I go to Wardrobe and get these shoes with nothing on them but drawstrings, talk about cold feet. I ask Snuffy what I was doing and he said I was doubling Sonny and there are going to be seven plaster statues that are going to be break away and I destroy them with my punches and kicks. "You do your chop suey on them," as he always said. I said okay no problem. So the next day I come on set to Warner Brothers and I walk over and see the seven statues on pedestals all lined up about five feet tall on these five foot pedestals. People start coming in to get ready for the shoot and I walk over to the statues and start examining them. I say to myself, these don't feel breakaway to me. I take one and tip it and realize it has some pretty good weight to it. I'm going hey, these aren't break away. These are real plaster. I put it down, no one is saying anything. They are watching, but not seeming to care. This got me thinking. The golden rule is you never touch the breakaway prop until you are actually shooting. It seemed to me something was up. So I go to find props and effects, see if they have the breakaway statues ready for the actual moment I break them. I walk over to the effects department on stage and I introduce myself as Steven Lambert who will be doubling Sonny Bono for Roy Harrison. I told them I looked at the statues and asked if they had statutes that were breakaway. They said nope. My mouth fell open. I told them I was supposed to kick and punch the statues. The guy looked at me and shrugged. He told me the real plaster statues were all they had and if I was going to break these with my hands and feet, good luck. I shook my head and turned back around. I could swear out of the corner of my left eye, I saw him smirk at me. Well, just great. I better talk to props about this, there has to be a bunch of breakaway statues somewhere. I go to the props truck and introduce myself again and ask if they have the breakaway statues somewhere. The prop guy shrugs as well and tells me no, what is out there is all they have. I told them I'm supposed to break these statues. He says no, only what is out there. I'm scratching my head. As I turn to leave, I swear out of the corner of my right eye, I saw him smile at me. I thought that was strange. Finally about an hour later, because I'm always early,

Snuffy arrives and I walk over to him. I say to him, "I looked at the statues and they aren't breakaway, they are real, did you know that?"

Tilting his head down, he looked at me over his glasses and said, "I know everything."

I told him I had also gone to effects and props and they both said that's all they had. Snuffy looks at me over his glasses and says, "right, we have no breakaway statues." I tell him they are plaster and heavy what am I going to do? How am I supposed to break them? He tells me I'm the big karate man and breaking plaster should be no more difficult than breaking boards and then smiles. So we walk on the set and we go over there and he picks up a statue and says, "you can't break this?" He turns it over and there is a hole right in the middle of it. I realize the hole in the middle leaves about an inch and a half of plaster. He tells me the hole makes it easier to break. I'm looking at him and the statue, mind you the statues weighs about twenty five pounds. Yeah, they are hollowed out but still an inch and a half thick at its thinnest and seven inches at its thickest. I was never one to break boards but I couldn't tell Snuffy that. As Bruce Lee once said, "boards don't hit back." In this case, I think plaster will. Not hit back, hurt back. Nevertheless, Sonny Bono comes and we say hello and thank you for doing this, you know familiarities. Snuffy goes over the scene and says you do one punch on this statue, one kick on this statue. One after the other without stopping in a line. I'm thinking in my head, this is going to hurt. The first statue he wanted a front punch. The second one a back spinning punch. The third he wants a roundhouse. Fourth one a back spinning kick. Fifth one a chop. The sixth he wanted a head butt. (Only kidding, that might have split my head open.) The seventh one he wanted me to jump in the air and scream and do a back knuckle.

Well I started with the first punch and in my head as soon as I made contact and started to move onto the second, I could feel the pain in my knuckles, but I couldn't stop the scene. I went to the second one, hurt my other hand. I was trying to alternate one hand to the other and incorporating my forearms into it to transfer the pain. Plaster flying everywhere. I went from punch, kick, punch, kick until they yelled, "cut." I look at my hand and my mind was going one hundred miles an hour through this trying not to focus on the pain. I just wanted to get through it. As soon as they yelled cut, I dropped down to the ground. My knuckles were cut up as well as my fingers and back of my hands. My shins, my feet, all cut up. Abrasions everywhere. I was a hurting little Jewish boy. First aid came over with a bag of ice for me. Snuffy walked over and instead of asking me if I was all right, he said that he knew I would need first aid and ice as soon as we yelled cut. I looked at him and he had a big smile on his face. It all flashed back to me. The smirking effects man, the smiling prop guy, Snuffy had set this all up. He knew what was going to happen. But I got through it and everyone clapped, I was very proud of myself. A proud moment when Sonny came over and congratulated me. He picked up a piece of plaster and put it in front of everybody and stated he couldn't believe I had done it in one shot. I was glad too, if I had hit it and it didn't break, I would feel dejected inside. I had no choice in my mind to go full force even though I knew I would be hurt. That was a proud moment and I knew I made Snuffy, one of my heroes, happy.

I gave a quiet thanks in my mind to Sil-Lum Kung Fu and Douglas Wong and proceeded to endure the pain. Ouch. It wasn't just on sets that we had a lot of fun with the hard work, but after the day was over as well. We would go eat at places called La-Frites, Tennessee Gin and Cotton and The Eggshell (who remembers those restaurants out there) on Ventura Boulevard, which I'm sorry to say, do not exist anymore. They were big stunt hangouts of the seventies and eighties. I remember one of the funniest moments that I have had in my life that came from my job was when I was meeting everybody from the show *Matt Houston* after wrap at La-Fritties. People like Lee Horsely himself, Mister Matt Houston. They thought he was going to be the next James Gardener, but it just never happened. Cool guy otherwise. The Director of the show Chris Bowles, the Second Assistant Kim Manners (who went on to direct the *X-Files*), Joel Kramer, John Meiers, Ronnie Rondell, his son Reed and Roy Harrison were all there. We were all having a wonderful time. Snowshoe, wild turkey and peppermint schnapps, that was my drink. The others, well you will just have to ask them. The place was packed with families. Kids, Moms and Dads. We were sitting at one big round table. We were having a good time partying. Me being a joe jock athlete, I had never touched a drop of liquor until I got

into the movie business. My first drink was a Snowshoe. Wild Turkey and peppermint Schnapps. Roy Harrison introduced me to that drink and I loved it forever. It's a skiing drink for winter but boy is it a potent drink. Not used to drinking alcohol, one of those would send me flying through the clouds almost as fast as that red headed guy Gene Lebell.

We were having a good time, making fun of each other and things that had happened at one time or another since we all have worked together many times. For instance, (let's tell a funny story within a story), the time a bunch of us were doing a car sequence on *Matt Houston*. Joel Kramer was in the lead car and right in the middle of the scene, my pal "Goyim" Kramer, stopped his car in the middle of the shot and got out. We all came to a screeching stop as we didn't know why he stopped the car and got out. Guess what? As crazy as it sounds, he proceeded to wave to the Executive Producer as he pulled up in his car to watch what was going on. We were all stunned and laughing inside. Wouldn't dare to laugh on the outside. You know why? The First Assistant yelled cut, everybody wondered what had happened.

Snuffy's reaction was, well let me tell you. He saw this and took his walkie talkie, banged it on his head a couple of times (yes on his head) and proceeded to throw it in Joel Kramer's general direction.

He was lucky he was too far away. Why he didn't wait until after the shot, who knows but it sure was funny.

(Roy Harrison. The look we all knew and love.)

Back to the restaurant. All of a sudden, someone and I'm not going to mention the name at this time, we will let you guess who it was out of all these guys I just mentioned, did something hilariously inappropriate. Should I mention funny? We are having a fun time as are the family's around us when one of us nonchalantly gets up. Hmm, you wonder who it is. That person decides to go to the bathroom, which we barely noticed because we were having such a good time. Half of us are making jokes, some of us are asking if we could come to the bathroom too (there are reasons for that), but this person goes in and about five minutes later, we forget that he even left. He comes back and proceeds to sit down and we are still having a great time, the restaurant is lively and more people are coming in to eat. Seconds go by, minutes go by and all of a sudden, Lee Horsely starts making funny faces and starts sniffing with his nose. He comments that something smells nasty and wants to know who farted. One by one everyone else started smelling it, wondering what it was. We were so out of it, everything was getting over amplified. All of a sudden, Lee Horsely stands up and reaches over into the middle of the table. There is a glass with a white napkin over it. He grabs the napkin and unveils the glass. What the hell do you think was in the glass? Fresh baked brown fudge. Being that everyone was in a good mood, upon seeing this new discovery, that all changed in a second. It was like we were all on a ratchet. I flew back into a table where a family with their friends and kids were sitting at. It wasn't just me. A lot of us fell into the unsuspecting tables full of families trying to eat their dinner in an effort to escape the sight and smells of this new addition to our meal. Dishes, food, cups, crashed onto the floor. The waitress was upset, the bartender was upset. The whole place was in an uproar. They are screaming, "there is a shit in the glass, who shit in the glass, who did this?" Within five minutes, the whole restaurant stunk. I looked over and there was the glass broken on the floor with our table turned over. Mixed with food from other people's tables that were turned over as well. I don't remember who, it might have been the waiter who simply put a napkin over it in a fruitless attempt to stop the chaos. Mothers started walking out with their kids and yes, I did feel horrible, but I must say it was funny. The manager found out who it is was and we were kicked out that night but the culprit was kicked out for six months. You asked who did it? All you stunt people out there just take a guess. Those who aren't will never know. But the people who do know the gentlemen at this table will know the culprit in a second. This is just one incident with many of the people I spoke to, many of the fun times like that. If I may say, they sure have many stories about me which you won't find in this book. They will have to write their own.

I remember one time I was sitting in the Eggshell one night with Roy Harrison. A stunt man named Jack Tyrese just passed away. He did a high fall and missed the bag. We were good friends. He was part of my Association. That was the first time I knew someone in this business that passed away. Roy Harrison and many others took it really hard. Especially Dori, Roy's daughter. Good times, bad times, you know. Once I was with Joel Kramer and had too much to drink. We were walking out of the restaurant and saw a telephone pole about twenty feet away. He bet me a hundred dollars I couldn't do a flying side kick and hit the telephone pole. I told him okay and I started to run. As I got closer to the pole, I saw three and I jumped and missed the real one by three feet. I have no idea how I missed it but I landed on my back and Joel got a good laugh. Oh, the things you do when you are drunk. Listen to this one. I was with John Meiers having dinner and I get beeped, back then we had beepers, and it was Joel Kramer. So I go to the payphone and call him. He says why don't you come pick me up. I had a Corvette, I just bought it from a stuntman named Dennis Madolone. Cost me about ten thousand dollars. We were roommates at that time and Joel had a big monster truck, it felt like when you got in you were ten feet in the air. I pull up behind it in my little Corvette. I go into the house to get Joel and he decides we should take his car. Joel just got back from a party and I had been partying and having a good time. So we get in the truck, he puts it in reverse and all of a sudden he hits something and the car goes into the air. We both look at each other with a look of confusion as our asses are up, just like the ass end of his truck. I look at him and ask what the hell happened? He didn't know. I waited in the car while he got out. Five, six seconds go by and I don't hear anything. So I yell. "Joel, what did you hit, man?"

He comes over to the driver's side, his head down like he was dejected. He looks up and pops a smile, his eyes widen. "Steven, don't get mad."

I shake my head in confusion. I asked him, "what the hell did you hit?" Well, he won't tell me. So he asks me to get out and look. I jump out and turn around and what do you think he hit? You guessed it, but I didn't, went right over my head. I look at Joel's monster truck sitting on my 1972 Convertible black Corvette, windshield smashed, the whole front end totaled. It was as flat as a potato pancake.

(Wouldn't this make you mad?)

I began to fume, fire appeared in my eyes. All of a sudden, I hear something and I look up and Joel is laughing! Well, that did it. I start screaming that I just restored the car and he begins to laugh even harder. I decide to go after him and he starts running down the street in the dead of night. I've never seen anybody run so fast and laugh so hard at the same time, which got me even more steamed. I go after him and finally catch up with him on someone's lawn and start punching him. I'm yelling and punching and Joel just keeps laughing and laughing. Finally, I thought what I knew to begin with, that it was just as much my fault as it was his. My playful rage stopped and I fell down laughing on my back with him. I ask him what am I going to do. He said don't worry, he'd pay for half. My friend Joel. He said it was my fault for not telling him the car was there. It was hidden by shrubs, that's how narrow our driveway was. We just laid there for fifteen minutes laughing on a stranger's lawn. Thank God the sprinklers didn't turn on. What a sight that must have been. I can't tell you the calls I got from that, yes of course it got around and like many other stories, it was part of the Stunt Fu Jew or the Radical Rabbi and of course Lambo (which were a few of my nicknames) conversations for years.

CHAPTER 12
(What Friends Aren't For And The Dancing Producer.)

Things were going good for me, professionally and personally. I was meeting a lot of Stunt Coordinators and getting a lot of work. Me and Debbie, now engaged, were doing well too. She was beautiful, a Meg Ryan look alike and it wasn't long before we decided to get married. I would take her out with the other stunt guys, wanting to share the experiences with somebody I cared for. Here comes a wild one. Some of the old timers might remember these two punk asses. Two of the people we went out with was a guy named Don Fox-Green, a former football player who was doing stunts on shows like *The Hulk* for Stuntman Frank Orsatti. He was a big dude. I also met this guy named Bobby Seargent who I also became good friends with. He was picked by Hal Nedham to replace himself, stunt doubling Burt Reynolds. He was a big deal then and everybody knew him. One day we decide to go out to dinner. It was Debbie and me, Bobby his wife and Don Fox-Green. It was an Italian restaurant on Riverside Blvd. We sit down, here are two good stuntmen that are working, two friends I met and hung out with. I grew up in one place until I was thirteen and I had the same friends. So in my mind, friendship has a meaning. We all sat at the table and had good conversation, laughing, telling stories and just having a good time. All of a sudden, Bobby's Seargent's wife has to get up and go to the restroom. So we get up and let her out and it just so happens I have to go too. I excuse myself and head to the bathroom, leaving my girlfriend alone with my friends. No big deal you would think. At the table is my girlfriend Debbie, Don Fox-Green and Bobby Seargent. I'm in the bathroom for a couple of minutes and I come back and Bobby Seargent's wife hasn't come back out yet. I get to the table and I see my girlfriend Debbie standing up. The closer I get, I see that she is hysterical and in tears. I ask her what's wrong. I'm looking at her and Bobby Seargent and Don Fox- Green and they are about as white as a sheep. I don't know what is going on and she is crying saying she wants to get out of there. I turn to Bobby and Don asking them what is going on. Debbie is grabbing my arm and pulling me to the door, she wants to go. So I follow her. I've been going with her for about a year and she knows my background, my Martial Arts abilities, etc. I ask again what the hell is going on, but I'm met with silence. She is pulling me harder now, crying in hysterics, desperate to leave. Bobby Seargent's wife finally comes out of the bathroom and asks what is going on as well. I reply, "that's right, what is going on? Why is my girlfriend crying," as Debbie drags me out to the car. We practically get into an argument over what happened, she just doesn't want to tell me. She knows if she tells me there, that something terrible might happen so she stays quiet. So we get home and we go inside and she finally spills the beans to me what occurred at the restaurant. They were trying to fix her up with Bobby Seargent. Right in front of me and Bobby Seargent's wife while we in the restrooms. How horrible is that? I was devastated. That's breaking the golden rule. Fox-Green trying to fix up Bobby Seargent with my girlfriend and Bobby Seargent is letting it happen and he is a married man and his wife is there?! I'm a moral, old fashioned guy. It was beyond my comprehension that two friends would do this. I was on fire. It took hours for her to stop crying and it took weeks to even halfway get over it.

I called up Fox- Green the next day. I left him a message and told him I knew what he did and how dare he try to set my girlfriend up with Bobby Seargents. "How could you do that? I can't believe it. She told me everything," I said. "When I see you, we'll settle it Cowboy style and I'm going to rope and hogtie you. In other words, I am going to kick your ass." He calls back and tells me that the next time he sees me, he is going to make me shut my mouth. Remember, he is a former football player with an inflated ego. I guess he hasn't dealt with anybody like me before. He is going to be in for a big surprise, I thought to myself. I told him to be ready and we'll see.

Then I called Bobby Seargent and he didn't answer the phone. Bobby Seargent lived five minutes away. Guess what I did? The next day I decide to go to Bobby Seargent's house. I go to his door and knock. I yell his name and tell him to come out, we gotta talk. His wife appears. Tells me to get the hell out of here. I said not until I talk to Bobby. I asked her if she knew what her husband did. She said, "get out of here or I'm calling the cops."

I said, "okay, let me tell you what he did. He tried to pick up my girlfriend while we were in the bathroom." I told her what happened and she said that wasn't the truth. I knew Bobby was in the house hiding. I yelled out, "come out here you coward, come out here!" She proceeded to be the person with the pants in the family standing up to me and Bobby became the person with the dress, just hiding in his room I would imagine. I couldn't believe that was Mister big shot Hal Needham's stunt double. After a few minutes, he just wouldn't come out so I left fuming. Before I did, I let him know verbally that I was not finished with him and that I was going to ground pound him when I see him. My last words were, "I WILL see you, Bobby." Fox- Green didn't deny it. My girlfriend has no reason to lie. I yell up at the house to Bobby. I say, "Bobby, you know I'm going to see you again, we run with the same crowd. I'm going to see you and when I do, we'll settle it then." That's how mad I was. So days go by and I don't see Bobby. I don't see Don Fox-Green. I start asking people, Stunt Coordinators if they have seen these people and they haven't.

The next day Roy Clarke calls me up and tells me he is doing a television show called *Emergency*. He tells me to come to Universal and he will leave a pass for me. He wants to talk to me about this job he has for me. He wanted to introduce me to Randy Mantooth who was the star of the show and Gary Jenson who was another stuntman to discuss what we were going to do on the show. I set out to meet him at the production offices at Universal which are in the back. I walk in and see the security guard Scotty (you remember him) and told him I was going to the production offices. He smiled saying come on in. Good old Scotty. I pull into the parking lot of the production offices and they are standing outside. Teddy Shields the Producer/Production Manager of the show was also there. Mind you he was a little Jewish guy, five foot one, eighty seven pounds soaking wet. He was a big hot shot at Universal at that time. I walk over and Randy Mantooth is there, Roy Clarke, who doubled the actor James Gardner all his career, and Gary Jenson is there as well. I walk over there and Roy Clarke introduces me to everybody in the circle. He starts explaining to everyone what the piece of action is and what we are going to do. He gave me a page with my lines and action and we are talking about the Martial Arts. Teddy Shields is asking about my "Martial Arts stuff." I told him yeah, talked about my Kung Fu and abilities. Teddy Shields is a very demanding hyper little guy. He reminded me of a poor man's Peter Lorre with a double breasted suit. Minutes go by and we are in conversation and all of a sudden out of the corner of my eye, I see a van pull up into the parking lot. We continue talking and in my head, I'm thinking, I know that van. The door opens, a guy gets out and takes off his cowboy hat. Guess who it is? Yes, it's Don Fox-Green. He starts walking over to me like the showdown at the O.K. Corral. Here I am with Teddy Shields, a huge producer at the time and the closer he gets, the more I feel that something is going to happen here. He comes forward and literally pushes Gary Jenson and Roy Clarke aside and he lunges at me. He grabs me around the collar and shoves me against the big glass double doors of the building.

Now in my mind, the golden rule is you never fight on the set or in the studio. That is the golden rule. I try to tell him as he is tossing me around that this is not the time or the place. He just won't listen. I quickly trap his hands. He's lifting me in the air and banging me against the door. Everyone around us is screaming. Teddy Shields jumps back and Gary Jensen jumps back, no one knows what is going on. We are up against the door and I know I can't hold him very long, I know. He's a big football player trying to flatten me. So on the fourth time that he bangs me against the door, I put my foot behind his body and he flies past me into the window. Then I release my lock and start pounding on him. Everyone begins to realize what is going on and they are screaming again to stop fighting. I'm not stopping. I'm upper cutting him and punching him like there is no tomorrow. Finally, he falls on the floor after about a dozen punches. Randy Mantooth grabs me around the neck, Roy Clarke has my arm and Gary Jensen is in front of me. They are all trying to stop me. They were holding me back as hard as they could. See the idea when you fight is that you can't just stop. Especially with a guy like Don Fox-Green who is a big football player. You can't just punch him and then stop. He will most likely come back at you and get a good punch in. Besides, the only thing that was on my mind is what he did to my girlfriend. So he is on the floor and they all have a hold of me. Little Teddy Shields is jumping up and down yelling, "let the little guy go. Let the little guy go. Let him kick his ass." That's all I see in the middle of this fray. At that moment I managed to get away without hurting anybody and get a few more shots in while Don Fox-Green is running away. Everybody comes and grabs me again. Don Fox-Green gets up all bloody and Roy Clarke is asking what the hell is going on. Don doesn't say a word, just heads for his van, like a beaten city Cowboy that just dropped his football. I explained to everybody what happened and they were all in disbelief.

I get a call the next day from Frank Orsatti, asking me to come to his set on the television show *The Hulk* to explain what happened. Little did I know, Don Fox-Green had told Frank and Charlie Perchurni and Tommy Huff along with some others that I had started a fight, but didn't tell them the truth. So I go to the set and see all these stunt guys and tell them what really happened and why I was so upset. They are completely on my side. After setting them straight, I left and faster than one of my punches, it was all over the industry that I was looking for Bobby Seargent. Three days later, I'm out and about looking for Bobby Seargent and Debbie doesn't want me to go. She is scared about what I'll do when I find him. I decide to drive by Bobby Seargent's house again and I see through the window the house was completely empty. That day I find out the word on the street was that he heard what I did to Don Fox-Green and he "adiosed" back to Texas. Now you have to understand, Bobby Seargent had it good here. He was doubling Burt Reynolds and was in very high demand in the industry. He was a so called big shot who had it made. Yet, because he was afraid of being demoted from a Seargent to a Private if he confronted me, he up and left. Instead of facing me, apologizing, or taking a beating, he left.

(Bobby Seargent, missing in action.)

Don Fox-Green was never the same after that either. His career dwindled. I didn't want any of this to happen, but it did. From then on there, weeks went by, days went by and I found myself being noticed. Everyone told me they heard what happened and all of a sudden, this situation began helping my career. I didn't know it would, but Stunt Coordinators wanted to hire the little guy that beat the big Cowboy. Teddy Shields would take me on, he loved me after the fight. He had told me when he was younger, he was picked on all the time by the bigger guys. So when he saw me fight Don Fox-Green, he put himself in my place and became filled with excitement. I smiled and laughed. Let me finish up this story by saying that a few months later, I asked Debbie to marry me. She said yes. We took off to Vegas and got hitched. A short time later, meaning a couple of weeks, I found myself having a meeting with her parents. A sit down meeting at their house. I couldn't believe it. They wanted me to quit my dream and get a regular job. Yeah, a regular job. Anything other than the movie business. I was stunned, I actually had to make a decision. Be happily married so to speak with a nine to five job, or divorce her. I couldn't believe it. It was a very hard decision to make. This would take me a long time. So the next day I called and just simply said, divorce here we come, and that's the end of that tune. That's how wild and crazy it can get behind the scenes.

CHAPTER 13
(Show business. Illegally Allowed.)

Speaking of wild and crazy, I had mentioned that I was an athlete before coming into this industry. Didn't touch a beer before I was twenty two years old. I found however, that everywhere I went was full of booze, marijuana, and cocaine. I could tell you from being there, people outside the movie business would not believe how rampant it was. I'm not talking about one celebrity or a crew member. It was Directors, it was camera, it was actors, it was Wardrobe, it was Effects, it was Stunts, everywhere you turned someone would be snorting cocaine. Nobody ever got in trouble, I had never seen anything like it. At that time, the President's wife, Nancy Regan was very against drugs. "No On Drugs," was her slogan. While a war raged over drug control outside the movie business, inside of it there was no war. Everyone was using drugs all day every day in harmony. It was all kept quiet. When you worked on a show on a regular basis, you would find out real quick what was going on. You'd see Effects was snorting Cocaine on the set, moments before they did their job. For example, Reid Rondell, Snuffy's son invited me onto the set of *Airwolf*. People don't know that after the first season, *Airwolf* became a closed set. Nobody could get on it unless you were working on it. Reid was doubling Jan Michael Vincent so I was able to get on. Well, what do you think I saw? I saw the star snorting Cocaine! That's why it was a closed set. Me being the new guy, quickly caught on to it. Now before you start thinking certain things, let me just say after about a year of it I stopped. I got sick of it. Cocaine keeps you up and after sitting in bed unable to sleep, watching the sunrise I said enough is enough. I'm miserable. So I stopped cold turkey, while over the years other people continued to do it. These were wonderful people, they weren't bad. But it was allowed and it was the thing to do. The movie people of today that weren't around when I started don't realize how pervasive the drug factor was. You put your life on the line with people behind the camera and in front of the camera and some of these guys were snorting left and right, they just weren't all there. You would just have to hope for the best. Some people in the industry after every cut, would literally go to their trailer and get their fix. Snorting cocaine was like having a soda. I had a close friend, who worked on a major television show. He was like a brother to me. During this cocaine era, my best friend was an addict. He was running a show and he got fired off of it because of his cocaine problem. His father wanted to kill him. He managed to convince the Producers to let him take care of the show until his son got out of rehab. After a year he became straight and his father gave him the show back with much love and affection that they both have for each other. I was there when he first got the show, they released Buddy Joe Hooker for some reason and called him up. He was so excited, he screamed.

Back to the drugs. It was normal, everyone did it and no one got in trouble. Even though the Regan's war on drugs was going full blast outside, inside the movie industry where they both had spent time, it was nowhere to be found. Let us take Jan Michael Vincent. I respected him for the great athlete he was, but then he became a hobo pandering for money on Venice Beach. I know this because I saw it and just shook my head at this very sad moment. That is what that stuff can do to you. 1973 to 1986 was the heart of the drug era in the picture industry. I know this because I asked. Moving along from one television show to another, it seemed like everyone remembered me from my encounter with Don Fox-Green and wanted to work with me. Whether I wanted it or not, this experience made everybody aware of me and my abilities and the jobs started to pour in.

Remembering a heart stopping moment, I get a call from a coordinator named Paul Stater. I knew his son Peter and became close friends with him. He put my name in to work on this army television movie. I was doubling an actor and a stuntman named Steve Kelso was doubling another actor. Paul Stater was an Olympic Swimming champion. Very famous person, tremendous athlete, used to double people like John Weissmiller (who was Tarzan), Douglas Fairbanks Jr., Earl Flynn and John Carradine. (David Carradine's father.) We go there and go to Wardrobe, get our hotel room, etc. We meet Paul and talk over the meal about what we are supposed to do and he tells me I will be doubling the lead and Steve Kelso is doubling the co-lead and Paul will be driving a big army truck in the middle of a city street in Arizona. The actor Steve Kelso is doubling is walking across the street and the truck runs a red light. I was supposed to rescue him or what we call a "bulldog," which was to run and grab him before he got hit by the truck. This is the night before, so we both know what is going on. I look at Kelso and we all agree it is no big deal. So we go to bed, wake up in the morning and go to Wardrobe. After that, we go on the set and the cast and crew are standing around getting ready for the shot. We are out in the middle of the street and transportation comes over with the army truck.

Kelso and I are hanging back, watching and listening. Paul Stater is explaining what the action of the scene is going to be to the actors and everyone else. The truck is going to come and almost hit, but the actor is going to be saved at the last moment and then dialogue goes on. Kelso and I are watching him explain and then all of a sudden, as if time itself stopped, he just freezes. Right in the middle of the conversation. Yep, you heard me. Freezes. He's frozen solid. No facial expression, no body movements. His hands are up in the air like he is in the middle of talking. Sounds crazy, doesn't it? Everybody is looking and all of a sudden someone shouts his name. Then another person. Soon everyone is screaming Paul's name. Paul is not moving. I'm looking at Paul and all the people. Everybody is afraid to touch him. Everybody gets hysterical. What's wrong with him? People are screaming in his ear. I've never seen anything like this. None of us know what is going on. In a matter of forty seconds, the whole set is in an uproar. I hear someone yell for an ambulance, doctors, paramedics. I look at Paul's face and it's a face of obscurity, like a mannequin. I don't know what possessed me to do this, but I broke through the crowd and grabbed him. I was pulling him away, actually pushing him away. Protecting him from the crowd. I walked him around the truck he was driving and everyone is following us. So yeah, he's walking but it is kind of a sluggish walk, his feet are being dragged. It's just me, him and Steve Kelso. I don't know what to do. Two, three seconds go by and I grab him and yell his name. I give him a good shake and by this time there are four or five people including the Director and the actors coming over. I give him another good shake again and suddenly Paul wakes up and he is continuing his dialogue! He comes back over like nothing ever happened. People are asking him what happened, why he froze, they had to call an ambulance. You could hear it arriving. Paul is continuing in his conversation and they tell him again that he froze.

Paul stops and blinks. "Oh, that happens sometimes," he says. He lifts up his shirt and proceeds to tell us his pacemaker stops sometimes and it freezes him. Everybody is freaking out because the pacemaker is visible. It is protruding out of his chest. You can actually see the shape. He tells the ambulance to go away and everyone listens to him. Fifteen minutes go by and I lose Steve Kelso. I'm watching Paul and all of a sudden, I hear Kelso whisper to me that he has to talk to me in private. I tell him not now, I want to watch Paul, make sure it doesn't happen again. He whispers again that he needs to talk to me. I relent and we walk away to a more private area. Kelso looks at me and asks me what we are going to do. I didn't know what he meant. He looks at me and says Paul is going to be driving the truck. What happens if he freezes again? I look at Steve almost laughing at him in amusement. He suggests someone else drive the truck. I told him no, let him drive. I see everything. If something happens don't worry, I'll get you out of the way. If he doesn't stop the truck and he freezes, I'll get ya. You see, let me explain. The difference between Kelso and me is that he was serious in what he was saying. I thought it was humorous.

"Relax, nothing is going to happen to you. Besides, we don't want to embarrass Stater. We can't replace him," I said. I'm arguing with Kelso that it will be okay, he is scared! What are you going to do, tell the Production Manager? It's going to get back to Paul. So I convinced him that I would bulldog him out of the way. We did it and nothing ever happened. That night we were going to meet for dinner and everyone is talking about what happened. Paul is telling everyone it happens all the time no big deal, all you have to do is shake him around and he'll snap back. Now before dinner, we go over and Paul is in the pool swimming a hundred laps. The guy is seventy something years old and now swimming a hundred laps with his pacemaker. True story, but I can honestly say that the funniest part about this was Steve Kelso being scared shitless. Things were going well and I met a lot of people. Stuntman Bob Bravler was a great guy who hired us but I could tell you one thing. He was a great Second Unit Director but when it came to stunts he would go overboard. Let me give you an example that I and every other person on the set found to be humorous. A stunt that would require only a few pads, he would put and I'll never forget this, dozens more pads than needed. When he came out of his trailer, he looked like the Michelin man or let me give you another visual, the Pillsbury Dough Boy or the Stay puft marsh mellow man. All padded up, with his pipe in his mouth. We often joked what he filled that pipe with. Regular tobacco or whacky tobaccy? He weighed about a hundred sixty five pounds but the way he looked, it appeared he was two hundred sixty five pounds. He was one of two good men that happened to be the cheapest paying men I worked with in my life. When I say one of the two, I'll let you know later on who the second one is. I never complained about getting a job and of course residuals came with it and we got an adjustment. We would get paid for what stunt we did and depending on how good it came out we would get money above the contract which we called an adjustment. It could be one hundred bucks, three hundred bucks or it could be thousands depending on the stunt. It could be any amount. The cheapest adjustment would be about a hundred bucks. Well Bob Bravler loved to give out twenty five and fifty dollar adjustments. Didn't matter if you cheated death itself. I'm sure everyone that worked with him loved him. Yes, we all admired and liked him and I will always be thankful for the work I received from him, but I say this out of respect, he was one of the cheapest son of a guns I've ever worked for at my job.

While we are at it, let's tell another Bob Bravler story. It was on a television show called *Eischied.* Joe Don Baker was the star. I put my wardrobe on, see Bob Bravler and I find out I'm working with another stuntman named Deny Arnold. For you stunt people out there, from the seventies and eighties, you know the name. Now

Deny was quite an unusual character, to say the least. He was a little off. To say the most, he was mashugana in the cup. That means crazy in the head in Yiddish. He invented apparatuses for stunts like the air ram, a machine that catapults you through the air. A very clever and nice guy when he is sober. So we were both working for Bob Bravler on the shoot. The morning was going slow and our work was to start after lunch. The shot involves using a helicopter. Joe Don Baker is on the skids up in the air and he jumps and bulldogs me in a field, as I'm running. Now it would be Denny Arnold that would be making that jump, stunting for Joe Don Baker as I am doubling the bad guy on the ground. It was a good piece of action. Now Deny Arnold has a history of doing wild and crazy things. On this day I remember sitting down with the Director and the Producer, Joe Don Baker and Bravler. Baker seemed like a nice guy always a smile on his face, yet he gave the look of being scary on the exterior, but he was a big teddy bear. Lunch comes and it's outside in this parking lot. Bob Bravler is sitting next to me as well as the Director and Producer and Joe Don Baker. The Director asks where is the stunt guy who is doubling Joe Don Baker? Bob replies he doesn't know. Mind you, there are about two hundred cast and crew eating lunch at this time, surrounded by honey wagons and mobile offices. We are all sitting down enjoying our food and having good conversation. Laughing and relaxing, when all of a sudden, we hear a faint noise in the sky. Now let's go back, mind you, we have all our food on paper plates with plastic utensils. The Director starts looking around, we start looking around. The noise gets louder and louder. We see a helicopter in the distance about a hundred yards coming right towards us. We then see a figure on the struts of the helicopter. The closer it comes, the louder the noise gets.

Well, speak of the Devil, who do you think that might be? The copter comes closer and the wind picks up from the helicopter blades. People start gathering their food items, hugging them to their chests like scared children. Here it comes, it roars right smack in the middle of the lunch area, literally about thirty feet above us. Food starts flying around, cups and plates join them. A tornado of craft services forms around us. People are yelling, the caterer looks like she is about to have a seizure. Some people are frozen, looking up at this guy in the helicopter while they are trying to hold their food. My eyes are dead set on it, in disbelief. The deafening noise joined by the flying utensils made for a scene from a movie. As the helicopter gets closer, we all realize it is Deny Arnold that is hovering there. He starts unbuckling his pants and drops them. Guess what comes next? You're right, his underwear. He pulls them right down to his ankles. And guess what is hanging there? Two meatballs. I guess because it was lunch time. His rear end appears as well, in the midst of this lunch

113

tornado, laughing hysterically. I look down at everybody at my table. Joe Don Baker is laughing his ass off. The Director and Producer's faces are open in amazement with blank expressions, while I found myself laughing at the mayhem around me. While everyone else is screaming or running or laughing, catering is raising their fists, screaming at Denny Arnold in the helicopter to get the hell out of here. It's then I looked over and there appeared my friend, Bob Bravler. He is sitting there in the fetal position shaking his head, with his elbows on the table and his head resting in the palms of his hands. Looking at his expression, I come up with the conclusion that it is a combination of sick to his stomach, angry, shocked and depressed.

(Bob Bravler)   (Wild man Denny Arnold)

When I hear him mutter, "why, why is this happening to me? I knew I shouldn't have hired him."

I reach out with my hand and put it on Bob's back and say, "are you okay?"

He turns his head towards me and simply says, "I knew if I brought him on, he was going to embarrass me. I'd fire him but the star, Joe Don Baker won't let me." I say to myself, I don't know, I must tell you that it's for sure not the right thing to do, but I sure think it's funny. After a minute, the helicopter speeds off and like that he is gone. Now let me ask you if this wasn't in the movie industry do you think there would have been a backlash? Oh yeah. People would be put in jail, the pilot would have lost his license. But we are in the movies. Not a single thing happened. How many cast and crew, how many pedestrians walking down the street saw the whole thing? At least a couple hundred people saw this. It was never on the news or in the paper. All because we worked in the movies. Ten minutes later, Denny Arnold came back to the set laughing his ass off. He has a heart of gold but he was insane. Don't ever invite him for a drink. People who knew him would never booze him. He was a wonderful guy when he was clean sober and dry. Needless to say, we did the scene without incident and his pants stayed on.

We are on a roll now, let's tell another Denny story. Talking about Denny Arnold, I'll tell you how whacko he was. There is a Stuntman named B.J. Davis, some may know him as the former husband of Linda Blair. She couldn't take him either, divorced him in the blink of an eye. One day he rented a huge mansion in the Hollywood hills, Mt. Olympus. I'm talking ten bedrooms and five bathrooms kind of huge. I couldn't figure that out. I wondered where this guy got his money from as he hardly worked. Of course, Linda Blair. He and Denny were running buddies and what I'll call nose buddies. They enjoyed inhaling the magical white sands of paradise. I was going out with my gal when B.J. and Denny invited me to a party at this mansion. They had valet parking starting at the bottom of the hill, for the party that was at the top. When we got there, there must have been five hundred people on the lawn. We managed to squirm through, going into the living room. People drinking on the lavish couches, marble table tops covered with plates of food and bottles of booze. We pushed on out to the patio which overlooked the backyard jacuzzi among games of horse shoes and volleyball. Smoke rose from several BBQ grills as the throng of people were having a very good time. Oh, I forgot to tell you, this is a daytime party. One O'clock in the afternoon. Thought you'd like to know that. There must have been a dozen or so people in the jacuzzi and I quickly recognized one as Denny.

He noticed me immediately. "Steven, come on in. Who is the lovely lady?" he asks. I tell him she is my date and explained we didn't bring a bathing suit. He looked at me with a big smile and a Devil in his eyes as he arose from the bubbles. "You don't need a bathing suit." To my surprise and noticing his schmeckle hanging out, my heart went up to my throat as my date turned around in shock. Before I averted my eyes and turned, I noticed three women and six bumps arising from the bubbles. (You get it?) That is when I also noticed blue uniforms spread out on the ground. A belt with a gun on the holster and handcuffs, a blue hat with a badge on it. Hey you readers out there, are you starting to realize what I'm discovering? "What are you doing? Get back in the jacuzzi, you are embarrassing me you idiot! Aren't you worried the cops are going to get called with the loud blasting music inside and everyone is skinny dipping?"

Denny laughed. "Nah, the cops are my friends, these are their uniforms, look at this." All of a sudden, he reaches down with each palm grasping the grip of two peacemakers. Some heads in the jacuzzi, who I assumed were the cops, turned and looked at him. Before they could act, he lifted the two pieces up to the sky and

BANG! One went off. BANG! The other went off. Those heads jumped out of the jacuzzi and to my surprise, they were also stripped to the bone! They grabbed the guns away from him and I remember as everyone was running away laughing and at the same time scared shitless as I was. I just grabbed my gal and we ran through the parted crowd to the patio and ran down the hill to our car. I gave the attendant a fifty dollar bill to point out to my car and get the keys and booked it as everybody else was trying to do the same thing but never going into their pockets. That is why I was the first one out. The next day I got a call from Denny Arnold who asked where I had ran to. "I ran the hell out," I said. "You shot guns and the cops were there, what the hell happened? Did more cops arrive?" I waited for his answer.

"Oh shit yeah!" he said.

Now I was very interested. "What happened? Did they arrest you? What happened with the cops in the jacuzzi?" I asked.

Denny laughed. "They all joined us! Wouldn't let us continue until we invited them." Boy, talk about house arrest.

Okay, get off the floor and stop laughing for a second. I got one more story about this guy. He gives me a call one day and asks me to come over and hang out, so I did. I got to his apartment and knocked on the door. I hear a muffled, "who is it?" I call out my name and he tells me to come in. I walk and there is a game playing on the tele. He is in this little bar corner when he says, "sit down, watch some football. I'll join you in a second." I sit down and watch. Thirty seconds go by, fifty seconds go by, a minute goes by and I am thinking he is making a drink or something behind that bar. I look at him and I look at him and he has a big shit eating grin on his face. His face was looking up at the ceiling and his eyes were glazed over with strangeness. And I continue to look at him. "Denny, what are you doing?" I ask. He reaches down below him and brings something up. No, not something, someone. A woman. A nude woman. I realize what she is doing and said, "I can't believe it, you're insane." Like a scared puppy dog, I said, "I am outta here." Now you can fall back on the floor and continue laughing. There's more of this but that's enough of Denny.

CHAPTER 14
(A Major Setback And A Major Comeback.)

The great thing about my job is you can always mix pleasure with business. For example, I decided to go dirt bike riding at a place called Pear Blossom, California which was dry desert. I went with a couple of friends. My main partner was stuntman John Meiers. Danny Weselis was also with us. I was a beginner at riding motorcycles then but loved to go out and ride. It's fun but also a tremendous learning experience as motorcycles are involved in action films. We had so much fun camping there, barbecuing, riding and just being together. Eventually at the end of the day, after riding for a few hours we decide to go back and pack up to go home. We were about ten minutes away when we came up to this patch of grass. Except unlike most grass, this patch was five feet high and as wide as a city block. Like a mirage in the middle of the desert, it called to us. We had to ride through it. So that is exactly what we did, back and forth, up and down at fifty five plus miles per hour. It was great fun. So it's getting late and we decide to go through it one last time before we head back. We all get in a parallel line to go through it and off we go. In the middle of it, we are laughing and going as fast as we can. I am going as fast as I can trying to keep up with these guys and enjoying myself when all of a sudden, my bike hits something and I go flying past my handlebars fifteen feet in the air like the graceful monkey I am. Unfortunately, my graceful flying was not as great as my graceful landing as I came down hard onto a boulder sticking out of the dirt, tucking and rolling on the ground. I'm on the ground, wind knocked out of me, the bike's wheels going round and round ten feet away. I'm trying to figure out what happened in my delirium. The guys come up to me and are asking what happened. I didn't know, as it all went by so quickly. They look back and see this five foot wide hole in the ground hidden by the grass. As they look around, they see other holes further away. Well wouldn't you know it, I was the lucky one. Again, why me? A punk kid from Brooklyn. I check myself out and realize my shoulder is hanging limp and boy am I in pain. So the guys pack me in their van and take me to Pear Blossom emergency hospital. They take one look at my x-rays, see I broke my scapula and clavicle and shrug their shoulders. Apparently, Pear Blossom wasn't equipped to operate on me. They gave me a shot of Demerol and from then on there I was a space case, laughing and feeling no pain. I was screaming, "let's go back and do it again!" John and the others were having a good time just watching me.

Exasperated but flying high, we packed ourselves back into the van and drove two hours back to Los Angeles. All the while we were on the phone trying to find a

Doctor who could perform an operation to put my poor shoulder back together. We found a stunt woman whose father was an Orthopedic surgeon. His name was Doctor Grant and he would see me the same day. He was one of the best in the United States. So we did surgery at Northridge hospital and he put two screws and two steel shafts in my shoulder. That was a bummer. A week later, we had a meeting and he told me I would be out for at least six months. This was a powerful blow to me. No shoulder, no stunts. In those days if you get hurt, it could show that you were inferior. Second, you just obtained a major injury so people wonder if you can come back from that. People would use any weakness, real or perceived to disparage a person and take their job. I sure hoped I could heal quick. Doctor Grant told me it would be up to me how fast I would heal and If I would make a full recovery. The more he explains this to me, the more I'm getting a headache and going into this migraine of reality. I was opening up all these doors, meeting all these new people and now I'm going to be out for six months plus? I couldn't believe it. He then tells me in three months I had to come back so he could take out the steel shafts. Then I would have to leave the arm alone and start with physical therapy for another three months. Then six more months to hopefully bring it back. It's not so easy after ripping your arm completely out of its socket in two pieces. Muscles, tendons, everything. I'm just looking at him thinking, oh my God, is this the end? So three months go by and God bless I have friends that help me. Rick Kahana is coming over to help me, John Meiers, Vince Deadrick Jr., Joel Kramer, Roy Harrison, Peter Stater, all these people I have met and became friends with. You can't go out and hustle when your injured, you stay secluded and try to heal. Hiding from everybody and not being able to do anything physical. I was a fish out of water. Can't do exercises, can't do stunts, can't do Kung Fu, can't hang out with friends else they talk about your injury to other stuntmen. It was horrible.

Three months go by and I have to go get the shafts removed. My friend Joel Kramer says he will take me, that's the sign of a true friend when they help you out like that. I'm sure he also wanted to see what would happen, knowing Joel. He packs me up in his car and takes me to Doctor Grant. We get there and Doctor Grant starts prepping his tools. Now you have to understand, I've had these shafts and screws in my arm for three months now. They have literally become a part of me. If you pressed on one of the shafts sticking out of my arm, I could feel it. Doctor Grant tells me that the following week they were going to take out the screws. Okay great, I am thinking. So today is just going to be a checkup for the surgery next week. Doctor Grant has all these instruments laid out and I'm thinking they are cleaning instruments. I'm not a Doctor so I have no idea. I'm listening to him talk to me about the surgery next week and when to come in, what is going to happen and so on as he is preparing the tools. Joel starts talking to me and we are laughing and having a good time. Before I know it, my bandages are off and I'm ready for the Doctor to clean my wounds as Joel is trying to make me laugh. I'm talking to Joel as my head is turned away from my Doctor and away from my wound. I'm laughing and all of a sudden, I don't know what the Doctor is doing, but I feel something latch onto one of my steel shafts. It feels like he is grabbing a part of me. I turn and in a split second, I see a pair of surgical pliers. He's grabbed a hold of one of these shafts and before I could say anything, he pulls. When he pulls, I flinch up. It feels like he's pulling bones, pulling my arm off. Before I can think, I go into shock. I can't breathe, the pain has taken over my mind. He hasn't numbed up my arm or put me to sleep or anything. Then he stops pulling and I realize it is only half out. How do I know it's only half out? (I barely remember this because my mind was spinning.) Because Doctor Grant opens his mouth and says, "oh this sucker is in tight." He hadn't pulled hard enough! The next thing I know I feel queasy as he is trying to get a good grip on this thing to pull out the first one. I don't know what happened next because the next time I opened my eyes I'm lying on the ground with Joel Kramer practically straddling over me laughing his ass off in my face. Wouldn't you know it? I had passed out! On top of that, the Doctor pulled out the other one while I was down for the count. Joel helps me up and sits me in a chair. I'm confused, angry and in a state of disbelief. I look up at the Doctor and I simply say "What did you do that for?" He shrugs. "What do you mean?" He replies. "You didn't even tell me or prepare me," I shot back. "I thought you knew," he said timidly. Well of course I didn't know! I hear someone laughing and I turn my head. Joel is still laughing as I am fuming inside. I ask him what he is laughing about and he points a finger at me. "You, Goyim," he says. I headed back home shaft free with Joel laughing the whole way back. What a pal, my good friend Joel Kramer. He made me laugh through the pain. What are friends for?

The next week I went into surgery and got the screws out. Everything went well. When I woke up, Doctor Grant told me to give him a call in the next few days so we can start physical therapy. I was excited about that. As the days and weeks went by with the therapist just trying to get some rotation in my arm, I knew if I didn't work at this hard, my arm wouldn't be the same. The physical therapist gave me some exercises to do that consisted of just trying to raise the arm, lift it forward and laterally. They would massage the arm and help me try to rotate it. A few more weeks went by and I started to get a little more rotation. I went to have a meeting with Doctor Grant. He tells me that it is going to be at least another three months. I thought back to what I was going to do. This was my life wasting away here. After three weeks of therapy, I inquired when I would be able to lift weights and do pushups. I was told not for another few months. I thought to myself and don't get me wrong, I always have been taught you should listen to the Doctor, but I also knew some things were mind over matter. I made up my mind to start progressing even though the Doctor said not to. I started lifting half pound weights. I couldn't even move it half an inch. This enraged me. I would do this up to twenty times a day. I would be so upset. I would lay on the ground and put my body into a lady push-up position with my legs flat on the ground and tried to push up my upper body. I just couldn't do it which upset me even more. I went back to the Doctor and told him what I was doing with the weight lifting and the pushups.

He tells me he doesn't advise that I continue. I said okay but I got home and I just felt like I had to continue my exercises. Doctor Grant was a great Doctor but he didn't understand, he couldn't understand how determined I was. My mouth told him yes, but my mind said otherwise. For days, hour after hour, I would try to do that one ladies pushup. I would try and fail. Try and fail. This went on for two weeks. I was getting nowhere but I had to keep trying. At the end of two weeks, I tried again and to my surprise, I finally got up. I screamed in excitement. I did a lady' s pushup! I did a lady's pushup! Happiness flowed through my body. When I went back to see Doctor Grant, I told him I did a lady's pushup. I told him I would show him and proceeded to get down onto the ground. He told me not to do it, but I wasn't listening. I got down on the floor and showed him. He shook his head and said I had better be careful. I told him I would, but in my mind, I was already thinking about trying to do a man's pushup. Nothing was going to stop me now. After another week I did my first man's push up. I danced around my house screaming that I did my first man's pushup. I knew if I could do that, I could get my arm healed. I start working my arm ten times a day for two more weeks. This was way ahead of schedule and now all guns were blazing. I started moving onto other things and picked up my Chinese staff. Slowly, I began to twirl it, getting my shoulder used to the movements. I was excited, I knew in my heart I was going to get my shoulder to where it was before the accident.

Then one day I was rotating the staff above my head and I heard a sickening crack come from my shoulder. Pain shot through me like a bullet on fire. I dropped the staff and it smacked onto the floor. I got scared, I thought I broke it. I was mortified that all my work, all my progress just vanished in an instant. I flew to the phone and dialed Doctor Grant. I told him I heard a crack like I never heard before and was in tremendous pain. He told me to come in and he would look at it. My mind was afire. Maybe I really should have listened to him and taken it easy. This whole time I was healing I was on Demerol for the pain. It made me feel wonderful and took away most of the discomfort. So I popped one and went to see the Doctor, feeling like my life was on the line. He took x-rays and came back in the office and I asked what the crack was. He said the crack was the same as when you get out of bed in the morning and stretch out. Everything was atrophied for months and when I worked it out, I opened up the shoulder. I asked him if he was sure and he smiled at me in disbelief and said yeah. He warned me to still take it easy and I said sure, sure, sure, whatever you say Doc. I went home as happy as could be ready to progress my healing even more. If you want a visual what this was like, look up the Jimmy Kimmel video on Youtube called, Guillermo injures his knee. Check it out. https://www.youtube.com/watch?v=jvYD0l-RPA0. So go take a look at that now. I'll wait. Let me know when you are done. Pretty funny huh?

I have one more Doctor story for you. This one will make you piss in your pants with laughter. It was around this time I had a problem with going to the bathroom. It wasn't that I couldn't go, it was that I went too much. I just couldn't hold it. I decided to avoid the Doctor, let it fix itself. I was that kind of a guy, hated going to the Doctor. Well, it didn't fix itself, and for six months it got progressively worse. Some of my friends told me I had a kidney infection. When one day, I am driving down Ventura Blvd. in Los Angeles and suddenly I got that urge and I looked down while I was driving. I said to myself, "hold it, hold it, hold it in!" But guess what? It didn't listen and it came out like a damn hose. I am yelling at it, but it's not listening. I find myself in Lake Lambert (it's a private lake) and my paddle didn't work. So I guess that's when I decided enough was enough. Time to call the Doc. I called my Doctor of about twenty years up and made an appointment and explained the situation. When I went in, I found my Doctor was absent. He was on vacation. They had a replacement Doctor instead who I didn't know. I thanked the nurse, who I knew well by now and went into the room. I get dressed in my gown and sat down on the table. Whoops, that was cold. The Doctor comes in and I explain to him my problem. He nods, takes some notes and asks me to turn around and bend over. Not understanding why, I do it anyway. The Doctor asks me a question. "I heard you were in the movies. Did you work with Chuck Norris?"

I nodded. "Yea, I-FINGER!!" Instantly, I flew over the table, doing a forward roll, smashing into the ground as I felt something going up my uh, uh, how should I say this? Okay, going up my butt! I get up in horror, looking at him from the other side of the table. Enraged I got up as furious as could be.

"What the BLEEP was that!?" I yelled. Flying across the table, like a crazed samurai, I grabbed the Doctor by his neck and shirt collar, slamming him against the wall. His face was white as a ghost as his mouth moved silently. "You think it's funny to stick your finger up my butt? What is wrong with you?" I blasted at him. The sound of footsteps entered the room as the nurse tried to get me to let him go.

"It's a prostate exam, Mister Lambert. That is how it is done, please let him go." The nurse was hysterical, I was furious and the Doctor was terrified. You have to understand, I am a punk kid from Brooklyn as I have and will continue to say, and I had never heard of a prostate exam. This Doctor didn't even have the courtesy to tell me what he was going to do which made me even angrier! I continued as the nurse is screaming in my ear, "let him go." I let Doctor Finger go, as a few of his buttons fell to the floor. I changed my clothes and left, still steaming mad. My Doctor called me the next day and I yelled at him too for not telling me what was going on. I felt violated. My personal bubble busted. I told him he should have told me what he was doing and then hung up on him. I wound up going to another Doctor, one who wasn't so hands on. He gave me antibiotics. P.S. I never saw my old Doctor again. I hope you got a good laugh out of that story, I sure didn't. All right, enough talking about the Doctor, let's move on. I had a friend who was a stuntman named Marvin Walters who was doing all kinds of television shows at Universal Studios. Physically at this time I am doing four to five pushups and it hurts but I'm doing them. A few weeks go by and I get a call from Walters who wanted me to come back and work a show. He never saw someone do action like I did, the way I did it. I told him I wasn't ready yet. He replied I would only be driving a car. I didn't know if I could, but I told him if he had confidence in me, then I would try my best. I figured if I did it, people would hear that I am back. So I took it.

There were about seven to eight stunt guys doing car stuff on that day. I was picked to drive a new Volkswagen Bug. He tells me I am driving the lead car. I look at him with my mouth open. You mean to tell me that all these guys will be chasing me and I have to steer to avoid them with one arm? He told me it's all slapstick driving, no one eighties or tight turns just weaving and turning the wheel. I'm beginning to get nervous. My arm wasn't fully healed and I didn't know how it would turn out. I was able to do a staff real slow and a couple of pushups, but I had no idea what might happen here with only about thirty five percent of my arm back. So now I'm in the lead car and six, seven drivers are behind me. I'm sitting in the car and mind you only the stunt guys knew I was hurt and semi recovered from the injury. Everyone else including the cast and crew had no idea. So we all get to our marks and they call action. Now I didn't drive the car over to my mark, transportation did. When I get in the car, I look and see it is a stick shift! Now I'm thinking about how I'm going to do this. My right arm has to change gears so how can I hold the wheel and change gears when they call action? My head is spinning. I can't get out of the car and ask transportation what I'm going to do, then everyone would know I was injured. Keep in mind I still had a sling for my arm. I just put it in my stunt bag and kept my left arm draped. I decided to put my arm inside the wheel using my knees to hold it while I shift with my left hand. As they roll camera, I take the shift with my left hand and decide to put it in second, thinking there will be less shifting. It's not moving. It's not going in gear. I'm trying again and again before they call action, but it's too late. I look up and I see the seven to eight cars going and I'm not there. Zoom! All the cars behind me race past me and coming across as I'm sitting there trying to change gears. The Director yells, "cut!"

The Stunt Coordinator and transportation runs over to me. They are asking me what's wrong. I tell them it's not going in gear. I'm showing them it's not moving. The transportation guy says that this is the new type of Volkswagen and you have to push down and then put it in gear. All of a sudden, I look up and see seven people looking through the window. Boy was I embarrassed at that moment. I didn't know all you had to do was push down. I'm trying to keep calm, not letting on that I'm hurt. I nod and tell them I'm ready to try again. I felt so small at that moment. It could happen to anyone, yes, but it happened to me. Again, why me? This time I'm ready and they call action. I push down and go. I'm weaving in and out, doing what I'm supposed to. It went like a charm. I never sweat during a stunt, I'm a cool cat. But here, I was sweating bullets. Not because the stunt was hard, or because I didn't know how to execute it, but because I had to be the one-armed swordsman. Luckily it went wonderful on the second take. I couldn't believe I had gotten away with it. Now I knew that I could keep doing jobs like this. If someone wanted me to do something that would involve my arm or landing on my shoulder, I would just say that I was unavailable and had another gig. This way I could still be back but have time to heal. Let's cut this story short. A month later I was doing forty pushups, fully recovered, ready to rock and roll and slam on the ground. I must say I went to the Doctor for the last time and I'll never forget what he told me. Simply he had never seen anybody heal so fast. Martial Arts had a lot to do with it, no it had everything to do with it. Sometimes you just have to be your own hero. Let's proceed.

CHAPTER 15
(Life's Decisions.)

Things are going wonderful. I'm finding myself not having to hustle. People are calling me now. I'm getting calls from Stuntmen's Association, Stunts Unlimited. I never thought it would happen but it's happening. Time goes by and stunt man Vince Deadrick Jr. comes to ask me specifically if I was interested in joining the Stuntmen's Association. There were five to six members in the Stuntmen's Association I became close with. This included Vince Deadrick Jr., Peter Stater, Mike Cassidy, John Robothan, Tom Morga and Tommy Rosales. I told Vince I would think about it and get back to him. I asked him if he discussed it with anyone else and he said no, just his father, Vince Deadrick Sr. who was a stunt double for actor Steve McQueen. He became like a second father to me and Vince Jr. became like a brother, that is how close we were. Anyway, getting back to being asked, I thought it was wonderful. He explained to me he needed five letters from people that worked with me if I decided to join. I asked him for some time and he said of course. So I went to Roy Harrison and discussed it with him as he was somewhat of a mentor to me. He was in Stunts Unlimited and I told him the discussion I had with Vince. He proceeded in saying that I had worked a lot in Stunts Unlimited as well and people thought highly of me there. He explained I should think about it and not rush to a conclusion. I looked at him and said are you telling me to wait and think about it? Of course, Snuffy replied with his classic look over his glasses. I knew he wasn't going to give me a straight answer. He told me I had to figure it out for myself. I replied that he had just told me that Stunts Unlimited might be interested, so what did he mean exactly. He gave me the look again and told me I had to figure it out. I asked if he would still hire me and he said of course but you must be loyal to your group and think of them first. He told me that if there was ever an opportunity, he would hire me but he also said I had to understand that there were people out there that didn't think the same way he thought. I had to take that into account as well. That was all I got out of him and the conversation moved onto other things.

I thought about this for two weeks and meeting with Vince Deadrick Jr. again, it came up. Well here were my thoughts. Stuntmen's Association was the original group that was started in 1961. Stunts Unlimited branched off. Ronnie Rondell, Hal Needham and Glen Wilder were originally members in the Stuntmen's Association before deciding to leave after a disagreement. They formed their own group called Stunts Unlimited. On their buckle, there is a symbol of three birds that represented them. From what I know now from both groups, that was a very smart thing to do, since the Stuntmen's Association isn't that smart and progressive as Stunts Unlimited turned out to be. With Stunts Unlimited, it is, "all as one and one for all." With Stuntmen's Association, it's more, "all for me and none for you." I thought about that. People like Chuck Roboson who doubled John Wayne, Harvey Perry who doubled Charlie Chaplin, the Three Stooges, Humphery Bogart, Bear Hutkins who drove Clark Gable (he would tell me stories of picking Clark Gable up and taking him to MGM) and Davey Sharp who was a favorite of mine had doubled people like Buster Keaton. I loved stories of the old days, the old movies, the old ways. All these people came from the Stuntmen's Association. Back then that group was great. Now Stunts Unlimited had people like Hal Needham who doubled Burt Reynolds, Ronnie Rondell, Buddy Joe Hooker, Alan Gibbs, even the first woman who became a member of a stunt group, Janet Brady. There hasn't been one since. (She later married Alan Gibbs and became Janet Gibbs.) We once had a meeting in the Stuntmen's Association about bringing in a woman, and can you believe it? All of them all went nuts except for a few. I personally thought it would have been terrific. They wouldn't allow it and threatened to quit, so that idea went out the window. Male Chauvinist pigs. It never happened. These were also people I looked up to and admired. Sitting back for a couple of weeks, I tossed around in my head which one I would enjoy more, which would be more exciting and beneficial. I thought back to the conversations of people I had from both groups. All this came into play. I turned to Vince Deadrick Jr., knowing there was no turning back and I opened my mouth. "Stuntmen's Association," were the words that came out. I had made my decision.

It was a huge decision. I really couldn't go to any family or friends to guide me in a situation like this. You see my family wasn't in this business and friends just might guide you the wrong way because they are dreaming about the same thing. I'm in a situation that people only dream of. It was unreal. I finally made the decision, wrong or right I had made it. If you ask me now, if I did the right thing, I would simply say, "HELL NO." Soon after one of my closest friends, Mike Vendrell called me.

CHAPTER 16
(Becoming Best Friends With Mike Vendrell.)

Here is a funny story of how we first met. It was on *Hart to Hart*. Stuntman Greg Barnett told me about a guy he met named Mike Vendrell. Greg would always call people Buddy. Hey buddy, buddy. He would always make you smile when he said that. It doesn't matter if he knew your name or not. So I always say, "hey buddy" when I see him. Now he told me that he had met and talked to a stuntman named Mike Vendrell who I hadn't met before. Among other things, he discussed that in Kung Fu, fighting came before forms. Meaning they invented all the fight moves before any of the forms were created. Crane, snake, praying mantis, etc. I told Greg that he was mistaken.

Forms came before fighting. They watched all these animals and insects and took their movements and put them into a series of movements which they call forms or Katas. Then they created fighting techniques from the forms.

A few days later I happened to see Greg again. He called me over and told me he had spoken to Mike Vendrell again about what I had said and Mike said that I was mistaken. It went back and forth over a period of weeks. Steven says forms, Mike says fighting, forms, fighting, forms, fighting. It was a playful see-saw, which I'm sure put a smile on our faces. Well if the pot wasn't stewed enough, Greg had an idea to stew it even more. Please understand that Greg Barnett is and was and will always be an angel.

He is one of the nicest and purest people I have ever met in my life. He is very religious, a man that everybody when they are young dreams to be. Honest and sincere. Finally, he said he wanted to get us together so we could hash it out. I told him sure, anytime.

A few weeks went by and I saw Greg who told me Mike would go to lunch with us. So we went to lunch and I will never forget this day as it was when I first met one of my soon to be dearest friends and a hero of mine. Greg didn't know what to expect but he was excited and maybe just a little mischievous as an angel can be sometimes. This came soon after my Don Fox-Green incident, so a part of me felt he wanted to see if anything would happen between these two disagreeing parties. We sat down and had lunch.

I would look at Greg every now and then and I could see the excitement in his face wondering what this was going to lead to. An argument, a separation where we never become friends? We started talking and the more we talked the more our chemistry mixed together. It built up the more we got into discussion. Greg's eyes were going left and right, left and right, waiting for some reaction or explosion between us. Then it was over. The result? We became lifelong friends. Greg couldn't believe it but I know he was very happy.

Mike and I just clicked. It didn't matter we were the same age. I found out he was one of the few in the industry that wasn't a liar or cheater or thief. It didn't matter if forms or fighting came first, we were past that.

We would begin hustling together and working together. This was about 1981 and I felt like I was on a high speed train, everything was moving so fast.

CHAPTER 17
(Actors Robin Williams And Jonathan Winters.)

I was getting calls from all kinds of television shows. *M.A.S.H., Dynasty, Dukes of Hazzard, Love Boat, Hill Street Blues, Magnum, Simon and Simon, Quincy, Greatest American Hero, Mork and Mindy, The Hulk*, etc. Let's stop for a moment and let me tell you *a Mork and Mindy* story. I got hired to work on it, stunt doubling a driving instructor who they dressed to look like Dracula. A stunt man named Buzz Bundy was hired to double Robin Williams who played Mork and a stuntman named Spero Razatos was doubling Mork's friend. The piece of action was Mork learning how to drive, can you imagine that? Buzz was a professional car driver and was going to ski a car, where you take it on the passenger's side on two wheels. So we get to the location in the backlot of Warner Brothers. Jonathan Winters happened to be there too. In the early eighties, skiing a car was a big deal and very rarely done by few people. Jonathan Winters was a funny man not just on television but in real life. I know this because a bunch of stunt guys would hang out and meet and discuss the current shows that were going on that day at this restaurant on Ventura Blvd. called Patties. A lot of stunt guys would get together and meet and we would have breakfast there about three times a week and guess who strolled by every morning? Yes, Jonathan Winters.

(Steven Lambert and Jonathan Winters, reminiscing about Patties.)

He would stroll by on his daily walk for exercise. We would say hello and he would stop and talk to us. He would tell us jokes and make us laugh. He was a very funny man. Now I see him on the set and ask him if he remembers me. He does remember me from the restaurant. He asks me if I was going to do crazy stunts today and I told him yeah, one of the stunt guys is going to ski the car and I'm going to be a passenger, while another guy is going to get outside the car and stand on it as Buzz Bundy is skiing it on two wheels. He laughs and says, "I don't see any snow around."

It took me a moment after I explained, that the light bulb went off and I got the joke. I told him, "no, skiing a car is putting it on two wheels."

He smiled and said that it was going to be quite interesting. So we talk in the scene, Mork drives on two wheels and his friend in the back gets scared and climbs out the window and stands on the top of the car. I'm not supposed to be noticing anything, just giving Mark some scores all the while keeping my eye on Spero, making sure he doesn't fall. Buzz Bundy was a small framed man, a man of few words with a good sense of humor.

He was very well respected. We begin and the Director calls action. I wanted to be as quiet as possible so Buzz could focus on driving and skiing the car. Distance, timing and coordination as I said before are very important. Everything is quiet and we are weaving in and out of cars in the parking lot, making sure I don't say a word, letting him focus on what he is doing. Now Buzz who is doubling Robin Williams is dressed like Mork.

High waisted pants, funny shirt and suspenders. Everyone who knows Buzz Bundy can imagine how hysterical he would look in the Mork outfit.

Everything is quiet, and he goes up on the ramp and starts skiing the car on two wheels.

(From left to right. Spero Razatos, Buzz Bundy and me wearing my James West hat.)

I cue Spero to climb out the window and get up on the car. Five seconds go by, ten seconds go by, everything is quiet. I could feel the concentration, so I thought. Then all of a sudden, Buzz Bundy turns to me and just simply says, "you know Steven, I am happy to do a show like this but I sure hope nobody takes a picture of me because

129

I look freaking ridiculous." My mouth drops open as his eyes are off the road and he is looking at me. To him, it was like walking, or chewing gum. It was nothing.

I laughed and he said, "go on, you can talk to me."

I was amazed. You would think he needed concentration, but Buzz had done this so much it was second nature to him.

There were very few people that knew how to ski a car and Buzz was one of them. After the scene was done and they yelled, "cut," Spero came back in through the window. Buzz brought the car down fifteen feet away from the crew, bouncing down from two wheels to four.

We got out and Jonathan Winters, Robin Williams and the Director get out of their chairs and applauded. They gave Buzz Bundy a standing ovation. Jonathan Winters sticks out his hand and says he had to shake his hand for that, he had never seen anything like it before.

Buzz thanks him and Jonathan walks over to the car and sticks his head in. Robin Williams asks what he is looking for. Jonathan Winters said the Whiskey bottles. He didn't think Buzz did that stunt sober. We all started laughing, those were good times.

CHAPTER 18
(Chinese Culture And Cowboys Don't Mix.)

Soon after I got a call from my now good friend Michael Vendrell. He said he was coordinating a movie named *They Call Me Bruce*. A comedy about Bruce Lee. The lead actor, Johnny Yune, dreams of being Bruce. He wanted me to play a ninja, doubling Margaux Hemingway who was the daughter of writer Ernest Hemingway, I thought that was very cool. I told him I would take the role and I asked him about doubling a female. At that time men were doubling women and it was allowed if you couldn't find a female that could do the action they had to do. Women were just starting to blossom and there were heavy discussions amongst the stunt women. It simply was not fair if the woman was able to do the piece of action. Sometimes the male Stunt Coordinator conjured up a reason or an excuse not to hire a female. I have always believed that women should double women unless in certain circumstances that were too dangerous or if they did not have an understanding of the activity. The same goes for a man. This was a time period where the female stunt performers were beginning to take a stand of having men double them.

If the women now were working back then, it would have been wonderful. There weren't really any women with Martial Arts knowledge in the Screen Actors Guild that stuntmen knew of. At this time, there were a lot of cases where men doubled women. Back in the thirties, forties, fifties, even sixties, there were very few stunt women, but here is one of the greats. Evelyn Finley. Let's get back to *They Call Me Bruce*. Michael Vendrell explained to me that I was going to do four to five weapons as a ninja and he couldn't find any females that knew these weapons. I told him no problem. I was just along for the ride anyway. I wasn't the boss so there would be no repercussions aimed at me. So I took the job, said thank you and we hung up. He called me back the next day and he asked me how many weapons I had. I told him about thirty. He told me to bring them all in so the Director can pick the four to five weapons he wanted to use. I packed up all the weapons I had. Long weapons, short weapons, Chinese weapons, Japanese weapons, everything. The next day I brought them on the set. I found Michael on the set and he asked me to lay them out. The Director wasn't there yet but Michael wanted to see them. So I lay out twenty to thirty weapons. Kwan Do's, sickles, staffs, swords, laid them all out nice and pretty. The crew would walk by and be totally oblivious on what these things were. Vendrell explains to me the set is like a Cowboy Bar. He's bringing in fifteen stunt guys to play Cowboys and the Director is going to pick four to five weapons to use. I asked him, where I was going to put four to five weapons? He explained to me that they were going to appear magically. Like if we used a staff or three sectional, he would open up on the hands and widen out to reveal them. "It will look like magic, don't worry," he assured me. I said okay.

So we proceed to hang out waiting for the Director when the stunt guys started to arrive. These are established well known stuntmen. They were mostly car guys and Cowboys, no Martial arts. They knew basic fights but no Martial Arts or anything like that. In those days, Martial Arts were kind of looked down on and seemed comedic. So they saw the weapons on the floor and they start looking at them and looking at them like they were objects from an alien ship or something. One of them, a big Cowboy named Bill Hart, famous for doubling Audy Murphy and working on many John Wayne movies, sees my three sectional staff and asks if he could pick it up. Bill Hart was a good friend. I used to tease him about being the only Jewish Cowboy. I always dreamed about being one. You see for some reason whenever I teased him about that, he would always deny it. I always thought that was strange, but I had a good time teasing him about it whenever I saw him. I told him sure he could pick it up. He picked it up from the middle and two sticks are hanging down from chains that make up the three sectional staff.

He turns to the other stunt guys and asks what I'm going to do with these broken sticks. The other stuntmen erupt with laughter. They said the chains would be rattling like a ghost in the attic when I used them. He asked me how to use it, so I showed him and did some unusual moves very close to him. Right away he jumped back. I asked him to try it and he began knocking himself in the head, almost knocked himself out. It was solid oak after all. He dropped it to the ground as if it was a rattlesnake. He knew he had made a big mistake. Another guy walked over and picked up a nine ring chain. Those are little knives connected by metal bracelets that are interlocked. At the beginning, they are held on to something that looks like handlebar grips from a bicycle with a swivel connecting the knives. He stared at it and started laughing. He commented on the little knives, stating he could make a nine course meal with each knife.

It was then and there I realized, really realized, how little the stunt and movie industry knew about Martial Arts. Sure, there was Gene Lebell, Doug Wong, Gerald Okamura, Bill Ryasaki, and a few others. But they were older guys and they were Martial Artists. You have to understand that the stunt community and the movie industry was still at its infancy when it came to Martial Arts in America. You had David Carradine in *The Kung Fu Series* and Bruce Lee in *Enter the Dragon*, but it was a whole different thing. All the stunt guys David used would laugh at him, thinking it wasn't very realistic. In *Enter The Dragon*, they used all Asian stuntmen.

You see back then, they were way ahead of us. Hong Kong, China, Japan, you name it. When it came to the Asian community and the Orient, they were hands down above us when it came to Martial Arts. That's a fact. Even today there are few Americans that know Korean, Chinese and Japanese systems. More now, but totally none then in the movie industry. Except for the people I mentioned at the beginning and a few others, that was mostly it. Anyway, they all made fun of my weapons and we laughed about it. Like I said they were Cowboys and car guys and were used to John Wayne style fighting. Using a club, gun or knife instead of a staff or sword. In their eyes, it was amusing. A few minutes later the Director arrived and was fascinated by the weapons. It was nice to see an American Director so engaged with these foreign objects.

(1982. It still amazes me that stuntmen of this day had no knowledge of Martial Arts.)

I explained to him which weapon was used for what and demonstrated how to use them. Ultimately, he picked out four weapons to use. A staff, a three sectional staff, a single chain and a nine ring sword. The Director asked me what the nine rings were on the nine ring sword. I told him the rings represent the nine stars in the Chinese solar system and were used as sharp shurikens that they pulled off and threw at the foot soldiers or the warriors on the horses. He was fascinated.

My old friend and nemesis, Gene Lebell, was there as well. I was excited to work with Gene because we had a fight where he smashes me into a wall face first once and then the second time, I run up the wall and do a backflip over him. He didn't know where I went and when he turned around to look for me, I used my fist and my forearm to run it up, right between his legs hitting the golden goose eggs.

What a ham he was. The expression on his face was classic.

(I told Gene Lebell I was better looking.)

I must say I was proud of beating him up, even though it was just in the movies. Whenever one of the car guys would make a joke about the weapons, he would say, "what do you know? You're just a bunch of car guys, all you know is how to fix a flat on your cars." That was Gene Lebell and of course they wouldn't say boo to Gene, otherwise he would put them to sleep. I gathered all the weapons up and put the ones I didn't use back in the bag. Mike brought the stunt guys on set and he began to put together the fight scene. Before then, I had just gotten into the Stuntmen's Association and a lot of these guys didn't know my abilities yet. It's a standard rule that you are supposed to hire in your group, which I will discuss later in this hopefully interesting book you are enjoying reading, but many did not hire within. During the choreography, the Cowboys would look at what I would be doing and say a good John Wayne left hook would take care of that. I would use the weapons and not expecting it to come so close, they would jump back and shout, "woah," knowing it would hurt if they got hit. Every now and then a Martial Artist has to show a Cowboy how to ride a horse so to speak. You have to stand your ground and tame them. Teach them that boards do hit back sometimes, teach them respect if you know what I mean. We finished putting together the fight and we get ready to shoot it, listening to their complaints on how these things hurt. I would scratch my head knowing some of them crash cars, some of them fall off horses, but they whimper about mildly connecting with a Martial Art move. All I would do is smile and tell them to put on their forearm pads.

You see where a Martial Artist would be used to semi or fully connecting, depending on where it was, an ordinary stunt man would flatly refuse or get upset if you would semi block or semi connect with a punch or a move. In their world there was no touching, it was all fake. That my friends, made a big difference in who you would pick to fight if you had a choice. It just was not done in the normal stunt world. You Martial Arts stunt people out there know what I'm talking about. Before we shot the scene, we had lunch. Mike invited me to sit with him and said he wanted to talk to me about a new movie he was Stunt Coordinating called *Revenge Of The Ninja*. He asked me if I was available and if I wanted to come with him to be his assistant. He told me there was lots of work in it and said he could really use me. I said, "are you kidding, of course I would." So we finish lunch and begin the shoot. The opening scene I found really amusing. I always felt they ripped it off from the show *Wonder Woman*. Margaux Hemingway arrives to this Cowboy bar and goes into an old fashioned telephone booth. She starts turning like Wonder Woman and a song comes on. All of a sudden, she turns into a ninja. When she turns into a ninja, it's really me in the costume spinning around in the booth. The Cowboys see me, her voice is dubbed over mine and the fight begins. I had a great time and it was a wonderful experience to show the Cowboys what I could do and they began to respect me.

Weeks later, going into a Stuntmen's Association meeting, walking into a hundred plus members, I got a lot of pats on the back. It made me feel welcome and feeling like I had found a wonderful family.

CHAPTER 19
(The Birth Of The Ninja. It Begins. Revenge.)

A few days go by and I get called again by my friend, Mike Vendrell. He wanted to know if I could have lunch with him as he had a big problem. He said he would tell me all about it then. I said sure and asked him where he wanted to have lunch. He wanted to go to Jerry's Deli on Ventura Blvd. I told him I knew that place. Now being the Jew I am, I knew how expensive that place was.

A sandwich was twenty bucks! If you had french fries, that would be another six. Coke would be another five. Dessert was twelve bucks! It cost, but it was always good. In those days that was a lot of dough. We met there and talked about the last thing we did together as we usually do, in this case, it was *They Call Me Bruce*. We joked about it and had fun. Then he got to the problem he was having. He said he was doing a movie called *Revenge of The Ninja* with Sho Kosugi and Director Sam Firstenberg. The Production Company was called Cannon Films.

I didn't know any of these people and it didn't matter to me. For me, it was another job. Mike Vendrell then told me the problem. He said he was offered another job. A television show called *Buck Rodgers* with an actor named Gil Gerard. It was going on at the same time and he had to make a choice.

A feature that would go for three months or a television show that could go for ten years. What would you rather do? Of course he wanted to do the television show. He was also offered to double Gil Gerard. So he explained to me that he made a phone call to Cannon and talked to Sam Firstenberg.

He told him he had a television show that he wanted to do and apologized he wasn't going to do the film. He then told him he had a guy that would be a wonderful asset as your Stunt Coordinator and he told him my name. He then told me, with a laugh first, that you guys were going to get along great. I asked why. He said you're both yarmulke heads. I laughed and said, "what do you mean, he is a Jew?"

Mike replied laughing, "yes."

That was a good one. Now that was funny. He continued to explain to me that Cannon films was an Israeli company, so we should all get along great. The laughing continued. Part of Michael's charm was his humor. He really could have been a comedian if he wanted, or a musician. He really played six, seven instruments very well.

I remember we used to live in a place called Fraiser Park. There were two sections. I lived in the Pine Mountain section. It was about five miles away, through the canyon. I remember whenever he wanted to talk to me, instead of picking up the phone and calling, he would get on the back porch and start playing his bagpipes. Yes, you read it right, bagpipes, just imagine that. Mike Vendrell, on his back porch playing his bagpipes. Guess what the song was? The theme from *The Kung Fu Series* with David Carradine. The sound would flow through the canyons, right up to my house. As soon as I heard it, I would just smile and laugh. I knew the phone call was coming next, and sure enough, it did. I remember once I was with him and David Carradine and we were on the beach.

They pulled out their harmonicas and started playing the theme from *The Kung Fu Series* and I played David walking in the sand. It was hilarious. Those were great times with Mike, I miss him very much.

Let's not forget he was also a brilliant Kung Fu practitioner, one of my closest friends and a hero of mine. Hero, that is a special word to me that I only use with special people. To give a job to a fellow stuntman, just isn't done. We are all competitors and most stuntmen wouldn't give you their show in a million years. They would let it go and leave it to chance. What Mike did was an example of a very altruistic action on his part.

Sam told Mike that he would set up a meeting to meet this guy, who just happened to be me. I was just overjoyed. Well, I guess now I have to pay this lunch bill at Jerry's Deli. Hahaha. This was going to be my first major Stunt Coordinator job. Sure, I had done a few things before on *Fantasy Island* and other shows, but this was huge. He gave me Sam Firstenberg's number and as soon as I got back, I called Sam Firstenberg.

You gotta understand to have someone give you a show is an ultimate dream. Especially given to you from a guy you only knew for a few months. No matter how good you were climbing the ladder, it would depend on the wonderful comments and work you got from other people that would bring you into the direction you were headed. Which of course, was hopefully up. You see, you could never do it alone, you always need help.

I explained to Sam Firstenberg why I was calling and he understood right away. He was very overjoyed Mike Vendrell gave him my name because he thought so much of Michael Vendrell.

Anyone would, after the first few minutes of meeting him. Sam and I talked over the phone and he asked me to call him Shmulik. Now in the back of my mind, I'm wondering what the hell is a Shmulik.

Yes, I'm Jewish but not that kind of Jew. I didn't know what a Shmulik was.

(Two wonderful people. Mr. and Mrs. Firstenberg.)

Nevertheless, I didn't care. I had the job. That day he set up a meeting to meet with him the following afternoon. After I hung up, I called Mike Vendrell and let him know that I was going to see the Director the next day. You see for all you new stuntmen out there, keeping the person informed who gave you the job, is the respectful thing to do. Never forget those kinds of people. Most of you out there forget where you come from and who helped you along the way. And for all those who are interested in the beginnings, I want you to know that if it wasn't for Mike Vendrell, I wouldn't be doing this well. Because you see, I did all three. *The Revenge, The Domination and American Ninja*. These movies put me on the map. Again I say, that's why he is a hero of mine. Thanks, Mikey. The next day I go to Cannon film's headquarters and meet Sam Firstenberg and Producer David Womark. Sam hands me the script and I casually open it up to look it over. I realize there are blank pages in the script. I had never seen a script with blank pages before. I decided to ask what was going on. "You didn't finish the script?" I asked. He shook his head and said those pages are where the action goes once we write it in. Write? They wanted me to write? It wasn't just a few pages, it was ten to fifteen in some places. It would say there was a fight on the golf course. I would have to think about what was on a golf course. Water, sand traps, eighteen holes, trees, and come up with the action for it. I told them I would do it. Half of me was overjoyed, the other half was scared to death. Who was I to do this and how was I going to do this, were the questions swirling around in my head. It's an awful lot of responsibility but I believed in myself, my knowledge and of course my imagination.

You see by now, paying attention and working with so many wonderful stunt and Martial Art people in the past, I understood the process, but at the same time, I had no idea how much in this film I was about to do. With that information and my Martial Art ability, I felt sure we were going to rock and roll on this movie called *Revenge Of The Ninja*. David Womark picks up the telephone and hits an extension. All of a sudden, he starts talking Hebrew to the person on the other end. How did I know it was Hebrew? I may not be the best Jew, but I'm Yid enough to know Hebrew when I hear it. Thanks, grandma Rita. Anyway, David Womark hangs up and tells me Menahem wants to talk with me. I ask him what's a Menahem. They start laughing hysterically. They tell me Menahem is the owner of Cannon Films. I said oh, ok. So I go upstairs and talk to the secretary. I tell her that Menahem wanted to see me and she points me down the hall. I walk down and come to a door with **Menachem Golan** in big letters.

I take a deep breath and knock on the door. Suddenly a booming voice echoes from behind it. "Yes, who is it?" It sounded like the voice of God or Moses. Just like Charlton Heston in *The Ten Commandments*.

"It's Steven, your Stunt Coordinator from Revenge Of The Ninja. David Womark wanted me to come and see you." I reply. I could not believe I am yelling this through a closed door, I think to myself. The voice comes again sounding like it was from a megaphone. "Good, good, come in, come in." So I opened the door and my eyes were met with Menahem Golan, the King of Cannon Films. I wound up doing eight movies for Cannon. You want to know what most people think when they work for Cannon? Take a look, I'll wait. Horrified? Good, I'll go on but it was fun and games for me. You see for some reason, Menahem treated me different than most. I got so much respect from him and enjoyed his humor as well as his personality that went all over the place. Whenever I needed something, he would agree and whenever I saw him, he never argued or yelled at me. Where most others, were not that fortunate. I will never forget the many times we saw each other, always the first seven words that came out of his mouth were, "Steven, Steven, you crazy man, come here!"

That always put a smile on my face and I would say, "YES MY LORD I AM COMING!" He loved that. He was a unique man and with all his wildness, craziness and the things that he put people through, I think people really did enjoy and love him in a strange way. Although now that I think about it, the ninety five percent of Israeli people on the show loved him, but the Americans - not so much. Lol. They just couldn't figure him out. And there was always a smile and a shake of the head in confusion when his name came up. Back to the story. He sat there akin to Louis B. Mayor or Samuel Goldwyn, he emanated power. He told me to sit down and he started talking. He spoke for five minutes, telling me how important it is. "Steven, this film is very important to me. I want big action, big, big, big special effects. I want it to be a big film that everyone talks about, bigger than Enter The Ninja. I want the greatest show on earth. Did I say I wanted it big? I do. Can you do that?"

Nodding, excited by his energy I told him, "you bet I can. This film will have lots of action and I will make sure it will be wonderful, every fight and every stunt will be big, big," I found myself shouting, just like Menahem.

He stood up and put out a big glove of a hand. I took his hand and shook it. By his shake, I could tell he was a very passionate and strong man that had been through a lot in his past. "You tell Shmulik and David you are going, you are the Stunt Coordinator."

I told him I would. He handed me a cigar. It was bigger than me. I felt like I was putting a flashlight in my mouth. I walked out of the office laughing and smiling. Looking at the secretary, I motioned with the cigar as I was passing by, acting like Groucho Marx. Here is another fine mess I got myself into. Menachem. Those who knew him will understand.

(My friend. The legend, Menachem Golan.)

I found Sam Firstenberg again and told him the meeting went well. He explained that I would be leaving with him in two weeks to go to Salt Lake City, Utah for prep. I left that day feeling I was given the dream job everybody would want. Nothing could stop me now, or so I thought.

CHAPTER 20
(Accidents Happen To Two Goyim.)

Arriving home, I found my roommate Joel Kramer waiting for me. I told him about the job and he was really happy for me. He also wanted to go get a water bed and wanted to know if I could drive him the next day. As James Cagney once said, "I am on top of the world ma," and told him sure.

The next day we hopped on my motorcycle and off we went to the furniture store to look at waterbeds. Two guys with shorts, shirts and no helmets. In those days, helmets were not required so we went without. Halfway to the furniture store, going about fifty plus miles per hour, we came upon an intersection. Approaching the intersection, we were zooming along through the green light. At this time, unbeknownst to us, a car had broken off from the others waiting at the red light on the intersecting street across traffic. The car moved up the yellow line, past the waiting cars and through the red light and right into me and Joel. I saw the car coming and tried to lock up the bike but it was too late. Joel jumped straight up off the bike and got hit by the side of the car, his shin smacking into the roof of the car. I went head first over the handlebars on my bike onto my back, right through the windshield. My legs stretched across the woman inside as she continued to drive undaunted by the man falling through her windshield. It looked like she was in her nineties and had a young kid in the backseat crying. I yelled at her to stop and finally she did, a half a block away from the collision. I got up and crawled through the windshield I had just crashed through and started walking back. I was thinking I had to get to Joel and see if he was okay. I shouted his name. "Joel!"

Finally, I heard back faintly, "Steven!"

I spot Joel who is lying on the ground, his shin split open in half and twisted to the side. It was horrible. That's when I noticed the blood. Not on Joel, but on me. I look down and see dozens of shards of glass embedded in my body. Blood is dripping everywhere. My left wrist and my left foot are hurting. Along with my right ankle. The most pain came from my crotch area. I look down and see a huge piece of glass sticking out from between my legs. Yes, the golden fleece area. Now my mind is off Joel and on my matzah balls and my kosher hot dog. Did the glass cut everything off? It certainly feels that way. I begin to undo my pants to see the damage when I feel hands start to push my head back. Bystanders have come over and are telling me to lay down and not move. I shout at them I have to take my pants off and see if my goods are still there. They just won't let me. They lay me down and the ambulances arrive. I tell them to take Joel first. He goes into one ambulance and I'm loaded into another. I keep telling them to check to see if my nuts are still intact. The paramedics tell me they will look once they get to the hospital. I have to lay there for ten minutes thinking about if Joel is okay and if I'm still a man down there. We get to the hospital and the Doctors finally cut off my pants. They took a good look and God Bless them, the glass shards missed everything by half an inch and are embedded in my upper inner thigh. Right next to those guys. I wound up with seventy eight stitches, a broken wrist and a broken ankle. Joel had x-rays and had completely broken his shin in half. He had to get seven to eight bolts in his leg. I felt horrible. I called him after surgery to explain how bad I felt and he told me it wasn't my fault and there was nothing I could do.

I knew Joel was out for at least a year and I was out for a few months. It didn't matter what happened to me, I was worried about Joel. He assured me it wasn't my fault and I'll never forget that. It's a sign of a true friend when someone can forgive you like that and say those kinds of things. So now he comes home with two steel shafts and is out for a year. I'm trying to take care of him best I can as I am on crutches and he is doing the same for me. We are both miserable but trying to keep ourselves in good spirits. There is one thing though that weighs heavy on my mind. I have a new show. I'm going to leave in a week. Now I can't do the show. I have to call Sam Firstenberg and tell him to find somebody else. I'm devastated. More than devastated. I'm gonna lose a great opportunity because of this ridiculous circumstance. Why me? I don't want to call him, but I have to. So I get him on the phone and tell him this elderly lady hit me on my motorcycle and I got seventy-eight stitches and a broken wrist and ankle with casts on them and I can't do the stunts. He understood and we hung up. I felt just miserable like the whole world was coming to an end. Moping the whole day. Thinking it's going to be three months before I come back and having three months of not working and people knowing I am hurt. How am I going to overcome this now, this wall life has put in front of me. I came back from one thing which I did when I hurt my shoulder and now I have to come back from this. I believed I would, but at this time I'm just completely depressed.

The next morning, I get a phone call. I pick up and it's Sam Firstenberg. I said hello and asked what was going on. Sam tells me it's more important I come to Stunt Coordinate and they can get someone else to do the actual stunts. He wanted me to put it all together and make sure everything was right. I said, "let me make sure I hear you correctly, I just have to set up the stunts and someone else can do it?"

Sam Firstenberg told me that was all I had to do.

I said, "yeah, if that's okay with you," astounded by what I was hearing. I started to celebrate. I felt like James Cagney in *Yankee Doodle Dandy*, tap dancing down the steps after he talked to the president of the United States. All you guys and girls who have seen *Yankee Doodle Dandy*, you know what I mean. Sam told me he would send the itinerary tomorrow of when I was going to leave. I thanked him and hung up. I went through my house walking on sunshine and crutches as happy as I could be. As the days go by, I start preparing and getting my equipment and luggage together to go to Salt Lake City on my first big one. I meet Sam Firstenberg at the airport and he sees me with one crutch, a cast on my wrist and my ankle. I explain what happened and he understood, but glad I was coming. We get on the plane and everyone starts helping me with things.

We get to Salt Lake City, Utah and get to the hotel. I go to my room and unpack. That afternoon around one thirty, I go down to the Production Office. I see David Womark and Sam Firstenberg in the office amongst everybody else. They are all standing around having a conversation with this girl. I guess they are talking about the movie. I can't understand what they are talking about and I finally realize, it is because it is all in Hebrew! Oy Vey! I'm a Brooklyn Jew and I don't understand! Finally, David sees me and walks over as if he had just given up on the conversation. He asks me, in English thank God, if I knew who the girl they were talking to was and I said no. He tells me she is Menahem Golan's daughter and her name is Naomi and she is head of Wardrobe. Sam Firstenberg comes over and explains she is driving them crazy. I'm thinking to myself, what does that have to do with me? But I listen. Firstenberg says she is driving us nuts. David agreed and looks at me. He said, "do me a favor and go talk to her, make her happy, introduce yourself and make her happy somehow."

I look at them and I say, "what do you mean make her happy?" Suddenly a light bulb goes off. I smile and tell them to watch this, before walking away. I get this bright idea and start walking over with the crutch in my hand. All eyes are on me, I can feel them on my back. I walk over to Naomi Golan and introduce myself. I told her my name was Steven and I was the Stunt Coordinator on the show. I told her I wanted to talk about wardrobe. She shook my hand and gave me a big smile. She yelled at me and said, "not now!"

I told her we would need doubles for the uniforms for wardrobe.

All of a sudden, her face changed. "Doubles, doubles!" she shouts. "Shmulik, David! Now I have to get doubles, where is this budget going to come from now?"

Well, this isn't good. I'm supposed to make her happy, not angry. My mind is racing, she is shouting at the top of her lungs at David and Sam. It is like I'm in

Martian land, the three Hebrews that are flying all over the place. I don't know what the hell they are saying, but it looks hilarious. So I did the only thing I could think of. I take half a step, grab her as Fred Astaire would do with Ginger Rogers around the waist, and flipped her around. I bent her over and planted a big kiss right on her lips. I lift her back up, not knowing what her reaction is going to be and all of a sudden there is a big smile on her face. She went from screaming at those guys about money and now she is like a little school girl, all excited. She spun me around and said, "we are going to get along great." She was laughing and everyone starts laughing as well. The situation was diffused and I thought I did it in a funny way. Little did I know the nightmare that I just started. I say goodbye to her and told her it was nice meeting her and we would talk more about the wardrobe soon. I let her go and I walked past David and Sam and I whispered, "okay boys, that's how it's done."

Sam replies, "Steven you're so smooth," a big grin plastered on his face. Let me tell all you readers out there, little did I know I had just opened Pandora's box. What do I mean by that? Stay tuned. It wasn't long before those blank script pages became full of just great action. Sam looked at it and said it was an awful lot and I told him we can cut out whatever we don't have time for. Well, they loved everything I came up with and the stunts I did. When I got back, I called a friend named Don Shanks who played Nacoma on *Grizzly Adams*. I called him up and asked him if he was available for a part. He said yes. I said can you come down to the hotel now, and meet the Director and the Producer. He said yes. I said can you come down to the hotel now, and meet the Director and the Producer. He said yes. I also told him I needed his help with something.

(Sho Kosugi always insisted whoever he killed would be me. Again and again.)

We hung up and not long after, he came up to my room and saw me in all my glory. He asked me what happened and I told him I got into a car accident and got seventy eight stitches and these casts on my leg and arm. "I need you to help me cut off these casts because I have too much action to do and I can't do it with them on. So let me call down to the lobby and ask if they have scissors," I told him.

He said we didn't need a scissor. He reaches down, pulls up his pant leg and pulls out a big ole buffalo skinning knife. I look at him and said, "you are going to cut my leg off with that thing." Laughing, I said, "Chief, are you serious?"

He said, "Steven, I'm an Indian."

So I said, "okay Chief." I put my leg on the bed hoping this didn't end with an amputation. He started chopping, cutting, ripping and in no time the cast was off. Then he started on my left wrist. Some more hacking and chopping, and that was freed too. I felt wonderful. My arm and legs were swollen, but at least I could use them. I have a right hand and left leg and that is all that mattered to me. My mind was ready, but I didn't know if my body was. You see, I'm painting myself in the corner. I'm not going to call anybody to do these stunts, I'm going to do it myself. Again, it's getting to a point where I'm putting myself in a corner, I better be able to perform and achieve because there was no way in hell I would let someone else perform these exciting things I came up with. I told Chief that in a couple of weeks I would have to get the stitches out and needed to find a Doctor. I took off my shirt and pulled down my pants and showed him my stitches. He nodded his head and thought to himself and told me I didn't need to go to a Doctor, he could do it himself. I looked at him like he was crazy. It's one thing to remove a cast, it is another to take out pieces of material stitched in your body. I said it to him, "you're no Doctor Chief."

He simply replied again, "I'm an Indian, Steven." He said all he needed was his trusty knife. He reaches down to his boot again and pulls out that Buffalo skinner and said that was all we need. I told him that the knife is too big to take out the stitches. He puts his finger on the point and explains to me he only uses the point to flick the stitch. My eyes popped out of my head and I told him to never mind about that now, I have two more weeks to decide before I get them out. I grab the two casts and bring them with me. You had to know Don Shanks, he was a real Indian, he was The Chief.

I introduce him to Sam and David and he gets the job. I guess I can say thank the Lord for me. I then was told that Sho Kosugi was flying in the next day and I had to meet him. The next morning, I got to the Production Office early and started talking to Wardrobe. (Naomi, remember her? You will.) Anything I asked her she said okay with a big smile. My conversation with her was very professional, but it seemed every time she spoke, it wasn't about wardrobe, it was about how cute I was and how she wanted us to go out on a date. LOVE. NOT ME, HER. I would smile and simply say, let's talk about this after work. Let's keep in mind, she was Menahem's daughter and simply wasn't my type and the last thing I wanted to do was get involved with the owner's daughter. Some people would, but not me, I just wanted to be friends. All of a sudden Sho Kosugi walks in. Mister ninja. I knew he was big in Japan and looked a little over his work in the first Ninja film. He used to do live shows at Six Flags Magic Mountain with samurai swords, did you know that? I knew that anyone who can do live shows can perform well, especially in front of people as there are no cuts. Everybody starts someplace. A few minutes into our conversation, Assistant wardrobe came over to us and wanted both of us to try on different ninja outfits.

We started talking about Martial Arts, he in broken English, every once and a while stopping to look for a word.

He said that he understood that I wanted to double him. I told him that was the plan. He said he was six one and a hundred and ninety five pounds. He asked me how tall I was. I said I am five nine and a hundred and fifty pounds in my wet feet.

He didn't understand that joke. He went, "UHH?" That is a Japanese word for what are you talking about.

He asked if I needed to get someone the same size as him and I told him no, I thought about it and came up with an idea. I told him, "I'll tell you what Sho." He looks at me waiting for my answer and I say to him, "It does not matter. Let me explain why. I am going to perform and act taller and you need to perform and act smaller."

That was kind of a joke, but again it wasn't. He looked at me, confusion on his face. Not sure if he understood the wits of this punk kid from Brooklyn. I smiled and walked away a few feet, turned and saw the confusion on his face. I said, "Sho, no one is ever going to know who is going to be your shadow."

He looks at me and says, "uhh?" Shadow?"

(We look so much alike. Don't we?)

So things are going wonderful. I'm having conversations with the crew, special effects, stunts. We get to a location called the Twin Towers in Salt Lake City. About a hundred twenty five feet across from each other. I had to come up with action at this location. Remember when I just said thank the Lord for me? I should also thank The Chief, Don Shanks. Let's explain why. We are all ready to go, twenty nine stories high. Cable strung from one tower to another, a hundred twenty nine feet across, hooked on the outside of the buildings. We have about twenty minutes of sun left. Five cameras set in different positions. I'm on the walkie talkie with Sam Firstenberg and David Womark. He is insisting we have to hurry, there wasn't much sun left. I planned to rehearse it with a hundred and fifty pounds of sandbags, but I am getting too much pressure from down below. All I am hearing on the radio is, "hurry up, hurry up. No time, hurry up." Being that The Chief finished his part in the movie, to make him some extra money, I put him on as my safety man. I tell him that we have no time for rehearsal with the sandbags, "I'm going." I radio down to my Director and tell him to roll cameras when all of a sudden, I am stopped by The Chief. He insists that we should rehearse this with the sandbags first. I explain to him that we have no time. "You hear the Gods downstairs screaming through the radio to hurry up." So I say, "move aside, Chief. I'm going."

He doesn't move. He repeats himself, "we have to test it first, Steven. With the sandbags."

Well, conversation turns into discussion. Discussion turns into an argument with me insisting, "I am going now." Now let me say, The Chief was in a competition called the toughest man contest. Before there was MMA. No holds bar. You know what that means? Anything goes. He took home the first place trophy. I tell you this, just so you know who I am dealing with. He was a badass but you'd never know it, he was so calm, cool and nice.

The Chief was insisting, "sandbags first."

Shmulik is screaming over the radio, "cameras are rolling, go, go!"

The Chief and I are one breath away from a physical confrontation. I am enraged that he is not listening to his boss, me. He won't let me go. I'm shocked. I unbuckle, grab the walkie talkie from the PA and yell out to my Director, "we are rehearsing it first, whether you like it or not." I look at The Chief and yell out to him, "test your sandbags. Go ahead and hurry it up." So he hooks it up by the window and he tosses the sandbags out. It goes five feet. Picking up speed, it goes fifteen feet, twenty feet, Bang! We hear a snap. I'm watching the sandbags descend. The cable broke. I'm still watching the sandbags. They hit the circus net that I have strung three stories above the ground. They go through it, smashing to the floor. I'm stunned for three seconds, trying to comprehend what just happened. I realize those sandbags could have been me. I turn, my eyes lock onto The Chief's. Don Shanks. Fright is registered in his face. I walk over with my arms extended. He reaches up as I say, "you saved my life." We hug each other. I repeat to him over and over and over again. "I'm sorry Chief, you saved my life. I'm sorry I yelled at you." I reach over and grab the radio from the PA. "Shmulik," I say. "Sam Firstenberg. Did you just see what happened?" There's a pause for a few seconds.

When I hear, "yes Steven, I'm sorry. I tried to hurry you."

I reply, "we learned a big lesson today, right Sam?"

He replies, "yes."

I nod and look at Don Shanks. "And that lesson is not to hurry and make sure everything is safe, right?"

I waited for his reply which was, "we understand and we're sorry."

(Don Shanks. He saved my life.)

The next thing I do is find that two bit special effects man, who rigged this whole thing for me. I went downstairs, we met up. He couldn't stop apologizing. I explained to him, "but that's not good enough. That could have been me. Apologies after the fact do me no good. Now you have to set this up again for tomorrow first thing. I want triple I-bolts. Not single, being that that's what broke. The I-bolt. And I want to see your work before I do it. I want to see the finished product on both sides before we do it. The word trust fell out the window, just like the sandbags. Understand?"

He says, "yes."

Should we have a moral to this story? You bet we should. Don't be stubborn. Listen, test and verify everything. If it wasn't for The Chief, there wouldn't have been no Steven Lambert past 1982. I thank God that you were there. Each location was a wonderful opportunity to let me create things that I never had an opportunity to create before. My imagination and juices were flowing. It was pure joy and happiness. Then I get a call from David Womark. He said he looked at the list of stunt guys I wanted to bring in. He said Sho Kosugi doesn't want me to bring in some of those guys. I asked who? He said namely, James Lew and Albert Leong. Now I had planned to invite them to come because they were such great friends of mine and the top of the line in talent. I had my own show so I now had the power to do so. I scratched my head and asked him why, but David couldn't give me an answer. He just told me Sho didn't want them on the show. Being very disturbed and upset, I couldn't wait to get back to the hotel so I could set up a meeting with Sho and ask him what that was all about. I got ahold of Sho when I got back and asked to come up and talk with him about some things on the show. He said okay and I went up and during our conversation, I managed to get in the only question that was only really on my mind. I simply said to him, "I understand you said no to James Lew and Albert Leong." He looked at me and with a frown on his face, just shook his head no. I asked him why. He told me to get other guys. I tried to get him to understand these guys mean a lot to me and will make the movie a lot better. He said no again. I asked him again in a different way. "Sho I want to bring these guys."

He shook his head and said no.

I tried to think of how to end the conversation, he wasn't going to budge and I didn't want to upset him. Should I walk out and say I understood or stay and talk about other things. I chose to stay and try to break the ice after that uncomfortable situation. In the back of my mind, I realized why. Jealousy. That's why. Insecurity. They are the real thing and he doesn't want the real thing anywhere near him. He knew their reputation and in my eyes, he was just scared that they were legends. I wanted to bring it up again but he was the star. I was just a Brooklyn Stunt Punk here. I had no power when it came to him except the power of persuasion and that wasn't working. When I left, I walked into the elevator and just leaned on the wall, hunkered over in despair. I knew what Albert Leong and James Lew could bring to a movie like this, but as long as Sho was the star it would never happen. To this day I never got a straight answer from Sho as to why he said no. Personally, my thoughts are, Sho Kosugi has never met neither of them so the only thing I can figure and I've always been confused about this, he is afraid about how good they are. I rest my case. When I got off the elevator, I headed back to my room. I opened the door and flicked on the light. I just couldn't believe why Sho was being so stubborn. I felt like my heart had been taken out of my chest. I needed to lay down. As I made my way to my bed, something red caught the corner of my eye. Turning, I saw drawing in what appeared to be red lipstick on my mirror. My eyes shot open. Someone was in my room? Who was in my room!? What the hell is this lipstick doing on my mirror?

149

I crouched down, waiting for any movement. Under the bed or in the closet. I shot down and peeked under the bed. Nothing. Yanked open the closet door. Nobody. That's when I noticed the drawing appeared to be words. They spelled out, "Steven, I love you," with a big heart around it. At the bottom, the offender had signed their name. Naomi Golan. Naomi was in my room! I was furious. You don't go into other people's rooms uninvited, let alone draw lipstick love letters on their mirror.

Well, enough was enough. I marched downstairs to the lobby and asked the front desk who had given her the keys to my room. They looked at me and shrugged, claiming they didn't know and they would have to find out. I went to the phone and called Sam Firstenberg who happened to be in his room. I asked him to guess what is going on in my room. He asked what happened and I told him, "there is in red lipstick, a heart that says Steven I Love You, and it is signed by Naomi Golan."

A second later, Shmulik explodes with laughter. I told him it's not funny, don't laugh. This morning I had a conversation with her about wardrobe and all she wanted was to go out on a date. That made Shmulik laugh harder. I asked him to talk to Naomi and tell her not to do that anymore, but I couldn't get him to listen to me over his loud laughter so I hung up. I called David Womark next and told him what happened. I walked into my room and somebody wrote on my mirror on my desk with a big heart and it was signed by Naomi Golan. A second later, David explodes with laughter too. I shake my head and tell him again, "it's not funny, you and Shmulik are two of a kind here. You gotta tell Naomi to cut it out."

David keeps laughing and so I hang up on him too. I decide to go look for Naomi and explain to her that this is the wrong path that she is taking. I find her room number and call her up and she is not there. I go to the Production Office and there she is. I told her we need to go into one of the rooms and talk. So we go in and I explained to her that, "I want to work with you and get along, but you broke into my room and you shouldn't do that." I gave an excuse that I had a girlfriend at home to try and get her off my back and said we could be friends but that was it. She wouldn't take no for an answer, she told me I could have two girlfriends and proceeded to sit on my lap. Okay, I'm going to stop this story. I know what you guys are thinking. Like when I told my story to my friends, you are thinking the same thing. Marry her and you will own a piece of Cannon Films. See the problem is, well let me just say, she was no Dorothy. She was more like the Wicked witch of the west, remember *the Wizard Of Oz?* So I told her, "no, enough. We can be friends." So she got up and said okay we can be friends and I told her yes, we can. I thought that was that and I asked her if she needed anything. She smirked and said she needed to talk to me about wardrobe.

We had a conversation about wardrobe and here again, every time I try to talk business, she is giving me gaga eyes. She's trying to sit on my lap and put her head on my shoulder, I'm trying to grab her hands which are going all over my body. I told her we would talk when other people were around and shot out of the office. I was embarrassed. Believe me, it's not the norm. I'm no Frank Sinatra. Women don't fall over me, especially when I start crooning, ha, ha. It was then time to meet and train Arthur Roberts who played the silver masked ninja. It would be our second meeting. He was a nice guy. The first meeting was an introduction where I asked him basic questions like have you ever taken gymnastics, ever taken dance or Martial Art classes. He said no to everything. He was just an actor at that. I ask these things to actors because it always helps me. I can contour and develop dancing or gymnastics skills to fight moves for the film. Usually, they know at least one of those things, but this guy didn't. I tried to teach him stances and punches in the first lesson. You understand their physical ability and comprehension right away when you first start teaching them. I mean to tell you, Arthur Roberts was one of the nicest guys I have ever met, but as far as being physical and having coordination and timing, he had none of those and his presentation, sorry to say, was the worst. I never met a guy I couldn't teach until now.

He would literally fall all over himself. So now I know I'm going to have to show him some moves that I need him to do for picture. These included quick shots, poses, punches and kicks as well as body language and he was able to give me none of those. I know I am going to have to use a fight double at every turn. I met him in the lobby of the hotel and we went over to the gym. I spent two hours with him and everything I tried to teach him he just couldn't get. His kicks were wobbly, his punches were all over the place and even the way he walked seemed unlike a jock. After two hours of training him, I had to go on a location scout with Shmulik and my cinematographer, David Gurfinkel. I knew I was going to learn a lot from David, he was a great guy. I knew I was going to learn about cameras and lenses and I would school him on how to shoot action, hoping the chemistry between us would be there and it was. After all, teamwork is very important. We sat down on a couch in the lobby about to leave and I explained to them the situation. I had given Arthur Roberts two lessons and although he is a great guy, he is not an athlete. Shmulik shrugged and said not to worry. I told him, "but he has to be equal to Sho Kosugi's character. I don't know where you got him or whose friend or family member he is, but he is not going to be able to do it." I made a kind of sarcastic and funny comment. "Where did you get this guy, who does he know? Is he working for free?"

Shmulik laughed and said, "oy, don't worry Steven everything will be okay."

I found throughout the picture, that would be one of his favorite lines with everybody.

"Don't worry, it will be okay." Shmulik to me, was and will always be a mensch. I've only seen him mad once in forty years which we will talk about later. So he told me not to worry, everything will be okay. I tried to explain how difficult getting Arthur to fight would be and he said not to worry again and again. You out there who know Shmulik and have worked with him, does that sound familiar? He is always one to calm you down and tell you everything will work out. The first day arrived and we started at the exterior plaza, you remember, it was the old Shuriken in the hobo's eye, falling into the fountain. I was very excited. The first shot of the day. I have already taught this actor how to fall and spin face first. It went well and he looked great. I had to show camera how he was going to fall. So unbeknown to the crew, I had a pair of swimming trunks on. I whipped off my clothes and played the hobo in rehearsal. Everybody laughed, it looked great. I turned to the actor and told him if you get anywhere near this, I will be a happy man and you will get a hundred dollar bonus.

That made his eyes light up. I turned to Wardrobe and asked for a towel to dry myself off. Guess who was holding the towel for the actors. You guessed it, Naomi. She starts screaming that she only brought one towel for the actor. I told her I understood and I took it. She yelled at me. I told her to be quiet and get another one. Guess what she said? Only if I go out with her. I smiled at her and stuck out my hand and she put the towel in it. Of course, I made the mistake and said no. She went crazy trying to get my towel back. It's too late, I'm drying myself off while she is screaming at me. I couldn't believe it. I'm having an argument about a towel. She created a whole big scene and caused Shmulik and production a good fifteen minutes of delay. I turned to her and could not resist and simply said, "you know, you're nuts." Big mistake, because that wasted another ten minutes while she proved I was right. And let me say, her tantrums were of course in Hebrew and directed to Shmulik. I would always wonder what she was saying.

Shmulik would always tell me, "you don't want to know." He also would comment we were just two love birds.

I would reply to Shmulik, "not even if she made the best matzah ball soup in town."

Shmulik laughed. It was a happy morning. We proceeded on shooting all the pieces we needed in the plaza. Reactions from pedestrians, cop cars, ambulances. The morning went wonderful. Now we are on our way to Salt Lake City's twin towers to do the interior with Arthur and the silver masked ninja, killing the bunch of bad guys that work for Mario Gallo who played Chifano, throughout the corridors. I had about five or six kills to do. Most of the action I planned, was going to be me in the silver mask, but I had to get Arthur to move like a ninja warrior and to give a presence, a look, a style. The rest I knew was up to me. It was the first time Arthur had the ninja outfit on. The first shot of the corridors was the killing of Keith Vitaly. By this time, I had the confidence of the powers. They seemed to listen to all my ideas, so I thought to myself, why kill Keith Vitaly? Let him live, I thought. Show up at the end of the movie with Sho Kosugi. Maybe they will make a ninja 2 with both of them. I mean this movie isn't set in stone. We are making it up as we go. Kind of. Let me hit Shmulik up with this idea. So I did. He didn't say yes, he didn't say no. But he asked Sho when he arrived. Sho shaking his head horizontally. I got my answer. Too bad, would have been cool.

You know, if you ask me my opinion, Cannon Films and Menahem made a mistake in not seeing the real and raw talent of Keith Vitaly. I'm glad others did.

(I tried my best Keith.)

The first time he put on the mask there were problems. Shmulik rolled camera and the walk didn't work, his movements didn't work, the killing didn't work. So Shmulik cut and called me over for a discussion. Sho Kosugi was there too. Sho mentioned that Arthur moved like a baboon. All of a sudden, Shmulik says, "I got an idea!" We looked and listened as he said, "why don't you play the silver masked ninja, Steven?"

I looked at him and said, "what!?"

He said, "yeah, you play him, no one will ever know with the mask on."

I looked at Sho and he agreed. Little do people know, that I was the silver masked ninja. Arthur Roberts, the lucky stiff, got to sit around for two and a half months doing absolutely nothing as the silver masked ninja. He was literally in three shots. Putting the mask on, taking it off, and at the end when Sho cuts open the mask and he is revealed. Everything else is Steven Lambert. It was a chance of a lifetime. You can compare it today, to a movie like *Spiderman*, where Spiderman's action double was on screen more than the actor was. I had no idea the blessing I had just been given and the cult status that this movie was going to bring. To me. It was another day's work and a chance to act in costume. I was very excited to act like this as I could do facial expressions and movements, that even though you didn't see my face, I could make it come through the mask and the uniform. Shmulik gave me the liberty to act with my body. This was the first time I really had a substantial part. People remember the silver masked ninja more than Sho Kosugi in some cases. I really had a chance to put to practice the things that I knew. My own style and make this memorable.

(Sho Kosugi. Finally victorious over Steven Lambert. Bring in the stand in, Arthur Roberts.)

The day went well and I had all kinds of kills in the corridors. Shmulik enjoyed it and so did everybody else. It was a fun day. I completely forgot about my broken wrist and ankle, even my seventy two stitches because I was happy and involved in what I was doing. Every time I turned around, I got congratulations from the cast and crew. I loved doing things the natural way, no CGI, or animated effects. Hanging, climbing, jumping, all real. Everything was going well and we wrapped at the end of the day. Soon I met with Grace Oshita, who played Grandmother Osaki. What a wonderful lady. It was like working with my grandma. On the set, I had a conversation with her about what we were going to do. There was a scene where I am on a ladder and she lassos my foot with a Martial Arts weapon, a rope with a weight on it. I'm about ten feet up this ladder, hanging down from a skylight and she ropes me and pulls me off the ladder and I drop to the floor. She didn't want to pull me off because she was afraid I was going to get hurt, how caring she was. I decided to do no rehearsal on it which made her even more nervous. I needed a good tug from her to make it look real and she was hesitant to do it. She reminded me of my grandmother asking me why I wanted to be a stunt man and not a Producer or Director. She was the sweetest. She was worried about me getting hurt. So cameras roll and I'm telling her to pull harder, harder! She just wasn't pulling hard enough. I shouted, "PULL!" Boy, did she pull then, let me tell you. I went flying off, surprised at the force of this little old lady and landed on a judo mat. Shmulik yelled, "cut" and she ran over with her hands on her cheeks, apologizing and asking if I was all right. Shmulik laughed and told her, "of course he is. That's what he does for a living, he's crazy."

I would smile and laugh at her, sweetest person on the whole show. Even sweeter than guess who, Naomi Golan, ha ha ha. I'm having the time of my life, playing non-descript ninjas and other characters, playing the silver masked ninja, coordinating stunts such as almost getting hit by a van, rolling over a car and landing on concrete. Every small, medium and big stunt there, it was me. Always tenderly landing on my non-broken wrist and ankle. Not that I was greedy, I just simply didn't have it in the budget to hire a stuntman to do the things I was doing, and besides I was like a kid in a candy factory, all the sweets were in front of me that I created. Anything I came up with, nobody said no. This wasn't only work. It was fun. I got reports back from Cannon on how wonderful the daily's looked. Shmulik and David would tell me how happy Menahem was, looking at the footage. I had the freedom to do what I wanted and people loved it.

(The Cho Osakai and Dave Hatcher show. Sounds good to me. Too bad it never happened.)

About two weeks into the movie, I got a call one evening from Shmulik. He says, "Steven, the accountant is coming in tomorrow. Whatever you do, do not talk to him."

I told him, "okay." Then I asked, "but what does the accountant have to do with me?"

He told me he's coming because he wanted to cut some stuff on the show. I couldn't believe it. I just got reports on how good it looked from Cannon. Shmulik didn't know why he was coming but he urged me not to say a word to him. So I hung up, wondering what this had to do with me and I think, what if they want to cut the budget in the action. Then I said to myself, there is no budget! Let me tell you right now, everything I did on that show cost $38,000 can you believe it? I think back now and if I was working for somebody in Stunts Unlimited doing this show, I would have made $300,000.

This is how cheap Cannon was, but I'll tell you right now, as far as I was concerned, I wasn't doing it for the money. I also got a call from Sho and he tells me not to talk to the accountant either. I said again, I wouldn't.

I call David Womark and tell him Shmulik and Sho told me not to talk to the accountant. David told me that he was coming in to try to cut some things but he doesn't know what. So the next morning, I get up and drive to set early. I was the first one there, along with Wardrobe and a few others.

I was waiting for Shmulik and Sho to arrive so we can talk about our work as we usually did. I'm sitting there waiting in the parking lot when all of a sudden, this guy in a fedora and suit pulls up. He walks over to me and asks if I'm Steven Lambert. I look at him and say yes and proceed to ask, "who are you?"

He told me he was the accountant and wanted to talk to me.

I forget his name but for our purposes, we will call him Mr. Pain In The Ass. With a smile, I say, "whoops, I'm not allowed to talk to you." I start walking backward as he walks towards me.

Again, he asks to talk to me. "Where are you going?" He asked.

I told him, "I'm walking away now, gotta get to set." I was still laughing as he's getting frustrated. I said, "I was told by Sam Firstenberg and Sho Kosugi not to talk to you."

He raises his voice and proceeds to tell me he needs to discuss the budget with me.

I told him again, "hear no evil, speak no evil and see no evil. Leave me alone."

He says, "I have to talk to you, Menahem sent me and he is the boss."

I replied that, "Shmulik and David are my bosses and they told me not to say a word. Is Menahem here to say otherwise?"

Mr. Pain In The Ass shook his head.

"Oh, okay then, have a good day," I blurted out. I quickened my backward walk and peeked over my shoulder to see how much room I had before I hit something.

Not much. The guy was closing in and I knew I had only a few more backward steps before I was trapped. Just like when the big guys were chasing me back in Brooklyn, only here I didn't have Arthur to save me. I looked skyward as if to ask for some heavenly assistance and wouldn't you know it, just then a car pulled up with Sho Kosugi and Shmulik Firstenberg. They had come together this time and Sho's son Kane was with him. Mr. Pain In The Ass turned his head and saw them get out.

Now he wasn't interested in me anymore and broke off his attack and headed over to them. I gave a giggle and said, "see ya, wouldn't wanna be ya," and watched him run over to the others. Then I had a great idea. Like a cowboy pulling out his pistol, I pulled out my trusty camera. (Quick draw). I took out my camera to take a picture of the accountant, Sho and Shmulik.

To this day I have never seen Shmulik upset or angry except in that picture. He just didn't want to talk to him. He put his hand up and said not a word. His face was unusually angry. Sho, I have seen upset during some scenes, as he had difficulty explaining something in broken English, but never Shmulik. The accountant would follow behind them during the day on set, and it looked so funny to me because they just flatly refused to talk to him.

Every now and then, during the day, he would try to talk to David Womark or Shmulik and they would turn around and ignore him. He hung around on set for hours but he never got a word. It was so comical.

We proceeded to do the action and he would just stand there, waiting to start a conversation. After we wrapped, we went back to the hotel and met a bit later for dinner. We met in the lobby and Shmulik says, "guess what, the accountant is on his way to the airport."

I asked if he got what he needed and Shmulik shrugged and said no. He wasn't going to get anything the next day either so he packed up and went home with his tail between his legs.

(Forty years knowing Sam Firstenberg, first and only time seeing him angry.)

Shmulik, Sho, David and I became like family on the set, so close we began to play jokes on each other. In one scene I am playing the silver masked ninja up on the roof of this building. Sho is trying to find me and I am hiding in a jacuzzi that is on the roof. I set up a gag where he is walking around the jacuzzi trying to find me and I had tied a piano wire on my ankle with special effects on the other end. When Sho gets to a certain part of the jacuzzi special effects is supposed to pull it to cue me to come up from the water and cut Sho with my sword. So we explained the action to everyone. Shmulik rolls camera and I take a deep breath and go under. Looking up, I can see Sho's shadow walking around. Ten seconds go by. Twenty seconds go by. Thirty seconds, forty seconds, I have no idea what is taking him so long. Sho has already made two trips around the jacuzzi, and I'm thinking to myself underwater, what is going on, why isn't effects tugging me. A minute goes by, and I'm trying to keep what little air I have left in me. I wasn't prepared for a deep sea dive here, what is going on up there?! Finally, I can't take it anymore and burst up to the surface, choking and soaking wet. I jump up gasping for air and look at Sho who has this look on his face of a child being reprimanded by his parents. I'm looking at him and he picks his hands up and says, "I don't know what going on," in broken English.

I asked him, "whaddya mean you don't know?"

He points behind me and I turn and blink. The entire crew of sixty plus people had vanished. No one at camera, no one on the piano wire. It was as if they all became ghosts and disappeared. I looked back at Sho and asked him, "where the hell are they?" At the same time, trying to lift my mask so I can see. Finally, they all came back out a few seconds later, laughing their butts off. They had gone inside while I was underwater to a building about fifty feet away. They couldn't believe Sho was still acting as everyone ran away, waiting for me to pop up. I realized it was a joke and that was one for Shmulik, he got me good. I asked Sho why he was still acting if they all ran away. He looked at me and shrugged. The funniest part was listening to Sho being asked by everybody why he was still performing. Again, Sho would just shrug his shoulders and look confused. He didn't understand American jokes, even if Shmulik was Israeli. Just watching Sho, it was hysterical. You should have been there. Of course it was Shmulik's brilliant idea, the first of many jokes to come. We rolled again and I told him the joke was over, and they finally stayed put. They did use the beginning part of that sequence where Sho walks around as the crew leaves, you can go check it out yourself. Now let's talk about everybody's favorite, the Rhinestone cowboy, John Wayne he was not. More like a fluffernutter cowboy. It was the big fight scene in the park with Sho Kosugi and Keith Vitaly. It is was what is now known to be the Village People. MACHO, MACHO MAN, I WANT TO BE A MACHO MAN. We needed four people for the fight sequence. I interviewed about ten people and got four guys I thought would be good to be interviewed by Sho and Shmulik and they picked all three. On the first day of rehearsal. only three showed up. The Illegal Alien (ha ha ha), the Japanese warrior and the gangsta thug from the hood.

The Rhinestone Cowboy was nowhere to be found. I'm supposed to put this fight together and only have three out of the four actors. After a of couple hours of training, I went over to the First Assistant and asked him where the Cowboy was. Shmulik overheard and told me he had somebody else in mind. I asked if he wanted me to pick him and Shmulik waved me off and said he had a guy that would be great for the role. I told him all right, but make sure the guy is an athlete. He nodded and told me in his usual way, not to worry, everything would go great. He told me he would be here soon. Come the next day the Mexican, Japanese and the gangsta from the Hood showed up, but no Cowboy! We are two days away from shooting! So I go back to the First Assistant and he tells me that this guy can only show up on the day of shooting. I say, "what do ya mean he can only show up on the day of shooting?"

He assures me the guy is great and won't have any problems learning the fight. I walk over to Shmulik and tell him, "get whoever you want but he needs to be trained."

He says he'll be here first thing in the morning. I asked his name and Shmulik shrugged and said he had forgotten. Before I could say another word, he walked away. I was getting really frustrated and worried that this guy wouldn't be worth a hill of beans. I didn't understand why this guy wasn't showing up. The day comes when we are going to shoot the sequence and I drive to the set and get there early. Right away I don't see the Cowboy. I ask Wardrobe where the Cowboy is. They tell me he is here. I figured he must be in his trailer. Well, I better go get him. Not only is he late but he's also lazy. I go to the trailers and take a look. I see the trailer for the Mexican bad guy, I see the trailer for the Japanese bad guy, I see the trailer for the Gangsta bad guy and then I come to a trailer that says "Cowboy bad guy/ Stunt Coordinator Steven Lambert." I'm thinking, no way, this guy needs his own trailer, he can't stay with me. I'm a loner. Like Marlena Dietrich says, "I vant to be alone." I find the First Assistant and tell him to take the Cowboy out of my room, to get him his own room or put him with one of the other guys. He looks at me and says that we don't have any more room for him. I shook my head and said, "put him in your room or the other bad guys room, I need to be alone."

He looks at me and says, "well, to tell you the truth Steven, you are alone."

I said, "okay, good you will get him out."

He says "no, we can't get him out."

How hard can it be? You just tell him to pack up and mosey on out.

The First Assistant says, "well, you see, you are the Cowboy."

I shook my head. No, absolutely not. Number one, the Cowboy shows his face. You see, even though I was playing the silver masked ninja, I had a mask on. To me, that's all body language, a different kind of acting. Secondly, the Rhinestone character was written as a feminine man. Now, Matzah ball man, Steven Lambert was not going to go out on set acting like that. No way in hell. I chose not to, and I'm trying to make every excuse I could think of. I go to Shmulik's trailer and he invites me in. As soon as I enter, he is laughing, he knew he had me played all along. Sho was there as well, this time he was in on the joke and come to find out, he was the originator of the idea. They were both in tears. I told them there was no way I was going to play the Cowboy. He laughs and says, "what, are you scared to act?"

I told him I know how to act, but not that way. I told him no and went outside. David Womark comes over a few minutes later and tells me I have to play him. Again, I tell him, I wasn't going to be laughed at by everyone on the set. I told David he should play him. David told me I was the actor here.

He tells me I have no guts.

I say to him, "I'm not playing a fruity cowboy with a feather in his cap and rhinestones all over the place."

I see the First Assistant laughing at me and other members of the crew. It was like I was surrounded by people calling me gutless, but I know their game. "Okay, I'll play him!" I snapped. So that is how I got that role. In rehearsal, I wouldn't play him the way I played him on film. I would just go through the motions, and Shmulik tells me I need to give this character personality, as well as saying my line and waving them off. I said to myself, okay, and I tried to smoke the cigarette as feminine as I could and did a little flick of my wrist as a feminine man would do. Let me tell you, my good friend Naomi was there with a big grin, speaking Hebrew to Shmulik. I can only imagine what she was saying by the expressions on their faces.

Well, it worked so well that the Camera operator had to cut several times because he was laughing so hard, he probably peed his pants. Yeah, very funny Shmulik, you got me good. I was self-conscious and nervous in that I had to forego my masculinity, but to tell you the truth ladies and gentlemen reading this, I did have a good time doing it. But don't tell anybody.

(Throwing David Womark a little kiss from the Rhinestone Cowboy. He won't have it.)

That took a lot of work physically and mentally. Luckily, lunchtime came and we moved on to eating and replenishing our energy. David didn't like spending a lot of money on food and I found this to be evident when I entered the lunch area. There were signs all over that told the hungry cast and crew that they could only take two pieces of fried chicken, can you believe it? Well, I was hungry. So when I got to the food, I decided two wasn't going to be enough. So I took five. The caterer caught me out of the corner of her eye, as I was surpassing the safe chicken taking limit. She picked up a big fork, reminiscent of a pitchfork and yelled at me to put three pieces back. I simply told her, "NO," and proceeded to walk away.

(I should have given her some of this.)

She came around the table, with the giant fork in her hand and started chasing me and I began running through the aisles. Everybody was cracking up once again, as I avoided getting forked from her kitchen utensil, trying to balance my chicken on the tray at the same time. I felt like a clown trying to balance bowling pins while playing keep away from the crazy chicken lady. I tried telling her I was the Stunt Coordinator and needed the food, but she would have none of it. David Womark told her to leave me alone and to let me have my chicken. She did, hesitantly, but kept an eye on me the rest of the lunch.

The next day, there was more food and no signs on the table. Everybody there applauded me, for causing David to get more food. I was the hero of the lunchroom, but not the chicken lady. She wanted to fork me like a piece of gefilte fish.

My next story is about Wardrobe. Now you might be thinking, why the hell would I want to talk about wardrobe for? Well, I had a very good friend in Wardrobe who you might recall. Yes, we are going back to the lipstick lady. Let me explain a little bit first about my outfits. I had two silver masked outfits, two Sho Kosugi outfits and three non-descript ninja outfits that I kept separate in the wardrobe trailer from all the other clothes. Now this might sound hokey, or funny, but amongst some others, you Martial Artists out there know what I am talking about. We have a thing called Chi, or energy. Every moment and every day I wore those outfits, my energy and skill would transfer out of my body into my uniform. Yeah, I can hear you laughing, but that was the way I felt. I was afraid if they were too close to another set of clothes, the energy would dissipate to the other clothes and I would lose the power of my uniform. Kind of like Jackie Chan in *Tuxedo*, where his tuxedo had super powers. In this case, it wasn't my ninja outfits, it was me. I had a very strict habit of keeping my chi infused articles of clothing away from the other wardrobes.

162

One fine day, the sweet, adorable Naomi Golan, learns of this information from one of her assistants. I could imagine that when she found out, the look on her face was a "eureka" moment. At the time, okay you ready for this? I was coordinating a fight sequence on the streets, doubling Sho Kosugi during the van sequence. By the way, I would like to mention how I came up with this van sequence. How many people have seen the movie *Stagecoach* with John Wayne?" There is an action sequence on the stagecoach, where his stunt double Yakama Kanuit, was doing all this jumping, climbing and dragging all over the stagecoach and horses. It was always a favorite of mine and in the back of my head, I always hoped to duplicate that in some way, shape or form. This was my chance and I molded all of my action ideas to that great sequence. Everything comes from somewhere. In this case, if you liked this sequence, let's both thank Yakama Kanuit for all the extraordinary ideas he has given stunt people of the future.

Okay, let's go back to trouble. I was setting up the fight with Sho, Shmulik and David. All of a sudden about fifty yards away, the love of my life - so she thinks, Naomi Golan appears. She had a cardboard box about 3x2, in her hands. We are not really paying attention to her, as we are focused on this choreography for the fight scene. Bam! She drops the box onto the street, a big grin on her face. She reaches into her pocket and took something out and started squeezing some sort of liquid into the box. I throw a punch towards Sho, demonstrating what the action is. I can't help seeing Naomi out of the corner of my eye doing something with her hands. She lit a match. I hope she doesn't walk over here. I have to get this scene done, I don't have time for her sweet talk. I'm talking to Sho and explaining moves, when she starts screaming at David Womark and Sam Firstenberg in Hebrew, fifty yards away. I turned and could see fire in her eyes. It took me a moment to realize the fire wasn't just in her eyes, it was in the box! Come to find out she was holding a matchbook. A blazing fire starts and smoke bellows out. David, Shmulik and about ninety percent of the crew, start yelling back in Hebrew at her. I have no idea what the hell is going on, but I know it not good. The wardrobe assistant comes over to join the conversation in Hebrew, and I still have no idea what is happening. All I can see is Naomi with a look of satisfaction on her face, giving me the fingers. David turns and looks at me and shakes his head. Shmulik looks at me and tells me, "oh no, you are not going to like this," as he laughs hysterically.

I'm scratching my head trying to figure out what is happening.

Shmulik asks me, "do you know what she is burning?"

Of course I don't! I haven't looked and no one has said anything in English!

Shmulik smiles and tells me, "it's your ninja outfits!"

In a matter of seconds, I just go berserk. Everyone is standing there or laughing, just dumbfounded. Like the Tasmanian Devil, I run down the street towards the burning box. I get there and look into the box, my outfits and all my CHIIIII are just being incinerated. I look at Naomi who has her nose up in the air with a smug look on her face. I have never raised my hands to a woman but at that moment, my fist flew up inches away from her. "You crazy bitch," I yelled. I'm not in the habit of cursing, but she just burned my uniforms.

She put her face an inch away from mine and said, "I am the Producer's daughter, you can't do nothing. I burned your ninja outfits, so what. I'm Wardrobe, I can do what I want."

I can't believe somebody would do that. If she was a man, she would be flopping like a fish on the ground. I say again, "you are literally insane." I look at David and ask him to say something. They tell me it's no big deal, they can get new outfits. I told them, "but my energy is being burned!"

Shmulik says, "energy, shmenergy."

Naomi is laughing and I realize they just do not understand. Sho is the only one not laughing, he understood because he was a Martial Artist and he thought she was a crazy bitch too. I must tell you, the look on Sho's face was absolutely dumbfounded. He simply turned to me and said she was crazy. I turned around and walked away, steaming so mad I could cook dumplings. I just could not believe it was really happening. As angry as I got, I just had to throw up my hands and give up. It was done, and no one was going to do anything about it, except get new outfits. All that time and energy and chi wasted in mere seconds. Naomi knew my energy was in there, her assistant told her. So she decided this would be a good way to get me back for snubbing her romantic advances. She had no idea how close she was to being strangled. It's safe to say that if I listened to David and Shmulik's advice to marry her, can you imagine what my life would have been like? Oy Vey, I have a headache just thinking about it.

Now what I am going to talk about was unexpected, frightening. Not so much for me, for David Womark. I honestly thought it would never happen. I was in the office with David, Sho and Shmulik. David, being the Production Manager, needed to cut corners where corners had to be cut, as it was part of his job. We all understood that, but that didn't mean we liked it. David was talking to Sho about cutting out a few things that he and I, really wanted to keep in the film. The conversation started to get hot headed between David and Sho. We were about a month into the film and things were going well, we were getting nothing but good reports from Cannon. Sho was feeling on top of the world. Sometimes actors can start developing thoughts in their heads that they are the say all and end all. This began happening to Sho. Sho, just like some other actors who didn't understand the cost aspect, but thought because they were the star, were entitled to have the final say when it came to decision making. Especially when we were getting phone calls from Menahem Golan on how wonderful everything was. David wanted to trim some things and Sho said, "no, we keep it." This conversation quickly became an argument when David said he was not scheduling any of it.

Let me just say, David probably never had gotten into a real fight in his life. He's a nice sweet, Jewish, Israeli man. Sho is a blackbelt, a man that people respect. If you are talking to an actor that's one thing, if you are talking to an actor who is a Martial Arts Master from Japan, that is a completely other thing. You have to talk to them in a certain way, a way in which they are used to, with respect. They both didn't want to let go of what they wanted.

One thing led to another and David said something to Sho that made him draw his sword, metaphorically speaking. David, in short, insulted a Master. David tried to tell Sho that he was a nobody when it came to these kinds of decisions and this kind of power. Sho got so mad that he reached up his hands and double palmed struck David, right in his chest. We call that a palm strike in Martial Arts. It's a punch. It sent David back so hard he went flying over his desk and fell down on his ass. I was shocked. Right at that moment, Shmulik yelled to me to stop Sho! "Steven stop him, Sho is going to beat him up."

I hear David, "help me, help me," as Sho is hovering over him.

I went over the desk and shoved Sho, screaming at him. "It's David, it's David! He don't know how to fight, what are you doing, stop it!" I manhandled Sho, pushing him away.

Sho finally snapped out of it and turned to me, his eyes lit with fire. I helped David up and his face was white as a ghost and I'm pretty sure he dribbled all over. For all you Goyim (non Jews) out there, look it up on your computer. It's a Hebrew word. It was a terrifying moment because I didn't know what was going to happen. Sho turned around and marched back up and ninja up to his room. They started speaking in Hebrew and I told them I would go up to Sho's room and talk to him. I explained he should not be raising his hands to anyone on Production and Sho shrugged it off. I told him that I would see him tomorrow and wished he would call David and work it out. He never acknowledged he would, but the next day I came on set and everything was fine. I never found out if he apologized, but it seemed something had happened. I thought David might leave the show, Sho was the star so of course he was going to stay. He had to realize he wasn't in the Dojo, he was on a movie set. That was one of the many things Sho had to learn but I was amazed they were friends again. It was a scary moment, you just had to be there and guess what? Sho got his way. Here is an ancient Jewish Chinese proverb.

Sometimes you have to go through a situation to find out the ending. Nothing was taken out. Let me end my experience on *Revenge Of The Ninja*, by talking about Sho's son, Kane. I found Kane to be very shy on set, not saying much and keeping a strict demeanor whenever his father was around. When I worked with him, I would always try to make him smile and laugh, to be a kid having fun. That is an important thing to remember, when you are working with children, always make it fun and you will achieve a lot more from them.

As I worked with Kane, I began to see that he acted in two different ways. One was when he was just with me, and the other was when his father was around. I knew that Japanese families have a very strict method of upbringing their children, but this was the first time I was witnessing something like this for myself. I never thought the Japanese method of parenting was effective as I was to find out years later with Kane.

Whereas my father acted the way he did because of ignorance, Sho acted the way he did because of tradition. For example, if Kane was doing a scene and he had difficulty with something, Sho would snap at him. I believe a father should gently help his son when he has difficulty, with a firm but loving manner. Sho treated his son more like a pupil than his own child.

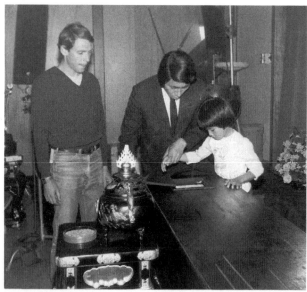

(A rare loving moment. Sho explaining to Kane Kosugi.)

I remember when we all took a picture together, and I got Kane to laugh, but when the picture was taken his mouth was taught and a seriousness had overtaken his face.

Sho stood behind him, his face just as serious. Kane knew his father would be upset if he smiled. If you want to see an example of Sho's strictness, watch the film *Aloha Summer*. In it, Sho plays a Japanese father who disciplines his son. You can get a sense of how he acted in real life with Kane. Years later, Sho and Kane stopped talking to each other. It hurt to know they had drifted so far apart, but it wasn't surprising due to his parenting methods. I made a promise to make sure I treated my own son differently and show him love and respect, and always take the time to communicate and explain. The most important thing is for a father and son to be friends. So let's move on to - wait a minute, what's that you say? Naomi? You want to know the outcome? We got married and had two wonderful children and I became head of Cannon Films.

April Fools! No I didn't, let me tell you what happens. About a week after she had burned my outfits, I came on set in the morning and talked to Shmulik and David as I usually did. The first thing they said was that Menahem Golan is coming next week to the set. They made it a point to tell me that he wanted to discuss the problem with his daughter and me, with a smirk on their face. My eyes went wide and I told them they were the ones that started this problem, asking me to go and talk to her in the first place. I don't have a problem with her, she has a problem with me. Why am I telling you guys this? You know it already. You guys should talk to Menahem, I don't want to talk to him about it. I'm innocent here, why do I have to talk to him? They told me I had no choice, Menahem was the boss and he wanted to speak to me. So a week went by and Menahem is getting closer to arriving. David and Shmulik and even Sho are telling me he wants to talk to me! Oy vey, this isn't funny! But they think it is. I think I might be getting fired and everyone else thinks it's a game. I don't find it at all funny and they keep reminding me every day.

Finally, Menahem arrives on set and I'm sweating bullets inside. I'm trying to hide from him as best I can. Avoiding him as an Orthodox Jew would avoid a large piece of ham. He comes on set and I'm watching him from afar, making sure I don't come in eye contact with him. Shmulik is in the middle of directing and Menahem tells him to move aside. I couldn't believe it. Shmulik had been directing for a few hours already. Menahem tells Shmulik to sit down and Director Golan takes over the whole set. Now, he has no idea what is going on or what Shmulik has shot and I am watching this all happen. The script supervisor, Ronit Ravitch-Boss is shouting at him in Hebrew. They start arguing and Shmulik sits there quietly like a child told to go to time out. After a few hours, lunchtime comes and I make sure to sit far away from everyone, by myself. Sho, Shmulik, David and Menahem are all together eating as a group, while I'm eating my lunch and hiding five tables over.

All of a sudden, I turn around and it's David Womark. He is laughing and asks me why I was sitting there.

I told him, "what do you think I'm doing, I'm eating lunch."

He says Menahem wants to talk to me.

I look at David and said, "I know what you're trying to do and I don't like being put in the spot like this."

He continues laughing. I said, "you know if you weren't the Producer and my friend, I'd put you to sleep and pull down your pants." He laughs and backs up.

Now mind you, I have a good sense of humor. I can understand why they think this was funny, but in a way, to me it was not. I guess if it was happening to someone else, I might be doing the same thing. Would you? David laughs again and says, "Menahem knows you are here. Go and talk to him."

So I man up and walk over to Menahem, put down my lunch tray and sit directly across from him. As soon as he sees me, I hear those magical words, as only he can yell them. "MISTER STEVEN, HOW ARE YOU? SIT DOWN, I MUST TALK TO YOU." Then, like a plague, everyone else gets up and leaves. Now it's just me and Menahem. I start asking him how his trip was and how he was doing. He brushed those questions away and gets right to it and asked me how I and Naomi were doing. Now let me tell you, your brain has two sides. The left is crying and saying "oh shit, I'm going to get fired." The right side is saying, "be cool, just explain the situation." I take a deep breath. I said, "listen Menahem, I think your daughter is a great girl and a wonderful help. The problem is, she wants to be more than friends." I kept repeating how wonderful she was and what a hard worker she was and how valuable she was to the production in a valiant effort to kiss Menahem's ass. Haha. My mind was racing, trying to think of excuses to tell him. "I'm engaged Menahem," I tried fibbing. I glanced at Sho, sitting five to six tables away from us, who was shaking his finger at me as if to say, "you are in trouble now."

All of a sudden Menahem says to me, "Steven, Steven, you are very valuable to this project, I want you to get along with my daughter."

I said, "I do too, but she is a very strong willed person. What am I supposed to do if she breaks into my room and burns my costumes? Shmulik told you about that didn't he?"

Menahem's voice boomed back. "I want you and my daughter to get along. Make up with her and be friends then." Menahem turns and yells out in Hebrew. "Naomi, Naomi! Steven, Hebrew words, Steven, more Hebrew words." He turns and does the same thing with David and Shmulik who burst out laughing. Naomi is at another table way down and she comes over and looks at me with a smug face, yelling in Hebrew. The whole lunchroom is staring now. I know they are talking about me. Menahem looks at me and says he wants me and Naomi to be friends. I get another bright idea and stand up to face Naomi and hug her while she is looking the other way. I apologized and asked her if we can be friends. She said something in Hebrew that made everyone laugh. I don't know what she said, but to this day no one will tell me. Sho didn't know. David and Shmulik would always tell me you don't want to know. The moral of the story is, when someone asks you to help them with a damsel in distress, turn and walk the other way.

Let me just end this story by saying, I did seven to eight pictures for Cannon after this one and if I were to work with her again, I would hope she would be more professional and we would both enjoy it. But as fate would have it, we never worked together again. Thank God.

One last note about *Revenge Of The Ninja*. When it came out in theaters it was a blockbuster. We couldn't conceive of the success of the film and the range of people, young and old, that enjoyed this film. This piqued the attention of MGM, who wanted to make a distribution deal with Cannon. This was the first time Cannon had a distribution offer with a studio and boy did Menahem take it! The only problem was, that when the deal was made, it was made so that MGM had to distribute EVERY movie Cannon made and that was the genius of Menahem and Yoram Globus. On top of that, Menahem decided that he wanted to use MGM studios to edit and they agreed. Aside from the Ninja films, they were also busy making movies like Lou Ferrigno's *Hercules* in Italy. These low budget B movies were nothing compared to the action and quality of a film *like Revenge Of The Ninja,* so MGM found itself in hot water quickly. Well using MGM's editing wasn't enough for the genius named Menahem, so he had the chutzpah (which means balls) to also just start using MGM's props, wardrobe, sound stages, film, publicity, the list goes on and on. What a deal it was, even if only Cannon knew about it. MGM had no idea how much Menahem was taking from them. Well after a year, Menahem called MGM to find out about where his profits were from *Revenge Of The Ninja.* "Where is my money? I want my money," Menahem yelled.

You out there who remember the inflection of Menahem can imagine that. He was told they would look into it and a few days later, the final amount the movie made was told to Menahem and Yoram, and their eyes went wide. Then MGM told them they discovered what they were doing and they owed money for using their studios! So the final amount went from $$$$$ down to 00000. Well, you can imagine Menahem just exploded with anger. The deal with MGM was quickly severed and that was the end of that relationship. Cannon still had got what it wanted however, distribution for *Revenge Of The Ninja,* and a few other films. *Revenge Of the Ninja* became the only successful Cannon film distributed by MGM at the time. What a special man Menahem was. By the way, a lot of people confuse the year this film came out as 1983. It was 1982! Just thought I'd set that for the record.

By the way, I read an article once. The headline was, "Ten things you didn't know about Revenge Of The Ninja." Most of them were wrong. It's funny how they write these things. You would think they would get in touch with someone who has been there. I will tell you the eleventh one and it is damn well the truth. I was the silver masked ninja in 99.9 and a half % of the film. No one else but me was in that suit. Never Sho Kosugi. And as far as anyone else stunt doubling Sho Kosugi? Just me. Alone. Yes, Kosugi says otherwise in articles and media. Shame on him that he would take away the art and the work of somebody who respected him and is a friend. He should be wise and tell the truth. That it was just a punk kid from Brooklyn. Me. By the way, let's jump years for a second. In 2017, after all the years of the silver mask being in my drawer protected in a towel, the silver mask and I were highly honored by Michael Matsuda and the Martial Arts History Museum. He accepted the mask and now you can go and observe it on a pedestal under a clear case. The mask I wore that was in 99.8% of the film.

(Martial Arts History Museum. 2319 W Magnolia Blvd, Burbank, CA 91506)

So after *Revenge Of The Ninja,* I returned home at the end of the month, knowing I have my first Stuntmen's Association meeting. I'm a member of the Stuntmen's Association and felt so proud of it. Think about it, who would ever think a punk kid from Brooklyn would end up there? A group that had everyone. From greats like Harvey Perry, George Robasin, Ronnie Rondell, Terry Leonard, Yakama Kanuit to Hal Needham, Davey Sharpe, Bear Hudkins, Glen Randall Jr. and on and on. I'm excited to attend my first meeting. I'm in the first established stunt group of motion pictures, started not really that long ago. In nineteen sixty one. I feel like I was born again. I thought to myself, how did I get into this position? I really didn't have an answer.

Was it fate? Was it hard work? Was it luck or was it God? Or all of the below. But I was there and I was ready for the ride and so very proud being in a group of stuntmen who did such great work and so many fantastic movies in the past. The legacy I belonged to now, I did not expect. So I'll ride the wave and hope someday my name will be spoken with the champions of the past. I was nervous and looking forward to it at the same time. I thought it was going to be very professional and run like a court proceeding, where everyone listens to the head of the organization speak, and there are group rituals and proceedings that take place that are all very organized and respectful. The first of the month comes when the meeting takes place and I drive over there.

Again, I couldn't believe they would take in someone like me who has no family in the business, who basically is a nobody. It was a great honor and I was going to do the very best I could to represent the group wherever I went. These were my thoughts on the way over. So I arrive at the building a half hour early. I knew there were approximately a hundred and fifty members in the group and I saw about a dozen stuntmen there waiting for the meeting to start when I pulled up. I walk up and introduce myself and they welcome me to the group.

Some knew me, most didn't. Eight pm comes and we walk upstairs. I look around and realize there were only about forty five members attending this meeting. I also noticed that none of the big shots were there. The stuntmen that were in the group who did the action on some great films. Where are they, I thought. I was very surprised. I thought everyone would be at a meeting that was being held by the first stunt group to ever be in existence, yes let's not forget that this was the original stunt group. The room was practically bare, except for two long tables on one side with all the board members sitting down behind it.

President, Vice President, Treasurer, Merchandise, Accountant and so on and cheap folding chairs for the members. It was pretty stale. Rinky dink I guess are the right words, with all due respect. I must say I've been up to Stunts Unlimited's office and they had a long beautiful old fashioned cowboy bar that they sat behind and Director's chairs for the members with everyone's names on them.

Mind you this was 1982. There were a few dozen members already in the room. Being very shy at that point in my career, I chose a seat towards the back just like I did in school. I was excited to hear about how we can get shows, who was doing shows, who to meet, etc. You know, like any company would do to try to further their business.

However, as time went by, there was no conversation about new shows that were coming up, what Stunt coordinators are doing what shows, or even who was working. People were just complaining about things, saying derogatory things about people in the business and even our own members. They were also discussing different ways to make money. Come to find out, they were more or less always in the hole. I didn't understand. When I first joined, we got a packet that talked about the by-laws and how you had to hire people in the group.

On *Revenge of The Ninja*, I made sure I gave out the majority of stunt work to my group. I wanted to show my morals, the common sense and integrity as well as especially loyalty, that was bestowed upon me by my relatives and my Martial Arts family. I was torn between hiring people who had hired me in the past and sticking to the rules of my own group. I knew I might make enemies, but that was the path I had taken when I signed with the group. Now here I am, listening to these members argue about other stuntmen not hiring each other, never once mentioning where to find work or how to help a member. To me, you should be happy if a member gets hired, we are a family after all. Instead, they began arguing about really nothing about nothing. It was like a *Seinfeld* episode. As the meeting came to an end, people came up to me and told me that the next show I do, remember to hire them. I was the new kid on the block and they were trying to reaffirm I knew the bylaws. I smiled and told them, "absolutely, I so appreciate you accepting me."

I remember driving home and just thinking it was just one of those things, the next meeting will be different. I shook it off, not wanting to read too much into it. I was lucky to be in the group and didn't think too much of what just occurred. Maybe the next meeting will have more information about hiring and work. Maybe this meeting was an abnormality and I walked into the wrong one for a beginner. Yeah, that was it. I'll just come back next month and get all the information I needed. I was young and star struck, and I had just figured that some people in this industry had slightly bent the rules in the group by not following the by-laws. I had no idea the amount of bending that was to come. A week or so goes by when I get a call from a Production Manager that I had worked with in the past, who asked me if I was interested in doing a television movie with Gary Coleman, called *The Fantastic World Of D.C. Collins*. I said, "why not?"

He asked me to come down and he would give me the script to break down all the action. This involved reading the script, knowing the story, putting together the action sequences and putting together a budget that represents the people and things I need. I went down and had a discussion with him about the script and he gave it to me. The following week I came down with the budget and met Gary Coleman and it was just wonderful. He was a very nice kid, but he seemed very vulnerable.

He had heard I was a Martial Artist and wanted me to demonstrate something. I didn't have my staff or sword or anything, but luckily the Production Manager had a pen on his desk. That's right, a pen! I leaned over and took the pen, a smile on my face. I asked Gary to put the pen in his mouth. He looked at me as if I just told him to go to the moon. I explained to him I was going to kick the pen out of his mouth. He shakes his head and says, "oh no, no, no, you might hit me in the mouth."

I laughed and told him, "I have been doing this for years, trust me. This is part of the demonstrations I used to do."

Reluctantly, he put it in his mouth. I explained to him to hold it softly with his lips, not with his teeth. He nodded and as soon as he put it in his mouth and before he could put his hands down or think about backing out, there was a loud smack! A quick whip kick sent the pen flying across the room. He froze for a second, his eyes not believing what had just happened. Slowly, a smile formed and he broke out laughing. "You got the job!" he told me. The next week we started working on it and it was a wonderful experience.

He was such a sweet and wonderful person on set. Good sense of humor and it was a joy to work with him. One thing that happened on this show was that I had a big piece of car action. The lead vehicle was a taxi, driven by an old man. I hired one of my heroes to stunt double him, Harvey Perry. He doubled Cagney, Bogart, the Marx Brothers, I could go on and on. Harvey was a quiet man, wouldn't hurt a fly. Never spoke unless you ask him a question. About five foot six and in his high seventies.

Have you ever seen the series *F Troop?* Well in the opening sequence you would always see this drunk guy going through town. That was Harvey. He was the town drunk. We got ready to rehearse the action. The Director spots who is driving the taxi.

He walks over to me and asks, "where is the stunt guy that is going to drive this?"

(On the Left, the legend Harvey Perry. On the Right, James Cagney)

I said, "you are looking at him, he is in the car already."

He says, "that is an old man."

I said, "that is not just any old man. That is Harvey Perry."

I proceed to give the Director his background and history. That shuts him up. We get ready to start the scene. Action is called and the taxi takes off with seven others following in the chase. Harvey is going sixty plus at times, old men can fly too, throwing nineties around corners. Sundown comes and it is a wrap. The whole day went beautifully. I went over to all the guys and explained to them where to park their cars for transportation on the street. They get back in their cars and do as they are told. As I walk over to the corner, jumping on a mailbox, remember those big blue and red mailboxes that were on corners? Right next to me is stuntman Roy Clarke. We are having a pleasant conversation when I happen to notice Harvey Perry parking his car. He is at the curb in front of three police bikes, some of our security for the day. Harvey is pulling it in reverse and parking when he accidentally just taps one of the cop bikes. Just hitting the front tire. That is when I see the three cops walk over and start yelling, "you hit my bike, you hit my bike." Harvey gets out of the car and this one cop is berating him as all three are hovering over Harvey like Grizzly bears as Harvey cowers and never says a word. As the berating continues, I see this happening and I jump off the mailbox. Here we go, the Tasmanian Devil comes out. Running across the street, screaming at the policemen. Saying, "don't you ever yell at this man."

The cop looks at me. "He just hit my bike."

I reply, "so what, he just tapped it, he didn't cause any damage. Why are you screaming at him? It was an accident."

The cop looks at me and tells me I had better be quiet before they pulled the permit.

I look at the cop and say, "you should be ashamed at yourself for yelling at an old man." I turn around and embrace Harvey Perry, walking him away. "They probably didn't get their fill of donuts today."

We both laughed.

CHAPTER 21
(Nicholas Cage, Sean Penn And Their Meltdowns.)

The last couple of days on this show I get a phone call from a stuntman named Victor Paul. Victor Paul was in the Stuntmen's Association and told me he was doing a period piece called *Racing With The Moon,* with two actors named Nicholas Cage and Sean Penn. He told me I could take my pick of who I wanted to double. I was surprised, that was the first time that kind of thing was ever offered up to me, a choice between the two lead actors. That is a big compliment when someone gives you that option. I asked him if I could have some time to look over the script before I made my decision and see the action. He said I could. I was excited to meet him and pick up the script. He asked me to meet him at the Stuntmen's Association and he would give me the script there. I was glad that a member had reached out to me. When I attended the Stuntmen's Association meeting, I didn't know what work was going on, so I was happy to be called up by a fellow member like this. By the way, I'm compelled to let you know, that at that time, I was the youngest member in the group. I was also the first Martial Artist in the group other than Gene Lebell. I was a kid and a monkey so to speak and he was an old man that wore a pink gi. Please don't tell him (once again), that I said that. I met him there and we talked a while in the office. He asked me about my past and I told him my main thing is fighting and Martial Arts. I told him I'm a monkey. He looked at me with his head tilted and asked what I meant. I told him I'm very physical and asked him if he wanted to go downstairs so I can demonstrate.

He said okay and down we went. I made a quick stop and went over to the secretary and asked her for a broom. She went and grabbed one and I can tell Victor is getting curious. We went down and I did a couple of forms for him, including a form I had just made up, the Sweeping Broom. I then told him I would use it as a staff and proceeded to do a kata for him. To make it more fun for him, I put in a few sweeps as if I was cleaning up, then went right back into the moves. I would whip it and stick it, an inch next to his face and he was just amazed.

I turned and saw a two story fence. I told him to watch and I threw down the broom and took four to five leaps and climbed to the top. It was about two stories high. At the top, I hopped down onto the solid cement below. Needless to say, he was hooked. I got the script and told him I would read it and get back to him on who I wanted to double the next day. I went home and that night I read the whole script. There is a little humor but truth in this part, so you have to understand. When I had to read a book in school, I couldn't even get past the first chapter without daydreaming. It would take me a year to get through it, haha. The teacher would tell my parents they couldn't get me to read. I look back on that and laugh, having read the script in one night. That's how important and special this business was to me. I thought about my decision on who I wanted to double and I ultimately picked Sean Penn.

At that time, I didn't know who the hell Nicholas Cage was, nobody really did as it was the beginning of his career but I had seen Sean Penn in *Fast Times At Ridgemont High*. If I had known then, what I had known now, I would have picked Cage. Because as all you stuntman out there know, when an actor says he likes you a lot and he is going to use you on his next show, ninety nine percent of the time, that is the kiss of death. You'll never see him again. That is exactly what happened with Sean Penn. It might have been different with Nicholas Cage. You never know. I told Victor my decision and he said, "I will bring in stuntman Mike McGaughy to double Nicholas Cage."

I told Victor I had met Mike and knew he was a Cowboy. At that time Sean and Nicholas both were pretty thin, so we could all interchange if need be. Everything was set and it wasn't long before I got my flying papers to head down to Mendocino, California. We were going on a private plane that fit about ten people. I was going with the Director, Richard Benjamin (who is an actor himself and a Director. Remember the original *Westworld*? He was a city cowboy with Yule Brener), Victor Paul, Mike McGaughy, the Producer, cameraman, Sean Penn and Nicholas Cage. We all met at Burbank Airport to get onto this small little plane. When Victor, Mike and I walked over to meet Sean Penn and Nicholas Cage, we walked over and stuck out our hands to greet them.

Right away you could tell they were a bit shy, maybe even embarrassed to meet new people. I felt a little wall between us and them, but I shook it off as this was our first meeting. I discussed with Mike that I knew they were the stars and we were just the stuntmen, we had to stand back and talk to them only when we needed to. I was schooled a long time ago that one of the reasons actors can get insecure of their stuntmen is because they are doing all the macho stuff. These days it's different. Doubles are respected and there are awards for stuntmen, but back when I started and before, it was taboo. Big time. So we get onto this small plane and Mike and I go to the back of the plane and sit down where we can observe everybody to the front of us. Since all the heads on this plane are above us, we were the low men on the totem. Stunt grunts. The plane starts and takes off. We are about ten minutes from landing and we were going through the canyons of Mendicino. We were close enough to touch them. All of a sudden, the plane drops out of nowhere, it seemed like ten feet, like a roller coaster. Everybody either screams or freezes. Everything not held down goes flying all over the cabin. I go flying, Mike McGaughy goes flying. We were sitting on the armrests of the chairs, in terror. I hear a high pitched scream, like a pregnant yak *from Remo Williams* (more on that film later) and turn towards the sound to see Nicholas Cage. His face is white as a sheet. I hear a lower pitched scream, like a wounded gorilla yelling, "HOOOSHIT."

That was the guy I was doubling. You guessed it. It was Sean Penn holding onto the back of the seat for dear life, also as white as a sheet. I'm clutching everything I can, if I had potatoes in my hands, they would be finely mashed. The propellers start fluttering as the plane drops again, rocking and rolling. Then comes back up and then drops again. I'm looking at everybody, eyes wide open, I truly thought we were going to die. The Captain turns on the seat belt sign and in a blink of an eye, Victor Paul puts on his seat belt. I've never seen anyone put on a seat belt so fast. I look over at Victor Paul and hear this weird squeaking noise. It squeaks for two seconds, then it stops. Then it starts again and then stops. I look at Mike and then back at Victor who is making these squeaks. I yell his name, "Victor, Victor!"

He ignores me and continues the squeaking.

It sounds funny, but it's the truth. It was scary watching Victor. The planes lurches and then drops again and I hear this loud, long scream. I look up and it is coming from Nicholas Cage. Sean Penn screams and the Director is yelling at him to calm down. It felt like minutes went by when it was only around ninety seconds. The Captain comes back on the loudspeaker and announces he is having a problem with the turbulence with major wind gusts and an emergency landing might have to be attempted. The screams get louder, the squeaking becomes quicker and quicker. This plane full of macho men has now become a zoo with roaring lions, shrieking birds and squeaking mice. Then the plane exits the canyons and the shaking and fluttering vanish as quickly as it came. Everyone looks at each other, shock and fear on their faces. The Zookeeper - I mean the Captain, comes back on the speaker and apologizes. He explains he had two choices, go around the canyons and avoid the turbulence, or go through the canyons which was faster, but risk the turbulence. He made the wrong choice and was sorry.

As soon as the Captain finished speaking, Sean Penn and Nicholas Cage went mad with rage. They called the pilot names and yelled at the Director for hiring him to fly the plane in the first place. I looked at Mike McGaughy and asked him if I should ask Victor if he knew why he was squeaking. Mike shook his head and said, "NO! Don't ask him why he was squeaking," as he was laughing at my comment.

That was a plane ride I won't ever forget. Between mice and men. They were the mice and McGaughy and I were the men. I mean, we didn't scream, except on the inside. Needless to say, when we landed, guess who was the first two to stampede off? That's right, the head longhorns, Penn and Cage. The comedy duo- I mean manly men. So we arrive and I go to the Production Office and get my per diem. That is the money you get every week just for living expenses. A few hundred bucks. Yes, this is my job. Can you imagine getting paid at work? Like the song Ethel Merman sang, "There's No Business Like Show Business." It's a wonderful life, just like Jimmy Stewart found out. We get our call sheets the next day and I find out I'm off and so are Sean Penn and Nicholas Cage. I get a call from the secretary in the Production Office who tells me Sean Penn and Nicholas Cage want to go on a hike the next day. She says the Producer would like us to accompany them just for safety purposes. I told them sure, tell the Producer I'll go. I hung up the phone and called Mike and he said he just got a phone call too. I said okay I will see you in the morning in the lobby, and hung up. Mike and I are in the lobby the next morning at nine, and low and behold the two Amigos never show up. Nine thirty comes and we call the secretary who calls us back in ten minutes and tells us they will be there at ten. Actors are always late. I can tell you new stunt people something I learned from my mentors. In most cases it is not the great stunt they remember, it's whether you get to set on time or not. Always be early. That is a sign of a true professional and the first thing your boss sees. He will admire that and never forget it. It ended up being ten thirty before they strolled into the lobby. We smile and welcome them and take off for our hike. We get to the trail and Nicholas Cage and Sean Penn start walking ahead of us about ten to fifteen feet. We are climbing up the terrain and we would shout back and forth every now and then just to try and create conversation. You can tell they wanted us there more or less for safety. We were trying to kindle a friendship, to be honest. They didn't seem too interested in that and kept up their pace ahead of us only to be ignored or turn around for a short reply. Unfortunately, sometimes that is how young punks are. Excuse me, that's the New York coming out of me. Director Francis Ford Coppola, Nicholas Cage's uncle. Director Arthur Penn, NOT Sean Penn's father. But he acts like he is. Those spoiled brats. Just a bit of information.

About forty five minutes later we reach the top of the mountain. Mike and I go over to the edge, looking down at the view. We see the small town we are staying in. We are pointing out our hotel, now a tiny speck. The forest looms in back of us, heavy trees block our view. The birds are chirping, the insects are deep in their winged symphony when a giant BOOM! erupts from behind us. Now I know the sounds of the forest and that was no bear. The sound echoed through the canyon as we both jump three feet into the air and spin around. The remains of a tree are smoking a few feet away from us. I blink and see Sean Penn smiling and holding a very large gun in his hand. My mouth drops open in shock. I look at Mike as Sean fires again! Boom, another tree explodes. I look and Nicholas Cage is telling Sean Penn that he wants to give it a try. "Lemme try," he said.

I find my voice and yell. "What the hell are you guys doing, where did you get that gun!?"

They ignore me.

I yell louder. "Hey, you better put that away." I couldn't believe it. They laugh at us and waive it off likes it is no big deal. I get really pissed off that they find this so funny and start to march towards them. All of a sudden, way down in the valley, I hear the sound of a siren as Nicholas Cage fires the gun. We look down and see a police car coming up the road about five minutes away. Everyone looks down at the car and begins to wonder if they are coming up for us. Sean Penn puts the gun back in his pants and puts his sweatshirt over it. The siren gets louder and we start walking down the mountain, as the cop car is coming towards us. We could have gone the other way and continued our happy trails, but I knew I wasn't guilty and I wasn't going to run away from what just occurred. If they caught us, I would automatically be guilty.

They would ask why I ran. My mind is racing a thousand miles an hour, wondering what we are going to do if they stop us. Sean Penn and Nicholas Cage are in front of us yelling at us to keep quiet. In my mind, I'm wondering what's going to happen here. If the cop stops us, I have two options. Lie and get in bigger trouble with the law, or tell the truth and take a chance that I might get kicked off the show. Sometimes when you tell the truth, it can get you in more trouble. As happened to me many times before and after this circumstance. You see, you have to walk a thin line. This isn't just for all you up and coming stuntmen, but for anyone who is in the business. You will come across instances where you will be put into a corner. You will be asked to turn the other cheek and go against what the right thing is to do. By doing this you will be able to keep your job, you will be able to keep the relationship you have with your co-workers and you will have future work. But I am here to tell you, you have another option. Yes, it may cost you a lot and affect your reputation, but it is at least in my case, morally and ethically worth it. If you were raised as I was, to be truthful and morally sound, then that is the only choice. When you are surrounded by powerful egos filled with obsession and greed, you cannot be pressured into making decisions that go against who you are as a person. I have found that when people who are high up on the totem pole make a mistake, instead of admitting to it, they will deny and deflect the truth. So be prepared for these instances and be ready to deal with them in the manner you see fit.

Getting back to the story, the siren gets louder. Nicholas Cage and Sean Penn are walking faster now and we lose sight of them. As we turn the corner, sure enough, we come face to face with the cop car. The policeman is out of his car in conversation with Sean and Nicholas, a seriousness plastered on his face. The cop yells at us to come over. Oh great, we are going to jail, I thought. I wonder what they told him. The cop asks what was going on. Mike and I were trying to concoct a story that was truthful without getting anyone in trouble when Sean Penn speaks up. "These guys wanted to shoot the gun," he said quickly.

I was speechless. I looked at him and he smiles at me as if to say, go with it. Well, you have to understand a few things here. Number one, there is no way I am going to get in trouble for something I didn't do. Number two, I could understand if he had made a mistake such as kicking a rock down into the valley and it hit someone down below, or if he had urinated on the Alamo like Ozzy Osbourne, but he was firing a gun! I looked at the cop and said, "Officer, I knew nothing about the gun, I didn't even know they had it. They are not telling the truth."

Sean replies, "Aw, come on. Nothing is going to happen just tell them you guys wanted to see it." Again, our mouths dropped. We just can't believe they are lying like this. The Officer can't tell who is telling the truth so he makes us get in his car. Guess who sits in the front? That's right, the two stars. The boys in blue rolled out the red carpet for them. The cop asked us where our Production Offices and Producers were and he takes us there. We get out and Sean and Nicholas storm right into the office. I'm trying to tell the cop my story. That I had no idea they had a gun. We walk into the office and Cage and Penn are chatting with the Producers about what happened. I spoke up and said, "no, no, it's not what we did, it's what they did."

Cage and Penn shrug and tell the cop if they need them, they will be in their room and proceed to walk out. I can't believe they just left. Now Mike and I have to explain to the Producers, and of course we tell them the truth. I had no idea they were going to bring a gun and shoot trees. If I had known, we would have never gone with them. The cop writes everything down on his pad and the Producers listen closely. They believe us and asked to talk to the cop in private. The cop agrees and we were allowed to leave. A few hours later I get called by the Producer who tells me not to worry about anything, they worked it out. I asked if he believed me and he said yes, Sean Penn and Nicholas Cage told them the truth. I thought to myself, "those two chicken shits." So that was the end of that (all's well that ends well, so I thought) and the end of our hiking trips with those two young guns. Haha.

Days go by and I see Sean and Nicholas on set. We would say hello but never really talked that much. My first stunt with Sean Penn is in this skating rink, with his girlfriend who is played by Elizabeth McGovern. The stunt is that I double Sean Penn skating in a roller rink and everyone grabs hands and makes a chain of about twenty people. Sean is the last person in the chain, whipping around in a circle covering the whole rink. The third or fourth time he lets go and goes flying across the room, out the door and down the stairs on roller skates. At this time, I was becoming very good at people watching, (I've always enjoyed that), and I began to notice that Sean Penn and Elizabeth McGovern had a little romantic relationship going and they were outside having a conversation. I was introduced to Elizabeth that day and she was a very sweet girl. The girl next door kind of woman. Cute, athletic and innocent. She was the kind of girl I wish I could have dated. She reminded me of Debbie Reynolds, Meg Ryan, you know the girl next door. So we talk about the scene with my boss Victor Paul and the Director brings Sean Penn in. The actor should always be in the room when their double is going over a scene so he can make sure the action is similar. The Director tells Sean what to do up until the stair fall and Sean gets this look on his face and tells the Director that he wants to do the stair fall. The Director shakes his head and tells him it is too dangerous. He could break his arm or hurt his head. Sean doesn't care and proceeds to demand that he do the stunt, rather than this guy. Yep, "this guy" was now the name Mister Penn referred to me as. I want to speak up as a friend and tell him that if I get hurt, they can replace me, but if he gets hurt, he cannot be replaced. Now this is sound logic and makes perfect sense. I'm a dime a dozen, Sean Penn is not in this case. Nobody says anything regarding that very important truth, so I speak up. I said, "listen Sean, it's not for me to say, but you have to understand I'm approaching this as somebody concerned about your safety. If I get hurt, they can call someone else and have them here in a few hours. If you get hurt, the Production has to stop the whole movie." I thought it was a very convincing argument. But Sean Penn, ever the bucking longhorn from day one, simply shook his head and smirked. Without ever looking at me, he said, "no, shut up. I'm doing it."

I looked at Richard Benjamin who looked like he was about to have a heart attack as the color drained from his face. "No, you are not," he stated. "You can do pieces where you hold on, but you cannot let go. We can film you going out the door and a separate shot before and after you fall down the stairs, but that is it."

(Director Richard Benjamin said, "no. Steven Lambert is going to do it. Penn wasn't happy.)

Sean Penn could not believe the Director told him no and simply stormed off the set. Richard Benjamin tells us to get set up, ignoring the drama that had just happened. Cameras and lighting get set and the extras form the whip. They call action and I skate over, pretending I don't know how to skate, and grab the last person's hand on the whip. I whip once, whip twice, and on the third time, I let go and time it just right. I fly through the door and into the hands of Mike McGaughy who tries to slow me down as I crash down the stairs. We cut. I go back into the roller skating rink to thunderous applause. Everyone thought I was going to crash into the wall and were amazed I didn't. Victor Paul and Richard Benjamin come over to shake my hand. Out of the corner of my eye I see Sean Penn. He has no facial expression whatsoever. As soon as the Director pats me on my back, knowing Sean Penn was there, I say thank you and walk away from everybody. You have to. You shouldn't and you can't let your actor see you get all these accolades.

Sometimes they get insecure and jealous. I was taught a long time ago to never let your actor see you get all that applause because you may not be back the next day. Most actors, unless it's a big scene don't get the applause. It's rare that a stuntman does a stunt that requires such precise timing, coordination and distance to complete, but these are the stunts I always get. Thank you to Sil-Lum Kung Fu and Douglas Wong. it's only natural that people can't help themselves but to clap and congratulate. To all you newcomers out there, you have to be very careful how you act after a big stunt. If you take all the limelight, you may not be back for the next movie or you may be let go that same day. The lead actor is the head honcho, so you have to remember that. That is why I turned my back and walked away. Now it is Sean Penn's turn to do the scene. All they want is for him to release from the whip in a full body tight shot as well as him going through the door. There are about seven people now in the whip with him at the end. He had literally three seconds of filming. When he goes flying through the door, who is going to be there to catch him? That's right, me. I can tell he isn't going to like that too much. I don't say a word to him before the stunt, making sure he has room to breathe. The first thing I do, as every stunt man should do, is I give him knee pads and elbow pads.

He put on the elbow pads and said he didn't want the knee pads and I explained to him that you don't want to break your kneecap. I asked him to please put it on and he finally said okay. We went on set and I told him I was going to catch him when he goes through the door. He casually looks at me and then turns towards the Director. We begin and Sean Penn is holding on for about half a whip. Instead of going around in a whole circle, he started about halfway from the door. They call action and the whip moves and Sean lets go. He pretends he is out of control and goes out the door into the arms of yours truly, the silver masked ninja. I take a knee down to stop him and look up at him. I immediately said, "great job, that is going to look great on camera."

That is what all you up and coming stuntmen should learn. When an actor does a stunt, after they are done you should automatically congratulate them. Whether they did it great or not so great, that is what you have to do if you want to keep your job and go on to future work. Sean looks at me and says, "thank you," before turning around and heading back out.

I was glad that he had said that to me, whether it was gratitude or just something to say, I was just happy he acknowledged me. As he walked back out into the rink, I heard him get an applause from everyone. I thought to myself that they were smart for doing that, but between you and me, my applause was bigger. A few days went by and I got called to go on set to location. I happened to see Elizabeth McGovern walking towards me and smiling. I wasn't sure if she was directing it to me or someone else. When she waved, I looked around. Why would this beautiful girl next door be waiving at a punk kid from Brooklyn? It didn't add up to me. When I realized she was indeed waiving at me, I walked on over, trying to ignore the tickle of excitement crawling up my spine. She made sure she remembered my name.

"Steven isn't it?" She asked.

I nodded, impressed she was interested enough to recall who I was. She smiled and wanted to congratulate me on the stunt in the roller skating rink.

She asked, "how long have you been doing scary stuff like that?"

I smiled again and told her a bunch of years.

We had a little conversation and she asked me where I was from. I told her Brooklyn and I had left when I was thirteen years old. Now I'm thirty one. She asked me what else I was going to do on the show and I told her maybe a fight, I had to do the scene with the train and some other choreography. She laughed and told me to let her know when I'm doing the stunts so she can come watch. I couldn't believe I was talking to her and inside, my heart just melted. She asked me if I was going to be at lunch and I told her yes. So we said goodbye and we went our separate ways. Unfortunately, come lunchtime, I didn't get to see her because my boss wanted me to go on location to look at the train I was going to be chasing and jumping on and off of with Mike McGaughy. Just my luck. The one time I had a beautiful girl waiting for me in the lunchroom and not some crazy, clothes burning, lipstick writing, romantically delusional girl (hint, hint. Cannon films), I couldn't be there.

A few days went by, going to locations and discussing all kinds of things. During the manly talks at the men's gossip hour, I discussed with my boss Victor, how I had the hots for Elizabeth McGovern and that I thought she was just wonderful, but Sean Penn and her had a thing for each other and were going out. Victor Paul suggested to me, that if indeed Penn and Elizabeth were going out, then I should stay away. I thought about it and agreed with him. At the same time, I would notice that Sean would never treat her very nicely. I didn't understand why. You should always treat someone you like with decency and respect. Instead, he would literally yell at her and call her names, berate her, which surprised me. A few weeks later I would see her walk away from Sean Penn, just in tears. I didn't know what was going on but I couldn't believe this girl who was as sweet as apple pie was being treated in such a shameless way.

Things that you simply don't say to a woman, let alone somebody that has a crush on you. I decided to stay away and whenever she saw me and waved, I would wave back and then pretend like I had to go work.

(The lady and the tramp.)

Every now and then I would see her and have a conversation. She even asked me if I wanted to go to the movie once, mentioning to me she would feel safe if I accompanied her. She seemed to be a very sweet and innocent girl with a great upbringing. I tried to stay smart about it and focus on the tasks I had at hand. One day I came on the set and heard a rumor about Sean Penn and Nicholas Cage. Where do you think I hear this rumor? On the street, you hear it from men in the gym, women in a beauty parlor. On set, I heard it from makeup and hair. As I was getting my Sean Penn wig put on, the makeup and hair woman asked me, "did you hear what happened to Sean and Nicholas last night?"

 I said, "no, what happened?"

She told me they trashed their room and threw their television out the window. I think I've seen this in a movie before. My mouth dropped open. She went on to say that they were both inebriated and got too crazy. I didn't know if I should believe her or not, so after I got my wig on, I went over to my boss and asked if it was true. He smiled and asked if I meant that our two actors went a little crazy last night. I nodded my head, eager for him to say it was. He said yeah, it was true. I asked if they really threw the television set out the window and broke it.

Victor Paul looked at me and said, "of course it broke, what do you think happens when you throw a television out the window?"

I was just stunned that they would do that. Sometimes that is just your typical actor. I asked if they got in trouble.

He replied, "Steven. Actors don't get in trouble. They just pay them off."

 For the readers out there, let me explain to you that there are two classes of people in the movie business. The people who get in trouble and the people who don't get in trouble. Even if they have a gun.

Need I say anymore? Days go by and the day came when we were doing the scene where we run with the train and hop onto it. We get to the location where they are going to shoot it (Nicholas Cage and Sean Penn decided to drive alone, go figure) and take a look at this steam powered locomotive.

We discussed how fast the train needed to go for us to hop on it. I asked them to rehearse it as I wanted it to go fast enough to barely be able to make it. I told my boss he could take it to the max and I would raise my hand if we needed it to slow down. I looked at my stunt partner, Mike, and he nodded his head in agreement.

We go about fifty feet back and the train starts to move. As it picks up speed we go faster and faster until we are sprinting, slowly catching up to the train. Now Mike McGauhy was a cowboy and built for fights and horses (cowboy stuff you know), not running at top speeds after trains. I start running at full pace and I make it up to the caboose.

 I look back and fifteen feet in back of me is Mike McGauhy! He is losing speed. Too bad he doesn't have Silver underneath him. I wave my hand under my chin, signaling them to cut. I walk back to Mike who is huffing and puffing.

"Too fast?" I ask.

He nods his head, trying to get his breath back.

So they put the train back into position and I asked them for the sake of my partner, to slow down the train a little bit more and we would animate our run to make it look like we were running faster. Let's see how that works. For you new stunt people out there, when you are working as a team, you cannot just think about yourself.

You have to organize and make whatever you are doing work so that all team members will achieve what needs to be accomplished. We start running again and the train starts to pick up steam. I'm going faster and faster. I pass the caboose, I pass the next car and the car after that. I can't see Mike across the way since he is running on the other side, as the train is blocking my view. I reach out and just barely grab the train car.

(On the right, me. Stunt doubling Sean Penn.)

I pull myself on board and am bombarded with noise. Screams, shouting, fast talking. I look around for Mike who should be right in my vision, across the way, but I am met with an empty corridor. I look to my left and then look to my right. No Mike. I start to hear Mike's name being yelled back and forth by the crew members. Then I hear someone say, "he tripped, he went under the train!" My heart sank to the pit of my stomach. I sprinted to the other side of the train and looked out. The train had stopped and people were shouting for Mike.

Finally, I see movement as Mike rolls out from underneath the train. Everybody's heart skipped in relief. He is bloodied and looks like he went through hell but he is alive. I went over and asked what had happened. He told me he tripped and fell underneath the train's carriage, his head inches away from the wheels. I shuddered to think what could have happened to him if he was any closer. We all took a moment, quite shaken up from what happened. On top of that, the shot would have to be redone. There was talk about me playing both Sean Penn and Nicholas Cage, but they needed both of them running in the same shot. The Director took Victor Paul aside and asked him if he thought Mike would do it again. He told him of course he would, he's a stuntman after all. So again we did do it. The train went extra slow this time and we had no problems. Major action acting in my run. It looked great. We then did the shot with Nicholas Cage and Sean Penn jumping onto the train. I assisted SFX in building them a little wooden platform to stand on as they pretended they were running and out of breath before jumping on. After what had happened with Mike, not one of them wanted to do that stunt themselves. Macho, macho, man. A few days later, I was outside on my patio, practicing my art when Sean Penn walked by. He saw me and asked what I was doing. I explained my background in Martial Arts and he became interested. He asked if I could teach him and I did.

This went on about three times a week, in private and an awful lot of times on set. Nicholas Cage even got involved. All of a sudden, this grumpy actor that referred to me as "this guy" was now my new best friend. It was a good thing. I always thought that was because when he saw me practicing, he might have thought if he got me upset, I would kick his ass. Of course I never would, but he didn't know that. At the end of filming, he told me he would definitely be using me again on his films. I became his "go to" stunt man and lived happily ever after. Just kidding, I never heard from him again. This sort of thing happens to us more often than not, consider yourself very blessed when you do get an actor that really appreciates you and tells the show that you are his stunt double and there is no other, so bring him on.

Let's move on with my life. After *Racing With The Moon*, I went back home, relaxing and looking forward to the end of the month, for there was going to be a Stuntmen's Association membership meeting. I began thinking, in the back of my mind, hoping this meeting would be better than the last one. Reassuring myself that it probably will and the last one was just one of those things, thinking I am overjoyed to be in a group that is the original with all the famous stuntmen of the past and present. I belong to an organization that was known all over the world. Me, a punk kid from Brooklyn.

CHAPTER 22
(The Day I Was Dominated By Lucinda Dickey.)

A few days later, I got a call from Sam Firstenberg. What a fantastic surprise. He told me Cannon was doing another ninja film and wanted to know if I was interested in coming back aboard. I thought about it for a second and answered, "is a frog's ass water tight?" I have a habit of making American jokes and sayings to people from other countries. In *Revenge Of The Ninja*, I would crack a lot of these jokes to Sho being that he was from Japan. In this case, Sam was from Israel. He thought about it for a few seconds and then asked, "

what are you saying?" I proposed the question to him again.

I asked, "is a frog's ass water tight?"

He replied, "yes."

I laughed and told him, "then yes, of course. Thank you so much, my friend. I'll take the job." Good old, Shmulik. I ask him if David Womark is back on board and he says yes.

I say, "terrific." Then I ask him if our D.P. David Garfinkel is onboard.

He says unfortunately not. He is doing something else. We have a new one whose name is Hanania Baier.

I hesitate for a second and ask him, "what's a Hanania?"

He says, "an Israeli."

I say, "oh God, not another one."

He laughs and I reply, "I'm sure I will have as much fun with him as I did with Garfinkel."

He tells me to come into the office the next day in the afternoon to talk to him and David. I go in the next day and Sam hands me the script. He tells me the title. *Ninja: The Domination*, about a girl who is a telephone repair woman who gets possessed by a bad ninja. At that time, my thoughts were on the action and the fact I was doing another ninja film for Cannon, not the title or anything else for that matter. I opened the script and again I saw more blank pages.

I look at him and say, "I think you guys would learn by now to fill in your own pages, don't wait for me."

He laughs and says, "that's your job."

This time I knew what I had to do. He told me that the woman ninja is played by Lucinda Dickey and that she was a dancer. I was excited about that fact, as anyone who is a dancer, gymnast, or an athlete, should pick up the movie way of fighting pretty fast. He told me to take home the script and come back with a budget. I asked him where we were shooting and he said Phoenix, Arizona. You see as a kid, I never got the chance to travel at all, which is why this is one of the greatest jobs on earth. It's free just like everything else in this crazy business when you are working. Free travel, free food and free money for your expenses. And should we talk about the salary you get for sitting around ninety percent of the time? I was excited it was a different location than the last Ninja film we did. I go home and read the script. For all you new stuntmen and even ones who are established, the first thing you do is when you read the script, you want to know what is going on in each scene. The reasons and whys for the action and the story. You never want to string together action just for the sake of having action. It needs to be smooth, make sense and flow with the story and the thoughts of what the Director wants. Communication with the Director and Actor is a must here.

By listening and learning, you will gain the experience and understanding needed to put together a wonderful sequence. Never be afraid to ask questions. Going back to reading the script, I realized it's a totally different script than *Revenge Of The Ninja.* That film had the good ninja and the bad ninja and "ND" ninjas. Here I had a female who was a protagonist, the bad ninja, and the ninja who rescues everyone. Now I have that to think about that and I realize in the script they have a lot more planned. They have cops with motorcycles and cars and helicopters. Chases and exterior locations all over the place. I can't double the main character and double a cop at the same time. I knew I was going to have to bring in stuntmen this time.

On the last film, I was used to doing ten to twelve parts a day, here I would have to do thirty, forty parts a day. I had no choice but to bring people in. This was going to be hard because the Producers saw what I could do physically on the last film and didn't understand why I had to bring people in when they could save money by just having me do it. Can you believe it? You have to understand Menachem Golan and Yoram Globus are two of the cheapest son of a guns I have ever met in the film business but as Producers, sometimes that is a good thing. Two very smart men. Anyway, I figured I am going to have to ask for at least a dozen guys. I'm trying to think about how I'm going to convince mister cheapskate David Womark to agree with this, so I come up with a plan. A few days later I call Shmulik up and tell him I had the budget and wanted to meet with him. He said to come in today in the afternoon and we would talk. I come in and give him the budget and he and David mention it's much higher than the last film. I told them of course it is higher, they have a lot more non-descript characters on or in vehicles in this film than in *Revenge Of The Ninja.* It was almost like it went in one ear and out the other as he proceeds to tell me that my salary is more than the last film.

I looked at him and said, "YEAH OF COURSE! It's only five hundred dollars more a week."

He shook his head and said no, he wasn't going to give me that.

I took a deep breath and put my plan into action. "David", I said calmly. "You saw how much money I saved you on the last film. This was due to the fact that normally when a person like me plays multiple parts, you get a separate contract for each one. I was doubling all of them and was on one contract." I was just happy to be doing the action, I wasn't worried about getting the most money. Sorry to say, I was never built that way. Throughout my whole career, I've always paid myself cheap. Always was thrilled when I was working for someone else, for that's when I would really get paid well for my services. I call that, a flaw in my armor. You new stunt people out there, don't make that mistake. I explained this to him and he looked at me with complete amazement. I told him I was going to do the same and more and he was going to like what he was going to get. For everyone who knows David, this was a fight to the finish and in the end, I couldn't believe he said yes. I was very happy. I then explained to him why I needed all these guys to play the cops. Keep in mind, the crew was relatively new to action and depended on me always. After explaining that I can't be chased by a cop on a motorcycle and be the ninja at the same time, and because it's too dangerous and too hard to hire someone off the street, I needed certain people.

At that time, most trained stuntmen only came from Los Angeles or New York. I told David I could get really good people that know what they are doing. I can't hire a guy I don't know, who doesn't know what they are doing and try to teach them in mere days. Especially when it comes to vehicles. It takes years of practice. You could literally kill people with some of these stunts. You out there, you must understand, that there were not stunt people all over like there is now as I explained. There was a mere handful. In today's times, there is a stuntman everywhere you turn around. David remained silent, deep in thought. Slowly, a small grin pulled at the corners of his mouth. He looked at me and I knew exactly what he was going to say. It started with a "y" and ended with an "s."

"We'll talk about it some more when the time comes," he responded.

Oh. Ok. Not quite what I wanted to hear. I told him we need to come to an understanding now, if we hire someone from Arizona or Utah, I can't teach them in time. David nodded and said to check with Menahem. I say to myself, oy vey. Wonderful I thought, I have to run it by the big boss. I agreed and we moved on to talking about the script and the ideas I had to put in the action. We all agreed it was going to be a great show and we were happy to work with each other. As we were walking out of the office, I blurt out, "what about Sho Kosugi? I thought he was going to star in the next ninja."

Shmulik replies, "no not this time. He only has a small part and he is not too happy about that."

I shrugged it off, knowing he had good action I was going to give him and said goodbye to everyone. I took the elevator up to the penthouse to see Menahem. I would see people like Boaz Davidson and Avi Lerner, big shots now but then just novices. They enjoyed my work and would congratulate me. I made my way to Menahem's office and the secretary saw me and I couldn't believe she remembered my name when she said hi to me. I was just tickled to death. I was so well regarded here after *Revenge of the Ninja*. She told Menahem I was here and it wasn't long before the voice of God boomed out from the intercom. "Steven, come sit down!"

I stepped into his office and boy was he was happy to see me. He sat behind his desk as he always did, with his larger than life personality right along with him. I sat down and told him it was good to see him again. He told me, "I can't believe what you did in my movie. You are a very unusual man. For this new movie, the Domination, we need BIGGER STUFF. More exciting action. You must make the Domination more money than Revenge Of The Ninja."

This was my perfect chance to let him know about the extra stunt people. I replied, "I will, but this time there are a few things I need Menachem." I then explained to him that because there were so many characters in this script, 10 cop cars and 15 motorcycles and different kinds of equipment that I needed, that my budget was much bigger. I couldn't double all of them at the same time in the same scene and needed to bring in more people.

He smiled again and said, "sure, anything for you Steven. You are Cannon Film's Jewish action man."

I laughed so hard and asked if he could make a t-shirt that said that for me. It was like the Red Sea had parted and I realized I could have anything I wanted because of what I did for him in *Revenge Of The Ninja*. I knew that I had to get a good girl or girls to double the lead and of course this was going to cost us money. The budget also went up for this movie, from a million to a million and a half! For all you greenhorns out there, even though the budget is bigger, it does not mean the money is for the action. I did explain to him the movie would be bigger and better due to the immense action involving vehicles and cops and bigger exteriors. He smiled and I asked about Sho. He frowned and said Sho is not too happy as the lead is a girl now. In my head, I instantly wanted to know more. I couldn't understand why they wouldn't bring Sho back again *after Revenge Of The Ninja* becoming such a big hit. That was the conversation we all had after the first two weeks of the movie. I regretted asking about Sho, but luckily it was a minor thing in the conversation. He stood and shook my hand and said to bring him fantastic stuff. Boy, was I going to.

So we go to Phoenix, Arizona and David calls me to come to a Production meeting the next day at nine in the morning. I get down there an hour early the next day and start talking to David. I asked him, "where is my bride to be?"

He looks at me and then realizes I meant Naomi Golan. He laughs and tells me that no, she is not going to be on this production.

Immediately, the music plays in my head and I break out into a "Happy Dance." I start dancing like Anthony Quinn in *Zorba The Greek*. Which by the way, he won the academy award for. More dancing with him later. Everyone in the office turns to look at me. David starts laughing hysterically. After my dance, settling down, I was told that Lucinda Dickey would be arriving tomorrow and I needed to get a schedule together to teach her before we start filming in two weeks. In my mind, I am thinking about getting a woman to double her, so I ask the secretary to look at Martial Arts and gymnastics schools in the area to see if we can find a few good girls to double her. As well as ask her if any stuntmen have stopped by to drop off a composite. She tells me yes. Then she turns around, opens her drawer and whips out an envelope. As we are talking, an Israeli walks in and David wants to introduce me to the show's D.P. We go over and the Hebrew starts flowing from their mouths again. Here we go again, deja vu, I thought. I had to wait until they were done speaking in Hebrew before they spoke in English. I waited patiently for them to switch languages and they finally tell me the man's name is Hanania Baer.

I start talking to him and find that he is a very intelligent man who understood my ideas for the action and got more excited as I explained them. We go into a big room and sit down. We go over the script and when we get to the action, Wardrobe is asking what I need, Props is asking what I need, Effects is asking what I need, and so on and so on. Eventually, everything I need is discussed and ready to go. A bit later we go to the golf course to scout the location. We go from spot to spot on the golf course looking at everything, I'm writing notes in my notebook. They liked my ideas and after three hours we went home, confident in what we were going to do. I hop in the van and am on my way back to the hotel when I decide to open up the envelope of stunt people that the secretary gave me. One picture I came across was a guy named Spanky Spangler. Including his picture, he had some shots with Eval Knievel and his son, Robbie Knievel. There is a one page letter explaining that he is a stuntman and has worked as a mechanic for Eval Knievel and is now Robbie's manager and equipment tech, with a mention he builds ramps and cages for cars and motorcycles. This was a wonderful find for me because my plan was to jump one of the cop cars over a palm tree into a golf course lake. After I got back, I went into the office, sat down and called up Spanky. I introduced myself and told him I was doing a movie called *Ninja: The Domination.* I asked him if he could come in and discuss building a ramp and putting a cage in a car. I asked if he could come in tomorrow to speak to me about this and he said yes. After I hung up, new ideas came into my head and I asked David Womark for a driver. He asked why and I told him I wanted to go back to the location and start putting everything together. I got back there and had some wonderful action planned. Cops, car chases, helicopters, swords, even getting shot more than a hundred times in a scene which I called the Elvis Presley.

You may ask why I called it that. After the movie came out, I took that piece of film and put it on my own personal VHS, which for all of you young people out there that don't know what a VHS is, it's what we had before DVDs. It had the song, "Jail House Rock." If you ever get a chance, put it together, it's funny and exciting. Movement and song. I also had planned climbing trees, mapping out a foot chase between the ninja and cop cars and motorbikes, high falls and of course, jumping a car over a palm tree. Everything you saw in the movie, the empty pages of the script became full. I start having meetings with wardrobe, props and transportation, when Spanky comes in. I explain the stunt to him and explain the measurements. I told him I wanted the ramp in two sections with a gradual rise from the ground to the top of the palm tree and asked him to come look at the palm tree on the golf course.

We go over to the location and I explain my idea, that I wanted a long ramp and slow rise. The palm tree is a good 25 feet high. I explain the sequence where I am on top of the cop car and the car will hit the ramp and go up and into the lake. Someone will be driving the car, his name is Vince Deadrick Sr., and I will be surfing the cop car on top of it. We will cut and I will switch costumes and become the cop driving the car and drive up the ramp and into the lake. I told him not only that I needed a ramp but I needed a cage put in the car for the safety aspect and gussets all around. A full cage including the doors and I needed the floor boards cut out for an alternate escape. Don't forget to take the back seat out. These are the precautions you take for another way out of the car in case the way out you have planned is blocked. He assured me he could do it all. I was happy I got that out of the way. I told him my height and weight and the rest of the measurements for the ramp and cage. He told me it would be done in two weeks and I thanked him, telling him there would be more stunts for him later on. That is what you do when someone is working with you. You always want to have a contingency, 10-15% above, depending on the budget and size of your action in the script. So everyone was happy. I told Spanky to get to work and make up a bill and bring it in for the secretary. He agrees and I'm feeling good about it. Late in the afternoon, I get a phone call from the secretary that Lucinda Dickey is in the office and David and Shmulik wanted me to come down. I get everything together and go on down to the office and see Shmulik there with Lucinda. He introduces me and we shake hands.

We start discussing the script and I commented that because I knew she was a dancer, I was going to use that to help with the Martial Arts in the film. For instance, when you do a dance and you lift your leg, that tells me something. I ask her to do it and she lifts her leg up high to the sky with style. I nodded and asked her to watch how I did it. I tried to mimic her, although she did it with a bit more grace and style, I have to say. I then asked David to stand up as I was going to demonstrate an outside crescent kick. He was going to be my dummy, but he wasn't no dummy. He started laughing, then Shmulik started laughing and I started laughing. One of my running jokes on *Revenge Of The Ninja* was that when I needed to demonstrate something I would always pick David Womark. That was my personal enjoyment of the day and as others seemed to enjoy it too like Sho Kosugi and Shmulik as well as anyone else who was around. He was afraid of getting kicked or punched and sometimes he did if I wanted him to feel it. These are the playful things we do. As big of a Producer he was and was destined to be, he was scared shirtless when it came to getting hit. That's what friends are for.

We proceeded with the meeting and discussed the different scenes she was in. David and Shmulik kept telling Lucinda about what I did in *Revenge Of The Ninja*, which was great. It gave Lucinda a sense of what I could do, but I wanted to talk about this film. So we concluded talking about the script and Shmulik mentioned he had the hotel ballroom booked out, so Lucinda and I could practice. I had gotten some pads from the local high school because David was too much of a miser to let me bring equipment from L.A. We agreed to meet after lunch at one o'clock the next day to start training and concluded our first meeting on a high note. We met the next day in the ballroom at one. After a couple of hours of practicing kicks, punches and stances, and talking about body language and the reasons and the why's you do certain things, she started picking it up pretty fast.

Her enthusiasm was flowing. Now let me say, I have taught and trained many people and I can tell you, I quite honestly never experienced this type of feedback which made me feel very uncomfortable in a good way. (Yee-ha, baby.) She would get unusually close as I was showing her the stances and try to mimic me very closely. To my amazement, her hand would brush against my thigh and legs to see how low I was and how strong of a stance it was before I jumped out of it. Up until

195

now, I've never had somebody respond to an action by making a corresponding one quite like this. She explained in dance, they are used to getting very close to the teacher when they are learning something, to feel and understand it. She told me she could feel the power of my muscles contracting as I went from stance to stance and it excited her, but I must tell you, imagine what it was doing to me. Okay, stop imagining.

There was a sense of enjoyment there, which I picked up on right away. This was very unusual for me as no one had done something like this with me before. But being a man, of course I wasn't too uncomfortable with the situation either. I liked it! Just call me mister happy boy. The session went wonderful, of course, and we said goodbye and see ya tomorrow. She shook my hand with a certain caress and when we went our separate ways, I found myself thinking about it for hours. Wouldn't you? I went to the Production Office and told David and Shmulik everything went well. David was glad and announced we were going on location so I can take Shmulik and Hanania Baer through the action. We got to the golf course and I started explaining all my ideas pertaining to the action. A few hours later we were all very happy with what we were going to do. I realized I was going to do things I had never gotten the chance to do in the past and I was very excited for what was to come. We hop back into David Womark's car and I lean over to David who is driving and I whip him with my hand, on his shoulder.

He looks at me and asks, "what was that for?"

I asked if he was happy that I had saved him money since we didn't need doubles anymore.

He smiled and said, "I'm sure you will find a place to use it."

We all started laughing and went back to the hotel. The next day comes and I'm doing some work in the Production Office before I go to the ballroom and set up for Lucinda. The time comes, and I head down to the ballroom. I find myself not fantasizing about stunts. Yes, you out there who are reading this, know what I am thinking. It ain't stunts. What do you want from me, I'm from the male species. I always find woman who are physical, interesting. It's not long before Lucinda enters the ballroom, a huge smile on her face. She prances right up to me and plants a kiss on my cheek, a few skin cells away from my lips. I asked her why she did that and she replied she was excited how wonderful a movie it was going to be and how happy she was to work with me. I agreed and we started with going over punches. As I'm in my stance, my fist is extended out to her face. I'm expecting her to block it, or move away. Instead, she takes my fist and puts it right up to her cheek and smiles. She starts caressing my fist and then kisses it. I pull away and take a deep breath trying to control my emotions and then smile. I told her that's not a very good way to block a punch. She smiles and laughs in a very amorous way. I asked her to block it like I had shown her the day before. I threw another punch and she blocked it, so we continued on with more punches and stances.

Then all of a sudden, she began to mimic my stances up against my back. Believe it or not, I got nervous and casually took a step forward to make some distance. She explains again that she needs to feel the stance to get used to how it feels. I smile and proceed with the lesson. I start to realize that she comes closer and closer as she mimics my moves. My face got red and her aroma was overwhelming. I was a punk kid from Brooklyn, I've never experienced this kind of activity. Elbow to elbow, cheek to cheek, thigh to thigh, it was all very unexpected but thrilling. Then I began to show her how to block and grab and push away. I pretended to be the bad guy and she did it to me. The third time we went over it, instead of blocking and pushing me away, she grabbed me and swept me into an embrace. Now instead of our thighs touching or our backs touching, our lips were touching! My heart beat a mile a minute, my eyes went wide. My mind was racing too. The ballroom door was wide open. What if someone walked in. Shut up, who cares! This is great! That was the voice in my head that was the loudest, so I went with it. After quite a few minutes, praying no one would walk in, we broke off. I told her we had better keep this quiet and she agreed. She told me her room number with a smile and exited the ballroom first. I waited five minutes, scared to death about meeting her in the hall.

So five minutes later I walked up to the Production Office and Shmulik was there in conversation. I told Shmulik I wanted to discuss how the session went. He said okay and we went into the office. I told him the session went great physically but my head is exploding. He looks at me and I'm trying to figure out how to word this. I'm a nice Jewish boy, this is brand new to me. I explain it to him carefully and he smiles and says his trademarked line.

"Don't worry, everything will be fine, don't worry about it. But let me give you a little word of advice. Don't let Sho Kosugi know."

I ask him why and he smiled saying, "you figure it out."

Not saying this is the same thing, but crazy things can happen. Hey, I didn't realize how fine it would be or how happy I would become. Shmulik shrugs and says maybe it will help the movie that we are love interests now. I didn't know if this relationship with Lucinda was going to go away or get more intense. I had no idea how crazy the domination was about to get and I am not talking about the film.

(Cast and crew of *Ninja: The Domination*)

As we got closer to the first day of filming, the meetings and training with Lucinda progressed well. I did my best to stay away from the happenings of the second meeting, with little to no avail. I could go into more detail, but it's not needed. I tried to stay away from things that would get us close together, not that she didn't try to get closer, she did. We would have lunch and midnight dinners together, keeping it secret from the cast and crew. If anyone saw us, we would pretend we were just talking about the script. The first day of filming arrives and it was the aerobics scene and it went well. Lucinda did her fight and it looked great on camera.

Then we moved on to the golf course. I bring six stuntmen from Los Angeles, including Joel Kramer, Mike Tillman, John Meier, Buck McDancer, Vince Deadrick Jr. and Sr. Now try to imagine this. We film the sequence when I'm playing the bad ninja and I'm on top of the cop car surfing it. Vince Deadrick Sr. is driving and in the middle of the scene, he throws the car into a slide and stops the car. I did everything I could to prevent myself from flying off the front end. He gets out and starts voicing his "old timers" opinion.

"In all my time doing stunts, I never thought I would be playing a cop driving with a ninja on the top of my car, down the road with a gun in my hand and shotgun in the car. I can just blow you away. Ninja, this."

He points the gun at me and we all started laughing, it didn't matter if we were rolling or not. That's one of the many reasons why I think he is the greatest.

(Death from above. Coppers Joel Kramer and Vince Deadrick Sr.)

The golf course sequence went great. All the chases and action were done beautifully by me and the stuntmen I brought along. Then came the helicopter day. I was doubling David Chung, who played the black ninja. David Chung was a quiet and timid person. Like actor Joel Grey once said to me, "you move like a pregnant yak," and that he did so I didn't use him in anything when it came to the ninja action. It was I in the ninja outfit. Let's talk about one of my favorite scenes. The black ninja climbs up onto a palm tree and jumps onto the struts of the helicopter. The helicopter starts flying away, right over the golf course lake. In the helicopter are stuntmen John Meier playing one of the cops sitting next to another cop who is played by Vince Deadrick Jr. who is sitting next to a pilot who is played by yours truly. I thought you just said you were on the helicopter struts, now you are saying you are inside too? Are you remembering this correctly, Steven? I can hear all you out there asking.

Yes, I was both places but I didn't need to bend time and space to do it. All I did was when I needed to change, I switched costumes and shot me in the helicopter and then changed back. Pretty smart for a punk kid huh? The scene was I, as the bad ninja, kills Vince Deadrick Jr. and throws him out of the helicopter. Then I go around to the other side and kill John Meier. Before I killed Vince Deadrick Jr., it was me playing the cop and when I switched back to the ninja, he took my place. I wasn't using any cables on the helicopter. I knew I could move more freely without cables and Shmulik didn't have to cut as much. If I fell, ninety percent of the time, I hoped,

I would land in the lake we were flying over. My hands were like vices when I needed them to be, and as loose as a dandelion in the wind when I didn't.

All this time, I had given the helicopter pilot certain palm trees to fly above, that way I could control how high we were and how safe I was in my mind. That is a needed practice, to feel secure in your mind while always doing action. Little did I know, when I was on the struts preparing to kill John Meier, which was about ten seconds, he was talking to the helicopter pilot, telling him to go higher. I had no idea what was going on. Let me say, John Meier one of the best stuntmen I have met in my life. I trusted him fully and looked up to him big time. So when I climb into the helicopter mind you, we are rolling, he is telling the pilot to go higher. From twenty five feet to forty five feet. As I'm fighting him, I look out the door and we are still climbing. I don't see the palm tree the helicopter is supposed to be above. I look again and there is the palm tree now over fifty feet below. I yell at the pilot, "who told you to go higher?"

He points back to John and says, "he did."

I look at John who smiles and says, "trust me."

Trust you!? It's now a fifty foot drop into a seven foot lake!

The pilot turns to us and tells us to hurry up. He has Shmulik screaming in his ear asking, "what are they waiting for?"

Now we have no choice. I look at Meier who smiles back.

He says, "let's go."

I look at him and say "F--- it." Can you figure out what I said? I take a deep breath and draw my sword. I slash my sword at him and we both jump out of the helicopter about fifty plus feet into the lake. I had every intention of landing feet first like a gazelle, while John twisted and turned like a flying squirrel. I hit the water and went down right to the concrete and dirt bottom of the lake. I hit so hard my chin smacked against my knees and I almost knocked myself out. I pushed up to the surface and came five feet out of the water in total disbelief we had actually pulled it off. I look over and see John Meier floating there, a big grin on his face. "That is going to look great," he said. I was glad that we did it, even if he took over my job, as it made the shot look better that we fell from that height. I was just glad I didn't wet my pants.

I was all wet, so if I did it wouldn't matter anyway as nobody could see. LOL. As we are swimming to shore, I didn't know whether to be upset or hug him. I chose the latter.

(The flying monkeys. John "bad" Meier and Steven lambert.)

Finally, the day where I jump the cop car comes. Spanky Spangler is coming to drop off the car and the ramp. I am very excited. I ask Joel Kramer and Mike Tillman to hang out and wait for him. I was out with the Director doing action on the lake. A few hours later I get a call on the walkie from Joel, saying with the humor only brothers can share, "hey Steven, you better come to base camp. Spanky just came with the car and ramp and I don't think you are going to like it too much."

I asked what he meant but he just insisted I come and look. Lunch came and we go to base camp. As we pull up, I notice this thing, this wooden thing. It looks like a wooden rocket ship ramp. The closer I got, I realize that it's MY ramp. Joel Kramer starts laughing as I get out and Spanky walks over. I asked him what the hell this was, and he replied it was my ramp. I told him this isn't what I wanted. I gave him dimensions and this ramp was nowhere near what I asked for. If I tried to hit the ramp, it was so short and steep, I would bottom out and my front end would go right through it! I was in total shock and couldn't believe he had brought me this. I was jumping a palm tree, not going to the moon. I gave specific orders that were just ignored. Diagrams and measurements. Suddenly, more laughing erupted from behind me. I look to see Joel who is waving me over to see the roll cage.

"Look at this Steven," he says while cracking up. I walk up and I see the cage and the bars of the cage. I realize as I try to get in, that he built the cage that would only fit Tom Thumb. For you out there who don't know who Tom Thumb is, he is a little person, a midget. Oh, I forgot I am not supposed to say that in this politically correct world. Hogwash. I can't even get in it, but guess what? Spanky made it a point to show me that he fit.

When he did, I looked at him and said, "dream on. Is that why you built the cage like this?"

Just then, I heard multiple laughs. Alongside Buck McDancer, guess who chimed in? Vince Deadrick Sr. and Joel Kramer. Now I had three of them hysterical.

I could say, great friends are allowed to laugh. I was ready to just snap. This was the biggest stunt of the show and nothing is right. Suddenly, I stop. I'm thinking, wait a minute, this is my mistake and it is my fault. He had this job for weeks and I trusted him. I shouldn't have trusted him and went down to check on everything at his garage at least four to five times. As mad as I was at him, I was also mad at myself. Now I have to figure out what to do. Spanky was 5'2. Am I going to let him do this jump? HELL NO.

So my stuntmen I hired got together and said if we could do it tomorrow, they can get some settling tanks and fix the cage. If they get some lumber, they can fix the ramp. Mike Tillman was the best of the best when it came to car jumps. Unfortunately, I didn't send Mike to Spanky's to check up on him. That was a big mistake.

All you out there who are going to do shows, no matter how much you think everything will work out, never assume anything. Double check. Triple check. I explained what happened to David Womark who wasn't happy. When these things happen, it causes a domino effect. Putting it off one day affects the Production Manager, the Director, the camera operator and all heads. It costs time and money and I caused it. So that was a tremendous learning experience. Again, we were like family and I was like the Captain of the ship. In this case, action. Thank God I had already proven my talents to them and they knew what they had and luckily, they understood.

I let my guys go to work and they were the best working their magic on the cage and the ramp. They made a secondary ramp to go at the beginning, so I could have a gradual climb up to this jump.

Spanky came back and I said thank you for your help and see ya. He asked me what day he was going to work. I apologized and said there was no room for him on this show. I stuck my hand out and he shook it and that was the end of that relationship with Spanky from *The Little Rascals*.

The boys spent the entire day and night going to Home Depot and the lumber yard and I was so proud of them and myself for bringing the right men. A TEAM. Now I could fit in the cop car and with the added segment to the ramp, I could accelerate slowly. We took out the gas tank and put in a tank that held a gallon of gas, which comes to find out, goes really quick.

So listen to this, we shoot it and I hit the gas, full throttle. No response. The car comes to a slow stop before the ramp. I hear on the walkie talkie, "cut."

(My three amigos forever. Joel Kramer, Vince Deadrick Jr. and John Meier.)

I unbuckle and jump out of the car, wondering what the hell is going on. People are looking at me like I chickened out. If looks could kill. They ask what happened.

"I don't know, the car just stopped. I lost power." As we were scratching our head, McDancer opened the trunk and realized we had used up all the gas in rehearsals. I soon felt vindicated, don't ever give me that chicken look. Well, as you can see from the movie, it was one hell of a jump. I reset and we are ready to go. I check in with Shmulik and camera one, camera two, up to camera five. I have an oxygen tank I can put in my mouth before I go. Joel Kramer is in the water as my safety diver. I wouldn't have had anybody else. I trust him with my life.

Shmulik yells, "ACTION." Then says, "Steven."

That's my cue. I hit the gas and I'm flying down the road. From forty to fifty to sixty to seventy, seventy five miles per hour when I hit the ramp. I come off the ramp looking up at the sky at eighty degrees. Everything is in slow motion as all I see is beautiful blue sky. Maybe I'm in heaven. Nope. All of a sudden, the weights in the trunk of my car kicks in and shift forward a little bit, causing the nose of my car to point downward to the hell beneath me. I slow up and the front end dips down towards the earth. I realize I'm literally a good forty five feet in the sky.

I can see a group of people a mile away in the distance. That's the goddamn cast and crew! I'm going straight down towards a seven foot lake. I hit the water and like Moses spreading the Red Sea, the water just opens up and I go down! Believe it or not, I could see the cement bottom. The window breaks and the steering wheel comes in onto my chest. I flipped over in the car with this tremendous crash.

Everything stops as I am face to face with the cement under the water. I then went from Moses to Pharaoh, as the water came rushing back in, engulfing the car and me inside.

As I hit the bottom, the concussion knocked the mouthpiece of the mini tank out of my mouth. When you are using a mouthpiece, make sure it is taped! I hadn't taped it and now I was in trouble. I looked over and felt the tank next to me. I put my hand on the tank and followed it up to the hose which brought me to the mouthpiece. I shoved it back in my mouth and breathed out. Now I can breathe, thank goodness. Always remember to maintain your composure, whenever something happens. An ancient Chinese Jewish proverb. Now I have to unhook myself and I quickly do that. I flip over to right side up and swim through the missing floorboards I had cut out. I spit out the mini tank and head up to the surface, when I feel myself caught.

I look down and feel I'm caught on my safety belt. I have to turn upside down and get my leg and half of my waist out. It feels like minutes are going by, everyone is going to be worried. Meanwhile, Joel Kramer, not able to see me, is swimming over to the car to try and find me. I get loose from my belt and swim up to the surface. I break the water to thunderous applause and screams from the cast and crew as well as reporters and guests that had come out to see this stunt. Around four hundred spectators. I wonder how long I was under there. It seemed like hours had passed. Yeah, right. Shmulik and David Womark run over and shake my hand.

Seconds go by. All of a sudden, a scream comes from the water. I turn and see Joel Kramer pop up from where the car was. I focus on his screams and I realize he is yelling.

"I can't find him, I can't find him. I don't know where he is!"

I raise my hand and yell, "Joel, I'm right here you moron!"

Joel is treading water as everyone starts laughing and he shakes his head in disbelief. He replies back, "I've never seen anybody move that fast."

I ask what he is talking about.

"You were in that car for five seconds. You must have jumped out before the car hit the water."

Everyone starts laughing around us. He expected me to wait in the car for him! No way Jose. To this day, if you ask him, he will tell you he's never seen anyone get out of a car faster. That is coming from one of my pals, Joel Kramer.

I go back to the honey wagons to change costumes for the next scene, while they are pulling the cop car out of the lake with a tow truck. I can't believe the whole front end is smashed up to the dashboard. I happen to look up and there is Lucinda

Dickey, running into my arms like a baby gorilla jumping up and wrapping her arms and legs completely around me, followed by a big kiss. Sucking lips. When after a few seconds, she drops her feet back to earth. I was shocked, but boy, she was a great kisser and just went with the program. We both stopped for some oxygen, long enough for her to say she had never seen anyone so brave and so crazy.

(After all that, thank you, Spanky Spangler for the rocket ship ramp.)

It excited her, she had a devilish grin and I must say my THERMOMETER rose. I mean my temperature. Then she said, "I want to take you to this lobster house tonight, after work." I had just come out of a lake and now she wanted to feed me seafood, but lobster was my favorite. I did hold the record for eating lobster tails on *Fantasy Island.* I said yes and thank you. She smiled and said I was so cute. I replied, "you are too. In more ways than one."

She laughed and asked, "what do you mean by that?"

I replied," your kiss was like sucking on a leech." You need to make a woman laugh. So I went on with my day and at about eight o'clock that night, I met Lucinda in the lobby and we went out to the restaurant. We ordered a bottle of sake with the dinner and had wonderful food and conversation. The sake was nice and warm and so was I.

We began feeding each other lobster and other things that would make an Orthodox rabbi faint. We finished the first bottle and went onto the second. After that, we went onto the third and fourth and fifth bottle of sake. I could have sworn I started talking Japanese by this point, my words were so slurred. Now, I am not the kind of person who is a big drinker, a bottle of beer and I'm ready to sleep. Let's just say at this point, I wasn't ready to sleep. Luckily, we took a taxi to the restaurant and were smart enough to take a taxi back. Not that we had much of a choice, but remember people shouldn't drink and drive. Five bottles of sake were good but wouldn't you know it, she wanted to take a take home bottle, one for the road or in this case, the jacuzzi.

We get back to the hotel and Lucinda decides we should take a midnight swim and a jacuzzi. The jacuzzi happened to be ten feet away from my room in the octagon shaped hotel, so I say "yes". We part ways to get into our bathing suit and I bring the sake into my room to wait for her to knock on my sliding glass door. I get into my high waisted baggy shorts which always doubled for a bathing suit. I decide that I was going to prepare for Lucinda's arrival in the hot tub, so I go get some towels from the bathroom. I walk over to the fridge and take out some cheese, crackers, candy bars and of course the sake with some glasses. I made a little picnic basket out of everything and set it by the jacuzzi. Romantic, aren't I? I felt like Romeo waiting for Juliet. I get in the water and wait for the female ninja to come down. Eventually she arrives in a white robe wearing a big smile. She asks, "are you ready for me?"

I say, "sure, the water is warm so come on in."

She takes her robe off and I see she is wearing a dark one piece bathing suit as the robe slides off her back and onto the ground. Boy, she was not only smart but wow, beautiful also. She comes into the water and sits right beside me, admiring the little picnic food I had set out on a white towel. She asked for a shot of sake, the fifth bottle having worn off, and I go to open it up when she stops me. I pass it to her and she slips it into the jacuzzi.

"Let's have it warm," she says.

The bottle floats in the water as she turns and embraces me with our lips locked. I thought I was dreaming. For some reason, I felt so shy and embarrassed. This kind of thing doesn't normally happen to this Brooklyn punk, but may I say, there ain't no stopping me now, or my little friend. He's got a mind of his own. A few minutes go by and I get this feeling. I begin to realize in my mind that we are in the middle of the hotel. With eyes upon us.

What do I mean by that? There are about three hundred windows facing us. Out of the corner of my eye, I notice one of the window curtains move from open to closed but I say to myself, it has to be my imagination. I look at another one, and another one and I realize it is not. The curtains are moving faster now, as my eyes dart around, my lips locked with Lucinda's.

I realize there really are eyes upon us! I tell Lucinda, after I separate from her, that we were being watched. She asked me what I meant. I said, "we got peek-a-books, lookie-loos, nosey bodies." I told her the curtains keep opening and closing.

A quick smile from her as she grabs the sake bottle. "Then let's put a show on for them, shall we?" She grabs a glass and pours the sake. She takes a big drink of sake and kisses me. I feel a stream of Saki flowing in my mouth. Damn is she good. At this point, I'm more embarrassed than excited as I realize people are watching. Not three or four, but forty to fifty curtains. She moved the sake from her mouth into mine, like a momma bird feeding her young. We start drinking and kissing away (boy can she kiss well. Her kisses had such magic, it made me forget about all the peeping toms around us) and I am completely oblivious at what I was doing. My innocence was revoked the moment she stepped into the hot tub. I move away and we both look at each other.

I glance up at the curtains and she follows my eyes. I wondered in my mind if she was finished for the night. She reached down and began to take off her bathing suit. I quickly determined that she was not and my innocence was in jeopardy. It was like I was mesmerized under a spell, it didn't matter who was lookin. Yes I know it's spelled with a "g" but that is the Brooklyn in me. "I'll give them a show they won't forget," she whispered. I shook my head like crazy and started to feel embarrassed, overly shy. I felt myself getting red in the face. "Lucinda, don't do that, everyone is watching."

She shrugs as if to say who cares and before you could say Mazel Tov, she was naked. Now that she had her bathing suit off, she was going after mine. I kept telling her "no" and moving away. I wasn't about to let Shmulik see my schmekel if he was watching. She keeps insisting and telling me not to be so shy. My head is spinning like a dreidel and my thermometer is higher than the jacuzzi. I finally give in, the Yang won over the Yin, haha. Off come the shorts.

Here we are, the Full Monty, in full view of the hotel clinging to each other like vines. Dozens of people start looking out. We were in hot water, literally. I pull away and say we have to go inside my room. Thankfully it was just ten feet away. I convince her to put a robe on while I slip my shorts back on underneath the water. She stands up in full view of the surrounding spectators like an unveiled statue, putting on her robe. My eyes are just glued to her as I clumsily try to find the opening of the pant leg of my shorts.

Once I get to the sliding glass door with Lucinda laughing behind me, I finally relax. I step in and close the door and the curtains. Mind you, I am soaking wet in my baggy shorts, so I excuse myself and grab a pair of dry shorts on my way to the bathroom. I turn on my radio and play some music and walk in. Meanwhile, without me knowing, Lucinda makes a phone call. After I get out of the bathroom, I see she is still in her robe smiling at me.

I sit down on the bed and things continue. We are having a good time, when after half an hour goes by, (yes you know I'm a man, so I'm not going to say five minutes), I hear a knock on the door. I jump up and yell, "who's that?"

A voice answers back through the door. "It's Lee. The prop guy."

The prop guy Lee? What?? Lucinda turns to me and says that she called him to come on down. He had a surprise for us. She urges me to let him in. Let him in? I don't want nobody in now! Sixty people just looked through their curtains, I don't want this guy in my room, while my head is spinning from the sake and love. I asked him "what do you want?"

He said he had a surprise and I should let him in. Lucinda asked me again to let him in, but I wasn't about to, so she gets up herself and opens the door. He walks into the middle of the room and like a ringmaster, he stands up straight, sticks out his arm in a fist and opens it. Guess what appears? The magical mystery tour.

Later, I found out he was her go-to-guy. I get upset and tell them, "none of this in my room, we will have to go somewhere else." Lucinda puts her hand on my chest and proceeds to put her arms around me, gives me a big kiss and says that we can all have a good time. My eyes bulged out. This certainly was not kosher! Not to me. This little Brooklyn Jew don't have that kind of fun. Oh god, just the thought of it made me sick. As the saying goes, no way Jose. Have I made it clear to you yet? Not this guy. Again, I say, "why don't you go up to your room and I will meet you up there." I look at Lee and say, "hit the road weirdo, get outta here."

Lucinda finally agrees and she gathers her stuff and heads for the door. I tell them I will meet them up there in a few minutes. They exit, I close the door and say to myself just like porky pig, "that's all folks." Too bad. I thought Lucinda was wild, but like no other woman I had met before. May I say she cared for me like no other woman I have had the pleasure being with before or after I had this blissful, beautiful encounter. It was something like you would only see in a movie with George Clooney or Brad Pitt, but it was Steven Lambert and it was real.

An experience I will forever be grateful for and my thanks goes out to Lucinda Dickey for giving me one of the most fantastic experiences in my life. My head was spinning and I decided after having happy time twice already, giving half the hotel a peep show, and having six bottles of sake, it was time to hit the hay, not the snow. (Oh, by the way, the next day, I asked Shmulik if he saw anything. All I got out of him was a big smile.) Lights out. I was dead tired.

Speaking of dead, that brings me to my next story on *The Domination*. The graveyard scene. I hated it. I tried to persuade Shmulik and the company to move it to a happy location. I repeated over and over, "how can you trample on people's graves, just to film a movie." I repeat, I hated it, but I was just a mere mortal under the command of Cannon Films. Every shot, I looked down to the ground and told them I was sorry. They asked me who I was talking to. I said, "the spirits of the graveyarrrrd." Doubling Lucinda Dickey when she was possessed by the ninja. Special moment. I was on set one day and a man drives up on his motorcycle and asks to talk to Steven Lambert. I was about fifty feet away and I turn around and ask, "who are you?"

He takes off his helmet and introduces himself as, "Robbie Knievel."

I say to him, "Robbie Knievel? Evel's son?"

He says, "that's the one."

I couldn't believe it. He asks if there was any work on the show and I shake his hand.

I told him, "hell yes, for you. Can you ride a bike?"

He laughed and said, "I was born on one, baby."

In my mind, I am thinking what a kick it will be to have Evel Knievel's son on the show. I mentioned I had just fired his mechanic, Spanky Spangler and he laughed. "Yeah, he always screws things up," he replied. Hearing that comment, from then on, we became instant friends. Robbie was such a great guy and we got along real well. He was a regular Joe with a little bit of a wild side. I gave him a stunt that I had to walk him through, he had never done anything quite like this before. He plays a cop on a motorcycle chasing me as the ninja. I sidestep when he catches up to me and grab him by the back of his vest and he goes into a wheelie on the bike. He falls down and as he gets up, I throw a flying side kick and his helmet splits in two as he goes flying back. A classic moment in the film. When I explained this to him, he looked like Roger Rabbit. His eyes popped out of their sockets. Three words came out of his mouth. "Are you crazy!?"

I laughed and explained to him that we were going to make it nice and safe for him. Making a statement, I say, "what do you mean, you are Robbie Knievel. You fell off a motorcycle at least a thousand times."

Three words came out of his mouth, "not on purpose."

I roared with laughter, listening to him say to me, "you know Steven what the hell, I'm crazy anyway. Let's do it!" I can tell you now, Robbie would have been a great stuntman if he wanted to. He did a fantastic job and I still miss that good time we had on the show.

(Robbie Knievel holds world records for jumping motorcycles, but he was scared to do stunts.)

All this was done in a cemetery we had permission to film in. I didn't want to film there, but it was in the script and I couldn't change it. Every time I would walk over a grave I would say a prayer in my head to the people beneath me. Okay, everybody who is reading this, it's David Womark time. Our Producer/Production Manager. In this graveyard scene, I was able to squeeze Womark for money to get some breakaway headstones. Originally, I had planned for three but unfortunately Womark only said yes to one. If I was able to get three, the plan was to put Shmulik Lambert and Womark on all three stones. So with only one, Shmulik and I decided to put "Womark", since he was too cheap to give us the other two stones we decided to make him the dead man on the stone. So if you freeze frame it, you will see his name. We decided to make him the butt of the joke. We made sure not to tell David and he was not to know until we shot it. We get to the scene and David is standing there and all of a sudden he sees the gravestone and saw his name.

He ran over and was very frustrated but found it funny at the same time. He asked why we put his name on it. Apparently, he had superstitions about having his name on a tombstone, kind of like me walking on graves. I made sure to yell "Womark!" when it broke but they cut it out. That was one of the many fond memories I had working with David. When they cut, I walked over to the disintegrated pieces of stone and scooped it up in both of my hands and raised my hands up to let it pour down over my head, yelling "David, I killed David!" Everybody roared with laughter, even Womark was laughing. I miss you, pal. So a few days go by and I am excited knowing that the office has told me that Sho Kosugi was coming in a few days.

Now David and Shmulik seemed as if they were not very anxious to see Sho. Before we came to location, they would explain that when they saw Sho at Cannon, they were not on the best of terms because Sho was not the star of The Domination. We hadn't seen each other since the screening of *Revenge Of The Ninja* and I was very excited to see him. You see, we built up a close friendship on *Revenge Of The Ninja.* A relationship that felt like we had known each other all of our lives. The joy that I felt we both had, working and communicating together was much more than usual. I felt the ties of friendship had a strong knot in it. The day came when I was working on the set and they come over and tell me Sho Kosugi has arrived. I turn around and ask where he is at. They point a few feet away. I just stop in the middle of the shot and like someone who hadn't seen their best friend in years, I felt such happiness coming over me as I couldn't move fast enough to get over to him. I stuck out my hand with a big smile saying how good it was to see him. I open up my arms to hug him and look at his face and it's just stoic. I say how great it is to see him and am excited. He just looks at my open hand with no feeling of happiness or joy. The only words that come out of his mouth were, "hello, Steven."

I could feel a reluctance and it took him a few seconds to shake my hand. I told him again how excited I was to work with him again and I could feel Shmulik and David watching us in the background. They are not coming over because they can feel the coldness coming out of Sho. I was devastated inside. I say to him, quickly trying to break the ice and thinking he was going to get excited, that we had a lot of good action in the next couple of days with him and am excited to go over the action to see if he liked it. What he said next wasn't just hurtful, it wasn't just surprising, it made me realize it was a whole new Sho Kosugi standing in front of me. He simply said back, "I will decide what action you will do with me." I was shocked.

I said, "sure Sho, of course, but is there a problem?"

He replied back, "no problem."

I knew inside myself he wasn't going to change much as far as I was concerned and I wondered why. The days went by and I had a discussion with Firstenberg and Womark about it and they said, "it's probably because he is upset at us and Cannon because he was promised to be the star of this film."

I said, "yea, but why is he upset at me?"

Shmulik said, "he's upset at the whole world now."

I was heartbroken that things with Sho weren't the same. To this day, I am confused about why he would be upset and have that kind of attitude with me when I had nothing to do with his situation. One of the few things I figure is that I still had a great relationship with Cannon and everybody in it. So maybe Sho felt a resentment, looking at it that way. Years later, he did a television show called The Masters. When I heard about it, I thought because of our relationship, I would have a chance to be the Action Coordinator. I tried and tried but it just didn't happen. In those days, it was easy to come onto the studio lots, so I went to see him to say hello, hoping and thinking I would get a different response from him. Thinking that the situation on *The Domination* was just a moment in time. When I arrived on the set of The Masters and saw him, we had a nice conversation but still got somewhat of a cold shoulder. I didn't mention working on the show to Sho but I did know the Stunt Coordinator. The great Gary Davis from Stunts Unlimited. He called me three times to work on the show but I was only available once. He told me on the phone that I was going to get beat up by Sho Kosugi. I said to him that was terrific. I said to "myself, myself, this is going to be interesting because I asked Gary if Sho Kosugi knew I was working."

He simply said, "let's surprise him."

We laughed. A couple of days later I arrive on the set. To make a long story short, yeah right, we go to rehearse and Sho sees me. With a surprised look, he roars out, "what are you doing here?"

I smile and say. "I'm here to get beat up by you."

He said, "oh, you one of the stuntmen?"

I say, "yes."

All I can say, it was a great fight. Yes, I did get tagged, but in a way, it was like old times. After it was over, we smiled and hugged and hung out with each other for a few hours, reminiscing. I sit back now and think about Sho and the great times. The laughter, the fun, the friendship and the work. I'll never forget him. He is a part of my life. We finished the film with great expectations. Although, to this day, I couldn't figure out how a female ninja that gets possessed is so appealing to everybody. That was the eighties for you.

The final entry on *Ninja: The Domination* is the greatest scene that never was. There was a scene in the script where Sho Kosugi's character goes to rescue his father from the bad ninjas. In the script, it simply reads two sentences. Sho Kosugi's father gets captured and killed by ninjas and Sho's character goes to rescue him and loses an eye. I asked my Director which eye? Shmulik as usual shrugged his shoulders and replied, "you pick."

(Twins. Who said a Caucasian can't double an Asian? You could then, you can't now.)

I ask you, what Director would let you choose? It was a common occurrence. That is why I adored that guy. After thinking for a bit, I thought how wonderful it would be to make it look like a period scene in Japan. Find some natural objects like rivers and mountains and place the action there, as it was supposed to take place in Japan. I told the powers my idea and they loved it. "Steven," Shmulik said. "We are quite busy with our schedule, so I am sending you out to do First Unit to direct this scene."

My eyes lit up. Excited I am. My directorial debut!? They asked me how long I would need to film it and I told them just one day. I just needed to tell wardrobe to get a dozen or so ninja outfits with swords and shurikens and I would be all set. A short time later, I find Sho and discuss my ideas and he was hooked. He was thinking we were going to shoot it modern day clothes and look, but I had a surprise for him. "Here is my thinking, Sho. It opens up on your father right by this river. He has twelve, fifteen ninjas surrounding him. He has two ninjas on each side with ropes and they are stretching him out. One is pulling one way, the other is pulling the other way. Your father has a look of desperation, agony and pain. Then we see cuts of you running through the forest. Like a mad dog, you arrive and the fight commences."

He reveled in the idea, especially that he got to sell Cannon more uniforms and weapons. Let's not forget that he was selling Cannon all the wardrobe and props. I call that genius. Some people call that a shyster. Soon after, we got to work. In the ballroom that I had booked in the hotel, I worked out the whole fight. I played Sho and demonstrated the choreography. Then I had Sho do it. It was cool, he was happy and put in his two cents. It goes with the territory. Always let them THINK that their wisdom is a big part of it. That is a must, to remember. The excitement built inside all of us. The next day we went to location with Sho, one camera with an operator and a dozen "ND" ninjas.

Don't forget Wardrobe, Makeup and a PA. And of course, a ninja outfit for me since I planned to insert myself every place I could. Yes, I had Sho kill me about ten times. I like to say, very few die like me I made twelve ninjas look like thirty, they were all over the place. I call "action."

Sho arrives, ninjas attack. Who do you think gives them the signal to attack? The Director of this scene. Me. Steven Lambert Firstenberg. In fact, I put myself in the scene. I jump off a boulder, thrust out my sword, land in a crouching stance and ninjas attack. The fight starts on land. Ninjas instantly consume him in a tornado of swords.

Sho Kosugi and his faithful double Steve Lambert on set.

Ducking, thrashing, and rolling to avoid death, Sho manages to kill multiple ninjas but others arrive. It continues until the action is brought to the river water. Knee deep, the action continues as Sho tries to reach his father. Closer and closer, the sword fight continues. Adding multiple Judo throws to the sword fight gave a unique effect as their bodies hit the water. Swords slicing through liquid and hitting bodies, slow motion all over the place. Ninjas flying through the air.

Luckily, I brought two mini tramps. Sho gets twenty feet away when two ninjas throw shurikens at him. One hits his leg. He blocks three with his sword. Then another hits his shoulder. The last, his eye. He goes down on one knee in the water, in agony and pain. He tries to get to his father before it is too late. He crawls through the water onto land as he suffers through the pain. I must say, it was an Oscar winning performance by Sho Kosugi.

(First Unit Director Steven Lambert: Feeling. Emotional contact. Yes, that's what I said to him.)

I had a tear in my eye. As Sho is crawling, we see three ninjas stick their swords into his father. Two are stuck in him. The other is thrown. By guess who? Me. As Sho gets fifteen feet away from his father, I walk over as the lead ninja and laugh at him before signaling the other ninjas to disperse into the forest. Sho Kosugi, wounded looks at his father with a sword in his gut, both in tremendous pain. Sho crawls towards his father. Ten feet, five feet. Sho reaches out, his father reaches out. Just as Sho gets to him, I do a separate shot of his father dying. Then a two shot of Sho's reaction, laying there and screaming into the empty air and the rushing river around him. Fade out. It was a scene that would never be forgotten. I went back to the hotel and sat with David Womark and Sam Firstenberg for close to an hour, telling them what great footage we got. We send the film back to Cannon and Menahem calls me in person to tell me how wonderful it looked. I treasure the words he spoke, to this day. I am on cloud nine.

Time moves on and we finish production on the rest of the film. Cannon sets up a private screening for cast and crew. I am excited to see the whole film. We arrive and for forty five minutes, people are praising Sam Firstenberg, congratulating David Womark. And me? I am just a fly on the wall. THE UNFORESEEN HERO. That's what they call us. The time comes. We take our seats. The lights dim and the film begins. People are cheering, electricity is in the air. I am enjoying the film. I notice that where my piece should be, it's not there! You see, when Sho arrives at the airport and we see him, that's where it should be. But it's not! I am sitting in the middle of all the powers who are just loving the film. I turn to my Director next to me and whisper, "when is the period death scene with Sho's father?"

Shmulik turns to me and gives a closed grin as if to say don't worry about it. The movie continues, but all I am thinking about, is where the hell is the scene? Now I am watching the end credits roll. Lights go up and everyone starts congratulating each other. I turn to Shmulik to ask him what happened to my scene. "Shmulik, I didn't see the piece I did. What happened?"

A booming voice cut in. "Shmulik! You did good!" Menahem.

I open my mouth when more accolades fly around me. I see everyone is in good spirits, so I keep my mouth shut. The next day I call Menahem up.

"Steven, what a great job you did! Everybody loves the film!" he bellows. "Your work is crazy. You're crazy. I loved it. You are a crazy man," he says.

I shook my head. "Menahem, what happened to the period piece that you said you loved so much. What happened to Sho trying to rescue his father? What happened to him losing his eye? What happened to the whole scene?" I waited for Menahem's answer.

"Steven, we only had ninety minutes, we had to cut things out."

I couldn't believe my ears. "Cut things out!? Menahem you could have cut many scenes out besides that one, which you said you liked so much. Why didn't you take out that ridiculous sequence with Lucinda Dickey dancing in the gymnasium? Or the fight outside with the guys picking on her? Or the stupid scene with Mister Hairy Chest?" I tried my best to push it, to get him to understand how much that scene meant and what it would do for the film, but Menahem didn't budge.

"The film is wonderful Steven, you did a great job. Be very happy. Everyone is going to love it, don't worry." That was the end of that. For those of you wondering what happened to that scene from various pictures scattered about, you can thank the marvelous maestro, Menahem Golan. The scene that never was. I get home one day and right away got a phone call.

It was to work on *Friday The 13th: The Final Chapter*. Jason Voorhees was such a big figure then, from the previous films so I was jazzed to work on it. You are always happy when you have a memory working on a cult franchise. I doubled one of the leads that gets killed in a barn by Jason. The double for Jason was a great friend named Tom Morga. Tom Morga was a multi-talented stuntman. We have worked together and I have hired him many, many times. I want you to understand something, when I use the word "friend," to me it is a very important word. To some people, it is just a throw away. I always thought that the word friend is a step below family. They should, and you should be with each other through thick and thin. Please remember that, as it will make you a better person in your life. Especially in the eyes of the beholder. We had a good time on the set and I was dead before I knew it. This was my first real Horror film and felt it was a big honor. A matter of fact, Tom Morga and I were on the "Tonight Show with Jay Leno," twice. We were Page boys. It was a kick in the pants, that means fun. When somebody went to the bathroom we would sit in their seat to save it. We both wanted to save the same seat and we got into a fight, right in front of Jay, the audience and on national television. The audience would not know what was going on and get frightened. Jay Leno would try to break us up, but keep his distance at the same time. It was hilarious. Tom once picked me up and dropped me into a glass table. Another time it was through the backdrop. Meeting Jay Leno was a lot of fun. Even though he did give me an autograph, I found him to be very aloof. Little did I know, a few years later I would be working with him again. This was a very special year for me, 1985. I call it the year of "My Hollywood Puberty."

WARNING: LIFE LESSON AHEAD. I learned a lot about people and how they go about getting what they wanted. I found everyone has two sides and most people are never what they seem, no matter if they are rich, poor, successful, happy, sad, or in between. That is how it was and is in this crazy world of cinema. Their egos and insecurities create a Jekyll and Mr. Hyde persona, that can be ruthless and unforgiving when it comes to a job. Perhaps now, people come to expect this from those in the industry, but back then I was a sweet innocent boy that had no idea how consumed with greed and power people could get and I must say, knowing what I know now, that has always been a trend. The movie business has the power to change a person's behavior, destroy ethics and evaporate friendships. I grew up in an era where your parents and grandparents told you what to do and what not to do. Here, the movie business was the parent, and it didn't care what you did or how you did it in most cases.

So this year taught me a lot of lessons which I will talk about, and forced me mentally to grow up and unfortunately, opened up my mind to the real world. I always try to tell the truth, and never put myself in a position where there is no need not to tell the truth and be a good person and make sure I stay a good person. That is how I was raised. My mentor Roy Harrison once said to me, "sometimes the truth can cause more damage, you should learn how to play politics."

Well playing politics is very hard for this kid from Brooklyn. You need to weigh the nature of the business versus the nurture of one's upbringing. Ultimately, I choose nurture. Please think about what I said, this is a big lesson here, it tis' a powerful one. What I say, isn't just for the movies, it's an everyday life lesson.

That year was a big adventure for me. My next big adventure was Pee Wee's. I was doubling Pee Wee himself, Mister Paul Reubens. He was a very unusual or different character. I would watch other people try to talk to him and it was like pulling teeth. You had to be there, but you couldn't figure out if he was shy, introverted, nervous or afraid. It was impossible to get to know him. Whenever I did a stunt for him, I got no reaction from him. The only other thing I can say about Paul Reubens, is boy, I am glad he didn't invite me to a movie. "Icky sticky." Figure that one out. There are certain special, humorous things you remember in a movie and this is one of them that I will never forget with my friend Mike Adams.

I did a show with him called *My Science Project.* Adams was the boss man. I was doubling a character running through a cave. He turns the corner and smacks face first into a wall and knocks himself out. When he wakes up, he is covered in around a thousand snakes, slithering everywhere. When I arrived, I was looking for my boss as I did not know exactly what I was going to do. I had no idea snakes would be involved. I start looking for Mike. Can't find him anywhere. The First Assistant and the Wrangler explains my action and when he gets to the snakes, I just stare at them. I said, "these snakes are going to bite me. Where is Mike Adams?"

The Wrangler laughs and says they are garter snakes and won't bite.

I reply, "who told you that, the snakes?" I look at him and say, "there are a thousand mouths there, how do you know what they are going to do?"

He shrugs and laughs. I see the animal Wrangler's assistants carrying big potato sacks over to the set. I know those sacks are filled with snakes and I shudder. They made a 10x10 coral and I'm supposed to lay down, while he pours the snakes on me and puts them in my pants, in my shirt, in my sleeves, all over the place. I walk over to the guy with the sacks and introduce myself. I ask how he was going to put the snakes on me. He tells me he is just going to dump them on me. I can't believe my ears. "Shouldn't we wire the snake's mouth shut?" I ask.

He laughs again and says, "no."

I'm thinking these snakes are going to bite my schmekel off. I have to talk to Mike Adams. I was told he wasn't there yet. A half hour goes by and everyone is set up and ready for the shot. They ask if I am ready and I say yes. So I run around the corner and body slam the wall. They yell cut and I am finished with that part. The only thing that was on my mind were those freaking mouths of the serpents, and wondering where Mike Adams was. Mike was a cowboy, bull rider, one tough sucker at that. I'm looking for him like crazy but can't find him. All of a sudden, I see the Production Manager. I ask where Mike Adams is and he tells me he is outside the door.

"He ain't coming onto the stage," he replies with a smile.

I'm confused. What do you mean he isn't coming in?

He says, "he is scared of snakes, he ain't coming in."

What? What is this all about. I ask to talk to him and they open the door. There is Mike, twenty feet away. I tell him to come in here, I wanted to talk to him. He says no way. I said I can't believe he is afraid of snakes. I ask him, "what do you do when you are in Cowboy country?"

He says, "I stay away from snakes."

I tried to grab him and comically drag him onto the stage, boy was that a bad idea. He put up such a fight and was ready to punch me in the face. I let him go and I started laughing hysterically with him right alongside me saying, "you take care of it, I don't want nothin' to do with those things."

Laughing, I say to him, "oh this is one for the Cowboy Daily, front page. Wait until people hear about this." Afterwards, they yelled cut and I picked up a reptile as the Wrangle is yelling at me. I head for the exit, snake in hand. I opened the door of the stage, run out and who do you think I see? Mister Mike Adams running away as I head for him yelling, "snake, snake."

With an audience of hundreds on the lot, everyone we passed was just pissing their pants with laughter as Mike barreled through the studio, trying to keep his distance. It's funny how everyone has their fear. Rest in peace, you rodeo loving cowboy.

CHAPTER 23
(Stunt Academy Awards)

If you thought lying on the ground playing dead with snakes all over you was tough, let me tell you about *Tough Turf*. At this moment in time, this show meant a lot to me. They were having the second year of the Stunt Academy awards and they had a category for best fight. Let's take a step to present day, today. I must say this. Beware, just food for thought, an opinion I am giving you that you might want to mull over. There could be people out there in stunt land who are on a mission leading the way to try and get stunts into the Oscars.

While this is a good idea, it could run into some problems. First thing to dwell on is that the Academy would need a group of stuntmen to help them determine in a number of ways, who should be nominated and awarded. Who would they turn to? Possibly, the handful of people who you, us, put front and center. Who are in the Academy's ear at this very moment. Second thing to dwell on. This gives these individuals considerable unchecked power, wouldn't you think? They may say they are fighting for you to get jobs when in reality there may be some that are fighting for themselves. If they get the responsibility and the control of the action in the Oscars, what could happen then, you could possibly ask. In a nutshell, the stunt people should be controlling and voting on the people who are going to represent them. If that doesn't happen, they are making a big mistake.

You know the saying. If you give a mouse some cheese. It's possible they will then accumulate enough control and power to eventually decide who gets work and who doesn't. Hiring only friends, relatives and people they like or have helped them one way or another. Us little people out there? Might be booted out in the cold. Remember, as it stands now there are really no rules in our business when it comes to who has the knowledge, who can do the stunt, who can put it together and who can direct it. It might be those chosen ones who make those decisions.

2nd Annual Stuntman Awards 1985

J.P. ROMANO   JOEL KRAMER
BOB YERKES   FRANK FERRARA
STEVE LAMBERT
REMO WILLIAMS

Be warned, if this happens you may never get a chance to dream. It is imperative the right kind of people are chosen for these roles, otherwise the power of the stunt industry and the Stunt awards at the Oscars could fall into the wrong hands. So beware my friends and good luck. Stepping back to the past and the Stunt Awards. My friend Vince Deadrick Jr. put me up for best fight sequence in *Tough Turf.* I was excited but found out a few days later that my friend Glenn Randall put my name in for best high work on *Remo Williams The Adventure Begins.* I thought to myself, wow awards. A punk kid from Brooklyn. Who woulda thought? Then I had a thought. Hey, I was Stunt Coordinator for *American Ninja,* I should put myself up. This movie will kick both of their asses. I put up myself. I thought, how weird. How many people put up themselves? I don't know but I guess I'll give it a shot. I might win one of these suckers. Now I am up for three things. About a week later I get a call from Vince Deadrick Jr. who tells me he saw I put myself up for *American Ninja.* He tells me that chances are, *American Ninja* would win over *Tough Turf.*

I said to my friend, "no shit Sherlock." Three chances for me to win, but when I reiterated that to him, he said he really wanted to win for his movie. So of course, I couldn't do that. I met Vince on a television show called *The Hardy Boys* where he soon became like a brother to me. I can't do that to somebody I think the world of. So as fast as I put *American Ninja* on, I take it off.

Now I'm worried that I might lose for best fight, but if I had *American Ninja* in there, I would have won by a landslide. Isn't that weird? But that was my thought. Everyone new out there, remember that sometimes fame has no business being near friendship. Always remember that, and you will feel better inside and life will be happier. As it turned out, I did bring home the trophy for best fight in *Tough Turf* in 1985 out of twenty others and best high work in *Remo Williams* out of sixteen other films. Deep down in the bowels of the ninja, I knew it could have won for the best fight, but I'm happy that I took the right path in helping my friend. Speaking of *American Ninja,* let's talk about the one. The only one, in my opinion of course, sorry to say, the only good one. Hold on, my phone is ringing. Its Shmulik! Well, this might take a while. More of this Kung Fu Jew, continues on in Volume 2!

CHAPTER 24
(American Ninja One. My Last Hurrah)

The only one. In my opinion of course, sorry to say, the only good one. A funny unknown fact. I get a phone call from the Shmulik, you know who that is by now, Sam Firstenberg.

He tells me, "guess what. We have another ninja film, but this time it is an American ninja."

I say, "what, they want to use me?"

Shmulik replies, "you know Steven, that is not a bad idea since in all cases, you are in it more than the star."

We both laugh and it's casually forgotten. He tells me to come see him in his office tomorrow and he would give me the script. The next day at our meeting, Sam turns around and reaches for a poster and puts it on the desk. He asks me to take a good look at it and see if I notice anything different or unusual. The poster is of Chuck Norris in a promo for the *American Ninja*. He is doing a flying sidekick and I looked it over and saw nothing unusual. Shmulik tells me to look at the picture and exclaims Chuck Norris is wearing the Ninja costume from the *Domination*. I couldn't believe it and ask Shmulik why they did that. He shrugs and simply says that is what they do. He then asks if I see anything else. I'm really scratching my head. My eyes are looking but I can't find anything unusual besides Chuck Norris wearing the *Domination* outfit. Shmulik finally says, "that's you! That is your body and they put Chuck's head on it!

I look a fourth time and it dawns on me that they took the shot from the *Domination* where I do a flying side kick to the motorcycle cop played by Robbie Knievel and inserted Chuck Norris's head. It was Chuck's head and my body fused together, like some sort of Martial Arts Frankenstein. As Doctor Frankenstein would say - HE'S ALIVE! At the time, I found it very amusing and quite proud, to find Chuck Norris's head on my body. After we laughed about that, we moved on and I realized that Chuck is very picky when it comes to certain things. I'm trying to find the right words to say. Finally, I tell Shmulik, if Chuck is doing this film, chances are I will not be the coordinator. Shmulik didn't understand and I explain. You see, Chuck has been doing movies for a while and he has his own people. He has a guy named Dean Farendeni and Chuck's brother Aaron Norris. I'm sure he would request, if not demand them to be on this show. I know from working on his films before, that is how it goes. Shmulik looks at me and says, "don't worry about it." I reiterate to him that he has to be prepared that I won't be on this film, I was very serious. Shmulik nods and says they are in negotiations and Chuck is deciding if he wants to do this film or *Invasion USA*.

I sure hoped he picked *Invasion USA* or I wasn't going to be on *American Ninja*

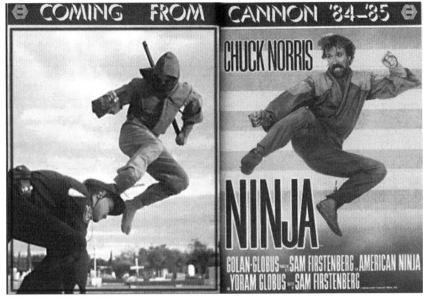

(The only time Chuck Norris wanted to be me. Can you believe it? Pretty funny.)

We discussed other things about the show and I opened the script and once again guess what? As usual, I found many blank pages. I ask Shmulik for a pen. He asks me why.

I said, "just give me a pen, Shmulik."

He hands me one and I go to the first blank page of the script. I write something on it. Then I go to the next, same thing. I write on it. Then to the next and the next and the next.

After a while, Shmulik asks, "what are you doing Steven?"

I close the script and hand it to him. I tell him to open it and go to the first blank page. I say, "read it to me."

That he does. The words, "me, action," came out.

He turns to the next blank page, "me, action" he says. He turns to the third blank page. "Enough already."

I ask him what it says.

He says, "me, action." We are in hysterics as he closes the script. "Yes, it will be you the whole time Steven."

I laugh and say, "there is your action for now. Some things never change. Scripts with blank pages, I can't believe they are still doing this to me."

Shmulik then tells me we are going to film in the Philippines. My eyes shot up. "You mean we aren't shooting in America?"

Shmulik says we are going to Manila. Here is a Brooklyn boy who has never gone anywhere outside the US and now I have a chance to go to a foreign country. I'm praying inside Chuck picks the other film, but at the same time, I have to stay in reality. I tell Shmulik if Chuck and his brother Aaron does it, he probably will be working with other people. That the budget and pay scale for Stunt Coordinator and stuntmen will be different because they will not be able to do the things I can do, so be prepared. Again, Shmulik tells me not to worry. I say goodbye and go home to break down the script. I did decide to go break down the script just in case things went my way but I had strong doubts. Even though Chuck and Aaron had been my friends for years, this is business. A week later, I got it finished and Shmulik said to come into the office the next day. I go in and we sit down. I happen to see the editor from the *Domination*, Michael Duthie, and we talk about how much fun it was to work on it. There has always been a part of me that is proud of it and there is a part of me that thinks it is pretty silly as far as the story goes. However, a lot of people liked it so who am I to judge?

When I met with Shmulik, the first thing he told me was that Chuck Norris had decided on *Invasion USA*. I was thrilled he had taken the other film, even though I did dream what it would be like if Chuck let me coordinate *American Ninja* with him in it. That would be very cool. Shmulik smiled and I snapped back to reality. I asked him why Chuck had not chosen this project. He simply said, "he doesn't really want to do a film at this point and time with a mask on his face."

I scratched my head and mentioned that he didn't have the mask on his face all the time. Shmulik just shrugged and we moved on. He then mentioned there were a few other people in the running such as Chad McQueen, Steve McQueen's son, Mike Norris, Chuck Norris's son and a new guy named Michael Dudikoff. Well, I have heard of Chad and Mike but said to myself and to Shmulik, "what is a Dudikoff?"

Shmulik said he really liked Michael out of the other two. He mentioned he doesn't know Martial Arts, but he reminded him of James Dean. I said if he reminds you of James Dean, the guy must be hot. He said they would decide in a couple of days who would be the star. So I told him that I was going to go home and work on some more ideas with the action sequences. Shmulik called me a couple of days later and said that Menahem didn't want Dudikoff, but through his persistence as a

Director, he got his wish so he was cast. I told Shmulik I wanted to discuss some new ideas for the action sequences and asked if I could come in. He said sure and we agreed to meet the next day. When I came in, he proceeded to tell me more about Michael Dudikoff. He said that Michael was excited to meet me and that Mike Stone was going to come out at Dudikoff's request. I looked at Shmulik and I asked him if he meant Mike Stone, the Martial Artist. Shmulik says yes, Dudikoff wanted him to come along and train him. I thought that was great. I didn't have to train Michael and I could focus on the action in the film. I was also excited to meet Mike Stone, who worked out with Ed Parker, Chuck Norris, Bruce Lee and other greats. I had also heard that he was one of the guys that had trained Elvis Presley in Martial Arts. It was really perfect. While I worked out big sequences like the ninja obstacle course, the motorcycle stunts and set up all the fights and action, he could be busy training Dudikoff. Perfect. Shmulik went on to say they had found someone to play the black star ninja. I asked who and he said it was someone named Tadashi Yamashita.

So we began to talk - wait a second, did he just say Tadashi Yamashita!? You mean that sword swinging, watermelon cutting, crazy Martial Artist we talked about a while back?? That was the one. My eyes popped out and I couldn't believe he was actually going to be on this film! Shmulik saw my excitement and asked if I knew him. I told him the story you all know well, about him in the gymnasium when he looked like Moses parting the Red Sea of people with his sword. He was just laughing and laughing. I couldn't believe my luck. I was going to meet a real legend in Tadashi and I explained to Shmulik that he was the real deal. I was so honored to be able to meet these great Martial Artists, talk stories with them and travel to a foreign country.

I was thirty years old, but I felt like a kid in a candy store. Every sweet I could think of was laid out before my eyes, just waiting to be devoured. But that is the thing about candy. As good as it looks and as delicious as it tastes, if you eat too much, it can cause your teeth to rot. Speaking of rotting, let's talk about Mike Stone. In just a bit. Shmulik also mentioned that another Martial Artist named Richard Norton was coming along to play a part as an MP guard. I said that I was very familiar with him and having another Martial Artist on the film was terrific. The more the merrier, I thought.

Maybe I can use him for doing stunts. Martial Artists do make good stuntmen. At least some of the time. Not this time. Shmulik also said that Michael had a thought, that Richard might double him sometimes if I needed him too. I wasn't used to hearing that. Wait a minute! They are coming down. The walls of Jericho. I said, "what!?"

He repeated himself and I asked him what he meant. Shmulik replies that Michael said they are similar, and if I needed Richard to double him, he could. I replied that was fine if I had my hands full and needed a double. Then if he can do the action I had planned, that would be no problem. Yet, I made it clear and said, "let me just remind you Shmulik about something we have talked about in the past and hopefully you have come to realize from past circumstances working with me.

That Richard and Mike Stone are Martial Artists not stunt people. Even if they are great Martial Artists, as you know and have learned, there are big differences between a Martial Artist and a stunt person. You need to learn how to perform in front of camera, you have to understand lenses and how to understand to put together action sequences, the reasons and the whys and the why nots. Not to mention, rigging, high falls, cars, motorcycles, being familiar with other departments on the show, understanding the script, understanding the Director and the actor's ideas to make sense of the whole thing, etc. And of course, fights. Yes fights. Just because you are a world class Martial Artist, doesn't mean you can do all this junk. I've seen it time and time again with Martial Artists. It doesn't mean you are qualified to be a Fight Coordinator. Shmulik replies, "but you are a Martial Artist too, Steven."

The words came out of my mouth in a very simple way. I said, "there are very few like me Shmulik."

He understood, smiled and we moved on with our conversation. I was excited that they were going to be there and knew I was going to find uses for them, but I had no idea what was to come. I showed Shmulik the action I had come up with and he loved it. I told him once we get to the Philippines and see the locations, I will be able to put it all together and make it bigger and better. That is always the fact. Until you get to location you really have no idea where your ideas are going to go. You must make sure that it all fits in. In this case, it was with the Shmulik and Michael Dudikoff, who I was very anxious to meet. I packed up my writings and ideas and Shmulik said he wanted to bring me into the new producer's office and meet Gideon Amir and Avi Kleinberger. I said, "oh, very curious." I remember walking out of the office saying to myself, this is going to be strange without David Womark. I'll miss him.

I walked into their office, sat down and started to discuss the movie and the action. Gideon had sunglasses on (indoors, can you believe it? I thought that was kind of unusual) and was very quiet and stern. He seemed to be a little...oh, hard nosed and big time aloof in this conversation. The reason why I point that out is that I knew then and there, he was no Womark. No enthusiasm, no excitement. All he wanted to talk about was the budget, which I realized was his job, but it had been

OK'd already. It is a very uncomfortable thing to talk about budgets because that means money and you have to fight for every bit of it, if you want the action and ideas that you designed in the movie to take place. And that was exactly what was happening. As I ran through it with them, there were a few hold ups in our conversation throughout. They didn't understand why certain action scenes needed more money than others. They told me that in the Philippines, you don't need to pay those guys as much as you would pay people in the United States. I said to them that I realized that, but as you see it is not a normal SAG daily. It is cut in half. They still were not happy with it, but I explained to them that this money would be well deserved.

We shouldn't take out anything or expect to take out anything until we get to the location and I can put it all together and see where this money needs to go. Reluctantly, I got them to halfway agree by Gideon saying, "we will talk about this when we get there."

For you beginners out there, remember what I said. It can help you in many situations. Avi on the other hand was a jolly fellow and full of excitement and curiosity. He asked me a number of times how I was going to do certain things in the action I was designing. I didn't know if it was a test or if he was just unfamiliar with the way Stunt Coordinators do their business. He said to me, "I have seen the other ninjas and the things you did in there were fantastic. Are you going to give us the same?"

I smiled and said, "yes. If you leave me alone." I found him to be very friendly and funny and easy going. After we discussed the budget, they asked me about the other guy I was bringing with me. I told them his name was Kenny Lesko and that he was a stuntman. I needed somebody I could trust, and when I ask him to do something, I have the utmost confidence that it will be done. Kenny was important because when I am doing something, I need eyes on the ground. Eyes that I can have faith in and that will put me ahead of everything else, including the people I have working for me. Meaning in front of camera and guys like you behind camera. Safety, that is what it comes down to. I explained to him that there were going to be an awful lot of times that I was going to be in front of camera, and I need somebody watching the things that were going on. Again, Gideon said reluctantly, "we will talk about it when we get there."

I want to remind you, gentlemen, I am going to a foreign country. I had no idea who or what they have in Manila, Philippines. They had said they had been there before. Reluctantly, I smiled and said, "okay, we WON'T talk about it when we get there. This is what is going to happen." I then simply said, "anything else my friends?"

They shook and bobbled their heads. I then went to speak to Shmulik and mentioned to him, "this guy Gideon, I think he's going to be a pain in my neck."

Shmulik laughed.

I then said, "Shmulik, I hope you are going to tell these guys what I do on this film and how important it is to let me work and leave me alone when it comes to your action."

Shmulik replies, "I'll tell them, I'll tell them. don't worry."

I say, "well it sounds like they are going to cut out everything. They don't understand what I do and how involved I am in the performance aspect with all the main characters. I am them."

Shmulik nods, "don't worry Steven." Typical Firstenberg, but you gotta love him. He then told me that the company will call me and tell me when I would be leaving in the next couple of weeks. Meanwhile, I asked him if Mike Stone was going to train Dudikoff while we were still in Los Angeles. He said he didn't know and wasn't sure. I said, "just remember. The more he knows, the more he does." I never got a reply back. After the meeting, I was overjoyed. Just walking into the sunshine on Sunset Blvd, I was happy as could be. 1985, Manila, Philippines, here I come.

The next thing I know I get a phone call from the secretary of Cannon Films who told me I was leaving the upcoming week. She also mentioned that Mike Stone would be on the plane as well. I thought, great I'll have someone to talk to on the plane, someone I respected and admired a lot. The guy's a legend. She said that Shmulik was going to be in Manila before I got there, and to meet up with him once I land. Again, I was excited like a monkey in a banana tree. I was in the business for eight years and it was my first time outside of the United States, after all. What an adventure it was going to be. It was a dream come true, that a punk kid from Brooklyn had the opportunity to film in such a beautiful and foreign place. I was anxious and overjoyed, couldn't wait to get there.

The day comes and I go to the airport and check in. I stretch my legs, knowing it is going to be a long trip. I still couldn't believe Mike Stone was coming. I look around and my eyes fall on him. He is looking around and just hanging. Mind you, I'm not sure if he knows me from atom. Very excited and happy in a sense, just thinking, "this guy is big time and it's going to be fun chilling with him." I go up to him and say, "Mike Stone. Steven Lambert, Stunt Coordinator, American Ninja."

He shakes my hand and I say to him, "it's nice to meet you."

In the mix of our immediate conversation, I mentioned to him that I saw him fight once. He smiled, enjoying the praise. He looks at me and returns the comment, saying it was a pleasure to meet me as well. We sit down waiting to board and I am thinking, boy, I have a lot of questions in my mind I would like to ask him. Questions relating to Elvis Presley, oh let's not forget Priscilla, Ed Parker, Bruce Lee and others. But I thought to myself, it's not the right time. Maybe in the future. We started talking and asked if he had met Shmulik and the Producers. He said he had, and I asked if he had started training Dudikoff yet. He said he hadn't and that he was going to wait until they got to the Philippines. I was surprised. This was strange to me, as I would start training someone right away as soon as I was assigned them. I thought to myself, that's surprising. You would think you would want your guy to know something on the first day of rehearsal, I thought. A week is valuable when you are training someone, especially when the person really knows nothing. Nevertheless, as they say, "that's NO my job." That's Mike Stone's worry.

A few minutes later it came time to board the plane and we got into our seats. Here I was, in the sky on my way to Manila, Philippines, sitting next to who I thought was one of the most well known Martial Artists around at the time. Once on the plane, we struck up conversation. I asked a couple of questions about Ed Parker and he mentioned that Ed was probably the fastest man with his hands he ever saw in his life. "Except for me," he said.

I thought for a second that was very egotistical of him and disrespectful. And to me, it seemed like he meant it because there was no smile or mention of joking. He went on to say that when Ed taught, he was very direct, and even the way he explained and spoke was very powerful and he liked to hit. I said to him, "that's a good thing. Most people don't know what it feels like to be hit. You must feel. Understand. Parker was right." I found it very confusing, how he told me many times that he, Mike Stone, said he was the best black belt out there. I then asked about Chuck Norris and he replied that they were very good friends. I mentioned to him that I had worked with Chuck and briefly explained to him that was more or less how I got into the business.

I exclaimed how great it was that he had grown up with these kinds of guys. People like Howard Jackson, Chuck Norris, John Natividad, Jeff Smith, Benny Urquidez and Joe Lewis. Great Martial Artists that I saw fight when I was a kid. I told Mike that just being there would put a smile on my face and he laughed. I was ready to ask him more questions about if he worked out with James Coburn, Steve McQueen and of course Bruce Lee. He replied that he had and they were all equals, but Bruce Lee wasn't a fighter. I looked at him strangely. In my head I said to myself,

I wonder what he means by that. He went on to say that Bruce Lee is just a showman, a fighter for movies, nothing like himself when it came to Martial Arts. I shook my head, thinking wow, that was an off color thing to say about Bruce since they were supposedly very close friends. I would think friends would compliment each other, just a thought.

Our discussion took a break and I sat back in my seat and relaxed. After an hour or so, I decided to do some work and took out my script. I had no idea we were about to hit some turbulence and I don't mean the kind that made Nicholas Cage and Sean Penn scream like little sissys. Mike Stone noticed what I was doing and I decided it would be a good time to explain to Mike, what I needed him to teach Dudikoff. So with my script out and notebook open, I proceeded in explaining to Mike Stone my thoughts on what I needed from him. All of a sudden, he interrupts me. "No, no, no," he says. He states very firmly, that there was no reason for my notes and ideas.

You know those times where you think you hear someone say something and then you realize you misunderstood what they were actually saying? I was pretty sure this was one of those times, so I waited for my ears to catch up to my brain and was ready for him to say something else that would make sense. He continued saying that he and Dudikoff had already sat down and filled in the blank pages with action of their own. Okay, I wasn't going crazy, he really did just say that. My mouth dropped open and I asked what he meant by that. Surely he didn't and couldn't mean, that they were thinking to take over MY job to plan out the action and waste weeks upon weeks of time I worked on the script!? This seemed very strange, especially without including me.

This was Mike Stone after all, a respected fighter in the world of Martial Arts, there was no way he could have done that, right? Wrong. I asked him if he went over all the fights and stunts and he said yes, they put it together already. I looked at him and said, "Mike, with all due respect, I am the Stunt Coordinator, the head of the action department. I really don't know where you are coming from and I appreciate your help. But I've spent weeks putting this together and am going to spend weeks when I get there making changes once I see the location, fitting my ideas into the story. On top of that, Sam Firstenberg has already given the okay. You see, this is my job."

Mike Stone replied that he and Dudikoff had talked to Sam, Gideon and Avi, and Gideon not only wanted Mike to teach Dudikoff Martial Arts, but he also agreed that Mike should be the Coordinator too. Per the strong request of Dudikoff. This was all news to me. I blinked, not believing these words were coming out of his mouth. I was just stunned. I explained that I was in charge on this film and I had spent a lot of time putting together the action and fights. I made it clear that this is my job by simply saying, "you're dreaming, MIKE. Let me fill your head with the facts. When Sam Firstenberg spoke to me, he had mentioned you were just coming to train Dudikoff and that was all."

He smiled a grin too big for his face and without missing a beat he said, "you're wrong and this is the way it is going to be."

I'll never forget those words and the cockiness of his presentation. I have never been in a situation where such a great so called legend in the Martial Arts world who was sitting right next to me, mind you, is telling me that he is taking over my job, so he thinks. How rude, how vicious his demeanor is to me. To my knowledge, he had only done one film and that was *Enter The Ninja* and from my understanding, that did not work out well. Now he's fantasizing that he is the boss? Are you kidding me? I am thinking in my head now, for you stunt people out there, can you imagine him saying that to stuntman Terry Leonard, Vic Armstrong, Alan Gibbs, Charlie Picerni? These are just a few of many high powered Stunt Coordinators that would put him in his place, right on the spot. Percini? He probably would have thrown him out of the plane, at least verbally. Yet, I am also a Martial Artist and there is a part of me that feels a need to give somebody like this, the utmost respect and there's a part of me that wants to smack him upside the head, but I'm a professional, so they say. I took a deep breath and told him with all due respect, that even though he is a great Martial Artist and equal with the best of them, "there is a difference between a Martial Artist and a stuntman. I am a qualified Stunt Coordinator, Action Designer and a fine Martial Artist, so they tell me. And this character, this ninja, I play them. As of the previous ninjas, I built a story behind this one." Graciously I say, "may I ask what have you done? Show me your work, Mike." I made it clear. I said, "Mike, if Dudikoff and you have ideas then I would be happy to incorporate some of them with my ideas if they are good and make sense. That is what you do when you work with a lead actor. It's called teamwork. Yet, I haven't spoken to Michael, and as far as I was told, you are simply his Martial Arts trainer."

He then replied, very rudely, that I was not the person going to arrange the action, that it would simply be him and Michael and that he had already written "my ideas." When he said "my ideas," I knew he meant him, Mike Stone. I asked if he went from page one to the end of the script and wrote all the action out. He said he did. I couldn't believe it. Well, it seemed like it didn't matter to someone like Mike Stone who did *Enter The Ninja*, as he so politely told me.

Okay readers, in my head I am thinking, this is a usual problem. When great Martial Artists think they know how to create action and do stunts. I have seen that film a few times already and it was super below par. He also made it clear to me in a very smug way, that Richard Norton is coming, not only to play a part but to double Michael Dudikoff. I said to myself, wait a minute, my head is exploding. This is one confused punk from Brooklyn. I told him, "please Mike, let me make something perfectly clear. Back off! I would be happy to work as a team on certain things, but when it comes to the designing and fight and stunt choreographing, I am the chosen one. Most importantly, I will be Dudikoff's double in whatever he does unless I say otherwise. The words Stunt Coordinator means knowledge and experience. Not famous Martial Art competitor. God forbid if anything happens, physically or production wise, then it all comes down on my head." I had hoped that had gotten him thinking, considering everything to the point where he might be dissuaded to continue his abrupt takeover of my on-set positions.

He simply smiled back and said, "you gotta big surprise then if that is the way you think."

I reiterated that, "I want you to understand that I am a team player and I appreciate your excitement, but you're in a fantasy land and it seems you don't appreciate what I do and who I am. Just as I appreciate you. This is a little bit much. All I would like you to do and all you are here for is to train Dudikoff. Please understand."

Mike Stone didn't want to understand and told me that Dudikoff wanted it this way, so this way it would have to be.

I asked if he had spoken to the Producers and he said he had. I'm thinking, wait a minute, I spoke to the Producers. I spoke to Shmulik and they never said anything about this. This is a problem with outsiders, this is a problem with great fight Martial Artists. Because they have achieved so much in their field, they think that it is easy to come in and take such an important position. They think that's all it takes to do what professionals do in the movies. You could say it's like telling Thomas Edison to sit down. Not to say that I'm him, but I'm trying to make a point here. Remember when I mentioned I had no middle? I went from calm, cool and collective, to fuming inside but I kept it together. All my work and effort was now in jeopardy of becoming meaningless. The wonderful dreams I had working on this film just came crashing down. Here I am, with somebody I respect so deeply, realizing he isn't the person I thought he was. For the next six to seven hours, it's quiet time. I reflect on everything that has happened and remember something from the past. Wait a minute, a light bulb just came on in my head. It's "Edison time."

I remembered when I was on *Revenge Of The Ninja,* I had asked Sho after meeting him a few times on set, what it was like working on *Enter The Ninja.* He said he enjoyed working on it very much.

I then casually asked how it was working with Mike Stone. Sho, who is often very serious and does not laugh unless he gets to know you, went from jovial to dead serious. All he could say was, "not a nice man."

I asked what he meant and he said that Mike didn't want to work together, he wanted everything his way, by himself. He thought he knew everything, but he really knew nothing. That's why he got fired. I nodded and it just went with the wind since Mike Stone wasn't on the project. I moved on with the conversation. Now I realize exactly what Sho Kosugi meant.

Mike Stone showed that he was very rude and very cocky when he spoke to me. Not the kind of guy that I would put on a pedestal, like others. I was crushed and disappointed. My conversation with him went from warm and inviting to ice cold in a matter of a plane trip. I've worked with a lot of great Martial Artists in my time. They were humble and first class. They were team players and they have respect for others and their work. They had something called honor, something that I would come to find out Mike Stone had none of. Eventually, you see, let me explain, the head of a department's job is to try to communicate and work it out with a discussion, so I thought and I did. I turned to Mike and spoke up and explained the same thing I did to Shmulik about the difference between a stuntman and a Martial Artist. A logical conversation one might think.

Well, he just snapped. Mike Stone just laughed and asked me how long I had been a Martial Artist and what had I done. I told him I was in the business for nine plus years and started to explain what I had done. I mentioned all my work and the things I had done and the great people I've learned from and worked for and told him I had one of the best Martial Art Masters in the world. He asked who and I replied, Douglas Wong.

He smirked and said he knew Doug Wong. I continued to mention other great stuntmen I had worked with. He smirked at me again and simply said that he had the greater experience in this case. I asked what he had worked on in the movie industry and he didn't answer. I gave him a long list of my work and people who I worked with, that to anyone else, without a doubt would qualify me for this position on *American Ninja.*

To Mike Stone, unfortunately, it meant nothing. Such disrespect from a man so highly regarded by many. I just didn't understand his behavior, wondering if he did the same thing to people like Bruce Lee, Chuck Norris and others. I sat back in my seat, staying mostly silent for the rest of the grueling plane ride.

I had no idea that this was going to start out this way. You need to understand that this job is not a game. An actor can get killed, a stuntman could get hurt, somebody behind the camera could get injured, let alone a spectator. Every stunt needs to be planned out by someone who is not just a Martial Artist, but a Stunt Coordinator with an understanding of each mechanism involved. It's a dangerous business and you should understand the responsibility and the experience from one who is qualified. It's kind of like me telling Vic Armstrong, Terry Leonard or even Bruce Lee, to sit down. You just don't do that. It's called respect.

From what I knew and had seen, Mike Stone just was not that guy. I'll tell you what that guy should be. Someone who cares about the beauty of all the work. If Michael Dudikoff had this idea in his head too, he is also part of the problem. This was too big of a responsibility for me to just sit back and let him take over. And if you give a little, they are going to take a lot and make a lot of mistakes. One of the many differences, I care. I understand. I looked at Mike out of the corner of my eye. His jaw was set and he looked dead ahead. He was a man with a mission, and that mission had me worried. Not for me, for the movie. All that was going on in my head was that once the plane landed, I. HAD. TO. SPEAK. TO. THE. SHMULIK.

Once we arrived, we picked up our baggage, met one of the Production Assistants for the show and got into his car. I asked him if he could drop me off at the Production Office and bring my baggage to the hotel's front desk. I needed to see my Director. The P.A. agreed and the next thing I know, I'm walking with all my notebooks under my arm, right through the front doors of the Production Office. There was a lady at the desk who I introduced myself to, and she directed me through another set of doors where everyone was. A large group of people with new faces, I was not used to seeing. A sea of strangers all around me. Then from across the room, I hear a voice. I look and see one of the most wonderful, intelligent women I have ever met on a show. My good friend Ronit Ravich-Boss, the Script Supervisor. She had worked on the previous ninja films and let me tell you, without her, there would be no films. She was the one that held everything together, making sure things were done correctly in the order which they were supposed to.

Continuity with Cannon Films was not at the top of their list of necessities, (just watch some of their other films) but thank God we had her. We discussed how strange it was working around these new people, some of which I heard were not accustomed to working on big little films like this if you know what I mean. I knew right then, I had to take the knowledge I had learned in the past and teach and apply it to this production, but the good part about that is that I found out they are all eager and terrific workers. You just have to make sure they understand.

She introduced me to the First Assistant and I explained I needed to see Sam Firstenberg. He took me over to his office and I opened the door. As I did, I saw Shmulik and the two producers, Avi and Gideon there. Well, great. I wanted to talk to Shmulik privately, not with the two Producers in the room! So I smiled and walked in, greeted Avi and Gideon and Shmulik like everything was hunky-dory. I sat down and they started talking about locations. In the back of my mind, I wasn't thinking locations, I was thinking about the conversation I had on the airplane. After thirty minutes discussing locations, the Producers and Shmulik wanted me to go scouting and check out the places they had found.

This wasn't anything new and was standard procedure to help me get the action on paper, integrated to the location. I told them I hadn't been back to the hotel yet and would like to go back there first and get some of my stuff. They all said okay, and I shook our Producer's hands. I looked at Shmulik and asked him he wanted to come with me back to the hotel, as there was a lot I wanted to talk to him about. He smiled and politely declined, saying he had a lot to do in the office. I smiled back, but inside I thought to myself, that could have been a good opportunity.

He was right there and I had to leave. An hour later, I returned to the office from the hotel and found Shmulik. I went into detail about what happened on the plane with Mike Stone, which for the sake of you readers out there, I won't go over again. I asked Shmulik before he could reply, "I'm curious to know why you didn't inform me that you saw Mike Stone and Michael Dudikoff and had this discussion where he is under the impression, through Michael Dudikoff, that he is the boss for this show."

I told him this was such a crushing blow to me because of how much I thought of Mike Stone, and it turns out my image of him in my mind wasn't what came to be when I met him. I told Shmulik he needed to nip it in the bud as Barney Fife would say, aka Don Knotts on the *Andy Griffith Show,* and talk to Dudikoff and Stone. Shmulik being Shmulik said he was very surprised and confused, but not to worry, he would talk to Mike about it when he came in.

"Don't worry Steven, you're the boss."

I say to him, 'it's not a matter of who is the boss Shmulik. It's a matter of having two different opinions. One right and one wrong. You gotta have a leader. A decision maker. Someone who knows. Look at what we did on *The Domination* and *Revenge.* Success. We want the same thing for this one, don't we?" I felt a lot better and decided to head over to Wardrobe. I told Shmulik I was heading over there and asked him to "guess what."

He asked "what" and I replied, "no Naomi Golan." We both laughed and all my worries were forgotten. I went to Wardrobe and told them I needed Joe's outfit, the Black Star ninja's outfit and a few non-descript ninja outfits, and John Fujioka's outfit (Shinyuki). I was going to do a lot on this film and was excited once again. She took my sizes, then looked at me and said, "but all the people you just mentioned are different sizes." I looked at her and smiled.

I said, "just do all the outfits to my size, that is the way I am used to working, the audience will never know." After I had my wardrobe order in, we went to location with the Producers. The first location was for the ambush of the caravan of army vehicles. Shmulik said that he found a long stretch of road with a mountain terrain on one side and jungle on the other.

We needed to see it since the main bulk of this action sequence I had planned would be taking place in a condensed area. As I got out and started looking at the side of the mountain he had picked out, I noticed there was no high ground there.

My idea was to highlight the Black Star Ninja, have him in the spotlight high above in order to signal his band of ninjas. My idea was to have the Black Star on high terrain mountain, while the ninjas would come down from coconut trees, out from the forest, the ground, and bursting out of the mountain. This spot was too low for that however, and I spotted another road. I told Shmulik that if we moved there, I could dig three holes in the side of the mountain, put greenery in front and have them exploding out of the holes in front, onto the flatbed truck we were using in the convoy. Shmulik cracked a big Israeli smile, as he has done in the past and it felt like old times.

He absolutely loved the idea. I started developing the fight with Dudikoff and the rest of his fellow army men, as the Black Star Ninja watches from above. That's when Dudikoff mentioned that Mike Stone and he had other ideas. I asked to hear them and with an open mind I listened. In a nutshell, I must say that in my mind, I said one word. "Boring." But verbally, I said to Dudikoff, "not bad Michael, but may I take the time to tell you my ideas?"

Since this was a Cannon Film, I always referred to the Black Star Ninja on the mountain like Moses with the Ten Commandments. So in that instance, whenever I spoke to Tadashi, I would say, "Moses get up there."

I always remember his big smile with the same comment he always gave me. "Just like Menahem, you crazy Steven."

This is a true matter of fact. Shmulik loved what I was doing and we fed off of each other's excitement. We discussed Joe in the opening fight sequence and the weapons they would thrust upon him. As usual, I and my ideas were very valuable to Shmulik and the ninja legacy, thank God. Needless to say, I was very happy with Shmulik.

By the way, Dudikoff liked my fight arrangements better. Believe me when I say that a Director like him for me, is once in a lifetime and now I have had him three times. As for my Producers, when I asked them, Gideon would just reply, "good, good," and that was it. You could never get mister sunglasses excited.

Avi on the other hand would always be clapping his hands when I did something impressive, with a big smile on his face. I explained what I wanted to do with the trucks, and whenever I did work with vehicles, I would always go back to Yakima Canutt doubling John Wayne in Stagecoach.

(By the way, let me give you a little historical information. Yakima got his name when a newspaper writing about him, mistakenly said he was from Yakima, Washington. Instead of getting upset, he liked the name Yakima so much, it stuck. He was really from Colfax Washington.)

I wanted Joe to run as fast as he could and take a huge leap onto the back of the truck. He would then proceed to leap on the truck like Fred Waugh on the television show, *Spiderman*.

One of the stuntmen I looked up to when I was just starting out. He would then go on the roof just like the silver surfer, surfing a big wave, or in this case, a big truck. Similar to what I did on the Domination on the cop car, but this time it was the good guy and not the bad guy.

Joe would throw a chain into the windshield, grab the wheel and roll the truck over before jumping off and what a jump it would be. Everyone loved the idea and I told Shmulik I needed to start casting all the stuntmen and Martial Artists for the ninja fight in this opening scene as soon as we got back.

Shmulik mentioned we had this guy named Renato, who was the head stuntman here in the Philippines and I told him that was great and we would call him up. That's what I did once we got back to the office and asked if he could come down. While I waited for him, I spent the day with props, wardrobe, sets, transportation, etc. During the day Hanania, our Director of Photography comes and we hug and greet each other, happy to be back together.

I sat down in his office and went through the entire script, action wise in regards to my ideas so he would get an idea of what he needed.

(The great stuntmen of the Philippines. See the guy with the hat? He called himself James Dean.)

Afterward, I head back outside and all of a sudden, I hear this squeaky voice and turn around to see this five foot three fellow walking up to me with a big grin on him. "Are you Mister Steven Lambert?" he asked in a high pitched squeaky voice.

"Yes, I'm Steven," I nodded, trying to figure out what this little guy wanted.

"I am Boom-Boom!" He smiled at me as happy as could be.

I said, "Boom-Boom? What does that mean?"

He puffed out his chest and pointed to himself.

"They call me Boom-Boom, I am the special effects man!"

I'm looking at him and thinking, Boom-Boom, special effects. That's a joke, right? I said, "great, just the man I am looking for. From now on we are connected at the hip."

He looked at me funny and asked what that meant.

I laughed and said, "that means we will be together all the time in Brooklyn, American. I need to sit down and talk to you about explosions and equipment I will need. There will be certain explosions and pieces of action that I need and I want to talk about the size of the explosions."

That made him smile even bigger and he said he knew all about explosions. I was glad to have him on my team, but a little worried. It's not every day you work with a five foot three, eighty pound Filipino that had a haircut like Moe from *The Three Stooges*. I had other things to do at the moment and we arranged to meet the next day. Later on, I met Renato and we sat down to talk. I asked if he was ever the head of anything on a film before. He said he had done a few Filipino films and some American films as well. I said that was good and explained to him that he was going to be my right hand man and anything he said to do came directly from me.

238

He was, as I would learn such a wonderful guy to work with as were all the Filipino people. The first thing I wanted to do was for him to take me to all the gymnastic and Martial Arts places. Any high schools that had pads. I then asked if he knew what a mini-tramp was and he said no. Then I asked him if he knew what a trampoline was. He said yes and I explained it was a small trampoline for one person. His eyes lit up and he said he had seen them before on another production. I asked if he had any and he said no. So I told him I needed three and I needed to find an ironworker to put them together. For all you out there, I feel I need to remind you that I'm not working for Universal Studios or Warner Brothers. I'm working for Cannon Films.

There is no way I am going to be able to order up equipment and bring it here. Cannon doesn't do that. I have to revert to the wonderful things that my mentors and the old timers had taught me. These are the tools I have to use now and come up with. Not only equipment wise, but setting up a sequence, the way Buster Keaton did it or Harold Lloyd did it. The way stuntmen Harvey Perry and Davy Sharp did it. These were some of the greats that did what I am doing now.

People I looked up to. I must say, if you ever get a chance, look up some of these people and watch their work. They are incredible stuntmen.

After our meeting, the next location scouting I went on, Hanania came with us. We looked at about two or three locations throughout the day, including the warehouse that is the main antagonist's base. Shmulik tells me all the actors are coming in next week and I am all excited. A week goes by and I am busy as a bee, setting up all the action in each location and checking with the heads of each department. Every now and then I think about Mike Stone.

I haven't seen him all week long. I asked Shmulik if he has seen him and he shrugged. He said he comes into the office sometimes, but as to what he had been doing for the whole week, we had no idea. Was he out training Dudikoff? I don't know. Is he preparing Dudikoff's action for me to look at? No, I haven't seen him. Just wondering. Truth be told, I am always ecstatic to be left alone, except for my good friend Renato the Filipino stuntman who was so nice and worked so hard for me. I made sure he got credit on the show, thinking that would be helpful for him when looking for future work. That's teamwork. I continued working on the opening action sequence, Joe and the caravan.

With all the elements and characters that were in this action scene, it was an arrangement that I was mighty proud of. I knew it was going to look amazing and couldn't wait to show Shmulik its entirety. A few days go by and the day comes when the actors arrive. I asked Shmulik to set up half hour meetings so I could meet with the actors one on one and I mentioned the first guy I wanted to meet was the mad swordsman, Tadashii Yamashita. Shmulik laughed. I guess one of the reasons was that I wanted joy and happiness in the morning with my coffee, black if I may say, no cream no sugar, just a dash of Tadash. I would find that would wind up being my nickname for him.

Guess what, the first actor was Mister Michael Dudikoff. Straight faced and introverted, he reciprocated by saying, "hey." I wondered if that was the James Dean Shmulik saw in him. We briefly discussed his family and his background and he informed me of a few films he had been in, including *TRON* and *Uncommon* with Gene Hackman, and of course the present day cult comedy, *Bachelor Party*. I had never seen any of them. I pulled out my script and my notebooks, spreading them out on the table.

We discussed the scenes Michael would be in, starting with the one I had just set up with the convoy. All of you stunt people and actors that are interested in doing a job like I do, this is part of it. Explaining to your actor what occurs in the beginning, middle and end of each action sequence, including the situations, motivations and the reactions they should start thinking about. This is very important. Most Coordinators don't do that.

You see, you should start giving your actors suggestions so they can start sculpting their character. It's a very important part of it. This way everyone is on the same page and can really build up the excitement for everyone involved. But be careful of the Director, sometimes they don't like it so you have to hide it and then they think it's their genius.

During this meeting with Dudikoff, mind you, I am not bringing up the situation yet that I had with Mike Stone on the airplane, thinking that being a Stunt Coordinator means not only going over the action with the actor but trying to show them the complexity and finesse needed to do these kinds of sequences. I asked Michael if Mike Stone had taught him anything before he left Los Angeles. He said he hadn't, but they were going to get together here. I told him I needed Mike to teach him stances, dodges, rolls, blocks, punches and kicks. All basic stuff. Dudikoff said he would tell Mike Stone to teach him those things and that was when I mentioned that I was having a little problem with somebody I think a lot of, who happens to be Mike Stone. "Since he is your guy, I thought there was a need to bring it up," I explained to Dudikoff. I explained to him what had happened, saying Mike Stone said he was the boss of the action.

Dudikoff looked at me and gave me another James Dean comment. "Yea. I also want to let you know that Richard Norton is here to double me."

I took a deep breath and tried to tell him that I was going to double him when needed. "I have no idea what Richard can do, but let me ask you, have you seen my work in the previous ninja films? Do you think Richard Norton could do that stuff?"

He replies, "Richard Norton is a great Martial Artist."

I say to Dudikoff, "yes he is, but I ask you again. Do you think he can do what I did in those films? I have to see Michael. Just because someone is a great Martial Artist, which he is, doesn't mean he can do the action that we need him to do. A Martial Artist is different than a stuntman and an action artist. So I will keep him in mind and give him a shot if that is what you would like, but I want you to know this is a very dangerous business and I must tell you, there are very few people that can do what we need and one of them is me."

He nodded and said, "I'll see."

I said, "yes we will." That's when I explained to him that there needs to be only one person in charge of the action on this show. I told him if he wanted him to be "your" Fight Coordinator and give me ideas when it comes to the fighting that you would like to do, I'm always happy to work as a team. But so far, he is batting zero.

Dudikoff asked me why I said that.

"Well," I said. "You showed me his ideas for the opening sequence and I showed you mine and you were much happier with my presentation. So there has to be some clarity here. I am the person that this company put in charge of these things and Michael, I want to do what is best for you and everybody involved. Let me tell you, I am more than just a guy that falls on my head. I have had an awful lot of experience and was taught by many great men who made a living doing things like this and Stone simply is a great Martial Artist who really has no experience in this field at all. Putting aside the safety aspect, as you know, this is a very serious job in many ways and I hope you understand."

Michael was very gracious and seemed to get it. Dudikoff agreed that he would let Mike Stone know. He mentioned he had a meeting before he came, with Shmulik and Menahem and saw that they thought the world of me. He had seen my work in the last two films and thought I was just unbelievable. I humbly thanked him and went on to explain to him some of the cool stunts I had for him. Including jumping over an army base wall with a motorcycle, going up against a helicopter like a matador and a bull, doing some great fights and jumping on top of a speeding army truck before surfing it down the road. I jumped up in the middle of the lobby and I started to mimic my ideas with a combination of the Ninja, Spiderman, and the little Brooklyn Kung Fu Jew.

I did all kinds of movements, that quickly attracted the attention of the hotel staff. Not to mention the "wahahaha women," the most beautiful women who were working there. Never mind, but on the other hand, I must tell you that all these women who worked at the Manila Hotel were all the daughters, sister and wives of all the Government Officials in the country.

This was a safe zone for the elite. The Manila Hotel. Dudikoff was quite amused and with his James Dean smile, I knew I had him hooked. He told me it sounded terrific and he was excited to see it. I also started to explain all the fights and told him there would be many and with his help, I wanted to give him exactly what he thought his character needed. I thanked him and we shook hands. I mentioned I was going to meet Steve James next and he nodded and said he had met him already. I told Dudikoff I would meet him in the morning the next day and take him to the first location with all the Department Heads and go through everything step by step.

(The American Ninja. That's not Michael Dudikoff shooting the arrow. It's me. Tadash did catch it.)

After Dudikoff, I met with Steve James, a hulk of a man with a big smile. I introduced myself and immediately found out that he was a jolly, happy, go lucky guy. He was full of excitement while I explained to him the ideas I had for him to do. I mentioned to him that I have it worked out where he is going to save the day at the end.

He will come up a set of stairs at the mansion, in back of a huge machine gun on an army truck, while killing his share of guys. I told him he was going to fight and look like a hero. As those words left my mouth, he jumped up with such joy and literally bear hugged me. I struggled to breathe as my feet left the ground and he twirled me around like a happy hulk.

We are both laughing as I am asking him to put me down. It was a wonderful meeting which would soon become a wonderful friendship.

Next up was the long awaited Tadashii Yamashita. I told Tadashii what an honor it was to meet him and explained my past in Martial Arts and stunts.

I told him who my teacher was and with a big grin, he said, "I know Doug Wong and his brother Curtis too. "Inside Kung Fu" magazine."

I nodded while he said they were very good friends. I mentioned seeing him slice and dice his way through watermelons, cucumbers and crowds at tournaments.

I asked if he remembered running up the bleachers with his sword and parting the people like the Red Sea to get to the hecklers that pissed him off and wouldn't shut up.

He laughed with excitement saying, "yes I remember." With surprise he asked me, "you were there?"

I told him, "yes."

He said, "people do that sometimes, they don't have respect."

I grinned thinking this guy was the greatest. I told him my ideas for him and that I was going to be stunt doubling him and I hoped that he didn't have anybody.

He replied, "no, I want you." He mentioned he saw the last two ninja films I did and said, "oh, I think you might be ninja in your past life."

We laughed and shook hands with each other. It was good to have him here. Lastly, I met Phil Brock, the Brock Man. The comic relief on and off set. I told him that even though he had no stunts, he would get beat up in the ambush scene. He was very anxious about doing anything physical and nervously asked how he was going to be beat up, claiming he was no stuntman or heavyweight boxer. I assured him he wouldn't get hurt and it would be fun. Of course, I didn't tell him exactly what I had planned for him after deciding I didn't want to scare the guy too bad.

After my meetings with the cast who had arrived for that day, I was energized and ready to start going to the first location to begin the walkthrough of the action, in this case, the opening sequence with Joe and the Caravan. Manila was about to be invaded by ninjas. That night I was going over all my ideas and was ready to put on a big show for Shmulik, Hanania and a large chunk of the cast and crew. We met up the next day at the location. I already had dug the three holes in the mountain and placed the mini tramps. A backhoe and a couple of shovels are all you need.

Yes, I made the mini-tramps at an ironworker myself. They weren't perfect, but they would do the job. I had four gymnasts and myself as the four ninjas bursting out of the holes. Shmulik, Richard Norton, Mike Stone, Dudikoff, and Jewish Judy Aaronson, uhh, for sure we will talk about "Judy Fruity" later. They are all watching. We go to demonstrate the action and when everyone was ready, I yelled "JUMP!"

Popping out like a jack in the box, front flipping onto pads on the ground. A big applause erupted as I walked over to Shmulik who had a big smile and said, "that was going to be terrific." I told Tadashii he was going to go up on the mountain and stand there like a God. Three other ninjas, one being myself, would slide down the trees behind him. You may ask how it is possible for me to slide down the tree and at the same time jump out from the holes. It is the magic of editing and cuts that allow me to be everywhere. Next, I show Shmulik the fight with the army men and the ninjas knowing that all eyes are upon me. (Dudikoff, Stone, Norton, etc.)

During the fight, there was one ninja with a spear that stabs an army guy and he wasn't doing it the way I showed him. Always remember, when you are putting together a fight, it is a performance and from your toe to your head if it is possible, it should look wonderful.

That is what makes it look interesting when it becomes formed in its entirety. Let me give you some examples. Gene Kelly, when he is singing in the rain. Elvis Presley doing the "Jail House Rock," James Cagney in *White Heat* and of course Bruce in *Enter The Dragon*. Now it is Steven Lambert in *American Ninja*. I hope you don't mind me putting myself in with all these great people, humor my friends. View some of these performances and watch their body language and facial expressions and hopefully, you will get what I am talking about.

As I always say, it's not the fanciest flip nor the greatest move, it should be poetry in motion. I went over and did the action with much more style and pizzazz. I turned around and saw Mike Stone and Richard Norton watching me like two hawks. I knew I had their focus now and they were impressed. By now I know that look and not a word was said. That's always the case. You must know and understand how to shut down your critics. I moved on to show Dudikoff more of the fight which he loved and started talking about the car roll. I looked at Phil Brock and asked him to come over so I could show him the action. I said to him, "guess what? I got a stunt for you, Phil. One of the rebels will throw your head through the car window."

I could hear his voice crack as he said, "you want me to do what?"

I looked at him and started to laugh. I had been through this kind of nervousness with actors before. It is very funny. I told him casually I was going to put his head through the window. He took a step back and I cracked a smile. I told him as I chuckled, not to worry, the window will be made of candy glass and break very easily.

He replied, "where is my stunt double?"

I grin and say, "I'm looking at him." I walk away as he is still trying to ask me questions as Shmulik and everybody laughed. I have been with actors who get nervous doing a little stunt like this and knew he had nothing to worry about. We moved on to when Joe chases the army truck and jumps onto it while it is speeding away. Dudikoff asked me how fast the truck was going to go.

I told him, "as fast as a gazelle can run with me doubling you, but when you are on it, the truck will go fifteen miles an hour with safety on the sides."

I told him I would show him what I was talking about and turned around. I called for the mighty Renato and said, "get in the truck and when I tell you to go, make it as fast as you can. Don't worry about me and what I'm doing." You see, little did they know, I have rehearsed this with him already. It is like my chess game. Always make people think you are making a move for the first time. Lesson learned. Everyone's eyebrows raised as I told them to watch me. I turned and gave Renato his cue and I walked twenty five feet back and yelled, "ACTION!"

He takes off with the truck and I wait a few seconds until he gets up to a good speed knowing that when I catch up, it will be barely and an unforgettable jump onto the back of the truck. When the time comes, I run full blast and grab onto the back and pull myself up. I hop to the top of the truck doing a forward roll, coming up like the Silver Surfer and as soon as I do, I grab the chain and start swinging it as Joe is supposed to do.

Now, unbeknownst to everyone down below, I have a little handhold up there. I grab a hold of it as Renato slams on the breaks at the stop mark at the end of the road. He slides the truck a good thirty feet at about fifty five plus miles an hour. We are hauling, I mean we're stopping, I mean we're sliding. Time for my magic. Anyone else would have gone flying, but I held on to the handhold posing like a stunt-fu ninja. (Fu is for Kung Fu, it's not what you're thinking.)

A few seconds later, I jump off as the truck is still sliding. I land in a bunch of carefully placed boxes down in a ravine and stand up to a great commotion. When we shot it, I had planned to be the one driving the truck as it slides and rolls over.

Yes, I was really everywhere, can you believe it? As I stood up from the pile of boxes, people are running over in disbelief, asking me how I hung on with the truck sliding so violently. I smiled and like a monkey, climbed back up on the truck. Magically releasing the carabiner and the handhold, raising it above my head like a Gladiator and his sword in the arena.

Everybody applauded. They were just stunned. In one swift leap, I jumped down from the top of the truck to the solid ground, putting some more amazement to my work as everyone watched. I turned and casually looked at Dudikoff, Stone, and Norton and uttered the magic words. "Do you want to try it?" Now let me explain to all you readers, the reason I asked him was, my Producers were there and I needed to let everybody know that there is a reason and a why I am here.

Since they wouldn't verbally listen, sometimes you have to physically show them and this is one way of demonstrating it verbally and physically. He looked at me and I looked at Mike Stone and then at Dudikoff in the five seconds of silence that followed.

Then I heard laughter and I turned to see Shmulik laughing. "No, no, only somebody like you can do this, Steven," he said.

(Mike Stone, Michael Dudkioff, Richard Norton. They simply said, "no thank you.")

Without any protest from anyone else, we moved on. Time went by and Richard Norton came over to me and said he heard I was having some problems with Mike Stone. He explained that he didn't agree with his behavior. He said to me that he wanted to be my friend and wanted me to know Mike Stone's actions had nothing to do with him and I was surprised that he apologized to me. As he stuck out his hand and I shook it, I thought to myself, this is a noble man, a man with rectitude,, dignity, a sense of what is right. Respect for others. As Shmulik and I walked off, they were all left behind for a moment. I knew at that moment, there was going to be no discussion about who was going to double who when it came to the action and the stunts. Shortly after, I called out for my FX guy. He appeared out of the crowd, eating a pickle half the size of his body. Let me tell you, it looked funny. He had pickle juice running down his chin, all over his shirt. That was Boom Boom. I must tell you, as crazy as this sounds, I wouldn't have traded him for anybody in the world.

I asked what that was and he said it was part of his lunch. Go figure. I said I needed an explosion when the truck rolls over.

He says, "okay Steven, how big do you want it? Do you want it BOOM? Do you want it BOOM BOOM? Or do you want it BOOM BOOM BOOM?"

I said, "what are you talking about, what does that mean?"

He simply explained small, medium, or big?

I asked him if three BOOMs meant a big explosion and he said, "YES!"

I said, "what happened to measurements?"

He replied, "WE DON'T NEED NO STINKING MEASUREMENTS."

I thought to myself, I think I heard that someplace before. Then I asked him, "is that how you determine the size of your explosions?

He said, "suuuuure!"

I told him I wanted three BOOM BOOM BOOMS. Big ones. Boy did I get it when we filmed. The stunt and roll over on the army truck went wonderfully and we all had a blast thanks to Boom Boom. A few days before we shot the scenes, I asked Renato to gather up the boys to see the choreography I had put in place between the army guys and the rebels. You see contrary to some rumors, I was the only person who put together the fights in this movie. As I'm watching it, I realize something isn't right. I turn to Renato and tell him this wasn't the choreography I had set up. Renato simply said that Mike Stone had come by yesterday after we had left and changed things around. I couldn't believe what Renato had just said. I looked at the fight again and none of it worked.

I told everyone to change it back to the way it was and told Renato if Mike says to change anything again, come to me and I will deal with him personally. In my head, I thought that was that and it was over. I needed to have another discussion with Stone. But it wasn't over and unfortunately, it happened three other occasions. This finally came to a head at the Black Star Ninja's warehouse. Each time, what he did, wasn't working in regards to camera position and certain elements I had set up. I might have worked some of his ideas in, but what he did was inappropriate and I was very disappointed by his actions. Again, I was having my Hollywood puberty growth spurt here as this was something I had never dealt with before and is just not done. He was adamant that he was working for Michael and regardless of the things I told Dudikoff to tell Mike Stone, he was going to do things his own way. I was getting upset over this and enough was enough. I told Mike just that and walked away just fuming inside. The lack of respect and rudeness was really starting to get to me. I guess he thought just because he was a world champion, taught Elvis Martial Arts and trained with Bruce Lee and Chuck Norris, he could do whatever he wanted.

I even honestly offered to teach him in a very sensitive and humble way, and he laughed in my face. "You can't teach me anything," he spat.

I replied, "Stone, I'm just trying to help. I'm trying to be a friend." I must say, these aren't made up words, these are the words he used. Something had to be done. That night I went out to dinner with Shmulik and Tadashii. I mentioned the problem I was having with Mike Stone and that was when Tadashii gave me a look like he has heard this before. "That man is not nice," Tadashii stated.

I was beginning to really get a sense of the guy, now that Sho and Tadashii had the same viewpoint of him. I asked him to please explain. He simply said, "these are the things that Mike Stone does, it is part of his reputation. Nobody trusts him. You be careful Steven. He will try to steal your job."

I looked at Tadash and smiled saying, "thank you, but I assure you that nobody is going to take my job, at least until I say I doubled you Tadashii."

He smiled and we continued our dinner. The next day we worked on the obstacle course the ninjas used to train. Oh, how I was looking forward to this. To me, this sequence was visually a piece of art. I had spent weeks putting this together with props and the set decorator and a hundred and fifty stunt ND ninjas. I got my ideas from watching old Chinese movies. I even gave Mike Stone a cameo in it. Here is when the Samurai Warrior comes out of Tadashii. You out there, who know Tadashii Yamashita, all I can say, his favorite thing is "let's do it for real." This is the scene where Tadashii demonstrates his skills to the investors and he is supposed to beat up a group of ninjas who attack him. I bring Tadashii over and I play him, going over all the moves that I had put together. He watches and makes a few changes and may I say they are dynamite and made my stuff look better. That is what you call teamwork. I told him to hang back and practice this fight with the guys and sharpen everything up. I told him I would be back in two hours with the D.P. and Shmulik. I went off and did some more business. A man of my word, I returned with my Israelites. I asked Tadash if he was ready to show me and the guys at full speed. He said yes. I walked back a couple of feet, turned and said, "ACTION TADASH!"

Well, all Hell broke loose and I'm watching in frozen amazement, whatever that means. I realize he starts really hitting these Filipino black belts and I mean hard! For real. I jump out like a Camanche Banshee yelling "cut, cut!" I said, "Tadash, what are you doing? I need these guys. You can't beat up on them like that."

He shrugged it off saying, "they are black belts, they can take it

I couldn't believe what I just heard. I started laughing, simply from pure shock. I said, "what do you mean they can take it? This isn't for real. This is the movies. I need these guys. They are my best." I look over and they all have their heads down like punished school children. I walk over and I pull off one mask and I see a big knot on his head. I walk over and pull off another mask and see a big welt on his neck. I turn to Tadash and I say, "if I take any more clothes off, I'm afraid of what I'll find." These guys were all banged up from the two hours of practice.

Tadashii shrugged, replying again, "these are black belts, ask them. It is okay I hit you right?"

I turned back and they were bobbing their heads up and down saying, "yes sir, yes sir."

(I felt bad for those guys. Yamashita beat the hell out of them.)

I looked back at Tadashii and said, "of course they have no choice but to bow and nod their head, you are Tadashii Yamashita, the master. They know your reputation. You scare the shit out of them."

He starts laughing at me which causes me to start laughing and everyone else joins in, except for the ninjas. They were hoping he would take it easy next time, but Tadashii never did, even though I begged him.

When we were doing the mansion fight scene with Tadashii and Joe, I came up with an idea with Shmulik to enhance the fight. I told Tadashii to do a punch, while Joe is on the roof. It was me playing Joe, and he looks at me and says, "you are too far away, why do I punch?"

I smiled and told him we are going to CGI in a laser that shoots out from his wrist and breaks a vase next to Joe.

He grinned and said, "Steven, you make me so powerful." From then on, he was always excited to see what I had in store. It was a grand memory.

(A special moment stunt doubling Tadashii Yamashita. A wonderful memory.)

When I wasn't doing the action scenes, I rarely had a day off. Shmulik liked to have me on set as I was always prone to come up with new ideas as you out there may run across as well. For example, in the opening scene, I saw Joe just standing by the army truck, watching them play hackey sack, just standing there. I thought to myself for a second and realized there is something missing from the scene. Here is an idea. I opened my bag and took out a butterfly knife and started switching it back and forth. Dudikoff took notice and I went over to him. I told him I thought it would be cool if he was playing with the knife. He loved the idea, as did Shmulik and after teaching him a basic move, he learned it quickly. That is how that found its way into the film and you may ask how I thought of it. All I say to that is thank you, Jeff Imada. The days I did have off, I enjoyed getting together with guys like Tadashii and Steve James. One time, we went on an adventure into the jungle.

At this time, it wasn't that dangerous to walk around, yet Cannon films went to the trouble to provide us with our own personal bodyguards. My guard was named "Boy." Yep, you heard right. That was his name. He was five foot nine, and built like Bolo from *Enter The Dragon*. He came straight from the upper echelon of President Marcos and his wife. At this time his wife was President. Every time I went out, Boy would always be by my side. He and I became good friends. So he, I,

Steve James, Tadashii, Phil Brock, Boom Boom and Renato all decided to explore one Sunday morning. Boom Boom said he would take us to special places. I looked at Boom Boom and asked, "what kind of special places?"

I jokingly told him I hoped we weren't going to a whore house.

He laughed and said, "nooooo Steven." He asked me, "do you want to go?"

I said, "no go. I don't want to get into trouble, I want to explore."

Everybody laughed. We spent about three and a half hours traveling through the jungle. We saw a stand where it looked like they were selling eggs. Oh good, I thought, I love eggs. As I get closer, I see they are cutting off the top of the egg shell with a spoon. Inside, instead of a hard boiled egg, I see a whole chicken embryo! I couldn't believe it. Renato explained to me it was a delicacy called Balut. Well, I "balut" had enough and turned away, watching them put hot sauce on it. Tadashii was laughing at me as Steve James started dry heaving.

Yes, the macho men couldn't take it. But we did say thank you. In this case, no thank you. After that, we went further into the jungle where we came upon this little village entryway where they had four or five monkeys in a cage. They had tied up one of the monkeys and brought out a long bladed knife like instrument with the end looking like an old time can opener. It was hooked. We were powerless to do anything except to watch as they put the monkey's head up against a rock. We turned away, but I saw what happened next out of the corner of my eye. They brought the blade down on the monkey's head horizontally, as not to make a mess if you know what I mean, and proceeded to ready the monkey for eating. The scream was unbearable. I thought it was the sickest and saddest thing I had ever witnessed in my life. We started to walk away as Boom Boom yells, "Steven, what's the matter? You never have monkey brains before?"

No, I hadn't. As a certain type of monkey, that being a stunt monkey, I would never eat my own kind. I was glad we got out of there fast and back to civilization. If that sight wasn't bad enough, I remember we were shooting the mansion scene at the end of the film with Steve James, Dudikoff and everyone else in that sequence. I called the scene, the Matador and the bull, me being the Matador and the helicopter being the bull.

(The bull fight. Grabbing the helicopter by its horns. I was just worried about the blades.)

That was the picture I painted to Hanania our cameraman. We were in the middle of filming and all of a sudden, a screaming breaks out from the other side of the mansion. As the seconds went by, it got louder and louder and we had to cut. The sounds started to echo around us and we were looking at each other wondering what the hell is that? It sounded almost human, the sound of an animal we had never heard before. We shut down everything and a few people began walking towards the side of the mansion and the unearthly sounds. A few more followed, including me and Dudikoff.

The sounds were all around us now, clearly the sound of something or someone that was from the bowels of hell. What the hell was going on here? We finally round the corner and to our disbelief, we see two of the security guards sitting on chairs around an open BBQ pit. In this BBQ pit, they had skewered a dog, through its mouth and out its rear end. This dog was half burned and still alive. The women screamed and we all started telling them to stop. Half the people who came to investigate the noises, flew back the way they came.

The dog is still screaming and the security men are being told by our crew to stop it and take it down. They did, but that dog was beyond any of our help. No one got in trouble or anything, they just got hungry and decided to cook a dog. It really taught me how people in other countries act and live differently than what we Americans are used to. This wasn't Coney Island where you could get Nathan's hot dogs. Here, they had real hot dogs and it shocked a lot of us. A moment in time I always try to forget, but can't. It's fried into my brain for eternity.

So let me move on to a more God like tale. Another time, we were shooting a jeep chase at night and all of a sudden, as it does there, it starts to pour. I mean pour so bad you can't stand beneath it, like a monsoon. We all stopped and ran for shelter. Everyone but me. I stood out there with my face up to the rain, just loving every minute of it. It felt like a cleansing. My arms extended, looking up to the sky with rain just pouring down on me. Shmulik is yelling at me to get under the shelter and I was about to answer him when the ground started moving. It started shaking! Everyone is pointing and I'm not sure what is happening. I hear them yell to look. I look down and these things start coming out of the ground. I don't mean five or ten I mean about twenty five dozen of 'em. There are these tiny mounds and they start bursting all around me. I realize they are small frogs just erupting from these mounds. I couldn't believe it. The joy that came over me was immense. It was then followed by a stampede of native Filipinos running out with potato sacks, trying to catch the frogs.

I yelled out, "why are you doing that?"

They said, "oh, we make shoes, we make belts, a lot of money from this."

I yelled out, "Nooo! Let me froggies go! Freeeeeedom for the frogs!"

Shmulik and everybody were on the wet floor laughing at me. It was a great moment in time I'll never forget. Just some interesting facts about the Philippines. I also want to mention stuntman Kenny Lesko, who had I brought along. Besides the stunt he did, he was also known for writing a funny poem every day at lunchtime, something that the whole cast and crew looked forward to. He would write a new poem each day, about craft services, prop guys, to me and Shmulik himself.

Everyone looked forward to Lesko's lunchtime poems and if anyone reads this book who has worked in this particular movie, I know you have a smile on your face reading this and remembering those times. A vivid memory I have at the lunch table (I know, there have been a lot) that has always confused me even to this day, is when Michael Dudikoff came over to me while I was eating with my Director, my actor Steve James, my D.P. and a few others. It was clear he was overly agitated. He spurts out that he heard I was putting together a huge "coming to the rescue" sequence at the mansion for Steve James and wanted to know if that was true.

It seemed like he was completely oblivious that Steve James was sitting at the table, or he didn't care. Looking up at him I said, "yes, of course." That was my job after all.

Well, Dudikoff disagreed with that train of thought and told me that I was his Fight Coordinator, not Steve James's. I was set back! I told him, "Michael, you must understand that I am everyone's Fight Coordinator. Cannon hired me for that purpose and our Director expects that function from me." Steve James was sitting a few feet away but said nothing. Just listened. I couldn't believe it.

Dudikoff explains, "I read the sequence you put together and it seems like you are making him the hero. Not me."

I explain to Michael that was the wrong way to look at it. All he is doing is assisting the hero fight the overwhelming force that he is up against. "Michael, I am going to show you being the victor. He is just a tool to make what you are going to do, greater. Just let it happen and you'll see. You'll understand."

Well understanding, he had none. He shook his head and said, "no. I don't want it."

I tried to explain to him, "Michael, it's not what you want or what I want. It's what the Director wants and what I put together, he wants. So that is what we are going to film. Please understand. This isn't about me, this isn't about you nor Steve James. This isn't about anybody."

Dudikoff turns and storms off. In my mind, I couldn't understand the reason. I looked at Steve James who had a look of let down in a sense of friendship. I asked him, "what was that all about?"

He explained, "we aren't getting along Steven."

I turned and looked at the Director, Shmulik. "Did you know about this?" I asked.

He said, "yes, Steven. But you have to understand. He is a little insecure."

"Insecure?" I ask. "About what?"

"You see," Shmulik says. "Steve James is an actor and it seems like it is making Michael a little insecure."

I've never had a guy tell me to only work with him when I was the Fight Coordinator for the whole show. This is a first. I have to say from the visuals, time after time that I saw them working together, my sense was that Steve James always tried for that sense of friendship and communication but unfortunately it was never reciprocated, nor understood why. In many interviews and magazines, it was stated that they were great friends. Unfortunately, this was not true. Speaking of getting along, Michael and I did. What was most important was that we respected each other throughout.

Every now and then people ask me what my favorite action sequence was to put together. I simply tell them there is not one that is my favorite. But I'll tell you which one was impressive and at the same time, a nightmare in *American Ninja*. The dreaded motorcycle jump. I had to figure out how to get Joe out of the army base without being caught. There was a huge sixty foot long cement ramp that was four to six feet away from the wall. It was perfect. I built a wooden extension, making the ramp six inches above the wall. I had already picked the motorcycle stuntman who was going to do this, two weeks ago. Why wasn't I doing it? I was the ninja after all. Here is why. My skills on a motorcycle were very basic at that time. The biggest jump under my belt was a baby jump. Four to five feet. Even a blind man could do that. So I got a guy from the Philippines. An hour before we do the stunt, I introduce Sam Firstenberg to my Filipino stuntman. Sam asks the guy how many times he has done a jump like this.

"A few times," he says.

I notice he had a nervous twitch, but I just brushed it off. I mean, I'd be nervous too. That's one hell of a jump. I go to the spot where the stuntman is supposed to land and start talking to the D.P. That's when I get a call on the radio from my Second Assistant. He tells me we have a problem and wants to discuss it in person with me. I head over to him and ask what's up? The motorcycle stuntman tells me he changed his mind and doesn't want to do the jump. We are about twenty minutes from the shot! I didn't understand why he was willing to do the jump since two weeks ago, but now at the last moment changes his mind. I discussed this with him and he tells me he is afraid, doesn't want to do it. I try to convince him it was normal to be afraid and I needed him as I had no one else to do it. He wouldn't budge. What can I do? I head back to my Director, all the while on my phone trying find someone to do this jump. I'm hoping I can find someone. I ain't doing it, I'll wind up killing myself. It wasn't long before one agreed and said he would be right over. I am very relieved. So we wait while Sam films some drive outs and closeup reactions on the motorcycle. My guy finally arrives. He gets in his wardrobe, drives around to warm up and I take him over to the ramp to do his stunt. He sees it and guess what? He says, "not me, not me."

I look at him and the only thing I could say was, "yes, you, yes, you."

He replies, "noooo. Not me."

Oh, shit. My Director comes over and I tell him the problem. He is asking me what we were going to do. My mind is racing a mile a minute. The pressure is on. It's building and building and then it bursts out.

"I'm going to do it," I say.

"I thought you said you weren't able to do this stunt, Steve," Sam replies.

Nodding, I said, "I fooled you."

I just ask him to set up cameras and I go put on Joe's outfit. This whole time I am thinking to myself, that I am nervous! I have done stunts a hundred times more dangerous, a thousand times more dangerous, but I've never had this feeling inside. It seems to be trying to overcome me. You ask yourself, do you have the will to do this, do you have the strength? Do you believe there is a doubt. You remind yourself you are a leader, how do you handle a position no one wants to fill. Do you stay a coward or do you step up. These thoughts flew through my head as I walked back to my Director. I made up my mind. I am doing it. I tell the crew I am ready and get the bike into position. I tell Sam that it doesn't matter if I crash or make it, just film the whole thing and he can cut away after. "Steve, you're crazy," Sam's voice came over the radio.

"Just get ready, Sam," I told him. "I'll see ya on the other side."

I take a look at the ramp and signal I was ready to go. I hear Sam signal to roll cameras on the walkie. I hit the gas and with a deep breath, off I go. I go from first gear to second to third to fourth. I'm going fast as I can. There's no thoughts in my head. As I am in the air, I remember what two great men told me in the past. Sit forward, raise off the seat and lean back a bit. Try to get your back wheel to hit the ground first and then lean forward into normal position. That's what I was taught by stuntmen Roy Harrison and Ronnie Rondell. That is exactly what I did. When I landed, I landed a little bit too flat. I came down hard, very hard. If you watch the scene, you will see Sam cut right before I hit. That's because I folded and my whole head smacked into the gas tank. Put a dent in my forehead and would need a couple stitches too. People surrounded me as blood dripped down my head. Sam Firstenberg asked me if I was okay. I looked up at him and simply said, "did you get the shot?" I cracked a smile as everyone went from serious to laughing. Sam nodded. He did.

(Steve James saving the day. He's the best.)

Talking of being the Fight Coordinator, that brings me to the climactic conclusion between me and Mike Stone at the warehouse. After finding out he made another change, we turned to each other on the set and I explained to him that we had gone over this before. I told him I have just had enough of him interfering and changing things around. Shmulik, Hanania and most of the crew were there watching us. Even they told Mike that he shouldn't do that because they had things set up as well. Mike Stone walks over to me and to my big surprise, he grabs my shirt and twists it into his fists. He starts to bring me up, yelling, "I don't give a CENSORED what you are, I am going to do what I want!"

Well, the minute he grabbed me and finished speaking, I went to my old style eagle claw. My left arm went over both his forearms and my right hand went to his neck and proceeded to squeeze and push forward. Now there are a couple of ways to escape that, but Mike Stone was in no position or thought of mind to do so and he finally releases me and I push him back. Immediately, I throw up my hands and step back. Shmulik comes running over, trying to break it up with his hands on Mike Stone telling him to stop, as a few electricians try to calm me down.

I turned to Gideon and Avi, the Producers and told them I had had enough. "Either he leaves the set or I leave. You saw him put his hands on me." I looked at

Mike and said, "you should be ashamed of yourself. You are supposed to be a somebody, but the way you act just breaks my heart. It's beyond belief. A man of your supposed stature. You are not the man I thought you were." On the outside I was furious, but on the inside I was heartbroken. To end this little moment in time, Mister Mike Stone simply "disappeared," never to be seen on this set again. If I ever saw him again, I would smile, put out my hand for a shake, say hello and with respect, keep one eye open just in case.

to steve
THANKS
SHMULIK

(Let's play "Where's Waldo," I mean Mike Stone. Sorry to say, not here.)

I would like to continue the discussion of friendships in a way - FLASH: Magazines, newspapers and videos say and print that there was always a strong friendship between Steve James and Michael Dudikoff on *American Ninja* one.

FLASH: I have news for you, the friendship wasn't there from the beginning. FLASH: It was more like two actors tolerating each other because they are on the same set. Not the fault of Steve James.

FLASH: New intelligence is telling you, that the friendship did not start until they both found out they were doing *American Ninja 2.*

FLASH: You ask me how I know this? Steve James and I did a picture about a year later called, *Behind Enemy Lines,* and he said Michael apologized.

FLASH: Reports that Steve James and Dudikoff were fellow actors on *American Ninja* one, and not close friends are now refuting the widely printed article and comments that always seem to be coming out of the star's mouth.

FLASH: Ok, enough with the flashes. Oh, one more. FLASH: We haven't talked about Judie Aronson.

FLASH: Spoiled brat.

FLASH: Pain in the tuchus.

FLASH: She had a crush on Dudikoff. FLASH: Then she went for me. FLASH: I don't like Jewish Princesses.

FLASH: Dudikoff thought she was a pain in the arse. FLASH: You could tell there's no love lost. FLASH: Dudikoff and her are friends now.

FLASH: Dudikoff gave up, lol.

(Judie Aronson. The Princess.)

That's it with the short flashes, let's go with a long flash. BIG FLASH: Judy maintains that at lunch, there were two lines. One for the Filipinos and one for the non-Filipinos. This is true. In the Filipino line, she says she saw them eating dog. This is completely fabricated and fake. We would all know if This was the case. She may have just wanted to make a scene after seeing the dog cooked behind the mansion by security guards. Not fair to my Filipino friends to state otherwise.

Sorry to say that even Michael Dudikoff and I didn't have a real friendship on set, it was more just business. When years later I got a phone call from Shmulik asking if I wanted to have lunch with him and Dudikoff. I said yes and it was only then we became close friends. Why you may ask? I always thought about that and maybe it was because the movies after *American Ninja* that he was in, didn't do as well. Or maybe it was just meant to be. In any case, it was a good thing our friendship grew deep.

Now sometimes people ask, email or text me about the end fight between Michael Dudikoff and Tadashii Yamashita. They ask why it was so short and so simple. I say to them, "I'll tell you why. Dudikoff unfortunately never trained in Martial Arts and the person that was brought over to make sure he understood

Martial Arts, never really trained him. He was more concerned with putting his nose and his business in other departments instead of doing what he was supposed to be doing. That person was Mike Stone who had already been asked to leave the show. Fired. When I started this major end sequence with my Director, we had so much on our plate, I just didn't have enough time to work on a sequence with a man like Dudikoff who is very inexperienced and slow to learn. So I did what I was able to do with what little time I had.

(The acting star with the action star.)

I have to take this moment to discredit a "fact" out there. Malaria and Dudikoff. He never had it, though he and others say otherwise. Look up the symptoms of malaria. Chills, fever, diarrhea. He had none of those. I was with him every day. The whole crew would have known. In interviews, Shmulik says he had no idea. He had no idea because it never happened! Actors, what hams they can be. Two weeks before *American Ninja* was about to end, I got a phone call from a very well known Stunt Coordinator and Second Unit Director named Glenn Randall Jr. He, along with Vic Armstrong coordinated the first Indiana Jones film. A little note here, they weren't big fans of each other. That is what happens when you put a hard ass cowboy like Glenn and a jolly Englishman like Vic together. More on this love affair later.

Ok, let's get moving. I called him back and he asked if I was interested in doing a movie with him called *Remo Williams: The Adventure Begins*. Randall was also part of the Stuntmen's Association and had heard of my past work. Remo had a lot of things in it that got me excited. I was tired of ninjas and had ninja on the brain. After doing three ninja films I had the strong thirst for something else and wanted to spread my wings or I could say spread my cream cheese on my bagel. I had heard through the grapevine that there was mention from Shmulik and the Producers that there was talk about *American Ninja 2*. I asked Randall if I could have a few days to think it over and he said yes. He went on to say it had a lot of action on the Statue Of Liberty. He explained Remo was a series of books in the "Destroyer" series, written in the seventies. He told me it has Martial Arts in it as one of the main characters is a Chinese guy and there is a style written in the book called Sinanju.

He asked me if that was a real style and I told him I didn't think so. It was most likely made up for the book. He told me the book said it allowed the practitioner to lift cars, dodge bullets and bring women to the height of sexual ecstasy. I knew then it wasn't a real style as I'm sure I would have heard about it. And used it. He asked me if I could come up with a style for the film if I took on the project and I told him I could. We hung up and I took a few days and thought it over. I had become family with Shmulik over these three films, so it wasn't an easy choice. My brain was going back and forth like two ninjas throwing shurikens at each other. It was a very difficult moment, but in the end, I hoped I could always come back to Cannon Films. When I returned to set, I casually mentioned to Shmulik that I had gotten an offer to coordinate a movie called *Remo Williams: The Adventure Begins*, and production started a day after *American Ninja* wrapped. It broke my heart and his faced changed and he looked at me with serious eyes. It was like telling a little brother you weren't going to be at his baseball game.

He told me that indeed they were going to do a second *American Ninja* and wanted me there. I told Shmulik I appreciated the offer but I explained what an opportunity *Remo* was going to be. Shmulik shrugged his shoulders and told me it was my decision. It hurt me inside to see him like this, we were like brothers and I knew how much he depended on me and I was proud of it in so many ways. Yet, I decided to go a new path and called Glenn Randall to tell him I was on board. The following day I broke the news to Shmulik and I thought that was that. A few days later I was in my room and got a call from Los Angeles and it was Menahem Golan.

I asked how he was and he said, "FINE, FINE, I HEAR WE HAVE A PROBLEM HERE." Again, anybody who knew Menahem and his voice, it was always a very special sound. I'm thinking there was a problem with the dailies we sent back.

He said, "SHUMLIK TOLD ME YOU ARE LEAVING. BUT YOU CANNOT LEAVE, WE HAVE AMERICAN NINJA TWO."

I was shocked. Here is the head of Cannon Films putting me in a situation that I simply had never been in before. You talk about awkward and in a way, heartbreaking. I said, "Menahem please, let me tell you this first. I want you to know how much I appreciate and value and even cherish the friendship and opportunities you have given me." I explained how gracious he and the rest of Cannon were to me, but I had made up my mind to do this picture.

"DON'T YOU REMEMBER THE GREAT ACTION YOU DID ON REVENGE OF THE NINJA?" The voice of God boomed back through the telephone. "WE WILL HAVE MORE GREAT ACTION, EVEN BIGGER ON AMERICAN NINJA TWO!"

I did remember the great times, but my mind was on the future right now. Mind you, Menahem wasn't cursing me out, he was just trying to figure out how to convince me to stay. He just wasn't the kind of guy to come right out and say it. He had more pride than that. Let's not forget he was a God. I didn't quite know how to take it but I told him again that my decision was made but I would love to see him in the future. Needless to say, the man was not happy and neither was I. He stated I couldn't leave, that I was part of the family. I thanked him for everything he did and hoped I would see him again.

He was very firm and said, "YOU MUST THINK ABOUT IT STEVEN. YOU SHOULD NOT GO." I took a deep breath.

I said, "thank you for everything." I asked him if there was anything else.

A few seconds later he said "NO," before he hung up.

I put down the phone and took a deep breath, bending over and putting my face in my hands. Fade out. At this point, I began to realize how crucial I was to Menahem and Cannon films. It was a wonderful feeling but at the same time, I gotta say I felt a sense of emptiness. Did I do the right thing? I guess it was that thing that they call Jewish guilt. What I didn't realize at that time was just how important I was. Having grown up with no direction in my life, no plans for my future, I didn't grasp what a great opportunity I might have taken. I think back now on what had happened then and the door that was wide open for me to walk into.

But I wasn't looking at the door, I was looking at the ceiling. I could have asked to Produce, Direct or even star, who knows? It was me doing all the actions in and out of the ninja suit, as well as all the movements and body language. I can honestly say 70-80% of the ninja films were all me and to have an opportunity to always write the action from empty pages will be something I will miss. But I wasn't taught in life, be it by parents, teachers or mentors to think like that. I never had the guiding light in how you progress a career. Everything was happening so fast that I just became a kid in a candy store. My mind was on the candy, not thinking about the business and how to further myself in my career. Menahem would have given me what I wanted without hesitation, but I just didn't have the mindset to think to ask. Just a punk kid from the streets of Brooklyn now lost in the halls of Hollywood.

Not much was said about it on set for the rest of the show. Dudikoff did come over and ask if it was true and I told him it was. He nodded, in his James Dean way, but said nothing. Even Steve James came over to me. Instead of a nod, I got a big hug. Again.

Lifting me off my feet, he was screaming, "you can't leave!"

What a great guy he was. I miss him. As for Shmulik, I felt an emptiness from him for the rest of the shoot. As much as this hurt me, I had made up my mind. I was leaving to do *Remo* in New York, and unbeknownst to anyone, and to my sadness, the future of Cannon's Ninja films would never be the same.

CHAPTER 25
(Remo Williams, The Adventure Begins. Back To Brooklyn.)

Homecoming. This is kind of a new beginning. You ask what I mean by that? A new beginning going back to my roots, seeing my old friends.

Breaking through the clouds, my plane descended. Then there she was. A woman who I had not laid eyes on for almost two decades. My eyes met hers and I couldn't help but smile. She was French, with beautiful features built into her. That's right, she was lady liberty. Then I noticed something different. She had scaffolding around her body, almost as if she was imprisoned. Her torch however, was untouched. The symbol of freedom rising above through the scaffolding. We land in New York and I can't believe I am home. I knew what an honor it was to work with Glenn Randall Jr. and I was excited to begin. I had heard comments in the past, about what a great guy he was to work with as well as comments saying he was tough to get along with. I wonder how this is going to work.

A hard ass cowboy and a Martial Art city boy. How's that mix for you? Keep in mind, I did have home field advantage. I also wanted to make a request to Glenn Randall to bring on Mike Vendrell and Joel Kramer which for me, asking would be a difficult thing since it was the first time working with him and may I say a bold request. But friendship was an important thing and I knew there were a lot of spots in the film and that is what you should do if you can. Always try to get a friend a spot. The worst thing that could happen was he says no and for me personally, I needed somebody to watch my back and keep me safe. I read the script and I noticed he was going to be bringing on a lot of guys so I had hoped he would honor my request with these two talented men. I was also excited to see my old friends from the streets of Brooklyn.

That's right. I mean Euguene Fish, Mordechai, Steve Ellis, what's left of the twerp twins, Jeffrey Elkins and Steve Lees. You see, Eugene had seen my name in the credits of a movie one day and set out to find me. When he saw a production going on in New York, he asked a P.A. if there were any stunt people on the show. The P.A. said yes and pointed to a few. He walked over and said, "hey do you know a Steven Lambert?"

They said yes and gave him a number to call. This number was good old Teddy O'tooles answering service. It was world famous. It was hard to get on, but if you did, you were a somebody. Buck McDancer is the one that brought me there and convinced Teddy to put me on. Buck had a way about him, all the ladies liked him, young and old. By the way, Teddy O'tooles is a woman, a grand lady. All the big and upcoming stuntmen were on Teddy's as well as Producers, Actors, and Directors. Teddy's had been in existence since the forties. She had a long list of well known names on her service. From Julie Andrews to Frank Sinatra, to Humphrey Bogart and Harvey Perry.

It was such an honor to be listed among their names on her service. Eugene called me up and left a message for me. He wrote me a letter as well and we stayed in contact for a while, waiting for an opportunity to see everyone. Well, when he found out I was coming to New York he said he was going to get all the guys together and we would meet up. It was a dream waiting to come true. I was almost more excited about seeing them than working on this movie. I mean, I grew up with these guys. A thousand memories and places to experience once again, how great it was going to be. I was going home, remembering the way everything was when I first left. But people and places change. And some don't change at all. I knew it was going to be different, but I was still excited. We land at La Guardia airport and as usual, I find my driver with my name on his sign. He told me they wanted to stop by the Production Office right away before going to set.

So we go to the office and I introduce myself to everyone. The Production Manager tells me to go to location right away to be introduced to Joel Grey to start teaching him Shininju. They tell me to look for a Korean guy there who they hired to teach Joel Grey Korean mannerisms and dialects. I got back in the car and they take me over to the set. Wouldn't you know it, it's Coney Island!

My first day back and here I am back at Coney Island. I'm looking at it and it dawns on me that all the rides are closed. The only thing open is Nathan's hot dogs. There was an old man as a security guard sitting at the Ferris wheel we were going to be using. He had been working there for forty years with all the keys to the rides. It was a surreal moment. The memory of thousands of people having fun was no more. But I can't be thinking about that for long because as we arrive, an assistant brings me onto the set.

(First Issue, Premiere Magazine. Centerfold, Steven Lambert and Joel Kramer.)

We walk over to this group of people and I see an Asian guy standing there. I'm thinking this is the guy, this is the coach. I start looking at him and he looks at me. A staring contest ensues and I finally walk over and introduce myself. I say, "hey excuse me, are you Joel Grey's dialect coach?"

He says "yes, my name is Joon."

I introduced myself.

He asks me if I would like him to take me to Mister Grey who is in his trailer and I reply that I would. He is talking to me like a very traditional Asian man like he was going to bow after every sentence. He is very erect with a slight lean towards me, like a monk in a monastery. He starts walking, taking small steps and I am staying back about seven feet as not to run into him. We start heading towards the honey wagons and he stops abruptly and turns around inches away from my face and I take a step back. In my head I am saying, what is wrong with this guy? He tells me he is going to take me to Mister Grey. Well good, I tell him, that's what I want.

He turns back saying, "follow me." He starts to turn away from the honey wagons and towards another part of the set. Moments go by and I am wondering if he knows where he is going. He kept looking back saying, "don't dawdle Steven."

I yell at him, "what the hell is your hurry man?"

Then as if a locomotive was coming to life, he starts to speed up. I began to walk faster after him, as he heads towards where camera is. I yell out to him that the honey wagons were on the other side. He just tells me to follow him again as I say to myself, this guy is a rice cake, he is a little weird. We arrive at camera where I notice Fred Ward and Guy Hamilton in conversation. Suddenly, Joon stops in front of these guys. They turn and look at me. Joon clears his throat and says, "I want to introduce you to my new friend Steven Lambert, the stunt man who comes from California to teach Joel Grey Sinanju."

I am standing there wondering how strange this is. Joon smiles and continues on. "He is looking for Joel Grey, do you know where he is?"

I got embarrassed as this was not what I had wanted. Firstly, Joon had said he knew where Joel was which turned out to be false. Secondly, I had no intention of interrupting the Director and main actor who were clearly having a conversation. Boy, I felt this guy put me in a bind. What was this guy doing? Now I have everyone on set looking at me, wondering what is going on. All of a sudden everyone around me starts laughing. I can't help it and start laughing as well. I don't understand what is happening but I laugh anyway. Joon puts his hand on my shoulder. He looks at me and in a Brooklyn accent says, "Steven you're not very observant, are you. It's nice to meet you, my name is Joel Grey."

I just went oh no, what an idiot! I can't believe it and we all burst into more laughter. They explain it was a set up from the beginning and I fell for it perfectly.

"Wow. What a great makeup job," I say. I even see Glenn Randall in the background laughing. The hard ass cowboy found it funny as well. After a few minutes of having a good laugh, we get down to business. They ask me if I am familiar with the book series and Sinanju. I told them I was a kid from Brooklyn and wasn't a big reader, but I went to the bookstore and brushed up on them and there was a lot. I said, "listen, I know a lot of styles and I can show you some ideas right now." Fred came over and introduced himself. I shook Guy Hamilton's hand and I spoke out, "how cool is this?"

He looked at me for a second and responded in his English accent, "how cool is what?"

I said, "working with the guy who did four James Bonds." He smiled. I asked Fred if he had taken any Martial Arts before and he said no. Joel was a dancer, but he hadn't any formal Martial Arts training either. I've already thought about it and I had realized that I could teach them all these styles and forms that I knew, but what would really make Sinanju special would be something I didn't know. Something very few people, if anyone, did. I was familiar with a style called Dim Mak, which is also known as the "Death Touch" through various readings.

It is supposedly an energy that comes out of a grandmaster's body with a kick, punch or even block. You could be five feet away and the energy would knock you down on your back. A single touch of the finger on a pressure point would send you into convulsions. Joel Grey's eyes lit up and Guy Hamilton nodded. "That's a masterful idea," he beamed. "Can you show me an example?"

Now I loved showing people different styles and techniques, but this was a tall request. I told him I could show him a fake example and he could look it up later.

Guy steps in front of me and asks in a deep authentic British accent, "if I ask you to show me, can you show me without hurting me?"

I responded with, "you know what they say Mister Hamilton-"

He puts up a hand, "oh, please call me Guy."

I said, "you know what they say Guy, sometimes you don't know your own Dim Mak power. I might have it without knowing it."

He looked at me strangely, before everyone broke out laughing. No, I told him I didn't have it, but I would show and explain. I reached down and touched him between his shoulder and arm and I told him the person would then go into convulsions. I had him touch me on my shoulder and that's exactly what my body did. Go into body convulsions. Then while I was wriggling, I had him touch me in the same place and I stopped.

Everyone loved the idea on the set, they thought it would be funny and it was easy and fast to "learn." Most Stunt people were not used to coming up with things like this, but due to the experience that I had on set and knowledge that I had gained from many Masters and pros in the Martial Art and stunt world, I had learned so much and became good at this kind of stuff. The moves were simplistic which made it easier for Joel to learn. I glanced over at Glenn Randall and was relieved when I saw he was happy with what was happening. When you're not the boss, you have to be careful you don't take the stage away from your Stunt Coordinator. Luckily, he was on my side and I knew I was on a roll.

"THE MASTER CHUN RAP"
(SINANJU STRUT)

lyric by D. Clark
music by D. Russo

NOW I'M GONNA LAY IT DOWN IN THIS FUNKY TUNE
ALL ABOUT A BAD RAPPER NAMED MASTER CHUN
BETTER WATCH WHAT YOU SAY, BETTER WATCH WHAT YOU DO
OR MASTER CHOON'LL CHEW YOU OUT WITH THE SINANJU

HE GOT A PRETTY TIGHT FEE FOR A DUDE SO OLD
CHECK HIM OUT, GONNA COST YOU TWENTY BARS OF GOLD
MASTER CHOON DON'T FLY IF YOU KNOW WHAT I MEAN
I MEAN THE CAT BE ONLY JAMMIN' ON A SUBMARINE

UNCLE SAM GOT A RACKET KEEP THE COUNTRY PURE
BUT THE YELLOW PAGES EMPTY UNDER NAME OF CURE
NO YOU WON'T FIND CURE AND YOU WON'T SEE SMITH
CUZ CHECK IT OUT, THE RACKET DON'T EXIST

SINANJU, IT'S THE MANNER OF THE MASTER, MASTER CHUN
SINANJU, Y'ALL KICK SOME BUTT ON KARATE AND NINJITSU
SINANJU, WELL, I'M RAPPIN' 'BOUT THE MANNER OF THE MASTER CHUN
MASTER CHUN, KICK IT OUT MASTER CHUN!

WELL OUR BAD KOREAN CAME TO TRAIN A DUDE
HE WAS KIND OF BRASH, HE WAS KIND OF RUDE
BUT CHUN DIDN'T LET BAD VIBES ALINGER
SET SOME ATTITUDE ADJUSTMENTS WITH HIS MIDDLE FINGER

MASTER CHUN'S GOT A GIG THAT HE DO SO WELL
HE BE DOOGIN' ON THE BULLETS LIKE A BAT OUT OF HELL
HE CAN WALK ON WATER LIKE JESUS LORD
HE CAN PUT A LITTLE HOLE IN HIS FINGER BOARD

SINANJU, IT'S THE MANNER OF THE MASTER, MASTER CHUN
SINANJU, Y'ALL KICK SOME BUTT ON KARATE AND NINJITSU
SINANJU, WELL, I'M RAPPIN' 'BOUT THE MANNER OF THE MASTER CHUN
MASTER CHUN, BWACKADOW MASTER CHUN!

NOW THE DUDE IS THE BEST, HE AIN'T GOT NO VICE
WHEN YOU VISIT HIS PAD ALL YOU EAT IS RICE
AND YOU'LL TRAIN REAL HARD DOING BREATHING TRICKS
IF YOU LIVE, HE'LL SHOW YOU LESSON '36'.

SINANJU, IT'S THE MANNER OF THE MASTER, MASTER CHUN
SINANJU, Y'ALL KICK SOME BUTT ON KARATE AND NINJITSU
SINANJU, WELL I'M RAPPIN' 'BOUT THE MANNER OF THE MASTER CHUN
MASTER CHUN, BOOGIE DOWN MASTER CHUN!

SINANJU, SINANJU, I'M RAPPIN' 'BOUT THE MASTER, 'BOUT THE MASTER "C"
SINANJU, SINANJU, HE BE LAUGHING AT A WOMAN LIKE MR. "T"

© 1985 Beef n' Brew Music

Steve,
We're looking for a couple million copies around Xmas '85!
Duane

(Here is a song by Producer Dwayne Clark. Son of Dick Clark)

After that, Glenn asked my opinion on what we should do for the obstacle course for the scene in Chiun's apartment. I thought that because it's in an apartment building in New York, we would only need a few things. We could put a railing up, as well as a pole with a couple of two by two posts with different sizes on a swivel. He also insisted on putting a harness and cable on me to hold me up and safety me. I told him that wasn't necessary and could do it for real. That's exactly what you see on film. I always carried a notebook with me and as bad as a sketcher that I was, I could always get my point across. Glenn loved my sketches and asked me to go to props and effects so they could start building them. I did that and then I went back to my hotel to check in.

Talk about a running start. The next day, we went to Coney Island and discussed the scene where Remo runs on the beach and his feet leave the ground as if he was running on air. Glenn told me they would be bringing in a crane. I looked at him and said, "I have a thought. What if we put some plywood down and put some tracks on the dolly with an extended arm and use that with me in a harness?"

268

He looked at me with a straight face and in my head, I'm thinking, uh oh. I knew I had said the right thing, but didn't know if I said it at the right time and the right way. Glenn locked eyes with me and slowly but surely began to nod his head.

"That's a good idea," he finally stated.

I relaxed, relieved he had agreed. "I hope you don't mind me giving you my thoughts, I learnt it in an old Harold Lloyd movie."

Glenn stopped walking and gave me that classic cowboy glare. This was his rodeo and I was just one of the riders, he explained to me. I smiled.

With a smile, Glenn says, "as long as it's not in front of people."

I nodded right away and said, "never!" I explained to him, "you are my boss and are the one that brought me here. My job is not only to perform but to watch your back as well."

He smiled again. We moved on up the beach and Glenn explained they were going to put a mound of sand in the path when Remo is running. He (meaning me) was going to jump through the sand mound and pop out on top. He said they were going to cheat it so when I doubled Remo, I would jump behind the mound. I said, "I have another idea."

He looks at me again strangely and I turn around to make sure no one is watching us - I mean Glenn and tell him my idea. "What about using those funnel slides, it's a plastic tube. What if you insert the tube flat on into the mound and then put another tube going up through the top of it like an "L." I can dive in like a monkey and pop up. You could have a big pot of sand in there and before I pop up, I will throw the sand up and then pop up."

He looks at me and says, "I think I got the right guy."

Right then I knew what people had said about him in the past was true. He was a good Second Unit Director and can coordinate stunts, but could never have an understanding of how to make something work, or put it together. You see, you really have to have had experience physically and mentally to come up with situations and to visually understand how to make things work. I realized he wasn't apt on understanding different ways to make things work and look a lot better, but I was very proud that he had approved of my ideas.

The next scene was by the Ferris wheel. This was the scene where Chiun was going to teach Remo balance, how to deal with heights and things like that. Glenn said he was going to rig a cable system with a few cranes so that I didn't fall when I was climbing it. I looked at the Ferris wheel and asked if we could get it to move. He called down to the set with his walkie-talkie and asked one of the assistants to get a hold of the one and only caretaker who had the keys. That same old man. He was cool.

The caretaker finally arrived and he turns it on and it starts to move. I watch the cable cars swing and move in a circle. At the top, I noticed the cars swing over and behind each other and I knew when I was up there, I had to be careful not to get knocked off.

I asked Glenn if I could climb up there and check it out. Glenn says he doesn't have the rigging and cranes yet and I tell him not to worry, I don't need it. He looks at me like I was crazy before saying, "knock yourself out." So I proceed on doing a Freddy Waugh. Back to the ninja without his suit.

I monkey up there and Glenn can't take his eyes off of me. I'm climbing every which way, experiencing and trying to understand where I can go and what I can do, as I head towards the top. I get to the top and remember back to when I was twelve years old with my sister who was screaming while I was rocking the cage.

Now, at the very top, the only thing screaming at me was the screaming of the wind. I could see for miles and the memories of stoop ball, stickball and skelly came flying back to me.

Then something else came flying at me. It was the adjacent cable car! Oh shit, I forgot about it. It came flying like a rocket. I jumped onto the roof flat, as it passed by, inches away. That was a close one. The cable car comes back towards the ground and as I get close, I jump fifteen feet onto the sand like the ninja. Glenn looks at me and before he can say anything,

I hear another voice. "Man, you are crazy!"

I look up and see it's the old caretaker. I start laughing and comment, "I love when people say that to me."

(Climbing like Spiderman. I mean lamboman. No cables or CGI.)

Glenn thought it was wonderful and I explained to him we don't need any cranes or wires I can do it that way and it will save money and time and I can give you more. He nodded and thought that was wonderful. As we were walking back down the beach, back towards the company, it was around this time that I gathered up the courage to ask Glenn for a request. I said, "I understand you are bringing a lot of stunt people on this show and I would like to recommend two people. Joel Kramer and Mike Vendrell."

He knew of them as they were in our group which was the Stuntmen's Association. I waited with bated breath for his answer and when it came, I almost missed it.

He had said, "yes."

I couldn't believe it! I knew now, I would have some friends who would be behind me on this show. Then he asked me a question.

He said, "we need somebody to double Chiun, do you know of somebody?"

I said, "yes, the chosen one."

He asked, "who is that?"

I said, "a guy named Bernie Pock."

"What the hell is a Pock?" he asks.

I proceeded to tell him who Bernie was. He said that later on today when we went to the Production Office, I should give them Bernie's name and get him on over here as soon as possible. I told him, "yes sir," and took care of it. I'll never forget the first time Bernie and Glenn Randall met. I was on the set taking care of First Unit for Glenn while he was busy doing Second Unit, when Bernie came in. We were in upstate New York in the mountains doing some inserts. Bernie placed himself on a huge boulder about thirty feet high. When Glenn came on the set and asked among other things, where Bernie was, I turned around and pointed and said, "that's him."

Glenn turned and looked over to the boulder and like a Buddha with his feet crossed in a full lotus position and his hands on his knees, there was the Pockman. That was my nickname for him. Glenn asked what he was doing. I said he wanted to reach Nirvana before he met you. Glenn gave me a look I'll never forget before I started to laugh. Glenn didn't have much of a sense of humor, but I was hoping he started to understand mine. The brownstones of Brooklyn. Lunchtime came, but instead of heading to eat, I went right over to props. I asked if they had any "pinkys" or "spaldeens." For those of you who don't know, they are pink rubber balls. Luckily, they had one and I went back to lunch and found stuntman Bernie Pock sitting down to eat. I told him my secret plan and we headed over to Joel Grey and

271

Fred Ward. I went over to where they were eating and said, "hey guys, I challenge you to a game of stoop ball."

Joel, who was eating, pushed his tray away and looked at Fred. "Let's go," he said.

I told them about a great stoop across the street and we went. Guess what? The whole company followed. It was me and Fred versus Bernie and Joel. I won't tell you who won but we all had fun. By the time we were done, there must have been a hundred people watching. There was no doubt about it now, Steven Lambert was back in Brooklyn.

After far too long, this punk kid was home. We won, whoops. I was on cloud nine as I went over to ask the First Assistant when I could teach Joel Grey. We set up the times, and in the morning I got to teach him on set. As I watching teaching him, I showed him a Tiger kata and at the end he applauded. He was fascinated by it and he wanted to learn it.

He said, "if I teach you a dance, you can teach me this Tiger form."

I agreed, having flashbacks to Neil teaching us moves for the school dance in this city so long ago. He decided to teach me a dance from the play he won a Tony award from, "Cabaret." In a week he wanted to go on set and he would show the Tiger form and I would perform the dance from "Cabaret."

He thought that would be hilarious. Especially when I realized that every time I practiced, he would sing.

After a week we each knew about twenty moves and we went on set at Coney Island. He went first and did the tiger form and it looked pretty good. Then I did the dance from "Money Makes The World Go Around." I had to make it a big show. I had secretly memorized the song, "Life Is A Cabaret," as Joel constantly sung it to me as I practiced and I started singing it in my beautiful Brooklyn voice. Well, everyone cracked up all around me, applause and hollers abounded on how ridiculous I must have looked. I can take. I looked over at Joel who was the only one with a straight face on and there was Chiun staring right at me.

(Joel Grey performing the Sil-Lum Kung Fu side step.)

After I had finished my song and dance routine, he looked at me funny and said, "I never told you to dance and sing, just to dance. You gotta listen to your Director! That wasn't even the right song." Laughter spread around me and I nodded and looked at him with a serious face before we both began to smile and exploded into laughter while he repeated a line that he used in the movie. "You move like a pregnant yak."

This created even more laughter and I knew this moment was one I wasn't going to forget. I tell ya, it's a good thing he didn't make me dance to "Ragtime," you know the musical where all those immigrants to Ellis Island? I only say this because I soon found myself on a tug boat with the other crew and cast heading towards this beautiful view of Ellis Island and that beautiful woman, lady liberty. She was magnificent, even with all that scaffolding around her, I thought about how majestic she was and how we obtained her.

Do you know out there? She was a gift from a French sculptor who declared that any monument would be a reminder of the joint efforts of the American and French peoples. She is a robed version of the Roman goddess, Libertas and bears the date of July 4th, 1776. And guess what, she almost didn't come. We couldn't afford to bring her. I caught a glimpse of her face above the scaffolding and smiled at her. I wish I could tell you that she smiled back, but I said to myself, honey, I'll see you in a little bit up close and give you a big kiss. And that I did. I thought about how she meant so much to so many, including some of my relatives. I thought how proud I was to be the first and only stunt man to ever work with this lady. We get to the island and we all hop off.

As a kid, I had been here many times, but today it seemed like I understood why she was here and how important she was in the past and just how important she would be to people in the future. Glenn wanted to go up and talk about where we were going to put the cables for the scenes on the statue herself. I looked at him and puffed up my chest. "Cables? I thought we went through this already, I don't need cables and I can do more without them," I stated. Glenn laughed and said he understood, but I was going to be over three hundred feet high at times. They were going to have catchers which was fine, but I didn't want any cables to get in my way. I can tell by his face, he doesn't quite understand what I mean. I knew once he watched me in action, he would see the freedom of movement I had without any wires on my back. I finally convinced him and we moved on. Don't get me wrong, safety is always first on my mind, but I knew what I could do and how I could do it safely.

(Lady Liberty was good to me. To this day I have been the only one allowed on her.)

Stuntman Joel Kramer and Mike Vendrell were going to be there too watching my back as well. I was so glad they were there, as it is important to me to always try and get people who have helped you in the past, onto a show in return. I was always brought up to believe you help others when they help you. That is an important thing to remember in and out of this business. In this case, giving my friends Joel Kramer and Mike Vendrell work. I felt safe and confident with them and I didn't have to worry about safety too much as I knew they had my back. I had a couple of off so I decided to sit on the cement base of the statue, about thirty to forty feet high. I looked down and watched production busy at work below and above me. I was thinking how wonderful the view was when I hear someone yelling up at me. I look down and see my boss, Glenn Randall. "Hey, I heard about what happened back in Los Angeles," he yells.

I put my hands to my mouth and said, "I can't hear you Glenn, do you need me?"

He yells back, "no, I just heard there was an accident on Airwolf. There was a helicopter crash and Reid Rondell was in it."

Glenn's words echoed up to me and on the third echo, it hit me what he was saying. I jumped up with shock and yelled out to Glenn. "Did I hear you right? There was an accident?"

He yells back, "yes, Reid Rondell died."

Now Reid and I were good friends. He came from a long line of stuntmen. His father and brother were famous stuntmen and it ran in his blood too. I ran downstairs to Glenn and he confirmed the worst. Like a sledgehammer in my stomach, I was crushed. For the first time, tears started running down my eyes uncontrollably as I remembered the good times we had together. Every time he had two jobs in one day, he would offer me one of the jobs as we were the same body structure and height. I stood there for half an hour just in total disbelief. It was the first time I ever cried for a friend. It was a very sad and unfortunate day on the base of the Statue Of Liberty. Moments like that are always etched into your mind. It goes to show how dangerous this line of work can be.

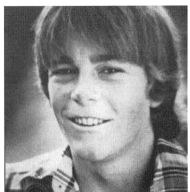

(Stuntman Reid Rondell, he was the best.)

I did have a funny and unusual happening on lady liberty though. Some may say it was funny, some may say it was sad and other may say it was unusual. Some others may say, okay fine, I'll get to the story. We were doing the sequence where Remo confronts the three construction workers high up on the statue in the construction elevator. One was action actor Frank Ferrara. I always thought of him as the stunt godfather of New York. He was a big man, with a heart that matched in goodness, humor and talent. I will miss him tremendously, the reason being that at this time in the period of my book, I have just received a little note that he passed away in January of 2017. It is always a sad day when a truly good person leaves us.

(Actor Fred Ward and his three Musketeers hanging out together.)

We get to the part where Remo is fighting the bad guys by the statue of liberty.

(Gene Lebell chasing Steven Lambert. Listen to this one.)

One of the funniest moments in the history of stuntmen that wears pink gi uniforms. I was picked with two others when they cut to get Gene out. So when they did, I ran over with the other guys and then I stopped them, pushed them aside. I could not help myself. Now for those of us who have wrestled Gene sometimes, he does not ask you to say the word "Mata", which means give up. Sometimes he asks you a question which is simply who is better looking and then you say, "you are Gene."

Since we always played with each other I knew I had him right where I wanted him. He was helpless in the cement. I looked down and just could not resist taking one hand, reaching down and tapping him on the face. Then the other hand.

Then I ask the question, "who is better looking?"

He just looked up at me and said, "no show, you are ugly. Now if you don't get me out of here, I am going to kill you."

I knew it was then time to get him out. So I reached my hand out, grabbing his and brought him halfway out. Then I released his hand, causing him to fall back in. Now he was really upset, so I pulled him out immediately. I quickly ran away as I knew he could not catch me in a foot race. My pal Gene. Much respect.

Now up on the statue, there was also stuntman Joel Kramer and oh yeah, one more stunt man. Let's call him "stuntman." Why do I say that?? Let me explain. Remo has to wrap a rope around one of the guys and tosses him out of the elevator cage. We had rehearsed this a few times before, all the way up to where he goes out of the cage two or three hundred feet high. At that height, if you fall, another hundred feet don't matter. He's on a double cable and we all made sure he was good and safe. So it got down to the moment we were doing it and Guy Hamilton and Glenn Randall called action from down below. I'm doubling Remo and have to knock him out of the cage. So that's what I try to do. Then I tried to do it again. And again. He just wouldn't go. I look at the stunt man and see his face is white as a sheet. His eyes are popping out of the sockets.

He has a hold of the elevator's cage door like a vice and won't let go. I say to him, "let go, J.P." Whoops, let's pretend I just didn't his name.

The walkie talkie on the floor comes to life and Glenn Randall asks what the matter was, as we went past our mark.

I turned back to the stuntman yelling at him to "go out, go out." He won't move an inch as I look at Frank Ferrara, trying to persuade him to let go. Then I look over to Joel Kramer and what do you think he is doing? He is laughing his backside off. I mean if you think about it, it was funny to everybody but Glenn Randall. Glenn radios back up and asks what is going on? I told him we had to cut, that we are having a problem. He cuts and I told him I would tell him what was wrong in a second. He came back on the walkie, pissed, wanting to know what was going on. I didn't answer him. I didn't want to get this stunt guy in trouble so I didn't tell him the problem. Joel, Frank and I all try to convince him and he says he'll be ready this time.

277

He said he was sure and we told Glenn we were ready to go again. In my head I'm thinking, this shouldn't happen on a movie. It may look scary, but if you have experience, it isn't. I keep telling myself, I didn't pick him, I didn't choose him. I felt bad for him at the same time, but he assured me he was ready.

I told Glenn we had taken care of the situation and we were ready now. The elevator goes back down to first position and we roll again. We get to close our spot and I go to throw him out. I try again. He doesn't go. I can't believe it. I told him he had to go, he would be fine. He said he would be ready in a second. I'm yelling we gotta go, we gotta go. We get to our mark and Glenn comes back on the radio and boy is he pissed. He is demanding what is going on! I tell him we are having a problem and he wants to know what that problem is.

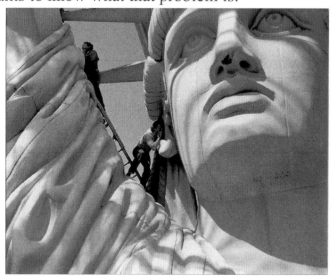

(Joel Kramer, whispering into the ear of Lady Liberty. That's a first and a last.)

I look at the stunt man and I tell Glenn that this stunt man isn't going out. Glenn wanted to talk to him and he tells the stunt man to do it with other choice words I would rather not say, they weren't good. We go back down to first position. We start to go up and Glenn radios me again.

He says, "Steven, if he doesn't go out this time, I want you to push him out."

Quietly, I replied, "push him out? Are you kidding? He's scared to death."

Glenn replied if he was all hooked up, just push him out. I knew if I was going to do that, I would have to do it when he least expected it and I wasn't happy about it. I knew it was the wrong thing to do, BUT, you know what they say, the show must go on. So as we got close, I put the rope around his neck and had to give him a palm strike that practically knocked the wind out of him before he could bring his hands down to grab a hold of something. He was rigged up so the worst thing that could happen was a heart attack. Don't laugh, I see you laughing out there. It went perfectly, luckily for me. That night, the stuntman called me up and thanked me.

I said your welcome, but I said, "stuntman (that's his name, not J.P.), I feel the need to explain something to you. I say this because you are a nice guy and my friend. With the utmost respect, if there are some things you don't have the heart for, just don't do them. Number one, you could hurt yourself and number two, you can hurt others. Number three, which is the only one who doesn't give a damn what happens and who only cares about time and money, is the company. Number four, which is the worst. You make Glenn Randall look bad. And now what you have done to yourself is put a bad light in front of your face and it is going to be difficult at times, to get work from other people. You see things like that spread. People talk. I won't, but other people do."

For all you people out there, remember to take the right path. The weekend was here, no work and all play. Locations are wonderful. A lot of benefits and time off and you get paid anyway. I set my sights on visiting some friends I grew up with. I was going to see my old pals from Avenue B and 96th street. First time since I left Brooklyn at the age of thirteen. Eugene, Neil, Harry, Mordechai, Steve Lees, Steve Ellis, and one of the Twerp twins. They would all be there. This is going to be extremely fun and fulfilling. We were going to have a catch in Central Park. I told them to bring their baseball gloves, as I always carried mine in my stunt bag. We meet up at one in the afternoon on Saturday and I am the first one there. Then they show up, all in Eugene's car. We all hug and I recognize everyone right away. The feelings that came over me are hard to describe, I hadn't seen these guys in eighteen years. We sit and talk about the old times and about life. Jeffrey Elkins, they couldn't get a hold of him, the twerp twins (one passed away, a bit of bad news.) It was wonderful seeing them. Eugene opens the trunk and they pull out their baseball bats, balls and Mordechai even had a boombox. But the one thing he did have, he was still a yarmulke boy. I couldn't believe it. I took it off his head and put it on mine and started my Baruchas.

Everyone laughed, even Mordechai saying, "some things never change, Steven." As a side note, we went back to Brooklyn and we took a picture of all of us in front of Mordechai's house and you can clearly see a half naked man cheering out the window. It was just like Mordechai's father used to do when he yelled at Mordechai not to go with us. How strange? It was like going back in time.

(Déjà vu. A moment in time. Eugene, Mordi and Neil.)

What an anachronism. Whatever that means, all I can tell you is get your dictionary out and look it up. Hours go by and we are having a great time playing ball. We decide to rest and get a bite to eat. We had Sabrett's hot dogs with New York onions and sauerkraut. I had three. We got back to the cars when we noticed the trunk latch was popped on Eugene's car. When he opened it, everything was gone. In my head I am thinking, oh man, that's too bad. The stuff was stolen. To me it was a sad thing, but not the end of the world. Then I looked up and saw the reaction each one of them had. As the seconds progressed, I realized that my friends around me were in utter shock and just couldn't take it. They got more adamant in the fact that their stuff was stolen and it just was the worst thing ever. It was just a few bats, balls and gloves as well as the boombox, but to them, it was as if they lost their most prized possessions in the world.

I said, "relax guys, it's no big deal."

They look at me with such confusion, I just didn't understand. They explained to me in such a way that really broke my heart.

"That boombox took me over a year to save up for," Mordechai managed to say.

"That bat was the only one I could afford, it's three years old," Steve Ellis cried out.

"We don't have money to buy new ones," Steve Lees admitted.

I realized I had said the wrong thing. Yet, I still didn't fully understand the gravity of the situation, the real reason, until the next day when we made plans to go out to lunch at a Chinese restaurant in Chinatown. The evening after we played ball in Central Park, I decided to surprise them from their loss earlier. I went to several sporting goods stores and bought all the guys a baseball glove, each a baseball and each a baseball bat. In fact, I bought two of everything. I went to an electronics place and bought Mordechai a boom box worth three times the amount of his old one.

It was twice as big with twice the features on it. It even had a microphone on it, it was top of the line. We met outside the restaurant the next day and they came driving up. I opened my trunk and I took out all the bags and gave it to them. There was such glory and happiness that came out of their faces like I had never seen before. To me it was no big deal, it was just a simple good deed for my friends. To them, it was everything. Like they had just received a million dollars each. I stood there as they hugged and thanked me. I had never seen anybody so ecstatic in my life over a bunch of bats and balls. We go into the restaurant, some of them have their wives and girlfriends and they are all thanking me. I tell them to forget about it, and we open up the menus.

Everything is going so wonderful and I felt so blessed. As we are looking at the menus I hear on my left, Neil say to Steve Ellis, "you want to share some chicken fried rice?"

Then on my right, I hear Mordechai say to Steve Lees, "you want to split some egg fu young?"

I hear this going back and forth and I look up and say, "hey guys, just order whatever you want on the menu. It's on me."

All of a sudden, Mordechai looks up and the air seems to change. Without looking at me, Mordechai turns to Eugene and asks if he wanted to split some shrimp lo mein. I said, "no guys, order whatever you want, whatever you want, it's on me. Don't worry about it. You have given me a huge gift. The gift of friendship, seeing everyone."

They look at me and say very firmly, NO. All of a sudden, we went from a happy go-lucky group of friends to a very serious and tense group of friends. As their conversation continues it is clear that they don't want to order whatever they want, they just want rice or to split one thing. They explain to me they don't have very much money and I told them to never mind about the money, I would pay for it. I still don't understand what the big deal is. I find myself arguing with my friends when we were in heaven a few seconds ago. Mordechai gets up and excuses himself to the bathroom. Then Neil excuses himself and goes to the bathroom, followed by several of the girls at the table. Eugene is sitting next to me and whispers that he wants to show me something outside.

We go outside and he explains to me that these guys are broke and they are embarrassed. They don't want me to pay because it would make them look bad in front of their wives and girlfriends. I said, "look Eugene, you are my friends. I want to pay for it." I go back into the restaurant and sit back down. I explained to them that I hadn't seen them in years and it was an honor for me. Please, let me do this.

I told them I understood things weren't going right but I wanted to do something to give back to them for all the things they did for me in the past. They began to open up and tell me that they don't have jobs, many of them don't even know what they wanted to be. They are thirty years old and still don't know what they want to be.

I thought to myself, boy if I was still here, who knows what I would have become. If it wasn't for my grandfather and grandmother, I would probably be in the same situation they were.

I felt terrible and it was then and only then I realized how really lucky and blessed I was to get out of a situation that may have never give me an opportunity.

(Brooklyn. Some of The Avenue B Boys.)

These guys were smart and talented. Eugene had the talent to be a comic book superhero artist when we were kids and could draw like anybody in the present day. Mordechai, who came from a religious background was a smart guy. Steve Ellis was a smart guy as well as Steve Lees. But realizing they didn't have the guidance and mentors like I had found in Doug Wong and Sil-Lum Kung Fu, realizing the string of fortunate events I had gone through never happened to the rest of my gang, that really struck me hard. I grew up big time at that moment. I opened the menu and ordered almost everything they had. It cost me six hundred bucks and I was glad to pay for it. We had a banquet and it made them feel better that we understood each other's positions in life. This was an experience I had never had up until then. At the end of the feast, I realized deep down the amazing opportunities that I had been given. I couldn't comprehend how much they were suffering until they told me then and there and it broke my heart. During that lunch, yes, we all broke down and gave each other hugs. I see now that I had nothing when we were kids, and now I have everything so to speak. I had developed a numbness on other people's situations, but now I have been brought back to reality and I understand that I am so fortunate. You out there, don't let yourself get that way.

Always stay humble and be thankful each day for what you have, because there are others who have much less. After the lunch, that was the last time we all saw each other. I tried to get everyone back for another meeting but it never happened. I think they were uncomfortable about seeing me again with the situations they were in. Punk kids from Brooklyn don't want to show their weaknesses, not even to their friends. A part of me understood that and a part of me was absolutely broken inside. In a moment I am going to ask you to stop reading. Yes, I am serious. I'll still have a ton of crazy stories when you get back. I want you to take a few minutes and think about the people that have had an impact on your life. Maybe it's your parents or your friends. Maybe it's your next door neighbor that gave you guidance when all was lost. I want you to take the time to reflect on how that person changed your life, and how their lives might have been changed as well. For better or for worse. Then I want you to thank that person, even if you think they don't need to be thanked. Because it is in that moment that you can stop and truly reflect back on the journey that has brought you to this very moment. You may be old or you may be young, but someone has brought you this far. Now is the time to show your appreciation, to give back what they have given to you. So go ahead and do that, I'll wait. Finished? Good.

You see, I had no idea that my past with my friends, running up fences, learning how to deal with certain situations, would give me something that I would be able to use to better my life. Now being here, where it all had started, I had come face to face with my possible future, had I not been whisked away to sunny California. I was home yes, but I knew now that home would never be the same place that I remembered so many years ago, ever again. As Snagglepuss in the cartoon used to say, "exit stage left."

Let's head south of the border. We were filming the rest of *Remo* down in Mexico. As I sat on the plane, I was going through a series of nettled emotions. Not because I hated flying, but because of an incident that took place when I was in my teens. Let me explicate. Hey, hey, take notice. That's a big word I just used. Thanks, Siri. I remember it now, clear as day. I was about eighteen years old and a few of my friends wanted to go down to Tijuana, Mexico to spend the weekend. We arrive and the first brilliant idea my friends have is to stop at this little hole in the wall cantina. Please, let me set this scene for you. We walk down this long narrow corridor, with just a whisper of light coming down on us. We are listening to noise in the foreground. I take one look at this place and know it is trouble. It looked like a prostitute bar, run down and hidden in the shadows.

I told my friends we should find someplace else to go, but when three guys outside the bar came over to us trying to coax us in, they took the bait. I had reservations at first and kept on insisting no, until I finally gave in with a bad feeling going through my body, thinking this was going to be a mistake. Intuition, that's a good Martial Art practice. I should have followed it. We follow this guy and he sits us down at a booth. Then proceeds to ask if we want a beer. Now at this time, I haven't touched a drop of alcohol in my life. I was a Joe jock athlete, pure as Russian rain and wasn't about to change that. Besides, to me, beer looked like piss. (Hey don't laugh I'm serious.) The bartender, a mountain of a man with a dirty mustache, walks over and yells out. "Gringos, how many beers you want?"

My friends nod yes and tell him. When his gaze finally gets to me, I take a moment and say to myself, I feel like I'm in a Humphrey Bogart movie. Then I say, "none for me."

He pauses a moment and nods his head. "Bueno. Quatro Cervezas, necesitas beber," he says.

Now I don't know a drop of Spanish, but I figure he understood me. I sit back and look around and spot several women in the corner eyeing us seductively. I shake my head and know this place is trouble. The bartender returns with a tray of beers. Four of them. He gives my friends three of the beers on the tray. Guess where the fourth one goes? In front of me.

I look up at the cisco kid and say, "I told you I didn't want any."

He looks at me with a glare and says in broken English, "twe nty doll ars."

I reply in perfect English, "I told you I didn't want one. I ain't given' you twenty dollars."

He demands again to pay up. "Ahora."

I shake my head even firmer and say, "I didn't order a beer, I ain't paying you nothin'."

The bartender clenches his fist and in a flash, strikes up at me as he aims for my face. I weave back out of the way, as his hand hits my breast pocket. Inside my breast pocket was an English-Spanish dictionary I had brought along. We both watched as it sailed out of my pocket, flipped through the air and landed smack in front of the cisco kid. He picks it up and realizes what it is, looks at me and laughs. He thumbs through the pages amusingly. He stops and his eyes scan the page vehemently.

He looks up and says, "you know what "Maricon" means?"

At the time I knew it was a bad word, but only when I returned back to Los Angeles did I find out I was right. I shook my head, at the same time trying to ward off one of the women who was making an attempt to sit on my lap. My friends quickly handed over their twenty dollars and proceeded to get up. I stood up too, but my wallet was closed for business. I said, "not from me, my amigo." I started walking over to the door as the waiter followed me. He was quickly joined by two other employees who were eager to start a fight. My friends trailed behind me, unsure of what to do. The waiter moved in front of me and blocked the door. I circle shuffled, spun between him and the door before he even knew I was outside. He immediately turned around and tried to grab and punch me as everyone else came piling out of the bar, including the two other henchman - I mean employees. One of the henchmen threw the first punch and I quickly blocked it and jumped back. More punches came and I spent the next few seconds, which seemed like an eternity, bobbing and weaving, dodging and diving. I managed to land a kick across his knee and the guy flew smack on his back. But you can only evade for so long before someone gets a punch in, and that's exactly what happened.

A fist to the back of my head. I spun around with a devastating left hook, connecting to his face. He instantly went down. Three others came from nowhere, now there are six. Punches flying everywhere and not one of my friends in sight. Just my luck, I'm hanging out with a bunch of cowards. I am screaming for them to help me and they are just watching the show. I decided enough was enough and proceeded with a flurry of punches on all six of them as I myself, was getting hit in return. When I realized I was fighting a losing battle, I looked up. Up ahead, across the street, I spotted a policeman. Oh thank God, I thought. I ran over, almost getting hit by two or three cars, and waved my hands to get his attention. I shouted my defense to him in English as these crazy bastards who had just tried to give me a beating, arrived behind me. They shouted things at the policeman in Spanish too. When they had finished, he looked at me and said, "listen to me. You do not fight back."

Huh? What did that mean? BAM! A fist landed in my side as the men converged on me. I wasn't about to give up. I blocked and evaded their punches at the same time, looking at the police officer, begging him to stop these guys. Yet, I was outnumbered and already bloody and swollen from the first confrontation. Then something heavy collided with my back and my legs gave way. I fell down, momentarily stunned. I turned on my knees, looking up and saw the policeman, his baton raised for another strike. I tried to get up but the pain was so intense, I couldn't move. I was battered but not beaten. I looked up at the cop who spit on the ground and leaned down to me. The smell of tequila was fresh on his breath.

"If you raise your hands again, you go to jail," he spat.

I looked at my friends through the blood and tears in my eyes and saw them watching, white as a sheet. I asked him, "what do you mean?"

He simply repeated, "you raise your hands and move again, you go to jail."

The policeman's words churned in my head, the word "jail" burning up my thoughts. Then the attacks came again. Pain seared through my body as I was helpless to protect myself. I had to get away, I had to run. Gathering what was left of my strength, I bolted past the oncoming attacks and flew towards the car. Wheezing and seeing stars, I looked back to see my friends behind me. Finally, seven to eight blocks away, I stop and turned to my friends who were trying to keep up and said the words, "let's just get the hell outta here, you freaking macho men!"

We made it to the car and we all got in and floored the gas pedal. When I caught my breath, I was screaming at my friends for just standing there, I was just ready to beat them up. I could have been killed!

They apologized profusely stating they had no idea what to do, they didn't want to go to jail. Our weekend long trip came to an end an hour after we had arrived and we all agreed getting back to America was the only smart thing to do. Ever since then, until today, I would go crazy when anyone ever mentioned going to Mexico. I didn't care where in Mexico, Tijuana was all of Mexico to me. Now here I was, returning to that despised land of previous beatings, where I swore I would never return. I think I'm getting a headache. I cleared my mind and turned to focus on the job at hand. The next few days filming in Mexico went well. I got to work with some canines as well.

The scene where Remo is being chased by the Dobermans, that was me. I decided to play a game. Cat and mouse, and see how close I could let the dogs get before they nipped me in the butt. Which, believe me, they did a couple of times. Not only the butt but the arm, the leg. It felt like I was being chased by that monkey in my grandparent's apartment building all over again.

Rats! You want to laugh? Picture this. For this next gag, I am happy to say that the audience who was the cast and crew, thought I was a barrel of laughs. They had provided me with a certain type of wetsuit for protection, but because I thought it was going to limit my movement too much, I just put a couple of long shin pads on without them knowing.

In this stunt, several rats are supposed to crawl up my pant leg and I was to put my hand down right on my upper thigh and stop them. As they began rolling, I tried to do just that, but the rats were faster than I thought and I was too late!

The next thing I know, I felt a sensation and it wasn't a calming one. This feeling was like needles going into my two hangin' matzah balls. I reach down to remove the rat, but this thing is on good. I'm supposed to fall backwards through this window, but I decide it wasn't the right time.

You see this feeling was coming over me, the pain was arising, so I decided not to. Below me they are yelling, "fall, fall."

I yell back, "rat has my balls, my balls!"

Laughter erupts from down below. I slowly kneel down and try to climb carefully down to the mat, my hand having a firm grip on the rat whose claws were more than likely shredding my manhood like swiss cheese. At the same time screaming. Glenn Randall is cracking up, I see his teeth stained with chewing tobacco.

I don't find it funny at all! I look around as I am in pain and everybody seems to be laughing. The only sound that is coming out of my mouth is, "OOO, OOO, AWO, AWO, IT HURTS!"

I start pulling down my pants as the trainer comes over to remove the rat. I turn around, not wanting anybody to see certain things and I am down to my underwear just struggling. The trainer tries to grab the rat, but I won't have it, he might touch my matzah balls.

I finally take the rat out myself, putting it in a chokehold and disarming the rat from my manhood, one leg at a time. I hand it to the trainer as I watched everybody crying with laughter.

I hear Guy Hamilton speak up with his English accent. "Steven, you are lucky the little critter didn't eat your worm."

The only expression on my face was horror at looking at little spots of blood down below as I held myself. I take a quick peek to make sure everything is still intact. It was, luckily.

(The Doberman was cabled and harnessed. Not I.)

They are shouting about having a medic take me to examine if there were any injuries, but I wasn't going to let anyone look!

I said, "give me some hydrogen peroxide," as I went around the corner where nobody could see and poured it all over. When I came out, imagine this, two shin pads on one leg and a pair of boxers looking like I went to the bathroom in my pants. The dogs got me from behind and the rats got me from the front. I was finished with live animals for that shoot. It was comedy central thanks to a punk kid from Brooklyn. P.S. I smartened up and put on the wetsuit for the next take. Print. The next day, Guy Hamilton comes out with a rat in his hand and asks, "Steven, you want to touch my pet rat?"

That was the last straw and I burst out laughing. That was a funny moment. We wrapped with the critters and headed to film in the wilderness of Mexico. The next stunt was not a difficult one, in fact, it was the easiest thing I could do. I had to double Remo Williams running. That's it. Piece of cake. The Second Unit was set up on a road on top of a cliff, looking down at the canyons below. I had to run from point A to point B, over logs and through brush and through ravines. Before I began to make my way down the cliff's edge, Glenn Randall waved me over and held up a small tank, not much bigger than a softball.

"Don't forget your three minute air tank Steven," Glenn said. He handed me the air tank and a walkie-talkie. I looked at him like he was crazy. I'm running, not jumping out of a plane.

"I'm a gazelle," I assured him. This had to be a joke, so I took the walkie-talkie.

Glenn tried to explain to me that the atmosphere is thinner at this altitude and breathing would be harder.

My comment was, "huh? What the hell are you talking about? Altitude? All I'm familiar with is a little attitude." Glenn shook his head and smiled.

He replied, "you're going to need this mister gazelle."

I replied, "are you mocking me? Watch this."

I headed way down the ravine over some heavy terrain. Took a good five minutes and arrived at my end mark. I left the radio there. Then I walked back keeping an eye on Glenn and when he raised a red flag, I stopped. That's where he wanted me to start. It was about a city block away from point B. He raised the red flag again and off I went. The camera began rolling and I started my run. Five seconds went by, running down ravines, jumping over rocks. Fifteen seconds went by, trying to find some wind as I'm hoping over a log, going through some branches. Twenty five seconds go by, sliding down embankments and wheezing sharply. Yes, I'm wheezing! I was gasping for breath! I say to myself, "what is going on?" A minute goes by and I find myself having to move in different directions and slow down to catch my breath. All while making it look like I was changing my path but really was trying to catch some wind in my lungs. Five more seconds go by and guess what? I am reaching down into my diaphragm, there's nothin'. I am trying to find O2. I look out to my stopping point, realizing I have another twenty seconds. I barely reach the end of the run and I collapse, gasping for breath. Rolling over, looking up to the sky with my mouth wide open and my nose dripping. I was drinking in the air. The radio comes to life and Glenn says, "great job, let's do it one more time."

Clicking on the walkie-talkie, I almost fainted! "Again!?" I had no choice at this point. I took a deep breath and guess what I said? "Hey Glenn, can you do me a favor? Can you send someone down with that air bottle?" I wait for his response, stars dancing in my vision. All of a sudden, I hear the switch on and then those words of wisdom come over the airwaves.

"Air tank? I thought you were a gazelle," I heard him say back. In the background, I hear the laughter of the crew. "There's no way we are coming down there, you had your chance."

I clicked the walkie-talkie back on saying, "pleeeeaaaase?"

The reply, "no. Go back to A mark."

I couldn't believe it. I picked myself up and walked back to the starting spot, which I prolonged as I was trying to gain my composure. Trying to put my ego back into my pocket and oxygen into my lungs. I threw both hands up in the air at camera, with two fingers showing. It t'was funny. I managed to do it two more times, barely. They printed it each time. And yes, of course when we got back to base, it was all over the place. For two days every now and then, instead of "hi Steven," from the cast and the crew, I would get, "hi, Mister Gazelle."

My friend Joel Grey saw me and said, "hey I heard next time you'll consider bringing that three minute oxygen bottle."

I laughed. A few days later, I find myself at Churubusco Studios in Mexico City. The beauty, the elegance of this studio and the history is breathtaking. Amazingly that it looks the same way it did long ago. A Mexican treasure. And by the way, so are the stuntmen of Mexico. Well learned from American stuntmen of the past. How do I know this? We had many conversations about it. People like Bear Hutkins, George Robotham, Harry Wills and of course Terry Leonard. Anyway, I'm doing a slide for life from the top of the balcony to the stage floor. I was sitting in a chair on stage, my Remo wig was being put on by makeup when a group of ladies walked by. Right away I notice one of the senoritas in the group. Boy, she was some hot tapatio. My mind started racing a million miles an hour as I watched her. The way she held herself, the way she looked, my heart was just fluttering. She walks over to another makeup artist and they start talking. I can't take my eyes off of her smile, her athletic build and her beautiful eyes. She was what I called, coming from good stock. It's a cowboy term. Little did I know, I would be often telling her that and she would laugh. I want to get up and introduce myself, but I was being called on set. This girl turns around and glances at me for a second time before she leaves. Shit! (How about that, my first curse word, whoops, sorry.) I try to follow, but I was called again to come on set.

I yell, "I am on my way!"

She turns at the sound of my voice and smiles at me. I go to the set and I'm thinking, aw man, I just blew my chance. I'm thinking maybe she is hanging out outside and I want to hurry with the stunt. The crew below isn't ready and I'm waiting and waiting until finally they yell, "Action!"

I slide down the wire to the ground, running quickly to the end and keep on going. I hear the Director yell, "cut", and applause erupts around me. I keep running and make a B-line to the exit door, hoping to catch her outside. I looked around and saw nothing and nobody. I smacked myself in the face, not literally. I ran back inside and found the makeup lady the girl was talking to and she told me that the girl was a soap opera star and she was her makeup artist. Remo needed another makeup artist so they borrowed her and the girl came to ask when she was coming back to her soap opera. I asked her the girl's name and she replied, "Cecilia Camacho."

I asked if she could introduce her to me and she said she would give her a call. Happy, I went back to work and proceeded with the stunts I had to do. A few minutes later I turned around and to my surprise, like an angel, there she was. I had no idea why she came back, but I figured she had another question or maybe those returned looks were the reason. I finally gather the courage to walk over to her and introduce myself. I asked if she could show me around the city since I was new here.

She said, "yes?"

Even that single word was so beautifully formed on her lips. She explained she did not speak English very well and I spent the next forty five minutes grabbing people walking by who spoke Spanish to translate. I got her to understand I was asking her for a date. She agreed and I was doing the Mexican hat dance. Hours later I open the hotel room door and find the call sheet for the next day. It had a note attached that I was to go to the logging camp the next day to take a look at the logs and location where Remo hangs on the tree trunk as it is transported a thousand plus feet above a canyon. Way up there. I get my harness and my pads, knees and elbows, and the next day we go to the location. The logs had a track in the middle of them with an I-bolt, going from top to bottom. Huge metal creations made to look like tree trunks. They have three, one is on the ground, one is hanging a few feet from the ground and the third was strung over the canyon with an octagon platform camera rig on top of the log to look down onto me. They were all thirty five feet long. My boss wants me to go onto the one hanging a few feet above the ground, hook onto the I-bolt connected to the track and slide vertically down from the top to the bottom. I had asked my good friend Mike Vendrell to come along with me. He was told he was going to play a part eventually in the film, but as of now had nothing to do, so I invited him along. I got my harness on in order to show the Director and the Director of Photography how the stunt was going to look. Mike pulled me over and explained to me that there was no bungee cord and that when I slide down thirty five feet, the ending was going to be a dead man's stop. "That abrupt halt is going to cause you some major pain, Steven."

I reply to him, "I know, but I don't want to embarrass our boss by explaining the right way to do this. All the head honchos are here." I look at him and tell him, "I got an angle on this. I am going to try to bear hug the tree the best I can with the inside of my arms and my legs and slow myself down."

Mike shook his head and replied, "I'm going to say something. I don't want you to get hurt."

I say, "Mike, this is my business. I appreciate your concern but I know the hazards and I want you to keep quiet. Don't say anything. Kung Fu promise?"

He said, "yes."

I get up on top with help from a crane, tie myself off to the I-bolt with the help of a carabiner, waiting for the word, "action. This is going to be a wreck, I say to myself. I suddenly realize that the log is too big in diameter to give it a strong hug. My ingenious plan went out the window. If I didn't slow myself down, the laws of physics would put my asshole in my mouth. That's what I call common sense. As Glenn Randall Jr. always said, "it doesn't take the brains of Churchhill to figure this out." I had to do it no matter what the outcome was. It's part of the game. Snug and secure in my harness, I was hanging there like a monkey and waiting for the stunt to begin. It was a mixture of stubbornness and pride at that time, that prevented me from admitting my mistake. I was hoping that my athleticism and flexibility would help me out of this somehow.

I was going to go through with it, knowing that this was going to, as they say, ring my chimes. I knew I got myself into it, but I wasn't going to be defeated by this miscalculation. That's what happens when you are from the streets of Brooklyn. You just do it. I hear the word, "action," and within a second, I tell my brain to let go. It says, oh no, but I don't listen. I try to squeeze, realizing it ain't working, but I'm going down so fast that I feel that my forearms being scraped. I dropped like a monkey out of hell, no bungee to stop me, not that I was given any when I asked. They wanted it all natural and boy was it natural. As I hit the bottom, I hit it going so fast and so hard that the air popped out of my mouth from my stomach. I let out a groan that echoed through the canyon. Michael Vendrell comes running over and unhooks me after thirty seconds as I'm trying to get breath. I fall to the ground in excruciating pain. Everyone looks on in horror as I hold my legs, trying to suck in the pain. It's like when you slam your finger in the door as the harness drove into my legs.

Guy Hamilton says, "my God, it looks like you broke in half, we don't have to do it that fast."

I say to myself, gee, thanks. Everyone looks at Glenn and I speak up, barely getting the words to sound coherent. "No, it's fine. I'm all right." I got up out of sheer will and stupidity and Mike and I walked over to the side behind some honey wagons and took off the harness. The moment I pulled down my pants, I could see black and blue marks starting to form from the straps pulling so tightly from the deceleration.

I look up at Mike and say, "I'm hurt and it's feeling worse as the seconds go by. I hope we don't have to do it this way again, but keep quiet."

My legs burned and pounded but I continued on. I knew I had major pulled muscles. My shoulders felt like a sledgehammer hit them. Thank God they were happy and they agreed later on after I said to my boss, we were going to use bungee cord and put on a tighter I-bolt, to do it again. On the day it went beautiful. Four times, different. Print. The next rehearsal and demonstration was where I was to sit on a log as it was pulled from horizontal to vertical and starts riding across the canyon. This time I put the harness OVER my pants and double shin pads in the leg areas. I was still in pain and I was going to do everything I could to limit any more suffering. They had another dummy besides me, a real mannequin, in case we needed it. This log, they had several I-bolts where you could lock it in and they wanted me in the middle of it. I was to ride the log like a wild stallion before it goes vertical. They had hooked it up directly across this sheer cliffside.

Now when something is that heavy on a cable, it bends and it swings. At this time, they were in a state of confusion as to who or what was going to try this out. The mannequin dummy or the human dummy. They strung cable for this log alongside a cliff wall, a hundred fifty feet high. This is what I notice. Why string the cable right next to this. When the log swings it is going to smack the upside of the canyon wall on its return. After much debate, they finally ask the chosen one, me. "What do you think, Steven?"

Hmmmmmm. "I'd like to see Mister mannequin do it first," I reply. "For a couple of reasons. I want to see if the log hits the canyon wall."

They ask what the other reason was.

I tell them, "so I can visually figure out what my movements are going to be. You see, you have to be one with the movement of the log."

So they agree and put the mannequin onto the log. I watch as the log is pulled into its horizontal position being dragged by a chain and the wire bends as the log starts to swing. Seconds go by as the log comes off the cliff. The weight of it is so heavy, it swings forward to a ninety degree angle closer and closer to the cliff. At its peak, imagine it reversing and going backwards. The weight of it stretches the cable. Smash! Boom! Crash! It hits, with the mannequin between the log and the cliff. Mister mannequin becomes Mister crunch like a pancake. I would have been dead. Huge chunks of rock and dirt explode off the cliff and the log bounced up and down like a slingshot, ripping the head off the mannequin as I watch it do a high fall. As

293

the rest of the crew is having a conversation on what they did wrong, Mike Vendrell and I casually walk over to the crash site and I spot what would have been my arm lying on the ground. Next to that a few feet away is my head.

Mike finds my legs scattered in some bushes. We start talking about it and we decide to go show everybody. I didn't have to say anything, they would understand immediately. They see us walking around the corner, my head in one hand, my arm in another hand. Mike comes around the corner walking my leg saying, "hi, my name is Steven, look at me walk."

I try to keep a straight face before I smacked him with my arm saying, "quiet, quiet."

The Director looks at me and says in his British, butler like way, "you were decapitated! This just won't do."

I said if we could move the cable away from the canyon wall and do it in two pieces, it would work with me on it. Glenn agreed and effects began re-rigging the whole thing. We went to lunch as I went to my room to change. When I came back into the lunch line, that's when I heard something alarming. I was in the back of the line, but when I got up to the front, it was imparted to me that there had been a big argument between Mike Vendrell and Glenn Randall a few minutes ago. All the stress and aggravation that had built up in the day and the fact that we were such close friends, finally took its toll on Mike and he just snapped. Apparently, Mike had gone up to Glenn who was with a lot of heads, including the Director and Producers and started shouting at Glenn that he had no idea what he was doing and anyone that was a good Stunt Coordinator would never have let that happen. He told Glenn he should be ashamed of himself and he had no business doing dangerous things like that and he was going to let everyone know when he got home. Glenn was humiliated and had no choice but to fire him right on the spot, so I learned in the lunch line. I was furious when I found out but understood why Michael did that. I learned Michael went back to the hotel and I went looking for Glenn. When I found him, I told him that Mike had no business doing that, but I would like for him to be forgiven and not be fired. I made it clear I was going to have a talk with him and it would mean a lot to me. I had become like a little brother to Glenn and I understood him. I think he kind of felt the same way and to tell you the truth, I was hoping that he valued me and my talents and succumb to my request. I realized this could cost me my job, but I was just asking.

As far as I was concerned, this was me, my body and my decisions and I appreciated Mike coming to my rescue, but I wouldn't have it. I told Glenn I had spoken to Mike about this before, but he just didn't get it. I asked Glenn to give him one more chance. Sure enough, Glenn had it in his heart to do just that.

When I got back, I went to Mike's room and we had a major conversation where I reiterated what I told him earlier and what I had said to Glenn. I thanked Mike for looking out for me but what he did was wrong. I told Mike to keep quiet and stay away from Glenn and just to do his part.

Mike stayed for another week, but I couldn't get Glenn to put him on film. I was very appreciative. It was a big learning experience because on one hand, it shows the meaning of friendship and brotherhood, which is few and far between with most stunt people. On the other hand, as Glenn Randall still says," it doesn't take the brains of Churchill."

And as I say, "to run a show."

The moral of the story is to keep your feelings in check. If you are concerned about something then by all means bring it up with your superiors. But do it at the proper place at the proper time. Don't let your emotions get the best of you.

That was a lesson we all learned that day. Needless to say, we made the corrections and the stunt went off without a hitch, and my body parts were all intact. I have to tell you though, when I was up there I heard this pinging sound. Ping, ping, ping, among the blowing wind.

(You bet I was scared.)

I radioed to ask what that sound was and they told me it was singing to me.

I asked, "what was singing?"

They told me, "the cables. That's what they do."

Oh good, I thought. It was music to my fears, I mean ears. Fred Ward and the rest of the cast and crew thought it looked great and we moved on. Also that day, being thousands of feet high, I found out the camera men on top of the platform were making bets that I wouldn't let go on the first take. Guess what? They lost a lot of money that day. A smart stuntman would have had a parachute on. I didn't. And here is another thing. A guy like me, unfortunately, never thinks about money. The art of the work, that's what I think about. God bless Glenn Randall, if I was working for somebody in Stunts Unlimited given that this log sequence took two weeks to complete, they would have paid me a hundred thousand plus. They know how. Glenn Randall? A total of eight hundred dollars. That's life. What an adventure!

If you were wondering what happened to Cecilia, if anything ever came out of our meeting, I can say not much. We just went on a few dozen dates together and we fell even more madly in love, but that's a story for another time which we won't get to for a while. A while being a whole paragraph or so. After *Remo,* I went home for a few weeks. I was glad to be back in the good ole' US of A. A few days went by when I got a call to work on the show *Big Trouble.*

I was going to turn it down, but then they mentioned it was starring Peter Falk. With a legend like him, I had to say yes. I was on set two days later in a scene where I was playing a terrorist and he shoots me and I go backwards through a window. I meet him in person, surprised by how small he was (5,7), and I introduce myself. Watching *Colombo*, I always found the way he spoke and his mannerisms to be very funny, but I realized it was actually the way he acted. We talked about the stunt I was going to do and I mentioned to him that I was from Brooklyn.

He said, "ah, I know that place well."

Then I asked, "Mister Falk, may I ask you a question? The film *It's A Mad Mad Mad World* you worked on, what was the funniest experience you had working with all those famous comedians?"

He told me he didn't remember because they were all drunk on that picture.

I looked at him funny. "Drunk?"

He nodded. "If only people knew, everyone on there was drunk! Everyday!"

I shook my head in disbelief. "Even Ethel Merman?" I asked.

He laughed. "She was the worst!"

I asked, "what about Spencer Tracy."

"If you only knew," he replied.

That was a fond memory. A one day affair that will always be on the reel in my mind.

CHAPTER 26
(The One And Only David Carradine. The Best And The Worst.)

I returned home and received a message a few weeks later from someone most unexpected. Guess who the hell it was? The supreme rabbi of Cannon. Listen to the message he left in a sonorous voice. "STEVEN! STEVEN! YOU CALL ME. IT IS MENACHEM GOLAN. ANSWER ME. PICK UP THE PHONE. YOU MUST CALL ME RIGHT AWAY. YOU ARE DOING A MOVIE WITH DAVID CARRADINE AND STEVE JAMES! YOU ARE GOING TO THE PHILIPPINES."

Then the message ended. I played it again to make sure it was really him. Nobody could duplicate that voice. It was him all right. I thought to myself, how about that service. I have a big smile on my face, thinking that was pretty amazing. He is demanding I take this job. Wouldn't it be nice if that happened all the time? I called Cannon and the secretary says that Mr. Golan would like you to come in and see him and pick up a script called Be*hind Enemy Lines.*

I agreed saying, "only if he has a plate of kasha and varnishkes waiting for me."

She said, "what's that?"

I said, "food. You're going to tell him that right? You want me to spell that for you?"

So I did and asked, "what day and time you want me there?"

The response was, "tomorrow. Two pm."

I ended the call by saying, "thank you. Don't forget to give him my message." When I hung up, right away I started doing my version of the Horah. The next day I go into the Director's office, thinking Sam Firstenberg and I are back together again! I knock on the door and call out, "Shmulik!" The door opens and I am met by the beautiful image... of sunglasses. Indoors. Guess who it is? My old friend Gideon Amir. He looked at me with a nod and I quickly glanced past him to see if Shmulik was behind him. When he wasn't, I realized the unavoidable truth. Gideon was the Director. I didn't have the best experience with him as Producer on *American Ninja*, those memories came quickly back, but my mouth started speaking before my brain caught up. "Giddy, what a surprise. How have you been? You are the Director on this film?"

He says, "of course."

I reply, "we're in trouble." But not out loud. Don't let those quotations fool you. It was only in my mind. We sit down and start talking about the script, budget and details about the movie. He tells me David Carradine is starring in it as well as Steve James and Phil Brock. I said, "ah, it's going to be great to see them again." We breeze through the script, stopping whenever there is a piece of action. Already he starts talking about money. "We don't have much money, Steven."

Yep, every time we stopped at a page where there was action, instead of talking creatively, he talked financially.

He said the sentence, "we don't have much money, Steven," over and over again. Nothing about the development of characters or the action. Just the gelt. For you goyim out there, that means money. At the end of our thirty minute meeting, I told him I was going to go home and fill in the blank pages of action, make up a budget and call him when I had finished.

"Not too much money," I hear from him as I leave.

Then I get excited. I am going to say hi to Menachem. Up to the penthouse I go. I walk in, seeing the secretary. "Steven Lambert for Menachem Golan."

With a smile, she says, "please be seated."

She gets on the phone. "Steven Lambert to see you."

A pause and then I hear, "SEND HIM!"

The secretary jerks the phone from her ear.

I laugh. "He's loud isn't he?" I ask.

She shakes her head in disbelief. "I still can't get used to that voice."

I walk in and open the door and there he is. When I shake his hand, he has a big grin on as usual and I immediately say, "WHERE IS MY KASHA AND VARNISHKES? WHERE IS MY FOOD?" He looks at me for a second surprised.

Then he says, "you still a crazy man."

I say to him, "you're still a wonderful man. But crazy too." I think he always admired the way I spoke to him. Like two friends jousting with each other. "Thanks for bringing me back Menahem." It goes over his head like it's nothing, but to me, it meant a lot. I wasn't so sure that I would be welcomed back after telling the head of Cannon I was leaving against his wishes the last time I spoke to him on *American Ninja*. Menahem starts talking about the film and the words, "bigger" and "better" were flung out into the space between us once again. He was excited I was back and I thanked him profusely. Believe me when I say I was dancing down the hall when I left. I read the script when I got home and I must say, if this wasn't a Cannon film, it would have been stellar. As a Stunt Coordinator, my job is the action, not the story, so I promised myself I would do the best I could.

The next day I gave Gideon and Avi, who was back producing, the budget. I explained that as usual when I can, I'll double all the guys so they can save money.

I had to bring in a double for David Carradine however since he was three times my size. He agrees to that and the budget so I go home and think of Joel Kramer. Joel would be great to double David and he was such a great pal of mine. Unfortunately, he couldn't make it. When great friends turn you down, it's always heartbreaking. Sharing experiences with meaningful people is what life is all about. But he mentioned and spoke very highly of another stuntman who was close to his body type named Billy Lucas. I had never heard of him at the time. Joel said that he was a newbie but a goody and that was good enough for me. He was also a former marine and one great stuntman.

How funny life is, for later on along with Joel Kramer, Billy Lucas was also Arnold Schwarzenegger's stunt double. Billy and I became close friends. I agreed to hire Billy, sight unseen, and Joel was thankful for that. An example of the true meaning of friendship. Little did I know how big Billy Lucas was going to become in the future. So now I know we are shooting in the Philippines, and now I am on a personal mission. When I was there shooting the *American Ninja*, the only one, I saw how unfortunate the people were there. Kids would follow us every day on the set, ripped up clothes, no shoes, begging for money. It was very sad and depressing.

So before I left, I went to Walmart and Target stores and spent fifty eight hundred dollars on shirts, jackets, shoes, underwear, socks, dresses and pants. I had five HUGE boxes of kids clothes. My plan was to find the kids on set the first day and do a deed that would end all deeds. It felt wonderful boxing the clothes up. I even bought three hundred dollars worth of school items. Papers, pencils, notebooks, erasers, tons of stuff. When I got to location, I brought the boxes in and I told everyone what they were for and how I was going to be like Santa Clause on the set for all the children. I decide on a Monday, that this was the day I was going to give the boxes of clothes away. The kids have been on set every day and I told them I had something special for them. Right before lunch I stopped in wardrobe and collected the boxes I had brought. I go to lunch and here come the twenty to thirty kids. I wave them over and open the boxes. I pull out pants and give them to a little boy, I take out a dress and toss it to a girl who I thought it might fit. Some shirts I size up and give to two girls who giggle with joy. I give some shoes and socks out. Kids are putting the clothes over their old clothes. Their faces are full of excitement, a few of the kids were actually crying. Mothers and fathers were there thanking me. I must tell you, it made me feel I had really done some tiny speckle of good in the world. They were talking in Tagalog and I got a few Filipino Production Assistants to translate. They told me what I already knew, that these kids were beyond ecstatic. Minutes went by and I handed out even more as new kids came over. I was the

Manila Santa Claus. I was just so happy, what a good deed it was. It wasn't that they got one set of clothes, some got four or five sets per person. It was such a good feeling I had that the day ended with me talking to God. I said, "I hope you are happy."

I actually said that, because I truly was. The next day the sun started to rise and I started to get ready. I got myself to the set and people started arriving to prepare for the day. The call time comes and I start noticing all the kids who always come in the morning for food or coins. I see two arrive, then four, then eight, then sixteen. I begin to notice that they don't have the clothes I gave them on! I walk over and say, "hey what is going on? Where are the clothes I gave you guys? Where are your shoes?"

They aren't answering my questions and just ask for money. I go into my pocket. I always have a pocket full of change. At the same time that I am handing coins out, I ask where the clothes are. "Where are the shoes I gave you?" Not one is answering me, they just want more money and more things. A Filipino Production Assistant comes over and tells me that I won't see them with the clothes on anymore. I asked, "what do you mean?"

He sadly explains to me that their parents take the clothes and sell them for money. They need food and rent more than they need clothes. I'm looking at these kids, their feet all cut up and have dirt everywhere. I just shook my head and realized on that day how common this must be. Just like when the government sends supplies and clothes to ravished nations, they just sell them for money. It's a revolving door of poverty. I learned a lot in that moment, thinking that this really does happen all over the world. As the rain began to drizzle down from the heavens, it just broke my heart. I spent the next few hours getting everything ready for the shoot ahead. I even see my explosive friend, BOOM BOOM!

I couldn't believe he was back. We were going to have such a great time together. I find Gideon and tell him that I have a guy named Billy Lucas to double David. Gideon tells me we have a problem with that and I shook my head.

"David Carradine called me and said he was bringing a friend to be his stunt double," Gideon replies.

I asked what he had done in the past and he shrugs. I told him Billy was the guy I needed to use, he is a real stuntman. I can't use David's friend and I won't. A few days later, David arrives and I meet David and his fiancé/agent. Also with him is this guy who he introduces as his stunt double. I look at this guy who is literally half the size of David. I shook his hand and told him we would talk more in a few minutes. I'm thinking, there is no way this guy is going to pull off doubling David.

He has a completely different body structure. David and I began to talk about Martial Arts and people we both knew, like Doug Wong, Tadashii Yamashita and Chuck Norris. I then asked him about his stunt double and he says he's done everything that he has done in his past films. I tell David that I was going to put him to a test and that is exactly what I did that night. Test results from one to five, five being the best. Zero. To make a long story short, he couldn't roll. He couldn't jump over a two foot wall and he couldn't climb a fence. I rest my case. He's your problem, not mine. He is not going to do any stunts let alone double you. We shook hands and David says he understands. He will use him as his stand in. As I'm leaving the office, I see something flying out of the corner of my eye and I look and it's a fist. It hits me square in the chest and I fall back as a roundhouse kick comes at my face. I double palm strike it down. I'm shocked.

David leans down, holding his shin and says, "gotta be on your feet, Lambo."

That was where my nickname was born. I said to him, "what do you mean? I just blocked it." He smiled before I got serious and told him that kick could have hit me in the face, to please don't do that again. I went outside and talked with David's stunt double. I soon realize what this guy was really here for. The real purpose of this guy. He was David's runner. What kind of runner you ask? I'll leave that to your imagination. Before long, Billy Lucas arrives and I was just in awe of the military aura he had. I liked it. Hard ass, but cool. "Ooh-Rah!" That is what he always said to me. I knew we would get along great and what a wonderfully wacky, crazy, and unexpected time we would have. Boy, was I right. Here are some of the untold Carradine Chronicles.

I spent three days working with five thousand gallons of gasoline and a hundred feet of prima cord we had to spread throughout a mountain. Please, take a moment and picture that. Me and Boom Boom were going to blow up this mountain in a giant explosion. David Carradine said he wanted a shot like Sylvester Stallone in *Rambo* where he comes up from this mountain with a big machine gun and a fireball in the background. I told him if Gideon said we could, I would do it. I talked to Gideon and explained how beautiful and fantastic it was going to look and how David really wants this shot in the film. Gideon said no but David said yes. Who do you think won? David. Gideon gives the okay and I spent three days on this mountain setting the gasoline and prima cord with Boom Boom. We would put red flags wherever we placed them and nobody was to go anywhere near the mountain as we had taped the whole mountain off. A half dozen guards would protect the mountain every night, it was all set up to be a great and dangerous masterpiece. I was excited about this shot with the star of the film since it was part of my Second Unit and nothing and nobody was going to ruin it. I found this hill where David can walk up and reveal himself. I told Boom Boom who was sitting behind me, that when I saw David's chin, I would give the signal to blow the mountain. This was a huge moment and I was ready for it. I had two cameras on it, one wide and one tight. I sent a Filipino Production Assistant down with David. I gave him a walkie to cue him to signal David when it was time for him to walk up the hill. This was the usual procedure. That was my first mistake and it turned out to be the only one I needed. The assistant understood perfectly what to do and I sat down in my chair and rolled camera. I called, "action."

I radio down to the assistant and call for David. I'm sitting there and I start to see David's helmet come over the hill, followed by his face and then his chin. I raise my hand and cue Boom Boom to blow the hill. KABOOM! The hill erupts into a huge fireball. We feel the heat of the explosion. I look at David and here comes, his machine gun by his chest and I'm thinking, something isn't right. His chest is followed by his lower extremities and now I KNOW something isn't right! Here comes David walking up the hill like Rambo, guess how? Butt naked! He wanted a Rambo shot, but here he is getting a Full Monty shot with a helmet on his head and boots on his feet. You got that visual your mind? I do. Forever. The fireball behind him is getting bigger, engulfing the whole frame. I look again and David reaches the top of the hill laughing his ass off! I jump up as his two lower grenades are swinging through the air back and forth for all to see. Do you get it?

I shout, "what are you doing David!?" I look at the cameraman who is dumbfounded and the few women on set who are clasping their mouths in horror. This wasn't Arnold Schwarzenegger, this was a pudgy wudgie David Carradine standing there in the breeze. The Production Assistant that I sent down with him, comes up from the hill and I said, "why the hell did you let him take his clothes off?"

The assistant shrugged. "He told me to be quiet," he replied."

I almost blew a fuse. "Quiet!? This is a movie, it's not a joke. I spent three days putting this together. What am I going to say to the Director?" I'm looking at David and he is five feet away from me in the nude. Not one person is laughing from the crew. I told him to turn around and get his clothes on and he just stands there doing the Kung Fu whooping crane, it was quite a sight to see. I tell my First Assistant to follow me, while others are helping David to get his clothes back on. He is putting on his underwear and pants watching me walk away and shake my head. Meanwhile, the mountain is burning beautifully, all for nothing. The First Assistant turns around and laughs at David. "DON'T LAUGH! This ain't funny!" I snap. He stops smiling, but in my head, I don't know whether to laugh or cry. This is what

David Carradine does to you. For all you people out there that have ever worked with him. Now it's time to inform the Director, I know the only one who is going to get in trouble is me. Not David, not that stupid assistant. Me. So I radio down to Gideon and ask if he was sitting down. He was. I told him what happened and he just said he couldn't believe it. He asked me to come back to set and talk with him. So I do and I explain to him it wasn't my fault. I asked if we should do it again or if we should scrap it. He told me we weren't going to do it again that way. He told me we couldn't afford a possible repeat. Instead, David would be on the truck, fully clothed, as it drove away from the exploding hillside. Separate pieces. I was glad we weren't going to have to go through that again. That night, I got a call from Menahem in my room and he wasn't a happy kreplach. (Yiddish.) I explained to him what happened and he told me I have to be more careful. I tried to make him realize I was an innocent bystander here.

"THREE DAYS YOU WASTED," he boomed back.

I told him I had no idea it was going to happen and assured him it wouldn't happen again. I found a different location and we did it with David on the truck. Everyone who saw the movie never saw the Rambo shot of David walking up the hill, it's too bad it was a hell of a shot. Maybe they should have kept it in. The movie would have made more money. The next time I saw David on set, he smiled and said, "got you, Lambo!" I let myself laugh. Understand, every time you are with David, you can't help but love him. He was just simply a wild man, but a very good one. Personalities make the world go around. I told him I didn't want to see his boobs again nor his flabby butt during the rest of the shoot. He nodded and said I didn't have to worry, it wouldn't happen on set again. Little did I know how carefully he chose those words.

(David Carradine insisting to carry Steven Lambert, not the actor. Distribution of weight is the key.)

I had a few days off so Steve James and I went into the jungle and saw a whole family of Pangolins and Tarsiers, it was wonderful. The next day as the work continued, I was off doing some Second Unit when I am told by my First Assistant that Gideon needs to talk to me right away on the radio as it was an emergency.

I asked him what was going on and he said I had to get down there quick, David Carradine is at home base sitting in a chair and he won't wake up. What do you mean he won't wake up!? That's what I thought to myself. I told Gideon to tell first aid to call for a Doctor and proceeded to head down there right away, telling my Second Unit crew that I would be back shortly. When I got to base camp, I noticed about a hundred and fifty people next to David's motorhome. I jump out of the jeep and walk over, curious and concerned. I go through the sea of bodies and all of a sudden, I get to the center and there is David slouched over in a folding chair, chin to his chest. I yell for everyone to back up and to give me some room. I put my hands on his shoulders and start to shake him.

"David, David, wake up!" I yelled. Nothing.

I advised them to get an ambulance immediately and some of the crew goes off to the Production Office to make a phone call. I get in between David's legs which are spread open and I pick his head up. I'm holding his head in my hands and calling his name, but he is not waking up! I'm getting scared and let his head down softly.

I've never taken first aid so I don't know what the hell to do. I take both hands and wrap them around his wrist. I feel movement in his wrist and I assume that is his pulse, but I don't know how to do it. I ask for a towel with some water on it and I pour the water on my hand and throw some on his face. Still nothing.

The Director and the Producer break through the crowd and have a Filipino guy with them wearing a white smock. He is identified as the doctor, even though he looks to me like an eighteen year old kid. I step aside and watch the doctor takes his pulse and open up his eyelids. No response. He looks at Gideon and says he is going to have to administer some medicine to wake him up. Gideon agrees and before I know it, this Doctor pulls out what looks like an elephant needle. This sucker is HUGE! I asked, "what the hell is that thing?"

The doctor just shrugs and proceeds to take out a coke bottle sized vial. He sticks the needle in and sucks up this clear liquid in the vial. I look around at everyone's stoic faces and finally break the silence. "Wait a minute, wait a minute, this just doesn't feel right," I called out. "We should take him to the hospital. He is not responding to anything. Gideon, where did you get this guy?"

Gideon shrugs. "He's a doctor," was all he could say.

The Doctor prepares to give the shot and I speak up. "Wait a minute, God Damn it! I just want everyone to know, I don't want this to happen. I say NO to this and I wipe my hands clean." Nobody else seems concerned or scared, but I was hoping to get through to my Director. Gideon takes a moment and then nods.

"Give him the shot," he commands.

I can't believe it! He totally ignores my pleas and continues on like it is no big deal. I step back and say again, "I'm telling everybody now, I have nothing to do with this." The Doctor injects David with the shot. It seemed to take fifteen seconds before he pulled it out. As the Doctor steps back, the crowd comes in. I asked the Doctor what he gave him.

He replied, "you want him to get up yes? I give him uppers to stimulate him."

Now like I said, I'm no Doctor, but I have plenty of common sense and this just doesn't seem kosher to me. Never heard or seen a Doctor conducting himself this way. I'm trying to get everyone back and I get down on my knees between his legs again and all of a sudden, he literally starts twitching. I jump back a little bit on my knees. My palms are on his knees and all of a sudden, his head pops up like a jack in the box. Next, his eyes open and he is looking right at me. Now as sure as I am a gazelle, his eyes literally started to propel themselves out of his sockets like a looney toon! It scared the hell out of me and I shuffled back a bit. He is staring at me with these protruding eyes and then just as fast as it happened, his eyes closed and he goes limp like a rag doll. In my mind, I am thinking that he is dead! I look at the Doctor who says, "excuse me."

He nudges me aside and takes David's pulse again. He turns back to Gideon and says calmly, "I guess I didn't give him enough, should I give him more?"

I jump up in shock shouting, "MORE? DIDN'T YOU JUST SEE WHAT HAPPENED!? IS HE DEAD?"

The Doctor tells me he isn't dead, he just didn't give him enough, that's all. Are you kidding me? I tell Gideon to stop this and get an ambulance and get him to the hospital where hopefully a real Doctor can look at him. Not an under aged intern. He tells the Doctor to go ahead with what he was doing, not even batting an eye at what I just said. Gideon was cold as ice, I couldn't believe it.

"You guys are out of your EXPLETIVE mind!" I yell.

I made it very clear once again that I had nothing to do with this. The Doctor sucks up some more liquid and sticks David again with the elephant sized needle. He steps back, I get in between David's knees and once again, he shakes, his head pops up and his eyes open. Only this time his eyes are even further out. A smile appears on his face without him saying anything for like five seconds. He looks like a zombie! Then out of nowhere he shouts,

"LAMBO!" He jumps up onto his feet, which knocks me back on my ass.

I stare up at him in shock as he rubs his hands excitedly. I didn't know what was going on and I tried to catch my breath.

"Are we ready to work!?" David called out to everyone.

I looked at him and said, "David, do you know what just happened? You were knocked out, the doctor gave you some upper medicine with a needle. Don't you remember that?"

"Oh, I feel great, let's go!" David replied as happy as ever.

I look at the Director and producer knowing the next shot is him and Mako driving a jeep when the Vietcong start launching mortars. I decided to double Mako and had mapped out a dozen explosions going off alongside the jeep. David was talking a million words a minute, pacing around, his veins popping out of his neck. I had never seen someone so excited to get to work. I told him there was no way I was going to let him drive, Billy Lucas would double him. David kept insisting to drive and I was afraid he would drive over a bomb.

Finally, I agreed to let him drive, but since I was doubling Mako, I was going to have my hand on the wheel and the gas pedal which couldn't be seen from the camera. So we do it and my hand is on the wheel and all of a sudden David starts pushing my hand away.

"Let me drive," he shouts. He starts pushing my foot off the accelerator. Then a bomb goes off. I grab the wheel again to try and maintain control and David pushes my hand away. We continue to do this all throughout the drive, past the bombs as the rest of the caravan is trying to follow us. This was not the path we rehearsed as David was trying to hit the bombs, but I winged it. How? Grabbing the wheel many times. It was a *Dumb and Dumber* moment. We reach the end and I am glad to be alive. David is laughing and keeps saying, "again, again." Nope. Print it. That's the end of that, we aren't doing it again. What a nightmare. A true story.

I enjoyed David as crazy as he was. There was something in him you just couldn't get mad at. At this part of his life on this film, he still thought he was Kwai Chang Caine from the *Kung Fu* series. Here is another doozy fer ya, imagine this. We get to an action piece where he goes up against six to seven Viet Cong and he is supposed to shoot them. David tells me, he doesn't want to shoot them he wants to engage them in hand to hand combat.

I try to explain to him that it wasn't possible as he would get shot by these guys with guns surrounding him. David insists, so I put a fist fight together while just shaking my head telling him, "all these guys have rifles and they are going to shoot your Kwai Chang Caine off. Or those two grenades that you showed me in the Rambo scene." I can't believe I'm doing this. There is this pool of water a few feet deep and David came up with what he calls, "a brilliant idea."

That's when you have to worry. He wanted to throw one of the bad guys over his shoulder into a puddle of water for effect. I get a guy about five foot three and came up with an idea to have David throw the guy over his shoulder into the water which was about eighteen inches deep, five feet wide. Mind you he has other guys coming at him and David decides to put his foot on the guy's chest while he fights off the other guys. I told him that was okay but he had to "play light foot" and asked if he knew what that meant. I wait for his answer.

"Yeah, I know what light foot is Lambo," he told me before throwing another punch at me.

I jump back and Wing Chun him away, laughing.

We rehearse it and it is fine and the day comes to shoot. We begin and David disarms two guys and kicks another guy and here comes the guy he is going to throw over his shoulder. He throws him over and into the puddle. As David puts his foot on the guy's chest, he sinks like a rock. David is standing on a slant now, his foot on the chest, leaning on the guy. He no doing light foot, he doing heavy foot. A few seconds go by and the guy is drowning, trying to get up. Ten seconds go by and I get a little hysterical. From behind the camera, I yell, "David, let the guy up!"

David is busy fighting the other guy and ignores me.

A few more seconds go by and I yell, "David let the guy up, take your foot off him. He's drowning."

The guy is flailing wildly trying to get up but David pays him no mind.

David has his whole weight on this poor stunt guy. All of a sudden that wildness gets cut in half and I realize this guy is losing consciousness under the water. I don't say nothing, I just run full blast into the shot, down the ravine and like a lion hitting its prey, I bulldogged him off the guy. We both hit the ground hard and he went flat on his back.

Gideon didn't know what to think as he yelled, "CUT!"!

I got up and I turn and look at the poor puddle man who has turned into a fish, rolling around and spitting water out of his mouth. I ran over and hit him on the back trying to get the water out of his lungs. Finally, it all gets spit out and he collapses. He tells me he is OK now. I look at David, who is as usual, smiling.

"It's a great shot huh? Let's continue on from there guys," he says calmly.

I blink in disbelief. "David, you almost killed the guy," I stammered.

David shook his head, "aw come on he's all right, you're all right aren't you?"

The stunt man looks up at David and asks, "do we have to do this again?"

I look at him and I look at David and I look at my Director and say, "I guess we have to do a pickup with him in the water, don't we?"

Gideon said that we did need a pickup. I asked the stunt guy if he would get back in the water but this time, I will be playing David. I'll put his boot and pants on. I angle the camera in such a way that you could only see a foot.

David walks off and I just can't believe how much David thinks he is still Kwai Chang Caine. I kept having to remind him this was not a Kung Fu film, but an Army picture. He never understood and gave me that David smile.

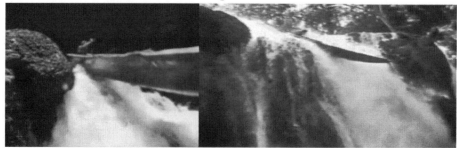

(I took one hell of a ride. My good pal Carradine wanted to do this. I told him he was crazy.)

I always loved Sundays in the Philippines. Everybody's day off. We were staying at the Manila Hotel, one of the top ten hotels in the world at that time. I got a call to come meet some of the crew and cast by the pool. It was a beautiful Olympic sized pool with a bar in the middle where you could eat and drink. Literally a couple hundred people were in and around this pool having the time of their life. People on vacation, kids playing in the water with all the toys. When I came out, I saw my Director, Cinematographer, Steve James and Phil Brock on lounge chairs. I sat down right between Gideon and Steve James. We are having nice conversations, watching everyone go by. A half hour later, I hear the magical voice of David Carradine.

I look up to see David and his agent and girlfriend beside him, both wearing white robes. We talk to him about the day and how beautiful it is out when David turns around and sees the bar in the middle of the pool. He looks at his agent and girlfriend and nudges her.

"Let's go in the water and go to the bar," he tells her.

They turn towards the pool as we stop paying attention to them and talk amongst ourselves. David and his girlfriend have their backs towards us and low and behold, they start opening up their robes. The robes drop to their feet and I am staring at two naked butts including one I've had the displeasure of seeing before. I look down at their feet, hoping they at least had socks on. No such luck. Within two seconds, we hear screams coming from all over the pool and people beginning to scatter. All of a sudden, I turn away from David and his girlfriend to see the hundreds of mothers, fathers and kids in the pool, screaming. Let me remind you, it's Sunday. Everybody's day off.

I look back at David and splash! They are in the pool! They are swimming over to the bar, parting the sea of people like a naked Moses. I'm telling you people couldn't get out of the water fast enough, as they flail over to the ledges. Mothers and fathers are busy covering their little one's eyes as the screaming has reached its zenith. In five seconds, I kid you not, that pool was basically empty.

From hundreds of people to just two, it was like witnessing a mass exodus. Their faces frozen in fear, trying to get away from the pool as David who is oblivious, swims up to the bar. Instead of sitting on a stool, he uses it as a stepping stone and climbs onto the bar, flopping down like a freaking beached whale. He helps his girlfriend/agent onto the seat. They are both nude with her on the stool revealing her pancakes from the waist up and him on the counter, revealing everything. This was a sight you never think you would see. David began leaning on his elbow with his head in his hand like it was a piano. It was romantic, touching and utterly horrifying.

Meanwhile, here comes two security guards, yelling at him to get out and put his clothes on. David ignores them and asks the bartender for a drink. The bartender is so afraid, he has backed himself into a corner at the other end of the bar. What does David do? He rolls over and gets behind the bar. He takes two bottles of liquor and starts pouring two drinks. All the people have vanished into the hotel lobby and into their rooms. The whole pool area has become a deserted wasteland. We are doing our best to pretend we don't know David. The guards decide to take off their shoes and belts and jump into the water. They pull them away from their drinks and get them out of the pool. They are yelling at them to put their robes back on. One of the guards looks at me and asks if I know him. I say, "no I've never seen this guy in my life," before walking away. I hear Phil Brock, the comedian that he is, threatening to take his bathing suit off too as I see Steve James laughing, grabbing Phil's bathing suit to keep it on his body. I must say it looked like something coming out of National Lampoon.

David and his girlfriend are finally taken out of the pool into the hotel lobby. I'm dying to see what is going to happen. Avi and Gideon vanished. They ran away, what cowards. I walk over with Steve James and Phil Brock and we start apologizing to the owner as the manager yells at David. David just turns around and says to us, "I'll see you guys later."

I watch as he walks to the elevator. To make a long story short, they forgave David and let us stay in the hotel. I heard a rumor that Cannon paid them money for the problems David caused and that might have made our stay a little easier. To this day I don't know how things like this never reach the tabloids. Well, I guess it might now. Here is the last story of the Chronicles. I get all of the department heads and actors together to show them a fight that takes place in a chicken coop cage, which is about fifteen by fifteen, water up to your shins. I managed to get most of the important people in, like the Director, the Director of Photography and a few other actors in. I'm trying to explain the fight to everyone, including David Carradine. We all have galoshes on except for David who is barefoot which was funny in itself. I turn to my Director and start explaining the fight I put together. Before I get my fourth sentence out- WHAM!

I see stars even though it's daylight outside. My knees buckle and my face goes right into the filthy, scummy water we are all standing in. My hands go between my legs in pain. I throw myself up from the water looking at everybody in shock and horror. Guess what, David just kicked me right square in my nuts. In agony and pain, I'm looking at everybody's face in surprise and confusion.

All Of a sudden, my eye line whips to David and I see his big smile and hear those all too familiar words, "GOTCHA LAMBO!"

I practically fall back into the water trying to regain some composure, when I look up at David and again hear him say, "I thought you were quick."

I simply say, "David, if you ever do that again, I'll hit you back."

He walks over and puts his arms around me, trying to make it seem like it was no big deal. I could tell you that he listened, but this is the kind of thing that I had to deal with all through this picture. I can honestly tell you, it didn't stop and I probably got away from or blocked eighty percent of them. Some people would get mad, but I understood David, for better or for worse. He was a very special guy.

CHAPTER 27
(Getting Engaged.)

Speaking of hearts, you remember that girl I met on Remo? Cecilia Camacho. I brought her over on vacation on this shoot. We were in the Manila hotel, one of the top ten in the world they say. How lucky I am, I have a suite with a jacuzzi on my patio. The surroundings were jungle like with beautiful huge flowers spread throughout. Big time romantics. It was raining, so we hopped into the jacuzzi. Love was in the air. Steam was rising as drops of rain were falling own, posing as rose petals onto our bodies. All of a sudden, I felt like I was in a movie. A love story. That's when I reached up and plucked a flower from the foliage above. I asked for her hand and laid the flower on her soft, gentle palm. Then I found myself uttering words. They were magical. "Will you marry me, Cecilia?"

Then she started crying. Yes, you heard me, crying. I was shocked and afraid. Afraid I had made a fool out of myself. I thought that meant "no." I apologized to her if I had said something wrong, but she shook her head and said, "no, no, I'm happy. That's why I am crying."

I wondered while I was smiling and asked, "are you sure?"

She jumped into my arms and said, "yes I am sure. Are you sure?"

I said, "yes, I am sure."

And then she said, "good, we are both sure." Then she kissed me. Fade out.

(Actress Cecilia Camacho, Maco, and Steven Lambert. The day I asked her for her hand.)

I'm on the plane with my bride to be, I convinced her to stay a couple more weeks in Los Angeles before she headed back south of the border to inform her family of the big news. She also had to go back to work on a soap opera she was working on.

CHAPTER 28
(Another Look At The Stuntmen's Association.)

Time goes by and I've been so busy out of town that almost a couple of years have gone by and I haven't been to a second Stuntmen's Association meeting. I find out there is one coming up at the end of the month. I should get excited, thinking this time the meeting might be constructive, but I heard from other members they never are. All they do is complain.

They are always trying to figure out how to keep themselves above water. The Stuntmen's Association never has money. Unfortunately, their version of progress is to argue amongst each other.

These are the explanations that I got. It always seemed helter-skelter. I wondered how could a business survive like this. I arrive early and here we go as usual. When eight o' clock comes, we all go in. I sit there and hear the different questions that members have and low and behold, it is the same as last time, everyone is still arguing. People were complaining about lack of jobs and bad mouthing the stunt people who got the job instead of trying to figure out what they did wrong and how they could do better next time.

It was like a bunch of well bred stallions not knowing how to team up and get themselves into their corral. I still couldn't understand the infighting that was going on. Growing up in Brooklyn, we would have arguments with someone one day and then the next day it would be forgotten. Here, the fighting spread like a cancer in the group and it was omnipresent. As the meetings went on, they tried making ground rules to bring it back under control. A rule was finally put in place stating that you had to hire 75% of your stunt crew from the Stuntmen's Association, which was cool but it was more or less in the by-laws to begin with.

So they were just reiterating a law instead of trying to get to the source of the problem. Hence, no one stuck to it as time went by. There were only a very few precious men that did in the group but they would hire the same fifteen to twenty all the time and unfortunately, it would leave out all the others in the group. I would come to realize that they weren't interested in helping each other become a Stunt Coordinator, get a show.

It wasn't thought of to help others. This business is more or less survival of the fittest, or you can say the greediest. The most selfish. There are no thoughts in most cases in helping your fellow man. That's so unfortunate and is not the way a brotherhood should run itself. But I must say, there are those few that have a great heart and a great sense of brotherhood and friendship, that help their fellow stuntmen and friends to learn and achieve a chance to hit a home run and have an opportunity to be a Stunt Coordinator of a show. As it happened to me.

I was very fortunate. Everyone always had an excuse which caused even more problems. On top of that, people were too afraid to say anything about it, because they feared they would lose a job if they spoke out. That was amazing to me. It seemed to take away their dignity.

They became like robots in a do whatever it takes mentality to secure that stunt job. In some cases, it was pathetic. In some, it was funny. Nobody discussed how to grab a hold of some shows so they can put more people to work. Or recruiting more Stunt Coordinators. What they do to pay the rent is bring in more stunt guys that don't run shows. Therefore, the problem grows.

I must say one thing. Stunts Unlimited? They have never had this problem. Every one of their guys are Stunt Coordinators, they run shows and it is mandatory to hire their own. Sure they argue, everyone does but they always seem to bring it back to reality. How do I know this? I have a few friends in Stunt's Unlimited. We talk about it all the time. Listen, I don't mean to always compare and put the two groups against each other, but I want you to understand that there is a right way and there is a wrong way. It was a lesson to me and I want it to be a lesson for you. Sometimes Stunts Unlimited goes outside when they find a good person but they believe in teamwork and they are all close friends. Another thing Stunts Unlimited has.

Women. Stuntmen's Association? They are not allowed. Figure that one out. Maybe if they did have a woman, she would have put them on the straight and narrow. Hoorah for women! Yes, everyone argues, it's normal. But they come back together. They have always been a smart group and a hard working team to this day. Anyway, I listened to everyone and thought to myself, there has to be a way to bring these guys together and work as a team. Better comradery. Then it clicked!

I would propose a softball game! Softball? Yea, I know what you out there are thinking. There's no way a bunch of big tough stuntmen are going to play softball. It would take a lot of balls to propose an idea like that.

Well luckily, after the ordeal with the rat on *Remo,* mine were still intact. I said to myself, let's wait until the next meeting that I am able to go to. I'll talk to another member that happens to be on the Board Of Directors and enjoys playing ball. His name was Rick Sawaya.

I took a deep breath and said, I hope I get enough nerve to suggest it. You see, believe it or not at this time in my life when it came to things like talking in front of people, I was basically really shy and introverted. In other words, scared shitless to stand up and be noticed and have everyone's eyes upon me. More on this later.

A week goes by and I am busy taking my fiancé all over. Chinatown, Six Flags, Knotts Berry Farm, Disneyland, we are having the time of our lives. You'd be amazed that when you are so enamored by a person and she doesn't speak English, something that would normally take thirty seconds to explain, takes thirty minutes. You know what I mean, that's a thing called love. You would do anything for it. Almost. The pleasure of explaining to somebody that caught your heart.

CHAPTER 29
(Arnold Schwarzenegger, Robert Davi And The Hot Spoon.)

That's when I get a call from Glenn Randall Jr. Remember him? That's the stunt man who hired me for *Remo Williams*. He asked me if I was available to work on a show with Arnold Schwarzenegger called *Raw Deal*. I said of course I am. He told me Joel Kramer says hello as well. I found out he was doubling Arnold and I was excited to see him again.

The remaining days with Cecilia went by quickly and we had a great time together. Like a gefilte fish chasing a taco, I gave her a kiss. There she went, back to Mexico (for now, la Cucaracha) and the next day I traveled to set. When I get my wardrobe fitting, I find out there are a lot of people I know working this show! People like Vince Deadrick Sr., Gene Heartline, Mike Johnson, Joel Kramer, and Phil Nielson. I met Phil on Remo where I was asked by Glenn Randall Jr. to pick three guys for a fight.

I'm always very proud. Most of the time when I am working for a Stunt Coordinator, they always ask me to assemble the fights. There was also Larry Holt, Peter Stater (the son of Paul Stater, remember him? Pacemaker man) the list of fine stuntmen goes on and on. Glenn always hired regulars on his shows and it was just wonderful knowing I was going to see everyone again. I also was excited to meet Arnold himself. I talked to Joel before I had left and he was excited to introduce me to him.

I found Joel on set and he brought me over to Arnold's huge beautiful motorhome. He knocked on the door and I heard this thick Norse accented voice, vibrating like a Viking roar. "Yaaa, woo is it?"

Joel replies, "It's Joel, I brought somebody I want you to meet."

I thought that was something very special that Joel did.

"Come in, you low forehead you."

First time I heard someone say that, but it wouldn't be the last. I started laughing and Joel opened the door. I step in ready to make my debut with Arnold Schwarzenegger. Joel moves aside and there is the man behind the voice. I blink my eyes, this can't be right. I've seen Arnold on television and in magazines many times and this ain't him! Before I could say anything, Joel spoke up. "Sven, I want you to meet somebody. A good friend of mine, Steven Lambert." I look up at this hulk of a man, as big a gorilla, and he looks at me curiously. He sticks out his hand and says hello and I stick out my hand and say hello. "Your name is Steven huh? My name is Sven Thoresen, you can call me Sven-Ole. You know, may I tell you something?"

I said, "Yeah, sure."

Sven smiled. "You know, you need to start eating and pumping weights, you look like a string I could break."

We laughed and I looked across the way and saw the man, Arnold, sitting down. He invites me over and we shake hands.

"It's nice to meet you, I have heard all about you. An amazing stuntman I hear. And you do Martial Arts too, I heard. Well, we will see about that when the time comes," Arnold joked.

I spot this other guy sitting quietly.
"This is Peter Kent, he is my stand in." Arnold informed me. "He wants to someday be an actor." I nod looking at him.

Sven laughs. "He's a moron. He's a God damn stand in!"

I don't know if I should laugh, not realizing yet that this was Viking humor. But as I see everyone else is laughing, I decided to join in. Peter Kent I learned, was part of the "in crowd" that little did I know from this moment on, I would have the privilege to be a part of. It was like a little rat pack, that thanks to Joel, they opened the door and let this punk kid from Brooklyn join them. It was in this group where I experienced many humorous, fun and unusual happenings. Every morning for breakfast, I was part of the elite few that sat at Arnold's table with Sven, Peter Kent and Joel and whatever dummy they got to sit with us. It was a table of six. At this table, in this group, there were always a lot of games being played. Both mentally and physically. We would always have an empty seat where someone would sit and say hello and talk to Arnold.

They liked to play a little game with these people. It was called hot spoon. They would be laughing and smiling at Arnold before the laughter turned into physical pain and you would jump out of your chair. Sven would take his hot spoon out of his boiling coffee and if it wasn't hot he would ask for another cup. He would have Arnold Joel talk to you, diverting your attention. Then he would put the hot spoon right on your neck when you weren't looking. He did it to me the first day. I sat down and I fell back right out of my chair. They distracted me and I went head over heels.

I was shocked and when I realized what Sven had done, I thought to myself, "oh well, I do have a sense of humor and it was funny." So I laughed right along with them. Sometimes a little pain with laughter goes a long way. It's all in fun. To most. Every morning there would always be a new unsuspecting victim sitting down and getting the hot spoon treatment. If they were after a particular person which usually was the case and didn't want anyone else to sit there, Sven would bellow, "you can't sit here, you moron. You weren't invited."

We would all laugh. Even if it was a Producer, he would say that. Only Sven can get away with that. One time it was even the Director of the picture. I just stood, kept quiet and watched. Guess what? The Director had no choice. He laughed. Why? Maybe because Arnold laughed too. That forced the issue.

What I want you to realize, is that after a while, Sven would call people up he wanted to sit in that chair and invite them to breakfast. The seat was to remain empty for the burning of the spoon, a special branding on the neck of our beloved cast and crew. My Yin thought it was humorous and my Yang thought it was not. Wait until you hear this. One morning, the actor Robert Davi came in.

Arnold yells out, "Davi, come over here. Sit with us."

Yes, I said Robert Davi. A full blooded New Yorker to the Big Apple's core. He thought he was a hard ass. Mister attitude, he was. Sven-Ole Thorsen is sitting right next to him and we are talking, everyone is having a great time. Sven gets up to use the restroom and when he comes back, my ninja senses lock onto him out of the corner of my eye. He is busy putting a big soup ladle spoon in a coffee pot of boiling water. Robert Davi was a big dude, so I guess Sven decided he needed a bigger spoon. Sven sits down briefly and joins the conversation.

"Oh Robert, you are such a funny man. And I have been watching you act. You are like Marlon Brando," Sven says.

I thought to myself, boy they are setting him up. Big time. Whenever Sven says something like that, you must know it's his way of making fun of the guy. He gets up and puts his hand on Robert's back.

"We are so looking forward to your good nature and understanding of humor, Davi," Sven says.

Robert puts his hand on Sven's and thanks him. Sven walks away and Robert turns back towards Arnold who distracts him. Sven takes the ladle out of the coffee pot of boiling water and walks over to Robert Davi. Like swatting a fly in the air, he brings down the spoon, SMACK, right on Davi's neck and holds it there for a second. Davi screams like the New York gangster that he is and falls to the floor like a rock, holding his neck. Everyone was laughing, but I wasn't. I looked at Davi's face and he was pissed off! Fire in his eyes.

He jumped up and said, "what the hell was that? I'm sick and tired of your jokes. Get up! I'm going to kick the shit out of you!"

Sven remains calm, sits down and simply says, "are you sure Robert, you want to do that? Can't you take a little joke, you moron, you?"

Everyone roars with laughter from the strange way Sven speaks. Robert shouts again for him to get up and he puts his fists up like a boxer. Sven smiles and gets up slowly. He comes three feet away.

Sven asks, "are you ready?"

Davi says, "come on."

As soon as Davi threw up his hands, like the gorilla that he is, Sven unleashes a massive front snap kick that would probably break a two by four and hits Davi right in the stomach. He flies back like he was connected to a ratchet and lands on the ground, trying to catch his breath. Mind you, Sven was a blackbelt. Davi is lying there trying to catch his breath and my eyes are coming out of my sockets like David Carradine, I was so in shock. Sven walks over and sticks out his hand, asking to help him up and give him some water. Davi gets up and storms out of the restaurant.

Sven looks at Arnold who replies, "guess he couldn't hold it in, had to find a bathroom."

A few hours later, I guess they made up. You could say Davi really didn't have any choice. Otherwise, he would have been miserable the rest of the show. Sven would have made sure of that. I walked over and saw Davi, Sven and a few others were sitting outside the motorhome having a good time.

I said, "Davi you made up with them. You are a smart guy."

That's Arnold, Sven and Joel Kramer for you. This was the first of many times to come, working with this gang and having fun, exciting and unusual experiences.

CHAPTER 30
(Menahem Golan Vs Tobe Hooper. The Showdown At The O.K. Corral.)

Some time goes by and I found myself getting a call from David Womark of all people. He wanted to know if I would be available to be the Stunt Coordinator on a show he was doing called *Invaders From Mars*.

Remember that show? This was a remake. The original came out in 1953. It was great, I saw it. I'll tell you right now, this was a piss poor copy of the original. I'll tell you what I thought in four words. A waste of money. Just imagine, working with big fat Martians. But I got to double an Academy Award winner, Louise Fletcher. She won for *One Who Flew Over The Cuckoo's Nest.* And now she is doing this. You know what they say, money talks. She must have got a bundle. You ask me now and I'm kind of embarrassed, but it was a job and some of the funniest memories that I have. Let's move on. I went to the set the next day and signed my contract, but I didn't receive the script. That should have been my first thought something was up here.

David greeted me warmly and then said, "Steven, I want to ask you a favor."

I nodded okay. What was he going to ask me, I wondered.

David went on to explain about this guy, we'll call him "Ed", who was the Stunt Coordinator on the project and they couldn't get him to leave.

I shook my head. "What do you mean he is the Stunt Coordinator, is this a joke?"

David clasped his hands and said, "well, let me explain. We just need you to do us a small favor. We need you to fire him."

My mind just exploded. Fire him? I said, "David, first of all, what does this have to do with me? It is not my job to fire people, you big chicken. You should. Second of all, I know this guy. He is a veteran Stuntman. I can't go and fire him. This isn't just some guy off the street. This is somebody I respect."

David shrugged. "We tried firing him, he just keeps coming back. You Steven, I know, you will make him stay away."

I shook my head and laughed, what was I going to do? So I looked at David and said, "you must be a manly man and try again. Don't ask me."

David insisted. Well, to tell you the truth, he begged me.

So I finally agree and said, "thank you very much, you yellow bellied jelly bean."

He laughed. I said, "David, man, I don't find this funny." I thought about it for a few minutes, normally you would think you would have some time to figure this out. But I didn't. I took a deep breath and went to go find Stuntman Ed. I knocked on the door of his trailer and he smiled in wonder when he saw me. "Hey Ed, how are you?" I asked.

"Hey Steven, what are you doing here?"

I took a deep breath. "May I come in and talk to you?" I answered.

He replied, "well, sure."

We sat down and I prepared myself. "I need to talk to you about this movie and what's going on," I tried to say as polite as possible. I tried to find the words as they formed in my mind. "Listen, I want you to know that I have such respect for you and I am grateful for all of your work on this show, but I got a call last night from the Producers, asking me to take over as Stunt Coordinator and they tell me you don't want to leave. I value your friendship and so admire your work, but please let's not have any problems or arguments. As somebody who is a fellow brother asking you to pack up your things and go over to the Second Assistant Director and sign out. Would you do that please? We don't want to turn this into any more of a problem than it is." I waited for him to protest, to yell, to say no. But he didn't do any of those things.

He just said, "Tobe Hooper doesn't want me to leave."

My eyes lit up. "Of course he doesn't. They tell me you guys are blowing in the same pipe."

Mr. Ed was shocked I said that, plus a few other things. But he agreed and left without protest. A true professional and a smart guy. I went back and told David he was gone and he thanked me. "You're welcome David," I said.

As we both turned away, I jump spun into a one eighty and went into a square horse stance with an intense face. David just shook his head. That was a job I had no intention of doing again. I was like an invader coming and taking over someone's world which any Stunt Coordinator doesn't like to do at the moment it happens. As strange and weird as that was, I was about to learn the real Martians were invading and it was about to get wild. I went home that day with script in hand. I stayed up all night and all morning reading the script and preparing a budget. The film involved the military and there were moments when I put four or five fire burns, I put explosions, ratchets, two jeeps doing turnovers and mid-air explosions, bombs going off, Martians destroying things with their beams. I even had a tank there with four or five men on it who would be lifted up in the air, caught on fire and explode into ashes. This was a big production and I thought I could do things with the military I never got to on *Behind Enemy Lines*, due to the lack of time and money. I knew this was a big production as it also had Karen Black and as I mentioned, Louise Fletcher.

They had Tobe Hooper as the Director. I mean one of the scariest movies I saw in my life, *Texas Chainsaw Massacre*, this guy was a legend. I thought working with Tobe was going to be such a unique experience. They hired Stan Winston to do the creature FX and his brother Matt. Stan just won an academy award for James Cameron's *Aliens* a few months prior. For a Cannon film to be this huge of a budget, and using these kinds of people, it was unheard of. I came back the next day with this brand new creation I had invented in my mind. I was overjoyed that I was going to do something so different than what I had been doing anywhere. It was going to be a 1986 version of *The Hurt Locker* or *Saving Private Ryan,* so I thought. I took this film very seriously. Even though the 1953 version was campy, it was laid out seriously. I sat down with David and the Producers and handed them duplicates of the budget and their eyes shot out of their heads. The budget I had proposed was over a hundred and fifty thousand dollars. On top of that, I had forty or fifty stunt guys working on the show, some multiple times. They told me they couldn't accommodate this size of a budget, they just didn't have the money.

I asked what they meant, I was told it was a big budget. They told me all the money is going to Stan Winston and his FX. Louise Fletcher had to be paid as well as the other big name actors and crew members. I told him I would cut stuff out but David put up his hand.

"All we need is the bodies, they will disintegrate when they get hit by the Martian's beam."

I asked about the final scene at the end with the military and tanks.

David replies that he wanted me to set it up, "in a simple way."

I asked if he wanted fire burns, but he said, "no they were too expensive."

He wanted to know what happened to the budget cuts I had done on past Ninja films. I told him we were hiring Americans, it's a totally different ball game and we are in Los Angeles. "My God," I spoke up. "You have Tobe Hooper here, don't you want great action?"

David shook his head. "No. We just need the bodies, that is all."

I asked what he wanted me to take out.

"All the expensive stuff," he replied.

Just great. All my dreams of putting together this dramatic serious army fight with the Martians was just disintegrated by David before my eyes! All my fantasies were just shattered. I was happy about hiring a lot of guys but it still wouldn't be the same. Little did I know as the days progressed, how foolish I realized that the show was. I watched many of the actors and actresses, including Louise Fletcher and couldn't believe it was the same actress and acting from *One Who Flew Over The*

Cuckoo's Nest. I'm not saying I am a critic, but I grew up watching a dozen movies a week back in Brooklyn with my father and grandfather. From love stories to dramas, I was enthralled by the performances. Here, something was just not right. It was just the worst performance I had ever seen to this day. She was even nominated for worst actress in the Razzie Awards when she had been nominated for Best Actress just one film back. Can you believe that? I couldn't believe the waste that is going on. David explains to me that Menahem all of a sudden has a desire to try and get an Academy Award and this film is how he plans to do it. I remember looking at him. Academy Award? For this film?

David just shrugged his shoulders. As the days went by watching Tobe Hooper, I realized there was something very wrong here. After every take, cut and print, he would head off to his motor home. As the days went by, there was a huge waste in time and tons of confusion. This was not normal. Tobe always had a Dr. Pepper in one hand and a cigar in the other. He must have had twenty five Dr. Peppers a day. I like Coke, but I ain't drinking twenty five cans a day. His breath smelled like smoke and soda and the stage reeked of it. It was a sign of the times, or if people just put up with it because it was Tobe Hooper. He was just all over the place. Again, whenever he had finished a scene he would rush into his motorhome. Why? You figure it out. I did and so did everybody else.

Weeks went by and take after take of watching the Producers and David Womark try to get Tobe Hooper moving, I finally asked David, "come on tell me, why is he taking a break and going into his motor home every half hour? This is strange."

David would simply act like he had no time to answer and turn around to go back to work. All I knew was that every time Tobe came out of there, he was like a happy jackrabbit. Eventually, I would hear bits and pieces from various crew that he was breathing in "pixie dust." Thirty times a day!? That just blew my mind. I found David and I cornered him.

I said, "I finally found out what he does for a half an hour in his motorhome."

David told me it was true. He also mentioned that he has never seen Menahem so upset and they were consulting with lawyers.

"Why?" I asked.

"Because we are trying to fire him too," he said.

I told him I would make him deal. "You asked me to fire one, I'll fire him too. Just give me the money you're paying the lawyers and I'll get rid of him for ya."

David laughed with impatience. We both agreed it was just a tremendous waste. David mentioned a small war between Menahem and Tobe. I was surprised by this but understood Menahem's intent. It seemed like Tobe just didn't care for this picture. Whatever scenes we had with action, he would always tell me to put it together and never seemed to want to change it. It went so far that when it came to action, I was directing the actors. His mind seemed to be all over the place. No direction from him, no setup, nothing. I knew he knew what needed to be done, he just didn't do it. It was a God damn free for all. Every department was taking advantage. Listen to this piece of work. One day we were shooting on the Martian cave stage and Tobe accidentally dropped his cigar down the vents in the cave. So like any normal person, you would think he would just go and get another, right? Wrong.

He completely stopped the production and had Stan Winston and the crew take apart the set to get the cigar back which took about two and a half hours. All the while, he went back to his motorhome to have a good time with himself. When he came back out, he had another Dr. Pepper in his hand, which I later was told that the sugar caters to the stars in his head. Brings back the pixie dust feeling. No wonder why he didn't care about *Invaders from Mars*, he was spaced out of the solar system. I was involved with Stan Winston a lot in this show since he was doing the Martians. David told me the Martians cost literally hundreds of thousands of dollars. Even though they had mechanics, I still had to hire a stunt person and little people to work them. I was also in the suits.

Imagine this. This is how the Martian suits worked. I would step in from the back and then a little person would go on my shoulders and would work the eyes and arms on top. To me, it was very amateur the way this worked. I would work the feet and the mouth. I would crawl into the opening in the back and the little person would go on my shoulders, you get the picture? There was no room to move around and no ventilation which was miserable. Especially for the little people. You couldn't even see, that is why the Martians just appeared and would be walking. Mind you, these little persons were fragile and every twenty minutes we had to stop and take them out for air as there were no air vents. After twenty minutes the little people would just about pass out. "Get me out of here," they would scream in agony. That took fifteen minutes.

Since they came out, I came out. Then another thirty minutes to get back in and believe me, the crankiness from the little people, I understood.

After the first day with these Martians, I had six little people and guess what, they all quit on me. I can see you laughing, me too, but at the time it wasn't that funny. You see, the word spread like wildfire and every little person we called didn't want to do it and I didn't blame them. I offered them more money and they still turned it down. Money wasn't the issue. The issue was the suffering and the pain that they went through in the Martian outfit. They were like a little clan, they all talked amongst each other. They had no air, no air conditioning, I felt so sorry for them.

They were just pouring in sweat, it was difficult. On top of that, being on my shoulders, sometimes the smell would get to me. Hahaha. Almost every mechanical thing Stan Winston used, they would always break down. Boy did he make a lot of money. It seemed like he had a system going.

Let's break down on purpose and make some more money. It's a good system if you can get away with it and he did. He had a twenty four hour crew of fifteen to twenty five people working every hour on the mechanics and the whole place. It was a tremendous waste of time and money. Every time I used the Martians, I would have to hire new little people. I offered them five hundred buck adjustments, but they didn't care and quit at the end of the day.

It was just a mess and I couldn't believe how a guy who won an Academy Award for *Aliens,* could have this happen every day and nothing would ever be fixed. This could only happen with Cannon films.

(Stunt doubling actress Louise Fletcher getting eaten by the Martian.)

They were making money so I doubt that they cared and it was just a shame. There was talk of getting Shmulik to replace Tobe to turn this around and I was excited to see if that would happen, but it never did. Now I want to talk about a crazy woman. A well known actress named Karen Black. The pictures that she had done like *Easy Rider*, with Jack Nicholson and *The Great Gatsby* with Robert Redford, were both great performances. On this picture, it was like she turned off the light switch. If I had to say two words to explain her, the words would just simply be, neurotic and delusional. Please look up the meaning of these two words and you will understand more. She would literally be unhappy with her performance in front of camera and she would throw a fit and talk to herself like she had multiple personality disorder. She would stop in the middle of a scene and get upset and then there were two Karen Blacks arguing with each other about the quality of the performance!

A voice would come out and it would be Tobe Hooper yelling, "you crazy bitch, stop talking to yourself and start acting!"

Can you imagine that? We would all try not to laugh, but it was hard. Karen would yell at him back or ignore him during her live debate with herself in front of us. This was a common occurrence that slowed us down even more. If it got really bad, she would storm off the set crying and go to her trailer. One time she even crawled up into a ball right in front of everybody, crying like crazy. Yes, this is true. She would even do some of these things in front of her son. Oh, which happened to be Hunter Carson, the main character of the film who was actually her real son. You would think a boy at that age would be well spoken, well behaved, well mannered and all around polite. Hunter was all of those things I'm sure, in his head. To everyone else, he was a spoiled brat. He would tell everybody to shut up, to wait for him, insult people, the list goes on. Okay, listen to this. I had hired a stunt woman who is very dear to my heart, a little person named Laura Dash, to double Hunter. I always wanted to do something different. A lot of men had doubled women, I have doubled women in the past, but when does a woman double a man or a boy? It don't happen often. To me, I thought that was a very cute and brilliant idea that could be spread around in the stunt industry.

Hunter Carson found out and was introduced to Laura without me on set and boy was the boy upset. David Womark found me and told me we had a problem. I had no idea what he was talking about. David told me the kid is pissed off because, "you hired a girl to double him and he is a boy."

I said with a big smile on my face, "so, he should be happy he has a girl willing to do the dangerous stuff his character does. Are you against women?"

David replied, "this is serious, stop fooling around."

I said, "I am serious, think about it, what is wrong with that David?"

He told me Hunter wanted a guy but I didn't have a guy that would fit the part. So Laura it was going to be. No one in the viewing public was ever going to know (until now hehehe). I made sure Laura stayed away from Hunter and we both had a good laugh. Here comes the day when she has to double him, and Laura comes on set to get ready. I am away working with other pieces of action when I get a tap on the shoulder and it is Laura. She is very upset. I asked what the matter was and she said Hunter and her had an argument.

"He doesn't want a girl to double him and he punched me in front of everybody!" Laura said he saw her and came over to her yelling, "what are you doing here?" Laura tried to explain to him that she was here to double him and make sure he was safe. But Hunter got so angry he punched her in the face.

I said, "what!? He punched you in the face?"

You have to understand how fragile little people are, on top of that she is a girl and Laura wouldn't hurt a fly. She is a sweet talented, wonderful woman. She stated again he punched her in the face. She showed me the red mark and I asked her to show me how he did it. She picked up her arm and swung it towards me and stopped, and I realized it was a hard punch! I took Laura with me to Hunter's trailer and knocked on the door. Hunter came out with his teacher and we went inside.

"Hey Hunter, I need to talk to you. I understand you had a physical confrontation with Laura. This is a little person, you can't hit little people just because you disagree with something. She is here to help you and work with you, she is putting her life on the line in some cases. She is looking after you and giving you pads to keep you safe. You should treat her with respect and it is okay to feel upset at times, but you must talk those feelings out. Use your words, not your hands. It would be a really nice thing, you know, to understand what I am saying and apologize to her."

I look at Hunter after I tell him all of this, and I thought I could see resentment and a bit of sadness in his demeanor. He looks at me with those baby eyes and I look at Laura who is right beside me, to hear the apology. I was glad this was all going to be cleared up.

"F*** off, I ain't apologizing!" Hunter barks and heads back into his trailer.

My mouth drops open and I look at Laura with those sweet eyes, just in shock. We both shake our heads and I tell her to follow me.

"What are you gunna do?" she asks.

I told her we were going to his mother. She is telling me not to get mad, but I assure her I was just going to explain to her what her son did. I knock on the door of the trailer and Karen invites me in, unaware of the situation. Laura tells me she will wait outside.

"That's what you think," I say. I grab her arm and tell her she is coming with me. I say hello and the usual greetings and before I can get a word in, Karen starts to ramble on how confused she is about today's work. Imagine this. she is sitting there telling her Stunt Coordinator about the process of the work she has to do to get ready for acting in the scenes today. I had no idea why she was talking to me about this. I am trying to figure out how to break the news about her son when after five minutes she finally stops talking.

I said quickly, "Karen, I came here to talk to you about your son. This is his stunt double, Laura Dash. She is a wonderful person and Hunter got very upset when he found out she was doubling him and she is here to protect him and make him safe."

Karen replied, "Hunter told me you had a girl doubling him and I tried to tell him that was a sweet thing to do, but you know how boys are," she replied. He doesn't want her. He wants a boy."

I tried to calm her down and finish what I had to say. "I appreciate that, but you have to understand that your son got upset and punched Laura in the face," I finished.

Karen looked at me wide eyed and replied, "so?"

I said, "So, again, she is a girl Karen."

Karen nodded and shouted, "I'LL TALK TO HIM."

Now Karen all of a sudden is yelling at me! I told her that it is not all right for her son to hit girls, especially a little person.

Karen raised her voice again. "I TOLD YOU I'LL HAVE A TALK WITH HIM. NOW LEAVE ME ALONE, I CAN'T HANDLE THESE PROBLEMS. I GOTTA FIGURE OUT WHERE MY CHARACTER ARC IS IN THIS SCENE, SO YOU ARE GOING TO HAVE TO GO NOW."

I looked at Laura and she couldn't get out of there fast enough. Once we got outside, Laura just said, "boy, I can see it runs in the family."

I looked at Laura and I said, "I'll tell you what. You are still on the show stunt doubling him and if there is another confrontation between you two and he raises his hands, you have my permission to hit him back. Only if he hits you first."

Laura replied, "really? We'll get in trouble."

I said, "no, we won't. Imagine if this gets out to the public. What are they going to say? Hunter Carson punches a stunt girl, a little person and gets beat up by her."

Laura looks at me, thinks for a second and then smiles and laughs. Well, a couple of days go by and what do you think happens? The inevitable. Hunter raised his hands again and hit her. Little Laura Dash went MMA on him. The whole cast and crew viewed Laura as a hero and she was championed as the one who stood up (literally) to the belligerent brat known as Hunter. As for Karen Black, yes I had a meeting with her. She wasn't too happy and she expressed it like the crazy person she was. You know what I said to her? "Miss Black. You know that song by Crosby, Stills, Nash and Young?"

She said, "what?"

I replied, "you know that song titled, Teach Your Children Well?"

She shook her head.

I say, "you should listen to that."

Well, she asked me to leave using her vocabulary of four letter words. We never spoke again and I am proud to say that Laura Dash continued on the show. One last wonderful tale about my dear sweet Laura Dash since we are talking about her and this one is very endearing to me. We were doing a stunt where Karen Black and Hunter Carson are running in the sand and they get sucked down into the Martian's caves. I was doubling Karen and Laura was doubling Hunter. We start running and the tornado like sand funnel starts spinning with us on top. Do you guys remember that scene? We go around and around until we are slowly sucked into the caves, into a metal container that catches us and the sand as well. We get ready to do it. They call "action."

The whole time I am thinking about the stunt, not looking at Laura at all as we spin around four or five times and drop down out of the shot. We cut and the machine turns off. In the distance, I hear Tobe Hooper complaining. I run back up and Tobe Hooper is shaking his head. He asks me to look at the playback and I do, curious to see what happened. He tells me to look at the girl. I look and there is little Laura Dash holding her nose as she goes down into the sand. I try not to burst out laughing, it was so adorable, holding her nose and holding her breath. You could see it clearly. Tobe tells me to redo it without her holding her nose. I go back down and tell Laura what Tobe said as I am laughing at her and as she is laughing at herself. Then I ask her why she held her nose. "

I didn't want to get sand in my nose or my mouth, Steven," she said with a smile.

It was a funny moment and to this day whenever I see her, I hold my nose in fond greetings. The coolest thing on this film was meeting Jimmy Hunt, who was the original boy in the 1953 *Invaders From Mars*. He played one of the police officers in the film and I told him not to expect anything like the original on this crazy set. The funniest moment on this show was when I was doubling Louise Fletcher when she got eaten by a Martians. Nobody knew and I told people to keep it quiet. When I came down to set with ladies socks, a dress and a wig, no one could tell it was me. Womark couldn't tell, the Producers couldn't tell and Tobe Hooper couldn't tell.

Tobe looks around and yells, "where is Steve Lambert? Where is Lambert?" I kept quiet, laughing inside.

"Get Steven Lambert, I need to ask him how it's going to be done," he yelled.

All of a sudden, I raised my hands and said, "you're looking at her! I mean him!" Everyone started bursting out laughing, it was just hysterical. Then there was the moment of moments on this show. Three quarters of the way into the picture, we heard that there was going to be a showdown between Menahem and Tobe Hooper and their perspective lawyers. All this time Menahem has been unhappy and had been trying to get Tobe off the show, as we were weeks behind and so over budget it was laughable. Lunchtime comes and lo and behold, a stretch limo comes driving up right in front of the stage. Everybody's hiding, but hiding in a spot where they could see what is going on. Including myself. Menahem comes out with four lawyers in suits and ties, I call them the suit men. David goes out and starts talking to Menahem in Hebrew. I could tell Menahem was upset by his gestures. Tobe Hooper appears from the other side of the stage, flanked by three of his lawyers. Menahem and his four lawyers are on the other side, it was like the showdown at the OK Corral. Menahem was like Wyatt Earp, Tobe Hooper was like Billy Clanton. They were about twenty feet apart, not one inch closer.

Menahem is yelling at Tobe. "I want you off the set, you are fired! I have my lawyers here with a contract that says I can fire you at any time!"

A few seconds went by as Tobe waited for the dust that Menahem's words had kicked up to clear, while he took a swig of Dr. Pepper and a puff of his cigar. He cleared his throat and took aim at Menahem. "EXPLETIVE you Menahem, you can't fire me. This is my set," Tobe fired back like a loaded revolver.

"You have two minutes to remove yourself or I will see you are removed," flew Menahem's words.

Tobe side stepped them calmly and swung a run-on sentence back at Menahem. "Get off my set, I told you that you cannot fire me, go back to Israel and leave my set alone, just leave and go back into your limo and take your lawyers with you, take off now I say, leave immediately."

Like Wyatt Earp and Billy Clanton drawing their guns and shooting, the bullets became words. Back and forth this went for fifteen minutes, not one of them daring to give up an inch of ground. All this time I am watching David Womark talking Hebrew with Menahem with beads of sweat coming down his forehead and his hand on his head going through his hair in misery. I don't know what the hell he is saying but just watching was hysterically funny. Every now and then, Menahem would turn to David and tell him to shut up. We were like the townspeople cowering behind wagons, our eyes darting back and forth to see who the victor would be.

Finally, Tobe has had enough and says, "I am going back to work, I am done with your craziness." Tobe turns around and takes his lawyers back to the set with him. Menahem is left alone as Tobe leaves the showdown. David, like old Doc Holliday, is trying to talk to Menahem desperately in Hebrew. Again, I have no idea what he is saying. Menahem turns around, gets in his limo and leaves. We all came out from hiding and I asked David what had happened. He shrugged his shoulders and said, "Steven, I don't know. I just cannot wait for this show to be over."

I start laughing. Believe me, I wouldn't laugh, but it's Womark, my pal! To sum this all up, Menahem's plan from what I understood, was to get an Academy Award in some way or form. He hired these award winning actors and actresses and visual effects guys and other heads of departments that were very talented to help him try to achieve these things. The picture went to theaters and won an award. It was no Academy Award though. It was the Razzie for the worst picture of the year! How about that! On top of that, it had a budget of twelve million dollars and only made six. The moral of the story is, don't throw money and big names together and expect a recipe for success. It's never that simple but as you know now, Menahem Golan never cared about that.

Invaders From Mars was unfortunately the start of the fall of Menahem and Cannon Films. Hey, if you were wondering what happened to that spoiled brat, Hunter Carson, he grew up to be a Producer. You can find him on twitter @work4producer2. Check him out and send him a few tweets. (I wonder if he would remember punching Laura Dash in the face and getting beat up. I'm sure he does.) Okay, enough with the public relations, let's move on.

CHAPTER 31
(A Genius Idea. Stunt Softball.)

A few days go by and I call up a mutual member in the Stuntmen's Association, Rick Sawaya and told him my idea to play softball and bring everyone together, which he loved. He could coach and I would be the manager. So at the next meeting, I waited for the right time and I proposed the pitch. Guess what? They loved the idea! This was the beginning of the Stunt Softball league, 1986, which is still going on to this day, 2019. I can call myself the Godfather of the league. Rick Sawaya is the Godmother, hahaha. I called up Stunts Unlimited and asked if they wanted to play us and they said they did! Now that's cool. I had a laugh when the secretary from Stunts Unlimited said they were going to kick our ass. It was a way we could all work together and hopefully get rid of the bad juju that had been present at the prior meetings I had attended. Well, we had the game and what do you think happened? They all fought with each other! We were outfield first and when Rick attempted to put people in positions, they started arguing. We could only have nine players on the field at a time, so we planned to rotate every two innings.

Well, that pissed some people off as there were around twenty six of us. A few guys who were not put in the first inning, or didn't like the position they were given, quit right then and there! They walked off the field, I couldn't believe it. It didn't get much better from there. The second baseman would miss a ground ball, the shortstop would call him an idiot. The right fielder would get a fly ball hit right to him, didn't have to move a step and the ball would come down a foot away from him with two guys yelling, "you are a stuntman aren't you?"

The pitcher would walk six guys in a row, the whole team would be yelling at him. This happened throughout the game. You know what they say, it looked good on paper.

CHAPTER 32
(Having Fun With Chuck And Aaron Norris.)

I then got a call from Aaron Norris. I had worked with him in the past at the airport on *Good Guys Wear Black* and was excited to see him again. I went down to Coahuila, Mexico to location and saw a lot of people I knew who were working on it as well. People like Rick Avery, Jeff Haberstaff who was doubling Chuck, the list goes on. It was great to meet Chuck again. It was also great to see Aaron Norris again too.

Aaron had multiple personalities and they were all fun, good and crazy. I could tell he really came a long way from when I first met him. There was one person working on the movie, who when I met him, I couldn't believe my eyes. It was Bob Wall! Bob was Bruce Lee's friend and student and was in numerous films with Bruce. He was the guy that came at Bruce Lee with the bottles in *Enter The Dragon*. He also was a good friend with Chuck Norris.

The first day I saw him I was nervous and excited at the same. Here is a guy that was a student, friend and in almost every movie starring Bruce Lee. I didn't say anything to him the first day, he was just larger than life. He had a chair, a Director's chair next to Chuck on this film. That's how important he was. Two days went by and I would still say hi, but not really have a conversation with him. My bit came up on the fourth day, Chuck gave me an action part in the film where I rush at him like a bull, then I turn tail and he rushes me back and kicks me in my back.

Bob Wall was there watching and we shot the scene and applause erupted behind camera. You know when everyone claps behind camera, you are doing something right. For all you new guys and gals out there, your audience is always behind the camera when you are performing. You can't hear the crowds in the theaters, but you can hear your crew behind the camera. So always strive to do your best and hear the reactions from them. They might yell, they might scream, they might cheer, so be prepared for that. That is how you rate your performance in your own little way. Not by the Director, by all the ordinary people behind the camera.

After the bit, Bob Wall came over to me and congratulated me on the great job I did. Thus began our friendship. Chuck and Aaron invited me into their inner circle on this picture, much like Arnold did and Bob Wall was part of that circle as well. That is when I got to ask Bob the questions I had been dying to ask. I had a chance to sit down with him and talk to him. I wanted so very much to ask him so many questions and guess who about?

Yes, Mister Lee. Bruce Lee. But I thought to myself, I have to wait for the right time. There has to be a reason, otherwise, I'm just another guy wanting to hear about Bruce. Bob was a nice guy, and I hungered for information. So guess what. I waited until he brought Bruce up and that is when I pounced and then casually asked him two things. Why Bruce Lee put him in so many pictures with him and why he was given so many substantial parts. He looked at me and I'll never forget what he said.

"Because I was one of his favorite dummies and most important friends. Bruce had many people that he worked with. And I was lucky enough to be one of those people he admired because whenever he did something with me, I took it to the hilt. He liked the way I did stuff and how it looked.

On top of that, I was a white boy and every China man needs a white boy to beat up."

We both laughed. I just shook my head in awe. These were things no one has ever asked before, information I had never seen on television or read in a magazine.

I said, "you mean he used you in Enter The Dragon, because you were his friend and because you made things look authentic?"

He nodded with a smile.

"You know, that is exactly what I try to do, take things to the hilt!" I laughed back.

Bob told me he saw that and when he and Chuck were in the motorhome, they were talking about me. It was like the ultimate orgasm to hear this. Bob was saying that Chuck thought of me as Bruce Lee thought of Bob. I was just overjoyed. Imagine this, here comes fantasy land. What if Bruce Lee was still alive? Let's see. I've worked with Chuck, I've worked with Bob, I've stunt doubled Brendan and have done so many other things, just maybe I would have worked with him. Bruce Lee.

My mind and imagination were going a million miles an hour. Could have happened, mighta' been a great dummy. I would have been proud to get my ass kicked by the man, the legend. Moving on. When we had downtime on the set, Aaron and Dean would invite me along wherever Chuck went. Most of the time it was doing something athletic.

Hiking for four or five hours for instance. I was invited to go "fun-yaking" with them. You know what that is? I didn't. It's kind of like a one man canoe. Small, about five feet long, three feet wide. It's fiberglass or plastic, you can carry it on your shoulder. Fifteen of us went and Chuck was just one of the guys. It was about a five hour adventure down the stream which consisted of stopping and like a bunch of teenagers, throwing rocks into the water and pushing other stunt guys boats over with our oars. Yes, a bunch of guys even attacked Chuck and his boat and knocked him over. That is when he really started to laugh and enjoy himself, dunking our heads into the water. It was a fun time. We even created little fight scenes. Nobody was around, it was just Chuck and his guys and his brother Aaron.

Eventually, we got hungry and we stopped to eat lunch. Aaron and Chuck brought a caterer who brought all the food in a canoe. Yes, there was an adult there. It looked hysterical with all of our food in that tiny canoe. He was always at the back of the pack. A couple of times we even threatened to throw him over into the water, but he had the food and nobody wanted soggy bread. In this fun and adventurous moment, you could really see the brotherly love between Aaron and Chuck.

(Team Fun yakking. The stuntmen with Chuck and Aaron Norris.)

I had heard in the past they didn't get along with each other, but now I could see their relationship has really come full circle. That's a beautiful thing. One time, we rented some four wheelers. Me, Dean, Chuck and Aaron decided to go for a ride in the desert. We were using the four wheelers for the shoot, so we borrowed these vehicles from transportation. They belonged to the company. Off into the desert we went, zooming around and having a good time. After an hour and a half, deep into the middle of nowhere, Aaron Norris told us all to stop. He had brought a red flag that he wanted to use in an emergency. He stuck it out and we all stopped. We looked at Aaron who pointed to about a Brooklyn block away, to see six or seven guys on horseback. They are on this rise, spread out, rifles on their thighs. "Banditos." It was like a scene out of a movie.

"You know what that is?" Dean asks.

"What is it?" Chuck replies.

"Those are Mexican Drug bandits. I think we are getting close to their territory where they have their drugs," Dean announces.

Aaron said, "let's get the hell out of here."

As we are talking, they are on their horses, walking towards us slowly. We started going slow and then picked up the speed as we got further away. I was thinking oh my God, are we going to get killed here or what. After we got far enough away, we couldn't see them and then we hauled ass. Now we could have made this a movie. You guys out there may not believe Chuck Norris ran away from a confrontation like this. I could make it up and say we hid behind rocks and bull dogged them and defeated the bad guys and took their horses, but NO. This wasn't a movie, this was real life. It was a scary experience that led to opportunities to work for Chuck many times in the future.

CHAPTER 33
(Gary Busey Tried To Kill My Director With Cocaine.)

I take my maracas and sombrero back home, glad to be back in Los Angeles. I get a beep, beep, beep, beep. We didn't have phones then, we had beepers. A beep from Teddy O'toole's answering service. I was out and about and I call them right up on a payphone. Twenty five cents. Again, they have a Stunt Coordinator they are not happy with and they have a huge fight scene to do. Here we go again. I asked who the coordinator was and wouldn't you know it, it was someone in my group, the Stuntmen's Association. I was told the Director was Richard Sarafian and he just wasn't happy with the coordinator. Now, let me just say, that doesn't mean the coordinator was bad. That just means he wasn't happy with him. Reasons unknown. I thought back *to Invaders From Mars* when David set me up and here again I was told yes, he was released. I said to myself, good, there is going to be no Deja Vu on this one. I go down there, thinking this is a Martial Arts picture, very excited and ready to work out the fights. I arrived on set at lunchtime. I was brought to Richard Sarafian's office and I'll tell you right now that I gave him a nickname too. I called him "Mad Dog." Want to know why? He was a straight up hard ass New Yorker. He reminded me of Edward G. Robinson, from his voice to the way he acted. He would always say, "yeah," after every sentence.

"You think you're so tough? I heard you are a good fight man. Are you gonna show me, yeah?"

I laughed and saw he was holding a cigar. I said, "why don't you put the cigar in your mouth and I will kick it out."

He stood up with that cigar right in his mouth and I asked him to lean forward and then said, "you sure?"

He called my bluff and just as he finished, my whip kick came. The cigar went flying across the room. I thought to myself, this guy has guts.

He looked at me and he said, "yeah."

That's how he would converse. Within minutes I felt a kinship with him. The movie was called *Eye Of The Tiger*. We talked about the action and as usual, I would break down the script and get back to him with ideas and a budget. I also found out this was a Drama, not a Martial Arts film, which was still fine by me. He mentioned Gary Busey and Bill Smith were in it. I heard and read stories that Busey was a little off, but I thought was going to be fun working with him. Bill Smith was a legend. I remember watching old movies with my father and seeing Bill Smith as a motorcycle gangster, so meeting him would be great. I went home and put together a rough draft of a fight scene that was first up, which happened to be the ending of the movie. When I met with Richard the next day, I went over it with him. The fight was between Gary Busey and Bill Smith and cocaine was at the center of it. I started acting out the fight for Richard which I always loved to do and found most coordinators don't do that. I did that with Sarafian and told him my ideas. One of those ideas was that Busey put Bill Smith's head into a pile of cocaine on a table, which was really baby powder in our case. Richard loved the idea. I proceeded to explain to him some other action including the cars and motorcycle action. I met Gary a short time later, sticking out my hand to greet him.

He looked at me and said, "I hope you have a better attitude than the last guy that was here."

I smiled saying I was there to please him and to make him look good. He looked at me and then shook my hand, a good ten seconds after I had offered it to him. I said to myself sarcastically, oh this is going to be fun. Then I met Bill Smith who was a warm, sociable guy. It was a pleasant contrast. We started talking about the fight. Gary was there too and it looked like he couldn't care less. I told Bill that I used to sit in front of a black and white television and watch him in these motorcycle pictures with my father and they were fond memories. He enjoyed that and we shook hands and headed off. A few days later comes the fight scene inside this junkyard. I hired a guy named Shane Dixon to double Busey and another guy to double Smith. I went over the fight with them on set. Bill Smith was very easy to work with and caught on quick. He used to be a weightlifter and had plenty of experience in fights, so he knew a thing or two about physical action.

Gary Busey on the other hand was a whole different story. He was always asking about the why, when and where. He needed motivation for every move and was more than surprised when I gave it to him. I had to explain to him how things would look in the fight, to make it more like a street fight than theatrical. He was very a moody guy and sarcastic at that. He had zero patience. He was a "NOW" guy. If you didn't get it on the first take, you weren't sure if you would get it on another take. He had no direction and didn't seem to care. He was all over the place. We managed to get by until we get to the part where Busey puts Bob Smith's head into the mountain of cocaine on the table and he pretends like he is choking. I explained that you don't do it for real, it is a lot of body language and facial expression. I used my doubles to rehearse those things and at times, sliding myself in playing Busey and Smith. I always worked this way when it comes to physical stuff because if there was one thing I understood, it was body language and I wanted certain kinds of abnormal movements from both of them at times. I always found most Stunt

Coordinators would never physically go over the action to show their actors. This is another little lesson to be learned for you guys that are just starting.

Busey looked at me, put his hand on my shoulder and pushed me away hard. "Don't tell me what to do," he snapped.

I looked at him and said, "Gary, please don't push me. If you want me out of your way, all you gotta do is ask. I'm just trying to help."

He ignored me, but everyone else heard me. After we rehearsed it a few times talking about it and going over the motions, as this is the kind of thing you can't do in rehearsals, we shot it. Gary put Bill Smith's head into the cocaine very gently, it all looked very phony. It just wasn't working.

Richard is shouting, "do it harder, do it harder!"

I could tell Gary just wasn't giving it his all and wouldn't listen to Sarafian. I got the impression they didn't like each other. Three quarters of the way through, Sarafian has to cut. He walks over to Gary and in his New York attitude, yelled at Gary. Busey wasn't happy about that and just gave him a stare, didn't say a word. Here is a California boy being yelled at by a hard nosed New Yorker. It was funny in a way. Second take, it was a bit better but still looked half-assed. We weren't really getting anything from Bill Smith either. Sarafian kept cutting and Busey kept getting madder and madder. He kept trying to explain it to Busey who clearly wasn't listening, or just didn't care. Like an earthquake, the pressure built up and when Sarafian and I finally walked over to Gary for a fourth time to demonstrate and explain, Busey had had enough.

Sarafian walked forward and said to Busey, "I'm going to play Smith. Smith, you watch me, yeah? I want to really feel you shove my head in that powder, yeah?"

As Sarafian turned, leaning over, I caught a smirk on Busey's face. Before I could say anything, Richard put his head over the powder, ready for Gary to stuff his head in it. He told Gary he really wanted to feel him shoving his head in because Busey kept saying he was shoving it and he didn't believe it! So Busey grabs Sarafian's head and just sticks it into the baby powder, a smile on his face. I look at Richard's head and five seconds go by, ten seconds go by, and Busey ain't letting him up. In fact, he is shoving him deeper. Sarafian is sinking deeper into the powder, his hands flailing all over the place. He is trying to get up but Busey won't let him. I look at Busey and he is looking at everyone around him with a shit eating grin on his face. He is laughing and just won't let him up. Sarafian is struggling, his cigar drops out of his hand. Sometimes his head goes up enough where you can hear him coughing and gagging before Busey shoves it right back down, even harder. I run over to Busey yelling at him to let him go. Just as I get there, Busey steps back and lets him up.

The cloud of baby powder erupts like a huge cloud and as it subsides you see the baby powder just all over Sarafian. In his nose and all in his mouth. He falls on his butt choking and gagging and everyone starts screaming save for Busey who is laughing. I'm yelling to get him some water and he is just coughing like crazy. His face is getting redder and redder. He turns over on all fours and drops to his stomach, head on the dirt in pain. Big time. Someone brings two cups of water. I grab one and lift him up a little bit and try to give him water. Before I can grab the other, Gary grabs it and starts drinking it!

I said, "this isn't for you Gary, it's to wash his face off." I reach out to take the glass. Gary moves his hand away and throws it into Sarafian's face and everyone is aghast. He wouldn't stop coughing, so to make a long story short, he went to the hospital. We were shut down for two hours! Once he came back, Bill Smith was glad he didn't have a heart attack, as we all were very concerned.

We call Busey back to the set to redo it and Gary has the nerve to ask, "do you want to rehearse it again with me?"

Sarafian takes a puff of his cigar, his face was smooth as a baby's bottom and shouts, "just F****** do it and do it right this time, yeah!"

With a big grin, he obliges.

Bill Smith turns to him and says, in a nervous fashion, "you're going to let me up, right?"

Mind you, I am watching this dialogue.

Gary laughs and says, "yes, I like you."

I walk over and say, "Gary, please, you are going to let him up, right?"

We shot it and it went perfect, which makes me think it was all a set up by Busey! A week or so went by and I had another sequence I needed to do. I needed Busey to jump into the shot and start the action. I got a six foot ladder right next to camera and asked Shane Dixon to get up four feet on the ladder and jump off to show Gary. So that is what we do and Shane finishes doing it. We ask Gary to do it.

Gary says, "I don't want to jump off the ladder, I just will run into the shot."

I explained to him that he was jumping off of something in the last shot, so I needed a lead up into this shot. He was still resistant to my idea and I tried explaining to him the action again when I hear a voice behind camera.

"Don't be a baby, Busey!"

I looked over and it was the freaking cameraman! What a mistake that was. Busey looked at Sarafian and walked right back to his trailer, never saying a word.

We were stunned as he walked across the field back to his trailer. I thought to myself, what a stupid thing to say, so uncalled for. The First Assistant goes to talk to him and returns a few moments later.

"Gary said he will be out in five minutes and when he returns, he doesn't want to see the cameraman. He's fired," he announces.

Without missing a beat, Sarafian turns to the cameraman and says, "you're fired!"

The cameraman packed up his bags and left just like that.

Busey returns to set, looks around and says, "anybody else want to say something to me?"

Well, I had to. I walked over and quietly said, "Gary, I really need you to jump off this ladder, would you do that for me please?"

Gary nodded and said he would. Boy was I happy I still had my job and I got him to do the stunt. A few weeks after the picture I met the previously fired coordinator and asked him why he left.

He took one look at me and said, "you worked on it, you should know why." The name Gary Busey popped into my head and I nodded and said I understood. It really was great working with Bill Smith and about ten years ago, I was at Gold's gym working out with Sven Thorsen when a guy appeared and said hello to me. I had no idea who he was but pretended I did.

Sven came over and talked to him saying, "hello Bill, how you doing you low forehead?"

We talked a bit and said our goodbyes. When he left, I asked Sven who the hell was that.

He said, "that was Bill Smith you idiot, I thought you recognized him, you low forehead."

I said, "Bill Smith, the actor?"

Sven nodded, "yeah, the actor."

I was embarrassed and stunned. He looked nothing like when I worked with him, he was skinnier than me! He looked sick and so fragile. The way some people change is mind blowing.

I remember one television show I worked on was called *Stingray,* starring Nick Mancuso. He had to climb a ladder for this one scene and he told me he was afraid of heights. He exclaimed this fact by doing a lot of unnecessary complaining and cursing. Not to anyone in particular it seemed, but more so to himself. It was quite comical. After ten minutes they got him to come up and do his dialogue. Then he started complaining he didn't have a chair to sit on and without a coat, he was too cold. When we did the fight, he would complain as well for no obvious reason, I bring this up because the next two shows I worked on with him, he did the same thing! Everyone on set took it too because he was the star. Amazing what you can get away with when you have your name on the first title card, but that was my memory of Frank Mancuso. He was a serial screamer and a nutcase. After this show, he never really worked again.

CHAPTER 34
(Actress Shelley Winters. One Crazy Lady.)

Driving along Pacific Coast Highway California, with some of my stunt buddies including one of my heroes, John Meier. Going surfin' USA and looking at all the honeys, whoops, I mean beautiful women, when my beeper goes off. I call good ole' Teddy's and they tell me it's the TV show *The Colbys*. They wanted to know if I was available to double someone and to put together a fight. I said sure, let's bring it on. Good ole' Teddy tosses me the number, verbally that is. I call them up and accept. No rehearsals, they just want to shoot it in one day. Work it out in the morning and film after lunch. I get down there and I meet up with the First Assistant. He explains to me it is a big party on set with most of the stars of the Colbys. Crystal glasses, fancy silverware and tuxedos. I am doubling one of the Colbys and there is a fight with two other actors. No big deal. You know, you would figure nothing to talk about, except when I tell you who the guest stars are. James Brolin, star of the TV show Medical Center. For those of you who don't know who the hell James Brolin is, he is Barbra Streisand's husband and he is also the father of the actor Josh Brolin.

Now let's get to the reason why I am telling you this story. Shelley Winters, an actress that was the star of big movies from the nineteen forties and fifties was a guest star. She was a hot momma then. Now? She is like a Jewish grandma. You look at some of the movies she had starred in the past, what a beautiful woman. Smart, talented, the face of an angel and a figure to go along with it. A very talented woman, but listen here, we are talking about nineteen eighty seven, not nineteen forty three. We are talking about forty plus years that have gone by. We were doing a scene where she is talking to one of the Colbys and James Brolin. As we are rolling, another bit actor is supposed to come up and say his line to Shelley Winters and happened to have a long stemmed wine glass in his hand. When they rehearsed it, it was fine. However, when it was picture time, they called action and this poor actor walks over to deliver his line and mind you there are sixty people on set. Actors, extras, four or five cameras, a huge party scene. This actor decides to sip his wine and improv, not realizing that he is putting the stem of his glass right into the middle of Shelley's face!

The bottom of the stem is literally two inches away from her nose. I don't know if the actor realized it or not but let me tell you, Shelley did. Shelley Winter's demeanor grew so cold, I began to shiver as she raised her hand and WHACK! The wine glass went flying out of the actor's hand and flew halfway across the ballroom onto the floor.

Shelley starts screaming hysterically at the top of her lungs at this poor actor who is now frozen with fear. James Brolin jumps back, fearful and confused at what he sees.

"HOW DARE YOU BLOCK MY FACE WITH YOUR GLASS! WHO TAUGHT YOU HOW TO ACT? WHAT THE F IS THE MATTER WITH YOU? HOW DARE YOU DO THAT TO ME! GET OUT OF HERE YOU ONE BIT CLUELESS FOOL," Shelly boomed.

Now mind you, James Brolin and the Director tried to calm her down but she is getting worse. She soon starts demanding at the top of her lungs that everyone gets out of the room, including the crew.

Everyone is shocked and is reacting with fear and confusion. I mean watching this, if you asked my opinion, she has a big time screw loose. The First Assistant and the Director ask everybody to leave for a few minutes, except the main actors in the scene.

Wine boy leaves, never to show his face again. They cut him out. I decide to stay because the actor I am doubling is in this scene.

Hanging back a little, I hear, "HEY WHO ARE YOU?"

I turn and see Shelley Winters ask me again.

"WHO ARE YOU? COME HERE!"

Mind you, she is yelling this to me, as you can tell and everybody is watching. I walked over and simply explained, "I am your Stunt Coordinator and I have a little fight scene to do at the party. If you think I should leave, I will leave too."

All of a sudden, she reaches out and grabs my arm. I get pulled over like a dog resisting its leash. In one quick movement, she grabbed my arm and sat me down on her lap. I try to get up, but she quickly puts one arm around my wrist and the other arm is around my waist holding me on her lap with force.

Every millimeter of a second, whatever that means, I am trying to get up but she has me good.

I don't want to hurt her so I just try to go with it while still trying to get up. Her old lady perfume clogged my nose big time, very disturbing. It was question time for me.

"Who are you?" she asked me again.

"I'm Steven, the Stunt Coordinator on the show," I replied trying to get to a standing position.

She looked at me and said, "You do those dangerous stunts on the show?"

I said "yes," again trying to get up as everybody is watching.
She smiled and put her head against my side just like my grandmom, Rita.

(If I had a choice, I would sit on the before. Not after.)

(Before)   Shelley Winters   (After)

"What is a sweet boy like you doing all those dangerous things for? You could get hurt," Shelley Winters near whispered.

I finally got up, answering the question. "Miss Winters, I enjoy this. It's my job."

I say this as she reaches up with her hand and softly strokes my cheek. I simply say, "thank you," as I step back to let the Director and First Assistant get this thing going again. You had to be there, folks.

CHAPTER 35
(Aaron Norris And My sixth Sense.)

Another TV show I found interesting that I worked on was The *New Perry Mason Show*. A remake of the original starring the same guy, Raymond Burr. Dean Farrendini was coordinating the show. He asked me if I was interested in playing a bad guy. I would be doing a fight in a bar, go through the window in the bar and do a car hit. I thought that would be great. I asked who I was doing the fight with and he said, William Katt. Listen to this little tidbit. Barbara Hale who was in the original, as Perry Mason's secretary is William Katt's mother. How cool is that? This was going to be fun. I asked who was driving the car that hits me blind and he said, Aaron Norris. That made me smile. Dean and Aaron were very close friends and worked together a lot. I knew for a fact that Aaron was a fine fight man, but this time he would be hitting me with a car and I don't see him coming when he hits me. So I go to set and meet Raymond Burr and let me tell you, Raymond was one of the widest men I had ever seen. Not fat, but wide. If you look at some of the minions from the film Despicable Me, his body structure was just like that. There was no roundness to him, he was squared off like a tank. It was amazing to me to see someone like this, someone who was built this way. We get ready to do this shot and I was under the impression we are going to do all this in separate pieces. Nobody told me that, it was simply elementary, as Sherlock Holmes would say. SO I THOUGHT. Film individual shots. Inside the bar and then outside on the street. That is until Dean came over to me and said the Director wanted to do everything in one piece. I told him he was going to have to cut from camera to camera. Camera A inside the bar can see the fight but won't see the crash out the window. Camera B won't see the fight in the bar inside and Camera C won't notice anything before.

"Dean, that is simply common sense," I said.

Dean shrugged and said, "that's what the Director wants."

One shot. I thought to myself, well here is an interesting challenge for me. I was to fight in the bar, explode out the window, I get up and palm past a truck in my way and step past the truck into the street and get hit by a car I don't see coming. Now remember, I never see the car that is coming until I get around the truck and then it's too late. That is the way they wanted it to look. I ask Aaron how fast he would be going and he tells me about fifteen miles per hour. Okay, good. I say to myself, if the timing isn't right, I can get away from a car going fifteen miles an hour. No problem. As they say, piece of cake. Simple as pie. Nothing to it. So I agreed we would do it in one shot. Time goes by and about an hour before the shoot,

I see Dean talking to Aaron. This happened about three to four times. Now what I'm about to explain to you, you may not understand. You may think I'm crazy. Let me tell you, there was a song written once and the title of it was "Hooked On A Feeling," sang by B.J. Thomas and that is truly the way I felt.

Each time it happened, my spidey street sense kicked in. Were they talking about me? Yes, that's the way I felt. What were they saying? I would go over and they would change the subject. I told Aaron that I wasn't going to see him coming as I come around the truck and emphasized it was important that he went fifteen miles an hour. He said he would and mind you, I have seen Aaron do a lot of things and they were all radical, crazy or out of control. Let me tell you there is nothing wrong with that, but in this case, it is something to think about. You know what I mean? Those out there who know Aaron Norris, like me, know he is a wonderful human being and a great guy.

Yet, there is always that other side. You know what I'm talking about? I had never seen him drive a car for a car hit. It can be exciting and the sense I'm getting from the conversations that I'm not hearing, tells me that he may want to go a little faster. I spoke to Dean about it and he assured me he had told Aaron to go fifteen miles an hour. It was all worked out, I was reassured. In my mind, I know that something is up, but what am I going to do? I can't go to the Production Manager and tell them I have a feeling that the stuntman who is my good friend is going to drive the car faster than fifteen miles per hour. He would look at me like I'm crazy, Aaron is a professional. Still, something was up, I just knew it.

I was stuck between a rock and a hard place, between two cactuses, icing between two Oreo cookies. Some would say that last one is not a bad thing. This was a multi-ton machine he was driving that could take my legs off. There is a certain way to do a car hit, not everyone can do it. You have to put your hands on the hood and jump up with both feet like a jack in the box into an almost rounded handstand. Timing is of the utmost importance. Otherwise, you can plant your face in the windshield. Especially when you are not looking. Most stunt people don't like that idea. Not looking, that is. So we go to rehearse it and I go into the bar. We throw our punches and I go out the door to the outside of the window and drop down approximately where I would have fallen. I get up and head into the street and palm the truck. I peek out and see Aaron going ten miles an hour. I jump up and do a half speed car hit, roll off onto the ground and everything is fine. Okay, you ready for this? No, not the song by Jock Jams.

We do it for real, cameras roll and off I go. I do the fight, get punched, run through the interior of the bar towards the front glass knocking people away. Chairs flying, tables going every which way. I explode out of the bar window and just eat the ground. I get up, dazed and confused and the truck comes out. I slam into the truck and palm around it erratically at full speed to the other side, not thinking about anything except what is about to happen. I'm not looking at where Aaron is with this car and I take one big hop away from this truck into the street and luckily at the last second, I see him out of my peripherals. Aaron Norris is literally two feet away from me. Not going ten, not going twenty, not going forty, not going forty five, but over FIFTY PLUS MILES AN HOUR. Yeah, you heard me. Now some of you might ask how I knew he was going over fifty. Believe me, you just know.

(Aaron Norris driving. I thought I was dead.)

Get into a conversation with a very physical stunt person who has done many car hits and understands situations like this and they will basically tell you the same thing. Out of pure desperation, I throw my hands up and like a rag doll, when my hands hit the hood of the car it propels me up higher. I completely go over the car three feet up, spinning like a dreidel as he goes whizzing beneath me. I come down and land right on my back. Slam my head, slam my wrist. I'm lying there in shock to catch my breath. The fall knocked the air out of me. I find myself asking, "are you all right Steven? Are you alive? Any broken bones?" All this while I'm gasping for air.

I hear the Director yell, "cut!"

I hear Aaron screeching across the intersection, joined by a death defying scream. I sit up, wind knocked out of me unable to speak. I would come to find out I had badly bruised ribs and a fractured wrist. I guess I looked pretty funny because I was still asking myself if I was hurt. I look over and see the scream came from the Production Manager. Yes, it was a man screaming, I couldn't believe it. He runs over as pale as a ghost and asks if I was all right. Guess what, this screaming man was also in tears. I'd never seen that before. Yes, you can laugh. I do, every time I think about it. Cast and crew, even Raymond Burr join in to see if I am okay. I couldn't speak which scared them even more. I watched and saw Aaron get out of the car, enraged at him. The look on his face was a look of a man that was surprised I was getting up to my feet. I guess, in his mind, he wanted to make the stunt more exciting. I'm going back remembering the chit chat between him and Dean and I shook my head, knowing my intuition was right. Even though Aaron got yelled at for going so fast, the scene was done.

It was cut and print, but the scar there was left. I walked over to him with a few expletives asking him what the hell just happened.

"You didn't go fifteen, you went fifty," I shouted.

I never got any real answers from them, just apologies. I decided not to take it any further and was just grateful I got out of there alive. This was one of two times in my life, I looked up to God and thanked him for keeping me alive. That is how dangerous it was. This is a situation in your life and in your business that there is just nothing you can do about. You just thank God that you came out of it. They were having a wrap party that night and I was invited. After that ordeal, I decided enough was enough and took a flight right home. I was so in shock and upset, that I couldn't bring myself to go to a party when I could have been badly injured if not killed.

CHAPTER 36
(Jogging With Meg Ryan, Dancing With Martin Short And Avoiding Dennis Quaid.)

In the sky flying over the Golden Gate bridge, there I was, coming in for a landing into the airspace, I mean *Innerspace* the movie. Starring Dennis Quaid, Meg Ryan and Martin Short, who I am doubling. I meet up with my boss and we go to have a cowboy meal. Steak and potatoes. It was good to see this hard nosed cowboy again. Glenn Randall Jr. It's always nice to have someone who appreciates your work and calls you back. As we talk, I realize there are a lot of opportunities on this show to bring in stunt people and that's what happens. I am asked to give recommendations. I mention Joel Kramer, my good friend as well as stuntman John Hateley to ride a motorcycle, one of the best riders I have ever seen. There is a respect between us at this point in our relationship and he nods his head. You see, you always want a few people around you that you trust and have faith in, who know you and your ability when you are working on dangerous pieces of action. Feeling a bit braver, I make it a point to bring up Mike Vendrell with a smile. I thought I would try to push it.

Glenn just simply looks at me and says, "you can lead a horse to water but you can't make them shit. NO."

I laughed. After our dinner we went back to the hotel, waiting for the next morning to come and looking forward for Randall to introduce me to all the actors and the Director. First, it was Dennis Quaid and Meg Ryan. Quaid mentioned he had heard I did Kung Fu and said he had dabbled in the Martial Art world for a while and would love to work out with me.

I said, "sure, we will find some time." Unfortunately, that never happened. Why you ask? Maybe you should keep reading and see if you can figure it out. As for Meg, we simply said our hellos as I became infatuated within seconds by her beautiful smile. She was adorable. Today? That's a whole different story. Two words for that. Plastic Surgery. It's a shame. Next was Martin Short and what a great, personable guy. He was very welcoming and full of excitement and energy. We sat and talked for twenty minutes about our lives and he even caught my Brooklyn accent, which everybody catches after they talk to me for a while. He started making fun of my accent, talking like Muggs Mcginnis from *The East Side Kids*, and I couldn't help but laugh, it was great. One of the pieces of action we had, was with Kevin Mccarthy, the lead bad guy in the film. Kevin Mccarthy was in the Body Snatchers in 1956, a cult classic and mentioned it was one of the most miserable shoots he was on.

"But it made me a star," he said. He explained that they were working around twenty hours a day and hardly got paid for it. He had no idea what a cult hit it would be and I completely understood, as it kind of happened to me with *Revenge Of The Ninja.* I always enjoyed talking to people from the old film library. (It was the only kind of library I visited often. The movies. No books. I didn't have enough patience to read.) Moving on to a very unique sequence that you don't have the opportunity to do, but once in your lifetime. I had to maneuver from a moving truck onto a convertible driven by Meg Ryan and her stunt double. No wires, no cables, I insisted. For me, that was always the way to go. Near misses with cars, straddling vehicles, transferring from one vehicle to another while motorcycles went underneath and through my legs, all the time knowing it must look comical and off balance. Buster Keaton, he we come. Which truly makes everything you do much more difficult. My boss asked me who would I like driving the truck. There were about fifteen stunt guys. I mentioned I needed a guy who I could trust. Who knew me and knew my work. Someone who I didn't have to worry about and had the utmost confidence in. You see, doing a sequence like this, it takes two to create a masterpiece.

So I said, "my favorite goyim."

 Glenn Randall said, "what the hell is a goyim?"

I said, "Joel Kramer."

I told him I needed somebody to go with the flow and not get worried or scared about what I am doing. You see, a lot of stunt guys would freak out and not go with the flow.

If they saw it was looking like I was going to fall, they would stop and cut. Not Joel Kramer. He knows me and I know him.

We have complete confidence in each other. You see, we did it flawlessly and got thunderous applause from the crew.

(Look ma, no cables. Stuntman Steven Lambert doubling Martin Short.)

At this time, I would notice Meg Ryan would come over and comment to me on how impressed she was by my heroics, not thinking much of it and just giving her a simple, "thank you."

She flashed a smile and feathered her hand, running it down my arm. Yes, I got the tingles. I can dream, can't I? Days went by and we would cross paths when she asked me if I wanted to go jogging with her, on her day off which happened to be the following day.

It was a large, bustling city and she said she could use the company, so I agreed. Wouldn't you? So the next day we met up and went out jogging an hour and a half in Grand View Park. We had a good time and we talked about our lives and how we got brought up. We stopped at a juice store and got drinks together, while she stopped to sign a few autographs. At times I felt like a bodyguard. At the end of our run, we said our goodbyes. She had asked if I wanted to join her again and I told her, "anytime."

I shook her outstretched hand and she gave me what I call the "Ryan Smile." Wow! Infatuated, who wouldn't be. You couldn't help but have an uncontrollable crush on someone like her, but you just laugh it off. Ha ha ha, and you leave. The next day on location, I am working on the vehicle sequence and the First Assistant comes over to me.

He tells me he needs to have a conversation with me and pulls me aside. He goes, "I understand you went out with Meg Ryan yesterday."

In my head, I am thinking, yeah, no big deal. He continues on, a really strange look on his face. I'm confused about what is taking place here.

He continues. "Well, I have to explain something to you, Steven. We all love your work and think you are a very valuable asset to this production, but I have a suggestion that would be good to follow. The suggestion is, I wouldn't advise you to go out with Meg Ryan anymore."

I looked at him, my mouth is open, my eyes are squinted and asked what he was talking about.

He said, "well there are certain powers on this show that heard about it and are not too happy."

I said, "what?? Not too happy about what? We just went jogging and stopped to get some juice. I felt more like her bodyguard, my god, what are you talking about? It was just innocent. She just wanted some company."

He leans in close and says, "between you and me I must say, my suggestion if she asks again? Politely decline."

I asked who didn't like it, I really didn't understand what was going.

He looked at me and said simply, "Dennis."

I said, "Dennis? Dennis Quaid? Why does he care?"

The Assistant looks at me and says, "they are an item."

Now I understood. Now you understand why I never worked out with him. On the other hand, can you imagine walking up to him, smiling, and saying, "hey Dennis, you want to work out?"

I wonder what he would say. I asked the First Assistant to tell Dennis it was completely innocent, I went with her because I assumed she was simply bored and wanted company. He assured me he would tell Denis (who never had the nerve to tell me himself it seems) and just wanted to stress that I take his suggestion.

I told him, "I got it." From then on it felt like there was a fence between me and Meg Ryan whenever we would work together. Dennis never spoke to me after that. Every time I saw him on the set he would give me a dirty look. Everything went fine, but knowing that occurred, it was one for the record books.

Very strange when you have to stay far away from a person when you are working with them. Quaid.

The last day I did the vehicle sequence, the Director, the Producers and Martin Short came over and gave me a bottle of champagne, Dom Perignon. I still have it to this day, never opened. Even though I got this bottle, it really does take two to tango and the guy driving the truck deserved it just as much as me. What we were doing took the utmost timing and coordination and trust between each other to work correctly.

I owe whatever accolades to Joel Kramer because he was the one driving the truck. One wrong move, I could have been badly injured and the trust I had for him was immense. A true professional at his very best.

Remembering Glenn had fifteen guys working on the show that day and when he asked me who I wanted to drive the truck, I couldn't get the words out fast enough. Joel Kramer.

Whoever out there enjoyed this sequence *in Innerspace*, I want you to know it was a team effort. Two goyim, Lambert and Kramer. You out there, you want to know what goyim means? A non-Jew. But we were Jewish. That was just our pet names for each other. Whenever we were on the set together and there were a bunch of people around, if we wanted to talk in private, we would call out to each other, "goyim! It's time!" We knew exactly what that meant.

(First issue of premier magazine. Centerfold: Joel Kramer and Steven Lambert.)

Okay, I do have embarrassing moments. There is a scene in the movie where Martin Short is drinking with Dennis Quaid who is inside him and he gets up and starts dancing to Rod Stewart's "Twisting The Night Away." Remember that song? He starts dancing all over the room and acting foolish, but it was funny. The DP asked him what he was going to do.

Martin Short says, "I don't know, just let it happen."

DP says okay, "let me see."

So they put on the music and there he goes. Everybody is gathering around watching and Martin Short starts dancing away. What do you expect? He is a comedian. Camera enjoys it and he finished the rehearsal. Everyone applauds.

I happen to be on stage in case there were pratfalls and they needed me. Martin goes to hair and makeup to get ready for the scene when the DP asks for him to go through the dance routine again for camera. Someone yells back he was in hair and makeup and the DP spots me on set. He waves me over,

"Hey Steven, did you see what Martin did?" he asked me.

I replied "YEAH," not sure what he was getting at.

"Why don't you go do that for camera?" he responds.

I shake my head and reply, "NO. I ain't going to go out and do that, it's ain't my job."

Glenn Randall Jr. is watching me closely and I didn't want to act like a fool. I had my tough guy image and didn't want to lose that. The Director chimes in his opinion and agrees with the DP that I should go do it.

I look at Glenn and he tells me to "go out there, Mister gazelle."

Now everyone is coaxing me to go out there. So I walk out to the set and the music starts playing. I find myself red as a tomato as I start doing this goofy dance and trying to mimic what Martin had done. And here I go. I start by swiveling my hips, throwing my hands up, flapping like a bird in the sky. Putting my legs together, like I have to go to the bathroom, I start hopping around doing the Kung Fu shuffle. Yes, everything reverts to Kung Fu in my life.

Trying not to look at people, I'm jumping on tables and the piano chair and I find myself doing the tiger and praying mantis forms. I start to run out of things to do! Everyone is laughing as I switch from katas to Elvis, trying to do whatever I could think of.

Please picture this in your mind. Twenty seconds go by when I feel a bump on my back and I turn and see Martin Short dancing with me!

I stop dead and walk away but he grabs me saying, "we are a good team!" I couldn't get out of there fast enough! Everyone is in tears. He tries to get me back by doing Muggs Mcginnis, but even the entire cast of *The East End Kids* wouldn't get me back dancing on that set! But it happened. He starts dancing, then stops. He points to me and says, "go, Steven!"

This repeats itself three or four times until both of us start together. Face to face. We are competing against each other to see who has the funniest dance moves. All of a sudden, money starts flying in. Coins. They are throwing money at us like two monkeys. I go to pick some up and yell out, "hey man, I'm Jewish. I see money and everything stops."

Martin Short tackles me to try and take away the coins I picked up. He knocks me on the ground. It's hysterical. Good times. Now that was embarrassing. It had nothing to do with stunts! Let's now bring back my good friend, John Moio. A man that has done so much for so many.

CHAPTER 37
(James Woods. This Was The Start Of A Beautiful Friendship.)

I get a phone call from John and he says he is doing a show starring James Woods called, *Best Seller.* He is a cop, a James Bond like figure and needs to act cool as a cat. The problem is, John explains, James is a brainiac. Not an athlete. That kind of threw me off and I asked him what he meant. This wasn't a fight or stunts, what did he mean train him to look cool? Nevertheless, I agreed, figuring I would show him stances and how to move, just like a Martial Artist.

At the same time, John also mentioned that he wanted me to teach him how to fight and the deal was made. He asked me to come down and meet James Woods and that is what I did the next day. Mister James Woods and I talked for a few minutes and he also realized I was a Brooklyn boy. We laughed and we got along great. Our schedule was to be four to five times a week of training where I began to teach him how to move powerfully, incorporating fighting movements in everyday motions to look cool. Long story short, we became good friends and often went out to eat together. I had this one activity that I liked to do with actors, stuntmen and even my partner of this book. That activity was to take them to Stony Point in Chatsworth, CA.

Stony Point had long been a prime filming location for everything from old westerns to Star Trek. There is a section that is all boulders and steep inclines and you climb up it to the top. Then when you go down, you rock bop to the bottom. That was my exercise, where you simply run, jump and bounce off the rocks down this mountain without stopping. You can play follow the leader with two or ten people with the goal of trying to get down the mountain in one piece. I took James Woods there as I did every actor that I have trained and suggested this to him.

He took one look at me and said, "you're out of your mind."

We still trained there and had a good time, discussing that actors from John Wayne to Roy Rodgers and James Cagney had worked out in this place. And now James Woods. People noticed us, I mean him and asked for his autograph. Always being gracious as I noticed then and all through our relationship, that he enjoys talking to people. It was here that he mentioned to me he had a good idea and asked me to double him for his stunts in the film. By then he asked me to call him Jimmy and I said, "I would love to do that Jimmy, but the Stunt Coordinator has to make that decision as I am just your coach."

And that was the end of that. So I thought. We went back to the Production Office and said our goodbyes. The next day I get a call from the Production Manager,

Jack Roe, who happened to be the same Production Manager on *Remo Williams*. We both got along great with him and his wife, who was head of Wardrobe on Remo and this show as well. Nepotism, isn't that great? We had a few laughs discussing the memories on that show on the phone before he asked me out of the blue to Stunt Coordinate this movie starring James Woods.

I said, "wait a minute, John Moio is the coordinator on this shoot isn't he?"

Jack clears his throat and says, "well Jimmy came into the office and had a request that he wanted you to double him."

I nodded slowly, thinking this through. "Fine, I will double him but you gotta get an OK from Moio, you know how that works," I stated slowly.

The PM answers back, "well you know we have a restricted budget on this film and if you could double him and coordinate at the same time, we could save a lot of money."

Now I was friends with Jack and prided myself on being a lot smarter than that and knew exactly what he was doing. "Wait a minute," I stammered. "You are just trying to save money here and it don't work that way. You are putting me in a difficult spot. Moio is my friend and he hired me. I will tell you now, no. You keep Moio, I won't do it. I will double Jimmy if that is Moio's wish, but as to coordinating, homey ain't playing that ball game."

So we said our goodbyes and hung up. The next day I met Jimmy for a training session and prayed this wouldn't be brought up. Everything went well and not a word about it was said. After we trained, I was grateful it wasn't brought up and went home quite relieved. I sat down on my couch to put my feet up when my phone rang. It was my very good, currently pissed off friend, John Moio. He starts screaming through the telephone and I ask him what he was going on about.

"YOU'RE TRYING TO STEAL MY SHOW. I GOT A PHONE CALL TODAY FROM JACK WHO SAID JIMMY WANTS YOU TO STUNT DOUBLE HIM AND NOW THAT WOODS ASKED FOR THAT, NOW JACK SAID HE WANTS YOU TO COORDINATE," he yells.

I waited for him to take a breath then quickly interjected. "Wait, wait, hold on a moment. Your cheap conniving friend, Jack Roe, is trying to play games here. Can't you see what he is doing? He is trying to pit us against each other. I told him I won't do it! So please relax John and stop yelling at me or next time I see you I will give you the Chinese monk death touch."

Moio however, did not fear death and screamed louder than ever. "HOW COULD YOU DO THIS TO ME?" He boomed.

I quickly began my defense again. "This is Jack's idea because he wants to save money, I had nothing to do with this."

John would not relent. "I HIRED YOU AND NOW YOU ARE TAKING OVER MY JOB, WHAT ARE YOU THINKING?"

I began to feel sleazy inside and tried to put a stop to this. "John, go tell Jack and Jimmy I said no, I am innocent in this, you have to believe me. I am telling you the truth. In fact, I don't even want to train him anymore. Get somebody else.

"I DON'T KNOW WHAT TO BELIEVE," John screams back.

I am trying to find the right words to say when laughing erupts from the other end of the line. "HAHA, I GOT YOU, APRIL FOOLS! I AM JUST FUNNING WITH YOU! I KNOW WHAT HAPPENED. Listen closely, I want you to take the job, you can have it."

My mind is racing in shock. "No," I said. "After all that, making me feel like a piece of dirt? I can take a joke but this is friendship man, you know?"

He tells me he has another show and I didn't believe him at first. This is one of the reasons my nickname for him is Doctor Jekyll and Mister Hyde, you never know what you are going to get from him. He finally convinced me to take the job as he did have another one and I took the reins from him peacefully. It was a beautiful thing that Moio did because that was the start of a wonderful career with Mister James Woods. Hey, listen to this. The first day I went to work on *Best Seller*, I go right to makeup and hair. They sit me down and they start their fix to my hair. Then they go over to a drawer and pull out an electric razor. I'm thinking it's to do a light trim on my hair, but the darn thing comes towards my eyes.

I jump back and say, "hey, what are you doing?"

"We gotta shave your eyebrows," they say.

"Shave my eyebrows? What for?"

She said, "James Woods has no eyebrows. Look at his picture on the mirror."

I look and she is right! He has no eyebrows. I look at her and say, "what does that have to do with me? I'm his stuntman, if you see my eyebrows then we're in trouble. I hide my face."

She replied, "we are going to have to tell the powers if you don't want us to take them off."

I think for a second and just bite the bullet. So they go and I look in the mirror, scared the shit out of myself! I'm not kidding. Hey, you out there reading this. Try it sometime. Look in the mirror and see what you look like. Mind you, it's not just for one day. They take months to come back. I had to wear sunglasses for two months. Every show after that, it became like a game. Sometimes I kept my eyebrows, sometimes I didn't. I never did mention it to Woods. I thought it might be embarrassing that I didn't like it. But when he did see me with no brows, never saying anything, I could tell by his expression that he was happy. Now Mister John Moio. I'll always love this guy even though he pisses me off all the time. There were days I was called to take another job on this show and was lucky enough to replace myself with people like Glenn Randall Jr. and Roy Clark, people who have worked me in the past. For all you newcomers out there, never forget the people who have helped you in the past. This was the start of a friendship between me and Jimmy that would make us almost like family. I met his brother and I met his mother who reminded me of my mother and you could tell she loved her sons to no end. His little brother looked up to Jimmy and so loved him as if he were an idol. They were such great people and that was the start of a beautiful friendship. There was one other person on *Best Seller* that became part of our little movie family and that was Debbie Figuly.

One time we were working out and Jimmy mentioned to me that he wasn't sure if he was going to use the makeup artist he met, named Debbie that they brought for him on this picture. I asked what he meant and he explained that her hair was three different colors, yellow, black and orange.

I said, "what?"

He said that on top of that, "she wears bracelets on her arm."

"What is wrong with wearing bracelets?" I asked.

Jimmy shrugged. "Nothing when you wear one or two, but she has about fifty on each arm."

I shook my head in disbelief. I asked if she came from Africa and Jimmy told me no, she was a New York Italian! We laughed and continued the workout. A few days later I met Debbie in a production meeting and saw her hair and bracelets and I thought she was great. Long story short, Jimmy and I took a liking to her and we became the three amigos. Jimmy began to ask for me and her whenever he did a picture. She was a really down to earth person and extremely talented. *Best Seller* was a great beginning with an actor who became almost like a big brother to me. That is how I felt towards him and that is how we continued to grow together.

How about this, another odd thing that happened on this set was Jimmy began to admire in a strange way, the way I dressed. To me, it wasn't strange. It was normal, even though all my friends always poked fun at the way I dressed. Some called me high pockets because I wore my pants almost to my solar plexus. I told him I like wearing loose clothes because they look cooler and I can move around better. I am such an active guy, I don't want to worry about being stuck in tight clothes. I hate it.

I called it a Martial Arts thing and took that style in the way I dressed. My clothes were always baggy. I liked to wear zoot suits when I had to dress up and enjoyed the freedom of movement I had.

Shortly after we talked about that, I attended a production meeting where all the heads of departments were there as usual. When we got to Wardrobe, the wardrobe lady began issuing her displeasure. At what you might say? At the small problem that she had with James Woods new decision. She told us she had bought over a hundred thousand dollars of clothes for him from socks to suits. When she brought them for him to try on, he said he didn't want them! Instead, he wanted baggy clothes.

As soon as I heard that, something clicked. Oh shit, I think I am trouble. She tried to talk him out of it and had no idea why he changed his mind.

He had explained to her that baggy clothes would make him look cooler and he could move around better. Oh no, I realize this is what I had said to Jimmy about why I wore loose clothes! I am keeping quiet, sweating bullets, hoping she didn't look at me and tell me it was MY fault that I had changed his mind. Luckily no name was mentioned and we endured her tirade on why she had to take back all these clothes. The next day I saw Jimmy, I told him what wardrobe said and he nodded, saying he took my advice and that is what he had told her.

I said, "Jimmy please whatever you do, don't tell anyone you got that idea from me." We both laughed and he promised that he wouldn't.

CHAPTER 38
(Kirk Cameron, The Pampered Prince.)

Time went by and I started working on more television shows such as *Matlock, L.A. LAW, China Beach, Dallas,* and *Growing Pains.* Ah, let us stop and talk about the only time I got fired and by who you may ask? The pampered prince himself, Kirk Cameron from *Growing Pains.* Yes, I came to find out that was his nickname, known to everybody on set except him. I get a call from a friend of mine, stuntman Buck McDancer who wanted me to double Kirk. I say, "sure" and I go on the set the next day.

I went right to hair and makeup and my hair wasn't right so they were going put a Kirk Cameron wig on me. As they proceeded to put it on, guess who walks into the hair and makeup trailer? Mister prince, but you can call him pampered. That's right, Kirk Cameron strolls in to get his hair and makeup done. A few minutes go by and I see him staring at me through the mirror. We are looking at each other, not saying a word, until I decided to break the silence.

"Hello Kirk, my name is Steve Lambert, I am your stunt double today."

He reciprocated back with a blank expression on his face. My street sense kicks in that something isn't right here, but it quickly goes away. A few minutes go by with more silence in the air, and as he finishes up his makeup and hair, I find myself saying it was nice meeting him.

He spoke up, as he seemed to be in a hurry, "same here."

They finished up on my hair and moments went by while I was just hanging out when I noticed Buck McDancer coming over with a frown on his face.

"I don't know how to tell you this Steven," he hesitated.

"Tell me what?" I asked.

"We are going to have to replace you," he said in a low voice.

I was thunderstruck. "Replace me? What are you talking about?"

I had just gotten here, haven't even done the stunt yet, why would they do that?

Buck averted his eyes but continued on. "Kirk went over to the Producers and he doesn't like the idea of someone older than him putting on a wig and doubling him."

I am just dumbfounded. "Why does that matter?" I stammered.

Buck shook his head, the frown sinking deeper on his face. "It doesn't and I tried to tell him that, but he just won't listen. He is the lead actor and he gets what he wants. I tried to persuade him, tell him you are one of the best, but he won't listen."

I shook my head. "Are you kidding me?" I replied.

Needless to say, I was told they would still pay me the daily, but they had to get someone else. I thought that was a rotten thing to do to somebody and was something Buck and I never forgot. I couldn't believe somebody with his stature and with a successful television show, would be so immature and insecure. I packed up my bags, signed my contract and left his majesty's kingdom.

That is the end of the tale of Kirk Cameron, the vain pampered prince. Or is it? Hey, guess what?

Many years later, I happened to be watching television and whose face do you think I see? Mister Prince!

Now he is not doing *Growing Pains*, but preaching as a TV evangelist! Here he is, telling people what to do and giving them advice as a purist when he himself is nothing of the sort! Watching him preach, I feel like I must find him and convince him to repent and apologize. That is a mission of mine. OKAY, a fantasy.

On top of that, a recently released article titled, "Kirk Cameron Is Still A Walking Talking Asshole," was published, criticizing his treatment of people and how they should behave. I'll say it again, "are you kidding me?"

Talk about a pain that is growing, that's Kirk Cameron for you.

(Hey Evangelist Kirk Cameron, is there an apology for me in that sermon?)

CHAPTER 39
(Legend Angela Lansbury Hates My Hairdo.)

Now we are moving on to another show you might have heard of called, *Murder She Wrote*, starring Angela Lansbury. THERE is an actress for you, from the forties and fifties. She goes all the way back to *The Picture Of Dorian Grey*, *National Velvet* and *Manchurian Candidate*. I could go on and on. She is an Academy Award winner. I was thrilled to death to work with her. I landed a great character role doing dialogue with her, playing a bad guy of course. I was in a scene with her, outside at the Getty Center in Los Angeles where I was eating, waiting for my boss. She was supposed to be spying on me from a couple of tables behind me. She comes onto set and I introduce myself and tell her what a big fan I was. I start naming movies she has done and explaining how wonderful they were and how I used to watch them growing up.

She opens her mouth to thank me, except the words don't seem quite right. "You have a very unusual haircut," she replies.

I smiled and said, "oh, thank you." My hair was in what I call the "Albert Leong look."

(Acting with Academy Award winner, Angela Lansbury.)

The only difference was I had my sides shaved, everything else was long and I was bald on the top and no fu manchu. I began to ramble on about how I was going bald and decided to comb it back, realizing that maybe I had said too much, as she gave me a tight smile. I finished and she told me how nice it was to meet me before she walked off. Under my breath, I muttered, "what an idiot, I am." I thought to myself, that was ridiculous. Why am I talking about my head? It's funny how you mean to say one thing but instead, something silly comes out.

CHAPTER 40
(Comedian Joe Piscopo And My Magnificent Seven.)

Okay, first there was a movie, *Seven Samurai*. What came from that? *The Magnificent Seven*. You remember that film? Yule Brenner, Steve McQueen, Robert Vaughn, Charles Bronson, James Coburn, great actors of their time. But now it's Joe time. The Magnificent Seven of Martial Arts. I get a call from a Producer saying he is doing a commercial with Joe Piscopo and asked me if I was interested. I say, "why not?" and I went down to their office and lo and behold, Piscopo is there. I am a big fan of Joe's work on *SNL*. His Frank Sinatra was incredible, what a great comedian. His Richard Nixon, Andy Rooney and Walter Cronkite were spot on. They told me they are doing a Miller Lite commercial and they want Joe Piscopo to play Bruce Lee. My eyes lit up and I asked Joe if he was going to really impersonate Bruce Lee. Joe said he would try to as he went on to tell me that he has the utmost respect for Bruce and he was really excited about this project. They gave me and explained the synopsis, saying that a bunch of ninjas are out to get Bruce/Joe and they wanted Joe to beat up these ninjas in a pizzeria, drinking Miller Lite Beer. It was going to be a thirty second spot. Well God knows I was so sick of ninjas at this point, thoughts just overcame me.

I said, "listen, having Joe play Bruce Lee is going to be big time, this could be memorable. But fighting ninjas, the same characters with masks over their faces, it just doesn't do it justice. You could create a whole story here. Have him fight different characters with different styles. Kendo, Kung Fu, Karate. Different faces and different costumes."

I finished my speech, hoping I didn't overstep my bounds. You see, I always consider myself not the norm, different. I would overstep and always try to change ideas for the better, even if they are completely different. I always found most Stunt Coordinators wouldn't do that, whether it was being nervous, not having enough guts or simply missing that creative input. In short, they keep their mouths shut and do as they are told. The words that came next were music to my ears.

"I love it," the Director said. They asked me if I could train Joe for three weeks and I said no problem. In my mind, this was a thirty second commercial, so my main aspect was to teach him the action acting portion of being Bruce Lee. As far as being fit, Joe had been lifting weights for a while and he was evenly distributed when it came to muscle. Man, he looked good. I didn't have to worry about that part. He looked fine like whiskey, MILLER LITE and wine.

For three weeks we trained together. We watched Bruce Lee movies in different theaters that were playing them. Everyone had become an expert in acting like Bruce Lee after his first film, *Fists Of Fury*. He would talk fast until he wanted to emphasize something. Then he would talk slowly. I did my best impression for him and he learned quickly from it. Soon after we had a production meeting with all the heads. Before we started, the Producer and Director called me into a private office. They told me they wanted me to do Second Unit on this and due to my knowledge of Bruce Lee and Martial Arts. They wanted me to take control of this commercial. We had the meeting and I decided to go from head to head and talk to each one. First was sets and being it was a pizza place, I asked for a few breakaway chairs for the scene as well as a few other things. "We are going to need them for Bruce Piscopo," I joked.

As soon as I said that, Joe who was in the meeting, broke out in laughter. He was soon joined by the Director and then the rest of the department heads.

Joe looked at me and said, "Bruce Piscopo? That's funny Steven."

I told him that was his new name for the show.

(I explain. You must be shapeless, formless, like water.)

I explained the opening shot would be Joe dive rolling through a huge piece of glass in the storefront window and come up behind this little wall, jump over it and start his dialogue. I was going to have a stunt double do it and Joe will be hiding behind the partition. So the double, whose name was Vince Deadrick Jr. and by the way let me say, Jr. made a comment after seeing Joe Piscopo with his shirt off, saying he was embarrassed to take off his. Pretty funny, I thought. I laughed and told him it was going to be so fast no one would have time to see his saggy titties. That just made him feel worse. For the record, they weren't saggy. I just said that to mess with him. He rolls in and stays down and Joe pops up and does his dialogue. We call that the old switcheroo. Everyone liked that and we moved on.

Then came props. I looked at the powers as I started speaking to the prop department.

I said, "listen, I have an idea. At the same time that we put together this commercial, we can pay homage to every movie that Bruce has done. At the end, when Joe Piscopo is sitting down, getting ready to karate chop the pizza, I'll have one of the Magnificent Seven of Martial Arts coming in to fight him. In the movie, Enter The Dragon, Bruce fights this character called Hans, the lead bad guy. In the film, he had one hand missing and had many hand weapon inserts to attach to his arm.

That is why he is called Hans, hahaha. One was a claw." I reached down in my folder and pulled out a picture of the claw.

(In Enter The Dragon, it was Hans. In the Miller Lite commercial, it was the henchman. Albert Leong.)

I asked them to make one of these up so we could use it at the table. Joe will be simply sitting down and this character with the claw will come up from behind him. Joe will lean as the claw goes into the table before he back fists him, punching him out of the shot.

Joe spoke up and said, "what a great idea," and everybody followed.

Then I said, "by the way, there is only one man that could do justice to the claw character. AKA, the Henchmen. Albert Leong." When we got to casting and wardrobe, I discussed how each character would have a different wardrobe.

(What do you get when you put together three Asians and a Jew? Dim sum and potato pancakes.)

I had ripped out pictures from Martial Art magazines and explained I would be happy to help them pick out the various wardrobes that would be appropriate for each style. Then the casting head asked me if I would help interview people that would play these characters, see how well they know Martial Arts.

"With your permission," I asked them and the Director, "I have been into Martial Arts my whole life and I know many well known Martial Artists that have great looking faces that would work well for these kinds of characters, so I would like to help you cast this."

They asked me how many people I wanted to cast and I told them seven. Why seven you may ask? They certainly did. I smiled and said, "in your original script you had four or five ninjas fighting Bruce. Well, I would like to shorten up the fights and bring in seven. I had envisioned it like Bruce Lee fighting the Magnificent Seven of Martial Arts."

All of a sudden, I hear Joe laughing in the background.

I turn to him and he says, "Steve, these visions you have, it's hysterical."

I said, "that's the way I think, man. Bruce Piscopo fighting the Magnificent Seven of Martial Arts." Everyone liked it and thought it was a great idea. Now in my mind, I already had three cast.

Who you may ask? Come on, after reading this far you should know by now. The first one is Douglas Wong, the second is James Lew and the third is Albert Leong. No matter what they said, those three were set in stone. I gave the Director and casting heads about twenty five pictures of well known Martial Artists. I put my Magnificent three at the top. I told casting that with all due respect, those three were cast. Three people who are very important to me. The other four you can cast, but I would like these three. (A little tip for you newcomers, you see the way I said, "I would like?" Always say, "I would like," never say, "I want." Ancient Jewish Chinese proverb that will help keep your job.)

They looked at each other before saying they trusted my decision and that they did have great faces. I let them know, these were three of the best I have had the pleasure of watching and they would not disappoint. We had a casting call soon after to cast the other four. Little did they know, I had the other four cast in my head already.

This is where stunt psychology comes in. Another possible teaching moment for you guys out there. They had about twelve to thirteen Martial Artists coming in to audition, which included my Fantastic Four of the Magnificent Seven.

Bill Ryusaki, Tadashi Yamashita, Jeff Imada and Gerald Okamura. Four great characters who I grew up with and admired in this career. You take the seven as a whole, I think the world of these guys and so does the world. All seven of these guys I have worked with over and over.

Extraordinary Martial Artists and action actors that I had every intention of getting into this commercial. The day we started casting, I was present and had a great plan to get what I wanted.

(The Magnificent Seven Of Martial Arts.)

"Bruce Piscopo Lee" Joe Piscopo Miller Lite Commercial

Steve Lambert hired seven martial artists to work on the Bruce Piscopo Lee Miller Lite Commercial. They were Master Douglas L. Wong, Master Tadishi Yamashita, Master Gerald Okumura, Master Jeff Imada, Master Bill Ryusaki, Master James Lew and Master Albert Leong. Al Leong is dressed in the ninja outfit covering his face, but you can see him in the commercial attacking Joe with the Claw.

When the first few people came in who weren't on my list of four people, I just sat there and let them do their thing. Then comes Bill Ryusaki and I spring into action.

367

I got up and shook Bill's hand and put my arm around him and took his picture from his hand. I went over to the casting person, slapped down the composite and said, "you see this guy? He worked out with Bruce Lee. He was Bruce Lee's friend. He worked out and taught Elvis Presley." Still having my palm on his picture, I said, "he is the fourth guy of the seven." I pushed the picture over to the casting person. I sat down as Bill introduced himself and did a few beautiful kicks and a little kata, then left.

The casting person looked at me and said, "you want him, don't you?"

I replied, "yes I dooo."

A few more people came in and I sat quietly, then comes Jeff Imada. Jeff, I was a little worried about since he is such a quiet and introverted guy. I got up, put my arms around Jeff, took his picture and put it on the table. I said, "see this guy? He is an original student of Bruce Lee. Danny Inosanto, Bruce's number one student, is Jeff's teacher. Jeff wrote a book about butterfly knives before anyone knew about them. Now, they are everywhere in the movie industry." I took my hand off the picture and sat down. Jeff did some Jeet Kwan Doon on me for them and left.

The casting person looked at me and said, "you want this guy too, don't you Steven?"

I said, "yes I doooo."

A few more people come and then Gerald Okamura and Tadashi Yamashita. What do you think happened? The same thing as the last two.

They asked me, "you want these guys also?"

I said, "yes I doooo, dooooo."

They got the picture and I got my Magnificent Seven of Martial Arts. Now to put the final touch to this story, while we were filming Tadashi Yamashita's part, I had given Tadashi two moves. A straight punch and a back fist. I had put him behind a huge round column where I had him pop out to surprise Bruce Piscopo. We rehearsed it and I had Joe do some Wing Chun, JKD style. It went fine. Come picture, we roll cameras and I call "action." Bruce Piscopo comes into the shot. All of a sudden, Tadashi pops out. Instead of throwing his straight punch and back fist, he has a pair of nunchucks in each hand, swinging them wildly. Joe Piscopo jumps back, looking like he nearly died from fright, as Tadashi is still swinging those chucks. I jump out of my chair and scream, "cut, cut!" I look at Tadashi and say, "Tadash, what the hell are you doing?"

Tadash looks at me as everyone in the whole room is frozen in confusion. Yamashita replies, "Steven, Steven, it look good. It only take a few seconds."

I looked at him and said "Tadashi, we don't have time for this. Besides, you gotta let me know." I turn and look at Piscopo, laughing my ass off as the whole company roars with laughter. It was funny, you had to be there.

(Yes, he really did hit me in the matzah balls. Accidents happen. But it still hurt.)

CHAPTER 41
(Sticky And Bloody. Where's My Money?)

The Norris's are calling. Aaron Norris that is, asking me to Stunt Coordinate their new movie called *Missing In Action*. Here is a Martial Arts legend in Chuck Norris, asking me to coordinate. The man I worked with on my first job in the business. The man that judged me in tournaments when I was a kid. I thought to myself, how cool is this? How blessed I am. It was also a Cannon film, so I was excited to be working for Menahem Golan again. The next day I go in and see Chuck and Aaron and we discuss the fun times we had on our last film together. Remember, fun yaking? I was so happy to see that Aaron was directing. I remember watching him grow from a Stuntman to a Coordinator, to a Second Unit Director and now a First Unit Director. We sit and talk and they both love my ideas, this is just a total dream come true. Then Aaron leads me to the Production Manager and tells him that I was the new Stunt Coordinator, drop a contract. Being the hands on person that Aaron is, I knew he would be very involved in the action just as he was going to be in his directing.

The weekend comes and my phone rings and lo and behold it's James Woods! He tells me he is doing a show called *Cop* that he is producing and is starring in. The Director I was told was a man called James Harris and Jimmy Woods wanted to know if I was available. For an actor like James Woods to call me was a big deal and I asked him if he wanted me to Stunt Coordinate the film.

"No, but yea. You can do that too," he laughs.

Now it has gotten completely over my head. I am a Stunt Coordinator, what did he mean when he said I could do that too? So I ask him.

"I want you to co-star, play the lead bad guy Steven," James said nonchalantly.

I asked him if he was joking, I wasn't an actor! A little bit here, a little bit there I could do as long as there was action involved and I felt comfortable, but a co-starring role was another story! I said to Jimmy, "if I have to straight talk with no action involved, I don't know if I can do it." I say, "is this a joke? Why me?"

He told me I only had a little bit of dialogue and he would coach me through it, the rest was all action.

"Jimmy, I appreciate it, but this is something I had never even dreamed of, it's way above what I am used to doing," I could only say.

Jimmy calmed me down and told me he would be there to help me through it all. They had six weeks until the shoot. I said, "Jimmy, I would enjoy it but I am already doing a film for Cannon with Chuck Norris that I signed a contract for." I knew Jimmy would understand and I hoped there would be opportunities to work with him again.

"So what?" Jimmy replied. "F*** Chuck Norris, just quit! You want to do a real movie, not that karate shit. We got six weeks, we have time to coach you. Think about it, every time I had a scene to do on Best Seller, they had you play me and had me watch you to figure out how to do it. You can do this."

I laughed and my mouth dropped open. Here I am talking to a big actor who wants me to do this film with him, sitting on my living room couch and thinking this is crazy. It's a dream, but it's not. "I don't know what to do," was all I could say. I asked him if I could have a day to think it over and he said yes. After a very restless night, I finally made a decision. I weighed both of the options and decided I could hopefully come back to Chuck Norris and work with him again. If I don't do Jimmy, he is not a Martial Artist and he is a big star, he might go with someone else. Look what he is offering me. Chuck is a Martial Artist and we have a deeper bond together.

So the next day, I call Cannon up and explain to Aaron Norris my situation. God bless Aaron, he understood fully. We talked for forty five minutes as I apologized a dozen times and he was just so understanding about the whole situation. A true professional. He said we would work together again and would let Chuck know. He let me out of the contract and I thanked him from the bottom of my heart. It was a wonderful ending and felt good he had intended to have me back. I then called up Jimmy on the phone and told him I was in. I explained I called Chuck's people and they were very understanding and I got out of the contract.

A brief silence issued from the other end of the line, when I heard Jimmy say, "too bad, we got somebody else!"

I near dropped the phone! Just kidding! He didn't say that, I just wanted to fool you. He said it was great and that was the start of our next picture together. So there I was, going up to Jimmy's house for six weeks to learn how to act. He would pull out old Richard Widmark films from the forties and fifties where he would always play the bad guy or crazy guy, the gangsters. He was insane. He would have this laugh and crazed look on his face that Jimmy would point out. He explained that body language and expression can communicate so much to the camera and the audience behind it. He would explain that you should always try to find something you can do that is different or unusual in a scene and never show it in rehearsal. I will get to this a bit later, when I talk to you about a movie called *Simone*, with Al Pacino. It really does work and here is where I learned it.

Finally, the time comes to start the film and I felt at ease for my first day. Why? Because I don't have any dialogue in the film except for the end! The scenes

I am in, there really is no speaking, it is all body language and expression. Almost like a silent film with Charlie Chaplin. Speaking of silent films, there are two scenes in this film that are so silent, you never see them in the movie. We had a scene where one of the serial killer's victims is hanging upside down, blood dripping everywhere and Jimmy comes in and finds her. Also in this sequence, we planned to do a moment where I kill her and we decided to shoot that after the scene with Jimmy, which also comes before. Get it? You understand? Call me up if you don't. They wanted to hire a beautiful actress to play the hanging dead girl, but I had a great idea. I suggested I bring a beautiful stunt woman in to play her, as she would be more experienced. I show Jimmy and the Director a few pictures of a beautiful girl named Lisa McCullogh. I call her up and she tells me she does circus work and hanging upside down is no big deal. I tell her she is hired and go back and tell Jimmy we got Lisa, no big deal. Fast forward to the day of the shoot, Lisa arrives and gets into her nighty. FX covers her in blood and we hang her upside down. Jimmy's scene is first and to make a long story short, we spent half a day filming it. All she had to do for twenty seconds was keep still, play dead while I danced weirdly around her.

Such a small thing. Upside down in a harness, covered in blood, any stunt person would love to do that. It is really no more than a glorified extra, as we in the biz say. One would think that was easy, but Lisa kept moving around! She wouldn't stay still. Jimmy and the Director would talk to her about it and tell her to stay still, she was supposed to be dead.

I just listened as she said, "it keeps pinching me and I'm too sticky and bloody."

Finally, after hours of aggravation, they gave up and Jimmy and goes back to his trailer. I couldn't believe it took half a day to do a five minute scene that we never got. They must have cut like twenty times. Needless to say, Jimmy wasn't too happy, nor was the Director. As for me, I was fuming. Now after lunch, it is my turn. I am supposed to have just killed her and am moving around like a maniac. I showed James Harris, the Director, my tiger and crane forms with two knives in my hands and he loved it, so that is what I was going to do. We roll camera and I begin my animal forms when out of the corner of my eye I see Lisa moving. The Director has to stop and comes over to Lisa.

"Listen, hun, we just went through a half day of this and I need you to stay still for the hundredth time," James Harris mutters.

I take her down and she apologizes.

Here comes her famous line again, "it pinches and it is sticky!"

I try and tell her all she has to do is stay still for ten, fifteen seconds and then she can move a bit. She agrees and here we go again. I start doing my forms and guess what, I see her moving. This is like the thousandth time today! I get close and whisper, "don't move. Stop moving." I can't do it too many times, or the shot would be ruined. I hope she gets the picture and I continue on.

All of a sudden I hear, "cut! That is a wrap, we are moving on!"

I look up and it is the Director. I walk over and ask him to shoot it a few more times and he told me he had already spoken to Jimmy.

"Jimmy said to give her one more chance, we did. We don't need this scene."

Jimmy came out and talk about being upset, and let me say, not really at me. I can't tell you the words he used expressing his frustration. Not of me, of the girl I hired. Now we have wasted a whole day. I apologized to Jimmy saying, "that she surprised me as much as you Jimmy. She is supposed to be a circus girl, a stunt woman. She had told me she could do it and the stunt was a nothing." I also told him if we had hired an actress we would have the same problem and I would have had to double her anyway. I had no idea this would happen. I calmed everyone down and went to Lisa's trailer. I knocked on the door and she is in her robe, with a frown on her face. I told her that we weren't going to do this anymore. I said, "Lisa, you embarrassed yourself. You embarrassed me, you embarrassed the Director and most of all, you embarrassed my friend James Woods. You said you could do this, it isn't that hard. You are wrapped. Go sign out."

She looks at me and says, "I was up there about fifteen times. I want five hundred dollars in adjustment each time."

I looked at her in shock. "Are you, kidding? First of all, we never got the shot. Second of all, it is not that hard of a stunt to do. Third of all, you want five hundred times fifteen? You are out of your mind, you know how much you get?" I put up my hand and showed her a big goose egg. "ZERO. You are lucky you get a contract after what you caused to this production," I stammered. I turned around and walked out of the trailer, thinking that is the end of that. I'm moving on.

An hour later, I get a tap on the shoulder from the Production Manager saying SAG is on the phone. "We have a problem with Lisa, she went to SAG and complained," he told me.

I called SAG up and told them what had happened and she wasn't telling the truth, you could ask anyone on set for the truth. How can you pay someone an adjustment when they couldn't stay still for longer than five seconds? I explained to them that an adjustment is something you deserve, but she did nothing. SAG agreed with me and that was the end of that. I learned to always double check who you hire.

Usually, you test the stunt person out, see what their abilities are. Yet, this was such an easy thing it went over my head that there would be any problems. Remember out there, you live and learn and sometimes it is just meant to be. Nothing you can do. I picked the wrong stunt woman and believe me, I was careful who I asked from then on out. Now Jimmy, having gone to MIT was an exceptionally smart guy who picked up on things very quickly. During the final scene where he comes to confront the serial killer aka Franco aka Steven Lambert, aka me, aka Jimmy's double, in the gym, he came up with a great idea. I was supposed to be out of breath from hiding and playing cat and mouse with his character and the first few takes, I just couldn't portray that accurately enough for his taste. He wanted something off center in my behavior.

So Jimmy says, "I got an idea." He turns to all production and asks them to give him a minute as he walks me outside the gymnasium. He points to the running track and suggests I run around the track for a few laps and not to stop until he gives me the okay. When he did give the okay, I was to come in, cameras rolling and deliver my lines.

I was a bit confused and looked at him saying, "what? What do you want me to do?"

He just simply said, "follow my lead."

I told him it would be no problem. Remember folks, he had no idea I was a gazelle. Haha. I start running around the track, first at a slow jog and I can see him watching me from the doorway. Every now and then he would pop his head out.

After a few laps, I ask him if I can come in and he yells back, "no, pick up the pace!"

I run faster and do a few more laps. This time, sweat starts pouring down my face and I finally hear him yell for me to come in during the eleventh lap. I run inside, finding Jimmy on his mark and I barely make it to mine from my exhaustion. I notice the crew around me quiet with blank expressions. They had a wandering look. Jimmy starts his action and I begin to deliver my lines, out of breath and tired from the impromptu run I just took. He hits me with the butt of his shotgun twice and with full energy, I take the hits and fall to the ground. Now I can barely get up, a crazed expression on my face from pure fatigue. We deliver our lines. I can barely get mine out. Then he blows me away. It was a one take cut and print from Jimmy and the Director.

(James Woods. My friend and acting coach.)

It worked perfectly and as you see in the movie, exactly what you see, is how tired I was after running around that track eleven times.

Jimmy smiled and said, "now that's acting."

I learned a lot at that moment and thankfully I was smart enough to take it with me.

CHAPTER 42
(Actress Doris Day, Wish You Could Stay.)

Now here is a quick and elegant tale. I was working on a television show at Warner Brothers Studios. Now here is a trick we used to do. Whenever I was filming on one stage, I would always make my way over to the adjacent stages to see what was filming and more importantly, if there were any Stunt Coordinators there. We would try to talk to them and see if we could get any work in the future. On this day, during lunch break, I happened to finish early and I casually strolled outside of the stage, when my ears came upon some chatter. As I look over, I could see this one woman surrounded by people. I soon realized they were fans. But of who? Looking harder, I saw she was signing autographs. A quick glimpse of her face and I couldn't believe it. It was Doris Day! My heart started racing as excitement flooded through me. I usually don't get excited around celebrities, but as you know by now, actors like her from the olden days make this stunt monkey go bananas. I patiently waited until she had finished signing autographs and the crowd around her had left. As she started walking back to the stage, I made my move.

"Excuse me. Are you Mrs. Day? Doris Day?" I asked.

She turned and looked at me. I was a little nervous as I was the only one around now. Had she seen me from afar, standing back like some stalker? The apprehension quickly went away as she smiled at me. "Yes, yes I am," she replied. "And what is your name?"

I reply, "my name is Steven, but you can call me one of your biggest fans. I gotta tell you the wonderful memories I have of you when I would be sitting with my mother and father watching you on a black and white television in one of my favorite movies, Calamity Jane," I told her.

She laughed. "Oh, that was a long while ago. When I was much younger."

This time we both smiled. She looked me up and down. "And what do you do?" she inquired.

"I do stunts. I am working on a show today," I said.

I could see her eyes grow wide with interest as she got physically excited. "A stuntman? Really? I remember I had a stunt double on Calamity Jane. I couldn't believe half the stuff she did. Her name was Donna Hall. It was so dangerous. Don't you ever get scared?" she asked while putting her hand on my arm. I blushed.

I couldn't help but laugh. "Nervous but not scared. I wouldn't trade it for the world."

I could see she was so joyful and interested, it was really a beautiful moment that I felt. The warm and loving Doris Day that we always see in the movies, I am witnessing right here. It was amazing.

I then said, "another movie I absolutely I thought you were great in was the movie you did with Cagney."

She says, "oh, Love Me Or Leave Me. Thank you so much."

I asked, "what was it like working with him?"

She smiled, "it was wonderful working with wisdom. He was the best."

I wanted to ask more but as she checked the time, she said, "I'm sorry dear, but I do have to be going now. It was a big tickle chatting with you."

I replied, "what?"

As she was walking away. she said, "it was fun, it was fun."

How cool was that, big tickle huh? Never heard that before. Big tickle. Thus ends the tale of how I met the great Doris Day.

CHAPTER 43
(Actor Tom Selleck And His Tipsy Sidekick.)

I get a call from the Boss of *Magnum P.I.* The Stunt Coordinator, Bob Minor. Bob was a great stuntman and a class one action actor. He asks me if I am available to come to the land of paradise, Hawaii. Surf city here I come, where the hula girls roam. Ye ha! Surfs up! I heard that Hawaii was like no other place in the world and now I will see for myself. He told me I would double Larry Manetti, who played Rick Wright, Magnum's sidekick. I get put up at the Colony Surf hotel in Honolulu, a suite overlooking the beach. I got to do five to six episodes, doubling Larry Manetti or playing myself. My first meeting with Larry on the set, I stuck out my hand and he shook it. As he was shaking my hand, he pulled me close to him, putting his hand on my back.

He leaned close, inches from my face. "You aren't going to be needed here, I do all my stunts," he just about whispered. His breath hit me right in the face and aloha Koloa and I mean the rum.

I simply said, "okay." You get the picture? I could tell he was a little tipsy. Next, I met Tom Selleck who loved and respected the stunt people, especially Bob Minor. As of my thoughts on Roger Mosley who played T.C., I found him only to be into himself and was told he was very demanding and unfriendly. And from my observation, this was true. Last but not least, HIGGINS. Higgins was a lot of fun and was amazed at the action, very polite and told old anecdotes about what we were doing which always made the whole cast and crew laugh. Working on this show was like a huge vacation, just magical. I had talked to Bob and asked him what I was going to do and he told me I was going to climb a tree and hide from bad guys who were chasing me. It was a very simple thing, but simple things I always liked. I was good at making simple things special.

I decided to climb the tree like a monkey, about twenty feet up. Bob told me that Larry had it in his mind he was going to do it, but they wanted to bring me along just in case and he was glad he did. Listen to this. On the day they had me do it first for whatever reason as Larry Manetti watched. It was a very old and big tree with branches sticking out of it. When they called action, I ran into the shot and took about a four foot leap. I caught one branch and swung up from branch to branch, hardly ever touching with my feet except to kick off and go onto the next branch. Chimpanzee, that is what you see. One take and it was beautiful. Who knew gazelles could climb. Let me remind you, I come from the "five animal style." When I got to the top everyone applauded and as I climbed down, I jumped to the ground from about ten feet up. Just like the ninja, always. That got me more applause and I looked at Larry Manetti who had a blank expression on his face. Tom Selleck came over and said that even the native monkeys can't climb as well as he had just seen.

I thanked him as Larry smacked me on the back and said, "good job." He went to his mark and as they rolled, he hopped onto the first branch and hoisted himself up. It took a long seven seconds before they yelled cut. Now that he was on the first branch, they called for a ladder. I was watching this, having no idea how much they were going to use. With all due respect, he looked more like a sloth than a monkey. Props comes with a twelve foot ladder and they put the ladder on the tree and Larry went up to the top and was told to lean back a bit. He hung from the branch and hoisted himself up before they cut again. In comes the ladder and here he comes back down. It was all inserts! I am looking at everyone's face, wait a minute, I can't see them because they are turning away with laughter trying not to make a big deal out of it. Then the Director cut and said we were moving on. Inside I was giggling. Bob Minor came over with a big shit eating grin and I couldn't help but laugh. Larry and the ladder, a tale that would be told again and again.

Having to leave Hawaii was like leaving a piece of Heaven and I had no idea when I would be back. It is the most extraordinary place. I couldn't imagine what summer in Hawaii was going to be like, wishing that I was there. But guess what, I soon found out.

CHAPTER 44
(Aloha Summer. Never A Thank You From Sho Kosugi.)

When I returned to the mainland, I began to get back into my normal routine when about a fortnight later, I got a call from the First AD, Brian Frankish, who was doing a new film and asked me to be the Stunt/Fight Coordinator. Guess what? It was in Hawaii! I was going to have an Aloha summer after all! The name of the film you ask? Why I already said it, *Aloha Summer.* You guys gotta pay more attention so I don't need to repeat it. Where was I? Yes, Aloha Summer. Ok, so I fly back to the Hawaiian flower girls with the lei's around their necks and head to the Production Office and meet Brian Frankish. He was a cool cat and reminded me of the hippies from the sixties. In the fifties, they were called beat nicks. You see, the word "hip" was coined in the 1940's as slang by the African American jive community meaning "sophisticated, currently fashionable; fully up to date." Now other slang words you may be familiar with are - wait, hold on, my co-writer just informed me I got off topic again.

Let's move on. In a relatively short amount of time, I came to realize he was a very smart man. I sure wish I had another opportunity to work with him, but that never happened although I still keep in touch with him every now and then. He kept everybody on the move. Good natured and a very hard worker. I met with the Director, Tommy Lee Wallace and we discussed the script. Little did I know how much this film would mean to me. A guy like me gets hired for action and in most cases, there is no strong story for the action. This film was taking place in the fifties and had a story that was so full of passion and nostalgia, I grew fond of it. For two to three hours, I spoke with the Director and how life was like in the fifties. He had such a vision for this film, if even a tenth of his vision found its way into the film, it was going to be a touching lesson in nostalgia. A movie that when you come out of it, you feel good. For those of you that lived in the fifties, it made you want to go back. For those of you who were born later, it made you wish you were there. I don't say it was the movie that made the most money or was the most memorable out there, but it is a special film to me with an endearing story.

It had a great cast, including Andy Bumatai who was a comedian in Hawaii, just as well known there like Don Ho. You know the singer who sang "Tiny Bubbles." He invited us all out for a luau and it was my first time dancing with real hula girls. We were all a little tipsy and Andy Bumatai was trying to teach us how to speak Hawaiian Pidgeon. It was hilarious, just imagine a punk kid from Brooklyn trying to speak Pidgeon with a Brooklyn accent. Everybody had a good laugh. They had a roast pig that I enjoyed, though don't tell my Jewish grandmother. It was wonderful. I had to get doubles for the surfing scenes and Andy directed me to some native pro surfers. I had a casting call and hired surfing doubles for everyone. A few days later, the actors arrived and I paired them up with their surfing doubles and arranged a time every day for the actors to be taught by them. We went out every day for a week, this wasn't work! This is a vacation! Andy took us to a botanical garden to see the Halona blowhole. He explained some people in the past jumped in, hoping they would be shot out like a cannon. Instead, they were sucked in like a flushing toilet and drowned. He then told me about Hanauma Bay, which I later found out, was the original name of Aloha Summer, before they changed it.

Now let's talk about the angel of paradise, in Aloha Summer. The wonderful Tia Carrere. Do you know, her real name was Althea Rae Janairo. What a beautiful name. I don't know why she changed it. So sweet, so innocent and very intelligent, yet very shy. This was the first film she had done. Tommy the Director, had to work very hard with her to get the acting just right. At times she seemed overwhelmed, but I was very impressed with Tommy who talked her through it and remembering that one of the most important things he said to her was "just be yourself." That showed his professionalism. As soon as he said that, it looked like she gained confidence and became more comfortable.

What you saw in the film was what you saw in real life, shy and sweet as a button. Yuji Okumoto who played Kenzo Konishi, what a fine performance he brought. His character was strong, confused, enraged, hurt but disciplined. He was wonderful to watch. We became friends and he was fascinated by Martial Arts. He was such a versatile actor. Here he was playing a traditional Japanese actor, and those who knew him, really know that he is just an ordinary Japanese American boy from Los Angeles, California. Now that I look back and see the body of work Yuji and Tia have done, I am proud that I got to see their beginnings. The lead actor was Don Michael Paul.

Tall and handsome, mister cool cat, I always thought he was going to get some big parts in the future. Yet, I never saw much of him. The memories I had with all of them was just one big vacation and a wonderful moment in time for all of us. By the way, one of the highlights for me in this movie was the aloha summer gang against the navy stunt boys down the main street of Honolulu. They were on their night out and run into the sailors who Kenzo had insulted and fought earlier. I had an opportunity that normally you don't have on a show.

I asked for twenty one stunt people for a week and the Producers said yes! I was in all my glory. Why you ask? Because there are few opportunities when you get to call twenty one people whose talent you admire, who have done a great job for you in the past or who have given me a job. I brought in great friends, like Mike Vendrell, John Meiers, Gene Lebell, Brian Imada, Bob Apisa, Joel Kramer, Bernie Pock, Kenny Lesco, Joe Dunne, Bob Ore and Steve Davison. All these people I had been connected to in the past in one way or another. I'll mention Gene Lebell, he played a drunk as an army officer. Now they say there have been two stuntmen who have performed the drunk routine the best. The first is Harvey Perry, the second is Gene "Hambo" Lebell.

Now remember I mentioned Gene once before being one loveable big ham, he had the whole cast and crew laughing. He did it so well the Director literally cut in the middle of the shot and told me to ask him to dial it down a bit. I walked over to Gene with a smile and told him to stop showboating. Now let me tell you, I'm no dummy, if I walked over to him serious, he might have put me to sleep right on the set and my friend Joel Kramer might have stripped me down to my underwear.

He laughed and looked around. "Where is that Director? I want to stretch him out real good."

I kept my mouth shut on that one. They were all glad to be there and I was glad to have them. I even had John Meier coordinate a fight while I was doing Second Unit. I mention that because those little things are important to show a great guy how much you value friendship. It was great fun and Joel Kramer always knew how to make it funnier. Picture this, spotlights down the middle of the entire street. I turn and see Joel Kramer, lit up in the center of the street, with his shirt off acting like guess who? Arnold Schwarzenegger at a bodybuilding competition. It was one big work party.

Now let's get into the meat. I want to discuss somebody I respect, Sho Kosugi, who played Kenzo. I happened to hear whispers that production hadn't cast the role of Kenzo's father yet and guess what? Two names popped into my head. Bill Ryusaki and Sho Kosugi. I thought, why not, let's give it a shot.

I had a meeting with the Director and the Producers and told him my idea. He explained to me that yes, they were having trouble casting that specific role. I mentioned I had a couple of people in mind and if they liked, I could get some footage for them to see. They agreed and I told them I had a VHS tape on Sho and could ask Ryusaki for his reel. The Director gave me the green light and I went to my hotel room and got the VHS, which was MY action reel which had the fight sequences from *Revenge Of The Ninja* that included Sho. On the roof with me, all those good scenes with him.

I called up Bill and asked if he could send me his action reel. Two or three days went by and I hadn't gotten anything from him. I called him and he said he was putting it together, but to make a long story short, it never came.

That was all right though, because the moment Tommy saw the reel with Sho, he got very interested. He called his agent and got Sho to come. He told me Sho was on board and I felt very proud that he chose my friend. He also happened to mention to me that when he spoke to Sho, he explained to him that Steven Lambert had made him aware of him. The day comes and Sho arrives. I found out he was on set and I headed down there from location. I saw him about thirty feet away and he was laughing and smiling with everyone. Then as I got closer, it was as if both of our energy's locked and his smile boiled away. He went to a very stoic face. I walked fast towards him and had my arms out to give him a hug. "Sho, it is great to see you," I said.

He nodded very sternly. "Yes."

I stuck out my hand and he stuck out his. I realized in seconds that the wall was still up from *Ninja: The Domination*. We were really good friends on *Revenge Of The Ninja* and then because Menahem went from Sho to a female ninja, something inside of him just snapped and broke. As the days went by, we would talk about old times but it just wasn't the same Kosugi. When we got to the Kendo fight scene, I had already put together the fights so it was a piece of cake for me. When we got to rehearsal, I started explaining to him the fight with the utmost respect, when he stops me and says he had some ideas that he wanted to do for the fight. I looked at him and said, "Sho, I have put the sequence together already but I'm more than happy to combine our thoughts."

He looked at me and said, "I do my thing and you do your thing. On my contract it says, I'm Fight Coordinator."
This came as a shock. In a second, very humbly, my reply was, "Absolutely, Sho. If you have ideas and I have ideas, we work together as a team like always. But I need to let you know, you are not the Fight Coordinator, I am. This is a different ball game, please understand. I don't get why are you acting so mean to me?"

He didn't answer. He just smiled. It was a cold smile and made me feel very sad. I had asked him what the matter was with him, why he was acting this way. I told him that we were friends and he didn't need to be so stern all the time. He grunted, turned and smiled before walking away. It really crushed me inside to see him changed like this. It hurt. Even though we spent only a few months together on the ninja films, it felt like years of friendship. Now it was like all that never happened.

I made it clear I had nothing to do with Menahem and the decision to cast aside Sho for a female lead, yet I feel like he holds me accountable. Coming from a traditional Martial Arts background as Sho did, you would think he would understand, but no, he held a grudge. My God, I was just the Stunt Coordinator, I had nothing to do with decision making.

It was a man called Menahem Golan.

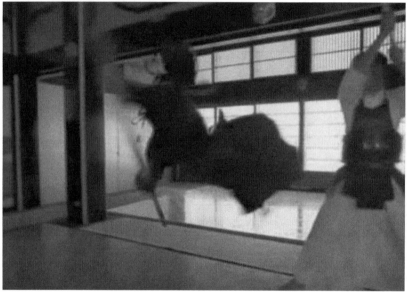

(Sho Kosugi, not a happy man fighting Steven Lambert.)

I would never ask for a "thank you" or a pat on the back from Sho, for getting him this job, but to get this kind of reaction really bothered me. Where is the gratitude? You would think that I would learn from my mistakes, but you can get burned by a match twice which you will read about later on. However, I was proud that I got Sho this job and an opportunity to do his first real American film. His performance was so fantastic and it really showed his acting ability. I will always be proud that I was the reason he got this gig. I thought he was going to be a big American Japanese star but for some reason his cinema work took him to another path. If I was his agent I would have stressed for better films after *Aloha Summer*, but that just didn't happen and Sho just faded away in the American Martial Art cinema.

Despite the negative encounters with Sho on the set, I wasn't going to let this ruin the fun I was having on this film. I got to double Yuji in the Kendo fight scene with Sho which was a surprise. Why? The whole thing was kind of for real. Sho went at me like a bat out of hell and I had to do the same thing in return. The fight routine was wonderful and real. With surfing, Hawaiian delights and a great bunch of people to share it all with, who could ask for more?

CHAPTER 45
(Vince Deadrick Sr. And One Wild Bachelor Party.)

1988 was a wonderful year. Working on TV shows like *L.A. Law, Midnight Caller and America's Most Wanted,* as well as movies like *Two Moon Junction, Traxx* and the film I thought I would be seeing double on. Until I found out it was Danny Devito. You guessed it, *Twins. Twins* was my second picture with Arnold. I did a week on the show doing some fight and car scenes. Watching Danny Devito and Arnold work together when cameras weren't rolling was like being at a comedy club watching two great comedians on stage making fun of each other. One day they were working and Arnold looks at Danny and says, "if you stick with me, I cannot do anything about your height, you little man, but I can work you out and give you muscles."

Danny takes one look at Arnold and makes a muscle. "Oh yea? You see these? These are street muscles. I don't need to lift. I can beat you with one hand tied behind my back. I can beat you with my brain."

Arnold laughed and said, "Danny, let me take you under my arm, oh never mind. I might squish you like a tiny bug."

Everyone started laughing. They were a great pair. Arnold would always bring a bunch of cigars on set. Danny Devito got one as did most of the stuntmen. As usual with Arnold, Sven Thorsen was on set. As Arnold's good friend, he went where Arnold went, always. Joel Kramer and Sven would always give me an invitation to be a part of the clique. I always felt honored. We hung out, ate together and even went bowling when we had days off. It was a great friendship that would only ripen over time. I was thankful for Joel for introducing me to Arnold in the past and was glad that he had allowed me into this inner circle, which so few people were allowed. Speaking of my friend goyim Joel, here is another story from the past. A wild and crazy one. Here is the scene, picture it in your mind. Are you ready? Camera one rolling. The event - Joel Kramer's bachelor party. The location - Santa Monica, California. It was a private party put on by Sven Thorsen and Arnold Schwarzenegger. It was at some international French type restaurant. I arrive with Vince Deadrick Sr. and we get there early and the bouncer comes to the door. It is no other than Sven Thorsen.

"Let us in," we ask.

He smiles saying, "you low foreheads are early. I can't open the door until eight o' clock. Come back later."

After we say it's us and curse him out, he speaks up.

385

"You want me to open the knob? No, not for you two. Come back at eight o'clock."

Yeah, he was messing with us as he turned around laughing. Vince mentions he knows a bar around the corner we could get a beer at.

I told him, "I hate beer it looks like piss."

He said it was just around the corner, so we stroll on over. We come to the bar and casually walk in as I follow him. The bar is pretty dark and there is a long wooden bar counter stretching down the way. I follow him to the counter, noticing there are some other tables in back of us. As we sit down, Vince calls over the bartender. Nature calls and I told Vince I had to use the men's room. As I'm trying to adjust my eyes, I ask for the bathroom and the bartender points in the back at the end of the bar. I asked Vince to order me a Sam Adams.

"A Sam Adams? That's a manly beer!" Vince calls out.

What the hell is he talking about? I just look at him funny before making my way to the restroom. I get to the end of the joint and to my right are two dark wood stained doors. I look up to find the men's room and blink. Two signs read "Men" and "Men." I find myself wondering and reading the signs over and over again, not sure which one is for me. I looked around for any other doors, but these two were it. I wondered if the "WO" fell off and now one of them just said "MEN" as that could have been a possibility. In my state of confusion, I look toward Vince and notice the individual tables behind him and the people that are sitting there. They are a bunch of guys! Noticing, as my eyes started to adjust, that they are very close to each other. Some are holding hands, some are about to kiss. Holy Mackerel! I'm thinking, I have to let Vince know. Now, I'll tell you what I am not. Homophobic. I will tell you what I was. Surprised, as I hold my number one in. I rush over to Vince who is talking to the bartender and like a little kid, get in his ear.

"Vince, Vince," I whispered all excited.

He looks up at me. "What? They didn't have Sam Adams, but they had Budweiser. Sit down and have your Bud."

As the bartender moves away, I continued in a panic as I could feel eyes on me.

"Vince, do you know what kind of a bar this is?"

He puts down his drink and screams. "WHAT KIND OF BAR THIS IS? WHAT?"

I try to quiet him down, "Sh, quiet. It's a gay bar!"

Vince opens puts down his drink before yelling, "IT'S A GAY BAR? NO SHIT! HEY BARTENDER, MY FRIEND HERE JUST INFORMED ME THIS IS A GAY BAR!"

I now feel the eyes of four to five couples on my back staring at me from the tables. I don't know whether to laugh with Vince or high tail it out of there.

"SIT DOWN AND HAVE YOUR BEER AT THE GAY BAR," Vince roars with laughter.

As I shake my head and call him a few expletives, I sit down. I tell him to shut up but he just keeps laughing as I try to down my beer in two gulps. I finish before Vince and tell him we should go. "HEY BARTENDER, MY FRIEND WANTS TO LEAVE IN AN AWFUL HURRY HERE."

I hiss at him to shut up and after a few minutes, I finally convince him to leave. He was just soaking the humor up that he got me and had set it all up.

As we leave, he turns around and yells, "BYE BOYS. MY FRIEND OVER HERE WANTS TO THROW YOU A KISS BEFORE HE LEAVES."

What did I do? I couldn't get out of there fast enough, while he was laughing.

I yelled at Vince saying, "they probably thought you were my sugar daddy, you idiot."

He laughed in a deep scruffy voice. Anybody who knew him loved his laugh. This got around like wildfire and was talked about for years. We went back to Joel's bachelor party and as to what happened in there? Well, unfortunately, I can't tell you, other than we had one crazy, wild and good time. Arnold and Sven, well if you want to know, you will have to find me and ask me personally and if you are over eighteen - I mean twenty one, then I MIGHT tell you. I could say that Vince Deadrick Sr. and I saved Joel's life and honor by bulldogging Arnold, Sven and Joel out of a pair of glass double doors. For the rest, use your imagination.

CHAPTER 46
(The Last Crusade. My Friend Vic Armstrong, Where Is My Credit?)

As the world turns in the Universe of stunts, there are many dreams a stunt man has, such as working with a big star. Working on an important picture, even working for a Director like Steven Spielberg. Those kinds of things might be thought about as a pinnacle of a stunt man's career. One day that dream came true. There's this girl I met. She does stunts. I worked with her two, three times and I was very impressed. She was new and had a lot of potential. I took her under my wing and worked very hard with her. We became very good friends over the years.

Always using her on my shows and always giving her name out to people, which was very rare for me to do because I found that most women have no business in the action world. But this one proved she did. There are only two women in this business that I wanted to spend time with, perfecting their abilities to fight in the movies. One was Dana Evenson and the other was named Luci Romberg, who is now very big in the industry. I worked a solid year with her as well. Twice a week, a couple of hours a day. She was extraordinary and has the gift to radiate her inner emotions to her body language and facial expressions. One day, which I'll never forget, I get a very exceptional phone call from Dana Evenson.

Dana explained she had a friend from England named Vic Armstrong who had done *Raiders Of The Lost Ark* and was now *doing The Last Crusade.* She said she had told them about me and my abilities. There was a scene where River Phoenix was playing a young Indiana Jones and she had put my name in to double him. I listened to her and told her I was thankful and said, "that is a very special thing for you to do Dana."

Inside, I really didn't expect anything to come of it, but I was very appreciative of her. What Stunt Coordinator in their right mind would hire someone who they had never seen in action before, especially for a movie series of this magnitude. Which is why, a few days later when I got a call from Vic Armstrong, my mind was in suspended disbelief. My ear was met by a jolly English accent who went on to ask me if I wanted to double River Phoenix.

I said, "you bet your bangers and mash I do."

He told me I would be heading to Moab, Utah. It was amazing how fast it got around. The stunt world is small and people began calling me and telling me how lucky I was. Like Tony the Tiger would say, I felt, "preeetty good!" When I arrived in Utah, I went from the hotel right to the Production Office. I met Armstrong and he brought me into Stevie Spielberg's office. You may ask me why I call him Stevie.

It is in memory of Vince Deadrick Sr. That is what he called him when they were on set. It was always very amusing. I was introduced to him and it was very cool. Steven was very lively and talkative. Another guy who noticed my accent. I could never hide it.

"Where are you from, New York?" He asked.

I said, "yeah, Brooklyn, Canarsie. Remson and Avenue B."

Our conversation was very intriguing. Whenever I spoke, he hung on and listened more than others would do. It's very hard to explain. He talked about the train sequence. Explaining that the character is running on the roof of the train cars. He mentioned in a very preliminary way, that I was being chased on top of the train. He wanted the character to grab a waterspout and swing around. Then he would drop back down onto the roof of the train, falling through the top into a lion's cage. I'll never forget the last thing he said which was, "and that's all I got so far."

I made sure he was finished talking before I spoke up and said, "may I give you an idea I have?" He looked at me with enthusiasm and said, "go ahead."

I told him, "as it reads, it seems to me that this could be a very visual sequence and I would like you to think about having River and myself play it like the actor Buster Keaton would."

Well, Spielberg jumped out of his chair. Then I watched him hop once up in the air and clasping his hands in enthusiasm he said, "that's a great idea!"

And so went our first meeting. After that, Vic and I went to scout locations. He mentioned to me that he was very impressed with what I said. He took me to see the train where River jumps on and is being chased by bad guys. He explained the basic action to me and I was excited. My creative wheels started to turn.

(Swinging three sixty, all in one shot onto the train.)

In the coming days, we go to the train and here is Steven Spielberg, George Lucas and the Director of Photography all ready to go. I come out with my boy scout uniform and my beautiful blonde haired wig on. It didn't take long before the other stuntmen started teasing me. They would take out their wallets and start placing their orders for girl scout cookies. I told them I was all out of cookies but had a few knuckle sandwiches left for free. I arrive on set and see the train is stopped so I get up on the ladder to go to my spot. All the animals are in place and I don't mean the stunt guys.

Yes, we had real animals as well as animatronic ones. It was supposed to be a circus train carrying live animals to the next performance location. My good pal Vince Deadrick Sr. is playing one of the bad guys along with stuntman Jeff O'Haco as the Indian.

My wheels are turning in my head as I wait for twenty minutes for everyone to get set up. I look around trying to think of something to do that would enhance the scene and the stunt. Being on top of the train, there is nothing you can really do prop wise so I went back to Buster Keaton and Charlie Chaplin and asked myself how would they portray this.

(From left to right See, speak and hear no evil. Freddy Hice, Steven Lambert and Jeff O'Haco)

How can I make something out of nothing and show it, not in rehearsal, but when the cameras are rolling. I decided I was going to give a performance with my body and this was the perfect scene for it. I am running across the train, told to go from point A to point B and had free reign to do what I wanted. The train starts chugging down the track and they call, "action."

The bad guys jump on the train and I start running. I begin action acting and would do little things like a circular stop as I came upon the giraffe, a quick look back at the guys chasing me as I hop onto another car and pretend to almost lose my balance. All Charlie Chaplin and Buster Keaton like in nervous and uninterrupted body language. I get to the third car and one of the bad guys catches up with me and I swing down like Tarzan in one motion into an adjacent car.

Spielberg yells, "cut!"

He comes over and wouldn't you know it, the first words that are out of his mouth are, "you look like Buster Keaton up there! It was amazing!"

I can't tell you how good that felt, that he had picked up on what I was trying to do. We were on the same wavelength. You know what they say, all Jews think alike. Ha ha ha. That was a joke, reader. He said that was wonderful to look at and I just said back.

"Steven, coming from you, that's big time."

He smiled and we went on for another take. We did one sequence where I fall back onto the train car and Freddy Hice is stunt doubling the character on top of me with a knife. Our commotion disturbs a rhino down below and his horn plows through the top of the train car, right through my legs. The effects guy has the lovely task of doing this and mind you we are not cabled off.

Vic Armstrong asked me if I wanted to be cabled off and I told him I didn't believe in cables except for maybe a great height and I know he admired that a lot. I could move around more and do what I wanted without constraint. Here I am on the train, the effects guy tells me not to move around too much as this horn is coming up through the breakaway roof, right by my crotch! I ask him when he is going to push the horn through and he tells me a few seconds after he hears Spielberg yell action. So we get into position and I hear the effects guy yelling up at me.

"Make sure you don't move your ass when we start Steven, or you will be like the Newlywed Game," he says.

Freddy Hice starts cracking up.

I look at him and say, "the Newlywed Game? What do you mean the Newlywed game?"

The effects guy yells out, "didn't you ever see that? You know, in the butt, Bob." Here- https://www.youtube.com/watch?v=2naTw9y7zsE.

Close enough. It was a fun time. We start filming and here comes this rhino horn smashing through the roof and I can feel it right against my crotch. I look and Freddy Hice looks and we start laughing as we are performing.

This thing is huge. I look at Freddy while we are rolling and say, "missed me by that much."

You may ask why I said that or you may not care, but I'm going to tell you anyway. You see, Freddy Hice's father is Eddy Hice. You may say, so what. Give me a moment and I'll tell ya. Eddy doubled Don Adams in the television show *Get Smart*. Would you belieeeeve?

Anyway, at lunch I got to meet River Phoenix on the first day. I found him to be really shy and reserved.

His mother was there with him and Armstrong told that they were purists and she was there to oversee her son. Watching River, through my eyes, it was almost like River was seeing the world for the first time.

Almost like a kid from another country. As the days went on, River found that watching me perform was simply amazing to him, so he told me consistently. He and Vince Deadrick Sr. became good friends. Every day on the set, River would ask where Vince was. Vince would tell him old stories about the old movie stars.

(Stunt doubling River Phoenix. Steven Lambert and Freddy Hice.)

Steve McQueen, John Wayne, Barbara Stanwick, the list goes on and on. They actually hung out together throughout the show. It was an amazing sight to see that old man Vince and River Phoenix all buddy-buddy.

(Vince Deadrick Sr. River Phoenix's hero.)

When he saw me, he would say, "Steven, Steven, where is Vince?"
I thought it was hysterical but wonderful and I understood because I loved this man dearly.

(He had a good soul. River Phoenix and Steven Lambert.)

He was like a second father to me. At this time, I hadn't met Harrison Ford yet, as most of the movie had already been filmed out of the country. When I first got to introduce myself to him, I found him to be very quiet. I said my name and how nice it was to meet him and that was pretty much it until the next day. The following morning, I came onto set with a Chinese long sleeve tee shirt, white baggy shorts, ladies long ballet socks, work boots and the River Phoenix toupee on. My style of dress, as you should know by now. That's one thing I could never figure out. Why people thought I dress funny. I always thought it was cool. Sure enough, Harrison Ford and I happened to cross paths and he stops and looks at me.

"Steven, right?" He asks.

I nod as he looks at me up and down.

"Those your clothes?" He asks me, not sure of what to say.

"Yeah," I told him.

"You dress different," was all he could reply back, but I was ready for him.

"Oh, you like these shorts? I get them in Venice, I can get you a pair."

He looks at me as if to say he wouldn't be caught dead in these kinds of shorts.

"If you like the socks," I continue undaunted, "I'll throw those in for free.

They are ballet socks." Just as he gives me another look, the still photographer snapped a picture of us. It was classic.

He just shook his head and said, "no thank you."

I laughed.

(Harrison Ford thought I was in my pajamas. He was just jealous.)

That would be the last time I saw him. So I thought. The next sequence I was called upon to do was me crawling on the horizontal ladder in the train car with all the animals and the bad guys following me. Remember that? The last thing Vic and Spielberg did before rap that night, was go into the train car to plan out the action.

Vic told Spielberg I was going to do a forward roll on the ladder flying off as it broke and come up into a sitting position with my feet in a barrel. Spielberg didn't understand how I could do it without falling off so I showed him that night.

They released the ladder and it collapsed horizontally like you see in the film and I rolled down sitting right above the barrel with my feet inside. The Director loved it and complimented me on my performance, which I thought was just wonderful. He decided that would be the first thing they would shoot in the morning and off we went to bed. The next morning, I get my boy scout uniform on and head to set while they prep for the scene. Once they are ready, they call me over and I get to my spot. They shut the little window door since I have to open it and yell, "action!"

I crawl along the ladder, it breaks. I do the forward roll and my legs go into the barrel and all of a sudden, this THING pops out of the water. I have no idea what it is as my heart stopped for a moment and I let out a scream like a hyena. Instead of falling into the box on the floor that I'm supposed to fall in, I fall to the other side screaming like a wounded animal. I turn around and I look up to see this big animatronic snake coming out of the barrel. No one told me that was going to happen! I had no idea!

(The joke was on me.)

I'm on the floor on my backside, my heart is pounding from fright, thinking what the hell just happened. I look at Vic and Spielberg and all the other laughing faces. It wasn't until I got up and see the whole crew is laughing at me. Only then I realized what happened. The joke was on me. In my mind I'm going, he set me up! Spielberg set me up! I was so embarrassed I just thought about the cowardly scream and how it sounded. But I ask you, wouldn't you do the same if you saw a freaking anaconda burst out of the water? Now you know why Indiana Jones really hates snakes. Because when he was young, his stunt double almost had a heart attack from one!

I look at George Lucas and even he has a smile on. George was probably one of the most timid men I had ever met. George was always the one watching and listening. If he needed to say something to Spielberg, he would walk away with him and talk. It was almost like the big brother looking after the little brother, Lucas was like the prodigal son. There was never an outward or verbal reaction from Lucas. It's hard to explain. He never said anything. A thought, an expression, an idea, even a hello was never heard or seen in public. It was almost like he was a wounded puppy. Afraid to say or do something. A fear in him. As I said, it's hard to explain. It really was amazing how extroverted Spielberg was and how internalized Lucas was.

As the hours and days went by, I realized what an incredible genius this guy is. Steven Spielberg knew everything about every department. He knew how to do things you didn't even know were possible. He was a man of many talents, from camera to props, to letting people work. Yes, that is a very important thing. Steven Spielberg and Vic Armstrong had the wisdom to allow me to have the creativity and freedom to pull off the scenes that you see in the movie today. I am always afraid I would have limitations by the Director or Stunt Coordinator for all different reasons, but here I had that freedom to do what I wanted. I have worked for and with a lot of Coordinators and some want you to do exactly what they want, some will give you a bit of freedom, but let me tell you that I have never had such freedom like this since the Ninja pictures.

That's why I could say, Vic Armstrong is a very smart man and a terrific Stunt Coordinator. He lets his people create and perform. That's the sign of talent that very few people understand. As time flew by, we move to another location. Remember the big cave in the opening sequence? A huge cave where young Indiana Jones tries to safeguard the artifact that was found from the conniving adults. Steven Spielberg has a throwaway line that he wants to give to one of the stuntmen, so he goes over and tells Vic Armstrong. Vic looks at me and says he has the perfect guy for it, Vince Deadrick Sr. and asks me to go get him. I go find the old pain in the ass and bring him to Spielberg who gives him his line.

"There he is! Go, go!" Vince says the line back to Spielberg and it's perfect.

We go on set and begin filming, mind you we are in this huge cave where everything reverberates. Echooo. Vince knew this and the ham he was, saw his chance. He said his line nice and loud, way too loud. It was as if the cave was erupting with his voice. Roaring up from the depths of the cave, it echoed multiple times. A few seconds later, Spielberg cut and raised up his megaphone. He always loved to carry a megaphone, which I found quite funny and fascinating. He has his baseball cap on, can hardly see his eyes with his sunglasses on. Everyone is quiet. He raises this megaphone and speaks into it.

"Vic? Vic? Vic Armstrong. What is your stunt guy's name who we just gave the line too?" His voice amplified by the megaphone bounced around the chamber.

Vic tells him it is Vince Deadrick and he calls for Vince on his megaphone. Vince pops up and looks up at Spielberg who is seated high up, as he usually is on set. "Yeah?" Vince calls back.

"Do me a favor," Spielberg replies from his megaphone. We all wait for Spielberg's reply, and then it comes bounding down throughout the cave. "Please, a little less of John Wayne and a little more like Myrna Loy."

Now you gotta understand what Spielberg just said. John Wayne was a larger than life cowboy with a big voice to match his personality. Myrna Loy was a silent screen actress before the sound era. So basically, Spielberg is telling Vince to tone his ass down by using film history! Everyone started bursting with laughter in the cave, save for the boy scouts who were too young to know who Myrna Loy was and Vince's face got bright red. On top of that, the people who know Vince, know John Wayne is his idol. So you can bet they were laughing and screaming all over the place. When the initial laughter died down, those who didn't understand, asked. After another 30 seconds of laughter echoed through the cave, things finally settled down.

Vince called back up to Spielberg saying, "you'd never have the guts to say that to John Wayne." All eyes went to Spielberg to see what he would do or say.

He took a moment, lifted his megaphone and said, "you're darn right pilgrim."

The cave erupted with laughter one last time before we got back to work. I could say it was one of those rare moments that somebody got the best of Deadrick. After we did one more take, Spielberg was satisfied and told Vince, "John Wayne would be proud of you." The next day at the cave was the last day of this cave sequence. Now this cave we were at was about six to seven hours away from our hotel. They had a bus for us, it looked like a school bus inside but it had a bathroom in the back. Guess what? They decided to put all the stuntmen and the little boy scouts with their moms and dads on this one bus.

I don't know who came up with this brilliant idea, but nothing of excitement really happened until the final trip back to the hotel after we had wrapped on the last day. Before I tell this story, I will preface it with an introduction of events in a passage by the man who wrote the book, "The World's Greatest Stuntman." Vic Armstrong. (Hmmmm, you don't say?) In his book, he writes - "We also went to Green River, Utah, for the scenes of young Indy in all those caves. The unit drove up there from the airport in one coach while the stunt crew had their own, and we bought Jack Daniels and coke and lots of other booze for the trip and it was an absolute riot. It was just a rolling party. We even ended up trying to lasso the driver as we arrived. One of the guys was so out of it we found him walking down the center of the road mumbling, I'm walking back to LA, I don't like this place.' LA was three days drive away! Everybody was talking about this coach trip, and at the end of the shoot, driving to the airport to fly out, the other coach was empty because everybody was on ours waiting for the party to start."

There you have it, wasn't that fun and exciting? I know what you are saying. As asked by somebody who reviewed his book, "where are all the details?" Well, my friends, let me tell you what happened from a person who was actually sober during the whole event in question and will not leave anything out for the good, bad or ugly.

You see, let me explain the truth. All the stunt people sat in the back of the bus while the boy scouts and their parents sat up front with a few rows in between us. I call that a segregation separation. It was odd to me for four to five days, why the parents where a little nervous until that last day where we gave them just cause. As we were heading back, we saw a small quick-e mart type food and liquor store. Vince Deadrick Sr. wanted to stop and get some drinks, so we all got off and shopped around. When he said drinks, my thinking was water, soda, etc.

Back on the bus we were eating our munchies and having our sodas when Vince pulls out a brown paper bag. I always sat next to Vince being that he is a hero of mine, a second father. I dig that guy, he always made me laugh. I ask him what is in the bag and he starts laughing. He reaches in the bag and like a magician pulling a rabbit out of his hat, he pulls out a Bean. Not just any bean mind you, but Mister Jim Beam. How do I remember it was Jim Beam? Knowing and seeing Vince for so long, he is a man of habit. The only hard drink he would ever buy is Jim Beam. Not Jack, Jim.

"What are you going to do with that?" I ask

. He looks at me like I'm crazy. "What do you think I'm going to do with it?" He takes the top off and starts drinking it.

Freddy Hice looks over and asks, "what is that?"

Vic Armstrong looks over and sees what Vince is doing and he makes a comment. "Are you Irish men always that selfish?"

Bob Jauregi passes the bottle to Vic. Then Freddy Hice takes a swig and Bob takes a swig and so on and so on. They pass it to Jeff O'Haco and me.

I say, "nooo, not this guy."

Jeff O'Haco follows suit. It looked like somebody had to stay sober on this trip. I was right, just keep on reading. It seemed like hours go by, and they are on their third bottle, the race was on. Vince takes a clear plastic cup and pours some Jim Beam into it.

"Watch this," he says.

Vince and Vic are feeling the happiest and I am just watching everything happen before my eyes. He leans the cup over to me and I look inside and I see these things floating in there. It takes me a moment to realize that it's his false teeth! I couldn't believe it.

"Hey Vic, I got some more for you in a cup," Vince yells over to Vic.

Vic is flying as high as Big Ben at this point and he takes the cup from Vince with a smile. Vic starts drinking and he notices the teeth in the cup. Now if it was me and probably you, the cup would have been dropped and liquid would have been spit out. What did Vic do?

He just took one look at the teeth and said, "it makes it mighty tasty." He proceeded to drink the rest of it and held up the cup to show the teeth were still in there. Vince smiled, showing off his gums as we all burst into laughter.

(Toothless Vince Deadrick Sr. makes for a wild bus trip.)

This has been going on for hours mind you, and all the boy scouts and their parents have begun to catch wind of what is going on in the back of the bus. When it first began, they were laughing with us. Now hours later, they are holding their kids closer and whispering to each other. They are scared out of their wits. We are getting pretty loud and obnoxious in a civil way (whatever that means) and things are getting out of control.

The people watcher that I am, I've noticed the last couple of hours how the parents aren't liking what is going on. But they are too scared to say something, which you have to understand, the visuals of all this were incredibly funny. It isn't long before some of the kids and parents have to relieve their concern. In other words, go to the bathroom.

You can see the parent's faces are white as a sheet. At the beginning of the trip, they would let the kids go by themselves. Now they accompanied them. Holding them close as if they were walking through the halls of a prison. We were the drunken inmates on both sides.

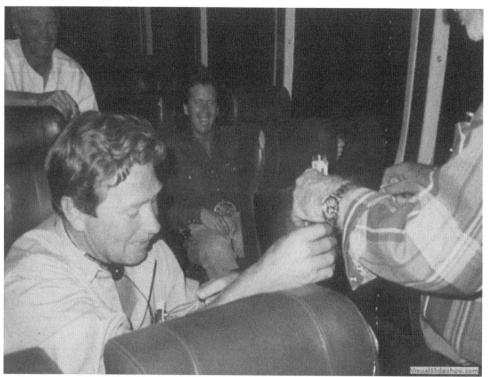

(All aboard, said Vic Armstrong. Pass the Jim Beam.)

The bus driver isn't saying a word during this, he is smiling too. In Vic's book, he mentioned lassoing the bus driver. Well frankly, I don't remember that. I give you nothing but the facts. We finally get back to the hotel and those kids and their parents couldn't get off the bus fast enough. Vince and Vic are two shit loads to the wind. Vic can't walk and Vince is a rocket ship on legs. Vince mentions he knows a bar around the corner and heads off the bus to find it.

Vic can hardly walk, so I take it upon myself to help him. All the other stunt guys run away. You ask me why? I just don't know. Vic's hotel room is upstairs and he can't walk and I'm left alone. I manage to get Vic off the bus. He literally can't walk. So I hoist Vic over my shoulder, all the while yelling at Vince to come back as he is stumbling down the street like a maniac. With every ounce of my strength, I'm preparing to walk up two flights of stairs as I hear Vic mumbling behind me.

"Put me down, I want to go with Vince."

I'm yelling at Vince as he is meandering down the middle of the street. "Stop, stop, Vince."

He ignores me. Everybody else has disappeared. No one to help me. Isn't that funny? I laugh and head up the stairs. I go to Vic's room carrying my boss with all my strength over my shoulder. I open his door, plop him on his bed, take his shoes off like a good friend and cover him up with his blankie and he goes night-night. Goodnight moon, goodnight Jim Beam, good night Vic. I rush downstairs and out to the street, high tailing it around the corner and I see no Vince, no bar. I spend an hour looking for him with no luck. The next morning I call his room and there he is. I asked him where he was and he said he met some shit eating cowboys in a car.

"Get out of the street," they told me, Vince recalled. He then asked them where a good cowboy bar was. So they took him to one!

I asked who took him home and he said they did. That's what shit eating cowboy friends are for. I just sat back and shook my head in disbelief.

"You're too much," I told him before hanging up.

You gotta admire Vince. When I went down to the lobby, I expected a backlash, a mention, something. Then I went to the set and not a peep from the boy scouts or the parents, which I thought was very strange and always will. Maybe they did say something but nothing was mentioned. All's well that ends well. Chugging along, back on the set with the train. The next day I meet up with Vic, my boss, and he is moving mighty slow. He asked me how he got to his room, he didn't remember. I refreshed his memory. We continued to go over the basic outline of this next piece of action. You see usually when it comes to a drawn out piece of action, they only have a beginning and end.

Where they want you to begin and where they want you to finish. That is why I so enjoy what I call story sequences. Anything in between, I have the liberty to join in the fun and create. This is something you should always take into account and know you do have that option, if you have enough understanding and most importantly, guts. Finishing up the sequence, there is a waterspout for the train on the tracks and I am supposed to jump on it and it swings around in a circle back to the train. Vic shows me a cable he has connected to the waterspout and he wanted me to put on the harness and try it out. I said I had an idea to make the shot look better. I hope by now you readers are starting to get me a little bit.

Vic asked what idea and I told him, "I could do the shot in one take without being cabled up and jump off, swing around and come back, no problem."

He looked at me with surprise and said, "what happens if you fall?"

Like a game of chess, he thought he had me, but I was ready. "I'm not going to fall, besides, worse comes to worst, I'll break a leg and you can just bring in somebody else. He won't be me, but he will have to do." Checkmate.

He smiled at me and thought it was funny and simply said, "I want you."

Those three words meant the world to me and I simply said, "it's a piece of cake for a stunt monkey like me." I knew I could hold onto it with a tiger claw grip and release like a graceful crane. Vic loved it and went over to Spielberg to explain what I was going to do.

"You can give me all of this in one shot," the excited Director said.

"Yes, sir. Not only that, but I can give you more."

He asked what I meant.

"Well, after I spin around holding the spout and come back on the train, you don't have to cut. I could land and fall down right in front of Paul Maxwell (Panama Hat) and crawl backwards before falling backwards into the lion's cage all in one shot. Buster Keaton wouldn't have it any other way. Would you Steven?" I replied.

He smiled and shook his head. "You can give me that?" He asks.

I speak, "sure I can. Without a doubt."

(Me and the Boss. We were like two little kids dreaming up a sequence.)

He shakes his head, smiles and turns to the D.P. "Let's go set up multiple cameras." He turns back to me and says, "I like your thinking." He gets the cameras set up and I get ready in my head.

I couldn't understand why they were so surprised, but I have always got that throughout my career. Something that I felt was so simple to me, was in other people's eyes, out of the realm of believability and I always enjoyed that.

Distance, timing, coordination, focus and most importantly, power of the mind. Said to me when I was a kid by Grandmaster Douglas Wong. We begin and I jump off on the waterspout and do a double kick to the bad guy played by Jeff O'Haco who is chasing me and swing all the way around back to the train, completing my three sixty and dropping back to the locomotive like a falling butterfly.

All the while, I'm trying to hide my face and you gotta realize that if you're doing something interesting, the audience is looking at the environment, not your face. It went perfectly and I got a standing ovation.

Even George Lucas as quiet as he was, ran up to the train and shouted, "now it's my turn!" Everybody laughed except Spielberg who said there was no way he was going to let George do that.

"That's a bunch of bollocks," Vic commented as George insisted.

After doing it a couple more times, (all prints) I stepped over to my boss and quietly asked Vic what the hell is a bollocks.

"It's an English word that means testicles, but we use it to say bullshit," he replied.

I laughed. (The more you know.)

After completing the stunt and finding a new word to use, bollocks, we moved on. Now let's go into the lion's den, yes the lion's den. Vic explains that the lion will be chained as I fall through a breakaway roof into the train car and come face to face with the lion.

The animal trainer said the lion would be secured and I had three feet of chain that would separate me from man's worst friend if I hit my mark. Whatever I did when I fell, I was not to go forward.

I replied, "ya think?"

My boss came over and explained he wanted to do it in cuts to put the pads in. I told him I didn't need pads on the floor and he looked at me funny again. "Bullocks! It's an eleven foot drop right onto your bum," he stammered.

My bum? Man, I'm from Brooklyn. We say tuchus. I insisted and he agreed. I told him we didn't need to cut there at all.

There are so many cuts that stuntmen do and have done, that I realized are not necessary if you know how to do things right. I made it a motto. The less cuts and cables, the better all the way around. I got noticed more and the immediate reaction from doing something in one take would always end in applause and admiration. I got such joy working with everyone on set, especially Vic for giving me the freedom to do that.

So I showed him how I was going to fall and we started filming. I did my crawl on top of the train, went through the roof and fell on my back perfectly. Now all I had to do was jump back and - LION! A huge maw shot out of the shadows before me and I jumped back like my life depended on it, because it did! I almost knocked myself out jumping back into the wall, I was so scared.

Got a big knot on my head.

The bad guys throw down the whip, I grab it and they couldn't pull me up fast enough. I mean it, they were too slow.

I look up and see that Deadrick laugh, as the lion grazed the back of my shirt with his paws. The only two who seemed to be pulling were Jeff O'Haco and Freddy Hice.

The trainer had asked me if it was okay if the lion touched me, I think I told him it was. Yet after the heart attack I almost had two seconds ago, I wanted to get up as fast as can be. And I ain't lion about that.

(Into the Lion's den I went, feeling the power of his roar.)

404

Now let's go back to the rehearsal with the bad guys pulling me up with the whip. We needed and I needed a test to see how fast they could pull me up. Now the guys who were doing that were O'Haco and Deadrick Sr. We are about to rehearse and I have a hold of the rope.

Suddenly, Deadrick yells out, "wait a minute, what happens if my back goes out?"

The thirty to forty people who are watching in close vicinity are quiet. I'm in the train car looking up, and I yell up to Deadrick, "this ain't funny. Stop messing around." I look up and see his false teeth protruding out of his mouth. I yell up at Jeff and say, "do me a favor. Let go of the whip for a second and kneel down. I want to see something before you grab it and pull me up." Jeff does what I ask and the minute he does, I proceed to tug at it with Deadrick Sr. the only one on the other end. I bring him to his knees, almost going through the hole, head first. Everybody starts laughing.

Moving on. Before I knew it, the job was over and what a job it was. A dream job, but not just any job. It was an *Indiana Jones* and a Spielberg job going on my resume. Can you imagine that? I took a flight home and just relaxed for a month, working here and there on TV stuff. But to my surprise the crusade wasn't over. One early morning on a hot summer night, I was waking up to go to sleep - tell me does that make sense? I don't know, but it sounds good. I get a call from the secretary of Amblin Productions. She tells me that Stevie Spielberg wants me to come to Universal, to Amblin and talk to me about another sequence he is shooting for *The Last Crusade*. She then told me that he would like me to coordinate it. I explained to her, "wait a minute. Vic Armstrong is the Stunt Coordinator on this. Why are you calling me?"

She explains that Steven knows that, but he had a talk with Vic who was unavailable. In his stead, he had recommended me. I couldn't believe it and immediately said sure. I did the electric slide, the Kung Fu version. The next day, I went into Universal and started my adventure towards the bungalows to find Amblin's Production Office. After a few minutes of searching, I finally found it. It was big time hidden, you would never know it was there. I opened these huge towering doors and walked inside. It was like walking into another world, very beautiful and ornate. Every poster Amblin had done was on the walls along with the awards that came with them. This office was one of a kind. I had been to many at Universal and believe me, with this one, let me say that you can tell who the head honcho is by the clothes he wears. In this case, it is the office he is in. Wow! An emperor's palace. I check in with the secretary who asks me to sit down and she would let Steven know I was there. All of a sudden, I got very nervous, almost overwhelmed with apprehension. Steven and I have worked together wonderfully in the past, but walking into his office and talking to him just face to face about things was daunting. Especially when I really didn't know what the hell was going on. As she led me to his door, I prepared my thoughts. I reached out and opened the door, a gush of air came shooting out hitting me in the face. It was almost like walking into the throne room.

Steven and I met eyes and the first thing he says is, "Steven, I can't wait until you see the things you did in the film, everything was cut together so wonderful. Buster Keaton would be proud of you."

I laughed and it seemed to put me at ease. I thanked him and sat down, still curious as to what exactly this meeting was going to be about. We proceeded in small talk, I discussed what I had been doing the past month and how I had been, when he finally got to the topic at hand.

"We have the film all put together," Steven announced. "I had a private screening at a theater in front of a special audience, which I usually do, to spot anything we may have left out of the film that would enhance it. We realized after we viewed it, that we are missing an action sequence."

I nod, trying to figure out what sequence it could be. He gets up and asks me to follow him. He opens up another door in his office and I head in after him, wondering where we are going. I step in and realize it is a little theater with about twenty four seats and a projector. A screening room he did have.

He looks at me and asks, "where do you want to sit?"

I find this question surprising and a little amusing, as I would sit anywhere Steven Spielberg tells me! "Eye line in the middle of the screen," I respond.

He smiles and I take my seat. Spielberg turns, looking up at the projection room. He yells out, "hey you up there, Reggie, let's get it going!"

The projector comes to life and it is the scene after Indiana Jones and his father are tied up in the castle. They escape and fool the Nazis by letting loose a boat and then come out of a wooden crate on a motorcycle sidecar and high tail it out of there. They kick two soldiers into the water, drive off and look at each other. That is where the projector shuts off. End scene. It was only a matter of seven to eight seconds. Steven looks at me and says that he realizes they need a big action scene in between. I nodded and asked if he had a synopsis I could follow.

He said, "no I don't have a synopsis, I want you to write the sequence."

I looked at him, not believing my ears and a little confused. "You want me to write the sequence and what happens?" I repeated, more for me than him.

"Yes," he said, his eyes locked on mine.

I say, "you mean everything? A whole little action story?"

He replies, "yes, as long as it is in the confines of the scene."

The wheels in my head started turning and when I asked and was granted a few days, my juices started flowing. I left just overjoyed and thinking of the sequence. That sequence, you can see in full in the film, which I wrote from top to bottom. When I had finished writing it, I went over it a few times and when I felt it was ready, I called up Universal again. I went back into Spielberg's office and had three copies of the sequence in my hand. I gave him one and he proceeded to read it. It was dead silence for five minutes while I waited for him to get through it. I felt like a schoolboy squirming in my chair as the headmaster looked over a report I had just written. It was about ten detailed pages and it seemed like it took him ten to fifteen minutes to get through it. When he was finished, he read it again, out loud. I tried to write as excitingly as I could and when he read it, it sounded so elegant and I hoped he was liking it. My question was answered as he began smiling and laughing at certain parts. No one had ever read something like this back to me this way. It was infectious as I found myself smiling and laughing with him as I heard my thoughts come out of Steven's mouth. Every now and then he would stop and ask me a question. Like for instance when the German pops a wheelie or when Sean Connery sticks the umbrella in the spokes. He thought that was a great piece. "This is great, you are an original thinker," he said.

I was overjoyed by that comment. When he had finished that, he finally spoke.

"I love that you used Sean Connery's umbrella in the sequence and I like the idea that Harrison takes the flagpole and uses it as a knight jousting on two horses. I love those ideas," he beamed.

I smiled and went on to explain how that would work with the checkpoint and the Nazi motorcycle coming around in front of Indiana Jones. He was wiggling in his seat he was so happy to hear these ideas I had come up with. He loved the ideas and asked me how many motorcycles I needed. I told him eight total should be enough as that would give us three spares in case we have breakdowns and then I asked him if I needed to build the motorcycles myself or would they be provided. Steven didn't know and called the Production Manager into the office to find out. As we were waiting, I said, "can I ask you something?" Taking a deep breath, I gathered my courage. "Being that Vic Armstrong is unavailable and you brought me in as your Stunt Coordinator, I would like to be added and credited on the movie as the Stunt Coordinator for this motorcycle sidecar action sequence."

Nodding, Steven instantly replied, "absolutely."

I thanked him and knew in the back of my mind what that kind of credit would mean to me and do for me in the future. The Production Manager finally arrived and we began talking. He liked my budget and my synopsis and left the bike buying and building to me. He asked how much time I would need to build them and I replied I would let him know, explaining that I am building the bike exteriors to be German bikes. I would need to hire a designer and builder of my own choice. You see, I also had five guys in mind I was planning on hiring that I had worked with before and were top of the line motorcycle guys. They were brothers Paul and Sean Lane, Jeff Jensen, Steve Kelso and John Hateley. Paul Lane was my go to guy. It's important for a mechanic to not just to know how to fix and repair them, but how to ride too. So in reality, I'm not just bringing five motorcycle riders, I'm bringing five mechanics as well. All you stunt people that are interested, remember what I just said. Hiring riders that are mechanics. You do that, you are gold.

Little did Amblin know, but that is the trick you can use. Get as much as you can out of the people you hire. I called up all of them and they were all available and tickled to death to be on this show. As the days went by, the story spread that I was doing this sequence.

Whenever I walked into the Stuntmen's Association, you would think people would be happy for me. But no, they seemed annoyed. I tried to stay away from the conversation as I knew I couldn't hire them as I had already hired my five (all from this organization), but they didn't know that. It really surprised me how most of my so called "brothers" acted when they found out I was doing that sequence.

But let me say, this doesn't only happen to me, this type of situation happens to everybody who coordinates a show. It is the usual practice. Jealousy. Not happy for your good fortune. I could actually say you could see it in their faces. I don't know about you, but I am always happy when somebody succeeds. I called up my friend and fellow stuntman Paul Lane.

He was the son of Bill Lane who had hired me many times when I was a kid. I asked him two things. Are you available and if he knew a mechanic who could work on the bikes and cosmetically make the bikes look German. He said yes, Doc Chabenaou Jr.

I said, "I know of him. His father was in the business."

So Paul Lane brought me down there and we went to his shop and explained what I needed and the time period with Paul's assistance. I had made him my right hand man.

You see when you don't have full knowledge, like in this case motorcycles, you always make sure you surround yourself with people who do. That's another sign of a great Stunt Coordinator. We make a deal on a budget and I get the eight bikes over to him and the build is on.

A few days go by as I am busy talking to different departments, working on my ideas and getting everything ready, when something dawns on me. I had stunt man John Hateley simply doing an endo on the motorcycle after Sean Connery sticks the umbrella into the spokes. It was going to be a big wreck and look good, however, we have seen endos before. Let me see, when you put a cannon in a car, it goes up into the air.

A cannon is a cylinder you put underneath the car on the inside with a piece of a telephone pole in it. It is propelled by Nitrogen and the piece of pole shoots out and forces the car up and over. So I thought, what if I put a mini cannon on the motorcycle, on the side. I wondered what it would do. I went over to the special effects supervisor, Michael Lantieri and spoke to him about my idea. I asked him if we could try it out with a motorcycle frame and a dummy and inquired if he had any around. He did, being we were at Universal and we set it up. I put the cannon right next to and in front of the back wheel and hoped it would work. I made an appointment to explain my idea to Spielberg, as you must do if you have any changes. I went in there and to my surprise, Lucas was there too. Or is it also? I don't know.

Spielberg asked me how far in the air it would go. I had never seen this done before so I told him seven to eight feet, I was winging it here. I wanted it to look real, no one had seen a bike go up that far before. They look at each other and finally decide they wanted to see it. A few days later, the effects guy is ready to test it. I let everyone know and we go to the backlot with the motorcycle and the dummy.

Spielberg and Lucas come driving up in the Amblin golf cart and hop out. This was an unbelievable moment for me. Having total control of a situation with two of the most powerful men in the movie business. I was the professor and they were the students. I brought them over and like a Kung Fu master talking to his students, I explain the set up that leads us into this situation as Spielberg and Lucas listened diligently. I explain how the shot was going to look and turn to Paul Lane.

I brought Paul because I wasn't sure how the dummy on the bike was going to start the bike and he had explained how you could lock the throttle. That's why you bring pros along. We get all set up and the effects guy is gracious enough to let me flip the switch to fire the cannon. I put the bike on a track, about twenty feet long.

I yell, "action!" The bike takes off from zero to twenty in a matter of two seconds and I hit the button and WHAM! This thing flies about twenty feet in the air as we all jump back. Spielberg and Lucas are running to get out of the way. This thing shoots up to the sky like a rocket ship. The motorcycle does a perfect three sixty and more in the air with the dummy on it, flipping twice, before it comes crashing down. The silence is deafening. I turn to the effects guy.

"Ho Ho Ho Holy shit!" I blurt out like a surprised Santa clause, raising my fist in the air. "Wow," I scream out before gaining my composure back.

Spielberg says, "I like it a lot."

George Lucas is clapping. "Amazing!"

A few more seconds go by and Steven says, "I'm not sure if that will be too much."

Before I can say anything, Lucas chimes in like an excited kid. "No, no that's great! That's just what we need."

Spielberg still isn't sure and they start having a conversation back and forth. It was the weirdest thing. I had never seen Spielberg unsure of himself. When I worked on the train scene it was the other way around. Lucas was the quiet one and Spielberg was the excited kid. Here, it was completely different. I explained to them that I could lower the height, it would be no problem.

"No, I want it to be exactly like this!" Lucas shouts.

Spielberg is not sure, and my eyes are going back and forth to George and Steven who just can't decide. They finally decided they would do it, but weren't sure of the height. They said they would get back to me on that. It was such a wonderful moment.

Moving on, Doc was busy getting the bikes ready and he had asked me if I needed to bring along a mechanic. Namely, himself. I told him that I didn't know. My real thoughts were, I had five. I didn't need anymore. My budget was also set. As days went by, it seemed things were not being done as fast as they could be. I had made promises that the bikes would be done in three weeks and needed to keep that deadline. I finally began to realize our mechanic wasn't what he used to be. I couldn't go to another because guys that do this kind of work are few and far between. I put Paul Lane on contract, deciding to have him work with Doc. I found out that our mechanic had mistaken the spark plug for spirits. I guess it had a twist off top. Nevertheless, things were finished in time thanks to Paul Lane and the day before we were to leave for Lucas Ranch to shoot the scene, I sent an eighteen wheeler over to Doc's place to pick up the bikes.

That day, Doc had called me again and asked if there was any chance that I could bring him along as my mechanic. I thanked him for his work but I told him I cannot justify bringing him with five guys who are mechanics who are already there. I didn't feel bad not bringing him along since he was getting a hearty paycheck for the work he did, so I thought. I asked Doc to help load up the bikes in the truck and thanked him for his work. As I hung up, I felt something was not quite right in the back of my mind, but I quickly brushed it away. I decided to call Paul Lane and asked him to go down to Doc's and make sure the bikes are all loaded on the truck and there are no problems. I needed to make sure all eight bikes were there. Paul agreed and went down there to load the truck. He helps Doc load them and says goodbye. Paul called me up and said everything was set. I fly to Lucas Ranch in San Francisco and meet up with Lucas and Spielberg. I picked out the spots for the checkpoint and where each stunt would happen. I tell them the bikes will arrive tonight for the next day's shoot and so will my men. The next day, I meet my five great stuntmen, load up in the van and we are off to location. I explain to everyone what they would be doing in the scene and we are all ready to roll. We get there and are greeted by the Production Assistant who tells them wardrobe and contracts are in their respective rooms. I look at them and say, "lets burn rubber boys." I meet Spielberg and pull out the shot list I made up with him and boy it was wonderful sitting down for hours, discussing and explaining shots with him. A moment I'll always remember. He told me the first one was all five motorcycles coming into the shot in the straight away. As I'm discussing this with him and others on the design of it, I realize Paul Lane is behind me trying to get my attention. I had told Paul to go take a look at the motorcycles and get them all warmed up after he put on his wardrobe. As I glanced at him, I saw a look of perplexity on his face. I couldn't help but think something wasn't quite right when Spielberg spoke up.

"We'll be ready in twenty minutes for the first shot," he said.

I replied, "got it." I walked over to Paul and said, "what's up?"

He replied, "you're not going to be happy. I just pulled all the bikes off the truck and all the wires are cut," he whispers.

All of a sudden, I go from Seventh Heaven to the depths of Hell. I said, "what? What do you mean wires cut?" I had to be dreaming.

"Doc cut the wires on the bikes," Paul repeated.

"I thought you were there loading up the bikes with him?" I managed to say while trying to stop a panic attack.

"He must have had a key to the lock," Paul said as he threw his hands up.

I look at him and said, "I have twenty minutes until the first shot with five of the motorcycles. Can you fix it?"

Paul thinks. "I'm not sure, but I'll try my best," Paul replies with a dumbfounded look.

I said, "okay, get all the guys together to help you. Whatever you need, go to FX and if you have any problems come see me." I told him he didn't need to fix all eight, all we needed right now was five. He said he would try his best. Now I know the first shot of the day always takes longer than the rest, but I was told twenty minutes. That is the way you have to think. (Otherwise, you get in more trouble. A tiny little lesson.) I also knew that and was told by Paul that this kind of work usually takes hours. I didn't have hours, I had twenty minutes before a very unhappy Spielberg shows up, as far as I was concerned. Paul assured me he brought his "shit load of tools" that I asked him to bring and he would try his best. I said, "Paul, I need your help. We have twenty minutes. Get it done please."

(Kneeling down next to me, one of the best. Paul Lane and the motorcycle gang.)

He takes off and gets to work and I'm watching the company set up and as I thought, as usual, it was taking longer than twenty minutes. Twenty minutes go by, thirty minutes go by and I haven't said a word to anybody. I stroll over to Paul and the others who are working vigorously on the bikes. I stay silent and watch them work, the clock ticking in my head. It was like I had a half dozen shots of espresso, I just couldn't stay still. Paul tells me they are getting close and I decide to go on set, play it like everything is going well. After forty-five minutes I get a tap on my shoulder and it's Paul Lane.

He says, "I got five bikes ready."

I look at him and like a little kid as happy as could be, I put my arms around him and say, "thanks. Great job." I think to myself, sure glad I brought him. Pat yourself on the back Steven. He goes back and brings the bikes out on set and Spielberg sees the bikes and smiles. I have to stop and give credit to Paul Lane. If he wasn't there, who knows if those bikes would have been fixed and ready on time or at all. This is what I call a true talent. Someone that simply cares as much as you do.

His father Bill Lane, would have been so very proud of him. Now let's get back to Stevie, the Director, as Vince Deadrick Sr. called him and let me say Stevie always acknowledged Vince. Big Time. If Spielberg were to find out, he would have been very upset. I mean, let me tell ya, the whole reason we were there was to film the bike sequence, it wasn't like we could move on to anything else. No cars, no high falls, no fights. It's a sequence with bikes, that's it. I was also lucky he liked my work and I had done the train sequence before this. If I was a new guy on set, I'm sure I would have been going home if I didn't have those bikes ready. Thank God for past performances.

I smile back at him, knowing he has no idea the chaos that just happened moments before. Now, I'm golden. For a few minutes, everything was going great again. Then, wouldn't you know it, I ran into an unexpected roadblock. Sean Connery and Harrison Ford came onto the set to see what was going on and I was introduced to Harrison Ford again. We shook hands and he asked me if Vic Armstrong was here. I told him he couldn't make it and said, "oh didn't you here? He is committed to another show and had suggested me to coordinate this sequence."

He nodded with certain uncertainty. He then asked me out of nowhere to my surprise, "what about Leonard?"

Terry Leonard was his friend and stunt double. Terry's one of a kind. A crash and burn guy. A man that everybody admires as much I do. I also told him no, he was unavailable, but I brought a great stuntman who would be perfect. Paul Lane. Harrison looked at me very seriously and I immediately took out Paul Lane's picture from my notebook.

He looked at me and asked, "you have books of stunt guys?"

I told him that in my room, I did.

He asked me to bring them down so he could look at them.

I said, "If I may ask, why do you want to look? Is it for another double?"

He said, "yes."

I took a deep breath and believe me out there, this wasn't a fun conversation. It takes a lot of guts, as I tried to explain to him that Paul is a perfect double for him and his motorcycle ability is extraordinary.

He just looked at me and said, "let me see the pictures."

I said to myself, okay, no more, I got his drift. "Okay, Harrison. You got it," I said. As I was going to my motor home, I thought, boy, this is the first time something like this has happened. Usually, doubles are set in stone before.

I had already talked to Spielberg before we left and he agreed. Now I'm thinking, are we going to have to put this off for another day to wait for a double for Harrison Ford. If that happened, I'm not sure Spielberg would be too happy about this, but I can explain to him this isn't my doing. I had no way of getting a hold of Harrison Ford and dealing with this issue with him before this. The company knew who I was bringing. Well, that's my excuse and I think it's a pretty good one if Spielberg looks at me and has any questions. I went up to my motor home and got all the composites and books I had. A book from Stunts Unlimited, a book from Stuntmen's Association and a book from ISA and many independents. I went over to Harrison's beautiful motor home and knocked on the door. I was invited into his kitchen and we sit down at the table.

I show him the independent stuntmen first and he breezes right through them. Every time he looks at a guy who he thinks might be right for him, I point a few things out. This guy doesn't know how to ride a motorcycle, or this guy is a bit too short to double him. I was gently herding Harrison towards a certain direction that dead ended with Paul lane. Each guy he was interested in, I explained why Paul Lane would be better.

He began to give me a look and I quickly stepped in and said, "you know Harrison, one of the reasons Vic Armstrong and Spielberg trusted me to do this sequence, is that they fully believe I know what I'm doing."

I wasn't sure how he was going to react to that and he did so with silence.

Harrison continues to look through the pictures and happens to stop at a stuntman named Diamond Farnsworth. I say that Diamond is great on a motorcycle. Even though he was an inch or two shorter than Harrison, you can't tell on a motorcycle. Harrison looks at me, then back at the picture, then back at me.

"Diamond," he says, saying the name out loud and shaking his head with a smirk. "Anybody with a name like Diamond, I don't want doubling me."

(I told Diamond this story, he didn't think it was funny. But I did.)

Quickly turning the page, Harrison moves on and I try not to let my inside laughter out. I found that so amusing. First of all, Diamond Farnsworth is a great stuntman, he doubled Stallone on the original *Rambo*. On top of that, his father is Richard Farnsworth who was nominated for Best Actor at the Academy Awards for a movie called *The Straight Story* and has been in many other films. Harrison knew his father, and I was afraid if I said that, he would pick Diamond instead of Paul. So I stayed quiet. I will never forget that statement coming out of Harrison Ford's mouth.

"Anybody with a name like Diamond, I don't want doubling me," he says. I can assume a couple of ways that name could be taken, good or bad, but little did Harrison know he was passing over a diamond in the rough, a talent, one of a kind. Even though Diamond was great, I still thought Paul was the best person to double Harrison. In the end, he took two or three pictures and told me he would think about who he wanted. Now, none of those pictures he took were of Paul Lane, but wait, I had one more trick up my sleeve.

As he walked away, I said, "Harrison, I've been told that you haven't had a lot of experience riding a motorcycle with a sidecar, so would it be all right if I had Paul Lane teach you right now?"

He said that would be fine and we went our separate ways. I went over to Paul and explained the situation to him and he understood completely. I told him to be cool, be sincere, just be yourself Paul and let's see what happens. I asked him to teach Harrison how to drive the motorcycle and that's exactly what he was going to do. I hopped into the sidecar and Paul drove me over to Harrison's motor home. I introduced Paul and Harrison, the latter being very introverted, and they headed over to the motorcycle. As they were walking away, Paul looked at me and I looked at Paul. A quick wink from Paul made me smile and told me he had it under control. I had no doubt that Harrison would fall in love with Paul, hoping Harrison returned with a different way of thinking. My confidence was instilled when half an hour later, they returned as happy as can be. Best friends, it seemed like. Harrison got off the motorcycle and walked over to me.

"We'll use Paul as my double," he said.

I smiled and thanked him. I went over to Paul and we hugged and laughed.

"Yeah, we had a great conversation," Paul commented. "We talked about my dad and other old timers, he knew a lot about him and we had a good chat. We also talked about Terry Leonard and how close we were and I threw a couple of funny stories in that Harrison enjoyed."

That made me feel good and I knew just being around Paul would do the deed. As for Sean Connery's double, I had a decision to make. Before I got there, I had three stuntmen I wanted to choose from, including Roy Clarke and Mike Vendrell. I thought about what they could offer, the opportunities and friendship they gave me and what they could offer as a whole.

It was very difficult. Roy Clarke was one of the old school stuntmen whom I ultimately decided on. I worked a lot for Roy in the past and decided on him because he was an elder and should be the first on the list since he was one of the first to hire me when I was a kid. I must say, it cost me about six months of friendship with a hero of mine and a great friend, Mike Vendrell.

He got very upset at me and had a heavy discussion with me on the reasons why he thought he should be there. It really broke my heart, but soon after we made up like it never even happened. That's the meaning of friendship. That guy meant a whole lot to me. I miss him big time.

I just hoped and prayed Sean wouldn't do the same thing Harrison Ford just did. I got Roy and Sean together and they talked and God bless Sean, he liked him. The whip crack of dawn arrives the next day and I am up and ready. I got my men together and we worked on the remaining three bikes with cut wires. What a lowlife that mechanic was. Once they were fixed, I got to set early and started getting things ready.

(Writer and Stunt Coordinator Steven Lambert, motorcycle sidecar sequence.)

Paul fires up a motorcycle with a sidecar and Roy Clark gets in and I hop on the back of Steve Kelso's bike and we head over to the location ready. The Location Manager brings us to the different locations and I explain to my men what formation I wanted them in. Sometimes three abreast, sometimes in back of one another, sometimes weaving in and out of each other, all different looks. Sometimes turns, these were all going to be two shots with the motorcycles chasing Harrison and Sean in the sidecar. I get to a fork in the road and we stop. I explain to Jeff Jensen where he is to peel off during the chase, up this hill and over the ravine where eventually he was going to be in front of the motorcycle sidecar. Harrison is going to be sandwiched like an Oreo cookie. How about an ice cream sandwich, or maybe even a nutter butter with the peanut butter between two crackers. Am I cracker-ing you up? And then I go over to John Hateley and ask him how long he can hold a wheelie. He looks at me and explains it depends on how the ground is when we do it. I explained to him he would be on the flat road for a semi smooth run and asked again how long he could hold it.

He goes, "well Steven, have you ever drunk four or five glasses of water and you can't find a bathroom? And then it's a miracle! Finally, you find that bathroom and you start to relieve yourself. It's going and going and going and you are getting impatient because you are urinating longer than you thought."

I look at John with a shocked and confused look on my face and so do all the other stunt guys. He has us captivated and intrigued, like five monkeys on a string.

I'm thinking this is going to be a profound statement, but I'm confused as to where it is going. "What are you talking about?" I ask him confused.

He laughs. "I can go as long as you can Steven."

We all smile and laugh. You have to know Hateley, he's a funny guy. For instance, listen to this, one time we were on a show working for Glenn Randall in Mexico City at Churubusco Studios on a Jay Leno and Pat Morita movie called *Collision Course.* Oh, I got a lot to tell you about that one later on. There must have been two hundred people on stage, including the actors, when Hateley gets one of his funny ideas. Little did we know.

He goes over to makeup and strips down nude. He puts on a g string, yes you heard me right, a g-string, only covering his private parts. That would be enough for most people, but not John. He then has makeup put all different colored sparkly sparkles all over his body. Red, green, orange, silvery blue and gold. Now picture that. He also has red hair that he hair sprayed straight up. He looked like an exploded firework. We had no idea this was happening as we were focused on filming on the stage. Glenn Randall, who we called, "Mr. Humor," (not the ice cream) because he had NO sense of humor, was on set. Get ready for this. The Director yells, "cut," and we hear this awful screaming.

Now picture this, we turn and here is John Hateley, running from one corner of the stage to the other, screaming his head off, looking like THAT. A shiny sparkling man, screaming like he was on fire running across the stage. Everybody just roared with laughter, except Glenn who didn't find it so funny as he shook his head in disbelief. So that was John Hateley's sense of humor. The next day we all get together and are going to do the two shots on the motorcycles. Everything is going great and lunch comes. We eat up and head back to set, ready to do the part where Jeff Jenson peels off and gets in front of Indiana Jones and his father.

We set up the guardhouse and the guard and get the motorcycles ready. I picked a person very dear to my heart to play the guard at the checkpoint. A stuntman named Steven Lambert. That's right, it was me! Bet you didn't know that! Harrison goes through the checkpoint and grabs the flag that breaks off. He puts it under his arm as if he were a jousting knight. In medieval times, it would be two horses, here it was two motorcycles. The flagpole lance connects with Jeff Jenson who goes flying head over heels on a ratchet. He was a big fellow. Hit that ground hard.

I hear Spielberg yell, "cut."

We print it and move on. Great shot.

(Stuntman Paul Lane as Harrison Ford, Roy Clarke as Sean Connery.)

Guess what, I was so happy that I brought a great friend named Phil Chung as my equipment specialist. Today there are literally hundreds of equipment specialists, back then there were just two and Phil was one of them. Phil was a good friend of mine who I trusted and admired and he was always a great help to me. He used to let me practice on his equipment for free when I first started. We moved on to the double endo. I was having Paul and Shawn Lane do these stunts where they would slam on the brakes and lock off the front wheel of the bike and they would go head over heels. They were both wearing long coats as that was part of their German attire. Producer Frank Marshall walks over and starts giving his opinion. I am explaining to Spielberg why we should shoot it this way and in this area when Frank speaks up. He wanted separate shots of the crashes while I suggested it would look better if they did it at the same time.

Well, Frank Marshall didn't like my opinion. That was a quote he expressed to me.

Spielberg turned and said, "we will do it your way, Steven."

I glanced over to Frank Marshall who had a not too happy expression on his face and that was my first taste of Franky boy. Nevertheless, we set up for the scene and this is where the unexpected happens. Unbeknownst to me, Shawn had left his long overcoat opened, unbuttoned. Nobody noticed and I didn't notice. I was busy with other things.

When everyone was ready, Spielberg calls, "action!" All hell breaks loose as the motorcycles come into the shot at fifty miles per hour. They lock the front brakes off and the back of the bikes start rising. They both come off the bike, Paul looks like Superman. I look over to Shawn and here he comes looking like a bat flying through the air with his wings spread. His overcoat is completely opened and he looks like Batman going through the air. Everybody is watching the shot and it's amazing. They crash down to the ground and Spielberg yells, "cut!" Spielberg jumps up and runs over to Shawn. "You were like Batman up there! Your coat was fully open!"

Everybody starts walking over to him and he doesn't understand if what he did was a good thing or not.

Shawn started to apologize, but Spielberg quickly spoke up in response. "Oh, no. Don't apologize, that was amazing!"

Shawn's hesitation turned into a grin as we all laughed. It was cool. At this time, we had Producer Frank Marshall on the set overseeing things. He would make comments on changing little things here and there. I didn't see any safety concerns or major problems, so I always said, "yes." You always want to give the people in power the freedom they desire to make certain changes, which allow them to know that you realize they are Producers and they have the power to do so. Especially if they have short men complexes. He wasn't short, but he had a complex. So why would you cause a problem? Use your opportunities sparingly, when there is a need to speak up. Life's lesson.

A funny and embarrassing moment arose when I was explaining to Harrison Ford the path I wanted him to follow with the sidecar. I was walking backwards, explaining the shot to him as he was following me intently and I didn't see a tree root sticking out of the ground. I tripped and fell right on my ass! I looked up at Harrison who had this look of concern and uncertainty on his face.

As if to say, "why is this klutz on set, are you sure they brought the right guy?"

I got up, quite embarrassed, as you always want to have an aura of professionalism around actors of such caliber as Harrison Ford. I continued on like nothing ever happened, but Harrison kept his grin on. Great, I'm thinking, when I heard the words, "nice fall." Now he'll remember me as the klutz who dresses funny. It was a most awkward moment that I wasn't about to let happen again. Distance, timing, coordination, power of the mind and now I'll add avoidance of tree roots. Let's move on. The second to last gag was the wheelie with John Hateley. We rehearse it once and he pops a wheelie for about five seconds before we cut. We are in the camera truck about thirty feet ahead of everyone. I am standing in back of Spielberg, who is sitting in a chair, as I am doing a semi-side horse stance with my feet. We roll camera and I clap, signaling John Hateley to break through the pack on his motorcycle. He comes out and is roaring forward. Visually, I am happy to say, Spielberg left most of the work to me and he had no idea what I was about to do. All of a sudden, in back of him, like a maestro with his wand in the air at the crescendo, I raise my hands. That's his signal. John Hateley pops his wheelie and here I am with my hands up as John gets closer and closer until he is about ten feet away. Suddenly, Spielberg senses me behind him and he looks up. I get worried that he is going to be upset seeing me direct this action and I look down at him.

He looks back at Hateley, then back at me. He realizes what I'm doing as we continue to go down the road with the wheelie. Spielberg keeps looking back and forth and is smiling like a kid in a candy store. He can't stay still as he jumps up and down in his seat. That's how Spielberg was. When he became excited about something, it was as if he became a little kid again. It's an amazing gift. When I felt Hateley getting to the end of his wheelie, I dropped my hand and he dropped the bike. It was perfect.

Spielberg yells, "cut!"

The truck stops along with all the bikes. Spielberg literally jumps up on his seat and looks at John Hateley and says, "that was great. I can't believe it." He looks at me and says," that's a winner Steven. Let's move onto the umbrella in the spokes."

I explain to John he has to move the bike over to the left side of the sidecar. I decided to put Roy Clarke and Paul Lane in the motorcycle sidecar as I had no idea what would happen with the umbrella.

It could bounce back and injure them for all I knew. So that is what we did and it worked out great. Then we move onto the final shot, the mini cannon on the bike.

While they are setting up the track, I walk over to Spielberg and ask him how high he wanted the bike to go. Should it go as high as it did in rehearsal or less? George Lucas is standing there along with Frank Marshall.

"I wasn't there," Frank spoke up. "How high in rehearsal did it go?"

"It went HIGH, man. It looked great. We should leave it like that," George Lucas insisted.

I looked at Steven and he had a look of uncertainty about him, but he ended up agreeing with Lucas. So we agree to put in as much powder as we did in rehearsal. I have Paul and Roy in the motorcycle sidecar since I wanted the explosion in one shot. I have the doubles in because again, just because the bikes went up in the air in rehearsal doesn't mean that's what is going to happen when we shoot it. I told Paul and Roy to keep those hats down over their faces as best they can. We are ready to roll and Spielberg hands over the baton to me to call, "action."

I had put John Hateley's stunt double on the bike, his name was Mister Dummy. Tied him to the bike with wire, legs feet and butt. I got the honors of pushing the button again as I offered it to Spielberg but he was too nervous. All of a sudden, I blow it and it goes WHAMO! Beautiful shot. It goes a few feet higher than it did in the original rehearsal back at Universal. Everybody was there watching and they all jumped back in fear as the explosion and smoke were just incredible. We put dust in the canon to add more smoke and the bike went twenty feet in the air. When it landed, Paul Lane went out of the shot with the sidecar and the Director yelled, "cut."

Everybody just roared with applause. It was like the end of a great musical play. It seemed to go on for forty, fifty seconds. All throughout the stunts on the train, Spielberg would be jumping up and down, excited like a little kid. I look at him now and again, it just wasn't there. He still just wasn't sure. Did he not like it because it was over the top? He has had over the top moments in his other films like when Jaws died in a huge explosion, when the scuba tank was punctured, much larger than what would happen in real life. Or E.T. riding bikes in the sky. That day at the end of wrap, all the stunt guys got together and we had a big party. A big celebration. I was glad I hired the right people to deal with these unexpected situations and things worked out. True pros. That's how you get future work, as I will talk about later on. The next day I went home and a week went by when I get a beep on my beeper. I go to a payphone and call Teddy's, my answering service. They tell me Amblin just called and wanted me to call the office. I'm thinking, are we going to do more, or did something go wrong? We left there in such good spirits. A half hour later, my thoughts ablaze, I give them a call and get the secretary on the phone. After I introduced myself, she told me that Steven wanted to talk to me. My heart pounding, I wait as she puts me on hold. I was nervous, man. Who knows what could have happened? I didn't. I hear a click and Spielberg's voice saying my name on the other line.

"Hey, what's going on Steve?" I ask.

"Oh, I just wanted to let you know that we put the sequence in and had another private screening. When we showed the sidecar sequence when it came to that, I gotta tell you that got the biggest applause of the whole movie. It literally got a standing ovation. Especially the motorcycle mini cannon in the air. I just want to say thank you, you did a great job and I hope I'll be seeing you in the future."

I took a moment and replied, "Steven, thank you very much. I hope so too." We both said to take care and hung up. Imagine this, I'm in the phone booth, just as happy as can be. I walked out of the phone booth and just for fun, I started strutting like Charlie Chaplain with an imaginary cane in my hand and a derby on my head. Pivoting back and forth, as happy as can be you see. Swinging the cane, with the derby on my head. I had no idea of the storm that was crossing the Atlantic. I'll give you a hint, biscuits and tea. See you all in volume three.

CHAPTER 47
(America Against England. Again.)

Time goes by and I am bouncing back and forth, working shows at Universal and Warner Brothers, when I happen to meet up with a few stunt friends of mine from my organization. The Stuntmen's Association. They ask me if I was coming to the next meeting and I told them I wasn't planning on it. They mentioned Glenn Randall was in town and he wanted to talk to everyone at the meeting.

I said, "oh yeah?" Then I asked them about what.

"We don't know, but we think it's regarding a certain stuntman from England," they replied.

I looked at them confused. "Stuntman from England? Joe Dunn? Vic Armstrong?"

One of them nodded. "Yea, Vic Armstrong."

I pressed for more information, but they had no more to impart. You see, in those times most American stuntmen hated foreign stuntmen. Yes, I know that's a strong word but unfortunately, it's the right word. Stuntmen from Hong Kong, stuntmen from England, Canada, anywhere but here. The reason being, they weren't from America. They felt like they were tourists. There was a tremendous insecurity and jealousy, even more so than their fellow compatriots. It was visceral to an extent. Vic Armstrong was not very known in America at this time. I was informed of an upcoming meeting that I know never changes. You see I don't want to sound negative but unfortunately, I have come to realize that is how these meetings are. Me, myself? I welcome men like Vic Armstrong. Greats from other countries mean more work for everyone.

That's what the Stuntmen's Association should be talking about. The good that could come out of it. You go thinking there is going to be creative thoughts, new visions, teamwork, comradery, and you wind up getting schmutz. Noun: schmutz. Dirt or a similar unpleasant substance. I go home and a few days later, before I know it, I get a phone call. Lo and behold, it's Vic Armstrong! He wanted to know if I was available to work on *Rambo 3*. I said, "sure, yea man. Thanks." It was just a breeze by conversation where I thanked him for *Indiana Jones* and I discussed how Spielberg called me and what he said. Vic seemed real happy about that and we ended our conversation. I was excited to work on a picture like this with Sly Stallone and looked forward to being with Vic. Somebody that I admired and respected a whole bunch.

I don't ask Vic about Glenn or the meeting at all. I'm not the gossip kind nor do or stick my nose in things without a legitimate reason to. I refuse to be like most stunt people. They gossip just to get a job and that causes more trouble. That's called street smarts. Just call it my Brooklyn street sense. The day comes and I go to the office where the meeting is being held. I greeted everyone and quickly found out to my not so surprise it was the same old. I figure by now I don't have to explain it to you again, do I? NO. I hadn't seen Glenn in a while and when he arrived everyone ran over to see him. He was the one doing a lot of shows in town and stuntmen in this organization couldn't wait to in a sense, kiss his saddle. Not me. Friendship is a whole lot different in my mind. It comes from mutual respect. After all the saddle kissing wouldn't you know it, he moseyed on right down and sat next to me and I was very proud of that. See, you don't have to kiss saddle. That's the meaning of friendship.

Figure that out you stunt puppies. You know who I'm talking about. I love it when the big guys sit next to me, it is an honor. He asked me how I was and what I was working on. I tell him without hesitation that I was going to be working for Vic Armstrong on *Rambo 3*. I knew Glenn and I knew when he had fire inside and all of a sudden that candle was lit. I didn't understand why, I wasn't going to lie to him, that wasn't my way. You see, I have always prided myself as a truth seeker. If I had nothing to be ashamed of, why hide it. But I knew why.

It was because I had mentioned Vic Armstrong. He had a spittoon in his hand, a cup. He was gnawing on Copenhagen and spitting it out like Clint Eastwood in one of his westerns. He lifted up the cup, spit in it and nodded. "Well, that's what I am here for. To have a conversation about Vic Armstrong and the English and I think you ought to listen."

I looked at him and said, "I love ya Glenn. I'm a good listener. Now let's see if I agree." I smiled as he gave me a stern but curious look. He was used to me respectfully giving him my thoughts and boy, was I used to that look and spit in the cup routine. Very few have enough spurs to speak to Glenn like that. It's just being honest. (That's why people love me. Ha ha ha.) The meeting went on, we talked about the regular problems and the normal complaints and grievances, upcoming events and the such. Come the time when the floor is opened up, Glenn jumps up from his seat and walks up to the front with his spittoon in hand.

"Listen, everyone knows me and everyone knows how tough it is to get jobs in the business," Glenn's voice boomed out to the room. "This is America and there are people trying to take our jobs from other countries and we need to put a stop to it. The Asians, the Canadians, the English. People like Vic Armstrong."

I winced as he said that name.

"We don't go to their countries and take their jobs, so we need to stand up to them here. We should decide in America who comes here to work. I know a few of you have worked for Vic in the past," Glenn continued.

Now, I'm thinking about the ten or more people from this organization that just worked with Vic on *Indiana Jones*. Glenn knows that I have worked on it and I'm sure he knows who else worked on it too. He proceeds to give a twenty minute speech on how these "foreigners are taking our jobs." Now I know that Glenn Randall and Vic Armstrong were dual Coordinators on *Raiders Of The Lost Ark* and to say the least, they didn't get along. How do I know this? At times, they both spoke about each other. The difference was that one spoke with respect and one spoke with anger, I'll leave it to you to figure out who said what. Glenn ends his speech, I'll never forget this, by saying, "anyone who works for Vic Armstrong will never work for me or anyone else I know."

That sent me back. I went from listening intently, to sitting back just deflated, angry and disappointed in my chair. People start talking amongst themselves when Glenn spoke up again.

"I want to see by a show of hands, everybody here who is NOT going to work for Vic Armstrong on Rambo."

A few seconds go by and twenty hands go up. Then twenty five hands. Then Forty, then fifty five. Finally, the whole room's hands are up. Except for three. Who were those three? Jeff Jensen, Ralph Garrett and little ole' me. Even the people who worked for Vic on *Indiana Jones* had their hands up. I guess I can't blame them, but it's hard not to. You see, it's taking out a piece of one's self. I thought to myself, Glenn, what are doing? Vic Armstrong promised everyone in the group work. There are so many people that are so in need and you can't see that. I was shocked. Three people with their hands down, fifty plus with their hands up. I tried to be cool, sweat was beading on my forehead. When the gavel hit the table, the meeting was adjourned.

Everyone flocked to Glenn Randall to pledge their loyalty. I walked away from the situation, disappointed and dazed at what just happened. I don't hold it against Glenn. I still look up to him and respect him. I give you this story as a lesson in life and an important one at that. Jeff Jenson walked over to me and asked if I had gotten a call from Vic Armstrong. I told him that I did and so did thirty other people. As everyone was kissing saddle, we walk out. Ralph Garrett runs in the back of us and says he also got a call from Vic too. I said, "well, either they are going to lie to Glenn and take the job, or they aren't going to take it."

You see, you gotta understand that this was a big deal. This kind of thought process was all over this town. Most thought that way, very few didn't. I wondered if Vic knew about this meeting and later learned on the set that he did. Two thousand seventeen, guess what? Stuntmen's Association? They all love Vic Armstrong now. They even made him a member. They got smart for a moment in time. A few days later I get a call from Vic who gives me the dates for the shoot. I said, "hey, I heard a rumor that you are inviting a bunch of people from the Stuntmen's Association."

He replied, "yeah I did and it was a bunch of bullocks because nobody is excepting it."

I pretended to let it just go over my head and acted surprised and told him I didn't understand why they would do that. I mentioned to Vic, "listen, you are a good guy and needless to say, very talented. I told them at the meeting they were making a big mistake. This isn't for any other reason but politics. Everybody is entitled to work where ever they can get a job. This is not truth, this is not justice, nor is it the American way." I mentioned that Jeff Jensen and Ralph Garrett were going and Vic confirmed that they were.

"That's okay," Vic said without missing a beat. "I'll just hire Stunts Unlimited and Independents. The rest of them, it's their loss."

I thanked him and hung up. Later that night, I called Vince up as he didn't go to the meeting, and told him what happened.

He was surprised and simply said "F_ _ _ Captain Fatty."

That was his pet name for Glenn Randall. I laughed, and Glenn wasn't even fat. Figure that out. He also was invited to go on *Rambo* but turned it down because he just wasn't in the mood. That was Vince for you. A hero of mine. I felt like brothers in arms with Jeff Jensen and Ralph Garrett as we headed off to Rambo. A bit in shock that we used our common sense to begrudgingly "defy" Glenn Randall. A few other stuntmen patted us on our backs, but I found it humorous as they weren't even going!

CHAPTER 48
(Actor Sylvester Stallone And The Look Of Love.)

The flight was interesting as we all talked about that meeting the whole trip. It was the main topic of conversation. This threat that was made by Glenn, we just couldn't understand it. It hurt people in many ways and it bothered me especially. I had a strong relationship with Glenn Randall and this really put me between a rock and a hard place. Taking away your right to work happens a lot in this industry, it is up to you what path to go down. Whatever path you choose, unfortunately, it is possible may be collateral damage either way but you have to choose the one with the least and which is in your heart. Hopefully, it is the right way. As the ten commandments say, "thou shall do the right thing." Oh wait a minute, that is the eleventh. There was no more room on the tablet.

We landed and met Vic Armstrong there and realized just how many stuntmen were on this project. Literally lots and lots. Stuntmen from everywhere, even Afghanistan! The first day was fun, full of action. I enjoyed sitting back and watching what everyone was doing and coming up with my own ideas. It wasn't long before I spotted a tank and the light bulb went off in my head. I went over to Vic Armstrong and asked if I could be on top of the tank with a machine gun and shoot everyone. He said it was a grand idea! I thought the word was funny. "Grand." You'd never hear anybody from Brooklyn use that. So we set up this final scene in the movie with horses, helicopters, tanks, just a massive battle. I get up on the tank and we roll film. It's moving along and I'm shooting people left and right when the tank starts to go up this hill.

I look towards the cameras as the tank rolls uphill, five feet, then ten feet, twelve feet. I'm not paying it no mind. It finally reaches the top at about two stories high. I was getting a nose bleed. I see cameras all around me, one is pointed right at me. A good lesson is to always know where the cameras are pointing, that way you can do something that will be memorable, unexpected. Play it for the camera. I was about to do something very unexpected. So unexpected that I had no idea I was about to even do it! As the tank reaches the top of the hill, it keeps going over the hill.
I don't realize what is happening as it begins to teeter totter and I quickly assume a square horse stance to maintain my balance. All of a sudden, the front of the tank whips downward like a seesaw and I go flying into the air, catapulted up. I flew up about fifteen feet in the air. Here I come on all fours speeding down to the ground and SMACK!

The Director yells, "cut, cut, cut!"

As I'm trying to catch my breath and figure out what just happened, I notice fifteen people running over to me.

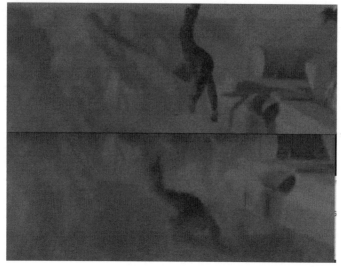

(Teeter Totter on a tank and I won, didn't get hurt.)

My knees, forearms and ankles hurt a lot as I tried to get up. Anyone else might have been seriously injured, but I was thankful my cat like reflexes had saved me from worse harm. I roll over and sit on my butt, letting them know I am all right, grateful I landed on hard desert ground instead of hard concrete.

"I hope we use that. It was fantastic!" The cameraman says.

Vic nods and explains what happened. "Steven, you were a human catapult."

I laugh as everyone else follows. If you thought that was a rocky situation, get it? Listen to this. Stuntman Jeff Jensen calls me up in my hotel room and says, "hey, Vic Armstrong needs your assistance."

I ask, "what are we doing?"

Jeff says, "he wants you and I to come with him to look at rigging on a helicopter." He mentioned all the important department heads like Directors, Producers, DPs and more were coming along as well. The next morning we get up and go down to meet and greet them. They have three vans ready to take us to the helicopter. All the big shots are in the first and second van and us little people are in the third van. It's me, Jeff Jensen and three others that we didn't expect. In other words, they weren't invited, they were what we call stowaways. How do I know this? I leaned over to Jensen and asked. They were Gary McLarty, Gary Epper and Andy Epper. Three terrific stuntmen. We arrive at the location and everyone piles out like a herd of Buffalo. Of course, all the important people head up first. As we approach the helicopter, I hear mumbling coming from Gary McLarty. As we walk up, it gets louder and louder as we near the chopper. I'm starting to hear words like, "who does he think he is!? God Damn it! Why didn't they listen to me?"

He starts shoving people out of the way as he leaves the back of the pack and heads towards the second group, breaks through and barges right into the first. I'm looking into the crowd of department heads who return his advance with stares of confusion, wondering who the hell this guy is. I am thinking the only people who know who he is the stunt guys. For all they know, he is some hobo off the streets, as they could think we are. They don't know any of us besides Armstrong. They don't even know that we are there, nor did they care, so I thought. The Whiz, yes that's McLarty's nickname, approaches the chopper and jumps inside as Vic is admiring the work, telling everyone how safe and correct the rigging looks. I watch from behind as a moment later Gary McLarty raises his voice to the tops of the surrounding mountains. What does he say? He bellows in rage with all kinds of foul language in between his dialogue to everyone around him about how the rigging and welding is all wrong. That someone needs to fix it, or he was going to tell Sly. I happened to look at Vic Armstrong. He is shocked. Neither he nor I had seen anybody turn on a switch and blow their fuse like this. You could say, schizophrenic. All the heads are confused, I know I am. Big time. They don't know who this guy is, they looked scared to death. A minute goes by then two minutes, he is still carrying on, explaining in his rant that none of it was done right. Everyone is backing away from the helicopter, wondering where did this guy come from, who the hell is he? This is what I read on their faces. Finally, he jumps out and makes a B line through the department heads in the first van and then the heads in the second van, to our van. He jumps inside and slams the door like an upset teenager, going right to the backseat. I look at Vic Armstrong who is keeping his cool which I thought was amazing in itself. Everyone stared in disbelief.

"That's all right, I guess we'll talk about it later, fellows. Everything looks fine to me," Vic says.

I hear a voice upfront ask, "who the hell was that? What the hell just happened?"

Vic replies, "Just a stuntman whose having a bad day, he must have had an argument with his wife." All the heads forced a chuckle. He goes on to explain the action of the scene to the Director and how safe it was. After Vic had assured the Director and said his peace, everyone piled back into their respective vans. I could tell they were just speechless. In our van, not a word was said except for Gary McLarty saying how he was going to talk to Sly Stallone about this horrible helicopter rigging and Vic Armstrong's unprofessionalism that he imagined he saw.

When we got back to the hotel, our driver was a genius to know to park far away from the first two vans. Andy and Gary Epper ask McLarty where he was going. Stallone was his destination, he told them. They decided to tag along and I just looked at Jeff and said, "what the hell just happened?"

Jeff shook his head and said, "McLarty happened. He must have had his own personal snowstorm again. We should have expected this from him."

We go back to our rooms when three hours later I get a call from Jeff asking me to come to Vic Armstrong's room.

"We need you for backup," he says. "Gary voiced his grievances to Stallone and Stallone called Vic Armstrong wanting to know if Gary was talking crazy or what the hell was wrong with him."

He explained that McLarty told Stallone that he was going to take over the show and was headed to Vic Armstrong's room to confront him. Yes, this stuntman that most people on set didn't even know, yet was a legend throughout the stunt industry, was going to try to take over the show. His blimp was filled with air and bravado as he marched towards battle with the big Englishman. Jeff and Vic were afraid there was going to be a physical confrontation and they wanted the Kung Fu Jew to come as backup. I hung up and in a matter of seconds arrived outside the room.

"Who is it?" Jeff calls out.

"Lambo," I say, and the door opens. Inside I see Vic and Jeff as they had just finished talking. A few minutes later, we hear a rumbling at the door. A pounding follows. Jeff asks who is there and Gary's angry voice answers back to let him in. Vic looks at me and asks if I was ready. I told him, "yea sure. Bring it on."

Vic looked back at Jeff and gives him the okay. I think to myself, boy, I hope this doesn't end up in a fist fight. Jeff opens the door and McLarty bursts in. Who follows? Walking in behind him is Gary and Andy Epper. McLarty's wingmen, I figured. I swear Gary went across the ten foot hotel room about thirty times like the cartoon roadrunner, amped up. He was repeating that he had talked to Sly and was going to take over the show and that everything was done all wrong on the chopper, screaming at the top of his lungs.

Vic interrupts. "I just talked to Sly and he thinks you are crazy and out of line."

No answer from McLarty as he continues his one man speech. McLarty looks at me and says, "we know why you are here, Steve. You're the Karate bodyguard."

I say nothing back, just giving a look at Gary and Andy Epper. McLarty's eyes flew from me to Vic to Jeff back to me, in a never ending tornado of glances.. Andy and Gary Epper are as stunned as I am at McLarty's outburst. Those two almost looked like they wanted to be on our side. We are all just listening, taking it in. He never went near Vic, just paced back and forth like the cartoon Tasmanian Devil using every curse word in the book. He told Vic how amateurly the show was run, which made no sense to me. Vic was doing great in my eyes and in many others. What McClarty was saying didn't make any sense. It was like he was in an alternate world making everything up. We call it opposite land. After five minutes, McLarty takes his last stride across the hotel room and opens the door, his last words being, "I'm going to put a stop to this!"

As he slams the door, the rooms shakes. We are all stunned. I look at Jeff, then Vic, then Andy and Gary Epper. That's right, McLarty forgot his wingmen (the look on their faces was pretty funny), his two buddies! They look at us sheepishly and say, "guess we'll see you later guys."

Jeff nods and says, "maybe so."

Vic Armstrong says, "see ya, mates."

I watch as they quietly make their way to the door and disappear. I look at Vic and ask what he was going to do.

"We'll see what happens with McLarty," he shrugged.

Jeff asked me to hang around for a few more minutes in case Gary came back for round three, but it never happened. The next morning I asked Jeff what was going to happen with McLarty and he wondered the same thing. As we went outside we happen to see McLarty leaving on his motorcycle. We head off to set wondering what happened. I heard through the grapevine Vic didn't fire him. Eventually we ask Vic what the story was, and he tells us McLarty wasn't fired and he's welcome to come back to work. Jeff and I look at each other and mentioned to Vic we had just seen him drive off on his motorcycle.

"He did?" Vic said with raised eyebrows.

We nodded as Vic told us he had talked with Stallone about McLarty. Stallone thought he was off his rocker and didn't pursue Gary's concerns. Two days went by without a word regarding Gary McLarty. The third day came and around midday on set, we look up and here comes McLarty on his motorcycle. He pulls up, takes off his helmet and heads to wardrobe. I look at Jeff and then at Vic who watches Gary walk over to get his outfit on. We walk over to Vic and ask if he wanted us to do something about Gary.

He shook his head and said, "no, if the lad wants to work, let him work. I didn't fire him."

This came as a big surprise to me and showed what a guy Vic Armstrong could be. As for Gary McLarty, I heard he never once apologized to Vic. He pretended like it never even happened. Not a word was brought up. It's quite a wild tale. If you can figure out why this happened, let me know. Because I'm still trying.

I have to do a scene in a jeep leading the caravan with Stallone's son. Transportation brings the jeep and I notice they leave it running. I get in the driver's seat as Stallone's son is in the passenger seat.

Transportation waives at me saying, "hey Steven, don't turn off the ignition. Otherwise, we have to jump it again and wait fifteen minutes to have it ready again." "No problem," I say. I watch as Transportation walks away and look over at the kid who is looking at the throttle and then back up to me. I smile down at him and decide to break the ice. "Are you having fun?" I ask. It's always important to make sure kids are having fun on set, especially when it's Sly's.

He looks at me, nods and in a split second, he grabs the key to the ignition and turns it. The car sputters and dies. I'm stunned! Transportation comes running over.

"Steven, why did you turn it off? I told you not to!" He says.

I quietly got out and walked over to him. I threw my hands up, I was an innocent man, man. "I didn't. It was the kid."

Transportation glances at Stallone's son briefly before whispering to me, "make sure he doesn't do it again, the little brat."

I nod and walk back to the jeep. "Please don't touch anything. You'll get me in trouble. Now they have to wait to restart the jeep. I understand you're bored, but please, hands off."

The kid looks at me, not saying a word. Transportation brings a jump kit and fifteen minutes later, we are rearing to go once again. I am waiting for them to start the scene, keeping my eye on the kid. I wonder what is taking so long for us to begin, so I glance over at the crew. Big mistake. Stallone's son grabs the throttle and put it in first. The jeep lurches forward and stalls out. I turn back around in shock as he turns the ignition off. Are you kidding me?! I about lost my top. "Hey! Why did you do that? I told you not to. Didn't you hear what Transportation said?! You were told not to touch anything, you didn't listen. Now they have to jump the jeep again. Do you know how much time you have wasted!?"

Well, that did it. He started laughing. I called for Transportation again as the kid bolted from the jeep. He ran past the vehicle, past me, past camera and right into the arms of his father. Sylvester Stallone. I am watching the kid for a few seconds, he is telling Stallone something, I think that something, was me. Stallone's eyes went right to mine. He locked on to me like a missile. Oh, crap. I'm thinking in my head, "that's not a happy face. He is pissed. I wonder, am I going to get fired? I upset the star's son. This is it for me." I didn't dare look over at Stallone as I could see his son explaining what happened a mere fifty feet away. Out of my peripheral vision, I felt the cold hard stare of Stallone. So cold, I found myself sweating bullets at the same time, trying to stay cool and calm. I waited for him to come over and say something. Luckily, he never did. We shot it a third time and thank God the kid stayed still. The rest of the shoot it was like walking on eggshells whenever I was with Stallone. Thanks, kid. Thanks.

CHAPTER 49
(It Breaks my Heart.)

After *Rambo,* I saw that *The Last Crusade,* had come out in theaters. Finally, I get a chance to go see it. I went to see it, excited to see everything come together. It was beautiful and the motorcycle sidecar scene got roaring applause, just like Spielberg had said. At the end of the movie, I stayed to watch the credits and looked for my name. I found it, but it was only credited once just as "stuntman." The title of Stunt Coordinator for the sidecar sequence that Spielberg had promised me, was absent. I was confused. Why, how come I am not credited? I guess mistakes can happen and that is the world of Hollywood. Or is it? Wondering what I could do about it and feeling dejected, I quickly put it in the back of my mind and went on my way. Yet as years went on, I realized that no one had mentioned my hand in that sequence. Not Spielberg, not Armstrong, not anyone. I would see Spielberg, Armstrong and others give interviews on this motorcycle sidecar sequence and not a word was said about me or that scene having to do with me. That is when I began to get a little unsettled and curious. I hope you can imagine how strange it felt that someone I looked up to and admired as much as Vic, wouldn't give credit where credit is due.

Not in any interviews, not in any public talk shows and not even in his book. Watching the scene, it gives the impression to the audience that Vic Armstrong did this piece, which was the motorcycle sidecar sequence. When you never mention giving accolades to the person who really did it, it leads everybody to think different. It gives the wrong impression and he is smart enough and wise enough to know that. I was very surprised. As this went on, I never made a big deal of it openly, yet I was dying to know WHY? There was snow on the roof, but a fire was lit in the chimney. You have to understand that my work is my mark, it's my life, it's what I have done, it's my memory and it's the facts. No one should take away what you have done. No one should claim it by staying silent. Such an important and talked about scene will stay significant, one could say, forever. So shouldn't my mark on it be as well? That's only fair since I'm the one who wrote it, created it, and mutually directed it with Spielberg. Much thanks to Armstrong since he originally put in my name for this sequence. But does that give him the right to take it away? Listen, I take pride in what I do. I like to think of myself as an interpreter of a scene. I put caring and love into what I do. It's true.

Nobody knows the days you have left, so who is going to tell my grandchildren and my great, great, grandchildren and the people of the future? Not I. I'll be gone. I was promised credit after all, which my contract stated. Stunt Coordinator. Motorcycle sidecar sequence. So many questions swirled through my head. Would Vic do this on purpose? Is he afraid if he mentions it, it would draw the attention off of him since it was said it was the most exciting scene in the movie? He doesn't mention me in his book, nor anyplace else. Why is that? I mention a ton of people that I worked with and looked up to in this book, including Vic Armstrong. He is a man that I will always admire. It should make you proud and honored. Vic is mentioned several times. Why not I in his book, "The World's Greatest Stuntman."

I just don't understand it. You work so hard on something and you expect at least a little mention here and there. Not dead silence, being that you know it's not your sequence. I wonder if it was done intentionally or just as a result of indifference and ego. It is amazing to me, even when you are one of the biggest Stunt Coordinators in the business, which Vic Armstrong is, that you would still take the wax off other people's cars to shine your own. But he's just a person, like me and you. Isn't that what God says? Fame doesn't mean a thing when it comes to what is right. It's a problem in the world. Perhaps one day I will get an answer, perhaps not. Until then, the fire in my chimney rages, wanting him to speak of these questions. Wouldn't you? Not only for me and my family but for him and his. My friend Vic Armstrong, why? It's a terrible thing to be taken away. My legacy.

CHAPTER 50
(Egged On By Corey Eubanks. The Fight That No One Forgot.)

After surviving my run in with *Rambo,* little did I know I was on a collision course with a movie called exactly that. How's about that? It was a Glenn Randall Jr. movie and he called me up and asked me if I wanted the job. I was surprised as all of you are, since that verbal show he put on at the Stuntmen's Association, but I guess you can't get mad at me. He always knew if he hired me, he was going to get something unusual and unique. So I took it. I was playing myself which is called ND. Non-descript player, if you want more detail, you got it. "Not a main character or a written situation, lacking distinctive features or characteristics in the script." I soon learned that this film was starring Jay Leno and Pat Morita, two funny and wild guys or so I thought. The people watcher that I am, I soon put on my stunt psychology hat and noticed Jay Leno to be a very introverted guy. He just wasn't sociable with the cast and crew. They would say hello and he would more or less mumble. They would smile, he wouldn't. Somebody would try to have a conversation with him. Somehow he was too busy. Boring, he was. Not a funny nor a nice guy off camera, which really was perplexing to me. Pat Morita was a different story.

Pat wanted to be an honorary stuntman and got closer to us each day. I always brought four or five stunt hats with me on every show, so I passed him one. He loved it and wore it almost every day. I also gave one to Jay Leno and may I say he never put it on once. He just gave me a forced thank you and that was the end of that. During downtime we would play "liars poker" on set which had to do with a dollar bill and the serial numbers on the bill. Pat would play with us and learned quickly. For instance, if you had three ones, that would be three aces. You would try to come on set with fifty to one hundred one dollar bills since you never wanted to use the same dollar bill more than once. Pat lost hundreds. He caught on and he decided to have a poker game, a number of times throughout the week in his room. Boy, were we glad to join him. It was wild. I never cared if I won or lost because the catering up in his room was fantastic. He would call down to the hotel restaurant and every half hour they would knock on the door and come up with three or four trays of food. One half hour it would be hamburgers, the next half hour would be chicken, the next half hour would be desserts, the next half hour would be appetizers, it would just roll from one meal to the other.

Oh yeah, drinks as well. Snowshoe, please? Wild Turkey and peppermint schnapps. I only needed one of those, as I would tell the bartender. Yes, the bartender would come up and make us drinks. Pat would always have plenty to eat and plenty to say. He would also have plenty to smoke. Yes, he was flying that kite high. He was dubie-dubie-doing just like Dean Martin. Even when you walked past his motor home you could smell him having a good time. As to his personality, what you saw in *Happy Days*, is what you saw for real. Pat was just a genuine caring, vibrant and fun off the wall kind of guy. Strangely, you never knew what he was going to say or do. I always found how a man portrays himself on set is his true being. In other words, it's not a put on. He always had a cigarette case full of wacko-weed in his pocket that he would wax on and wax off and save the buds for later. Was Jay Leno ever at that poker game? Hell, no. It just seemed like he didn't like being with people. I know you are asking me how can Jay be so introverted and be a very talkative, funny, engaging host as he was on *The Tonight Show*? But I found there was a difference.

Let me explain. I don't know. Maybe the fact that he had a script and a dais full of people that knew what each other was going to say is what gave him the ability to feel comfortable. Or maybe he was just acting on camera. There is nothing wrong with not talking to people. But when it is a daily occurrence, minute to hour to days, you start to ask yourself is he that unfriendly on purpose or is that just him? To each his own, I always say. I think that is a real interesting difference. There was no hanging out with Jay. He would say, "hello." That would be it. He didn't seem to have the social skills nor maybe want them with us, to advance beyond the initial greetings. Hearing that is strange I know, but that is in the eyes of the beholder. He never seemed to be bothered by his lack of personable skills, at least to my knowledge. I guess you could say he took it on the chin. It's oversized.

My second to last memory on this show was indeed a collision, some may even call it a wreck. I got dressed one morning and went out onto set which was dressed like a farmer's market for the scene we were about to do. Fruit and vegetables everywhere. We were going to do a car chase and foot chase through the market. There were many stuntmen on the show. Guys like Manny Perry, Larry Holt, Bob Apisa, Corey Eubanks, Gary Wayton, Greg Elam, William Lane and others. As I strolled on set, I noticed all the stunt guys grouped together in a line. As I casually walk closer, I see Corey has four or five eggs in his hands. Getting even closer, I could now hear Corey saying, which seems to be jokingly, he was going to throw these eggs at the stuntmen. Suddenly to my surprise, from about fifteen feet away, an egg goes flying and splatters all over one of the stuntmen. Everyone was laughing except for the guy who got egged. It wasn't over, as Corey proceeded to repeat his antics. This time at one of the others who were laughing. Now he wasn't laughing, but the other ones were. This happened three or four more times as I walked up.

The people laughing would stop as soon as they got hit, while the ones who were egg free, kept it up. The ones who got hit just hung their heads in humiliation, they didn't fight back and asked him to stop. This my friend, is where politics come in. That is an important aspect in this story. He wouldn't listen and that is what annoyed me. That is called disrespect when somebody asks you not to. Least to say, if Wardrobe sees it, they are not going to be happy. That seemed to be the modus operandi with the stunt people. They would do what they had to. Anything to draw them closer to people who could give them a job and they just didn't want to offend Corey and risk losing work in the future. Politics, ain't it fun? It could ruin a good man. You could see the hesitation in their eyes, but they were forced to laugh if they wanted work from Corey or anybody that was fond of him. This is what I got out of this situation which has been the same since the beginning of time. Some things never change. As the son of Bob Eubanks, he was "put on a pedestal."

Unfortunately, this kind of relationship between stuntmen was something that I would see all too often. Corey and I worked together once on a television show. Guess what we did? We boxed. We had choreography, but there were some moments where you could ad lib and we did tag each other a few times. My character wound up beating his and I guess it seemed to me that it bothered him. Why? I'll leave it up to you, I mean it is just a television show. I was constantly polite and congratulating him on moves that he did. As I get closer to him and the egg game he is playing, all of a sudden, he spots me and simply decides it is my turn to taste "Corey Eubank's scrambled eggs."

The first words out of his mouth were, "now it's your turn, Lambert."

I kindly smiled, looking at my clean outfit wardrobe had given me and simply said, "no, please don't do that Corey."

"What happens if I do?" he shot back while raising his arm, egg in hand.

I told him again, "don't do it, Corey."

Again, he challenged me.

"Listen Corey, if you do it, it won't be any fun for both of us."

He smiled hearing this and tossed the egg up a few times in his hand before raising it over his head in slow motion. Like a minor league pitcher, he winds up and throws the egg right at me. I quickly threw a roundhouse kick and hit the egg as it was coming towards me, lightly tapping it with my toe so I wouldn't break it. I channeled all of my chi and changed the momentum of the egg, directing it back at Corey. BAM! The egg went all of his face. Cool scene, right? Well, that's what it is, just a scene because in reality, all of my Kung Fu instincts failed me and I did absolutely nothing. BANG! The egg hits me smack dead in the chest. I look at it, as it is dripping down my wardrobe. I look at him with anger for a split second. My natural instincts, but then I smile and casually walk over to the egg department. Oh yes, I knew what was coming next for my pal Corey. I soft style tiger palm grabbed five eggs, turned and smiled at Corey. I walk over to Corey, eggs in my hand like a waiter, showing him the omelet Chez Lambo was about to prepare. I get about a foot from him and we smile at each other. He doesn't move or run away, he just faces me. Instantly, like an eagle swooping down and grabbing its prey, I eagle hook the back of his neck bringing his head towards me. I take my left hand and tiger claw palm strike the three eggs into his face as the eagle claw is bringing his head to the tiger palm. The eggs splattered all over his face. I don't let him up as I push and pull, making sure he gets a big taste of his own medicine. I always seem to overdo it, but never start it.

I finally let go and step back before I am forced to weave left and right as he throws blind punches at me. Other stuntmen are in shock as he throws another punch, this one almost connecting. I quickly block it and throw an inverted upper cut, tagging him on his head. Then a right hook tagging him on the other side of his cranium, before putting him in a headlock and all the while knowing full well the golden rule is never to fight on set. Too late. My thought process was a little slow. I squeeze him in the headlock telling him to stop as he is trying to get out. Two or three stuntmen come over and try to pull us apart as they are yelling at me to let him go. It's very hard for me to stop when I start, I am in the heat of the moment.

"Let him go," they scream in my ear.

Finally, I wake up and let him go as Glenn Randall walks on set and demands to know what is going on. I explain to him what happened and how Corey started this whole thing. Now my motto is, it doesn't matter who you are or who your daddy is. If you do something wrong, you do something wrong. The way I was brought up, there is no special privilege. Glenn wasn't too happy and sent us to our dressing rooms to get dressed as we were told we were finished for the day. When I say we, I mean Corey and I. I walk away very pissed off. I told Glenn that I wasn't upset that he threw the egg at me, I was furious that he humiliated the other stunt guys and got away with it as usual. I told Glenn, I'm sorry but it wasn't my fault, but man he wasn't too happy. I got to my trailer and took off my shoes and shirt. I had hip pads on and was about to take my pants off to return them to Wardrobe. Now I want you to picture this. My back is facing the dressing room door. I'm pulling down my pants and hip pads down to my ankles, when all of a sudden, all hell breaks loose.

My door flies open and I hear a bang! Before I could turn around, I am bulldogged from behind by someone. We both go flying across my room into these bunch of chairs that were on top of each other. I still don't know what the hell just hit me. I turn around and realize it's my pal, Corey Eubanks. "What the hell are you doing?" I yell as he tries to greet me with a barrage of punches, that I quickly block and evaded. I tell him to stop fighting, that we were in enough trouble. I am trying to crowd him and hold him to convince him to stop, but he keeps going, the spoiled brat that he was. So I do the only thing I could. I start swinging back. Connecting three or four times to get him the hell away from me and make him stop. I get him in another headlock saying, "are you going to stop fighting?"

All he says is, "let me go, let me go, no."

I wasn't about to do that until I was sure he was going to stop. The trailer is rockin' and rolling. Bouncing from one side to the other as we ram into the walls. Or should I say Corey's head rammed into the walls about a half dozen times. You see I decided to knock some sense into him, Brooklyn street punk style. He finally says he gives up, but I'm not about to let him go with him right next to me. I throw him backwards and he lands on his ass. That is when I see the trailer door is open and notice half a dozen guys looking in. Corey jumps up and walks to the door.

"Let's take this outside and we will decide this," he yells.

Man, this guy just doesn't get it. I walk over to the door and see all the people around him watching. I found out later these were a bunch of extras. Now I had two options. I could go take this street fight out into the street, or I could close the door and leave Corey to his anger. Now you may ask which choice was the best one? Closing the door and ending it then and there would be, I can hear you all shouting. You're right. That's what I should have done. As I told you once before, once I start, it is hard for me to stop. So like the Brooklyn idiot I am, I don't close the door. Instead, I hop out ready to confront Corey. Not Bruce Lee style, but Lambo style, haha. I suggest to him that it is enough, but he says no.

"Put up your hands and fight," he says. He has his hands up in a boxing stance. He is known to be a great boxer.

I asked him if he really wanted to do this and he was adamant about it. I lift my fists, Kung Fu boxing style. All the extras around us were watching us with eager eyes. Some were concerned and didn't know what to do. I could imagine some in their head calling the fight.

"In one corner, from the Hollywood Elite comes the mighty boxer, baring the great name of his father, the mighty son, Corey Eubanks. In the other corner, hailing from the streets of Brooklyn, the no nonsense punk kid, Steven Lambert."

Of course, they didn't know our names, at least not yet. I'm just juicing this up for you readers, but the juice is factual. I look at Corey and ask, "you ready?"

He says, "yes."

I quickly did an "SL." Not a Segal and Lebell, but a Steven Lambert! I threw a fake jab and his hands went up to block and that's just what I wanted. Here comes the combination roundhouse lift kick, right smack in his yankee doodles. It was dandy. That's right, "in the butt Bob, I mean the balls, Bob, I mean Corey." I lifted him a few inches in the air and he went right to the floor. All the extras watching jumped over to me and held me back. There was nothing I could do with four or five guys holding me. I wasn't about to hit them too. That's when the First Assistant and others came over and told us to go back to our trailers. The brawl was over but the war unfortunately, didn't end there. But I wasn't the only one in a collision on this show. We were doing a fight scene in a bowling alley, a dozen or so guys.

Great stunt man Bob Apisa was a real physical guy who was a part of this fight sequence. He was a big ex-football player from Havaii, yes Havaii. In other words, a big kahuna. Strong and crazy. His piece of action was to be thrown or punched straight into a candy machine. You know those machines you put in a quarter and you get something. Whaddaya want? A Milky Way, a Snickers, a Kit Kat or a Baby Ruth? The machine was real, the hooks that were holding the candy were real but it was only the glass that was fake. It was called candy glass, but don't try to eat it! Now the plan was for Apisa to lower his knee as he went into the machine. Either that or place both hands on the side of the machine to slow your momentum and to stop you. Common things a stunt man should do. But instead, when they called "action," he took off like an angry bull twenty feet back and plowed towards the machine. As he gets there, instead of using his hands or his feet to slow down, he uses his head. CRASH!

Right through the candy glass and into the machine he goes. Tearing through the twisting metal rings that hold the candy and through the metal backing of the candy machine itself. Everyone is shocked. That wasn't supposed to happen. He went in one end and halfway came out the other. They ended the scene and he tried to get out of the back of the vending machine as he was half in, half out. Knocked out. He didn't know where he was. He looked like you could just turn the machine around and mount it on a wall. Instead of a Hawaiian pig, you would have the rare and elusive Apisa as a trophy. We run over to him and the first thing I saw was his bald head. There was a huge gash on top of his head, blood pouring out. We were surprised he had intended to run through the machine like that, but like the crazy man he was, he just tore through it. He shredded it and it shredded him. Off to the hospital he went to get stitched up.

You can't stop an Apisa volcano. Let's get back to the candy machine. Now I had two choices. I needed to choose the right one. I could either get a Milky Way or I could get a Baby Ruth. I chose the Ruth. Free candy, I mean when you are working for Glenn Randall, he was a cheap guy! Never gave much in adjustments. What happened to Bob? Bob is one tough son of a gun. He came back ready to go. Wardrobe threw him a hat. Let me tell you how tough he is. For instance, we were once playing softball in the stunt league. He was on another team playing my team, The Stuntmen's Association. There were always arguments going on and that day one of them involved Alan Graf, a big ex-football player. He and Bob got into an argument and they wouldn't stop. It quickly escalated and I knew it would lead to fisticuffs.

I ran over while everyone else just watched and shoved myself face first between them and said, "Alan, listen to me. You raise your hands to Bob Apisa and that will be the last thing you do. A big mistake, man. He'll wring you out like a wet towel."

I knew both of them very well and knew Bob would come out on top of this fight. You see there is a difference between a so called big tough guy and a real fighter. Luckily, Alan listened to me and reluctantly backed off. Bob was one tough coconut. Fast forward to the plane ride home. I'm thinking about what happened with me and Corey Eubanks. I was hoping Glenn wouldn't still be upset, after all, I was an innocent bystander. Corey started it with the eggs and bursting into my dressing room. I guess I could have handled it a better way, sure, but I handled it my way. Most people would never stand up to Corey as they would be afraid to lose a job. Unless you are people like John Meyers or Roy Harrison or Ronnie Rondell, Charlie Picerni, Vince Deadrick Sr. and a few others, you don't take that kind of bullocks as Vince Armstrong would say. You have morals and ethics and you stand up for them regardless of what politics are going on around you. At least that is the way I saw it. I've never been a suck up like some others. That my friend is one of the reasons why people may not like me. I am me, not what they want me to be. I finally get home and after a couple of days, I turn on my message machine, realizing I have a ton of messages.

I listen to a few of them and I hear people saying, "hey I heard about what happened on set, you got into a fight." Another said, "I heard you got beat, everyone is talking about it."

WHAT!? All of a sudden, I jump up like a soldier saluting a commanding officer. Got beat? Who is dreaming? It was the other way around. I start calling these people up and explaining to them what really happened. The truth. I must have called about a dozen people whose stories needed correcting. I asked, "where are you hearing this stuff?"

They replied, "we heard this from stuntman Gary Baxley."

Now I began to understand. Mister innocent troublemaker, I called him. He always enjoyed needling people. Baxley was a good friend of Corey Eubanks. Gary came from a very successful family in the business and had some unfavorable traits that were similar to Corey's, but even more a spoiled brat in a nice way. Most of the time. Gary was always an instigator and trouble maker, that's just who he was. For instance, one time at the Stuntmen's Association there was a good stunt man friend of mine named Bill McIntosh. Bill was down on his luck lately and needed a job desperately. Gary and I were in the room with him when Gary said he needed people for a job and started spitting out sizes that he would need people to fit. Well, wouldn't you know these sizes were exactly Bill's measurements. I spoke up and told Gary that Bill would be perfect.

Gary looks at Bill and shakes his head. "Nah, he ain't the right type," he says with a big shit eating grin on his face.

I looked at Bill and he was just crushed. Without a moment's hesitation, I turned to Baxley and said, "you asshole. You know that wasn't nice." Maybe I shouldn't have said anything, but I so dislike evil. That was me and that was Gary. Now you know. So the next day I go to the stuntmen's office and my fight with Corey was everywhere. Even the Board of Directors in the stunt group I was in, wanted to hear what had happened and wanted me to come up and speak to them. I said, "no problem.

You are bringing Corey up there too right?"

They told me he would be coming in a different time and that got me laughing.

I said, "why? Why don't you bring us up together?"

They say, "no we can't do that."

I said, "what is he afraid of? That way you can see who is telling the truth. Have both men on the stand and go through exactly what happened and then see what happens."

They say, "no. That was discussed. We think it's a bad idea."

I laughed some more. I didn't like the fact that I had to go up, but I felt it was my responsibility to try and set the story right. As time went by leading up to this meeting, I quickly found this story was all over town and when I say all over, I mean all over. It spread like wildfire. To a bunch of yenta stuntmen. Poor Corey Eubanks was attacked by this crazy stuntman Steven Lambert and Corey gave him a beating he won't soon forget. Nobody knew the truth. It was almost like Segal and Lebell, no one would tell the real story. After a week, I had enough. I thought a day or two about it and then I wrote a letter, explaining the truth with an open challenge and gave it to our secretary at the Association. Before I did that, I called up the man, Gene Lebell. I told Gene what had happened and told him I was going to put out an open challenge to Corey Eubanks and Gary Baxley.

He said, "good, can I be the referee?"

I said," hell, yes. You can even wear your pink gi."

I wanted to have a no holds bar competition at the Olympic Stadium. Now Gene grew up in the Olympic Stadium, his family owned it at one time.

I asked him and his response was, "hell yeah, I want to see this."

Then I get a phone call from stuntman Wally Crowder, who heard what happened and I explained I had written this letter and I was going to bring a hundred copies to the Stuntmen's Association. Think that is overdoing it? Wait, I'm not done. I told him I was also going to bring a hundred copies to Stunt's Unlimited and then a hundred more to the women's group and even more to a few others. The letter was an open invitation to Corey Eubanks and Gary Baxley to come fight me, one after the other. I told Wally this and as soon as I said Gene was going to referee, Wally had an idea.

"Let me sponsor you," he said, excitement in his voice. "I'll make it an event and we'll sell tickets. It will make a fortune," he continued. "It will be like Ali and Fraiser."

So I say, "let's get it on."

Crowder assured me he would handle everything. I decided on a hundred dollars a ticket, with fifty going to a charity and fifty going to the winner. So that's what I did, went to all the groups and handed out letters to everyone I saw that was a stuntman and even all the answering services including Teddy O'toole's. Within a couple of weeks, the word spread throughout the lands, until it finally reached to Corey Eubanks and Gary Baxley. The chosen ones. Weeks went by with no answer until finally Teddy's called me and mentioned to me that Corey just called and wanted me to call him.

I said, "why?"

She said, "I don't know, he just would like you to call him."

I called him up and guess what? He apologized.

"I don't want to fight you, Steven," he admitted.

"Then you better start telling everybody the truth," I warned him.

He agreed and I said goodbye. Now I knew everyone who wanted a job was going to side with Corey. The only difference is that I would never tell someone not to give Corey a job, but I felt he had told people in some shape or form, otherwise with me. How do I know? It's simple. Friends become no friends. Sometimes you are told and sometimes you just feel it. That is the movie business. You have a job for them, they will do anything to get it. You movie people out there, you know it is a fact. If Confucius wrote Gary's epitaph it would say, "I asked God for a bicycle but I know he doesn't work in those ways. So I stole a bicycle and asked God for forgiveness." That was Gary wrapped up in a nutshell. I put out the word that Corey apologized and waited to hear from Gary Baxley. As days went by, I would go to the Stuntmen's Association and I always hoped I would see Gary there, but he was in hiding it seemed. Hey deja vu, this kind of reminds me of Bobby Sargent, except Gary didn't leave the state. Remember that?

One day I was in the stunt office and again the secretary told me I had a phone call. Gary Baxley was on the line. Oh good. I picked up that phone and started talking a mile a minute. "Hey Gary, how are you? Did you hear? We have the dates for the fight. Now the 24th I have to go grocery shopping and the 30th I have to buy a new pair of tennis shoes that I can wear in the ring, but the first is the fight, it's all set up. Hey, guess what, Lebell is the referee and Wally Crowder is sponsoring it. Are you available to get your ass kicked that day? Remember this is for charity and on top of that, you could make a lot of money. It's a hundred bucks a ticket. Fifty goes to charity and fifty goes to the winner and I'll tell you what, I'll only use one hand for you. No feet."

I waited for his response and when it came, I smiled. "I don't want to fight you, Steven. I'm sorry," he stammered.

"Well Gary, you don't want to fight me but you can spread fairy tales?"

He simply said, "please let's forget about the whole thing."

I simply said, "I better not hear any more stories that are untrue because I will find you and de-spine you."

He quickly agreed and we hung up. I called Lebell and told him the fight was off.

"Shit, I'm not going to see Lambert kick the lies out of Eubanks and Baxley? No blood? Well, damn. What can I do to get it going again?"

Gene said. I found that funny. "I want to see you put him to sleep," Gene replied.

"Sorry Gene, it's off," I said.

I told Wally it was off as well and he was just as disappointed. It would have been the fight of the century, but Corey and Gary just didn't want to walk the walk while they tried to talk the talk. Damn shame. If and when they read this, if they'd like, we can always bring it back. We can put it on Corey's internet talk show. Which by the way, I am available to come on and tell this story, the real stunt story. Let's put it on. I'm just a phone call away. But we are friends now. (REALLY?) I haven't heard from him since. I wish them both well. What happened then, we smile and hold no grudges now. I will always respect the great stuntmen that they are. That my friends is the difference. I rest my case. Now that the fight was off, who you gonna call? *Ghostbusters*. Number two. Kamikaze Kramer Joel, asked me if I wanted to work as he was the Coordinator. I said, "I'm afraid of no ghost." And off I went. Dan Aykroyd and Bill Murray were two everyday Joes on set. They made you laugh until you cried. I don't have too many stories, but I remember when I met Bill Murray. Joel called me over and introduced us. Bill looked at me up and down, unbuckled his belt a little bit and grabbed both sides of his pants. He picked them up to his chest and retightened his belt. He looked at me and stuck out his hand.

"Nice to meet you," he said, as Joel Kramer instantly was laughing in the back.

I asked Bill Murray and pointed to Joel, "he put you up to this, didn't he?"

Then he jumps into a Martial Arts stance and says two words that surprise me. They were, "Bruce Lee."

I thought to myself, it's amazing. So many big stars like Bill Murray know of this legend and for them to mimic him in any way, shows the profound impact that he had on the ordinary and the extraordinary people of the world.

CHAPTER 51
(Actor Rutger Hauer. Homie Don't Shuffle That Way.)

As I think I had mentioned before, some of my finest memories were going to Chinatown and practicing Kung Fu at Grandmaster Ark Wong's studio and then after, going to a movie. You know, of the masterpieces, in my mind, happened to be *Zatoichi*. A blind swordsman who could hear a butterfly coming by the whisper of the wind and strike with perfect accuracy. I say this because guess what, my next movie I was to coordinate was inspired by it. But instead of Shintaro Katsu as the blind swordsman, it was starring Rutger Hauer. An American dramedy.

They called it, *Blind Fury*. I get a telegraph by electric wire. I listen in one end and talk into the other. It's called a phone. It's Production Manager Mister Dennis Murphy. He said I was highly recommended and wanted me to come in and meet with the Director. He then proceeded to say he was going to send the script to my house. My house? That was a first for me and quite a surprise. I felt "Juyo" (it's a Japanese word, look it up. Don't be lazy, learn.) I read the script and liked it a lot. How much? As you remember, sometimes it would take me weeks to read a book in school. Sometimes it would take FORNEVER. (Don't laugh at me.) I read this script in two hours. My imagination went wild. I broke everything down and did my budget. The next day I went into the office and met Dennis Murphy. Straight forward, no humor and doesn't like anyone but himself kind of guy. He reminded me of Poindexter. Remember him from "Felix The Cat", the cartoon? Who is he you ask? Again, look him up. :) We talk a little bit about some of my ideas and I presented him with the budget.

"Too many guys you're bringing over," he says.

I say to him, "where are we supposed to get them? LA is the closet place. This is the amount we need. If the ideas change and we don't need certain things, then we save money. That is part of my job too. To look out for you."

He stared at me not knowing what quite say. So he didn't and we moved on. Before long I was brought to the Director, Mister Philip Noyce. I was surprised how small his office was for such a big, cool, overbearing man, as he seemed cramped behind his desk. Six-four and he was hilarious. Big dude. To his right stood, guess who, Rutger Hauer. An accented voice boomed over to me.

"Steven, how are ya, mate?"

I looked back and realized it was coming from Peter Noyce. The Australian accent made me smile and I walked over and shook his hand.

"I want you to meet the star, Rutger Hauer," he continued.

I then shook hands with Rutger as well and said," the Hitcher. Rutger, The Hitcher was one of the scariest movies I ever saw. You scared the shit out of me. Is that how you are in real life? If it is, I quit right now."

He started laughing, Philip started laughing, I was trying to be funny but at the same time, I wasn't. He had a scary aura about him! Go see the movie! After that, the questions started from both of them and I sat down and explained my background. Where I grew up, how I got into Martial Arts, even mentioned my John F. Kennedy Award I got in gym. We moved on to talking about the script and he went right to the first sequence where Nick Parker goes to get something to eat in the restaurant and meets up with these tough guy gang bangers and he beats them all up. I thought, well, he isn't going to pull out his sword and cut them to pieces, so what about using just the cane without pulling out the sword and make most everything look like an accident. Peter and Rugter looked at me in thought. Maybe it was watching old movies with my grandfather, or going on adventures with my gang, but I would always come up with creative ideas to incorporate into the action. Most of the time, the Director only has a rudimentary idea (really nothing) and doesn't know which way to go or what to do. So this is a chance for you to guide him and have an opportunity to show what you have in your head more than other Stunt Coordinators. This is where I always thought of myself as an interpreter of action performance. I explain to him what we could do with him in this scene. As I was explaining, I watched Phillip reach behind him and pick up a cane. He said he wasn't sure what I meant and asked me to demonstrate.

I said, "okay, let me show you out front, there is more room. Follow me."

We went out of the office to the lobby and I asked Phillip and Rutger to be the gang bangers. They were nervous so I told them, "don't worry, I won't hit ya," as I flung the cane around to warm up as they looked at me and smile. I demonstrated the moves, what you see in the film is a lot of the stuff I came up with and showed them. I made it a point as I was demonstrating, that the moves should look accidental and at the same time sharp. I looked at Rutger and I asked if he was listening. "This part is up to you," I say. "Your body language and facial expression need to give the impression that it is not on purpose. At the same time, your moves must be fluid and non-directional since you are blind. So we must practice this a lot and part of my job is to guide you. We have to work hard and put a lot of physical time in." He agreed to commit.

(Stunt double Shane Dixon with Rutger Hauer trying to give me a circumcision.)

At the end of the demonstration, they absolutely loved it. Whenever Phillip liked something, he would begin speaking very fast and excitedly about it, putting ideas together out loud. I was in a tornado of words as Phillip took what I had shown him and constructed the whole sequence right then and there as if he was giving a speech. I was just the catalyst, but boy what a fire I sparked in his mind. Rutger was standing there amazed and amused. We both looked at each other. Noyce briefly explained to me that he was somewhat of a boxer in his younger days. He asked if he could throw some punches at me and inquired how I would block it with the cane. I explained to him that it might hurt since he didn't have any forearm pads on.

His reply was, "I can take it."

I said, "okay, throw whatever you want." I stopped his left hook, bringing up the cane. Then I stopped his jab, with a pivot. Then he lunged at me with two hands and I whip spun the cane right across the back of his forearm.

"Ouch," he says. Rutger screams out,

"I thought you could take it." I didn't hit him very hard, just hard enough for him to feel a little pain. "You asked for it," I said as he rubbed his arm. "That's enough. Let's quit while we are ahead. I'm not fired am I?"

We all laughed. We went back into the office and continued discussing the script and finally finished after an hour and fifteen minutes. It was a record meeting for me and we all left very happily. The next day I called Poindexter, I mean Dennis

Murphy, thanked him and asked him to let me know who Philip and Rutger decide on to coordinate. Dennis told me they were still interviewing potential candidates and he would get back to me. I hang up and I am thinking in my head, what if they are calling other talented stunt Martial Artists. All these names popped into my head and as doubt always creeps in, I began to wonder if I really would get the job. But I always said that on the other hand, they are my friends and great guys, so more power to them. I would be happy either way. A few days later, I get a call and Dennis Murphy tells me the job was mine! It was imparted to me that I was the only one that came up with unique and creative ideas and demonstrated. Rutger and Phillip were very impressed with what they saw. So that put me on the top of the list. He wanted me to set up a training session with Rutger and teach him Martial Arts and the sword. I agreed and went into the office to talk with Rutger. I asked Rutger if he had any Martial Arts training, gymnastics, dancing or anything like that. He said he had played soccer for most of his life.

That was great, as he had some notion of distance, timing and coordination. I am given eight weeks to train him and we decide to work out five days a week, three to seven hours a day. Now not only do I have to teach him how to use the sword and achieve the grace of a Martial Artist, but I have to get him to lose about forty pounds. He was on the thick side. Big boy. Nothing like in his previous films. Getting someone to lose that much weight is serious business. I was not a dietician but had enough common sense and knew how to get the weight off him. Train baby, train. Exercise. It was really up to Rutger because I can work him to the bone, but he can go home and eat chocolate cake and french fries and gain it all back. That was exactly what I told him. "You need to focus and we need to work as a team," I told him. I think he was impressed by the way I spoke to him.

Phillip understood that as well but left it to me to do my job and fulfill my promises. The first week I worked out with Rugter, he was just a natural. He was wearing shorts. His calves were as big as my head and his thighs were something you would see on a cornerback football player. He had a powerful lower gait. By the way, let me explain the meaning of gait. Our body has three of them. Everybody has a lower gait, middle gait and upper gait.

Lower, from the toes up to the thighs. Middle, from the waist to the solar plexus. Upper, from the solar plexus to the top of your head. They all move together or individually. There I go talking about Martial Arts again. Another learning moment in the life of a punk kid from Brooklyn. As I trained Rutger in shuffles, stances and movement of his body before he ever touched the sword, he was so strong and so powerful in all his gaits that he was just coming along wonderfully.

450

Like many other people and actors that I have trained, exercise is key. And of course, Stoney Point in Chatsworth, California was part of it.

Rock bopping, Rutger loved it. You head to the top of Stoney Point and race down, going from boulder to boulder. Some two feet away, some ten feet away. All different and challenging. Such a natural talent for someone who has never done Martial Arts. Weeks went by and training was going wonderful. He was like an eager bear cub learning how to hunt. His progression was more than I could hope for. He was shedding weight like a snake sheds its skin. Fifteen pounds he lost and I was amazed at his hard work. Everything was going perfectly and then the strange, I guess you could say humorous to some and unusual happened. One time I was teaching him and I jumped into a square horse stance.

To my surprise, I looked up as Rutger extended his hand and noticed it was coming towards my buttocks. Yes, my rear end, you read that right. I quickly back shuffled away and stood up straight like a matador and looked at him. He smiled, I was confused and more or less laughed it off like it was a joke. Hmmm. We went on with the lessons and the next day I found myself in another stance, a crossover stance. Again, he was right next to me and again he reached out. This time he managed to brush his hand against my thigh as I twisted out from the stance to avoid what was at hand. He smiled as I said, "what's up with that?" He just smiled again and we went on with the lesson, but I was confused about what had happened. After the training, I went home and began thinking what the hell was going on? Was it a joke? Was that part of his humor? Who the hell knows, I don't. I couldn't make heads or tails of what that was all about, but I decided to forget about it. When I had a meeting with Phillip Noyce, we discussed his training but I never brought the hand thing up. I wonder if I had, what he would have said.

"Take it or your fired?" (Haha.) Or, "come on mate, you gotta be kidding." Either way I am glad I didn't say anything. The next day I met Rutger at the gym and we went over some stances and swordplay and about an hour and a half in, guess what, deja vu.

Well you know what they say, three times is a charm. I looked at him silently for a moment as he smiled, before saying, "listen, Rutger, I gotta tell you something. It's a great honor to be working with you on this film, and I am very much excited about it. But what's this all about? I'm not judging, but I'm not like that. To each his own." In hindsight, I felt it was a very stupid thing to say, but it was the first thing that popped into my head and I tend to be honest as you know by now.

I watch Rutger as he smiles and takes a step toward me. Then another step and another step. Not knowing what he is about to do. Here comes his hand again, slowly rising up towards me. I watch it as it rises up to my shoulder. He places his hand on it and looks at me. His stare felt inches away.

(Mini me. The laughs were many when I came out to double Rutger.)

In my head, I'm thinking, "am I going to have to punch him out? It looks like he is going to try to put a wet one on me."

Then I heard, "Steven, I'm sorry. I won't do that again. I promise." He reached out his hand as I did mine and we shook hands, smiled and went on with the training. Never to be brought up again until now.

Rutger progressed very well and I was getting calls from the Director who wanted to come and see what he had learned.

I explain to him, "give me another week, as I am finishing up a sword routine between him and me to show you."

We argued in fun like two friends trying to get their way, back and forth about it, but would agree in laughter. Even though he would call me up and tell me he was coming down to see him. I told him, "no you're not! You have too much to do at the office." Luckily, he waited. I put together a show, a two man set, sword versus sword. About thirty moves. Dennis Murphy and Phillip loved it.

By the way, this routine was the same one I used for the Sho Kosugi, Rutger Hauer fight where Rutger puts his hand on Sho's face and says, "Japanese, huh?"

Sword fight coordinator Steven Lambert handled the look and training of Rutger Hauer's swordplay. Lambert, a member of the Stuntman's Association, won a Stunt Academy Award in 1986 for best high work in "Remo Williams: The Adventure Begins ... ," and won honors for best fight work in "Team."

Lambert and Hauer started working out with physical, martial arts and sword exercises three months before "Blind Fury" began filming. For two hours a day the two would go through routines of demanding bodywork and intricate footwork, a schedule that was kept up throughout the 10 weeks of filming. Before he faced the camera for a day of shooting, Hauer had already completed two hours of heavy training.

(Rutger Hauer, the best non-Martial Artist I ever worked with.)

Ancient Lambo proverb. Never throw away a good thing. Use it.

Moves were learned, forty one pounds were lost and Rutger was ready to unleash his blind fury. Hey, guess what school I trained Rutger in? A school called Sil-Lum Kung Fu. Owned by none other than Grandmaster Douglas Wong. The energy from that place transferred right to Rutger Hauer. By the way, Rutger went to school for the blind, two weeks. And guess who else had to go? Yes, me. Philip Noyce and Rutger both insisted that I need to know what it felt like being blind.

I resisted for a moment, thinking it wasn't part of my job but then immediately realized that they were so right and it was important for me to know and understand. God Bless the blind. We fly to Reno, Nevada and start working on the shoot. It wasn't long before I got a call from Dennis Murphy who explained Phillip had about six professional ex-football players in his office and he wanted my help to pick out which ones would be good to play the bad guys.

I had that day off, (that's a showbiz term, you never really have off) so I told Dennis I would be there right away. I head into the Production Office and see all these football players in this HUGE office.

I have nowhere to sit so I stand and look at all of them up and down. Phillip is sitting behind this desk that dwarfed him. Big difference from the first one, I gotta say.

(Rutger Hauer giving me an ultimatum. School for the blind, or die.)

He says, "Steven, I want you to pick six of these guys. Talk to them and find out which ones would be best."

So we start talking and we discuss what position they play, their backgrounds, etc. Phillip is listening in and let's talk about Phillip Noyce for a moment. My hands on Director. Like I said, a very physical guy. As we are talking, he comes up with a blooming idea, as he would put it. (Remember kids, the British say Bullocks, the Aussies say Blooming.) What was this great idea? He wanted to test out the physical nature of these already very physical football players. I was listening. How you might ask? His brilliant idea was that he wanted the football players to run at me, wrap me up and slam me against the wall. Oh, okay. That sounded great.

I looked at Phillip and chuckled. "You're out of your mind! They don't know how to do it safely nor stuntly and they are going to come running at me like I am the freaking quarterback, they are all linemen!" I knew I had to explain to these guys quick on how to perform and to make it look real without it actually being real. Not one of them had a clue. Phillip didn't want to wait. He gets up and practically pushes me aside.

"Well, if you don't want to do it, I'll do it!" he shouts.

I said, "what? No, no, I can't have the Director get his bell rung. Okay, Okay, I'll do it! Relax, sit down." Everyone starts laughing and I get in place as he sits back in his chair. I pretend there is an invisible me across the room and show the football players how to do it and make it look real without hurting the man they are running at. ME, in this case. I take a few steps back and run like I am about to tackle someone and ease up slightly as I wrap my arms around them, stopping at a mark. They all watch and I can tell it is going in one ear and out the other. Dumb ass football players, but they were all nice guys. We get ready to go at it. I stand a few feet away from the wall and look at Phillip with a big Aussie kangaroo smile on his face as he asks, "are you ready Steven?"

I say, "bring it on," shaking my head in reluctance. Not showing it of course. Phillip yells, "action."

Here comes a Samoan a bull with fire in his eyes, ready to take out whatever is in his way on a twenty foot run. My mind quickly says to me, "hoooly shit!" My heart is stopped. I get ready to spring off the hit and watch him closely. Now being a Martial Artist, I know when he has to start getting ready to try to slow down the hit and right away I notice, he ain't doing that. There is no way he is stopping. The locomotive is at full throttle. Now he is about two feet away and I realize I have no choice but to quickly do a back fall with a half twist log roll slip and slide. I think that's what it was, it happened so freaking quick. I barely get the hell out of the way, just as he flies past me and hits the wall, which shook like an earthquake. I rolled out of the way just in time and saved myself from being broken in half. I'm telling you readers, I would have been a pancake on the wall. It took everything I had. Phillip jumps out of his chair, just laughing hysterically. I'm on the floor, my heart is pounding.

He comes over and I hear, "why did you move out of the way?"

Still on the floor, I look up at him and say, "I would have been broken in half. Are you kidding?"

I get up and he said, "all right. If you don't want to do it, let me do it."

I couldn't tell you the joy on his face, the excitement in his eyes. As I'm amazed at his looney toon behavior, I said, "no Phillip, I can't have you get hurt. Who acts this way man, calm down. I'll do it. Just give me a moment to show them how it is done."

He does. I brushed myself off and explain it again, how to do it. Only this time I decided I was going to demonstrate by running at the football player in front of the wall.

We get into place and Phillip yells, "action."

I run at the football player and as soon as I get close to him, I start faking it and make contact. The guy doesn't move! I bounce back a little bit. I start yelling at him in his ear to "let me a little, let me a little!" It felt so comical when he finally let me, and he hit the wall like a train coming to a stop at a station. Slowly.

Phillip looked at me and said, "what was that?"

I shook my head and said, "let's just do it." I pointed to another football player and told him to get on the mark. I looked at Philip and told him to call action as I stood five feet away from the wall. CUT. At the end of the day, they had to call in a plaster repairman to fix the holes and dents in the wall from the half a dozen times I got pounded against it. That day I got a gift from my Director. A female masseuse. Two hours of pleasure. Wait a minute now, get your mind out of the gutter. Let's move on. We all had lunch. That first week, all the actors came in. I was unfamiliar with them except for Nick Cassavetes. I said, "Cassavetes? Any relation to John Cassavetes?"

He said, "yea. John is my father."

I told him how great of a character actor his father was, that he was a badass.

That got a smile. "Yea he was, he whipped mine a bunch," he says.

CHAPTER 52
(Actor Tex Cobb. The Doobie Man.)

It was also going around that Randall "Tex" Cobb was going to be coming on set soon. Word was he was a little crazy. If you ask me, it was big time crazy and cool. He didn't care what anybody thought of his actions or behavior. I knew a little bit of him from his fights. He fought boxers like Holmes, Spinks and Shavers. When he arrived, I was introduced to him by Rutger and I started talking about my background. Well as soon as I mentioned Martial Arts, his eyes lit up. In less than a second, he throws a roundhouse kick at me. Both arms go up, open handed double palm blocking his kick. I jump back as two punches came at me. I was far enough away to evade the first one, it seemed like I jumped back a mile, his arms were so long. Then the second one came a left hook, it was. I threw up a boxer's block while it went around and his forearm connected with my arm. The impact was so strong, it threw me sideways a couple of inches. I jumped back as he looked at me. "That was pretty slick," he said. "What's your name again?"

I told him, "just call me the man who evaded Tex Cobb."

Tex smirked and looked at me up and down. "We're going to have some fun," he said.

I said, "I'm sure we will, but right now I have to go train Rutger."

Tex looked at me and back at Rutger. "Can I come?" he asked me.

I said, "no, it's private, but if you want to do some workouts, I'll be happy to do that."

He gave a satisfied grunt and nodded. That was my first experience with Tex Cobb. But not the last.

(Me and the man after a little boxing workout.)

Guess what? It looks like I have another David Carradine on set. Was I going to have to watch my back like I had to on *Behind Enemy Lines*? Only time would tell. We had a good first few days and everything was going smooth until Dennis Murphy called me over and explained he was bringing in a Stunt Coordinator for an upcoming car sequence. I looked at him curiously and reminded him I was the Stunt Coordinator, what did he need another one for? He told me that he thought I had my hands full with the fights and had a very good coordinator he was bringing in, that Phillip had given the okay for. I shook my head not fully understanding what he was saying.

"First of all, this was not what we agreed on. I already put together the vehicle sequence including putting a roll cage in a vehicle. I have everything mapped out and everybody has seen it."

Murphy replies, "no, no. You're doing fine. The guy we are bringing in is a car guy and a friend of mine. You Steven, I believe know him. Dick Ziker."

I nodded. "Yes, I know him. He is excellent, but this is news to me and we need to have a conversation about it." So sure enough, I met with Dennis and Phillip and I explained my thoughts on this matter. But before the meeting, I thought to myself, this is Dick Ziker. He comes from Stunts Unlimited. Very well respected by me and all his peers. It's not like he is a wannabe, I say to myself. My argument is limited, being who he is, but that doesn't make it right. So I told them I was fully capable of doing the car sequence and the fights without any help. Dennis, however, had a very hard nose and pressed for his friend Dick Ziker to come on set. I couldn't win this time, so I relented and wouldn't you know it. Dennis Murphy assured me that everything I designed for the car sequence would still be used, but he was going to turn everything over to Dick Ziker.

My reply was, "sure. I do all the work and he gets all the play." Let me explain, these are things you have to contend with when the bosses have their favorites, it's a done deal. It is not that one is better than the other, talent isn't the question. Sometimes it is just a matter of friendship and politics and you can't beat that in the movie business. I finally agreed on the condition that I got to speak to Dick first and explain some things to him. So that day I called Dick and told him how great it was going to be to have him on board. "I have to say though, I would like to make an agreement with you and show you how I work as a team. A sign of friendship," I told Dick. "Ninety percent of the action on this show is fights, I'll make a deal with you. I'll let you bring in fifty percent of the fight guys and I also designed a car roll for this show, I would like to do it."

He agreed saying, "sure Steven. I understand."

It was a wonderful chemistry and we each had a great time. I had a fight sequence to do with the casino boss and all the football players as his henchman in a gymnasium. I wanted to allow Dick to use his expertise in this scene, the legend that he is, so I told him I would let him bring four guys and I would bring four guys. Lucky for me, one of them was Jeff Dashnaw. A great stunt man and a great guy, full of humor.

CHAPTER 53
(The Snowman On A Horsey And A Prostate Exam.)

Speaking of Jeff Dashnaw, get your milk and cookies ready because it's storytime with Steven again. I will tell you a funny tale about Jeff. I was working for Jeff one time on a television show where I played a drug attic on PCP in a house. The cops break into the house filled with drug addicts and they hear somebody in the bedroom closet. They open the door and there I am. I happen to find a little snowman on a horsey, like a little Christmas ornament. It was wood. Now when we rehearsed it, I didn't use it. When we shot it for real, I decided to improv with the snowman on camera. When they opened the closet, there I was, playing with the snowman. Petting his head and making him move on his horse, saying, "snowman on a horsey, snowman on a horsey."

Nobody knew I was going to do that and it just gave the scene and character way more life as the other actors performing as cops, loved it and went along with it. One of the actors even repeated what I said.

That's when you know you are working with pros. After that, I jumped out of the closet doing the praying mantis form, attacking the cops. It looked hilarious in my underwear. Towards the end of the show, there is a scene where around fifteen cops come into this one bedroom and fight the main bad guy who was me.

(Say no to drugs. And snowmen on horsey. Unless you're in a movie.)

.Jeff Dashnaw and I began to choreograph everything, this guy throws a punch here, this guy gets tackled there, all hell was going to break loose. Until Jeff Dashnaw steps out to talk to the Director.

When he came back in, to my surprise, he says with that easy to read mischievous smirk, "we have an idea."

We all stop and listen. He decided we were going to ad lib. That's right, he was going to open the door, the cops were going to storm in and whatever happens, happens. "To hell with the choreography," he says.

My reply, "say what?"

He turns to me and asks, "can you handle that Steven?"

I think for a moment, finding it humorous and say, "hell yeah. But let me understand. You mean it is going to be a free for all? Let's do it." Now you have to understand that Jeff is a Master of Mischief. He enjoys seeing the unexpected happen. I asked him how far he wanted me to take it and he said, "all the way."

I say to him, "no punches, no kicks correct? But everything else is okay right?"

He says, "yes."

So I point to one of the stunt guys and say, "I can grab him by the crotch and pull him the f down, right?"

Dashnaw looks at me and says, "yes you can." He knew I wasn't serious, but played along in an instant. But all the guys? I got them scared, they thought I was serious and that's just the way I wanted it. "Mind games." I asked him what he meant and he replied, "they are just going to try and get you down and you try to stop them. Whatever happens, happens."

I ask him, "when do you want me to stop?"

He says," I don't. Until they get you down."

I shook my head knowing all hell was going to break loose. He turns to the guys, all fifteen of them and says, "I want you to all pile on top of him. Don't let him up just don't cover his face. We are going to bring a handheld camera in at the end and Steven, you keep screaming."

I looked at the fifteen guys, all drooling like a bunch of starving hyenas, ready to pounce on the little Kung Fu Jew. This seemed to give them an opportunity in their minds, to see just how bad ass I was. I could see it in their faces and they are having conversations trying to work as a team to get me down. They were talking about strategy, it was hilarious. I just sat back and watched until it was time. I say to all of them in a playful way, "you guys think you can get me down?"

Now let me speak about this one particular stunt guy who was playing one of the fifteen cops, Jimmy Nickerson. Jimmy was an ex-boxer and he thought he was a hard ass. He was involved in the first *Rocky* movie, teaching Sylvester Stallone how to box. Now let me tell you a little bit about Jimmy and our situation. It's pretty funny. I think so. A bunch of years ago, Jimmy had gotten into a verbal confrontation with my friend Joel Kramer. He and Joel were doubling the same guy on a television show, *Matt Houston*, starring Lee Horsley and one thing led to another and he threatened to beat up Joel. You see, Jimmy just didn't like the idea of another guy doubling the same actor. It was simply the ego factor. A little jealousy there. He just didn't want to share. So I decided to come to Joel's rescue. It became that type of situation for me to insert myself. That's what real friends are for. I called Jimmy Nickerson up and first tried to persuade him how wrong it was to want to get into a confrontation for reasons such as this. Well, he didn't want to hear it and called me a couple of unfavorable names and said it was none of my business.

He also said if I don't back away, well, let's just say he threatened my career. At this time, Nickerson was big potatoes and I was a small fry, as some in the movie business think. I just simply and very calmly, explained to Nickerson, if you raise your hands to Joel, I am going to do ten times more to you than what you put upon my friend. Do you understand that Nickerson? He blurted out a few more unfavorable words and abruptly hung up. Needless to say, he never did anything to Joel Kramer, it must have been our conversation. It was nice to see us all working together in a friendly sort of way on many tv shows after that. As for Nickerson threatening my career at that time? When it got around what had happened, to my surprise it made me more liked amongst my peers. More well known. Pretty funny. Back to the Jeff Dashnaw story. So all the cops get into the hallway and I am in the room throwing around a female cop who is trying to get me with her stun gun. I do the praying mantis around her which the Director loved and even asked me what I was doing. I told him it was Kung Fu. That all the movements were blocks and strikes all put together looking like the arms of a mantis. The Director was just crazy about it, Jeff loved it too. I asked to demonstrate it on Jeff Dashnaw. I told him to throw a punch. He did and I blocked it. While he stood still, I went crazy on him. Everyone found it humorous, while Dashnaw stood frozen while I threw a barrage of twenty mantis moves all over him. I was very fortunate. This is why I got hired a lot. People knew I was going to do crazy different stuff. We get ready to shoot and I look in the doorway and see Jimmy Nickerson leading the pack. I say to Jeff, "look who is in front. Jimmy Nickerson."

He sees Nickerson, laughs, and says, "that's your problem."

I look at Jeff and say, "watch what I'm going to do to him." Problem or not, I was ready. We start the scene and the Director calls, "action." The door slams open and there is Nickerson in front, leading the pack. Well, wouldn't you know it. Like a fricking Tasmanian devil, here comes Jimmy Nickerson, right at me. He fully extends his hands like he is going to give me a bear hug. Like a tornado, I cross over and spin out of the way, grabbing his arm and his shoulder. I then direct his head and shoulder into the wall where he thought I once was. Hard. Continuing my spin, uninterrupted, I get on top of him and put him in a neck lock. I turn him around and use him as a human shield while the other cops are after me. I whisper in his ear, "you missed me, Jimmy." Then I take him down on his knees and his chest and step on him a few times while I am dealing with the others. Here we go, I'm running around doing Aikido, Judo, arm locks and evasions. Many arm sweeps to the back of their legs, slamming against the walls and screaming like I had PCP superhuman strength. Cops are falling over each other, walls are shaking, as the Lambert Hurricane wreaks havoc on them. Grabs were missed and kicks were stopped as the cops were strewn throughout the room like dirty laundry. It seemed like minutes went by, I was losing steam. The hurricane was petering out. It was time to relent.

Fifteen cops jump on me and I hear the Director shout over my screaming, "don't cover his face, don't cover his face."

All of a sudden, the bodies part from my face and I am screaming bloody murder. They cut and I see standing applause from the crew. I am on the floor as everybody gets off of me. Jeff comes over to help me up as he is laughing hysterically. I ask, "do we have to do this again?"

He says, "no, we got it."

I happen to turn and guess who I see? Mister Nickerson. I said, "what happened? You missed."

He puffed out his chest and said I was lucky.

I replied, "I guess I was. Too bad we are not doing this again."

Nickerson looked at me. I looked at him and I spoke. "That one was for Joel."

He walked away. We move on to the next shot. They establish me being carried out of the house. Jeff Dashnaw and Buddy Joe Hooker are playing the cops carrying me with two others. I have plastic ties around my hands and legs as they carry me out, face down like pallbearers. One of the cops opens the door in preparation to throw me in. The door is now blocking the camera, keep in mind. Buddy Joe Hooker throws me in, face first. Problem is, he didn't throw me far enough and two thirds of my body are sticking out with only my head on the seat. I mumble to them, "you have to come around, you didn't throw me in enough."

They aren't listening and they push harder. All of a sudden, I feel something very uncomfortable and strange. Something where it's not supposed to be, in no man's land. I feel something pushing into my ass. Yes, you read this right. My ass. Dashnaw is behind the door, laughing hysterically. I managed to turn my head enough and realize Dashnaw has his finger pushing up my rectum and it seems to be traveling. That's how hard he is trying to push me in. I'm yelling but at the same time, trying not to be heard. "Dashnaw, what are you doing!? Get your f-ing finger out of my butt. What are you doing? Get it out! What the hell are you doing? Quit it, you idiot." He is pushing and pushing and laughing and laughing as I try to wiggle away. The camera can't see this going on, as I try to avoid becoming a finger puppet. After about ten seconds of me screaming at him, the Director yells, "cut!" The Director walks around and leans over to me. "Print! That was great Steven," he said. "But this time, don't curse if you want to ad lib."

My mouth dropped open. He had no idea what just happened. I look at Dashnaw and back at the Director. I told them to untie me and Dashnaw erupts in protest. Dashnaw is laughing hysterically.

"No, no Steven, don't hit me."

With a grin on my face, I said, "no, I'm not going to hit you, I am going to do the same thing you did to me, so untie me."

He apologizes profusely saying, "sorry Steven, I couldn't resist. I thought that would be the fastest way."

What a genius, I thought. Second take, no prostate checkup from Doctor Dashnaw. Although I did look to see where his hands were a couple of times. Thank God. Let's travel back and talk about *Blind Fury* some more. We were about to do an interior scene with Tex Cobb in the house, we are waiting for him to come back from his motor home. All of a sudden, we hear arguing outside. It is quite loud. We go to the front door and there is Tim Matheson, one of the Producers. Or in his mind, a God. But he is just a man with a bad attitude. By the way, he is also an actor, but not in this show. I see him screaming at Tex Cobb. In Randall's hands, guess what was in them? It wasn't a cup of coffee, it wasn't a script. You could say it was a prop. Maybe for another movie, but not this one. It was something called a doobie. A doobie doobie do. Not the Dean Martin kind. A colossal doob. That's right, a cigarette. Not just any cigarette mind you, but a homemade one. What he had done, is he had taken rolling paper the size of the front page of the New York Times, opened it and rolled it up with what had to be a few ounces of whacky tabac-e in it. It was the size and thickness of a baseball bat. He held it with two hands. This is in front of family and kids, the public, watching outside mind you. In 1989, this just wasn't done. Especially in Reno, Nevada, or anywhere for that matter. He is being obliterated at by Tim Matheson who is telling him amongst other things, to put it out or be fired. Mind you, Tex Cobb is six foot three and looking down at Tim. Tex takes a big drag and laughs.

"Settle down Timmy," he says. "This is just for my high blood pressure. You look a little tense. You want a hit?"

My mouth dropped hearing this discussion. That did it. Tim yelled over to two security guards and told them to escort him back to his trailer. They grabbed Tex on each side of his arm, who quickly brushed them off like flies.

"You can take my cigar, but don't touch me," Tex said.

With trouble brewing, I ran over to Tex and asked him if we could talk in his trailer. He agreed and we went inside. For some reason he listened to me, I guess there is always a certain kind of respect between Martial Artists. I sat him down and asked him what the hell he was doing, coming outside with the monster cigarette, especially with all the people around. He could get the whole production in trouble. I had to say something.

He looked at me and nodded before saying, "Okay. You want a hit?"

I said, "Not now. I'll put my gloves on later."

He said, "No, I mean of my cigar."

I said, "let me ask you something, crazy man. Were you ever stoned when you fought professionally?"

He replied, "ALL THE TIME." He roared with laughter as I shook my head and smiled.

"You are a true piece of work," I said. He understood and we had no more problems. As I was walking out, I turned to see if he was going to throw a punch at me. He always did the same thing Carradine did to me, except Tex hit harder. God bless David, but getting hit by Carradine was like getting hit with a wet towel. Good memories. Now a particularly proud memory I have in the things I have given this film was in the scene where the casino boss asks his henchman to get an Asian fighter to deal with Rutger's character. I was on set and came up with a great idea. "Why don't you say, get Bruce Lee?" I told them.

Phillip Noyce loved the idea and so what you see in the scene, the dialogue, "get Bruce Lee. Bruce Lee is dead. Then get somebody Asian, they are always badass," was all my idea. So little gems like that happen on set from time to time. I couldn't believe they accepted it. Between you and me readers, I said it more or less as a joke. When the Director respects you and values you enough, they will listen to your ideas and incorporate them into the film. A similar instance happened on *Remo Williams*. They needed someone to teach Joel Chinese calligraphy and they were going to send out for somebody. I told them, "why do that? You have somebody here."

They asked me, "who dat?"

I spoke up, "Bernie Pock is your guy." He was half Chinese, his mother was the famous Chinese actress, Nancy Kwan (*The Flower Drum Song*) and he knew how to do that stuff. The Director was overjoyed and used him to teach Joel. Now Phillip Noyce and I got along real well on *Blind Fury*. So well, he would invite just me out to dinner with him after wrap. We would discuss what we needed to do in the days ahead and how to prepare for it. Tim Matheson wasn't too happy about that. He expressed it a couple of times during our many dinners together. Yes, he always invited himself. The topic of the Asian bad guy came up one day, over sushi and sake go figure. Phillip mentioned he hadn't found an actor for the part yet. I said to myself, wow, it's happening again. Let's see if I can do this. A light bulb went off in my head.

I said, "if you don't mind, I have a really good suggestion. Someone I know real well, an actor and a supreme swordsman, Sho Kosugi. He would be perfect for this. I could show you some footage." Phillip agreed and so the next day I had someone go to the video store and get some DVDs, I mean VHS tapes, of *Revenge Of The Ninja* and *The Domination*. Phillip and I watched the tapes of Sho and he insisted to know details, like who is the silver masked ninja. I was very honored and humbled when he mentioned to me that the portrayal of the silver masked ninja was his favorite character in the movie, it was great.

He said, "your movements are very strong and poetic."
I'll never forget that evening. Philip Noyce was like a teenage kid, just laughing and enjoying himself while we watched *Revenge Of The Ninja*. The next day he came on the set and mentioned to me,

"Revenge was good, but the Domination was one of the stupidest films I ever saw in my life, but I liked Sho's character. How do I get in touch with him?"

I didn't know his agent's number so I called a man who did. That man being Sam Firstenberg. So that is what I did and the rest is history. I had a sense of joy and happiness in my heart and soul that I was able to give two wonderful opportunities to Sho Kosugi on two of his only American films. Here's to you, my friend. Movie, *Blind Fury*. The first day on set with Sho Kosugi. I was excited. Phillip happened to mention to Sho Kosugi that he should thank me as I was the one who recommended him. Guess what I got? A look and a nod from about ten feet away. I could say that is Sho's way of saying thanks. But is it? I'll leave that up to you readers to decide. You would think with our past friendship that there would be a little more warmth there, but he was visibly rude. Not only then but all through the time we spent together on the show. It was very, very sad to me. I was disillusioned with our friendship and what I thought we meant to each other. When I say we, I mean him. I admired the guy. Thought the world of him. I thought I proved my friendship many times. Our relationship was just not ever the same after *Revenge*. I hope someday we see each other again and we smile and talk about the good ole' days. Now it was time to do the big fight sequence at the jacuzzi with Sho and Rutger. I had planned it out already. It was all set, as I had already played Sho and worked out the sword sequence with Rutger, but Sho insisted he wanted to change it. We had a big argument between me, Phillip and Sho over the sequence. We didn't want to put it together again when it was already so beautifully finished. Phillip was happy with it, Rutger was ecstatic with it, I was happy with it, but Sho was not. I told him he could change a few sword moves, but the main sequence was set. I had to explain to Sho that he had little choice in the matter as he was not the star and the Director was happy with it. On top of that, when we were discussing his double for the fight, he wanted to know who his double was.

I waved my hands in the air. "I'm your double," I told Sho. "Somethings never change." I thought he would be excited about that. You know, just for old time's sake. But he wasn't. He shook his head in disagreement and I was just shocked! I said, "Sho, I doubled you on previous films, why change it up now?"

Sho stayed silent and adamant. "With all due respect, I don't have time to find you another double and I want to double you, so I am going to do it," I stated.

Sho just turned and walked away. It hurt to see him like this, but what could I do? During the actual fight, Sho was stunned a couple of times seeing how impressive Rutger was with the sword in his hands. He saw the natural ability that Rutger had and it made me proud knowing I taught him.

(Stunt doubling Sho. He says no. I say, here we go.)

As they went through the fight, there was a moment where Rutger reaches out his hand and touches Sho's face. "Japanese," he says. The look on Sho's face is his real expression as he had no idea Rutger was going to do and say that. Guess what? During one of our breaks, I had mentioned to Rutger to do and say that to Sho without letting him know if he thought it was a good idea. Remember stunt people, you are allowed to suggest if it has to do with action. After he did it, he had congratulated me on my improvisation skills and I told him I had learned it from James Woods. It was really fun seeing things like that happen. Just like the little snowman on the horsey. Going back to the beginning of the film, we are in the forest with the Vietnamese natives (by the way it was my favorite scene in this movie, you see it doesn't have to be all about action) and we are there for about four days.

The first day I notice that Rutger and the focus puller are getting along quite well. They are hanging out with each other, enjoying each other's company, by the way, the focus puller was female. Figure that out. The second day goes by and Rutger and her are getting more friendly. The third day comes and lunch time arrives. I'm sitting with the crew and all of a sudden, they start talking about this focus puller. I start to hear pieces of conversation.

"I guess she got a black eye. I heard he got rough."

I'm saying to myself, what is going on here? I ask them and they explain things got physical (Olivia Newton John style) and she developed a black eye.

I said, "whaaat?"

I asked them, "well, what is going to happen now? Have you seen her? Is she mad? Is she gonna sue?"

I really didn't know what to say. I was shocked.

They said they had seen her and she didn't look upset, just a little embarrassed. I asked if she was going to continue working and they didn't know. The next day comes and I am at the catering truck having breakfast when out of the corner of my eye, I see the focus puller. Boy does she have a shiner! I can't believe she came on set with a black eye like that. Nobody said anything, but I could see the relationship between her and the actor was different.

I never found out what happened but when I told Phillip Noyce about it, he shrugged and said, "that's show business."

Speaking of Phillip and show business, there was one moment where Rutger is confronted by two henchmen and he picks up his cane sword with his foot and tosses it up to the henchman who catches it.

I was showing this move a few days before to Phillip Noyce, to get his approval to use it in the scene.

He stood in front of me and asked me to demonstrate to show the D.P. how it would look. Now I must have done the move two dozen times that day without a mistake, but at that moment for some reason, I got lazy. Instead of going straight up, it went forward and flew right into the forehead of Phillip Noyce. SMACK!

He went back a couple of feet. It hit him hard.

"You did that on purpose!" he said, holding his head.

I was trying to hold back my laughter. It was an honest mistake, I told him.

(Why would I do it on purpose, you're a nice guy. It was an accident.)

Thank God there was no blood, but there was a big knot right smack in the middle of his forehead. First Aid came over and gave him an ice pack. Boy, was I embarrassed. Nevertheless, I did it a second time for the D.P. This time, I made sure I caught it with Phillip several feet away, holding the ice pack on his forehead. This time, everybody was laughing, but also staying far away watching me do it five times in a row. I hear Phillip in the background, "I still think you did it on purpose."

I yelled out, "I was innocent, man!"

Philip Noyce had a great sense of humor. That sounds familiar.

CHAPTER 54
(The Jet. Benny Urquidez And The Prison Yard Knockout.)

A movie called *An Innocent* Man starring Tom Selleck. Let me tell you about the greatest show on earth like Barnum and Bailey's Circus but in this case it was a movie with the greatest story you will ever hear with the one and only Benny Urquidez. Yes, the Martial Artist, Benny "the Jet." As I say, the one and only. One of the greatest real fighters I have ever seen. I was there doubling a snitch in a prison, doing a fire burn, getting a balloon filled with gasoline popped on my head.

(Working for John Moio. Always the hard way.)

But this story believe it or not, is not about me. Now understand this, real life, we are in Nevada State maximum security prison with killers, rapists and arsonists. Picture this, we have to wear orange vests and the guards there always have to make sure we are all together. We are guarded by security everywhere we go. It's scary. So Moio mentions to me he is bringing in Benny Urquidez and asks if I know him.

"Of course," I say.

He explained to me it was for a boxing scene in the middle of the prison yard. I was curious to know who he was going to be fighting. To tell you the truth, at that moment, I was hoping that it might be me. But come to find out, to my surprise, wait until you hear who he is fighting. Moio said he would be fighting one of the prisoners.

My mouth dropped open. "A prisoner, he is a real prisoner?" I asked in disbelief. They are putting a boxing ring on the other side of the yard and they want a real prisoner to box with Benny? Are you kidding me? Moio had his mind set and that night Benny came in. Moio starts talking to Benny, telling him that they told this prisoner the fight was going to be make believe. Their punches would connect but it was going to be light. Benny sat back just listening, not saying much, which was the usual Benny. I was sitting straight up in my chair, thinking about how many guys this prisoner has killed or how many women has he hurt or who or what has he set on fire. Not Benny, he was cool as could be, just listening. If you were the nicest person or a cold hard killer, it was all the same to Benny. Benny came from the streets and learned how to fight several people at a time. Everybody who knew Benny back then, if you thought there might be a confrontation and you saw Benny, you crossed the street to avoid him or went the other way. So the next day I go with Moio and Benny to the Warden's office. Walking through this high security prison with Benny Urquidez was a memory for the ages. We get to the meeting and there is the prisoner in handcuffs seated by the Warden. Moio stands up and begins describing how the fight is going to go down and I just can't stop thinking about the fact he is using a real jailbird. Why he didn't bring in a stunt fighter, is beyond my comprehension. Moio asked me to stand up and demonstrate the boxing with him. They had boxing gloves there so Moio put them on and proceeded to demonstrate. He asked me not to block and proceeded to throw a few light punches, but I couldn't resist myself and so I did block a couple. Typical Moio. He yelled at me and Benny and I laughed as I said, "you are lucky I don't hit back."

Moio grunted. "That is how hard you hit," he said to the prisoner.

The prisoner is asked by Moio if he understood and he says, "yes, sir."

Then I hear the Warden. "Do you fully understand!?"

The inmate stands up and yells out, "yes sir!"

I looked at Benny. He is smiling. Not I. I had never seen anything quite like that before. The meeting lasted about five minutes and as we were walking out, I still couldn't believe what was going to happen. I have never heard or seen a real prisoner being used in a scene like this in all my years, nor have I heard it from old timers. I remember going to my room and calling my friend Mike Vendrell and telling him what was going on here. A little gossip session amongst friends. He was laughing and wanted me to tell him what happened. I had hoped nothing unexpected. The next day we get bussed to the prison, put on our orange vests and head for the usual meeting place, the prison cafeteria. I see Moio talking to one of the guards and I walk over there and overhear what they were planning. He wanted three hundred of the worst of the worst up on the catwalks on the first, second and third stories overlooking the boxing ring like the Roman Coliseum and a hundred or so chairs around the boxing ring on ground level. Real prisoners. Real killers, rapists, thieves, cutthroats, did I say killers?

They are also talking about fifty plus guards, some with machine guns, some with rifles up on the catwalks and around in the ring amongst the crowd to protect us. Three hundred crazy people and the cast and crew are only protected by fifty guards. This was wild man. My thoughts here? If there was a situation, and a fight broke loose what is the chance one of these bullets will hit this punk kid from Brooklyn? I was never a star student in math or statistics but those numbers didn't sound good and this was unheard of. At least it was until now. I looked at Benny and he was carefree as they come.

It was kind of funny and kind of horrific at the same time. I've heard stories of prison riots and god forbid that should happen here. Car stunts, fire burns, high falls, I would do any day of the week, but being surrounded by a sea of serial killers and mad dogs? That gave me pause. As we go inside to wait for them to get the three hundred prisoners in place for the scene, I overhear one of the guards mentioning that they told all of these inmates just who was going to be in the scene. Benny "The Jet" Urquidez. They all knew who Benny was and his reputation. To his surprise, the guard mentioned that having Benny inside the prison, for the inmates, was like having Jesus walk past their cells. I fully didn't grasp what he was saying until after all the inmates were in place and ready. We were going to do no rehearsals which I must tell you my friends, that was a shock to me. No rehearsals with a maximum security prisoner? I look over to Moio and say, "no rehearsals with a real prisoner? Are you kidding?"

Moio tells me to, "shut up."

I laugh, just shaking my head. He said it would just be like two inmates tapping each other. I just listened while I was taking this all in. Moio has put himself and me in a prison outfit as we were to play Benny's seconds in the boxing ring. Listen to this, Benny has this huge cowboy hat on, I'll never forget it. It was beige and made out of straw. Oversized. Tall in the cap. In other words, the hat looked bigger than him. It was great. This prompts Moio to ask him to take it off.

Benny looks at him and says, "I will, but I am going to walk through the prison with it on. I will take it off once we get into the ring and before we shoot."

Moio didn't think anything of it, nor did I think anything of it. All of a sudden, we hear on the walkie, "we are ready for you guys."

The door is opened into the yard by a guard and we are escorted out. A guard goes first. Moio comes out next and the prisoners are looking at him, not saying anything. No one is saying anything, no one knows or cares who he and I are in this

472

prison. Then another guard comes out followed by another. Finally, Benny comes emerges, walking out like Muhammad Ali. I follow him with a guard in back me through the dead silence into the yard. He takes five steps and from that dead silence, the entire prison breaks into a chant.

"BENNY, BENNY, BENNY THE JET!" I couldn't believe it. Benny's chest comes out and all of a sudden not only the people on ground level, not only the prisoners who are up on the catwalks but the other hundreds more inside of their cells hear what is going on and their voices join in. I look at my feet as I feel an earthquake of sound hit us. The whole prison feels like it is vibrating by the sound of what they are saying. "BENNY, BENNY, BENNY THE JET."

I realize this was not planned, it is not being filmed. This is real. Benny walks up to the ring, makes his way through the ropes and walks into the middle of the ring. It is then and there that he takes off his hat and holds it up. The place explodes into even more roaring cheers. The greatest show on earth put into a prison, countless inmates seeing someone who they would normally never see. Five minutes of cheering and roaring as he is walking around the ring like a rodeo champ winning first place, sucking in all the applause from murders, rapists and arsonists. Here comes the good part. He throws his hat out of the ring, watching it land into the arms of one of the inmates who put it on. Okay, here we go. The lights are about to come on, the toilet is about to flush, in other words, the bell is about to ring. They bring in the prisoner and before we roll cameras, Moio brings them into the center of the ring with the head guard and I follow being his cornerman. Moio tells them to spar lightly and to remember this is not a real fight. They both nod in understanding and they go to their respective corners. Remember, this boxing practice is going on as part of the background in the film, that is what makes this so incredible. We get in place and they roll cameras.

The bell rings, the fight is on, loudest battle royal in Benny's history. The inmates are roaring. They are trading punches and I see that Benny is hitting lightly, but after ten, fifteen seconds, I notice the prisoner is getting in some good hard hits. After a few seconds they cut and Moio goes over to Benny and I'm down below listening. "You want some water, Benny?" Moio asks.

Benny shakes his head. "No, I don't want water, I'll tell you what I want. This isn't supposed to be real, right?"

Moio caught on quickly. "That guy is hitting you for real, ain't he?" Moio says.

Benny nodded.

Moio tells Benny he will take care of it and goes over to the prisoner. He once again explains that the fight is not real and to only give light punches. I see the prisoner chuckle and smirk as he looks across the ring at Benny.

"What is the matter? Is he a pussy? It's too much for him?"

I look up at Benny who I can tell is shocked hearing that comment, but he doesn't say a word. But boy, does his face change. Moio stresses again that it is not a real fight.

"Yea, I understand. I won't hit hard, he can't take it," the prisoner says.

Moio walks back over to Benny and tells him he won't get hit hard anymore. Benny shrugs his shoulders, like it is really no big deal. Here it comes, round two. Cameras roll again and ACTION! Benny gets in the middle of the ring and they start boxing and here we go again. I see Benny hitting soft but the bad guy is still going in hard! After thirty seconds they cut again. Moio walks over to the prisoner and tells him not to hit hard.

The prisoner nods. "Okay, okay, I thought I wasn't hitting him hard! The Jet can't take it, huh?" Benny hears this and smiles. I notice the smile and something inside of me says "uh-oh."

Moio walks over to Benny, looks back at the prisoner and says to him real quietly, "if he hits you hard again, I give you permission to hit him back the Benny way."

Benny's face lights up and he grins, he is coming alive. I hear Benny say three words to John Moio. Three words.

"Thank you, boss," Benny says.

I'm wondering what was going to happen in the third round. You out there reading this, are you catching on? They go out there again, the bell rings for the third go around and they start boxing. Ten seconds go by exchanging shots. Then, can you believe this, the prisoner side steps and hooks Benny right in the side of the face, a good hard shot. Benny steps back and shakes it off. The prisoner moves in again to uppercut and all of a sudden, there is a barrage of hook and uppercuts from Benny. Shots that would shake the roots of a tree. BAM! Guess what? Come on, guess? What do you think happened? Down goes the prisoner, knocked out cold. A roar of cheers erupted even louder than before, as Benny is hovering over him bouncing up and down with his hands in the air. Benny is looking down at him giving him the sign of the cross, blessing him. Don't ever mess with Benny Urquidez. The roaring from the inmates is so extreme that I have to put my hands over my ears. "BENNY, BENNY, BENNY THE JET," the crowd roars.

I look up, noticing some of the guards with the weapons, wondering what the hell was going to happen now. This is how crazy the inmates got. I could see the guards had a worried look on their faces. What a sight to behold. We later found out the word in the prison was that the prisoner had told everyone he was going to go in hard on Benny and knock him out. In fact, they had bets going. Knowing Benny was going to hit soft, if he could land a good punch and knock him out, his reputation would spread throughout the prison. Everyone was expecting this kind of end to the fight to happen. Someone was going to get knocked out and of course we all knew, including you readers, it wasn't gonna be Benny.

(Benny Urquidez. Pound for pound, the toughest man around.)

As he stood there in the applause, chants and deafening roar of the prison crowd, it was obvious to me that this was the greatest, the most memorable and the most earth shaking story about Benny Urquidez. If they ever do the Chronicles of Benny Urquidez, they ought to slip this story in it. It was if a God from the outside came down into the prison and was challenged by a mere mortal. And of course, the God won. A moment I will always remember.

(Benny and I. Dragon Fest 2018. I just reminded him of the story.)

CHAPTER 55
(Movie: Always. Actor Richard Dreyfuss, John Goodman And Holly Hunter.)

Why don't we talk about *Always*. A movie by Steven Spielberg. That was my next big thrill. Amblin calls me and to my surprise, Spielberg is calling me in to offer me another flick. I thanked the secretary and literally mentioned, "what about Vic Armstrong? He always works closely with Steven." I was always brought up to remember the people who have helped you and assisted you in the past as I hope you know by now.

She told me that, "Vic was unavailable and he requested you, Seven, to do this project."

I owe thanks to Vic for that moment and bring up again that I never really had to hustle. I always found it strange. Work always came to me. You can call that a blessing or lucky, but this was the way it seemed to be throughout my whole career.

So the next day I came in and got the script, knowing where to go this time and as I was leaving, she told me Spielberg wanted to speak to me. I hadn't seen him in a while, I was nervous, so the butterflies followed me into his office. He had a smile on his face. He brought up my work on *The Last Crusade* and that made me feel like a somebody. I reiterated to him how thankful I was to him and Vic Armstrong and he replied back, "what a wonderful job you did for me, Steven."

It was at this moment, I knew I had the perfect opportunity to bring up something that was personally important to me. Vic Armstrong and I talked about while shooting the breeze on *The Last Crusade*. Among other things, his brother Andy Armstrong got brought up and Vic briefly mentioned to me that Andy didn't have his SAG union card to work in America yet. You see, Andy was also a stunt man in England. So I ask, "Steven listen, Vic Armstrong has a brother who is a stuntman in England. I would like to bring him on the film, but he doesn't have a SAG union card yet. I would like to show my appreciation to Vic and bring him here and get him his SAG card and need your approval."

Without a slight hesitation, Spielberg says, "yes. And if you have any difficulty just let me know."

I stick out my hand to say thank you. He does the same. I close my hand. He does too. Fist bump. How many stuntmen can say they fist bumped with Spielberg? These are the things you need to do to show your appreciation and I must say, on my part, a genius move. I'll always be gratified that I was able to accomplish that for Andy Armstrong.

(My stunt firefighters. From left to right. Mike Vendrell, Mike Johnson and Andy Armstrong.)

You see, this is another learning and teaching experience. These kinds of things should always be a part of your life. To find a way to reciprocate for people who have done good things for your life and career. He told me to read the script, it is a film about airborne firefighters starring Richard Dreyfus, Holly Hunter and John Goodman. He asked me to come up with a budget and a couple of ideas. He explained to me that this wasn't an action piece, more of a love comedy drama. A dromedy. I took a week to break down the script and brought it into him with my ideas and questions. I was excited, as there were seven or eight non-descript firefighters that I could bring stunt people in for. The rest of the show was more safety and security than stunts. Frank Marshall and Pat Kehoe were there. Frank was producing and Pat was First Assistant Director. I never met Pat before, but as soon as we met and had a conversation, I had an instantaneous connection with him. Little did I know we would become great friends.

Every Sunday we had off, we would go fly fishing, he taught me. I found it extra exhilarating as I whipped the pole back and forth letting out the line. You fly fisherman know what I am talking about. Kehoe taught me and gave me high praise for catching on so fast. I told him that was the Kung Fu in me. He didn't understand so I showed him, using the pole like a spear, flying around. From then on, he called me the Kung Fu fly fisherman.

I always thought that would make a good title for a movie. I was also informed as we discussed the budget, they had an Aerial Coordinator named Jim Gavin who happened to be in my stunt organization. That was fine with me, planes were not my expertise and I thought he would be a big help to me. Little did I know how little of a help he would be with him wanting the whole show for himself. The greedy vulture that he was. Let's drift back to Spielberg.

Steven mentioned he wanted me to go to firefighting school. I was excited as it was something I could put in my bag of tricks and learn what real firefighters go through when fighting fires. I could then impart that to my stuntmen and create a great scene. It would be perfect. I also suggested several firefighting scenes I had come up with, of which he only chose one.

Unfortunately, we had no time for the others. It was of a humongous log going down a hill on fire. I wanted the firefighters to be all stuntmen and he agreed. He also wanted a comedy bit with John Goodman, so I came up with a good wet scene. Yes, wet. I'll keep you dry for now though. During this conversation, Spielberg kept mentioning how important it was that I go to this firefighting school, every day for a week to learn the exact procedures firefighters go through. That is when Frank Marshall, or as the crew called him, the mob boss, spoke up and casually stated that he was going to bring in some real firefighters as well. I was fine with that, figuring they would be background and extras and help me as far as being on my safety team. Towards the end of the conversation, Spielberg mentioned he would like to bring one of his friends, Ted Grossman along.

I knew Ted was in my stunt group and I already learned how famous he was with big stars from the fifties and sixties. Ted was a good stuntman but missed his calling as a comedian. He was hilarious. I found out later from Pat Kehoe that he was Spielberg's good luck charm ever since Ted had coordinated the original *Jaws*. I saw no problem with that and said okay, thinking I would make him one of the firefighters. After the meeting, I called Vic Armstrong to let him know his brother would be working here in America. He was overjoyed to hear that and I simply said, "I was glad it happened."

I called Bernie Pock who I picked to double Richard Dreyfuss and Janet Brady who would be Holly Hunter's double. After a few more phone calls, I called Ted Grossman and gave him the dates. Listen to this. It turns out he was unavailable. No good luck charm for Spielberg. Oh well, no big deal I thought. A week later I found myself in Montana. The first thing we did was set up hundreds of trees, logs and greenery that we were going to set ablaze for the forest fire scene.

Five to six hours a day, special effects and I would place trees and shrubs to create this scene, it was a Herculean effort and boring at that. Happily, I was able to go in and out throughout the hours. My time was needed in many other places.

(Aerial Coordinator Jim Gavin tried to take my job. Failed, big time.)

I was happy about that. Setting trees and bushes got boring after seven and a half minutes. I was also involved in some heavy machinery. A scene where this small vehicle gets turned on and drives wildly by itself and crashes into a porch. Spielberg wanted it to hit the corner and that meant it had to zigzag. I suggested I could be hidden with a tarp and blind drive it. Then at that moment, it was Jim Gavin voicing his opinion which by the way, was rude and wrong. He said it was not possible to control a vehicle like that, to make it go exactly where you wanted it to.

Here is a learning lesson, you never want to say something that you think cannot be done on set. Never go against a fellow worker. Especially someone like me. I have to say, he really had no idea who I was and what I was capable of doing. You get together as a team and discuss what the best thing is to do. Besides that, what he was doing was trying to make me look bad and if you are a team player, that is a big no no. I mean it's like me telling him how to fly. He is the Aerial Coordinator. I am the Stunt Coordinator. We show respect and that is the golden rule. On any job.

Needless to say, the pressure was on. Little did they know, before we shot the stunt, I had come in early and practiced it. When we filmed, I crashed it within an inch of where Spielberg wanted it. Everyone was speechless. I walked over and put my hand on Jim Gavin's shoulder, smiled and walked away and Spielberg saw that. And guess what? He smiled at me. Right then and there I knew it was one for me and zero for Gavin. Guys like Jim Gavin, there are many. Selfish and self centered. Later in the day, among my many conversations with Spielberg, I just happened to mention that his friend Ted Grossman wasn't available. I didn't think anything of it. Spielberg gets all antsy.

"He's not available? Did you tell him I asked for him?" Spielberg said.

I nodded. "Yes, Steven. He said he wasn't available and he apologized."

Steven's eyes darted back and forth nervously. "Next weekend, we have a scene with a bunch of firefighters up in the tower, make sure he is here for that," Steven replied.

I saw him starting to think, getting a little uppity in a serious way. I thought that was strange, I didn't understand at the time what it really meant to him. Okay, no problem I thought. The next day, Sunday morning came and Pat Kehoe and I went fly fishing. As I was reeling in my line, Pat told me something he had heard and seen. I said, "what's that?"

He said, "just look out for Jim Gavin." He said during a scout that he had seen him asking Spielberg to replace me, that he doesn't need two Coordinators. I looked at Pat and shook my head.

Pat said to me, "don't worry, I told Spielberg that you understand and are better at action than Gavin is."

No matter how nice of a person you are out on the street, when it comes to work, it is a dog eat dog world. Regardless if they are in your group, if they are your friend, or at times, even your family. "It never ceases to amaze me," I told Pat. "Besides, Spielberg knows my work."

Jim was world renowned and yet he still is petty enough to try and steal a show and my job. He told me Spielberg wouldn't have it. I knew how much Spielberg liked me and it was going to take more than someone like Jim Gavin to get me out of here. Little did I know, that person was already on set. When I got back to the hotel, I kicked off my shoes and thought to myself, it's time to call Ted Grossman. He picked up the line on the other end and I spoke. "Ted. Are you available next week? You gotta come. Spielberg is getting a little weird. I hope you are available because if you're not, it may put me in the shitter. In other words, he may not be too happy."

He laughs and replies. "Tell him I'm not available, I can't make it," Ted says.

"What do you mean you can't make it? What are you doing?" I ask.

"I'm on my way to the yacht club, going sailing. Just tell him I am busy and that I'm sorry. I'll catch up with him soon."

I said okay and hung up in defeat. The next day, I tried to hide from Spielberg but I found that to be impossible. Why? Because he sent a runner specifically for me. I had no idea why, but I thought it might be serious because this was a first. When I went to see Spielberg, I walked over and our eyes immediately locked. Having no idea what he wanted or needed, the first words that came out of his mouth were, "did you get ahold of Ted Grossman!?"

I told him with a hesitation, "uh, Steven. I hate to say this, but Grossman still isn't available." Spielberg got serious. He turned to me and our eyes locked. "What do you mean not available? I want him on the show, you tell him to get down here!"

Well, I was flabbergasted. Shocked and just a little scared. Wow, he was adamant about this, as I had spoken to Spielberg many times and had never seen him so aggravated. I think I'm up shit creek without a paddle or a Ted Grossman. I better get him here. I tried to calm Spielberg down and explain to him what could I do if he is busy?

Spielberg simply said, "get him here."

Taking a deep breath, I nodded. "Okay," I said." Leaving the set, my mind was going a thousand miles an hour thinking what the hell just happened. Ted Grossman, you must be a God in Spielberg's mind. So that night, I was back on the phone. Begging him to come. I remember one of the first things I said. "Ted, my ass is grass if you don't come and I am serious. Your friend is neurotic about it, I am telling you. He wants you. You know Steven is very direct with what he wants, you must know what I am going through. Please come. I can't tell him you are not available a third time. He wants you here, he needs you here. You're his freaking good luck charm. You gotta save my ass and save the day." Yes, I said all that before he even spoke. I listened. The sound of beautiful music flowed into my ear.

"Yes, tell Steven I'll come," was the reply.
I felt a calmness throughout my body as he said that. I was prepared and I gave him the dates. "Thanks, Ted. It means a lot. I'll see ya in a few days." I hung up, feeling like I had just scored a touchdown on third and long. The next morning, I told Spielberg the good news. He nodded and just smiled like it was no big deal. I said to myself, is that all I get after all this?

Sometimes you have to jump through hoops to get a nothing burger. You always want to please your Director, especially if his name is Steven Spielberg. The day came where we were to do the scene I had come up with involving John Goodman. What a great guy. He is on his lounge chair, listening to the radio and drinking soda and sitting on this hill and waiting for his recruits to fly by and put out a fire as a test. One of them flies by and dumps water right on John's character.

I hear Spielberg tell me he is not sure if we were going to do it. I asked why. He told me Jim Gavin had mentioned he had heard about what I was planning and said it was too dangerous.

"If you dump that much water on someone at that height and speed, there is a possibility the force could kill him," he explained.

I shook my head thinking, "there he goes again," completely disagreeing with Jim's assessment. In my mind, I know this will be a great stunt. I already called Jeff Jensen to double John. I don't want to lose it. I had a private meeting with Spielberg explaining to him that it can be done and I would like to do a test myself and videotape it to show him. Spielberg agrees.

Without anyone knowing, I get a helicopter to dump the water from a dump tank underneath it. I played John and sat up there and had a flag in my hand. I waved the flag and signaled the chopper to start flying. Mind you, I have a P.A. filming all of this on a camcorder down below. The water gets dumped and it hits me like a ton of bricks. I go flying, still in my chair, down this hill. Tumbling and turning, I reached the bottom of the hill. I'm soaking wet as I get up and I look up and smile at the camera, clenching my fists together in victory. It was specular.

"You got all that?" I asked the cameraman.

"Yea, it looked wild and hilarious," he replied.

I thought to myself, gotcha Jim Gavin. Great. I get changed and head into a production meeting where Spielberg is discussing the stunt among other things.

"Sorry Steven, I think it's just too dangerous," he tells me.
Now everyone is at this meeting including the one and only Jim Gavin who put me into this situation.
There is also Pat Kehoe, who is in on what I was doing. He was the First Assistant. I needed his approval after all. I said, "excuse me, Steven. It can be done and safely."

Steven looks at me over his glasses. He spots me taking out the camcorder from my bag.

"Take a look at this," I say.

He takes it and looks into the lens as it plays back. It was a moment I'll always remember.

(Jeff Jenson doubling John Goodman. Sorry Jim Gavin, you were wrong. It worked.)

Always. A film by Steven Spielberg, who is at the moment watching a scene by Steven Lambert. I forgot to tell you I had a fat suit on and a cigar in my mouth, imitating John Goodman.

Picture this, the scene is a good minute and a half long. Spielberg is straight faced, calm as could be. But the moment I got hit with the water, you could tell.

Steven starts wonderfully laughing jumping up and down saying, "holy shit, holy shit!" You could even tell when he got to the end, he said, "wow, Steven, you did it, you are fine! We are doing this Steven!"

I walked over to Jim Gavin and guess what I did? I Put my hand on his shoulder, smiled and walked away. And guess what Steven did? He saw it and SMILED. I thought to myself, two to nothing. When we did it with Jeff Jensen, it looked wonderful. He was four times the size of me and he bounced down like a rolling boulder. Spielberg loved it and Jensen got a roaring applause.

Meeting all the actors was great, especially Richard Dreyfuss. He really is one of those good guys. So real and comfortable to talk to. Come to find out, he is a major American history buff. He would discuss history on set for hours with us. I learned so much, it was really meaningful and we became good friends. Little did I know, I would work with him later on as an actor.

(Two old friends. As soon as Richard Dreyfuss saw me, he raised his fist. Good to see ya, Lambo.)

John Goodman was a wonderful guy too, really loved and respected stuntmen. Holly Hunter was a great gal too, but sometimes we got a few surprises. Let's talk about one incident. She was riding a bike in this scene, going as fast as she could through the forest. Suddenly, the chain falls off and the bike goes erratic. The prop guy and I come running over to help, grabbing her and the bike.

"Are you all right?" I ask. Look at me, saving a damsel in distress. The hero of the day, I thought. The prop guy held the bike and I started to put the chain back on as a good person would do when BAM! I jumped up startled. Holly started screaming at us! I looked up in shock while she was reprimanding us for helping her put the chain back on the bike. Yes, you are reading this right. She is yelling at us for helping her. This is a first for me.

"I'm fine! You guys get away. I can do that myself you hear!? What, you think just because I am a woman that I don't know how to do it?"

I looked up in disbelief. "No," I stammered. "It's just part of my job." I looked back and saw half the crew laughing and half the crew not sure if she was serious.

Steven came over and diffused the situation by saying, "let me do it. I don't want your hands to get all dirty."

She stood back as I held the bike and Steven started to put on the chain. I looked at her and smiled. Just to break the tension I said, "you can be on my stunt crew any day, Holly." She took a step towards Steven and hip checked him to the ground. There is Steven in the dirt, looking at her in amazement while she proceeds to put on the chain.

Steven says, "I didn't know it meant that much to ya. Excuse me."

Holding the bike, I hear Holly say, "you men are all alike."

I proceed to lift the back end so I could rotate the chain. She looks at me as if she was about to say something when click. The chain connects. Everybody is walking on eggshells when she asks for a wet towel to wipe the grease from her fingers from the bike chain. There were no towels, so guess what? We had to wait twenty minutes so she could go back to home base to wash her hands. Obviously, she wouldn't have had to do that if she had let me. What a strong wonderful woman she is. What a gal. Tough cookie.

Okay, let's be like water and flow forward. I was never much for water and certified I wasn't, but it was one thing I took pride in. Common sense. I practically had no experience Stunt Coordinating underwater work, but I knew what had to be done. Considering I had watched other professionals do it for years. I knew if there was an accident, they would for sure find out I wasn't certified and I and the company would be in big trouble.

You see, I want you to understand the risk I was taking. If someone got hurt underwater and they found out that the person at the top was not certified, well, all I could say to you is that would be a terrible situation. But if you use your head and hire true professionals on your team who could give you the answers, everything will be fine and you'll be sipping a bottle of wine. And that's exactly what I did. As I always say, if you hire the right people, they can guide you along the way and make you look like you are the king of the hill. So, let me get to this penultimate story.

Hey, you out there reading this, you know what the hell I just said? Penultimate, my writing partner mentioned that. (Hi guys.) I asked him, "what the hell does that mean?"

He explained, Penultimate: Second to last. Now the punk kid from Brooklyn knows a new word. Here we go. There is a scene with Holly at the end of the movie, where she crashes the plane into the water and Richard Dreyfuss's character rescues her. I was nervous, as this was my first big time major underwater sequence and I better get it right because there are literally lives on the line including Holly Hunter and Richard Dreyfuss. It was a major deal. I had Twenty five professional divers on this team, just for this scene. We put the plane underwater in this Olympic sized indoor pool. I got a safety diver for everyone who was going to be underwater. Dreyfuss, Hunter, my stunt doubles, the D.P. and his crew. Even the gaffers. Everyone underwater was certified. Except me. But please be quiet, don't tell anybody. My SCUBA guys knew I wasn't and they let me. Trust was a major factor. They liked me and they knew I was serious. It was a very big deal. What made this great for me, is that I could communicate with everyone via headsets.

It was very intense since I was verbally controlling everything, including Spielberg's direction. By the way, I gotta tell you where Spielberg was sitting. I found it oddly entertaining seeing Spielberg with his megaphone above everybody, sitting twelve feet in the air on a lifeguard chair. You just had to be there. On rehearsal, I had Bernie Pock jump in as Janet Brady emerged from the cockpit with Bernie's help. They grasp hands and start swimming towards the surface as the sunlight streams down. Just a beautiful shot. Everything worked wonderfully throughout the rehearsals. A few days later, Spielberg came on set and we were ready to shoot it for real. I was confident it would work perfectly. We begin the scene. Bernie swims down, grasps hands with Janet and they swim up. It's beautiful. Cut.

I see Spielberg call me over. A big smile is on my face and I am pretty sure he is going to tell me how wonderful it looked. He brings me over to the monitor and starts playback.

"You see anything wrong here? Look close," he says.

I look and shake my head. "No, Steven. I don't," I reply, confused.

He points to the screen. "Look at your stuntman. What is wrong with your stuntman?"

I look. I say with uncertainty, "Steven, I don't see anything."

Steven jumps up laughing and puts his finger up Bernie's nose on the screen. "Bubbles, Steven. He has bubbles coming out of his nose. He is supposed to be dead! He is supposed to be a ghost."

I look at Steven, I look at the screen. It finally hits me. "Oh, you're right." I start laughing with him. I went to Bernie and told him that he couldn't have bubbles coming out of his nose, it was okay for Janet, but not him. We try again and this time instead of twenty five bubbles, there were three. Still not good enough. Spielberg wants zero bubbles. In my mind, I am thinking we can just CGI the bubbles out. Of course, I don't have the guts to say that to Spielberg between you and me.

I don't know why he didn't say it himself, but nevertheless, I had to figure a way to eliminate all bubbles. Cotton, I thought. It will fill up both oraficesesesesesesses. Lol. In other words, I'll shove cotton up his nose. Hopefully, no air will come out. I go over to Bernie with that idea and shove it up his nose. We painted it brown and went for another take. It worked wonderfully. No bubbles. Not a one. But it was hell getting the cotton out. Long tweezers. Now we have to do some of the scene with the actors. I ask Richard if he would mind putting cotton up his nose. He said he didn't, as long as it wasn't a finger up his rear end. I laughed, remembering when that happened to me and told him the story.

Guess what? I couldn't put the cotton up his nose until he stopped laughing. He found it so funny he had to call Spielberg over which attracted the rest of the cast and crew and I had to retell the finger up the butt story with the Doctor. It took fifteen minutes for the laughter to stop before we got back to order. Richard wanted to do it himself and I told him that it might be a little bit uncomfortable since we needed a lot of cotton to stop the bubbles. He puts some in and I look at it and I can tell it is not enough. He puts some more in and I start feeling his nose and find it is pretty flexible.

"This is getting uncomfortable Steven," he says in a nasally voice.

I find some holes and say, "I'm sorry Richard, but we gotta put some more in."

He nods. "Okayyy," he said.

I shove some more cotton in and now his nose is packed. We go to do the shot with Richard and Holly with the plane moved closer to the surface. We shoot it and it worked beautiful, no bubbles and Spielberg was happy.

CHAPTER 56
(Producer Frank Marshall. My Guys Vs. His.)

Okay, let's finish up with this movie, *Always*. Mistakes, life is full of them my friends. Then you learn and move on. The story I am about to tell you may be a mistake to some, to others it would certainly be the exact opposite. I will let you decide. The big fire scene is about to take place. All my hard work in placing the shrubbery and logs is coming to a blazing end. It takes forty five minutes to set up cameras, as we prepare to set a square city block on fire. I have set up a scene with Spielberg where my stuntmen go into the flames and fight the fire and come out the other end after Holly's character rescues them with the dump plane. I get my men all ready, physically and mentally for this upcoming battle going through the fire with flames, a hundred plus feet high. They are surrounded. Everything is looking good, when the Producer, Frank Marshall walks over and asks to speak to me. He tells me he wants to put the professional firefighters he got, in the scene.

The ones he had insisted to bring over and that I had given the okay to use in the background. He wanted to use these men and women, (he brought a couple of women. I had all men, but maybe bringing a woman wouldn't have been a bad idea) for this scene. He goes on and insists that we are going to use these firefighters who have been training all their lives to go into the fire and put it out, just like Spielberg wanted. In the back of my mind, I know what he is saying is completely wrong. I let him finish and then I speak up choosing my words carefully.

"Listen, Frank. You sent me to firefighting school for a reason. One of the things I learned is that these firefighters don't go into the fire while it is still a big blaze. They wait until the dump planes come and reduce the fire to a few areas, then go in to finish it off. The embers, small sections. My guys are professional stunt guys, they are used to being in fire."

Frank looked at me and it wasn't like it almost went in one ear and out the other, it really did. As soon as I finished, he said, "Steven, I am the Producer. I tell you what to do and I want you to use my guys. Understand?"

I shook my head saying, "Frank, these people won't be able to do it."

He just didn't care. "I told you, use my guys Steven."

I finally agreed and went over to my guys to explain the situation. I told them to do everything they could to keep these people safe. They all agreed and we got ready to shoot. I could tell by the real firefighter's faces they are scared to death. They all agreed to do it, be it ego or whatever, but I could tell inside they were terrified. I showed them the path, which mind you, wasn't much of a path as the flames would whip across. I did this before we set it on fire and put safety guys all over. We have three dump planes coming to put out the fire, these things are very expensive to put in the air. Hundreds of thousands of dollars for each one and time consuming to fill up. Nevertheless, we are ready to do the shot. Spielberg is up in the tower and has no idea what just occurred on the ground. Spielberg takes his megaphone and yells down to me, "are you ready Steven?"

I tell him I am. Before we rolled camera, the dump planes were already on the way. A minute away. I look at the firefighters. In my eyes, I saw fear from these fighters. I asked them if they were okay, "Are you sure you want to do this?" I asked.

They say, "yes." Hesitation in their speech. Thirty seconds later, I cued the FX guy to set everything on fire. Flames roar everywhere. It is HUGE. A hundred and fifty feet high. I look at Frank's firefighters who are white as a sheet.

"Action! Send your men Steven," Spielberg calls down.

Frank's men start running towards the fire. A few of them take a few steps and then stop. Some go in before coming right out. They look back at me and I'm yelling, "get in there, get in there!" Two or three go in while the rest back up. The heat is tremendous. I'm yelling to go in, but as soon as they enter, they pop right back out. My guys are slapping fire gel on them and trying to give them confidence to get back in there, as I am doing. It is a nightmare and embarrassing. They keep looking at me as Spielberg yells in his megaphone.

"What is the matter with your guys Steven? Get them in there, the dump planes are coming. What about that one, what about that one, get them there!"

I try my best, but it's a losing battle.

Spielberg yells down again. "Why are they at the edge? Get them inside!"

This goes on and repeats itself in a vicious cycle. Nobody is going to stop these dump planes, they are five seconds away.

I am yelling, "get in there, get in there." Not one listens.

Spielberg is yelling at me, "get them in there Steven."

These guys are horrified, they don't want to go in there. The dump planes are right over us. The bottoms open and I see the three planes dumping thousands of gallons of water over the area. Cameras are rolling, the water hits the fire. The fire goes out in some places, it is still burning in others. Now would be the time for the firefighters to go in, but this is not what we set up.

Spielberg yells, "CUT!"

(Free falling log. Almost took my head off.)

Guess what? Nobody is in that fire.

Spielberg puts his megaphone to his mouth. "Steven, what the hell is the matter with your stunt guys? Why didn't they go in?"

Now, remember what I told you at the beginning about mistakes? I'm a punk kid from Brooklyn, I always try to tell the truth but sometimes the truth doesn't prevail. The minute Steven yelled at me, I looked up at him. Now, a smart political guy would have shut his mouth and took the blame. But the point is, it is not just my guys getting into a fire. Not just any fire mind you, but a gigantic one that is going to take half a day to set up. This was also my reputation and principal on the line here, I thought.

I look up and I say, "Steven, you need to know. These guys that were just in there, they are not my stuntmen. Those were Frank Marshall's guys. He came over to me and demanded we use the real firefighters. Steven, I explained to him that real firefighters don't go into the fire until it is almost out. My guys are over there. These are Frank's guys. He didn't listen. I explained to him that you sent me to firefighting school to learn. And I explained that the real guys aren't the stunt guys. My guys will go in. Frank's guys as you see, won't." I was frantic trying to get it out. And again I say, was I smart? Did I do the right thing? That is for others to decide. Spielberg is listening, in fact, the whole crew including Frank was listening as I yelled up to him. Steven hesitated, thinking for about three to four seconds.

He brought the megaphone up to his mouth. "Those are your guys over there?"

I yelled up "yes."

Spielberg continued. "Okay, we are going to reshoot this in a few hours. Steven have your stunt guys ready, not Frank's guys. And Frank, you stick to the producing."

I nodded. "Yes, sir."

Pat Kehoe looked at me and gave me a wink saying not to worry about it. I shrugged my shoulders knowing in this industry a mistake is a mistake regardless of who did it. I turned as I see Frank Marshall casually walking towards me. He stops and more or less whispers into my ear. Now I know you are anxious to hear what he just whispered. It wasn't an apology. It was one quick sentence coming out of his mouth.

"Steven, you will never work for Amblin or Steven again," he snapped.

I looked at him and I said, "Frank, I'm just trying to help."

He said, "you heard me."

I walked over to my stunt guys and told them what Frank just said.

I remember one reply from Andy Armstrong simply saying to me, "don't worry about it. That is a bunch of bullocks."

A few hours later, second take with my stunt guys. Action! Fire blazing, stuntmen going through walls of fire. Here, there, everywhere. Cut! Standing ovation. Spielberg on the megaphone. "Your guys were beautiful Steven, let's move on!"

I debated with myself, the whole rest of the show whether I should have a conversation with Spielberg on what Frank Marshall said to me. I ultimately decided not to bring it up to Spielberg and just let it ride. What could I do? It's Frank Marshall, he is his number one guy. I would have just made the situation worse. Needless to say, that was the last time I ever worked with Spielberg. Thanks, Frank Marshall. I still have a wonderful memory and it's not of you.

CHAPTER 57
(Total Recall. Director Paul Verhoeven. What A Moron.)

Okay, let's tell another Arnold Schwarzenegger story. They are always compelling. The movie, *Total Recall.* The whole gang was there. Joel Kramer, Sven Thorsen and Billy Lucas and others. I was playing non-descript characters for a while until Joel asked me to play a nice innocent guy with a backpack going up an escalator. That is the way I saw my character. I mean since it wasn't in the script, I can define who I am, right? Who cares? I do, so hear me out.

I go to makeup, they powder my nose and tell me I am alright. I go put on my wardrobe and finally go to FX. They have a shirt and vest for me with squibs. These are not just any squibs, they are shotgun squibs. Triple loaded shotgun squibs. Let's talk about it. Three in one, triple the force in one load. They mounted about ten squibs on the vest.

Each squib is triple the impact on my body. It is like somebody hitting me with a sledgehammer. I'm going to feel these, but that's alright. No big deal, just give me more to react to. I go to set and met up with the Director, Paul Verhoeven and Vic Armstrong who was Stunt Coordinating and my buddy Joel Kramer, who was always there if Arnold was involved. Let me give you the skinny on Paul. Paul reminded me of some people in those documentaries from the mid nineteen forties, if you get my drift.

You know those guys who reach for something in the air with their arms and talk loudly? We get ready to rehearse and here we go. Wait. Paul sees something he doesn't like.

He calls up to us in a very Gestapo way and says, "stuntman! What are you wearing under your shirt? It makes you look too big. You, I said, what's underneath your clothes? Step forward."

I spurted out the most intelligent thing I could think of at the moment. "What do you want?" Armstrong and I explain to him that it is my vest to protect me from the squibs.

"I don't like it. Take it off," Paul says.

I blinked in surprise. "Paul, those are triple shotgun squibs, if he takes the vest off then he has no protection from the impact," Vic tried to say.

FX speaks up. "The only place else to put them is on his body and that is going to hurt."

Paul shrugged and said again that he wanted it off so I went back to FX and asked a simple question. "If I took the vest off would the impact be safe?"

He replies, "kinda."

I say, "okay let me ask you this way, is it going to hurt?"

He said, "yes."

I said, "on a range from one to five, five being the worst, give me a number."

He said, "five."

I shook my head in anger and said, "put them on my body."

So I decided to give it a try and please my Director. We roll cameras, there are about six of them and call action! The bad guys are running after Arnold as he makes his way up the escalator. There, I appear. Arnold grabs me, using me as a human shield and he is fired upon and the bullets strike me. Bam, bam, bam! The squibs explode, each one feeling like a full on sledgehammer, immense pain. Aw, that hurt!

(Two goyim and a Schwarzenegger.)

Now after three go off and in excruciating pain, I decide to play dead. Then, here comes the other three, one at a time. Bam! It hurt so much that it looked like I woke up. Bam, bam. So much pain, you could say they woke me up from the dead. The squibs are still going off as more bullets fly into me as my eyes are closed. Most people playing dead don't move. That was my intention, but the pain racked my body and I couldn't control it. I grimace and wince in pain, but the performance was wonderful. I played it. After we cut, Paul called me over and I thought he was going to congratulate me on the scene. Instead, he screamed at me. He just couldn't believe I wasn't keeping still.

"What are you doing moving around and making faces?" he asks. "After the first three shots, you looked like you were dead.

Then the others came and you woke up and then played dead again." I looked at him and started to explain. "Yea, Paul. Because they hurt. I didn't know when they were coming. Without the vest, those triple shotgun squibs feel like getting hit with a ton of bricks. Why don't we pretend I just wasn't dead yet or the concussion shook my body? To be honest, I think it looks realistic." I tore off my shirt and revealed huge red welts on my stomach and chest.

Paul squinted his eyes. "Well, look at this. This guy is trying to teach me how to direct!"

I shook my head as this wasn't the first time that I had heard that before. "No, no," I said with a big smile and a small giggle.

You see I found it humorous that a man like him who is supposed to be so intelligent would think and say something like that. They come in all kinds of packages, I guess. "I am not trying to teach you how to direct Paul, I just think it works and without the vest, there isn't much I can do, there is nothing anybody can do PAUL. Nobody is going to not be able to move. That is a fact." I glance over to my boss, Vic Armstrong. Nothing said, he is silent. I look at my friend Joel Kramer. He is laughing his ass off. Oh by the way, so was Sven Thorsen. He showed up too. "It's going to hurt. There is going to be movement," I said.

Paul didn't seem to care as he yelled at me to keep still again. "If you can't do it, just bring in someone else!"

I looked at him and said, "I'll tell you what Paul, if you show me how, then I'm sure I will be able to do it."

He looked at me confused, speechless for a moment before I told him what he got was what he got. He printed it and as far as I'm concerned, if you print it, you like it. When I saw that scene in theaters, it looked wonderful, movement and all. But over the years, I have come upon some articles that friends send me every now and then from magazines. They always make fun of me saying "that's the guy who didn't know how to die." Little did they know the real story. At the end of the stunt, Arnold picks me up and throws me on top of the bad guys and other people on the escalator. If you think that was bad, listen to this.

During another scene where bullets were flying and squibs were exploding, an Irish stunt man named Bronco McLoughlin (a fine and funny man he is. Good natured.

Great stuntman. Armstrong brought him over from England) had his arm too close to a squib went it went off. Guess what, we were doing a scene with about twenty five guys taking bullet hits all over the place. At the end of the scene we went over to him and our eyes went wide.

His arm had a clear see-through balloon like swelling on it. It was the size of a softball. You could literally see through it and the chunk of flesh beneath was sickeningly visible. The tendons and veins were on display. About two inches deep. It was bad and Bronco was in pain. Anyone would completely understand if the production was stopped and we waited while medical treatment was administered. Paul Verhoeven, Mister no compassion, was not just anyone.

"What is the hold up?" he did say, as he looked right at the injury. "Get him off the set, we don't need to deal with this. Get somebody to replace him, let's go again. Quick. Move him!"

I couldn't believe what I was hearing. It was one of those moments where you wonder where someone's humanity went.

(Steven, let's make fun of Paul Verhoeven today. He's a moron.)

Let's turn the page on a heartwarming story on this movie, *Total Recall*. I was on set ready to take some bullet hits off a second story balcony. I was being shot at by Arnold of course when a Production Assistant came running up literally twenty seconds before we rolled camera.

"Steven? Steven Lambert!?" he called out.

I waved at him and the look on his face told me something big had happened.

"That's me," I said.

"We just got a phone call. Your wife, she just went into labor! I was just told," he yelled.

My wife had been pregnant with my first child, my daughter for a few months now. I looked at Joel and Arnold standing side by side. I call out to Joel, "what am I going to do? I am in the middle of a scene. I'm all squibbed up."

Arnold just yells out, "we'll just replace you, go now. Get to the airport."

Paul Verhoeven screams out, "what is the hold up? We must finish!"

Arnold yells to Verhoeven, "shut up, you."

Joel says "go to the Production Office and they'll get you a flight right away."

Arnold says, "just make sure you call us when you are ready to come back."

I couldn't believe what I was hearing. I looked at Arnold who put his hand on my shoulder. "Steven, this is a great honor, do not worry. They will fly you first class."

I smiled and shook my head. "You don't have to do that Arnold," I said.

"No, I want to," he replied.

I went to my Director and told him what had happened. He congratulated me and told me to go see my wife immediately. That is what I thought he was going to do.

Instead, he looked at me and said, "why are you telling me this? Get to places, I don't have time for these minor things." That was Paul Verhoeven for you. The dirty rat.

Nevertheless, I soon found myself on a flight back to Los Angeles and saw my daughter be born. It was a once in a lifetime moment. I called Joel up a few weeks later when I was ready to return to work and I came back right away. When I got to set, Arnold greeted me with a box of cigars as a present. I hear Sven Thorsen in the background.

"Steven, you low forehead. Now you have proved you are a real man," he laughed. "But let me look, let me make sure you have something down there, let me look at it."

I tell him to take a hike while we all laughed and I passed out the cigars. Speaking of cigars, here is another Sven Thorsen story. Now you have to know him to understand. I happened to be at his house one day admiring his antique ashtrays.

Sven said, "Steven, do you like them? I know where to get them."

I said, "sure."

He said, "it is a cigar place called The Tavern in Los Angeles. We will go tomorrow."

Well, we did. When we got there, he introduced me to the owner. You could tell they were very close. I went through the place admiring many ashtrays when Sven took a moment and walked up to me. He asked which ones I liked. I showed him my three favorites and then he asked me to walk away. I said, "why?"

He looked at me and said, "you idiot, just listen to me."

I shrugged my shoulders and I did. Then I turned and was shocked at what I was observing. Sven, putting these huge glass ashtrays in his pants, underneath his jacket and in his pocket. I looked at him as if to say, what the hell are you doing? He put his finger up to his lips and motioned for me to be quiet. We went on for a few minutes, looking around the store before saying our goodbyes to the owner. We got out to the car and he handed me the stolen merchandise.

I said, "you stole these. Why?"

He looked at me and simply said, "I wanted to see if I could do it. Don't worry, Steven. I'll come back tomorrow and pay for them. I do it all the time. Look at the cigars I took."

I watch as he pulls out a handful of cigars. That's Sven for you. A few days went by enjoying many evenings playing tennis with these guys, including Arnold. You see there was a tennis court on the roof of the hotel, all caged in. We would play at least two to three times a week. Most of the time I was on Arnold's side against Joel and Sven. I've been playing since I was about sixteen years old and Arnold always wanted to win. The arguments were hilarious. We all made fun of each other. They were really moments that will always be extra special to me because for two hours a night, we would all be like a bunch of kids. Playing, laughing and doing goofy things in that cage on the hotel roof. Get this. One night goyim Joel Kramer called me up and invited me to go have sushi with Sven and Arnold. We walk about five or six blocks through Mexico City to the sushi place. We sit down at the bar, Joel, Arnold, Billy Lucas, Sven and I. There is a stranger to my left who is already eating. A few minutes go by and we are enjoying our yellowtail and salmon eggs, which everybody ate except me. This is one guy that hates that stuff. There we are sitting in a row eating roe (fish eggs). You find that one funny? Do ya? When before long, this stranger sitting right next to me at the bar, pulls out a pack of cigarettes, takes one out and lights one up at the sushi bar. Picture that. Now there is a time and place to smoke, but inside a little sushi house where you are having fish? That is unheard of except maybe for in a movie. Our raw fish was quickly becoming smoked salmon. I look up and see everyone to my right making faces, clearly bothered by the smoke. Okay you readers, you ready for what is coming? Sven shoots his eye line at me. It is a look. The look of trouble coming. He speaks up to the sushi smoker

and says, "hey, you over there, excuse me, are you a moron?" I see everybody's eyes light up in amusement as mine lit up as well. We all knew something was coming from Sven, but we didn't know what. The smoker moves around grains of rice on his plate, ignoring him. With a little more gusto in his voice,
 Sven yells, "hey you, we are eating here, what's the matter with you?"

The sushi smoker turns to Sven and stops. He reaches up towards the cigarette, takes it out of his mouth...turns and puts it back in! Sven leans into the table with his huge head looking like he was about to go Viking and I see Arnold smile. Sven's head disappears as I see him slowly rise up from his chair. The funny part is all through this, Arnold was always looking straight ahead. He never turned his head to look at what was going on, but you could see the humorous expression on his face. Sven passes Arnold, he passes Joel and he passes me as I look up at him. He winks. He walks behind the smoker just as he goes to take another drag on the cigarette. With perfect timing, Sven's hands rise up. One towards the lit end of the cigarette, the other to the back of the smoker's head. BAM! Like a vice, he clamps his hands together, Sven's hand smothering the man's face and the lit cigarette. I can see the vibration, it is almost like he is squeezing a coconut. My friends are jumping out of their chairs laughing while this guy is struggling to remove his head from Sven's Viking grip. I still can't believe as six seconds go by, he has his hand crushing the lit cigarette against the guy's face. Finally, Sven releases his grip and the guy goes crashing to the floor. Sven gets up into a semi square horse, ready for the attack, as the sushi smoker rises to his feet. He goes past Sven, right past the four of us, and out the door faster than you can say sashimi. We look at Sven and start laughing.

I say to him, "let me see your hand." He turns it and I see a burn mark. It's red and I can tell he has burnt a bunch of skin.

I ask him, "do you want some ice??"

He looks at me and says, "Steven, that's so sweet. You want to kiss it too?"

I throw his hand away and say, "let's get out of here." Okay, this is my last and final story on *Total Recall*.

As Arnold would say, "it's a good one." Some of you are going to find this very hard to believe, like I still do, to this very day. But it's a hundred percent true. It is, I promise you. I was out walking down the pink zone of Mexico City, with Arnold, Joel and Sven. We went to eat some enchiladas and tacos. Mexicana food with a little rice and beans and maybe a cerveza. O'le. We had a wonderful conversation about life on set. Watching Sven Thorsen sing with the Mariachi band was fun to see. You should have seen me play the matador with Sven's fingers up on his head playing the bull. He would come at me and I would duck and dodge and hit him over the head with my maracas. We had Arnold laughing the whole noche. It was about eleven at night when we started walking back to the hotel. We were staying at a beautiful and traditional hotel, an A list hotel, in the heart of Mexico City. One of the best. It just so happened to have four foot high hedges all around it. We were walking across the street from the hotel. Mind you, streets in Mexico City are not that wide, so we were close and in sight of everything that would be going on. All of a sudden, I see some movement in the bushes. Hey you readers, you ready for this? I speak up to the boys, "what the hell is that in the bushes?"

I hear Sven say to me, "where?"

So I point. We stop and we are all looking at these bushes.

I hear Sven yell, "what is that?"

Arnold goes, "it's people."

Joel speaks out, "what are you doing in there?"

Sven calls out, "we see you. You come out or we are going to come and get you."

All of a sudden, we see a head pop up. It seems like it is looking up to the sky and bobbing up and down. We still couldn't make out who it was but I realized it was two somebodies in the bushes.

"What are you doing back there?" Sven calls out.

The bodies straighten up and my eyes focus in and I can't believe what I am seeing. Was it a monkey? No. Was it a bunch of kids? Nope. It was a Verhoeven. A Paul Verhoeven! The Director.

I turn to Arnold who steps forward and calls out, "Verhoeven?"

The head looks at Arnold and another head pops up. Guess what? It's a Mexican stunt woman working on this show.

"Can you believe it, I can't find the earring," she says.

Sven roars with laughter. "You liar, you are full of big stories tonight. We know what you are doing. You moron, go upstairs and do that. I can't believe you are having a party in the bushes when you have a beautiful room." Sven smiles at us.

Well just like that, Paul and the stunt woman run out of the bushes like speedy Gonzalez. What were they doing? It sure looked to us like they were having happy time in the hedges. We couldn't stop laughing all the way back to our rooms. None of us could figure out why Paul, who had the second most fancy suite in the hotel had to go out into the bushes to do the hokey pokey. I went to sleep thinking about what would be said the next day. Joel and Arnold kept quiet, but not Sven.

"Tell us what you were doing in those bushes. Is that what you do in your neighborhood," Sven would ask Paul. "Verhoeven, where you going, don't run away from us. You told us you were looking for an earring. You lie. Maybe you had to go pee-pee and she was holding it for you." Sven kept this up throughout the day.

Paul would ignore him and scurry off. Now you may ask, what happened to the Mexican stunt woman. Like that ancient Mexican City, El Dorado, she just vanished. Never to be seen again. You never heard this story in the tabloids, did yea? Moving on. Oy vey!

CHAPTER 58
(Charlton Heston. Holding The Heavy Bag For Moses.)

I get a call from another knish, an Israeli one. They seem to be attracted to me even though I don't wear a yarmulke. It's Second Assistant Leo Zisman and he tells me he is doing a film called *Solar Crisis* and asks me if I'm available to come in.

(My first spacewalk with Andy Armstrong. On our way to craft service to have some bangers n' mash.)

I say, "sure, but I hope it's not on the Sabbath."

He laughed. The Director is, guess who? My good friend "Mad Dog" Sarafian. I go in and see Richard and he mentions the Busey film. Amongst other things, he called him a drunk and a whacko. That's Sarafian for you. He never hides his feelings on whatever he is thinking. That's why I always called him mad dog. He had the face of a pit bull and the attitude of a nineteen thirties gangster. After I got the script, I got up and looked at him. "Mad dog," I said. He looked at me and laughed.

"Get out of here," Sarafian replied. He liked my nickname for him.

"Not before you give me one of those stogies, you cheap bastard," I shot back.

I think he liked me more than most because I gave him that Brooklyn, rough and tough and brash attitude. He seemed to enjoy it like he was back in the streets of New York. Every once in awhile, when I would have a discussion with him, I would bring my arms up, spread my legs and brush my forearms against my sides doing my version of Cagney. He would just give it to me back. He handed me a cigar and I left. A few days later I went to set confident of what I wanted to do. One of the things I did was double a guy in an explosion with an air ram in a very narrow tunnel. Sarafian didn't want me to hit the walls since he needed the tunnel for other scenes. Sure enough, I went right through that sucker like an arrow, as explosions ripped through the tunnel behind me. The last story on this show is of Godly significance to me. Working with Moses, Charlton Heston himself. *Ben Hurr, The Ten Commandments, Planet of the Apes*, the list goes on and on of the films he has done. I don't usually get excited to meet actors unless they are throwbacks and old style actors. Charlton Heston sure was one of them.

There is a scene where he is in the space ship recreation room hitting a heavy bag as he is being given a report. I had assumed I needed to instruct him how to hit a heavy bag. The First Assistant escorted me over to Heston's motor home. We knocked on the door and I hear an echo.

"Who is it?"

A big smile appeared on my face and in my head I said, there he is. The guy with the two tablets. My man Moses. He freed my people, he parted the Red Sea and then he closed the sucker. He opened the door and we were introduced. He invited me in and I proceeded to explain the reason why I was there.

I said, "Mister Heston, in this scene, you are going to hit a heavy bag. I would like to rehearse it with you."

He listened and then he said, "call me Chuck."

We continued our conversation leading into what I assumed I had to teach him. I asked him to come on stage so that I could go over some punches with him on the heavy bag.

He smiles and says, "okay kid. You lead and I follow." He begins following me to the stage. Then I hear his voice from behind me. "You know, I had a great stuntman."

I replied, "I know."

"Did you ever meet him?" he asked.

I said, "yes, in a barber shop. The old fashioned kind. Five bucks for them to use a scissors on you. I happened to walk into this barber shop and there he was, getting a cut. I sat down in the chair right next to him, stuck out my hand and told him it was an honor to meet him."

Heston then went on to explain to me, that Joe's father, Yakima Canutt, directed him in the classic chariot sequence in *Ben Hurr*.

I said, "I know."

Then he reached out and put his arm around me.

I said to him, "this might seem kind of corny, but it really is an honor to meet you. You are larger than life." It was too bad I didn't have a cell phone. It would have been the perfect picture. I said, "I can't tell you how many times I sat with my grandfather and father watching all of your movies on a black and white television." The hand over the shoulder became a big hug. Can you imagine that? As I opened the stage door and we walked in, it was a magical moment. We go to the heavy bag and without thinking, I say something very naive. "Have you ever boxed?"

He takes his hand, extends it passed my chest and literally pushes me back. It was as if I had just questioned Moses if he could find the way out of a desert in forty days and forty nights, as he walked over to the heavy bag and started throwing punches. I smiled. The punches were beautiful. I look at him and apologized. "I just want to make you look as good as possible and was ready to teach you, but I see there is no need."

He smiled, turned and threw two or three punches at me. I stood there not reacting.

"Get your hands up," he said.

I replied, "what do you mean?"

"Let's spar a little bit," he replied, his hands up. He proceeded to throw and I proceeded to block. Chuck said, "you're very good."

I simply said, "Kung Fu boxing." Then we walked off. I think he had no idea what I meant. After lunch, it was time to do the scene. They were rehearsing and I see this extra holding the heavy bag for Mister Heston. Suddenly a light bulb went off in my mind, a firecracker. I thought to myself, the extra ain't holding that bag for him. YOU are Steven! Now listen to this genius plan. I ran over to Wardrobe and told them I was going to have the extra come over and when he did, to have him take his clothes off. Wardrobe agrees and I go over to the extra and send him to Wardrobe. He leaves and I hold the bag for Charlton Heston. The First Assistant sees me and walks over.

"We got someone to hold the bag Steven, you don't have to do that," he tells me. I replied that the extra was changing his clothes and I was just holding it in the meantime. Charlton starts hitting the bag a few times and before long, he turns around to rehearse his dialogue with the other actor. Now here is my chance. I run over to Wardrobe, peeling off my clothes. I arrive at Wardrobe in my underwear and ask for the extra's clothes. Wardrobe hands them to me and I quickly put them on. I have about thirty seconds left before they shoot the scene and I sprint over to the set. The First Assistant walks over and he is giving me a funny look. "Steven, I told you we got somebody to do this," he says.

"No, you don't. I put on his clothes. Surprise, now I am doing it. So shut up get away from me and go play First Assistant. This is my chance to be in a scene with Charlton Heston. I want to hold the bag," I blurt out.

He asks, "does Sarafian know?"

I say, "he is going to know soon enough. He won't care because it's me."

The First Assistant looks at Sarafian and asks if it was okay.

Before Sarafian could say anything, I scream out, "say yes Sarafian."

Sarafian takes the cigar out of his mouth and says, "it's okay, let him do it."

And that's how I got to be on film with the one and only. Charlton Heston.

Yea man.

CHAPTER 59
(Air America. Mel Gibson, Robert Downey Jr. And My Friend Joel Kramer.)

Home one evening when my phone rings. I hear a voice.

"Hello Steven, how have you been?"

I hear a voice. "Hello Steven, how have been?"

No, I didn't just repeat myself, that is what I heard. "Who's this?" I ask.

"Andy," the voice replies.

"It's Vic," I hear it say.

"I thought you said you are Andy," I asked confused.

"It's both of us," I hear back.

Finally, it clicked. There were dual Armstrong on the line. Double the fun. It was pretty funny, to what do I owe this honor? I said, "what's going on?"

They told me they were working on a movie called, *Air America* and wanted to know if I was available. Well of course I was! I said, "thanks, guys."

They mention it was starring Mel Gibson and Robert Downey Jr. Not only that, they had a ton of stunt guys working on it. Thirty three to be exact in one scene, and I knew every one of them. A great bunch. After coming to set, the next day after breakfast, we were told by the Second Assistant, "go put your wardrobe on."

So I drifted over to my trailer. I take it off the rack and I instantly get concerned. Not because of the style, or the color, but because of the size. I notice they are jeans. Not just jeans, but bell bottoms. Not just bell bottoms, but hip huggers! I look at the size, size twenty seven. Right away my temperature starts rising. Too freaking small, I said to myself. I pull the shirt off the hanger. It is a t-shirt, size extra small. I squeeze into it and pull on the pants. I look in the mirror and I see I look like I had been hit with a shrink ray, but only my clothes shrunk and I stayed the same. This ain't happening. I don't wear clothes that I have to peel off. Where they hell are my baggies? This sucks. I was debating what I should do. I decided to go to Wardrobe and ask for a bigger size.

I go to my stunt bag and get my excuses out. My hip pads, knees pads, elbows, all of them. I had no idea what I was doing, but I had to come up with some reason to get bigger clothes that fit. I would explain to Wardrobe that I wouldn't be able to fit the pads under my clothes. I'm preparing the conversation in my head. I put all the pads in my hand and walk over to my door. I'm pissed at these tight clothes. I throw my door open. I jump out three feet onto the ground and as I'm landing, I look up and realize there is a shit load of people looking at me pointing and laughing. Then I realize it is more than just a crowd. It is between a hundred and a hundred and fifty people. Suddenly it dawns on me as I spot Vic and Andy Armstrong. Not only them but my old stunt friends. Billy Lucas, Vince Deadrick Sr, Mike Vendrell, Ralph Garret. You know who else? Burt Reynolds! I've never met Burt in my life but there he was laughing at me. Mel Gibson? Robert Downey Jr.? They were all laughing their asses off. Guess who is in the center of everybody making sure they got a peek and a good laugh? My good buddy, Joel Kramer. Everyone knows how I am with clothes.

Andy Armstrong comes over and says, "I did it to you. Joel told me to set you up."

They are pointing and laughing. I began to walk away from my fashion show when I hear a voice behind me.

"Where do you think you are going?" Andy asks.

"To wardrobe to get this stuff off," I yell back at him, smiling.

"Oh no Steven, we aren't letting you change," Vic laughs.

Wardrobe speaks up, "sorry Steven, we don't have any other clothes for you."

I stopped in my tracks. "Okay, you guys can have your laughs," I said. So snug in my hip huggers and extra small t-shirt, we shot the scene, the laughter of the cast and crew still ringing in my ears. Because they were still laughing. Only this time, in between my suffering of the clothes I was wearing, I was laughing too. And wore those suckers the whole day and hated it. I hid from everybody. They got me.

CHAPTER 60
(Actor Michael J Fox. Spoiled Brat.)

Hey, guess what? I'm going to have some of my favorite foods. Brooklyn dogs with New York onions, knishes on a cart and the best pizza around. It's the water I tell ya. New York, here I come. I get a call from one of the funniest stuntmen I know. The man that at any moment you can turn around and see a red clown nose on his face, he always had one in his pocket. A clown nose. Not only was he funny, but Conrad is an excellent Stunt Coordinator. Why do I say that? He is the rare kind that works as a team. If you have great ideas, he'll use them. I think that's one of the reasons he hired me so much, because of my ideas. He gives me a call and tells me he is doing a film called *The Hard Way*. And guess who is starring in it? He tells me, "your buddy James Woods and Michael J. Fox."

I say, "great, I am excited." The last two words I say to him always seem to be so simple, but in my mind, they have always been the most important. And they were "thank you." A few days later, guess who calls me up? Mister James Woods.

I pick up the phone and I hear, "is there a rabbi in the house? Is there a guy who can rock the dreidel?" Right away I know who it is.

I ask, "how are you, I miss you."

A warm voice responds. "Hey Steven, we're doing a new film called The Hard Way and I told them to bring you onboard. It films in New York and has a lot of action in it," Jimmy says.

Wanting to give my good friend the gratification of letting me know since Conrad already told me, I said, "sure, I'll see you there. Thanks, buddy."

Before we hang up, he mentions to me, "you will be staying in my hotel."

I explained to him, "Jimmy, I have to go to the hotel they tell me to stay in."

A pause on the other end. "I'll handle it", Jimmy stated. He always did that, he always wanted me close by.

I relish that. If you ask me, I call it real friendship and most importantly, trust. He knew he could count on me in every way, shape and form and I felt the same. A week went by and I flew to New York. Came in with a few stunt friends at the time including Richard Hancock. You can call him Dick, as we did jokingly. Dick Hancock hahaha. He is a great friend and stuntman to boot. Peewee Piemonte and good ole' Bruce Barbour. Yes, Peewee Piemonte. Funny name, but you should see him. He is a bodybuilder. Bruce Barbour, a timid man who owns about forty seven different types of guns. That may be a little bit much, but he sure has got a lot of them. Richard told me on the flight over that Conrad was having him double Michael

J. Fox. I thought that was great as I was doubling James Woods. Richard is always a good man to work side by side with. I got in and the next day went to set. One of the first things I notice is that Michael J. Fox has another double named Charles Croughwell who had doubled Michael on *Back To The Future*. When an actor like Michael requests someone, they get them.

Now there was a big car roll stunt in this film during the first week of the show, that Michael J. Fox's stunt double had to do. Now Conrad didn't know Charlie Croughwell, but he knew Richard and his abilities and very much trusted him to do exactly what he needed. And that, my friends, is very important. Conrad assigned Richard to do the car roll, but come to find out there was only one problem. Charlie Croughwell found out and he told Fox.

Charlie told Michael that Conrad was taking away from him, one of the biggest stunts in the film. Fox had a meeting with the Producers and Conrad, demanding Charlie do the car roll. This is what Conrad told Hancock and me. There was a big showdown regarding this and because the Director who was John Badham, thought so highly of Conrad, he listened to Conrad and went with Richard. Well, Michael J. Fox was furious. The Director went over Michael J. Fox's head which surprised me as Fox was in high demand after his *Back To The Future* films were a hit and he was the lead on this show. Nevertheless, Richard did the car roll and it was just fantastic.

At the day's end, it became much clearer that the friendship between Michael J. Fox, Charlie Croughwell and Conrad Palmisano had drastically changed within a day. When Conrad and Richard said "hello" to Michael or Charlie, they would just ignore them. Guess what? For some reason, I got the same thing! I figured Charlie told Michael that I was close to Conrad. Being that Conrad made Hancock and me his right hand men, I was caught up in this feud as well. Why me? A punk kid from Brooklyn.

As days went by, it kept getting worse as we began to work with each other more and more. It quickly became clear that there was only going to be one way to settle this. The hard way. Example number one. There is a sequence where Michael J. Fox is fighting ninjas in his character's action movie. Conrad asked me to put together a scene and I thought up a wonderful sequence. In the beginning, Michael J. Fox swings down from a vine to save a damsel in distress.

Now, I have put together this fight sequence already, rehearsing it with Michael J. Fox before this whole car situation occurred. I have already rehearsed this dream sequence with Michael several times and showed it to the Director and the Producers. Here is a little fact that will bring us to a special moment later on. When

I showed it to them, I had a little visit with Rob Cohen and he was nice enough to say to me that he didn't know I knew Martial Arts and was very impressed. He commented that his next project was a Martial Art movie. If I was interested, he mentioned I would be a good fit to be the Action Coordinator.

Like a quick breeze going by, I said, "sure, thank you," and went back to work thinking how many times I have heard that before. In other words, most of the time, it is BS. Conrad asks me to get the harness so we can see how Fox looks swinging in on set, into the group of ninjas.

Conrad came over to me and asked me to get Charlie Croughwell and go over to Michael J. Fox's trailer to help him put on the harness. So I did and went over to Charlie's trailer. I knocked on the door and Charlie opened it. When he saw it was me, guess what he did? He promptly shut it.

I start yelling through the door, "excuse me. Excuse me. Conrad wanted us to put this harness on Michael J. Fox." I am met with silence. Yoo hoo, anybody home? I knock on the door again and Charlie opens it violently.

He looks at me and says, "you want that harness on Michael? Go put it on him yourself!"

SLAM! Well, I was in complete shock. So what do I do? I had no choice. I went and explained to Conrad what happened and he was as shocked as I was. He told me to get the Second Assistant and go to Michael's trailer and help him put him on without Croughwell's help. So that's what I did. I knocked on the door and I hear Michael ask who was there.

"Stuntman Steven Lambert. I have a harness Conrad asked me to put on you," I replied.

I see the door open and there is Michael. He looks at me, looks at the harness and guess what? Slams the door in my face too! The Second Assistant looks at me in shock and asks what happened.

"I think he is a little upset," I say before explaining to him what happened with Michael, Charlie and Conrad. He was just as dumbfounded as I was, so I had no choice but to go back and tell Conrad what had happened. I'll never forget, with harness in my hand, seeing him. I couldn't help but laugh, watching the expression on his face as I come over to him. I don't even have to explain.

He knew already by simply saying, "he don't want to put it on, right?"

Then I explained in detail. I simply told him, "that little fidget did the same thing Charlie did to me. Slammed the door in my face."

Conrad takes the harness and tells me to follow him, so that's what I do. We arrive at Michael's trailer and Conrad knocks.

"Who is it," the voice inside calls out.

Conrad tells him and we are met with silence. I looked at Conrad with eyebrows raised. It was the perfect "told you so" moment. Conrad knocks on the door again saying that we needed to put this harness on to see what it looks like.

Michael opened the door and said, "if you want it on me, give it to Charlie. I don't need your help." Can you believe the lack of understanding this guy has? Making it personal. Conrad gave it to a Production Assistant to give to Charlie and promptly went on to talk to the Producers about this problem.

I discussed it with Woods later on and he said, "F that munchkin and his superiority complex."

Apparently, Fox and Jimmy were having problems on the set as well. I understood right away and realized there was more to this story between Fox and Woods as he went on to explain to me. As the days went by, we start doing the stunts on the giant mannequin billboard of Michael J. Fox's character in Times Square. I was surprised at the lack of safety set up for this stunt, especially since my boss Conrad is so focused on a safe environment.

I would be a hundred and fifty plus feet up in the air, keep in mind. I have to stick a wire inside the giant head, to an I bolt and hold on tight. I'm expected to fall down this giant fedora, no net, no crane, or secondary safety cable.

As you should know by now, I hate cables. I don't like to be connected, I can't move the way I want. But in this case, if I fall, I can't fly away like Superman, web-sling like Spiderman or get so scared to turn into the Hulk in the middle of my fall. And the five thousand New Yorkers screaming up at me, "fall, fall," would simply step aside and I would be as flat as a piece of matzah.

So it would be nice if we had a crane up there. I wouldn't mind removing the crane and cable in post, but it never happened. And face it, if I would have asked, I probably would have got it.

I always find it difficult working nights as it's hard for me to sleep during the day. Even when I had the chance to sleep, I was too excited! Why? Because my wife and kids were coming into town! One night after working on that giant hat, we went out and celebrated. Everybody came, save for Michael J. Fox and Charlie Croughwell.

What party poopers. I ordered steamed clams and we all had a good time. That night, knowing I had work in a few hours, I woke up at two in the morning. Immediately I realized something wasn't right. I was burning up! I had a temperature of a hundred and four, and couldn't stop throwing up. I was in PAIN! That was the last time I ever ate something non-kosher. At least for that week. I called Richard Hancock and he came to my room with Bruce Barbour and another stunt guy.

They saw how sick I was and asked if they should contact Conrad. I didn't want to bother him, so I asked them to take me to the emergency room. They had to carry me out as I literally couldn't walk. The hospital told me I had food poisoning and gave me a shot of antibiotics. I went back to my room and we discussed what we were going to do. We decided to call Conrad and he came up to the room.

Sick or not, I was determined to work. "I'll manage," I told him when he asked about my inability to walk.

Conrad nodded and after a few tense seconds, gave me the okay. So Bruce and Richard help me down to the lobby and we went down to the van. Once we got on set, they didn't take me to the trailers. No, they took me right on set in front of the Producers, the Director, Michael J. Fox and James Woods. They open the doors as I am resisting being assisted out.

You see, I don't want anybody to see me weak. I literally couldn't walk. I tried to present myself as normal. I don't mean mentally, I mean physically. I hope you agree. I was shocked and embarrassed. I look, not understanding why we are on the set. The Director John Badham and the Producers come over, see the situation and say something I will never forget. This whole night was filming all me, keep in mind. I realize they know I am sick, assuming the obvious - that Conrad told them, but I keep telling them I am ready to work.

"Listen, we think the world of you Steven," they say. "We are willing to shut this night down." Now I am thinking I have to be very careful here. It would be great to go back and rest, but this is a whole production night they would have to scrap. On top of that, I wanted to work, that is how I am built. On the other hand, I knew if I said to scrap it for that day, they might tell me it was no problem but inside they would be saying, "that son of a bitch, he's shutting us down for the night." So there was no way in hell I was going to say shut it down.

I told them I am here to work and if something happened to me, they had other stunt guys to take my place.

So that is what I did. Richard would help me to my spot, I would roll down the hat and hang and climb back up. No legs needed. No one would dare come out on that hat, so I would have to climb back up and then they would help me once I got to the door. I'm getting to the moral of the story here as I am working nights, not getting enough sleep and now I have food poisoning. On top of that, within the next few nights, my wife and children are coming in.

(New York City, Times Square. No CGI here.)

Within the next couple of days, finishing up different angles on the hat, working with the stunt woman, and the actress Annabella Sciorra, and James Woods on some pieces of the hat they recreated on stage, I find myself being told to put a harness on Annabella. I knock on her door, introduce myself and hand her the harness to put on. It is obvious she has no idea how to do it, so like a fine gentleman, I tell her I would go get the stunt woman to help her.

She looks at me and says, "it's okay, you can help."

A second later, I find myself watching her strip down to her underwear and bra. Man, blue was pretty on her. My jaw dropped as she turned and looked at me.

"Well, stop staring and put it on me," she laughed.

I did, happy as could be. This happened a couple times a night. Everyone would ask me why she would only ask me to put it on.

I said, "I don't know, but I'm a guy. I don't mind. Doesn't take much to make me happy." One of the times I was harnessing her up, she asked me if I wanted to hang out. I shoulda, coulda, woulda, but I didn't. I had to explain to her that I was married and faithful. Life is a bowl of cherries, sometimes you can't have the whipped cream.

CHAPTER 61
(Never Yell At A New York City Maid.)

Then the night came. Wait a minute, that doesn't sound right. Let me put that another way. My wife is finally arriving with my children. Doesn't that sound better? Production let me stop at two in the morning so I could pick up my family. That was a wonderful thing. So two o'clock comes, I'm still not feeling well and probably only got five hours of sleep in the last three days. I pick up my wife with my driver I was given and we go back to the hotel. I'm carrying one child in my hand. I'm tired and miserable and I realize I forgot the key to the door which happened now and then. I left it back on set. Wait! Lucky for us, I see a maid in the hallway. Thank goodness, here she comes to the rescue. I know this maid, as she had let me into my room a few times before when I had forgotten my key in the past. "Hey, how are you?" I ask with a smile. "Can you open the door?"

I look at my wife, happy the maid was there. But wait again, I see the maid shake her head as if to say no. Surely, I was seeing things. "You know me," I said. Please, I just want to get into the room." Again, she shakes her head no. "What do you mean, no?" I shot back, my patience quickly ending. It's early morning and I am in no mood for this. I got babies in my hands. I get annoyed and start reprimanding her. I turn to my Hispanic wife and ask her to translate what she says.

The maid still says, "not allowed, no more."

My first mistake. I pop my cork and start yelling at her. I don't say anything dirty or inappropriate, but I am extremely frustrated. She knows me and what I am doing here and she won't open the door. That is exactly what I am telling her. I scold her so much, after five minutes, she opens the door. I never cursed her or anything but I was just yelling at her for not doing something she had done before without incident. I got my wife and kids inside and abruptly closed the door. A stupid mistake one might say, even my wife was surprised. But I wasn't going to take the time to think about it. That was the second mistake. I was sick, tired and physically exhausted. I put my family to sleep and off we go to dreamland. An hour or so later my phone rings and my wife answers. She wakes me up and tells me it is Conrad. I get on the phone and ask him what's up.

"Steven, you are going to have to pack up and leave the hotel," Conrad stated.

I'm half asleep and I find myself laughing. Mind you, Conrad is a big practical joker, so that is why I am laughing. But Conrad wasn't.

"No, Steven. I am serious. You need to pack up and get your family and leave the hotel I am not joking. We have a new hotel for you, but you have to leave this one."

I asked him what he was talking about. Leave the hotel? Why?

"The Maid Union of the hotel called the production company," Conrad continued.

I started laughing again and I didn't know what the hell he was talking about and asked him to stop joking around. He assured me he wasn't. He simply stated that the Maid's Union had talked to the Producers and the Producers called me. The union told them I had scolded a maid to let me into my room. I feel the blood rushing to my head and I realized she must have gone down and talked to the manager.

"She was in hysterics," Conrad said.

I shook my head, "what? She wasn't crying."

Conrad takes a moment and says," Steven, Steven, it doesn't matter, this is where we are now. Either you leave, or the maid's union, ten thousand strong, is going to go on strike."

I looked at my wife and turned back to the phone. "Bullshit," I stated.

"No, I am serious Steven," Conrad said back. "The whole New York Maid's Union is going to go on strike if you don't leave the hotel. You want that in the newspapers?" (STUNT MAN FROM A MOVIE COMPANY CAUSES NEW YORK MAIDS UNION TO STRIKE)

Well, now I was starting to believe him. "Can't I apologize? I feel horrible Conrad," I tried to say. I told him what happened and he understood it wasn't intentional and that I wanted to apologize but his hands were tied.

"No, Steven. I suggested you apologize but they want you out now," I was told.

I packed up my wife and kids, big time embarrassed, frustrated and ashamed. Boy, you should have seen the look on my wife's face. I never did find that maid as much as I went back to the hotel to look for her. The guilt was just eating me up inside. I was embarrassed that Jimmy Woods was going to find out, the whole production crew was going to be privy to what happened. I tried to tell my side of the story to anyone who would listen. Even the van driver that would pick me, just me, up from the new hotel and take me to set. He understood, it seemed everyone I had been talking to did, but it didn't fix the problem one bit. We get to set and I run to my room and get dressed. I jump out and go to where we are shooting and start seeing everyone. I was hoping no one knew what happened, but deep down inside, I know the truth. Everybody knew what happened as I emerge from the van and I quickly started apologizing, trying to explain. No one says a word, they would just laugh. Then the Director and Producer Rob Cohen walk over, I was shaking in my pants.

John Badham speaks up. "Steven, we have been working with you for a while now. We know you, we know your work and we know that isn't like you to act that way."

I started hugging and thanking everybody. A few seconds after the tension, here come the jokes.

"Make sure Steven's trailer is unlocked, I don't want to get yelled at," they would say and we would all laugh.

This reinforced a lesson that would always stay with me. No matter what the situation is, what the causes, you should never let yourself personally get out of control like that. Always have respect and however the situation turns out, always learn to deal with it and do what is right. No matter how tired or frustrated you may be, keep in mind the other person has feelings too. Sticks and stones may break bones, but words can cause the whole Maids Union of New York to go on strike. By the way, Woods found out and like a great friend, he understood. That didn't stop him from calling me names like "Jewish American Princess." Here's another bit of history on Michael J. Fox's face in the fedora, or as my friend Jimmy Woods would say every time he saw that billboard, "I can't believe I have to look up in the middle of Times Square and see that narcissistic midget."

Jimmy had a rare way of bringing his humor out in such an off tempo and surprising way. In the way he said his words, it would just make you laugh. I found he would use this tactic in his acting as well. This tale involves me, Michael J. Fox, James Woods and Richard Hancock as well as my boss, Connie. Let's not forget Charlie Croughwell. There was a moment where Michael's character is trying to open the door on the hat and he is unable to initially get it open. Conrad asked Richard Hancock along with me, to go on the outside of the door on the other side of the hat on stage and told us to push against it when Michael tried to open it. He wanted to prevent him from getting through. He said he didn't mind if it opened a little bit, but it should slam back right away. We get into place and roll cameras. They call, "action" and I feel Michael try to open the door and we push back, preventing him from opening it. A few seconds of pushing and preventing go by and we find ourselves in a game of tug of war. Boom. Michael hits the door. We push back. BAM! The door gets hit again and we push back stronger, not aware of what Michael was doing. When I think about it now, I guess nobody told Michael what we were really going to do, specifically. Kaboom! We feel Michael slam into the door, the door inches open and we double slam back.

This goes on over and over again until finally, the Director yells, "cut!"

Not once, but several times as the war on the door is so loud. We hear screaming and here comes Michael, walking around the scaffolding. "

What the hell are you doing holding the door so hard!? I hurt my shoulder!" Michael yelled looking directly at me.

I shook my head in surprise and disbelief on how angry and neurotic he was. "I was told too," I said calmly.

He said, "who told you too?"

I said, "it doesn't matter."

Now he is angrier and clenches his fists. A little note to you readers, I'm just trying to protect my boss.

Michael stepped back. "What, are you stupid? You're a dumb idiot, is that it?"

Well, that did it. Again, why me? I was just doing what I was told and Michael is calling me names. Then I thought of something brilliant to say. Or maybe not.

"Have you ever heard of action acting?" I shot back. "I can teach it to you if you like," I said with a smile on my face.

I watched Michael's face change from anger to shock and back to anger as everybody arrived on set. Woods spoke up and said, "Michael, Steven was just doing his job, he was told to hold the door."

(Michael J. Fox, he whines more than my daughter in my hands.)

Michael looked at Jimmy, fuming for a second before his mouth began to move. The words I heard were two. Simply, "fuck you."

Jimmy replied in kind. "Fuck you too, you homo-sapien munchkin."

Michael promptly turned and marched away, back to his motor home. We all stood there in disbelief. I looked at Croughwell and caught him with a big shit eating grin on his face like he enjoyed what just happened. Then he turned and followed the Fox right into the henhouse. I mean motor home. That is where Fox stayed until they got him out. Nothing was said, nothing was spoken, but something inside was definitely woken. These kinds of confrontations and situations, big and small, unfortunately continued on throughout the picture. It seemed like Michael was very insecure. I would get into a number of conversations with the powers on the set, listening to them whisper to me about Michael's small man complex. You see those things aren't talked about on a megaphone if you know what I mean. Gotta be careful. I guess we became so close that they would just confide in me and tell me things like Michael was very uncomfortable and he felt that James Woods was overshadowing him. Even though he had a giant head on a billboard, it wasn't enough, I guess. There are some things I have found that start out as nothing but turn into something picture changing as I said once before. You may ask what picture changing means. Simply, a discovery that affects a piece of a movie. I was doing a sequence where the bad guy, the party crasher, jumps on the tow truck and James Woods takes off after him. Originally, there was really nothing to this scene.

The party crasher, Stephen Lang, jumps in the tow truck and James Woods jumps on and they wrestle before he gets knocked off by Nick Lang's billboard's cigarette. It was that simple. We go to rehearse it and I jump on the truck and we start driving down the street, passing by cameras. Stuntman Dana Bertolette was driving the truck (when he came out he was quite crabby, that's because he told us he had the crabs from Wardrobe.

By the way, he told that to his wife too. He insisted that, but we all knew better. We all laughed), doubling Stephen Lang, when halfway back to the first mark, I decided to hop off. We are going twenty five miles an hour and when I hopped off I expected to run with the truck, but instead, I went sliding like I was at a water park. I felt like Sonja Henie at the Olympics! I looked down and realized I was hydroplaning! I started thinking for a moment. That looked cool! This is where I want to offer up a lesson to my readers. I decided to talk to my boss Conrad and asked to show him what just happened. I told him when I jumped off the truck, I slid and if it was possible to make it more than what was in the script, it would look great. I had a feeling he would like it and I told him to come watch. What had happened was that transportation had watered down the streets and the water froze, becoming like ice. I was wearing rubber shoes and that is why I slid.

So I took the truck halfway down the block and told Conrad to wait and I would show him what happened. We began moving down the street, heading right for Conrad as I was on the side of the tow truck and Dana started speeding up. Twenty miles an hour, thirty miles an hour, finally forty miles an hour. I moved from the mirror to the side of the door and told Dana to make a hard right around the corner. He did and my feet went up and I'm flying like the American flag. A few seconds later, he hit the brakes and I let go just before we passed Conrad. I started sliding and continued right up to Conrad who looked at me with his mouth open.

"I've never seen a physical stuntman do what you do," Conrad said. "Best thing I ever saw." He was just in awe and to me, the words that just came out of his mouth were the kind of comments I always longed for. Admiration was the reward of my creative juices flowing like a thousand points of light. Thank you, Conrad.

(Hanging with the party crasher. Fifty five plus. Street skiing. Slipping and sliding. No cables.)

He decided to show Director John Badham and we did. He loved it. The lesson is to never take away what could be done better or greater, no matter how small or insignificant a stunt or action is. Don't be afraid to speak up and offer advice, you never know what could happen. The icing on the cake on this film was when we needed James Woods to do some shots on the truck. As wonderful as an actor as he is, gods bless him, he is no athlete since that is what I am there for. He would be apprehensive about doing these kinds of things.

That night, I was under the impression they were just going to do close ups of Jimmy, so I went to my trailer to get some shut eye. I'm in dreamland when I hear a knock at my trailer door. I wake up a bit alarmed and shout, "who is it?"

Two voices respond back. "It's John Badham," one voice says.

"It's Conrad," says the other.

Now I have been working on this film for a month and a half and I have never seen those two come for me together. This must be serious! I flick on the lights and squint as my eyes adjust. I tell them to come in and ask them what is going on. A few seconds of silence go by and I pinch myself to see if I am in a dream. OW! No this is real. Finally, Conrad speaks up.

"We decided to do some scenes with Jimmy and he got hurt, smashed his finger pretty bad on the giant billboard cigarette. Now he won't come out of his trailer."

That's right, a few hours after I went to my trailer, they wanted to shoot a few scenes with Jimmy and the truck, where the Party crasher throws him off the truck and into the giant cigarette, and they decide to shoot a few shots of him without me. Jimmy loses his balance and he falls and smashes his finger on the cigarette, bruised it pretty good. You could say he broke it. I shook my head, reminding them I had warned them to wait to do any action with Jimmy until I was present.

"We made a mistake," John admitted.

"Now I need to ask you a favor," Conrad said looking at me with a bashful grin. "Can you help us get him out of his trailer? He's been in there for half an hour."

My response, "what? Are you guys crazy? It's not my job." My mind was going a mile a minute trying to figure out how I was going to get Jimmy out. I look up at them and simply say to Conrad and Badham, "what, do you want him to get angry at me too?" I'm still half asleep here.

Conrad says to me, "but he respects and listens to you."

I look up at Conrad and I say, "so you want that to change?" Conrad laughs but Badham is serious.

"Please, Steven. He listens to you," John says pleadingly.

I shake my head in disbelief thinking in a manner of seconds, okay I have a choice here. Make them angry at me, or make Woods mad at me. Which is it, I say to myself. Myself answers. Okay let's give this a shot Steven but I just feel I'm being set up either way. Oy vey. We go over to Jimmy's trailer and discover it's empty. A Production Assistant tells us he went to the makeup trailer. Jimmy always liked to talk to the makeup people because they would listen. That's the case with a lot of actors, they often require a lending ear to makeup and hair.

We head over there and you have to understand when you open the door to the makeup trailer, you are met by mirrors. Anyone sitting in the trailer can see who is coming up the steps. The mirror reflects the people coming in. Badham goes first, followed by Conrad and followed by me. I see Jimmy sitting there through the mirror and we lock eyes. I have known Jimmy long enough that I can discern whole sentences from one glance. I say to myself, oh boy this is trouble. I know that look very well. Here his eyes were saying, "I know what they are trying to get you to do, don't do it, Steven."

I close the door and wait for the two heavyweights on this film, John Badham and Conrad to start talking. But they don't. Seconds go by as Jimmy is looking at me and I am looking at Conrad who is looking at John who is looking at Jimmy who is still looking at me. Hall of mirrors and I want out of this funhouse. I felt like I was one of the Marx Brothers. The circle of silence continues until all eyes shift to me, so I decide to speak up. I didn't know what to say.

"Jimmy, it was an accident, I have an idea to make it safer. I'll be there this time, please come back to set," I managed to say.

Jimmy looked at me before saying, "I told them it was dangerous and they didn't listen. Now they need you to bring me out?"

With encouraging glances from Conrad and Badham, I continued. "I know Jimmy, but we are all part of a team here." Long story short, he agreed and said he would be out in a moment. I still couldn't believe Conrad and John never said a word. It was like I was an animal trainer trying to get a tiger to come out of the woods. Jimmy Woods that is. I said to them, "hope you learned your lesson guys." They sure did. I told Conrad I had an idea. I asked him if we could build the floorboards out so I could lay down and hold onto Jimmy's feet as the truck is moving. The cameras wouldn't see me and he would feel safer. He agreed and that's what we set out to do. Right before we roll cameras, I look up at him and say, "Jimmy, you understand the position they put me in, I had no choice."

Jimmy says, "I knew that you Matzah Ball."

I knew everything was all right when he said that to me.

(Hair department wanted to cut my ponytail off. I said no. So they sent James Woods.

So here we are in the middle of a very busy Times Square, thousands of people on the sidewalks watching what is going on. As we come back to first position after the third take, I am lying down relaxed when all of a sudden somebody jumps on the floorboard and starts screaming.

"Hey Woods, hey Woods!" I hear.

Mind you, we are in the middle of New York, I have no idea who this person was. I look up and who the hell do you think I see? Christopher Walken!

He looks down at me and says, "hey guy, I hope I'm not stepping on you now."

I smile as he continues to talk to Jimmy.

"I saw you across the street, thought I'd say hi," Walken says.

Jimmy replies, "I'll call you tonight, we'll go out to dinner."

I move around as best I could, trying to keep Walken from walking on me. I feel weight leaving as Christopher Walken jumps off the floorboard. I told Jimmy how unexpected and nice that was and he nodded.

"You never know what kind of nuts you will find worming their way through the Big Apple."

I look up at Jimmy and I ask, "tell me the real story about Robert Wagner, Natalie Wood and Christopher Walken."

He looked down at me, smiled and said, "he was there."

For those who don't know what happened, just look it up.

CHAPTER 62
(Actor Miles O'Keeffe. Tarzan Meets The Viking.)

How about this, let's swing to the next tree. Hey, let me ask you something. Remember Johnny Weissmuller? Tarzan the ape man, king of the jungle. That was long ago from the nineteen forties and fifties. He was an Olympic swimmer, a triathlete. One hell of a physical human, a terrific athlete. Well, I got his alter-ego. The Tarzan that never should have been. The joke was on me. Miles O'Keeffe. Movie, *Relentless 2.*

You could say Miles looked macho, but I put him in the category of the tin man. He had no heart. In other words, he is a big chicken.

He was just one of those guys I guess, whose whole life was so gawked upon because he looked like Adonis, that he didn't have to do anything physical. In other words, it was a mind blower that he was so fragile. But he was a nice guy. I can't believe I was going to work with the latest Tarzan. Bo Derrick as Jane, remember them? Miles, a macho guy, I thought. I mean, Tarzan. Running through the jungle, jumping from boulder to boulder, fighting alligators, being in command of elephants. He was one tough guy. I mean his best friend was Cheetah. Boy, was I wrong.

Macho, he was not. Nor brave. Needless to say, he was an apprehensive ape. Michael Schroeder was the First Assistant Director on one of the "Ninja" films and how about this, now he is my Director. Well, guess who I got to hire to do a featured fight in the movie. The one and only. The Viking, Sven Thorsen.

Needless to say, when I brought him in to meet my Director, my Director fell in love with him as everybody does. Some people say it's his charm. Some people say it's the way he speaks. Some people say it is a certain type of presence he portrays.

What do I say? I know the real Sven. They are all fooled. He's all that and more. The big moron. I bring in the big man about a week later to explain the fight I put together and start the rehearsals. I ask him to find Miles and introduce himself as he was excited to meet Sven.

I was busy finishing up something else. About an hour later, Sven finds me and tells me Miles is very excited to work on the fight with him. I said that was great and we would start tomorrow.

A few minutes after that, Miles stops by to say hello to me, so I thought. But instead, he asks if we can talk in private about my stuntman. I say, "yes, but he is not my stuntman. He is an actor, a character lead on this movie." We shuffled off to his motor home and we went in had a seat.

"I met your actor Sven, and I am a little nervous working with him. He is coming on quite strong," Miles said.

I smiled and laughed and said, "I know exactly what you're going to say, so say it."

Miles took a deep breath. "The guy scares me."

Looking up at his face, I was shocked to see beads of sweat coming down. Yea, he was really scared of Sven.

He asked me why I am laughing.

"That is just Sven," I said. "That is just his persona, it is the way he jokes around. Believe me, there is nothing to worry about with him. You guys will get along just fine. He may seem intimidating, but don't worry. He is harmless."

The conversation went on. I couldn't convince him otherwise, but I had enough power in this movie to tell Miles that Sven was staying. Reluctantly, Miles agreed and I assured him that I would talk to Sven and they would be best friends. All the time, laughing inside. A short time later, as in the next day, Sven appeared.

In my poor Arnold Schwarzenegger imitation, I called out, "Sven, you low forehead. Come here. I want to talk to you." I asked him what was wrong with him, scaring the shit out of Miles. The whole time I am laughing which causes Sven to laugh. I said, "yea it's funny, but only to us. You got Miles scared shitless that he thinks you are going to hurt him."

"Sveetheart, don't worry," Sven said. "I will give him hugs and kisses."

I knew whenever Sven started talking like that, that mind of his was hard at work at mischief. "Don't give him hugs and kisses, just don't make him so nervous," I say.

Sven laughs. "Don't be such a moron Steven, here have a cigar." He pulls out a cigar and I take it, but I tell him to make friends with Miles.

"You got him so scared, he doesn't want to work with you. In other words, he wants to replace you. And that ain't happening. So please do me a favor, make nice to him and stop clowning around." Now for all you people who know Mister Thorsen, I am sure you are laughing while you are reading this.

So he says, "okay Steven, I'll behave myself."

I glance at him giving him a look. "Sure you will." The next day, I see Sven again and ask him if he is behaving himself.

Sven gives a deep laugh. "Tell Miles not to worry, I will love him."

I shake my head. "No, Sven, you tell him not to worry. We are going to be rehearsing in about an hour, so be nice because I insisted that it's you and nobody else but you, my sveetheart," I reply.

522

We both laugh. I just don't know what to do or frankly, what exactly is going on between those two but we head over to set. There is Miles and his eyes go to Sven and then back to me. "Miles, don't, Sven won't hurt you," I try to calmly say while trying not to laugh.

"Are you sure?" Miles asks.

I push Sven, forcefully, to the front. "Tell him, Sven," I say.

Sven smiles and says, "I am a butterfly. I am a sheep in wolf's clothing. Miles, I want to show you something."

I turn to him with a frown.

Sven walks over to a bunch of two by fours and picks one up. He goes over to the wall and places it at an angle against the wall. He drew his foot back and went to a hammer kick, shattering the two by four in half.

He turned to Miles. "Don't worry, I won't do that to you. You are king of the Jungle and I am your Jane, my sveetheart. I want to be your friend."

Miles turned white as a sheet and nodded.

I couldn't help but laugh. Here is the tag to this story. Miles O'Keeffe as nice as he was, he was very difficult to work with in a physical sense.

I'll give you two examples. In this fight sequence, you see a chain. Ninety-nine percent of the time, that was a real chain that weighed a couple hundred pounds.

In fact, I can tell you with all honesty, the only shot that was a fake plastic chain is when we dropped it around his neck when he looked up. Sven took a lot of abuse for two and a half days (and I thank him for that) where Miles, every shot he hurt his fingers and was worried about his face. It was a very difficult scene to make look good.

(Steven, you moron. The chain's too tight.)

All this time the fight that was going on with him and Sven, Miles would come over to me and say, "Steven, Sven is going too hard. Can you ask him to ease up?"

To comfort Miles, I would walk over to Sven and whisper in his ear. "You need to go harder."

Sven would turn and look at me and say, "okay."

I would walk back to Miles and tell him, "I told him to go easy."

He would thank me but for some reason it continued. The second example was fighting me in a scene playing an electrician in a construction site. In the opening shot of the action, he drops upside down like a bat.

Originally, I wanted that to be a full shot. Show you he is hanging by a two by four with his feet. I spent about an hour trying to get him to do it. Finally, I gave up and had two grips hold his legs.

(Miles O'Keeffe nearly pissed in his pants fighting Sven Thoreson.)

When you see it, you only see from the waist up, upside down. It was hilarious when he spoke out.

"I can't take the blood rushing to my face. I can only stay like this for six seconds." Miles might have been king of the jungle, but on this set the rare Sven-Ape was king.

I love that guy. As crazy as he is. It's a great crazy and I always enjoyed myself whenever I was around him.

(As I said, he ain't no Tarzan.)

CHAPTER 63
(Actress Dolly Parton And Her Twin Towers.)

Now let me give you some *Straight Talk* now. Starring Dolly Parton and James Woods. They were great friends. Everyday Dolly and James would have fun on set. James would always complain that his acting was hampered by Dolly's "breasteses." That's what he called them. Everybody from the Director and the P.A.'s would love and laugh at James Woods's humor.

They all knew it was in good fun as Dolly would make fun of his private parts saying, "I've seen those before and they ain't anything special."

James would retort, "I can't memorize my lines with your breasteses right there, Dolly. They keep poking into my thought process."

(Steven Lambert with the real Dolly Parton. She gave me a big hug and they sure felt real.)

That just shows you how much fun they had with each other. Jimmy and Dolly's friendship, I mean. Not Dolly's breasteses.

CHAPTER 64
(Actor Lou Gossett And His Boxing Debut.)

Um, let's move on, shall we? Remember *Diggstown* with Lou Gosset and James Woods?

I get a call from Mister Woods and he says, "I want you to coordinate. I'm putting your name in, so call them tomorrow."

As usual, I say my thank you. I called the Production company who then told me they already had a Coordinator named Jimmy Nickerson. Now I knew Nickerson from way back, the PARTY DAYS. You might know him from when he trained Stallone in *Rocky* and if you do some research on the web you can find some more about him and let me say, IT AIN'T boring.

I was simply told that I would be doubling Jimmy Woods. That was fine with me and six weeks later I went to get fit for wardrobe and found out Nickerson was on set rehearsing with Lou Gosset.

I went over to see him and we discussed his training for Gosset in the six weeks he was given before I got there. Nickerson said to me that they were training hard. Gosset was getting in great shape. Come time to film, that day I walk on set excited to see Lou Gosset and what he has learned over the last six weeks. I see him walk in the ring, take off his robe. Fat belly, flabby arms, is what I first noticed. I watch ten seconds of rehearsal in the ring and realize it is not going very well. Lou is not remembering the moves Nickerson has rehearsed with him.

After a few moments, Lou has to stop. Gasping heavily and slightly bruised, it is clear he was not ready for this kind of fight, or any kind of fight to put it bluntly. As Nickerson scrambled to get him to remember the moves, time went by and we hear the First Assistant scream out that they were ready for picture. They had to stop the first take as Lou was out of gas after just ten seconds. They tried again and this time they had to cut after fifteen seconds. He just couldn't remember the moves and looked like he was ready for a long nap. He was exhausted.

As they tried to continue to film over and over again, it became clear in the minutes ahead that after six weeks, Lou wasn't in any shape to do this fight. He had no endurance, his arms were flappy, his gut stuck out like a bullseye and he wasn't able to stay in the ring for more than fifteen seconds, let alone remember what he was supposed to do. All his punches and all his movements were simply horrific. Within a minute they had to cut four or five times.

This happened repeatedly, over and over again.

Finally, I'm watching as the Producers and Director storm into the ring and start to argue at Nickerson. You had six weeks, what have you been doing?"

Nickerson stayed quiet as he took the abuse. I guess it was obvious to me now that there was no training with Lou Gosset, he is the lazy type. But it is up to Nickerson, whether the guy likes it or not, to get him into shape. That was his job and he didn't do it. Everyone knew it. As this is going on, Lou shrugs and can you believe it, calmly walks off to his trailer.

But not before he says, "call me when you guys figure this out."

It seemed to me that he could care less. Jimmy and I are standing there half laughing, half in disbelief when he turns to me.

"I told them they should have hired you," he laughs.

I couldn't believe it. Six weeks and he wasn't physically ready and didn't know any routines or basic boxing moves. They fired Nickerson right then and there in front of the whole cast and crew. Talk about embarrassing. They decide to call it a day and move onto something else. An hour later, Jimmy tells me he talked to the Producers and to expect a call from them.

"Okay great. Thanks, Jimmy," I reply. I'm expecting this phone call and nothing happens the rest of the day on set. I go to my hotel room and fall asleep, my phone never rings. The next day I go to set and find out they hired someone else. What a surprise! I see a friend of mine that we all know in the Martial Art world. It is Benny "The Jet" Urquidez. He tells me they flew him in.

"Steven, good to see you," Benny says. "I have no idea what they want me to do, I can't create magic. I need time to train him. Haven't even met him." He asked me what Lou Gosset is like.

I look at Benny and say, "I just got to wish you good luck because you are getting ready for a nightmare situation. Lou Gosset can't do anything, no matter who they bring in."

Benny says," I can't train a guy while they are filming."

Like I said Benny, good luck. He asked me to help and we tried to do our best to try and get Lou to throw a punch. As nice as Benny was, he simply said to the Director and Producers Lou was too old, too fat and too tired to train day by day.

Just like that. It was great. Benny, the truth sayer. So I went on to assist Benny in his impossible task as you can't work miracles, teaching and filming the same day. If they had a good trainer from day one, it would have looked great. So that is why what you see in the movie doesn't look anywhere near as good as it could have been. They should have listened to Jimmy or got somebody else who was able to take control of Mister Lou Gosset.

CHAPTER 65
(Hoffa. Actor Jack Nicholson And Stuntman Mike Vendrell.)

Heeeeeeerrrrre's Johnny! Jack. Nicholson that is. The movie *Hoffa* starring Danny Devito, Jack Nicholson. Now hear this, we were on the set where we were doing a scene where Nicholson walks through about two hundred extras playing angry dockworkers.

Andy Armstrong who was the boss man went over to my good friend Mike Vendrell who was on set and asked him to be Nicholson's bodyguard in the scene. Jack had a habit of going where he wanted to and Andy didn't want him getting hurt. If someone got too close, Andy wanted Mike to push them away.

That put a big smile on Mike's face. We get ready to do this scene and the Director arrives and it's Danny Devito, who is also starring in the film. He asks Nicholson if he wants a rehearsal.

Jack smiles and says, "some guys may want a rehearsal, but not me." Jack laughs as we join him.

Mike walks over to Jack and says, "I'm Mike Vendrell, I'll be playing your bodyguard."

I'll never forget Jack's response.

He goes, "you think a guy like me needs a bodyguard? Who is going to protect you?"

Mike starts laughing. "Only in the film. And don't worry about me. I know Kung Fu." Mike turns and looks at me with a wink and I laugh.

"You mean like that guy David Carradine? I know that guy very well," Nicholson says.

"So do I," Mike replies.

Jack laughs. "We've smoked some good shit before."

Mike laughed even harder. "So did he and I."

Nicholson looks at Mike and asks if he has any good shit.

Mike replies, "yes."

Nicholson tells him to, "look him up later."

Mike Vendrell turns to me and in a Jack Nicholson voice, he says, "I'm gonna smoke with Jack." We both start laughing. I tell him to take a few pictures, I'd like to see that. The scene begins and they jump down into this sea of Dockworkers and it's hard to follow them. Then lo and behold, I spot a Dockworker being thrown aside, another one being redirected and another fall on his behind. After twenty, thirty seconds I hear DeVito yell, "cut."

I asked Mike what he was doing down there.

"It was fun, Steven. I was practicing Kung Fu, redirection," Mike said. It was wonderful, the Dockworkers didn't know what hit them. Nicholson was impressed with Mike's Kung Fu. "See Jack, you need not worry with me here," Mike laughed.

(The stunt crew of Hoffa. George Fisher said it couldn't be done. But I did it.)

CHAPTER 66
(Don't Ever Doubt This Lambo, Mister George Fisher.)

We had about two dozen stunt people working on this film. We have a truck sequence coming up and Andy gathers all the stuntmen in one bunch, almost in a line. He tells us he needs someone to drive the truck and someone to jump on the outside floorboard of the truck while it is moving with a baseball bat and break the window, while the driver goes up a ramp and rolls the truck. Andy asks Gary Baxley if he wanted to drive the truck and of course, he does.

Then Andy looks around and says, "Steven. You want to do this?"

I said "Hell yeah." I start walking over to the truck as Baxley does and start laughing, knowing that I was going to be working with Gary. I look up at him and say, "how about that Gary? Me and you. Too bad we are not fist fighting like I would with Corey Eubanks."

He just smiles.

I love those little inside jokes, all good fun. Some people there knew Gary and I weren't the best of friends as you know by now. I can honestly say it wasn't my fault. I tried my best in the past to be friends. He is a very good stunt man but as a human being, it was WAYYY DIFFERENT. What upset me was he could be a very nice guy, but he had another side to him that was mischievous and evil. It seemed that he would cause individuals hurt. Reread what happened with him in the Stuntmen's Association if you need to. Remember the Jim Wilkey discussion. Andy says that he is going to cut right before the truck rolls and they would do the second part in a separate shot. I know Andy knows me and I feel comfortable giving him suggestions. "Andy, why do we have to cut? I can ride the thing like a surfboard and fly off once it gets on two wheels. I'll do a forward dive roll way up in the air and crash in front of camera. It will look great."

I could see a smile as Andy thought to himself. "You could do that?"

I nodded firmly. I reeled my friend into doing my idea, but I seemed to have snagged somebody's ego. It happens a lot.

"You can't do that. It's too dangerous," a voice shouted out.

I turn around, shocked. I've never heard those words before. The guy keeps talking. My eyes dart back and forth at all the stuntman until they land on the one talking. It's stuntman George Fisher. I resented what he was saying and spoke up.

"Who are you to tell me I can't do that? You know what I can do. I'm sure you have heard. How dare you say something so absurd." Now listen readers, I wouldn't have spoken up in that manner to George, but as you see he started that. If he didn't believe I could do that, it should have been a private conversation. Not in front of the cast and crew, it showed total disrespect and gave doubts, which you should never do.

"No George. I won't get hurt. It's all about timing, disTANCE, foCUS, coordINATION aND POWER OF THE MIND, GEORGE! THINGS THAT YOU DON'T HAVE." I was real proud saying that because it came from my lessons in Kung Fu and I said it in a Sven Thorsen way, YOU MORON! I was furious. Everyone started laughing, while George continued on like an on set medic. I can understand if he was concerned, but I told him I would be fine and now he was giving my boss and DeVito doubts. Then the power of the Gods spoke, his name was Mike Vendrell. I hear his voice laughing.

"George, you don't know Steven. If he says he can do it, he can."

I hear another voice yell out in agreement, then a third voice and a fourth.

"You see George, people believe I can do it. So shut up," I finished caustically. I was pissed that he caused this whole situation, let alone telling me I can't do something that I said I could do.

Andy looked at me and said, "I believe you can do it. I've seen your work. Let's do it." We go to rehearse it and Danny DeVito is excited.

"I heard you are going to do this in one take. You aren't going to get hurt now are you?" He asked nervously.

I smiled and told him that, "I would be fine." We rehearse it and we stop right before the ramp and now we are ready for the big take. I tell Gary Baxley to go about fifteen miles an hour and make it look like I just make it onto the truck. Once I get on, I told him he could accelerate as fast as he'd like. "I will bash the window in and then ride you like a wild Bronc," I told Gary. We roll cameras and here comes Gary. I see he is going a bit too fast and I am saying to myself, "Gary wants me to miss the jump." So what do I do? I turn on the Kung Fu afterburners and jump onto the truck. Nailed it. He goes faster and I smash the window with the baseball bat. The glass shatters. One hand holding onto the mirror, the other, bat in hand. Here comes the car ramp. We are on two wheels. I surf for a second or two and then I leap off, flying through the air like Batman and hit the ground hard doing a single roll, crashing down in front of the cameras. I play dead and they cut.

"Magnificent," Devito says.

It was a hard fall and I get up slowly as everyone comes running over.

"Are you all right? That looked incredible," the crowd shouts.

I get up and who do you think I'm looking for? BINGO. I zero in on George Fisher and walk right over to him, feeling vindicated. "Well George, whaddya think?" I asked.

He smiled. "That looked great Steven, sorry I doubted you," he replied.

I forgive him and before I turn around, I whisper to him, "don't ever let your ego get the best of you and never doubt me." I walked off like a cowboy who just defeated a renowned bandit brushing off the dust from my clothes. Thinking in my mind, "that hurt." But I'm not going to let anyone else know as Mike Vendrell runs over and hugs me.

CHAPTER 67
(Robocop 3. Call me Conehead.)

Now how would you like to play a splatter punk? I did and this punk kid from Brooklyn became a punk from Detroit in the future, on *Robocop* 3. I had long hair then if you can believe it. I called it my Albert Leong cut. Some of you may know him as "The Henchmen." Some of you may say, who the hell are you talking about? My hair was all the way down to my back. I went to Wardrobe and left with a punk rock looking outfit. Then I went to hair. Hair thought my hair was perfect for this. For what you ask? They started to comb my hair straight up like Dan Aykroyd in the *Coneheads*. They sprayed it with cement glue to make it stick. It felt like it was three feet tall including my head. I went to props and got a pair of nunchucks. I asked them if I could bring my own, but in case something happened they had to use theirs. I knew that but thought I would give it a shot. You always feel more comfortable with your own. We went on to set to rehearse some things and the whole cast and crew burst out laughing at our hair. I asked Conrad if I could use my hair as a weapon. He laughed and said only if Robocop could swing me around by it. I said, "no, he'll pull it out. Bad idea, bad idea."

I'll remember that always, it's pretty funny. You had to be there. I fought Robocop after all. I beat him up and down with the nunchucks and then he takes me out with one shot.

CHAPTER 68

(Actress Rosie O'Donnell And My First Fifteen Thousand Dollar Weekly.)

Still on the wrong side of the law, I become an actor now in a movie called *Another Stakeout*. I am back with my pal Richard Dreyfuss playing a bad guy in a nine minute opening scene. He was happy to see me. It is also with Emilia Estevez and Rosie O'Donnell. It was great to see Richard and he was delighted with the part I was playing. I remember him saying, "I never saw a Stunt Coordinator turned actor."

I said, "don't forget, I'm Jewish too."

He laughed and said, "you are a mashugana in the cup also."

I said, "that's a good thing, isn't it?"

He said it was. We had built up a good friendship on *Always*. Every day on the set, I would teach him a simple form called the salute form. He so looked forward to it. Now, Emilio Estevez was an okay guy but very quiet. Rosie was the exact opposite. She wouldn't stop blabbing. I would use the word talking, but that's how annoying she was. You might ask me what she was saying. Nothing but jokes and they were bad at that. She got on everybody's nerves.

They called her the loudmouth. A surprise I got when I went to the office to sign my contract and when I read it, my mouth dropped. The weekly amount was fifteen grand, man. Yep fifteen thousand smackers. Dollars bills. American. Something wasn't right here. Stuntmen usually get paid around thirty five hundred a week. This had to be a mistake. I got up and went over to the secretary, showing her the amount and questioning its validity.

"Well, that is what they put down," she told me.

I asked to speak to the man. The man that brought me here. Conrad Palmisano.

(Richard Dreyfuss asking Conrad Palmisano how many more times we have to shoot this.)

She got Conrad on the phone and he told her it was correct. I'm in the dark as to what is going on here. I told her if it was a mistake, don't blame me. I made sure to check. A few hours later, I see Conrad in the hotel and ask him, "what was the story on that salary on my contract?"

He smiled and said, "there is no mistake Steven, I fought for that amount for you. You are acting on the show, this is what you deserve."

I thanked Conrad for that, just thankful for his friendship. We had many great times in the past. Most good, some strange, but I could tell he really had my back and I always had his and proved it a couple of times as he did me. I have worked for many Stunt Coordinators in the past and none of them took care of me as well as Conrad did and no one let me perform the things I wanted to do more than he did. In other words, he left me alone.

Always with class. That meant a lot that he appreciated my talent. I'm into my acting part on this movie. I'm crazed, in the moment and getting ready to do a four story high fall and there is no stopping me. I'm bulldogging Richard Dreyfuss out a window of a fire escape in one shot. They have hired a stunt man to double Richard, who has come from New York.

(Richard says, "first comes the Academy Award, then comes fighting in garbage. What next?")

I know nothing about him, he was hired by a guy I trust. There is a danger in that sometimes. You have to make a choice. Another lesson that I am offering you. I talk to him and ask if he knows how to come off after I bulldog him, how to release. You can't move around in midair. If we hold onto each other, there is no way to release in time.

He seemed nervous, but I trusted my boss for hiring him and trusted myself to stay away from him. When we did the scene, I saw the fear in his eyes as I ran at him full speed. I couldn't and wouldn't stop.

I hit him and immediately release him. I don't even grab him so to speak. Out the window and off the fire escape we go and the first thing he does, terror plastered on his face, is grab me. The one thing I told him not to do. He holds onto me and there is no stopping us now. This continues and now I can't redirect myself in midair.

When- Bam! He took me right into the fire escape. My head hits the fire escape and it looks like my head is torn off. Well little did the audience or even me for that matter know was that my arms were extended and that is what hit first, keeping my head enough away from the steel edge to avoid causing too much damage.

We didn't have an airbag, we used porta pits. I came down feet first as I had no choice, he was still holding onto me, can you believe it?

Not only did I hurt my head and hurt my arms, but I broke my ankle. I was in some major pain.

(Inexperience at its worst. He held on to me all the way down.)

Bernie Pock was there, doubling Emilio Estevez and he helped me out of the porta pit. I was wearing boots and he had trouble getting it off, my foot swelled up so fast! I had some choice words for the stunt man from New York who I knew now wasn't as experienced as I thought. But to tell you the truth, I knew it before, too. That's why I mentioned that last lesson. He could have literally killed me, but like the Aaron

Norris hitting me with the car, they would have looked at me crazy if I would have voiced my concern before. I mean nothing ever happens before, so they would have thought I was going nuts. That was the last day he worked on the show. I was asked to do the high fall two more times, broken ankle and all. However, this time it was Bernie Pock doubling Richard Dreyfuss and I had no doubt these two takes were going to be a success and they were. I refused to go to the hospital. I knew they would put me in a cast and tell me I couldn't work for weeks.

Well, that ain't happening. Luckily, Bernie Pock knew Chinese internal healing. For hours at a time, Bernie would try to get the swelling down with some herbal pack medicine that he got from New York's Chinatown. The stuff stank like rotten eggs, but it worked. Some of you may laugh and say that stuff doesn't work. Some of you might know first hand that it does help and that it did. I was on set for the rest of the week, luckily not working much and having Bernie continue to work on it along with hot baths and ice. Eventually, I had a running scene to do and by then my ankle was strong enough to get through it. A special thanks to Doctor Bernie Pock. Rest in peace. But the funny part about it is a couple of weeks after the show finished, the Producer called me up very excited to tell me. With laughter and joy, he says, "guess what? We are going to use the shot where that stuntman almost killed you. It's so scary looking." I laughed and said, "hey, whatever works."

CHAPTER 69
(Dragon. The Bruce Lee Story And The Queen Bee.)

Hey, let's reflect back in time when Rob Cohen mentioned to me that he wanted me to be Action Coordinator on his upcoming project back on *The Hard Way*. Remember that Martial Art picture he talked about me doing? Well, how about that? Some things do come true. His secretary called me and I go in to see him at Universal Studios. After waiting for a few minutes, he calls me in. I enter his office with a smile. Rob Cohen. I park myself and we chat for a bit about old times as he reaches down and opens a drawer. It's a script. He flops it down on the table and says, "this is the movie I want you to Coordinate. Dragon. The Bruce Lee Story." I stand up and I reach out and pick up the script and I can't believe what's going on. I'm shocked, utterly shocked that this punk kid from Brooklyn is being asked to take part in a story about the life of Bruce Lee. Here I was being asked to insert myself into the life and legacy of the great Bruce Lee, the legend. Rob asked me to read the script and break it down and asked me how long it would take me to read it.

I looked at him, mouth still agape and said, "I'll finish reading it tonight and give me a week to give you a budget." I couldn't believe all this was happening. "

Great, you got the job," Rob said. "I'm going to give you a call in a few days and I want you to come back in and meet Executive Producer Raffaella De Laurentiis and three guys that have the possibility of playing Bruce Lee, that I would like your help in choosing."

I was just stunned by those comments. Little did I realize that he was actually asking me to help in his decision to pick a star. Not only a star but something that was bigger than that. A Bruce Lee. I put the script under my arm, like a Roman gladiator being given a scroll to me by Caesar, to be read and delivered back when finished. I was so honored to be chosen. I said, "Rob, this is a biggie. A great task, but I promise I will make you proud."

Rob laughed. "I've seen what you can do on the Hard Way Steven and I have had many inside conversations with people about you. I know you can pull this off." He stuck out his hand and I stuck out mine and we shook. Like Rick Blaine aka Humphrey Bogart once said, this is a continuing of a beautiful friendship. Okay, I changed it up a little.

I got that return phone call from Rob Cohen and he asked me to come in the next day. I went into Rob's office and shook his hand. I turned my head and saw who I assumed to be Raffaela De Laurentiis sitting in a corner with her legs crossed, leaning back on a big Queen's chair. Rob introduces me to the lady who was who I thought she was. I wait for her to get up to come shake my hand. Seconds go by and I realize, this woman isn't moving. Like the Queen Of Hearts in Alice In Wonderland, I was a subject to bow down to her.

Yes, my friends, that's what it felt like. That's how she made me feel. Like a peasant. Come to find out, she treated everybody like that. I approached her outstretched hand, palm downward, with uncertainty. I wasn't sure if I should shake it or kiss it being that it was in the kissing gesture. Shake it I did instead of slapping it like James Cagney or stuntman Charlie Picerni would have. I introduced myself. She asked me to please have a seat, sit down. I did and we started talking for about forty five minutes to an hour on how I would go about training one of these three actors, one of whom would be chosen for the part of Bruce Lee. I explained the first couple of weeks we had to work on getting him physically fit for the role through Martial Arts and other activities.

Gymnastics, tennis, rock climbing, weight lifting, running, the list goes on and on. All these things were important to get him as close as possible to Bruce Lee. I also stressed how important it was to have someone from production get as many interviews and films of Bruce Lee as they could so we could start creating a likeness with the actor. Raffaella spoke up first.

In her royal tone, she asked, "why do we need to get all of this material of Bruce Lee?"

I explained to her we need the actor to watch and learn from this footage every day. Not just to imitate his physicality, but to interpret and translate his mental process. Without doing this, you aren't going to get what you want and what the actor needs. To become as much as Bruce Lee as possible and we all know that's impossible because there is only one. So we must work hard.

Rob Cohen jumped out of his chair and exclaimed, "told you we got the right person!"

Raffaella pursed her lips and said, "I still like my people better."

I looked at her in that awkward moment, realizing there must have been pre-existing conversations as to which person would do my job.

CHAPTER 70
(Steven Lambert Is The Casting Director.)

We ended our conversation with high spirits and Rob asked me to come back at one thirty to meet the first actor who was auditioning for Bruce Lee. Raffaella was still in her chair, a few feet away. She stuck out her hand and like an obedient lapdog, or Action Coordinator, I stepped over but this time I kissed it. Yes, even I kiss ass sometimes. The moment arrived and I went in to meet the first actor. I played the question game with him and asked things such as if he had taken any Martial Arts or gymnastics, was he familiar with Bruce and his long history and how agile and flexible he was. He told me he knew Shorin Ryu Karate. I was familiar with that as I am with all styles. That's important. It was a very hard style, not to learn, but just in its display and katas. I asked if he knew any soft styles like Kung Fu and he did not. So we moved on to the workout part of the audition. I spent about three hours with him, looking at his movements. I tried to show him the way Bruce would throw a punch or a kick. Bruce practiced hard and soft style, but even his hard style would be graceful and have a flamboyance to it. I had him do some pushups and handstands and wasn't very impressed. I asked if he could imitate Bruce Lee and he said he could. I watched him do what many fans of Bruce did, which was scream and pose. His scream didn't impress me nor did his pose, but we could always work on it, I thought. After the three hours I thought he had potential but would need a lot of work. I walked him over to Rob's secretary so he could talk with Rob and told her I would be back in twenty minutes. I didn't want to be there when Rob spoke to the actor.

After twenty minutes I came back and told Rob my thoughts, that he had potential but the choice was entirely up to him. I felt like a Casting Director, which in one way I didn't mind when it came to the action part of the person. But we were also talking about the acting part of a person. I mean my God, who gives that kind of responsibility to a punk kid from Brooklyn. I wasn't necessarily enjoying it. Rob Cohen is asking me not to just pick out a star, but pick out a Bruce Lee. I had a lot of weight on my shoulders. Day one was done and I came back the next day for the second actor and went through the same process. At the end of the day, brought him to the secretary and came back twenty minutes later. Again, I told Rob he had potential and left it up to him. A few hours later I was meeting the third actor. He introduced himself as Jason Scott Lee and I joked that it helped he had the same last name as Bruce and we all laughed. I began to go through the same questions as I did with the other two. Yet, it appeared the third time was the difference because Jason's answers were not repetitive like those before him. Nor were his everyday movements. It appeared to me that he had seen Bruce's first interview he had done that was televised and was trying his best to imitate Bruce in his answers. I was shocked and impressed as I continued asking him questions. He continued trying to imitate Bruce's mannerisms, it wasn't perfect, but I found many things we were going to be able to work with. He had a touch of attitude. The expressions, a little bit too hard, he needs to relax.

His body language, he followed direction wonderfully. I was very impressed with his mental knowledge of The Dragon Lee. He said he took Karate a while ago and one semester of basic gymnastics which really consisted of nothing. After our talk, we moved on to the working out phase and I looked at his punches and kicks carefully. I had him take off his shirt and just like the other two, saw his body structure was unimpressive.

He needed a lot of work. He was skinny and wiry with no muscle tone. I asked him to mimic me Bruce Lee and I was impressed. He did pushups very fast and his handstand were not bad. We went over Bruce Lee walks and stances to minute gestures as well as punches and kicks, attitude. After two and a half hours I saw tremendous potential in Jason. I even tried to get him to dance the Bruce Lee way. Rhythm, he didn't have much. I needed to give him guidance. After all, I've been imitating Bruce since his very first movie. This time after walking him to the secretary and leaving him, I looked at her and said, "I'm not going anyplace this time."

She smiled and got on the phone to call Rob. We went in and sat down and Rob looks at Jason and asks, "how do you think you did?"

Jason smiled and replied, "you will have to ask Steven about that. All I can say is that I learned a lot in a short amount of time and had fun."

I nodded, knowing that was the perfect thing to say. A few minutes later, we all stood up and shook hands. Rob told Jason he would be in touch and we began to walk out. I hear Rob ask me to stay, so I shake Jason's hand and give him a smile and a halfway salute. Jason smiled back, unsure of what to make of it and I returned to Rob.

I said, "Rob I have to tell you. The difference between him and the other two is like a stealth fighter to a biplane. He has got tremendous understanding, mentally. He understands Bruce and his extraordinary personality and he threw me some Bruce Lee lines. Remember that interview Bruce did, be like water? He did that whole thing for me. It was beautiful, you should ask him to see it. He has tremendous potential both mentally and physically. If you ask me, if it's just between these three and you don't have anyone else, my choice is Jason."

Rob seemed to take this all in and promised he would give me a call in a few hours with his decision. I went home and that night I got the call.

I pick up the phone and the first thing I hear is, "Jason Scott Lee."

What? I hear it again.

"Jason Scott Lee. That is who we are going with."

I smiled as Rob asked me to come in the next day to discuss Jason's training schedule. I knew it was going to be fun and rewarding working with Jason and opening up the potential he had inside. I also knew that Bruce would have been happy with this choice. Okay, let's stop.

Now let me burn a hole in this story to tell a tried and true version of what came out of Rob Cohen's mouth. It set me on fire. I get a call years later from a friend, asking me if I had seen the new Blu-Ray version of *Dragon: The Bruce Lee Story*. I told him that I had not. He went on to say they had a screen test with me and Jason Scott Lee with commentary by Rob Cohen as part of the DVD's bonus footage. A few days later, I see the screen test and the commentary and am just aghast. I'm listening to a man who I view as a good friend and one of the nicest guys I have met in my business, saying on the commentary that when he first found Jason, he had the body of a God and was an extraordinary specimen. I'm hearing Rob Cohen say this, knowing that simply was not the case. That was simply B.S. Please excuse my language. I thought my ears were lying to me, but that wasn't the case either. It was Rob Cohen not telling the truth to the audience. Fabricating history and doing it so well. Mind you, I am not in the habit of taking offense. My whole career I have let many things go by. But this was too important to not explain what really happened. Don't forget that when you die, nobody is out there to let you know what really occurred. That's why, while I am still alive, I'll tell you what really happened. THE TRUTH.

Jason was wiry, skinny and lacked muscle tone as I explained above. I don't want to make this comical, but he didn't even look like Poppy BEFORE he had his spinach. The reason why I am so adamant about this and upset is because I for three and a half solid months, six days a week, up to seven hours a day, mentally and physically trained him in all ways, shapes and forms. I MADE him a body of a God with his hard work and me right beside him showing and explaining to him what to do. I dedicated myself to sculpting every inch of him to look like Bruce Lee. It was my mission. For Rob Cohen to say he came in like that simply isn't true and I hope Rob somehow someday corrects that total misstatement. I'm pissed off. Hurt. In the movie business, everybody loves to change the story to suit them at the time. Okay, I said my peace but I don't think I can ever get the comments that came out of Rob Cohen's mouth out of my head until I hear otherwise.

Okay, I took twenty minutes to calm down now. Let's get back to the story. I met with Rob and made a schedule for Jason. Monday through Saturday. From Sil-Lum Kung Fu workouts, personal training (climbing mountains, Pilates, Martial Arts, Venice Beach, etc.) to mental preparation and visual teachings, we trained six days a week. Looking at everything Bruce did every day. I would meet with Rob and Raffaella every day and explain the process. One day they called me in and said we needed to put together a screen test. A fight between Jason and a bad guy so the powers in the black tower at Universal can see Jason act like Bruce Lee. I didn't understand why, so I asked. Rob Cohen said to me that in order for this movie to get the green light, the okay, they want to see a screen test. I was told I have six weeks more to put it together. That was all well and fine and Rob asked me who we could get to fight Jason as Bruce Lee. I smiled and said, who better else than his teacher, me. Rob Cohen loved the idea and I told him I would get working on it right away. I asked if he was going to make Jason aware of this and Rob said yes. I asked Rob if he would keep it quiet for a while so Jason wouldn't be nervous and he agreed. I started the fight sequence I was making up with Jason, who didn't understand what I was doing. I told him I wanted him to get used to repetitive moves so that when he did the fights in the film, he would be used to them. That seemed to calm him down and in a week's time, we put together a routine with about twenty moves. The following week it accelerated, finishing the routine. I knew it couldn't be anything big time. My thought process was just to get some elements and reminders of Bruce's essence that we have all seen in the movies. The basics.

That's when Rob broke the news to Jason that we were going to be shooting a screen test and everything weighed on how it looked. I saw Jason get nervous, his whole body language changed. Rob and I jumped in and explained how he would be fine and gave him the confidence he needed as Raffaella watched in silence from her Queen's chair.

She never got out of that seat. Jason's confidence grew by the end of the meeting and we continued our training. We would discuss Bruce, his family, his writings, books, paperwork. What he liked, what he cared about and who he cared about and why. His philosophy and his writings. Jason was desperate and thirsty to learn these things to get them right for the screen test and the film itself. It showed you how much he truly cared.

Now I will tell you something very personal. Usually, you don't hear about things that are so dear but I am telling you this because it just showed how much it meant to Jason and how it affected me. It made me realize how important to Jason this was.

But then I thought about something bigger and that was of the importance to the world. Three times Jason broke down in tears, overwhelmed by the monumental task of becoming Bruce Lee. I would spend the rest of the day getting his courage back and restoring his confidence in those that believed in him. It was quite a chore. Incredible moments that drew us closer. Coordination, distance, focus, timing and the most important thing, the power of the mind. This is what I stressed to Jason and we got through the tough times. They were beautiful moments and he fought every step of the way to succeed and I was right beside him to guide him.

Six weeks went by and he worked tirelessly. It got close to the screen test time and Rob Cohen was trying to figure out where we could film it. Then, like the rising sun, it dawned on me. I wondered. I thought. Could it be possible? Is it there? Ark Wong. Grandmaster Ark Wong.

He had been dead for many years but I wondered if his school was still open. I thought nah, impossible. Then I remember hearing a rumor that his family still maintains the school as a shrine to him.

I racked my brain trying to think of how I could confirm this and find the family. All of a sudden, it hits me.

My Master's Master was Ark Wong!

How about that. Let me give Doug Wong a shot. I call Douglas Wong and explained to him what I was doing. He confirmed my suspicions about the school saying it was exactly like it was twenty years ago. I told him it would be a great honor and add such a mystique to what I was trying to do.

He loved the idea and said to me, "let me see if I can make it happen. I'll call you back."

To my surprise, that's what he did, to tell me the family would let us use the school. I was overjoyed. I asked him how he did it. Connections he says. Chinese connections. He gave me the information and his blessing. Now, I had floated in my mind and dreamed about giving this wonderful surprise of location to Rob Cohen.

The next day I met with Rob, I asked him to sit down and put his feet up. I stood in front of him like a ringleader in a circus. I said, "picture this. Grandmaster Ark Wong's studio.

Someone who knew Bruce Lee. He is no longer with us, but his studio still exists as it did when it closed in nineteen eighty seven. It's a shrine now." I described how lucky we were to be allowed to use the school as a setting for this screen test. Can you imagine that?

"And what's really cool is my master Doug Wong learned from his master, Ark Wong and now I am bringing it back full circle." How about that?

I thought it was fabulous and that's what we did. We met at the school in Chinatown and we met Ark's family and I'll never forget. They were so gracious and thankful, they even brought food. Bao.

Rob slowly walked through the school, amazed and fascinated. Looking at the different pictures on the wall, he turned to me and said, "I can feel the energy. This screen test is going to be great."

(Steven Lambert was Jason Scott Lee's original Martial Arts teacher. Even though Jason won't admit it.)

"That it is Rob," I said smiling back.

Rob asked questions about Ark Wong and we spent hours telling stories and learning about the school. We all huddled in a circle at the end, all of our foreheads touching with Ark Wong's family in the background as they actually said a prayer wishing us well. Half in English, half in Chinese. It was a moment of pure understanding, love and commitment and Ark Wong's energy was flowing everywhere to help make this screen test a success. And that it was. Rob Directed it, I was the lead bad guy and Action Designer and Jason was Bruce. Before we rolled film, I gave him a surprise. Keep reading, it's funny. I took off my sweatshirt. I had

546

a body like a Jewish Bruce Lee in those days, haha. All of a sudden, Jason's face changed.

"Wait a minute," he said. "I think you should have your sweatshirt on."

I explained to him it would look cool if we both had our shirts off. I said to Jason that you would see the strain in your body language.

Jason replied, "the only strain I want to see is from my body language."

Rob agreed and we all laughed. Personally, I think Jason didn't want to be upstaged. But between you and me, that's okay. ;) I put on my sweatshirt and we rocked and rolled. There were two situations where he got me and you could see it in the screen test. They were for real. The first time was the back handspring and he hits me in the chin and I go back six to seven feet on my ass. He halfway knocked me out. I shook my head a few times to try to get rid of the stars knowing that it was really my fault. To make it work, I had to get close. Trouble was I got too close and it hurt. My fault. I knew if I wanted it, that's the way it had to be. Second, was at the end when he threw his flying sidekick. I thought I could parry away but one time I didn't. Hit me right upside the head. That double hurt. Rob and I went into the editing room and cut it together. It took us a couple of days while we gave Jason time off to relax. Rob brought it back to the black tower and on the third day, I got a phone call. Rob said they were unbelievably happy with the screen test and the movie was on.

Now with the story I told you, don't you think they had a little help from a friend? I don't think I have to tell you which friend. I ask ya, how come we never get the credit. The reasons, the whys. The pre-making of the movie. How people are able to do what they do when it comes to movement. The action. Stunt people. We are unimportant We are trivial. That is to say after they get what they need from us. Then we are afterthoughts. The next phase was to get him ready for the film itself. A week of training went by and I began thinking. The more I was thinking about what I was thinking about, this thinking thing began to grow as the days went by. It was a very important thinking thought, when I realized, I had an epiphany. I asked myself, Steven, you must be realistic. How much further can you go with Jason to where it is not repetitive both mentally and physically. Sure, I could teach him move after move and make it look like Bruce, but I wanted and I needed something more than that for him. Not Jason, but Bruce Lee. I've always wondered why Rob didn't originally hire people that worked and trained with Bruce for this job, but I'm sure glad he didn't! You see, I never met Bruce, I only copied his style and philosophy as many others had as well. This was an important realization that really smacked me in the face so to speak. Wait. I had heard that some of his black belts he taught were still in California. I thought long and hard about how I could contact them.

CHAPTER 71
(Linda Lee Lends A Hand.)

Not coming up with anything, I went to Rob Cohen and explained to him an idea I have. I explained how wonderful it would be to have others on our team working with Jason. People that worked with Bruce, that knew his personality, his body language and mentality. Someone that had lunch with Bruce, talked about all his writings with him, that laughed, played and cried with him. Good friends. He thought it was a great idea and I said, "we had a conversation once. You told me you talked to Linda Lee. Why don't you call her and ask if she knows any of Bruce's blackbelt friends?" I watched him open up his phone book. He went to the "L" section and there it was. Linda Lee, Bruce's widow. I thought to myself, boy Steven that speech you gave was pretty impressive. I got him to do it. So he called her up and put the phone on speaker. I proceeded in introducing myself and telling her my idea to find these friends of her husband. To my surprise and delight, she gave me six names. Those names were Herb Jackson, Richard Bustillo, Danny Inosanto, Bob Wall, Jerry Poteet and Ted Wong. She explained they were all friends with Bruce and six of his black bets that Bruce knew very well. I wrote their names and numbers in my pad. Not my Ipad, my note pad. Don't forget, this was the nineties. I told Rob Cohen that I was going to go home immediately and get in touch with these six apprentices. I left the office and I'll never forget. I took out the note pad, opened it up to that page and I read off these six names. I just couldn't believe I was going to hold court with these six guys that were some of Bruce Lee's best. I flipped the pad closed. Wow.

Weeks went by and you talk about a kick in the gut. That's when one day I was called into Rob's office and watched as he walked over to a closet and took out a cardboard box, two feet by two feet. It was big. He tossed it on his desk, opened it and reached in. He took out a handful of letters and drops them on the table.

"Do you know what this is?" He asked me.

I shook my head, completely confounded. "No, I don't," I stated.

"These are letters," Rob went on.

I said to myself, okay.

Rob continued. "From black belts to monks, to friends, family, politicians and from Asian grandmasters all over the world."

I said, "alright," unsure of why he was showing me these.

"You know what they are saying?" Rob asked.

I had no idea.

Rob tried to make his answer a joke. "They are saying, who the hell is this white boy training Jason to become Bruce Lee? I know you are a great Martial Artist Steven, but they don't know who the hell you are and think you are not qualified. I have read a hundred and fifty of these letters and they are all saying the same thing."

I get up and walk over and lean over to the box. Holy Moses. There must be a thousand letters in there! I ask, "how long have you been keeping these?"

He replies, "they have been coming in for a month now. Every day."

I look up at him. "Can I call them fans?"

He almost fell to his knees in laughter.

Then I say to Rob, "okay, who cares. Do you?"

Then it came. "I don't, but Raffaella, your Executive Producer does."

I ask him, "in what way?"

Rob says, "well, she wants to get someone that people will accept." Then Rob made it very clear that in his mind, I had the job. I had the job, yet for weeks he was getting letters and phone calls asking where did I qualify to teach Jason. He also said that Raffaella was also very upset at this and there were whispers about replacing me. "

What are you going to do, Rob?" I asked, just floored by this new information I was receiving.

Rob raised his eyebrows. "I have an idea. Why don't we have a meeting with Linda and Brandon Lee? I have already told her about you and how much I believe in you. They are coming in a few days from now, we could set that up then."

Well, that was a wonderful idea. I must give praise where it is due. Even though you were an asshole on the commentary for not telling the truth Rob, you were a genius coming up with the idea to call Linda Lee. Even though I thought of it. I don't know whether to love or hate you. So I think I will do both. I agreed to meet them and left the office with a thousand thoughts running through my mind. I understood this was Bruce Lee, and he was the closest thing to a God in the Martial Arts world. Even doing a John Wayne story wouldn't be bigger than this.

Like I said, Bruce is the man. For three days, I barely slept. Now you gotta understand. We all do this. I conjured up the whole imaginary dialogue in my head between Linda and me. She would say this and I would reply with that. She would ask me about my qualifications and I would tell her this, this and that. It was easy. I finally had it worked out in my mind how it was going to go. On top of that, I was going to spend some cash on a big bouquet of flowers. Guess what? Just my luck. On the fourth day, I walk into the office with the huge bouquet of flowers. They were so big you couldn't even see me behind them. First person who sees me, I mean the flowers, was Raffaella The Queen Bee. The scent of the flowers must have drawn her from her queen's chair. She asked me who the flowers were for, her eyes flying from petal to petal as if she was intent on killing each flower with her looks.

"Well, I am meeting with Linda and I want to make a good impression," I tell her.

She takes one more look at the flowers and says, "don't you think youshould have brought me flowers too? I didn't want you for this job in the first place, but Rob Cohen convinced me."

My mouth dropped. She was pissed. Shew threw her head back and muttered a comment I was glad I didn't hear, before marching off back to her hive, I mean office. Talk about embarrassing. I stirred up the hornet's nest now, I thought to myself. I took a deep breath and headed to where Linda would be waiting, flowers in hand. I just hoped she would be more like a butterfly than a bee. As I discussed with you already, I had all these plans of what to say in my head.

But to my surprise after I presented her the flowers, which I might say she was very happy about, I mentioned to her, "Linda these flowers aren't what you call a routine. It's something I feel in my heart. It really means something to have a chance to meet and sit down with you."

These were the words I used almost verbatim and by her reaction, she was delighted and I felt she understood. We went on, having a discussion on exactly the things I thought and expected we were going to talk about. We talked about my Martial Arts, my stunts. We talked about what I thought of Bruce and how he affected my life like he has many others.

Until about twenty minutes into the conversation, then there was a complete left turn. She started asking me questions that had nothing to do with the movie, with Bruce, or discussions about my work. That left turn became questions about my childhood. How I felt about my family, my father, my mother, my grandparents. What it was like growing up in Brooklyn, New York. I was thrown off track, big time. I realized I was talking about things in my life that made me very uncomfortable, such as my father and life situations. It was causing me not just to be uncomfortable, but to have tears in my eyes talking about things I tried to throw away decades ago and she noticed that. Locked onto it big time. In fact, she put her hand on mine at a moment she saw the first tear in my eye. This went on for about thirty minutes until all of a sudden, the questions came to an abrupt hold which REALLY CONFUSED ME.

The questions became a long statement. About Bruce and his childhood and how he grew up. After about a five minute speech from Linda, explaining the similarities of how my childhood echoed Bruce's childhood in their circumstances, in other words, Hong Kong to good ole' Brooklyn, I was simply astounded. They were a lot alike in Bruce's childhood days. We moved off that for about another fifteen minutes and she was asking me what I thought of the script. A key moment, I thought that very much helped my situation when she asked.

I simply said, "you know Linda, it's really not what I think, it's what you think." I also made many comments to her about how I would try to present Bruce in this movie, in not only the action but his behavior. Caring about people, individuals, situations that life puts you through. "Some of these examples are shown in the script and I feel that is very important to you and everybody who loved Bruce," I said. She asked me about Jason. I assured her that he was coming along fine. I told her that I was really impressed he was working hard not just physically but on understanding Bruce. I asked her if she had seen the screen test where I played the bad guy and fought Jason who played Bruce.

She giggled while she said, "yes."

I asked, "what would Bruce think of me?"

How she answered, I would never forget. She said, "Bruce would have enjoyed fighting you, but he would have kicked your ass."

We both laughed. We continued for a minute or two when she stood up and said, "Steven, as far as my desires, I would love to see you continue on this movie."

I looked at her and stood up and said, "does this mean I got the job?"

She smiled and said, "I will tell everybody how happy I am with you."

I thanked her as we walked out of the office where Rob Cohen was waiting.

"What do you think?" He asked Linda.

"He's got my vote and Bruce's too," she says.

As we were talking, Linda gave us a quote from Bruce which was, "Bruce loved and respected all styles of Martial Art and fighting. He mentioned a number of times that what he does for the movies is simply called performance art."

I smiled and thanked them both. Wow, what a moment. After having a conversation for a few seconds, they went into Rob's office and I left mentally exhausted. The next day I opened my notebook and called each of the six guys Linda gave me, one by one to ask them for their assistance. The first one I called was Herb Jackson. After having a conversation with him, he came on board and said yes. As did Ted Wong. I was just elated. I set up meetings with each one of these guys to explain the film and how much it would mean if they could teach Jason. Bob Wall, I explained and he said yes. I went on to Danny Inosanto. EEEEEERRRRR- I hit the brakes.

I can't believe it. Inosanto said no! I stated again how much it would mean to Jason's training, but Danny was adamant. I continued my persuasive methods and finally only got him to agree to teach Jason one time for a couple of hours, but that teaching would simply be conversation. Everyone else was meeting him twice a week for three months. I kinda understood why he didn't want to, he said he was worried about what kind of film this was going to be.

I assured him the movie would be done correctly and Linda Lee was on board with it, but that still didn't change his mind. That one time was very precious and I made Jason aware that he should try to get all the information he could from Danny, as he and Bruce were very close. I was nervous about asking Richard Bustillo after that, but to my relief, he said yes.

We met at his school and he agreed to help. Then I called Jerry Poteet and he agreed. I couldn't get off the phone with him. I couldn't get him to stop talking. In fact, during our conversation, I mentioned that Herb Jackson and Ted Wong were on my team and in a roundabout way, he more or less tried to convince me that they weren't really needed. I kind of let those comments go in one ear and out the other. I also brought on Doug Wong as he was a crucial teacher in my life. I knew his extraordinary talents could help Jason as well as he had helped me.

By the way, I also brought on Olympic player, Mike Washlake the first week we started training, to teach Jason gymnastics. Nine people training Jason including myself and I redid the schedule with these special men by my side. Let me open up your mind to a treasure chest of stunning realization that came upon me. It was almost an enlightenment, but it could also be my imagination. I'll leave that up to you. This is why I am making this statement. Let me tell you how special these men were. First to Bruce and then to me, Jason and Rob.

First up, Herb Jackson. I learned Herb wasn't what you would call a physically talented man. No, he didn't have the physical ability, but he had the passion and the heart, the true love for Martial Arts and especially Bruce. He had the internal endurance like a honey badger. He had the strength of a Brahma bull. And a heart of a Lion and a grip of a gorilla.

He was also a tinkerer. He was Bruce Lee's equipment maker. Let me explain. He loved to build things for Bruce. Wing Chun dummies, punching bags, the list goes on and on. Bruce loved and used his creations because they helped him train harder. It also brought them closer. The first week went wonderful and we had a lot of discussions and gained a lot of knowledge from Herb as he worked out with Jason physically. Teaching him certain moves Bruce loved. I'll never forget his discussion about Bruce's one inch punch and I was the dummy. When he put his fist on my solar plexus, it looked like a sledgehammer and it felt like one too. Falling back about six feet on my ass.

Jason got a kick out of that. I mean a punch. And it bruised my bony ass. The second week, we sat down. Herb loved to tell stories about Bruce. His face would completely change. There was a glow. Almost a forgotten sense that Bruce was dead and he was talking about him like any second, he was going to come to the door and validate the story.

Herb told us a story of an experience he had with Bruce. He recalled a time when Bruce asked him to do a movement. When he didn't do it the right way, Bruce scolded him. Herb took it so personally, he had tears in his eyes. Bruce saw that Herb was so upset and stopped scolding him. Instead, he took Herb in his arms and hugged him. He recounted that Bruce was actually crying with him and apologizing for yelling at him. As he is telling us this story in his backyard, guess what he started to do? He started to cry. I looked at Jason as the seconds went by and then found myself crying! It wasn't long before Jason had tears and we both got up and sat next to Herb and cried together. And that's the truth.

Let's move on to another great man I grew to admire, care about and understand like Herb. All this happening in the short amount of time and experience that I had the pleasure of associating with him. His name was Ted Wong. Ted was a little aloof at first which made Jason and I a bit nervous. You see after every workout, Jason and I spent hours talking about each and everything that had occurred. Finding out later on, Ted was just a quiet and private man.

So I started asking Ted questions about Bruce's body language. As I have said before, when I teach body language, I break it up into three different categories. Lower gait, middle gait and upper gait. Put them together, they are all one. I was explaining this to Ted and as I did, I noticed a smirk from him. This smirk knocked me back and I stopped talking. I had seen that smirk before. That was Bruce's smirk that he flashes so many times in his films. It was as if he was saying, "you're telling ME what this is all about?"

I smiled back and said, "Ted, I gotta tell you. You looked just like Bruce right then."

Ted laughed and it just broke the ice right then and there. I started talking to Ted about hands, blocks and punches. He went right to the lower gait. He was explaining feet movement. The why the how and when. I would try to bring it back to hands and blocks. I got up to demonstrate and threw an inside opened hand block, posing like Bruce. I talked about his open fingers as he always blocked with open fingers. I asked Ted if my hands were right and if he could teach Jason that. He ignored what I was saying, his eyes on my lower gait and feet. I didn't get it at first. I tried to bring him back with subtlety. Look at my hands.

He went right back down to my feet! I didn't realize how naive I was. I was thinking to myself, "what, are you deaf?"

I didn't understand and had no idea, but I would soon come to realize as the days went by, that Bruce's gift to Ted was the art of the lower gait. Foot movements. I must tell you, Ted loved to move. If you just focus in from the waist down on Ted, his feet moved just like Bruce Lee. It was beautiful to watch and to hear Ted explain, you could see Bruce Lee. Thirty minutes went by. An hour went by. An hour and a half went by. Every time I tried to change the focus to the middle or upper gait, he went right back to feet work! It was like he was playing a verbal footsie game with me. Three hours go by and it was all about footwork. I was amazed he had that much to teach about it, and it was wonderful stuff!

It was Heaven and Jason and I absorbed a tremendous amount both with movements and mental understandings. Ted always told stories as Herb liked to do, and the same glow that I saw with Herb was present on his mug. One of Ted's many stories. Listen to this. He explained when he was younger, Bruce took him to see a movie of his. Bruce had to hide his appearance. He would enjoy going up to people and ask them questions, sometimes tripping in front of people, incognito. Just by putting on a wig or funny sunglasses or a hat. Sometimes a mustache. He always got a kick out of that because it tickled his nose. It made us all laugh. As they were walking out, Bruce asked Ted what he thought. Ted stayed silent. Bruce took him by his shoulders and looked into his eyes.

"What's wrong? Don't be afraid to tell me," he said.

Ted looked at him and said," I am afraid I am not going to see you anymore."

Bruce moved his hands from Ted's shoulders to his head and said, "we will always be brothers, don't forget that."

Ted finished the story, holding back tears. You could tell how powerful Bruce's words were to him. It really choked us up and moved us big time too. Jason and I. Again, I found myself with tears going down my face and I'll never forget that moment when Ted saw my tears, it was almost like looking into Bruce's eyes.

Then came the one and only Bob Wall. We met him on Ventura Boulevard at an empty store he owned. I thought that was a very funny and weird place to meet. He was sitting at a desk. In fact, the only thing in there was a desk and a few chairs. Jason had a big smile on his face, which surprised me as he was nervous during the first two meetings with Herb and Ted. And boy, was I excited. It was a lot different meeting Bob Wall. Maybe it was because Bob was more flamboyant than the other two. He sounded like a ringmaster as he welcomed us in. He also did everything with Bruce and was just about in every movie. As we sat down, he saw me looking around before I began discussing the schedule.

"You like the store? You can have it," Bob spoke up.

I looked up at him, trying to understand.

"To train. You can have the store to train. It will be empty for a long time and if it gets rented, I'll move you to another store, no problem," Bob said with a smile.

I was about to graciously thank him when he took out a key and threw it on the table. "In fact, here is the key to the store. Whenever you want to use it go ahead and when you want me here to help train, let me know."

I couldn't believe the hospitality Jason and I had just been given. I thanked him again and we moved on to telling a few stories. He told me one about the story I think we all know, but nevertheless, it was fun to listen to coming from him. It was about a gigantic punching bag that he and Chuck Norris, Darnell Garcia and a few others got for Bruce. It was going to be a surprise.

This bag was about ten feet wide. They saw Bruce in the parking lot and told him to put his hands over his eyes. They walked him in and when he saw the bag, he was shocked. He looked like a toothpick in front of it. Bruce walked over to it and stepped beside it. He picked up his fist and he tapped it. It didn't move. Everyone was quiet as Bruce turned around.
Then he faced the bag again. He hit it once, twice, dropped his hands and hit it harder. He turned back to see everyone smiling. Then he started dancing around it, jabbing at it until he disappeared behind the bag. Five seconds went by, ten seconds. No Bruce.

All of a sudden like a madman, he jumps out saying how much he loved it. Kicking and punching the bag all excited and thanking everyone for the wonderful gift.

After Bob had finished, I said "now I want to ask you a question about a story I heard. When you went after Bruce Lee with those two broken bottles you smashed together, in Enter The Dragon, you accidentally cut Bruce with those broken bottles. Is that true?"

To my amazement, he said, "yes and furthermore, he was mad at me. I took a lot of verbal abuse but a few days later, all was forgotten. Just a little tease every now and then."

Jason and I looked at each other. "One more question," I asked. Bruce was so pissed that you cut him, that the kick he threw at you in that iconic scene, was that real?"

Bob smiled and nodded and brought his hand to his stomach and said, "when I think about it, it still hurts. It took a couple of weeks to get over that pain."

We all laughed. Bob Wall. One cool guy. By the way, Bob owns three huge blocks of Encino, California. He's one rich dude.

The next guy was Mister escrima himself, Danny Inosanto. I knew we had one shot at this and I'll never forget driving up across the street from Danny's dojo in the evening and having a talk with Jason for about ten minutes. I discussed with Jason such things as the closeness that Danny and Bruce had with each other. It was very unfortunate that this was a one shot deal.

I was thinking to myself that maybe during this conversation with him, I could convince him to see us again. You see, when Danny joined Bruce to train, he was already a black belt. It was a very unusual relationship because Danny came to Bruce's school as a pupil, not a teacher.

The time came and we walked across the street to the dojo and met Danny.

(So honored to have met Herb Jackson and Ted Wong. Bruce lee's Blackbelts.)

We sat down on chairs and Danny sat down on a mat on the floor, crossing his legs. I felt like we were in a monastery talking to the Dalai Lama. I started off getting Danny to speak about meeting Bruce for the first time and how it came about teaching Bruce escrima sticks and if that was true. Danny told us that he kept his escrima stick skills quiet until one day he started practicing with them on a heavy bag in Bruce's school right after a practice. Bruce walked over and never having seen escrima sticks before, asked Danny to teach him. One thing led to another, meaning the student had become the teacher and Danny explained to us it was a trade off.

Continuing the conversation, I realized that is what made their friendship even closer. There weren't many things you could teach Bruce and he liked the escrima sticks so much, he looked at it as an extension of his hands. Danny explained that

Bruce thought it was an amazing weapon. That he thought it extended parts of his body. It extended his shoulder, extended his bicep, his forearms and his hands.

I watched Danny explain to us and listened with exuberance. Danny said that was the way Bruce Lee looked at it and explained it. During this conversation, I stood up a couple of times, going into a pose with my hands, at the same time trying to walk it out to the mats. But guess what? He didn't take the bait. He wouldn't budge. He was too smart. Danny was very master like and his expression told me this meeting was strictly business. He had that seriousness Bruce had in his interviews or some of his films, that unshakeable composure.

Look up that interview when he is talking about water. As Jason and I progressed in conversation, the feeling of the aura in the room was nothing like the ones we had with Ted and Herb and even Bob Wall. While the others were very open and sharing knowledge left and right, Danny was very metered in his words. He was like a soda bottle where you have to pop off the cap with your fingers.

Now don't get me wrong, I understood why he was very weary. It was strictly out of love and concern for Bruce. His friend.

(So honored to have worked with Richard Bustillo. One of Bruce Lee's black belts.)

Towards the end of the session, I had an idea. I told Jason I was going to leave him and Danny alone for a few minutes to talk amongst themselves and would meet Jason back at the car. Jason was very surprised at this move as he had no idea it was coming. I went back to the car and forty-five minutes later, Jason returned. I asked Jason what they had talked about and he looked at me as I looked at him with plain expressions on our faces. All of a sudden, he bursts out in roaring laughter. "I'M NEVER GOING TO TELL YOU!" he says laughing.

He never told me and I never asked him again out of respect. A few days later I picked up Jason in the afternoon and we drove to Richard Bastillo's dojo. We walked in and boy was it a beautiful dojo. It was huge. We started talking and Richard was very open, which I thought was great. I began asking him about Bruce's kicks. How did he get into his kicks from his shuffles? I wanted to know that and hadn't got into that with anyone as of yet. Did he use certain shuffles that led into certain kicks or did it matter? We were on mats right in front of mirrors and it was the perfect time. I went into a shuffle and kick to show him what I meant. Richard comes over and instead of looking at my feet, starts telling me how Bruce's hands would be when he threw a kick. I listened and corrected my hands. I moved on to another shuffle ending with a kick. He would come back to me and put my hands in another place. I asked about foot movements when Bruce did a punch and one thing led to another and again, he started talking about punches and blocks.

Then we found ourselves talking about nothing but punches and blocks. A light bulb went off in my head after thirty minutes, that like Ted With feet, Richard only wanted to focus on upper gait. The more I got into it with him and the more time went by, watching him perform with his arms and hands, the more I realized it was like looking at Bruce throwing punches and blocks. For Richard, it was all upper body and Ted nothing but feet work. It was amazing to me. Next up was Jerry Poteet.

I had a conversation with Jerry, letting him know I was teaching Jason Wing Chun and Chi Sau sticky hands, and I would like him to continue. He agreed. He invited us over to his house and when we arrived, he introduced his wife, Renee. We sat down and I began to ask Jerry questions. Every few minutes, however, it would be Renee who would interject useless knowledge to me. She did not understand that I needed it to come from Jerry. This would happen multiple times and I would do my best to let her know I wanted to hear from Jerry.

I wasn't here to interview her, someone who knew nothing about Bruce but sure thought she did. I had no choice but to become more forceful in a respective way and I noticed she didn't expect it. It became clear to me that she wasn't used to being told to button her lip. To put it lightly, it became clear to me she was yenta. She would constantly portray like she was part of Bruce's life. She was also a Martial Artist, I guess, as over and over again she told us. You know the kind.

During the training sessions, Renee would always be there and have her input which caused quite a few problems. I tried to be as polite as I could, but it was clear she wanted to be the center of attention. Needless to say, Jason wouldn't like it either and would inform me.

As we continued training with Jerry and the other six, something very special happened. I arrived with Jason to train with Ted Wong one day when he said he had a surprise for us. We went to his backyard and there was Herb Jackson. Ted felt comfortable enough to bring him in and do a session together. I thought that was unbelievably cool, having two of Bruce's students teaching Jason at the same time.

We spent about three hours of nonstop training as I sat on a tree stump and watched with awe.

How many people to get to experience this, I thought. And Jason agreed. Thinking how special this moment was, it truly was a gift from Bruce. They trained Jason mentally and physically and it wasn't long before we got into conversation.

At some point in our jovial chat, I casually mentioned I had Jason training with Jerry Poteet. All of a sudden, the happy grinning faces of Herb and Ted fell away, vanishing into nothingness in a mere instant. Both Jason and I saw this occurrence and I was surprised, didn't know what to say. Did I say something wrong?

Herb looked at me and said, "so you are training with Jerry." It wasn't a question, but more like a sad statement.

"Yeah. What are your thoughts on that? I can tell something's wrong," I replied a bit confused.

Ted sighed and looked at Herb before looking back at me. "We'll talk to you later about it."

That they did, when Jason went home. Herb looked at me and said, "since you are here for knowledge, let me impart some. Bruce wasn't fond of Jerry Poteet."

As I raised up from the stump I was sitting on, Ted continued with Herb listening. "There were a lot of internal conflicts with Bruce and Jerry. Bruce felt he was in it for all the wrong reasons. That he would take privileges and not listen to Bruce," Ted explained.

He went on to say that he caught Jerry in many a lie and he would constantly be angry if Bruce booked anyone other than him a job.

He was a very selfish guy and Jerry wanted to always be front and center with Bruce and there were a number of times that in fact, Bruce asked him to leave the school, only weeks later returning and appealing to Bruce's selflessness. Bruce would feel bad and always let him back in.

(Ted Wong and Herb Jackson teaching Jason about Bruce Lee's footwork. It was wonderful to watch.)

Ted and Herb made it very clear there was no friendship between Bruce and Jerry, as a number of magazines they read stated otherwise. Herb explained to me that Jerry was always willing to do interviews and make up his own fantasy world about him and Bruce. I asked them why they never mentioned the truth about Jerry and Bruce and Ted simply looked at me and said the word, "respect". This was completely opposite of what Jerry Poteet told me.

I took this information in, thanked them for their thoughts and we moved on in the conversation, unaware that they were trying to warn me about Jerry. I took what they were saying as a matter of fact. As the weeks went by, however, Jason began to talk more and more about the five out of six guys who were training him, minus Jerry Poteet, and not in a good way. Whenever I brought Jason to Jerry, I would notice more of a possessive type of friendship, it was very odd and come to find out, there was secret training going on. Poteet managed to get Jason's telephone number and they were meeting privately. I thought it would be better just to let it happen. No big deal. Comments were made about the other five guys and how inferior they were.

First, they came from Jerry. Then they began coming from Jason. Little did I know that Anakin Scott Lee was turning to the dark side. It got so obvious, that one day I asked Jason what the matter was. He told me he felt the other guys weren't teaching him anything. I shook my head and told him that if I felt they weren't teaching him anything I would have intervened. Everything they were teaching was golden. I couldn't understand where Jason was coming from or what he was going to do next and I told him so and more as I tried to convince him that this was a mistake. Until one day I got a call from Rob Cohen's secretary. She tells me that

Jason spoke to her and mentioned that he does not want to work out with Herb anymore. I asked her why he didn't notify me directly and she told me that she thought he was embarrassed. Scratching my head, I hung up and called Jason who was adamant. He wanted to learn other things and after four weeks with Herb, he felt he was finished with him. I had no choice but to adhere to his wishes as he was the star.

On top of that, in the same breath, Jason tells me he also wants to stop working out with Ted Wong. I became more confused and a bit angry inside. I asked him what his thought process was on this and he just wouldn't answer me. I hung up and called Ted and Herb to cancel our sessions. I thanked them for their time and told them my plan to have all six of them on the credits. The next meeting with Jason was with Jerry Poteet at his house, that's where all of our sessions were with him. During our training, Jason out of nowhere turned around to Jerry and said, "I got rid of those guys."

I looked up in shock as a slow smile spread across Jerry's mouth.

"Good, you don't need them," he assured Jason.

I am watching this from several feet away as the joy just emanates from Jerry's face. The coldness and satisfaction were akin to that of Emperor Palpatine himself. So when we left, I asked Jason bluntly if Jerry had told him not to work out with those other guys. Jason confirmed that Jerry had convinced him it would be better this way. Well, I had a long talk with Jason explaining what Jerry said was wrong.

"You were having a great time, loving every second of Ted and Herb's lessons a few weeks ago. Now you aren't?" I asked. It just didn't make sense and I was very upset at Jerry Poteet. I tried to explain to Jason that the only reason Poteet is trying to get rid of these guys is that he wants to be the chosen one. This is what you should to think about and realize.

The next lesson we had was with Richard Bustillo. It went wonderful. For four hours, Jason was pouring sweat and learned so much in that time. I was so happy. I was thinking maybe I shouldn't have been so hard on Jason. Ted and Herb were a little slower, a little different than Richard or Jerry's way of teaching and I was trying to rationalize his actions in my head. The next day we met with Bob Wall. He started talking about Bruce's way of dancing around and throwing punches. I wanted to know where he came up with that.

I asked him, "Bruce Lee loved to dance in his fights. Muhammad Ali loved to dance in his fights. Did he get it from Bruce or did Bruce get it from Muhammad Ali?"

Bob smiled and said, "he got it from Ali."

Jason just loved that as did I. Remember that, it's coming from Bob Wall's mouth. Four hours after we left, I get a call from the secretary again saying that Jason doesn't want to train with Richard Bustillo or Bob Wall anymore. I blew my top, and to who? To the secretary. She tried to calm me down and said even she asked Jason where this was coming from and he wouldn't tell her. I called Jason right after and the same thing as before happened. He wouldn't tell me. I called Jerry Poteet, just furious, but managed to calm myself down. I asked Jerry if he had been talking to Jason. He tried to play dumb, but I wasn't having it. Jerry finally told me that he discussed with Jason that working out with too many guys could be confusing and he would be better off working with one guy to get direct answers.

"That is not true," I shot back. "And who do you think you are telling Jason who he should and shouldn't train with, without talking to me. I brought you on to help me, not to dictate what he does and doesn't do. I am ashamed of you and I let Jason know I am ashamed of you and you should be embarrassed for yourself." Let me just stop and say here to all the magazine interviewers and writers in television and print from the past the present and the future, let me make one thing clear to you. Listen, Jerry Poteet was NOT Jason Scott Lee's teacher on this film.

It was I, Steven Lambert. It was Herb Jackson, Bob Wall, Ted Wong, Richard Bustillo, Mike Washlake, and Doug Wong who taught Jason. Not Jerry Poteet. The crap you see that Jerry proclaims he taught Jason in the movie, looks horrible in the film. I made Jason what you see in the film, not Jerry. I was Jason's foundation. I don't like saying the word "I", but I don't like people who lie. Ask Rob Cohen in front of me, mention my name, see what he says. Even though Ted, Richard and Herb have passed away you can ask Grandmaster Doug Wong, Bob Wall and the dragon master, James Lew. I brought James Lew on to train and get in shape Lauren Holly who played Linda Lee and to double Jason Scott Lee. Unfortunately, he got a job he couldn't refuse.

They will set you straight and tell you the truth that it was I. Me, Steven Lambert. Not Poteet. Again, he is a liar and I am sorry to say that. I feel bad that Jerry passed away but the false history he spread must be righted. I am calling out all the magazine writers who failed to do their research on this matter. Call me, write me, and I will speak TRUTH.

(From left to right. The dragon master, two sour apples and me.)

Shame on Rob Cohen for not speaking true in the past. Since I am on this path let me say, that this is the problem with individuals who become stars with the help of others. They forget. Or maybe it is just insecurity or selfishness. Some kind of jealousy, I am sorry to say. Who the hell knows, only they do. It would be nice if they all had the integrity, decency and respect as Martial Art actor Keith Vitaly, actor James Woods and actor Fred Ward. But I'll tell you who the hell cares, I do and hopefully everybody else out there. It is a shame that actors such as Sho Kosugi, Michael Dudikoff, Jason Scott Lee and stuntman Vic Armstrong, purposely forget who really did the work. I mean I think the world of these guys. They are all terrific in my eyes. But they do many, many articles, magazines and television interviews and not once have they mentioned the truth along with my name in anything. I don't get it. We were friends at the time and they all give other people credit when it's not true. They don't tell the truth, but I dare them to start. In fact, I dare YOU to start. All you fans, you so called interviewers. Grill them on what you are reading and see if they tell you the truth. The real story. But THIS is, so keep reading.

Before I hung up, I told Jerry Poteet we would discuss this more in the near future, "but let me tell you now. What you did and what you caused to these great men is unforgivable. They were supposed to be your great friends, brothers and you went behind their back and set up a situation with Jason Scott Lee convincing him that they were no good and got them fired so you, Jerry Poteet, could be the chosen one. How selfish. Bruce would turn over in his grave. Just once and knock the hell out of you." How I wanted to fire Jerry Poteet right then and there, but I knew Jason favored him and would be upset if I did. He got rid of all the other five guys and Jerry was his favorite. Being the star, I couldn't take away the one person he wanted.

If I did attempt that, I'm sure Jason wouldn't be happy and it would cause a problem for me, so I had no choice in my mind but to let it ride and I bite my tongue. I can't tell you how difficult it was going to Jerry's house for our next lesson and not saying anything when I very badly wanted to inside. I even went to Rob Cohen and asked for his help. I explained that now Jerry was controlling what Jason did instead of me, and I had seen this before and knew it wasn't a good thing. Rob had too many things on his mind however and I just couldn't get through to him. He just didn't get it. He had too much going on to be bothered about these personal things. As for the Queen Bee, she seemed delighted with my unhappiness with the situation.

Later on, I found out Jerry Poteet and Raffaella De Laurentiis were in cahoots with each other. As I was leaving, the Production Manager, Wan Allen, told me to hire a stunt guy named Merritt Yohnka. I knew of him but didn't want to deal with that with this going on. I asked the Production Manager for help but he was no help either. Still, I was extremely proud and grateful Jason and I got to work with five of the closest and most cherished people to Bruce. I was so enlightened spiritually that I got to see this and realized that this could have been Bruce Lee's plan from the beginning. Many people around the world are looking for Bruce's teachings, both the physical and mental parts of it. What I came to gather, through meeting and learning from these five men who were Bruce's students and friends, is that Bruce planned that. He imparted a portion of his knowledge, some physical, some mental to each of these guys who I mentioned above. While most people are going to one Master seeking information and style and life knowledge about Bruce Lee, as if they were trying to find a hidden treasure of knowledge, I realized something. I realized my friends, that it is not one man that holds the answer, but all FIVE of them.

You see, each person Linda named and each one I got to talk to and understand, it occurred to me that all of them, minus Jerry, (that weasel. Meaning treacherous, carnivorous and he eats his own friends) together make up Bruce in his actions, movements, thoughts and behaviors. Together, they are the God himself, alive and well and sitting before me at different times in different bodies. What a delightful piece of history I get to live with. Herb Jackson, Ted Wong, Bob Wall, Richard Bustillo. And a special thanks to Douglas Wong and Gene Lebell.

(Great men who I brought on to assist me in training Jason Scott Lee. One bad apple, Jerry Poteet.)

By the way, I took Jason Scott Lee to Gene Lebell's house one day. They sat and talked for hours about Bruce. Then it was time to get physical and of course, I took the abuse. Jason Scott Lee and my friend John Meier videotaped it and had a good laugh.

(I'm the only one living, that Gene Lebell lets on the mats with tennis shoes.) NOW YOUTUBE IT. https://www.youtube.com/watch?v=ZDRmvKWcSi8 Thank you so much for the love you showed to Bruce Lee, the help you gave me and the joy you guys bestowed on my soul. Moving on, why me? Let me tell you about the next problem I had on this show. One day Rob called all of us, including Jason into the office to have a meeting. I had no idea what it was about as we all sat down and started talking about all the aspects of the movie. We would talk about props, sets, wardrobe, choreography and any questions he had about Bruce Lee. I would always have an answer that he liked, even in the prior meetings we had.

After about forty minutes, out of the blue Rob states, "I want to make clear the chain of command on this set. I am the Alpha. Steven Lambert over here, he is second in command. Any question for any department goes first through me and then Steven Lambert."

I looked at Rob, not believing he was saying this as Raffaella's eyes locked onto me like a missile ready to fire. Rob reiterates this before moving on to other departments. An hour later, we adjourned the meeting and I sat down at my desk in the office thinking about what just happened. A few minutes later I got up and asked to speak to Rob.

I went in and the first thing I said was, "Rob, what did you do, what did you say?"

He looked at me funny. "Steven, what are you talking about?"

I threw my hands up in disbelief. "You made me second in command."

He nods. "Yeah, so?"

I couldn't believe he didn't see it. "If you want to do that, you do that between you and I. But you don't tell the star, you especially shouldn't tell the Producer, Raffaella De Laurentiis and Production Manager that. Now they hate me more than they did before. They didn't like me to begin with."

Rob tried to tell me how important I was to the film and I acknowledged that but stated, "you don't say I'm second in command in front of these people who have big titles and even bigger egos. Big mistake, Rob."

Rob shrugged it off, thinking it was almost humorous how upset I was. I took a deep breath and just shook my head at the nightmares around me. Not just with what happened here, but with Jerry and Jason too. Speaking of nightmares and demons, I decided to discuss with Rob a demon who was in the script, who was a major villain to Bruce in the film. I knew that Rob was still deciding who he wanted to cast and found this a perfect opportunity. I said, "Rob listen, I got the perfect guy for you to play the demon. I've worked with him many times. He is a great action actor."

When he asked who, I smiled. "His name is Sven Thorsen. He has worked very closely with Arnold Schwarzenegger in the past and has a great and powerful presence."

Rob scratched his head. "Thorsen? That doesn't sound Asian."

I shook my head and said, "Rob, he has a mask on he doesn't have to be Asian!"

Rob was intrigued and wanted to meet him.

(Few people know that there's a Viking behind that mask. Sven Thorsen. The Demon.)

I also spoke to him about the Demon's weapon. Originally in the script, it was a sword, but I mentioned to Rob, a sword would be too small for a giant demon with a God like presence. I had another weapon I wanted to bring in called a Chinese Kwan Do. I explained to Rob that a Kwan Do has a long staff and a three quarter bladed half moon on one end. On the other end, it has a four corner spearhead. It would be perfect. He said he wanted to see it. For you readers out there, I knew exactly which Kwan Do I was going to show him. It was the most beautiful one I had ever seen. This Kwan Do belonged to Grandmaster Douglas Wong. He had this Kwan Do for over forty years. I called Doug up, asked if I could borrow it and to my delight, he said yes. I showed it to Rob and he loved it. We made three duplicates. So whenever you see that Kwan Do in the movie, just remember it came from the School of Sil-Lum Kung Fu. I left the office a bit happier than when I left the meeting as I knew Rob would love Sven as soon as they met and this was a great opportunity for my dear friend Sven. I called him up and explained the part to him and he loved it. I reiterated that I really wanted him to get this part, so he should be on his best behavior. All of you reading this by now, know how Sven can be, so I was a bit nervous for the interview. Sven wasn't.

"Don't worry Steven," Sven laughed. "I will make Rob Cohen love me like a Viking's wife."

The day comes and I'm in the office to make sure Sven behaves himself. He comes walking in, greets me and turns to Rob's secretary.

"Who is this beautiful slice of strawberry shortcake?" Sven asks.

Already, I start shaking my head. Oh no, I say to myself, here we go. Let me tell you that if I had said that to her, she would probably have gotten upset. Yet, the way Sven says these things, women just seem to love it and she was no different.

She smiled and chuckled like a little school girl and let Sven kiss her hand. I just laughed, knowing that was Sven.

I introduce him to Rob Cohen and Sven sticks out his hand and they shake. I look at Sven and ask, "are you going to kiss his hand too?"

Sven looked at me and said, "don't be such an idiot." Sven always loved to call the people he loved, names. Idiot and moron. Even Arnold Schwarzenegger. Imagine hearing out loud, "Arnold, you moron, sit down. Come over here, shut up you idiot." Arnold would do it and say, "okay."

It was hilarious. Sven looked at Rob. "I can tell right now, I need to put you on a weight training program," Sven comments.

Rob nods and says, "yeah, I need that."

I shut the door, leaving them alone to talk, thinking I have no idea what is going to happen. Ten minutes go by, fifteen minutes go by, twenty minutes go by, forty minutes. I am thinking, what the hell is going on in there? Finally, the door opens and I look up to see Sven and Rob with their arms around each other laughing, two huge cigars in their mouths!

Rob Cohen takes the cigar out and says, "he got the job, Steven!"

I smiled as Sven chimed in. "I told you not to worry, you idiot." Sven turns to Rob. "Make sure you take your vitamins and next time I see you I want some meat on those bones."

Rob laughed as I went with Sven, still in disbelief he could say those things and get the job. I probably would have been fired if I said half the things to half the people Sven did. What a great guy. I love him. As the days went by, I found myself busy with meetings, training Jason and going over things with Rob.

CHAPTER 72

(Actress Lauren Holly, The She-Devil.)

By the way. I brought on the dragon master, James Lew to help train Lauren Holly who played Linda Lee. In the original script, there was talk about her doing a sword routine with Bruce in the bedroom. Remember that intimate moment they had? But it never happened. It was supposed to be very sensual. Lauren wanted to be physically fit even though she didn't have a whole lot of action in the film. Of course, when James had something else going on, I would be the one to step in and train Lauren. James was always a busy boy and being a friend, you would never deny somebody an opportunity. That happened over and over again and I quickly learned what kind of person she was. She would talk about her then husband, Jim Carey at every training session.

I would open the door for her and she would mumble, "I wish Jim did that for me." I would bring her drinks and she would say, "I wish Jim would do that for me." All she talked about was Carey, it was a very uncomfortable situation. On top of that, it was always a problem working out with her, in that she never wanted to keep the set schedule we made. I made her aware of the things I had going on and gave her a choice of days and times and she would pick out the best ones for her. Two days would go by and she would want to change. That made it very difficult for me, as I would have to cancel meetings with people that sometimes only could meet once with me.

I tried to explain to Lauren how much missing meetings would not just affect me but affect everyone further down the line in the Production. She didn't really care and kept up her complicating ways. I had children and only a little time to eat with my family. Lauren loved to call during this time or when I was in an important meeting and demand that I train her at that moment. Rude and abusive she was. I would have to get up from my dinner table or the meeting and go meet her demands as she was the co-star after all. I tried to insist that she stick to her schedule she had agreed upon, but she simply would not. This went on and on until one day I was at a celebration meal with my wife. Lauren called me in the middle of it and demanded that I come right away. I explained to her I had taken my wife out and we were in the middle of our lunch to celebrate a special occasion. She didn't seem to care too much. She, listen to this, threatened me.

"If you don't come and train me right now, I will go to Raffaella and Rob Cohen and tell them to get rid of you."

Seconds of silence go by on my end. "What?" That was all I could say before I got my wits about me. "Lauren, you don't have to do that. This has been going on for weeks, we set a schedule and you always change it. I am spreading myself thin here, I have a lot to do."

My words fell on deaf ears and Lauren insisted she was going to the office if I did not come at that moment. What could I do? Leave my wife in the middle of lunch? I told Lauren she could do what she wanted and asked her to call me back when she wanted to train at a later time. She slams the phone down on me and I am left in shock. Now, I know I am head of a department and in this business, you must conform always to the status quo, which is simply kiss ass and do as your told. But sometimes the punk kid from Brooklyn gets to me.

An hour later, Rob Cohen calls me and wants me to come to the office. I asked if it was about Lauren. He said yes. I asked if Raffaella was going to be there. He said yes. I asked if I had to come. He said yes. I suggested they have the meeting without me. I knew this was going to be trouble. I had tried to explain to Rob before about Lauren's scheduling habits but he took no action. Going into the office, I knew Raffaella would be in ecstasy seeing me in this position. I sat down and Rob told me that Lauren was very upset with me and that she had even called Jason, who was now against me.

"You don't treat a star that way," Raffaella says to my right.

I just couldn't take it and tried to explain to Rob that I was having problems from the get go. "Jerry Poteet turning Jason to the dark side and now I have Lauren Holly who I am treating like a queen and in no way disrespecting, calling me at all times, RAFFAELLA! I've told you these problems before and have gotten no help from you, Rob. What am I supposed to do? I've gotten no help from anyone so, I guess I'll pack my bags and ride off into the sunset."

Rob looked at me and said, "well why don't you try to fix the situation and apologize to Lauren." Apologize!? For what? For not leaving my wife in the middle of a very special meal to adhere to her unreasonable demands?

I got up and said, "if things change, let me know."

Rob shook his head, "don't leave, Steven."

What could I do? "See you later Rob," I replied. I walked out and never saw him again. However, after the premier I got a letter from Rob Cohen thanking me for all my hard work and explaining that he was going to give me credit in the movie. That was nice of him.

April 6, 1993

Steve Lambert
P.O. Box 2224
Toluca Lake, CA 91610

ROB COHEN

Dear Steve:

I felt it only fair that you receive credit for the hard work you did in preparing Jason for the long journey.

If you should see the movie, I hope you enjoy it.

Best wishes to you and your family.

Regards,

Rob Cohen

(It was such a pleasure and a wonderful experience, working with Director Rob Cohen. Thank you.)

A couple of unknown facts before I leave this story. I have video footage of all six of these men that I used, that nobody knows about. Number two. As far as what I think of the action in this movie? I was disappointed in every fight. The party fight with the military - bad. The fight in the ring - sloppy and poorly done. The fight in the back of the restaurant - too ridiculous, too comical.

The only fight I thought was wonderful was the ice house fight. Whoever put that together, my congratulations.

CHAPTER 73
(Bruce Lee's Cup. It's Mine.)

A few months later, I receive a phone call from Linda Lee. What a surprise this was.

I hear a voice say, "hi, Steven. It's Linda. Linda Lee."

I had no idea why she would call me, but I was thrilled. I didn't know why until she explained.

"Steven, I am having an auction of all of Bruce's collection. His stuff. Are you interested?"

I think for a second. "Yes, Linda. What is going up for auction and may I ask where you are you going to have it?"

I listen and the answer comes. "Beverly Hills, August seventh," she tells me. "If you give me your address, I'll send you the catalog that has everything that is going up for auction."

So I do. Then I try to make small talk. I ask her if she has seen the movie yet.

She replies, "no I have not but I had heard that they had changed some of the story and facts and that's not what I agreed on. If that is so, I am not going to be very happy."

I apologized to her and said I'm sorry.

She went on talking and said, "Steven, that isn't your problem. You have nothing to worry about."

I said, "I know that, but if you are disappointed, I would feel so bad since you and Bruce and the movie meant so much to me."

She said, "thank you. It means so much to me that you would feel that way." I also thanked her for the names she gave me. Herb Jackson, Ted Wong, Bob Wall, Danny Inosanto, Richard Bustillo, Jerry Poteet. I said, "thank you. I put them all to use. Believe me, it was extraordinary, the moments that Jason and I had with these men. It helped both of us spiritually and physically, tremendously. I only had one problem and I'm not sure if I should mention it to you."

She asks, "what was the problem? Don't be afraid Steven, I won't get upset."

I reply, "I mean this with all due respect, but the problem was with Jerry Poteet. To make a long story short, it turned out that he got all these guys fired, lying to Jason Scott Lee. In a nutshell, telling Jason that these guys were no use to him They weren't the real deal. Poteet said that he was only the real deal and convinced Jason after four, five weeks, to fire them. All of them. Except himself. He convinced Jason to make him the chosen one. I even had an agreement with the Director Rob Cohen and the Producers, that every single one of them would get credit and Jerry

Poteet put a stop to that, convincing Jason to demand that they would not be on the credits. Only Jerry Poteet would get credit. On top of that, I also had James Lew, Doug Wong and Gene Lebell instructing him also. I also brought them on and he got rid of them too."

She said, "oh, you brought on Gene Lebell? Bruce really respected Gene. They were good friends."

I said, "yes, I knew that."

And then she apologized. "I should have warned you about Jerry Poteet. He was that kind of a guy. Bruce wasn't fond of him either. There were a number of times that he got Bruce so mad, he would kick him out of the club. He would come back, begging Bruce to let him back in. A number of times." Bruce was such a softy that he did."

I understood and we said our goodbyes and told her I would see her at the auction. I hung up. Two weeks later, I received the catalog.

(The catalog of Bruce's prized possessions.)

Page one to sixty seven. Sixty seven pages. All kinds of stuff it had in it. Letters, clothing, pictures, ranging from when he was a kid until he was an adult. All kinds of identifications. Drawings, equipment that he used. Even some that Herb Jackson made for him. They even had what he wore on *The Green Hornet* as Kato. Hat and gloves. Original scripts. I had my choice of hundreds of things. From hundreds to thousands of dollars. What shall I choose?

I realize it's an auction and an item that may cost hundreds may turn out to bring twenty times more than it says in the book.

So I sit back and think hard. What should I choose? I got it. A cup. A ceramic coffee cup that somebody made for Bruce Lee on *The Game Of Death.* That he used. He drank out of it. The bidding price? One to three hundred dollars. It may go over. But even if the bid is a thousand dollars, I can still afford that. That's what I'm going to get. I hope.

Come the first of August, I'm excited. August fifth, I get a phone call asking if I am available to work for a week starting August seventh.

I can't turn it down.

Why?

Because it's working for James Woods. I've been with him for like fifteen years and never turned him down. I can't. Because if you do, you take a risk of never coming back, no matter how close you are. I think. What do I do? I'm so upset. I got it. I take the job and I call Linda Lee and explain to her what is going on. I ask her if it is okay to send my wife, Cecilia Camacho to bid on the cup. I want the Bruce Lee *The Game Of Death* cup.

"I'm going to send my wife, but she really doesn't understand how to bid at an auction, what to do. When she gets there, is there any way possible that she could look you up and you could have somebody help her?" I ask.

She replied, "yes. When she gets there, have her find me, introduce herself and remind me it's for Steven Lambert."

"Oh, that's wonderful," I say to Linda. "I can't tell you how much I appreciate this. I really want that cup."

She said, "okay, just have her find me when she gets there."

We say our goodbyes when on August seventh, she arrives to the auction. It was called The Bruce Lee Collection. My wife, when she gets there, she finally convinces somebody to help her find Linda Lee. Cecilia introduces herself to Linda Lee and says, "I am here for Steven Lambert to bid on the Bruce Lee *The Game Of Death* cup."

She turns to Shannon and introduces Shannon to my wife. "This is Shannon. Our daughter."

They also shake hands and say hello.

Linda says, "oh yes, follow me." Linda leads her into this room, so I am told in detail by Cecilia. I had her tell me exactly what went on. She walks over to this table and picks up a box that says, "ceramic cup. *The Game Of Death.* "

(With the name Bruce Lee, made of solid gold leaf.)

And hands it to her.

My wife shakes her head in confusion.

"I don't understand, don't I have to bid on it and pay for it?" My wife is Hispanic, she doesn't speak good English.

Linda says, "usually yes. But this is a gift for Steven. No charge."

My wife told me that she thanked her and said, "this is going to mean so much to Steven. And he is very much going to appreciate this."

They shake hands and Linda asks her if she was going to stay and watch. She says yes. But between you and me, she doesn't. She mentions to Linda and Shannon, "Steven would like very much for you to sign the catalog for his daughter Natasha."

And she does. Even Shannon signs it. She goes home and she calls me right away. Finally, she gets ahold of me. Before she even spoke two words, I interrupted and said, "did you get the cup!?"

She said, "yes, she gave it to me for free."

I was stunned. "For free? You mean you didn't have to pay for it?"

She told me, "no, Steven."

I was surprised. How wonderful that was, I thought. And then I thought again.

"Oh Cecilia, I say. "I wish you would have called me when you were there."

She asked why. I told her, "I would have paid for something else. Who knows, maybe I could have gotten something else for free."

Cecelia laughs and apologizes. How sweet she was.

I said, "no, no. I'm not upset. I'm just greedy. I just would have got two things instead of one."

She laughs and I laugh with her saying, "it's okay. What you did for me was terrific."

And that's the end of this story.

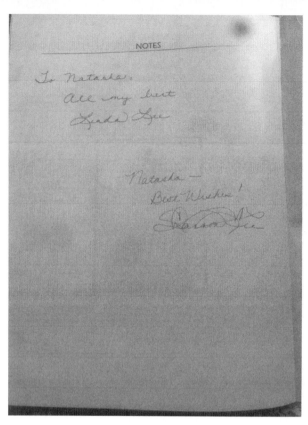

(Autographs to my daughter. Natasha Lambert. Linda and Shannon Lee.)

CHAPTER 74
(Actor Alec Baldwin And Kim Bassinger. Two Of A Kind.)

The Getaway, that was my next movie. No, not the original with Steve McQueen. I'm too young for that one. This was with Alec Baldwin, Kim Bassinger and my pal James Woods. It was a two week gig. I was doing a fight with James Woods and Alec Baldwin.

Alec, to put it mildly, he was, how should I say this? An ego maniac.

Everything had to be about him. Situations, conversations and even camera angles. At times, Woods got a little disturbed and made some comments such as, "you think this movie is about you? Without an actor like me in this scene, the film would be shown just for bachelor parties and clown functions."

Everybody exploded in laughter. Even Alec did. Woods always had great thigh slappers, always in fun. On top of that, I wish, one of the most beautiful women I ever saw and guess what? Kim Bassinger. All she would do on set is nag, nag and naggity nag. She needed chairs, she needed drinks, she needed shade. She needed makeup every five minutes. She needed her phone. What a kvetch she was. That's a Yiddish word, look it up. Alec would always call her, "Dear."

I mean it was so obvious after a while, everybody in the crew was dry heaving. What a pair. The most amusing thing being there, was with James Woods and the things he would say about those two around the crew and in front of them. They were good friends. It was hilarious and Jimmy always got everybody through the day with his humor.

He would say things like, "now ladies and gentlemen, here is Ren and Stimpy."

Boy, did they have foul mouths. Now moving on, let's talk about a class act.

CHAPTER 75
(A Fantasy In My Head Comes To Life.)

The name is Norris. Chuck Norris, that is. Now I have worked with Chuck Norris many times in the past. He is doing his television show, *Walker Texas Ranger*, which I have worked on many times before either playing myself or stunt doubling someone. One day I get a call from the crazy man. Now, in this case, crazy isn't bad. Crazy means wonderful. Remember that word in the sixties? That was a beatnik word for one cool cat. Aaron Norris, I say.

He is so much fun to work with. You never knew what was going on when it came to Aaron and I enjoy it that way. He asks me if I was available to play a part that they had for me. I would never turn down a show working for any Norris, so I jumped at the chance. I was told by Aaron they would send me the script. The very next day, I get a knock on my door and it is a carrier with the script! How about that? In those days you didn't get a script via email. I started reading the script and got excited, realizing there was more to my character than what meets the eye.

What I have here on my lap is magical. You could say miraculous. Momentous. At least in my head. You Martial Art people will understand what I am going to explain to you now. I practically had a part from Bruce Lee's *Way of The Dragon*.

The character I am playing resembles the kind of character Chuck Norris played in the film, to get rid of Bruce Lee. In my head, I am playing Chuck Norris in the scene and Chuck is playing Bruce Lee in the scene. This is the way it reads. Now in the script, there is a scene coming out of the jet being greeted by bad guys, a scene where I am keeping two women hostage and a fight scene that simply says, "HUGE FIGHT."

I am visualizing this scene from *Way Of The Dragon*. I am surprised but at the same time confused. This is a version of exactly what happened more or less in the *Way Of The Dragon*.

It also reads I have a briefcase. Inside it, a pair of swords. I wonder what kind of swords they have. All these thoughts are swirling in my mind for the next few days, wondering how much they are going to let me do.

(Chuck Norris and Howard Jackson. I saw them fight when we were young, and now I work with them.)

That question is just what I ask to Aaron Norris when I arrive on set and go to the Production Office.

He said, "you are a featured character on the show Steven, you can do whatever you want."

I told him I wanted Kung Fu double swords if they had them and he said he would get to props right away. I ask about wardrobe.

He started laughing saying, "I'm sure you will surprise us, Steven."

We shook hands and I was in seventh Heaven. I then headed to Wardrobe. I tell the lady there what character I am playing and she brings me into the costume room. She stops. I look at her and she looks at me.

Then I ask her, "what do you have me wearing?"

She smiles and she says, "my kingdom is yours, go pick what you want."

I blink and think to myself, self, did I hear that right? She flashes a smile and tells me to go down the aisles and pick out what I think would work. God knows that was music to my ears. Anybody who knows me knows that is a fact, Jack. I went up and down the aisles. Got some high waisted baggy pants, a very colorful baggy shirt. An eye catcher. And ohhh let's see. HOW ABOUT THIS.

I found a nice scarf, to go with my ensemble, you don't see very many bad guys wearing scarves do you? And oh, what do we have here? Looky looky, the hat department. I look up high to see a rack with hats and I take a hat and place it on my head. Perfect. As soon as it touched my head, it was like Michael Jackson with his silver glove. It was like Judy Garland with her red shoes in *The Wizard Of Oz*. The mighty Thor and his hammer. But in this case, it's a fedora on my head. I put it all on and look at myself in the mirror. I am thinking, there is no way in hell wardrobe, let alone the Director and Chuck is going to let me wear all this. But what the hell, let's give it a shot. I walk out in my new costume and find the wardrobe lady.

"What do you think?" I ask.

She looks me up and down and I know what she is going to say. "You look great," she replies.

Okay, that was unexpected. She asks me if I wanted anything else and I told her no, I was all set. Just like that, I had myself a costume. An Academy Award winning costume. Hahahaha. I'm on top of the world, ma. One down, two to go. Let's see what Chuck and the Director say. I go to where we rehearse in full costume and I see Chuck. We greet each other with happiness and I tell him it was so great of him to think of me for this role.

He shook my hand and said, "you were the perfect guy, Steven. We will get started on the fight soon. By the way, I love your wardrobe."

I crack a smile as he said, "only you Steven, only you."

We laugh with each other. Props comes over with a briefcase. I open it up and see the double swords. They are perfect. This whole thing is set up to be golden. To be continued. Ready to continue? Okay, good. The first scene I shot at the airport was fantastic. I made sure to make it memorable. When I made my debut revealing myself walking out, I stop in the doorway of the plane knowing I'm like a subject in a framed painting. I made sure I stood there looking at everyone for at least six seconds. James Woods taught me that.

He once said, "if you are ever in a doorway, make sure you stop and take it all in. That way you command a presence."

When I went to shake hands with all the bad guys, instead of going in order, I crisscrossed around. When the door of my limo was opened for me, I made sure I handed over my suitcase, took off my fedora and stepped into my coach. That my friends is how you stretch and command a scene. In the next couple of days, we finally got to the scene with the two singing women. We rehearsed it where the Director told me to just stand behind the two women while they sang. I did and it felt awkward, I felt like a statue. Something was missing.

I took a deep breath and went over to the Director and told him, "you know, I have an idea to enrich this scene and give it substance. Make it scary."

He looked at me like I said something foreign to him.

"I have this suitcase and everyone wonders what is inside. Instead of waiting for the Chuck Norris fight, why don't I reveal them now and swing them around close to them so it would look menacing."

The Director thought for a moment before asking me to show him what I meant. I call over props and ask for the suitcase with the swords. The D.P. then followed me as I laid the case flat and explained to them, "now you have the camera on the suitcase and I open it to reveal the swords." I picked them up, I turned and said, "now you follow me as I walk behind them as they are singing."

He did and then I started doing moves, three sixties, one eighties, around the girl's heads as they started acting and singing (for real) nervously. The Director stood up and actually applauded. I asked, "you like it?"

He replied, "hell, yeah."

The ladies wanted to know what moves I was going to do so every time they would be ready to expect certain things. I told them I was going to change it up every time, that was the whole point so that they didn't expect what was coming and give more realistic reactions from them. They looked at me like I was crazy, but I promised I wouldn't hit them. "It will be slow and scary so don't be wary," I told them. And that my friends, is how it's done.

I tell you from a teaching frame of mind, don't ever be afraid to think, to fantasize and suggest ideas. When we finally got to the fight scene with Chuck, boy, was I excited. This was the moment. Bruce Lee fighting Chuck Norris. No, Steven Lambert fighting Bruce Lee. No, Chuck Norris fighting Steven Lambert. *The Way of The Dragon.* I can fantasize, can't I? We rehearsed it a few times, Chuck and Aaron giving me total freedom to do what I wanted to do. For this is a fight, staff versus double swords. Then when we finally got to the moment, which is picture, I did something unexpected. Something that took a lot of guts.

I heard the word, "action."

I took off my scarf. I walked over in position, got into my fighting stance and I slowly reached up and took off the hat on my head and slowly tossed it, gliding through the air, landing right on a standing microphone. A Fred Astaire move if I ever saw one. I waited for the Director to yell, "cut", but it never happened! So I continued the scene, fighting Chuck. Then halfway through the fight I tried my luck once more, this time knowing Chuck was going to say something. I land a punch to Chuck's face. He takes it and goes back. I spin, doing a three sixty. Coming out of it, I LOCK INTO A POSE.

I bent down low and motioned for Chuck to come at me, picking up my hand and waving my fingers, EXACTLY as Bruce Lee did.

Well, would you believe it? He said NOTHING.

I was shocked, improv my friends. It works. We continued on until the end.

The Director shouted, "cut, print."

I stood up looking at Chuck, waiting for him to come over and say to me, "Steven, leave that hand gesture out when we do it again."

To my surprise, not a word was said. I was still in shock that he let me do everything I wanted to do. Remember, this is the Chuck show, not the Lambo show. Yet I made it the Lambo show, someway, somehow and they let me. I went up to Aaron Norris after and said, "Aaron you know what we just did?"

He asked me what I was talking about.

I told him, "we just replicated the scene from The Way Of The Dragon with Bruce and Chuck."

Aaron looked at me and simply said, "I know."

It was such a blessing and a surreal moment to be able to again do something so closely related to Bruce Lee and Chuck Norris.

CHAPTER 76
(Actor And Rapper Ice T Steals My Head.)

After that, I got my head chopped off in a movie called *Surviving The Game*. My buddy Bob Minor calls me up, wanting to know if I wanted to do a part in the opening sequence of the show. Of course! He tells me Rutger Hauer and Gary Busey will be on it. I said, "oh, I'll see a couple of my old wacko friends!"

He laughed. "Yea."

I love doing acting parts and when the limo greeted me to bring me to my first class seat at the airport, I was even more thrilled. I get dropped off at the airport and I sit down to wait for boarding. A half hour later, here comes Ice T walking past me. "Ice T!" I yell.

He looks up nervously and asks who I am. I tell him my name and that I was working as an action actor on this show. I tell him I get my head cut off and we discuss the sequence. We start talking and he gets comfortable, but every now and then he keeps looking nervously all around us. I ask him, "you looking for somebody?"

He said, "no man, I'm afraid I'm going to get jumped or popped."

He explained in street talk vernacular. "Man, ever since I did that cop killer song, I've been gettin' threats on my life, gotta watch my step, bro."

I'm listening to this hardcore rapper talking about being nervous everywhere he goes and I am amazed he felt comfortable talking to me about it, someone he just met, but he had a way about him that was very cool. It was like he was two people. On the box, he is Ice T. In person, he seems like an ordinary guy. Facades, anything to make money, how about that? We board the plane and we continue to discuss our lives, childhood, etc. When we arrive, I call the secretary and ask her to let me know Rutger Hauer's room number and when he was coming in as we were good friends from working on *Blind Fury*. I wasn't about to ask for Gary Busey's room number after the events on *Eye of the Tiger*. He is a mad man. The secretary refuses to give me his room number but luckily there was the First Assistant nearby who contacted the Producers who contacted Rutger on set. Rutger agreed that I could call him that evening after he wrapped. I was very excited to see him again and it was he who called me first. We talked a bit and he invited me over to dinner with Busey and a few others. I met him at a steak house and there is Rutger sitting at the table. Along with him is Gary Busey and F. Murray Abraham. I walk over and Busey looks at me and says, "I know you!"

I nodded and said my name to him and mentioned, "mad dog! Mad dog Sarrafian. Remember the baby powder?"

That was the perfect thing to say because he starts laughing and asked me to sit down. We start talking about all our past movies, eating and having a good time. I even mentioned the time Busey fired the cameraman and he burst out laughing at the table. It was a great dinner amongst friends. It was hilarious. I survived the dinner, but I knew I had no chance of surviving the game. The next day I found out a stunt guy I knew was coming in. Guess who? George Fisher. Remember THAT guy? He calls me up and asks me downstairs to the hotel's restaurant to have breakfast. I say "why not?" I go down and get a table and wait for George to arrive. A few minutes go by and I look up to see, not George, but F. Murray Abraham.

"Hey. Great time the other night, Steven. A lot of great stories flying around. Mind if I join? I'm starving," he says.

I nod and said, "Sure. Help yourself."

He smiles and sits down. We start talking and he asks me what I'm having. I simply told him, "breakfast." I thought I'd give him a little New York attitude. That is when I feel something on my thigh and my leg. I quickly realize it isn't a dropped fork or a waitress putting a napkin on my lap. It is a hand. F. Murray Abraham's hand. I'm what the FFFFF Murray Abraham is going on!? I look at him and say, "if you don't remove your hand from my leg now, I'm going to break your face."

He jumps back in shock and I get up, pissed off. I decide to walk out of the restaurant and as I am leaving, I pass George Fisher.

"Where are you going, Steven? Breakfast is this way," he calls out to me.

I looked back and said, "I'm out of here, go have fun with your other half."

George looked at me confused, as I headed back to my room to get a clean pair of pants. Yeah, I know we heard he's married, but what the hell does that mean? Let's move from hands to head. My head. For the scene where I get my head cut off, I had to take a plaster cast of my head. Was it fun? No. You had to stay very still for a long time. Hours, with two frickin' straws up my nose so I can breathe. That is why I grew attached to the prop once it was detached from my body. After shooting my sequence and getting decapitated, I went back home. But before I did, I asked the FX guy if I could have the cast of my head when the show is over. He said yes, to call him. A few weeks later, I called the FX Coordinator on set to inquire about getting my ugly face back. The FX guy had bad news.

"I'm sorry Steven, he took it," he told me. "

Who took it?" I shot back.

"Ice T took it. I told him several times I had promised to give it to you but he is the star and he practically confiscated it."

I couldn't believe he took MY HEAD!

(Stuntman Bob Minor and Ice T. Guess where we are going? Lunch. Soul food, baby.)

What could I do? I couldn't get mad at the FX guy so I hung up dejected. A few months later I just happened to be on my couch eating a Fatburger in front of the television and what do you know and what do I see? Me. An interview with Ice T comes on for *Entertainment Tonight*. The only reason I'm watching is because that blankety - blank stole my head. They are in his house and he is showing the cameras around. He goes into his playroom and shows off his things. They happen to pan full screen on a fish tank. I almost dropped my Fatburger on the floor! There was my ugly head in this fish tank! My Head! With my hair floating all around and the fish swimming in between trying to bite it.

The cameraman asks, "were we supposed to see that?"

Ice T smiles. "No, no man that's fake. Don't get me in any trouble. That is some dude that got his head cut off in a film I did," he explains.

So that is where my head went, I thought to myself. A few months later I soon found myself working on a television show called *New York Undercover*. Guess who was on it? Ice T! The first thing I did was find out where his motor home was and went right over like a hawk to its prey. I knocked on the door. A voice comes through.

"Who is it?" he calls from inside.

"Steven Lambert, an actor on the show," I respond.

Silence. Then the door opens and Ice T looks down at me with a who-da- hell-are-you face. I point right at him.

"YOU STOLE MY HEAD! I saw you had it in your fish tank. I want it back. It was promised to me and you had no right to take it," I tell him seriously.

He shakes his head, "aw, man. That thing? Man, that dissolved in the water and ended up killing all my fish!"

A smile appears on his face and I smile back before we burst out laughing and gave each other a fist bump. It was good to see him again, even if he stole my head.

CHAPTER 77
(Actor Jean Claude Van Damme Takes It Out On me.)

My next risky venture was a movie, *Timecop*. A Jean Claude Van Damme film. I'm playing Lansing, a great character role.

(Me and my sidekick.)

I'm in the last fifteen minutes of the movie. The last two people you see is Van Damme and me. In the middle of the scene, I have a big fight with Jean Claude. We need to put it together. Good ole' Glenn Randall. Three times, he sets up rehearsals and Jean Claude doesn't show up. You see, Randall was told by Van Damme that he puts together his own fights. Not the Stunt Coordinator. Glenn tells our Director, Peter Hyams, a day before we are supposed to film this fight that he had made three rehearsal times with Van Dame and he never showed up.

Our Director simply said, "eff him. You guys put together the fight."

So Randall and I did. Got ahold of Van Damme's double, who was Mark Stefanich and we put together the fight. The next day when we are supposed to film it, Jean Claude finds out that the fight is done already. All choreographed, put together. Well, Van Damme gets a little aggravated. He's pissed. He wants to put together his own fight. We are on stage and he is arguing with Glenn Randall. Randall insists that the fight that he and I put together, stays. Van Damme is infuriated. He tucks his tail between his legs and he goes and complains to Peter Hyams, the Director.

Peter says, "you do the fight that we have all together already. There's no time."

Van Damme resists.

Peter says, "if you don't do it the way it is now, then we cut it out."

Van Damme ain't happy, but he concedes. We have to do this in pieces now. No time to teach him and do it all at once. During the fight, I have a gun and Van Damme disarms me and the fight is supposed to continue. But when he disarms me, he decides to keep the gun in his hand and slips another unscripted punch in with the gun and splits my eyebrow wide open. No, that wasn't planned. Most people say he did it on purpose. I say that they are right. You can tell by a man's expression when something is deliberate. He didn't even apologize as blood is dripping down my face. It hurt. I wanted to punch him in his face. But we all know, that's part of the territory. You just gotta suck it up and move on. The Director wanted to take me to the hospital.

I ask him, "why?"

"Well, you are bleeding all over the place," he says.

I laugh and say, "it fits. Just let me finish the scene and then I'll go to the hospital. It looks more realistic this way. Just give me a wet towel so I can clean my eye." I found it extremely funny that Jean Claude was nowhere to be found during this conversation. When he was called back to film the rest of the sequence and we stood face to face, he asked me why I wasn't going to the hospital to get my wound stitched up.

I looked at him and said, "I'm tough. And if you hit me again, I'm going to get rough."

CHAPTER 78
(Stuntman Walter Scott And His Brilliant Idea.)

I smiled. What's next you ask? Well, James Woods was working on a TV movie called *Next Door* with Randy Quaid and like a good neighbor Jimmy is there. He brought me on the show to be the Stunt Coordinator and I met the Producer and Director. I had been told by the Production Manager that Walter Scott was in line for the show and mentioned that he was from my group and was a good guy. You should always show respect to people even if they are in line for your job. Competition is always healthy and I knew anyway, even if I wasn't coordinating, I would be doubling Jimmy. I told them if I coordinated and doubled the lead actor, they would save a lot of money. A little enticing trick I talked about before. A few days later, I was told by the Production Manager that the Director and Producer are thinking about Walter Scott. I went back in and tried to convince them otherwise, using my experience with Jimmy and my budget cutting ideas. They said they would get back to me and that they did. The choice was made and Walter Scott was his name-o. When I told Jimmy this, he was not happy. He told me he was going to go into the office and as the lead, put his foot down and demand that I be the Coordinator.

I thanked him, but said, "listen, Jimmy, even if I am not coordinating, I am still doubling you. This way two people get a job and I am happy I am giving work to a member in my Association. Yes, he is in my stunt group. Brotherhood." I knew I could get the job, but I thought to myself, this is an opportunity to be nice and giving. This calmed Jimmy down and he decided to let it go. Most Stunt Coordinators wouldn't do this. About a week goes by and I see Walter Scott on set and say, "hey, Boss." I mention to him, "now there are two of us working, Walter. I asked Jimmy to back off."

Well, it just went right over his head and he went on like it never happened. As time went on, it was awkward working with Walter Scott. I would put together the bulk of the sequence, especially with Jimmy but still let Walter take the credit for it, which was normal when it comes to me when I am working for most Stunt Coordinators. Until one fine day, we were doing a basketball sequence. Get ready to laugh, this is a good one. James Woods played the good neighbor and Randy Quaid played the crazy neighbor. This was a basketball contest between them and their sons. Randy's character played ball the New York way. Body checks and illegal moves, to name a few. Okay, let me set this up for you. Jimmy's character would get more frustrated until Randy's character body checks him to the ground as he is making a layup. The Director suddenly decides to have Jimmy fall out of the shot and onto the ground. Now Jimmy had hip, elbow and knee pads on which I put on him, but since he was flying out of the shot and onto the ground, he asked for a small falling pad to land on. He requested it and was met with silence.

"Hey, guys. I need a pad to do this," Jimmy reiterated.

The First Assistant shook his head and asked FX.

The FX guy shook his head. "I don't have any. There was no call in the production meeting to bring them and besides, it's not my job unless I am asked. Do props have any?"

The prop guy shook his head, saying the same thing. No pads unless I am asked. The prop guy looked at Walter Scott.

"You are the Coordinator, aren't you supposed to have pads ready?"

Walter Scott, wearing his cowboy hat and having a half unlit cigar in his mouth, shrugged. "What do you want from me. I had no idea he was going to fall out of the shot. He has hip and elbow pads, what's the matter? You soft Jimmy?" He says this in front of everyone, the whole cast and crew, loud and clear. Big mistake. All of a sudden, there was conversation of where this pad would come from when I spot Walter Scott break away and go over to a lounge chair. Sorry for the laugh, my writer heard it. I just find it hilarious the stupidity of the situation. He picks up the pad from the chair, walks two steps and says, "hey, Woods."

Everybody stops talking and looks at Walter Scott. From ten feet away, he flings this pad with two hands across the set, full blast. The pad hits Jimmy's legs hard. We are all just agape that Walter Scott practically assaulted a lead actor.

Walter takes the cigar out of his mouth and says, "here is your pad, now stop whining." We were all stunned. James Woods, fire in his eyes, spoke.

I said to myself, "oh, shit. Here it comes."

(Third one from the left, Randy Quaid. Looney tunes.)

Jimmy stepped forward and flung his words even harder than Walter Scott threw the pad.

"You shit eating, cigar smoking, ten gallon hat, phony ass looking John Wayne that you're not. You're out of here." Jimmy walks off set and goes to his trailer. Still, everyone is quiet.

Walter Scott tries to break the ice. "Well, jeez. I don't know why he got upset. He is only falling down. I gave him a pad."

Well, picture this. Walter Scott became like the bubonic plague. The Producer didn't want to talk to him. The Director ignored him. The cameraman turned his back on him. The more he tried to talk to people, the more people turned away. Everything is shut down without Jimmy as the Producers scramble to figure out what to do now. I'm just an innocent bystander watching this chaos unfold. As I always do on every Jimmy show, I explain to everybody. Be nice and don't do anything stupid. Come to me with your Jimmy problem. They never listen. A half hour goes by and I am standing by craft services when I spot the Director and Producers heading straight for me. I have a feeling of what this is about.

"We can't get Jimmy out of his honey wagon, would you help us?"

Talk about Deja Vu. Again, this had nothing to do with me and if you remember what I said to the powers on *The Hard Way,* it was basically the same thing here. So I go to Jimmy's trailer, I shout out my name and am invited in. Right away, I got a death stare. I know his looks by now and this stare is saying, "you better not say the wrong thing." In any case, I tried to explain to Jimmy that he should give Walter Scott another chance, everyone makes mistakes. Well, the stare has come to its full power which is the voice.

Jimmy went ballistic on me, saying it was, "your idea to let Walter Scott have the job in the first place. Listen, Steven, what he did is not only unprofessional, it was unacceptable. It would be one thing if he brought the pad over, laid it down and said that's the only thing we have, can you work with it, Jimmy? But the way he went about it was beyond uncalled for. That phony ass Roy Rogers is done and you are taking over the show and that's that."

Right away, I knew this was serious. Jimmy was just disgusted as this was the first time that he ever yelled back at me.

I told him, "okay, whatever you think."

He told me he would be out soon and I left him be. As I walked back to set, I saw the Producers coming to me.

"Steven, we got this handled," they assured me. "We are going to move onto another scene and we have talked to Walter Scott and told him he wasn't going to be on the show anymore. He gave us another name, so Stunt Coordinator Max Kleven is taking over."

I was shocked at what I was hearing. You would think after all the work they saw me do, putting stuff together, coming up with ideas and even coming over to me a few times saying, "we know you thought of this Steven, it's a great idea," they wouldn't even consider turning it over to me? That's common sense, basic decency. I mean as another Stunt Coordinator friend once told me, "it doesn't take the brains of Churchill to figure that out."

Yeah, I know I have said that already. But here is another situation where it is true. I reminded them I was in the running for Stunt Coordinator and let them go with Walter and now they are hiring Max Kleven!? They are not showing me the respect I deserve and going over my head.

"Well, we know Max Kleven and Walter Scott highly suggested him," the Producer tried to explain to me.

"Right now I am talking to you, I'll talk to Walter in a moment. I want this job and I am upset you are completely painting me out of the picture," I shot back.

The Producers talked to themselves for a moment, then decided they would discuss it with the Director. As they turned to leave, I marched right over to Walter Scott. He had a new cigar in his mouth and waved cheerfully at me.

"Hey, Steven. You don't need to worry. I told 'em to use Max Kleven."
I was just amazed he was saying these things.

"Don't you remember it was me who told Jimmy to calm down, that I helped you get this job? You frickin' donkey riding cowboy, I'm pissed. You see what I did for you? You should have done that for me. Automatically. You of all people, Walter!"

He shrugged. "It's no big deal, Steven. Calm down. You still are Jimmy's double."

I couldn't believe this guy. "Of course I am Jimmy's double, nobody is going to change that. I am talking about Stunt Coordinating. Walter, look at me. You know something? YOU'RE FIRED! And guess what? I'm going to be the Stunt Coordinator."

I watched him take a puff of his cigar and threw my hands up in disgust. He thought I was going to hit him. He flinched back.

"You went over my head. I showed gratitude and friendship. Where is the reciprocation?" I turned around and walked off. Where did I go? Right to James

Wood's trailer. He was on the phone and I told him I would wait. When he got off, I told him what had happened. He started laughing and laughing.

"This is how a friend, a team player, a member of your group pays you back?" He asks me. Jimmy was right. No good deed goes unpunished in this business it seemed.

"I'll handle this," Jimmy says.

I told Jimmy, "Jimmy, please. I need to be the Stunt Coordinator. It is a matter of principle now. Not Max Kleven. If that happens, I'll feel and look like an idiot."

Jimmy looked at me and said, "I'll take care of it right now." He exits his motor home and heads over to the Producers. I would have gone with him but he said he could handle it himself. An hour later, the Producers find me and tell me I am Coordinating the show. End of story. Full circle. P.S. Max Kleven arrived. I fired him with style and grace. I told him to go home, he is not needed. Speaking of loyalty, stuntmen have very few ways to secure a job. Hustling to locations, getting your demo reel out there, word of mouth. All these things take years to come together so that you are working on a regular basis. Then there are the wonderful actors that request the same double on every show they do. They are merely a handful, but their names live on. John Wayne and Yakima Canutt. Clint Eastwood and Buddy Van Horn. Arnold Schwarzenegger and Joel Kramer. James Gardner and Roy Clarke. Harvey Perry and James Cagney. Burt Reynolds and Hal Needham. Then you have James Woods and Steven Lambert. That is truly something special.

CHAPTER 79
(Actress Sharon Stone Throwing A Hissy Fit And Other Tales)

Uh oh, Sly's back. This time without his son. In the movie, *The Specialist*. It was starring Sly Stallone and Sharon Stone. That's a lot of stones, they need some Woods. James Woods, that is. I was told the Stunt Coordinator Alan Graff would be calling to give me more information. I knew Graff. He was from my stunt group. I think he tried to be a professional football player turned stunt guy. He was an okay guy, I thought. A little rough around the edges. Maybe somewhat of a big man's complex, but we all have our own personality. We always had pleasant conversations and worked together in the past when we were kids. Let me tell you one story with Alan and myself. It's quite comical. We were working for Stuntman Gary Baxley. Let me set the scene. Apartment, brownstone building. Second story window doubling the bad guy. I get punched out of the window. Alan Graff is right below reading a newspaper. Guess what happens? Baxley tells me he wants to do it all in one shot.

I say, "you mean you want me to free fall right on top of Alan? I might hit him in the head. I can break his neck. It's best to do this in two shots. One falling out the window, one falling from a six foot ladder and I will hit him in the back. He doesn't see me coming, he's standing there reading the newspaper right below."

Baxley tells me, "I already spoke to Graff and he said it was okay."

I said, "you did? Well, let's go over and talk to him. If he says okay, fine. But let me tell ya, that's a little off in the way of thinking." That is exactly what we did and sure enough, Graff agreed to do it. I asked him how many concussions he had from football.

He said, "a few."

I said, "get ready for a possible 'nother one." I looked at him and explained, "I'm going to try and hit you as soft as possible, but there is always a chance I could break your neck."

He seemed worried, little sweaty raindrops were coming off his forehead but I knew he was just trying to impress Baxley.

I asked him, "are you sure? It's fine with me if you are sure."

He said, "yes."

I mean we all do some crazy stuff, but this is downright stupid. I explain to him again, "Graff, I'll try to hit you in your back, but I can't guarantee it. Your head is above your back, I can't avoid it. Just make sure you lean your head forward. You're the one that is going to take the brunt of this. I am using you more or less as a pad." Let's just cut to the chase. Cameras - Action! I get thrown out of the window, glass shattering, and came down like a sack of potatoes. A hundred and fifty five pound sack. Seventy five percent of my body hits him right where I want, in his back. Twenty five percent of my body hits him in the head, couldn't be avoided. Knocked out cold Graff was. I get up and I try to put him in a sitting position while first aid comes over and I look at Baxley. He's got that big shit eating grin on his head. A head I've seen before. He is a not very smart, sadistic son of a gun. BAM! Guess what? He was knocked out cold. I tried my best. Baxley came running over, he thought it was funny. He had that big shit eating grin on his face. Nobody else did. A classic memory.

Now this movie, *The Specialist,* that we are working on was about to start filming in a couple of weeks. A week goes by and no phone call. I decide to call Graff and got him on the phone. We exchange greetings and as we are talking, I feel a wall between us and ask him what is going on. I hadn't received the script yet and time was running out before the start date.

"Well, to be honest, Steven, I don't know if there is any action in the script and I'm not sure if I am going to use you," he says. He tells me this very rudely.

I explained to him I was requested by Jimmy and didn't understand why he was being so condescending to me. He tells me he would get back to me and we hang up. Another week goes by and no phone call. So I call Jimmy to say hello and to small talk. In the middle, he just happened to ask me if everything was set and when I was coming. I mentioned to him I hadn't heard anything yet and that Alan Graff said there wasn't any real action for me.

"Not much action? The whole script is filled with action," Jimmy said. "I'll remind him, Steven."

I thanked Jimmy and hung up. A day before the show is about to start, I still haven't heard anything. Now I'm wondering what is going on. I try to call Alan but no luck. I call Jimmy, but no luck there either. A few more days go by and one afternoon I get a call from Jimmy and he is upset! Well, actually, he was mad. No, he was furious.

He tells me on the phone, "what do you mean you are not available!? You told me you are available! I told the Producers you were coming up!"

I took a few moments to process what was going on. "Jimmy, what are you talking about, who said I wasn't available?"

I hear from the other end of the line, "the Stunt Coordinator."

I am stunned, I don't know what to say. A few seconds go by. Finally, I speak up. "Jimmy, what are you talking about? I never said any such thing. I'm waiting to hear from the Stunt Coordinator." I waited for his reply and it came quick.

"I talked to the Stunt Coordinator and he told me you said you weren't available and that you got another job."

The name Alan Graff rose up in my mind like a menacing shadow. "Jimmy, that's a big lie. He is only doing that because he is insecure. There are only a few reasons why people do that. Number one he wants somebody else. Number two, he doesn't want an equal there. Number three, he doesn't want the actor telling him who to use. Number four, he's jealous. You want a number five? Never mind. What a horrible blatant lie Alan Graff told you. I would never do that to you, Jimmy," I said.

Number three was the key as far as Jimmy was concerned. I repeated myself, "he lied to you, Jimmy. Now regardless if I go up there, I just want you to know that he lied to you. I would never turn you down. I appreciate everything. We are pals. The guy was in my group, I don't understand why he would sabotage a job for a fellow member. He went over my head with a lie and don't you think I would talk to you first Jimmy?" I waited for his answer, my mind going a mile a minute.

"You still want to come up? Are you available?" Jimmy asked.

"Yes, of course," I blurted out.

A few seconds later, Jimmy responded. "I'll take care of it, Steven. You will be getting a call soon. I'll make sure of it."

I said, "thanks, man. I do appreciate it, Jimmy." Sure enough, guess who called me?

Mister Alan Graff. He asked if I was available to come up tonight.

"You bet," I said.

He told me the office would call me with travel arrangements soon. Before we hung up, I asked him what the deal was.

His reply, "what deal?"

Now, let me explain it takes a lot for me to be upset and say what is on my mind. I let it all hang out and people who know me, know that I ask for the truth. So much so, it sometimes turns people against me. People who want their version of the truth to prevail. I tell the truth and that is exactly what I did to Alan Graff.

"Where do you get the guts to flat out lie to my actor? Where does that come from? Why would you say that? If you didn't want to hire me in the first place, you should be a man. Have some courage. Lie to me, not to my actor. How stupid you are, couldn't you figure out he was going to get in touch with me? I would think that's common sense. Oh, I forgot. You're a football player."

I finished my tirade and now he had some words.

"If you got guts to come up here, let me tell you, we are going to battle."

I smiled to myself saying, "just make sure they tell you what room I'm staying in because I'll be expecting you. I'm looking forward to it if you are," I say to him. I hung up and knew straight away, if Alan Graff was serious about fighting me, I would be sure to give him another concussion. This time on purpose. Only in self defense, of course.

(Don't worry Steven, you know Kung Fu.)

I always make sure I let the other person take the lead. Sure enough, I get my tickets and got in late at night. Everyone was in a hurry to get me fitted and get my contract signed. I went to see Jimmy on set and he introduced me to the Director and Producers and Stallone, who it was great seeing again. We talked about the good times on *Rambo* and what he was going to do to me in this film.

"We got a fight to do Jimmy, and I'm going to kick your ass," Stallone joked.

"You're not going to kick my ass, you're going to kick Steven's ass," Jimmy replied.

We all laughed. Two days go by and I haven't seen Alan Graff yet, but guess who does show up. Stallone's double, the wonderful and talented Mark De Alessandro. Now here is something that always tickles my fancy. I had been hard at work trying to avoid Mark De Alessandro for eight years now. Yes, eight years, can you believe it? You must understand my way of thinking. It wasn't because I didn't like the guy, we were close friends and I respected the hell out of him. It was because I found myself in a sticky situation. Sticky, sticky, sticky, bloody and sticky. Remember that woman I hung upside down on the film, *Cop?*

"Take me down, I'm sticky and bloody, and don't want to do this anymore," she said. Her name was Lisa McCullough. Well, she and De Alessandro were now married. Engaged at the time. Because of what had happened and what came down with her on set, I always thought De Alessandro was going to be royally upset. The third day on set I see him, and I am ready to throw my fists up if a fight is what he wanted. Instead, he walked over to me and said, "Steven, I know you have been hiding from me for a long time over the situation with my wife. Let me tell you that I am not upset at you at all. I love you brother. I know she was the one in the wrong. I know her, unfortunately, these kinds of things have happened before with her and I know you, Steven. Even though she lied to me, I found out the truth a couple of years later from your special effects guy on the show when we worked together and he told me it was her at fault."

I just stood there in shock. Nine times out of ten, even ten times out of ten, the husband never says the wife was wrong. Most guys had better be on the wife's side, but here he wasn't and I was shocked. He hugged me and I hugged him back realizing all these years of hiding was for nothing and proved to me what a good person he was. He explained to me his wife is a handful and gets in trouble quite a bit, but he still loves her. I told him I understood and was glad we were still friends. I sit down and explained to him exactly what happened.

"Did your wife tell you that?" I asked him.

"No," Mark said. "She did not. But that's how she is."

By the way, need I not say, divorce was on their tray. Soon after. The next day I met Mark for breakfast and we began discussing the script. Well, I told you I never got one and to my surprise, he never got one either.

He asked me, "what's the deal? We are doubling the lead actors, we need to know what's was going on."

I felt the same way. "Alan Graff doesn't want us to have a script," I replied.

"What's that all about? It's not done that way, we need to have a script, we are doubling the leads," Mark added.

I couldn't believe it. "Didn't you ask for one?"

Mark shook his head no.

"I will then," I told him. I get to set and say good morning to Alan. I always try to be polite regardless of what had happened in the past. I mentioned to him I never got a script and he told me I wasn't getting one and he would tell me day by day what was going on. I didn't understand this way of thinking, but if he wanted it this way, I had no choice. But I told him to be sure to tell me everything each day so I could be prepared for James Woods and myself. Alan also mentioned he didn't want me and Mark De Alessandro on set unless he needed us to be. Again, I asked why that was but he wouldn't give me a straight answer. He just shrugged and shook his head before asking if, "that was all." I said it was and he walked away. The day came when he called me over and told me I was going to do some action. I wanted to know what I was going to do, but he said he would tell me right before we did it. I was shocked, I know for a fact that is not a proper practice. Nevertheless, I went to set prepared for whatever it was I had to do. I've always thrived on the spur of the moment. He takes me to a car and tells me the buildings behind me are going to explode and the force of the blast will drive me over the hood of the car. Okay, no big deal, simple thing.

"We aren't shooting until the afternoon, so go back to your honey wagon," Alan said.

I thought that was rude of him and he only brought me over for his, "there, I showed you what you are doing, now get out of here" moment. To each his own, no skin off my back. You're the boss. I went and got dressed in my elbow and knee pads and went back to the set that afternoon. I got into my position and they roll cameras and call, "action." Boom! The whole restaurant explodes. Fire everywhere. Explosions. I had no idea it was going to be so big. The force sends me back over the hood of the car. Cut! Print! Big applause, just what I always look for. I hear clapping from the crew which always excited me until I see the Director storming over to me.

"You went over the car the wrong way," he shouted. "You ruined the shot for this camera."

I didn't understand. To me it was perfect.

"You were supposed to roll the other way, you ruined the shot," he tells me.

I looked at the Director and told him, "that is what I was told to do."

He shakes his head, "by who?"

Suddenly, I realize there is silence all around me as he continues to yell. The golden rule is never to argue with your Director. Even if your Stunt Coordinator is wrong, you keep your mouth shut. That is what I did, but I looked at Graff and waited for him to say something. I needed an explanation of what was going on. Silence was all there was. He let me take the abuse. I move aside as effects reset the explosions for a separate piece. I spot Jimmy and walk over.

"Jimmy, I have to tell you something. Alan Graff told me to stand in the wrong spot and he didn't say anything. He set me up."

Jimmy asks, "how do ya know?"

I say, "because he told me what to do and said not to talk to anybody before the shot."

Perplexed, Jimmy responds, "didn't you read the script?"

I threw my hands up. "I was denied a script."

Jimmy asked why.

"Beats me. I've never heard of such an unorthodox practice. He refuses to give me one. On top of that, he refuses to tell me what action you have until the last moment so I don't know what the hell is going on."

Jimmy tells me he will get me a script by the end of the day and that he would speak to the Director and Coordinator. I quickly told him I would take care of it. The stunt was no big deal to reshoot and just wanted him to know, "I wasn't at fault." Sure enough, they roll cameras and the second take was even better than before and the Director loved it. I made a B line to Alan Graff and spoke up. "Alan, you had to have done that on purpose. I'm standing in place for five minutes and you could have told me to move to the other side. The Director didn't know why I was standing there but I guess he assumed I was going to work magic and fly to the other side. No one asked why I was there, but you knew exactly what was going on."

Alan smiled at me and said, "that's your problem, Steven."

I said, "You are a coward. I don't know who you think you are or why you have been doing this from the very beginning of the show, but you are a coward."

He looked down at me. "Coward, huh? Tell me that at wrap and I'll beat the shit out of you."

I hid a laugh. "You're going to beat the shit out of me, Alan? I am ready and willing and able. At the end of wrap look me up. Knock on my door. Come find me, I'll be waiting."

He said he would with a mighty snort of a hog and walked off. Wrap came and I hung out with De Alessandro. I stayed on set for half an hour. No Graff. I was tense and ready for him to pop out at any moment but he never showed. On the way back to the hotel, I talked with Mark De Alessandro about what was going on with Graff and he agreed that he had no class and that Stunt Coordinators just don't do that to their people.

We happen to have a few days off. The first day off, every now and then I would be somewhere in the hotel, casually looking over my shoulder for the moron. But that moment never came on the first day. In a way I wanted it, but deep down inside I was glad it didn't happen. The second day off, Mark De Alessandro and I agreed to meet at the hotel gym and we started working out. I'm lying down benching some dumbbells when I hear Mark say, "holy shit. Look who is coming, Steven."

I look up and this gym has huge glass windows and two swinging glass doors and you could see whoever is coming. Outside the doors, I see Alan Graff coming full speed ahead. He pushes open the glass doors and walks in like a cowboy into a saloon, eyes on me. The doors crash closed and Mark jumps up and heads towards Alan, well aware of what's about to happen. A fight. I drop the dumbbells and stand up. Fire in his eyes, Alan is shouting at me at the top of his lungs.

"I'm going to beat the hell out of you."

I go, "come on." I'm standing my ground never moving as Mark puts his hands on Alan to hold him back. The old hold the bear back trick. I wasn't scared a bit as he continued yelling at me, telling me he was going to kick my bottom, to put it mildly. I would reply with a smile, "I'm waiting. Don't let De Alessandro hold you back."

Alan takes two steps forward and is pushed one foot back, the uncertainty shuffle.

"Come on Graff, you can do it," I say.

His verbal abuse went on for ten seconds when I said, "you are a coward, Alan. And if you come one foot within my range, I will tear your ears off. If you don't believe me, throw a bob or a weave on the man that's holding you back! Stop taking the two step. You and I both know that is a common thing to do when you are really a yogi bear, not a Grizzly bear."

That enraged him even more. Mark is busy going hither and yonder with him, dancing back and forth as if to keep a bull in his pen.

"First I'll tear your ears off and then I will punch your nose in until it breaks open. You are not a man, you're a liar. You have been lying and trying to get me in trouble from the very beginning and if you want to go to the emergency hospital, then stop looking for picnic baskets and make your way around Boo-Boo. You know you can, but you won't," I replied. I raised my hands ready for a fight. I knew if I could get around him the fight would be over as I would have a clear shot at his ears. If he got too close to me however, his size and girth would be very dangerous and have the advantage. One of the first things I learned about fighting back in Brooklyn is that you want to say something strange and really mean it in order to stop a person, like tearing your ears off. Alan went back and forth for a minute and a half, shouting at me before he finally decided he wanted to keep his ears and turned around and walked out the gym doors. He knew my reputation and that was a smart thing to do.

I looked at Mark who said, "I can't believe what just happened." I sat back down.

"Me either, buddy. I hope that was the end of that," Mark sighed. He was more shaken than I was.

"I hope to the good Lord you are right," I echoed to him.

We went back to working out, wondering what else was going to happen in the next two months of shooting. After the workout we went back to the hotel to take a shower and went about our day exploring together, still dazed about our crazed Coordinator confrontation. Remember when Stallone joked about beating Jimmy's ass which was really my beautiful behind? Now it came time for that scene. Mark De Alessandro and I worked out the fight moves. Graff? He didn't know what to do. For me, there was nothing special about this fight until the dialogue started. Moments before the fists fly. Right before we filmed this fight, Stallone and Woods have dialogue together. The Director calls, "action." A few seconds into this scene, Stallone is constantly making mistakes in his dialogue. The Director is forced to cut and reset. This continues to happen as the Director is getting frustrated.

That's when James Woods says, "let me have a minute with him." James Woods takes Stallone for a walk as they stroll off set. I had never seen Jimmy do anything that in my eyes, that was so strange and unusual. Ten minutes go by and they finally return to the set. They roll cameras and dialogue starts coming out from Stallone and it's perfect. Everyone was curious about what happened but Jimmy nor Stallone never said a word. After the day was over, I went to Jimmy's trailer and we started talking about the day and I asked him what happened when he took Stallone off set.

"What the hell did you say to Stallone when you took him off set?" I ask.

Jimmy smiled saying, "I taught him how to act."

We both laughed and I asked what he meant.

"You saw, I just took him aside and I became an acting coach. I explained to him what he had to do to get it out correctly. Take his time."

I was amazed at how well Jimmy was able to coach other actors. He made me sweat, running around the track and got Stallone to speak, after all. How I would have loved to be a fly on the wall during that conversation with Stallone. I never thought of Stallone as someone who would take advice like that so calmly and easily, but he did and it was just wonderful to witness. I could see that he admired Woods a lot and it was mutual. Days went by and we continued working. We got to a scene that I always called, "kiss my cheek with the gun." Let me explain. This is a moment that I talk about now and laugh, but it wasn't very funny when it happened. James

Woods and Sharon Stone. They are arguing. Jimmy is supposed to take out his gun (silencer) and stick it in Sharon Stone's face. I happened to be towards the back of the crowd on set and watched as this was happening. He was a little too close and the tip of his silencer gave her a little kiss on the cheek. A little love tap, if anything. Well, it was like a bomb going off on set. Sharon Stone exploded into a rage, all directed at Woods. Boy, was I glad I was hiding in the crowd. She starts cursing off Jimmy, shocked and enraged he hit her. It was only a mild tap, but she went ballistic.

She finally finished her tirade, during which Jimmy never said anything but, "I'm sorry, it was an accident."

Then she decided she was going to take it to the next level. From verbal to physical. She raised her fist and guess what she did? Punched Jimmy right in the face! It was an attack, a hard smack. Jimmy jumped back. Again, I'm glad nobody can see me, I was hiding. Lucky me. I mean understand that when something like this happens, you don't want to be seen. At least I didn't. Sharon Stone turned and walked off set, cursing at Jimmy all the way to her motor home. I stepped back further into the crowd, just speechless. Jimmy looked around at everyone with their mouths hanging open. Then Mt. Woods erupted. You can't believe the amount of cursing and insults that flew, this time from Jimmy to Sharon Stone. He took off and went to his trailer as upset as could be, holding his cheek.

The Director started talking to the Producer, no one knew what to do. Who's going to try and get Sharon Stone out? Who is going to try to get James Woods out? I know what you readers are thinking. You think they came to me. Not this time. I slipped away in the crowd and like a bat out of hell, high tailed it to my trailer. I prayed they wouldn't come knocking on my door to ask for help getting Jimmy out and thankfully they didn't.

Eventually, they got both out and did the scene again which I heard went fine. I wasn't about to go back on set for that scene after that wingding. After wrap, I went to Jimmy's trailer and he asked me if I saw what had happened with Sharon Stone.

Well folks, I could have won an Academy Award. I played like I was shocked. I played amazement.

"How could Sharon Stone have done that?" I say. I acted so well, I even fooled the teacher! He told me what happened and said he was never going to work with that beautiful woman named Sharon Stone again. He really didn't say beautiful, but it did start with a "B."

You get the picture. This last story on this film, I find difficult to think about. Not so much for me, but for someone who would do anything for his lead actor. Someone who cared about people and always tried to do the right thing.

This person was Mark De Alessandro. What I witnessed was something very confusing and just not cool and to this day I don't like to recall it. It just simply upsets me. We were on location on the set with a big crowd. The public. Stallone has these bodyguards around, big guys. Even bigger than Dwayne Johnson, the Rock.

(Sly Stallone. The best fight actor ever to work in motion pictures in my opinion. Great talent.)

Mark and I are hanging around on set, talking and having fun. A few hours go by and Mark strolls off but we are both in the vicinity of the set. Soon after, I hear a commotion. I happen to look across the way and notice Mark wrestling around with two guys. I look closer and realize that they are two of Stallone's bodyguards. Mark is trying to get away and the bodyguards keep catching him and one bodyguard slams him down to the ground! Now things are turning very physical. Mark is trying fruitlessly to get away as one of the bodyguards grabs Mark's foot and rips off his shoe. The other has Mark around the neck and slams him down on the cement ground. It is getting brutal and I have no idea what is going on, but I felt something wasn't right. They weren't simply playing. Mark manages to get up as a bodyguard grabs Mark's shirt and proceeds in tearing it off.

Mark is really struggling and I can see this is not fun for him. Mark manages to get away but only for a moment as he is caught again and put into a bear hug and body slammed right to the floor, again! Mark is struggling for his pride and the bodyguards are laughing as is everybody else who is watching. Including, to my surprise, Stallone. The Director, Producers. Everyone. The whole crew. Watching everybody find this humorous, I found myself getting angry. It seemed like I was the only one that wasn't laughing as Mark was being dragged around on the ground. I felt bad for Mark as he was being humiliated. I finally realized what their goal was. They were trying to strip him nude, take off all his clothes. Then the bodyguard began to pull off his pants.

"No, stop, no, stop!" Mark yells.

I look around and see Stallone laughing. I see the Director laughing. Like they are watching some sort of comedy stage show. I wasn't laughing. Mark certainly wasn't laughing. I didn't find it funny and Mark wasn't laughing and to my surprise, he wasn't punching either. I always thought, if the shoe was on the other foot, I might have. NO, I WOULD HAVE PUNCHED AND KICKED. The bodyguards bring Mark to the floor and get his pants and socks off. That wasn't enough for them. They went for the underwear next with Mark fighting with every muscle in his body to stop them. He was outnumbered and out muscled. The more he fought, the more energy he lost. Like a fish out of water, there was no escape. Helpless, he glanced at me a few times. It was all happening so fast that I didn't know what to do. The crowd was roaring with laughter at the sight before them. I was disgusted. Mark was pleading, praying and begging them to stop to no avail. Wow, finally, they left him on the ground. In his underwear mere feet from where I was standing. I could tell De Alessandro was humiliated. I felt his pain.

As Mark rose to his feet, shaking and exhausted, he looked right into my eyes and almost reading my thoughts said, "Steven, what am I supposed to do? I want to keep my job."

I looked back and said seven words. "I guess I have to understand, Mark." It was such a shameful act and I felt so bad for Mark as he went to pick up his clothes thrown all over the set. I couldn't understand how Stallone thought it was funny when you could see that it truly crushed Mark, but nobody saw what I saw. I said to myself, was I the only understanding one? After all that, he was still loyal to Stallone. It goes to show you the abuse of power that takes place in Hollywood. It disappoints me whenever I think about it. I hope you readers understand. It wasn't a good time for Mark De Alessandro.

CHAPTER 80
(Actor Keanu Reeves And My Herman Munster Boots.)

Vamos, vamos, it's El Guapo time. Viva El Mexico. Remember him from *The Three Amigos*? He is directing a movie called *A Walk In The Clouds*. I went down to the set and met that handsome man, (you get it? That's what El Guapo means in Spanish) Alfonso Arau. A macho man. We talked for about fifteen minutes. He was just like he was in the movie, very boisterous in an elegant way. You could tell he was a very proud man from a very great country. "Mexico is a magnificent country," he tells me. "Beautiful women," he says.

I say to him, "I know. I married one. Her name is Cecilia Camacho. She's an actress."

With excitement, he says, "I know Cecilia and her father. He is a great screenwriter in Mexico."

I say, "yes, he is a great man like you, Alfonso."

He smiles, his chest goes out proudly. I think to myself, I know how to stroke people. I also mentioned, "I took a car there once, got to explore the countryside. The people are beautiful. The trip was exciting and a tad bit dangerous. Went under an overpass, some guys threw a huge rock off. Went over it. Thank God for the safety pan. No damage." Anyway, I was then told I was going to be doubling somebody. I went to Wardrobe to get my measurements and they started measuring me.

"Oh," they said. "You are a lot shorter."

A lot shorter? What were they talking about?

"He is six three," Wardrobe told me. Six three? I was five nine!

"Who am I doubling?" I asked. The answer surprised me.

"Keanu Reeves," I was told.

(Stunt doubling Keanu Reeves. I got my Herman Munster boots on.)

I asked for a picture of him and quickly came up with an idea. I found out from them he was wearing boots. I suggested we put three inch soles on the bottom of the boot to make me look taller. That is just what we did. I find out Anthony Quinn is also starring in the film. I thought, now this is cool. An old time actor from the forties and fifties, always excites me, dontcha' know? I get the information on what I am doing. Doubling Keanu Reeves and rescuing Anthony Quinn. Not bad. The scene is at night, someone lights a grape vineyard on fire and I have to rescue Anthony Quinn and put him over my shoulder to carry him out of the fire. I found it funny that Keanu didn't want to do this, wanting his double to, but Anthony Quinn was excited about it and agreed to do it. Nevertheless, I tried to stay away from Keanu, not wanting him to see my short stature and my boots with three inch soles glued into them. That went well for a while until the Production Manager told me Keanu wanted to meet me. I tried to stand as tall as I could and went with him to meet Keanu. When he saw me, he looked me up and down and I could tell he was thinking, "who is this midget they hired to double me?"

I quickly assured him that I would have soles in my shoes to make me taller and it was going to be dark with fire all around. It would be hard to get a good look at my height. Keanu shrugged his shoulders and more or less agreed. I sit here and ponder if this was the Keanu of *The Matrix,* would this situation be different? That night, I put on my Herman Munster boots and walked onto set. Keanu looked at me, now equal with his height, but his eyes were on my shoes instead of my face. He just shook his head in disbelief.

I just had to laugh along with him and say, "it's night, you'll never see it." When we were shooting this, the Director wanted me to jump on and off a wheeled cart. It felt like I was wearing women's stilettos and I tried hard to keep my ankles from buckling. You try running with high heels. It was hysterical in my mind, even though no one saw the trouble I was having with that and especially trying to pick up Anthony Quinn. After I put him down, an applause broke out. More so directed at Quinn than me. He would always get an applause after everything he did, it was as if he was getting an Academy Award. It was great to watch. Like a movie within a movie. He would raise his hands and dance around. It would look like a scene from *Zorba The Greek.*

(Rescuing Anthony Quinn. I think it's time to take a photo with old school.)

In fact, it was a spot on replication. What was funny about it, was that many followed. I even found myself doing it. All we needed was the Zorba music which someone in the crowd would always mimic.

CHAPTER 81
(Actor Anthony Quinn And The Photo Op Fiasco.)

Realizing he was in such a good mood, I decided it was time for a picture of a real star. I walk over to my stunt bag and open it up. I grab my camera and have a big smile on my face, I was just so excited. I discussed how great it is working with older actors before and Anthony Quinn was no different. Every time I talked to him, it was like talking to his Majesty. It was very dramatic. I walk over to one of the background players and hand her the camera.

"I'm going to walk over to Anthony Quinn and when I do, would you take a picture of us?" I ask her. She agrees and I walk over to Anthony Quinn, just having saved him from the fire and say, "Mister Quinn, can we take a picture together?" Before he could answer, I walk over and get into position. I knew he would say yes and my excitement level was as high as could be. What a memorable picture this was going to be! I turn around to the background player who puts the camera to her eye.

I crack a smile when I hear from above me, "no! You cannot take a picture. I forbid it!"

I look up at him thinking he is just joking around. I turn back to the girl and tell her to go ahead and take it. The voice booms from above me a second time.

"Did you hear what I said!? No pictures!"

I look at him and he starts moving away.

I realize this guy is serious. I told him I just wanted to take a picture for a memory.

"I do not take pictures!" He yells back as he leaves.

I'm standing there shocked and slightly embarrassed, as the Director walks up to me and says, "Steven, remember. Just because a horse lets you walk up to him, doesn't mean he will let you ride."

I nodded back, half laughing and half in shock and asked, "is that a Mexican proverb?"

Alfonso replied, "no that is a universal one."

We all laughed. Lesson learned. Okay this next situation, let's just say, no way in hell. I wasn't going to bees there. Where? Everywhere on my body. Not me, Jack. There's a dream sequence in the film where Keanu's character is tied up and the next thing you know, he has bees swarming all over him from head to toes. I had told the Production Manager to be sure he got a bee master and to have him bring a double for Keanu. Six three, a hundred seventy pounds. He said he would take care of it.

The day comes and the bee man arrives. I had made sure that everyone who was allergic to bees was told to stay off the set. The bee man came with a huge truck with thousands of bees loaded on it. I mean thousands, enough to cover multiple people head to toe. I had a meeting with him and I made sure to have him come to me, away from his truck. We started talking and I asked him where the double was, who was going to play Keanu for this scene. You know, have the bees all over him. He looked at me and told me he was never told to bring a double.

"Didn't the Production Manager speak to you about bringing a double?" I asked.

He shook his head, knowing nothing about it.

I went over to the Production Manager and asked him what was going on.

"Oh yeah, I already talked to him, Steven. He is going to double Keanu," he told me.

I stepped back in surprise. "He'll double him? The guy is about eighty years old and five foot two. That ain't going to work, the body structure is all wrong. Besides, I already had a conversation with him and he told me he's too old to do it anymore. He can't get stung."

The next words I heard were even more surprising.

"Why don't you do it, Steven? You are big and brave."

In my head, I am thinking, "big and brave maybe, but again, why me? This punk kid from Brooklyn don't go bothering bees." I told him to buzz off it wasn't going to beee me, I don't do stunts with bees. I went back and spent a couple hours on the phone, trying to find a stunt guy that would put bees all over them. They all said no. They were all cowards, just like me. I mean I couldn't blame them. I didn't want those little suckers to sting my pee-pee. Finally, the old bee man found a guy. One of his friends. He was coming to set. We were able to shoot it and let me tell you, it is an amazing thing to watch. Alfonso Arau, Keanu and I sat around watching this extraordinary process. After the guy got all the bees on him, thousands of these buggers, it literally took hours to get the bees off with a few smoke machines. He even got stung about two dozen times. There was no way in Hell I could be still long enough to get the bees on and off if I tried to do that, but in the first place, I wouldn't. As I said, ain't no way in Hell. Coward

CHAPTER 82
(Hey Man, Hang me. Don't Drop Me.)

I get one of those phone calls that always keeps giving. Jimmy is doing a period film called *Killer: A Journal Of A Murderer*. Period films are the best. They take you away from today and show you something that once was and now is no more. The past. I give the company a call at Jimmy's request and introduced myself. I explain that I had doubled and Stunt Coordinated shows with Woods for a long time and James Woods informed me that he had talked to you about me being the Stunt Coordinator. They told me they would call me back and I hung up. A week later, I still hadn't heard from them. I thought to myself, here we go again. I know that feeling, they aren't interested. So I reached out to them again and that is when they told me they had hired a Stunt Coordinator already that was local. Michael Long. This came as a shock and I tried to explain to them that I had coordinated many of James Woods's shows and worked with him extensively. Any kind of problem on set in regards to him, I can help with no problem. But you know they never understand. They always have to learn for themselves. If Woods stays true to what he has done in the past, I'll get there one way or another.

James Woods is the kind of actor that needs someone there to listen and understand him, someone to lend an ear so to speak. Someone he trusts when it comes to action. It went in one ear and out the other, and they decided to stick with the Coordinator they had hired already. I told them if they needed anything in regards to Jimmy they could give me a call and left it at that.

Yet, something inside me didn't want to leave it at that. If you let things like this go, you'll never get anywhere. Well, Jimmy and I had a mutual friend named Alan Haft. I called him up and told him the situation and he said he would talk to Jimmy. I told him how delicate the situation was, I didn't want it to come across like I was begging to be on this show. I just really cared about Jimmy's well being. Alan told me he would give me a call the next day. The next day? It usually takes a week to get a hold and talk to a star of Wood's status. That shows you the friendship of Mister Alan Haft.

Yet, the next day he did call me. "Jimmy said he will take care of it," Alan tells me.

Woods calls me soon after and explains that the production says they don't have much money and this Coordinator was all they could afford. "Here's the story Steven, let's let them do what they want to do and see what happens. Don't worry.

Everything will turn out fine. If I don't see you this show, I'll see you the next time," he tells me.

My heart sank hearing this, but I hoped in my heart of hearts that there would be other opportunities coming up to work with Jimmy. I thanked him and told him I would give him a call mid production to see how much fun he was having. We would always talk about the fun we were having on set. We hang up and a week goes by when out of the blue I get a phone call and it's Michael Long, the Stunt Coordinator on the show. He tells me I have to come down right away, they have a problem.

"What is going on?" I ask.

He tells me they were doing an outside scene in the prison with Jimmy when he did some minor action with another actor. "Jimmy hurt himself and went ballistic. He stopped the scene and went to his trailer, demanding that they bring Steven Lambert on set before he works again."

Inside I was surprised and laughing at the circumstance before me. I assure Michael Long, "I'm not laughing at you. Just the situation." I was going to come and told Michael Long that. "I just want to make it clear, that you can be the Stunt Coordinator but so am I. We can work together as a team," I added. I heard relief in the voice at the other end.

"That's fine, Steven. Just come down here as soon as you can, please."

I continue laughing and I hear Michael doing the same. I say to him, "I'm glad you understand Michael."

He says, "I do Steven, I do." Michael was learning that when you have a plumbing problem, you call a plumber. When you have an electrical problem, you call an electrician. When you have a Jimmy problem, you call Steve Lambert. Sure enough, I got on a plane that night and went to the set. I arrived and headed to Jimmy's room and it was like our previous conversation never happened.

"I told you I would get you here and you would be Stunt Coordinating and doubling me, Steven. You will always be here," Jimmy says.

I just smiled and shook my head, happy to be there. "You're the best Jimmy," I say. "You're the top banana. You're the cream of the crop."

He looks at me and says, "shut up yarmulke boy."

We both laugh. I ask him how is his injury. "Let me see," I say.

He smiles and says "it was nothing. I'm a good actor."

I smile back at him and say, "what a guy."

As the days move on, I notice Jimmy having little conversations with the Director. Until one day, I see something I have never seen with Jimmy before. He asks the Director to sit down and he starts directing! I'm watching and thinking it is just for this scene. Minutes go by, hours go by and Jimmy is still directing. The whole day goes by and he is directing.

The next day goes by and he is directing. This continues on for days and now Jimmy is more or less the lead actor and the Director. Tim Metcalfe, the real Director, was a very nice guy. I thought Metcalfe was doing a good job, but now his assignment is to sit and shut up. Jimmy is directing the show. I then realized he was just as great a Director as he was an actor.

He had discussions with the actors and gave him his opinions. I would watch this and Tim would watch this.

It was a great learning experience for all of us to watch Jimmy work his magic in directing and acting. Soon after we start setting up the last scene where Jimmy's character gets hung. We are doing the old rope and harness trick where I would have enough slack to avoid being choked to death. They are building these huge gallows, sixteen feet tall.

Come time to do it, I put the hood over my head and am shackled by the hands and feet. We put the harness on as I get into position above the trap doors. Right before we roll, Jimmy is in his chair watching everything. He always likes to watch what surprises I would do when we rolled camera. We are ready to go, cameras begin to roll when I hear Jimmy shout out, "sometimes it's the gas chambers, sometimes it's the gallows, Jew boy."

I know he is talking to me and I'm laughing, shaking under the hood.

I hear the Director Of Photography shout back at me, "stop laughing Steven, stay still. This is a serious scene."

I compose myself and with muffled words say, "fine! Quit it, Jimmy! Hurry it up, you Hoosier bastard! I could kill a dozen men while you're screwing around." (Those were the last words of Carl Panzram, the character I was doubling).

I hear laughter from my left side but before I can reply again, the doors open up below me and I plummet downward. Seconds go by and I am still falling. It feels like it is taking forever for me to stop. I am thinking to myself, what if this sucker doesn't work? I tested it a day before, I didn't drop but I hung there. It is always in your mind, what happens if something goes wrong.

Two more seconds go by when I feel the rope going taught and I bounce up a little. A second later, I feel something beneath my feet and it is hard. Then my butt hits something hard. My head goes to the side and it hits a hard surface. Still unable to see, I surmise that I had fallen to the ground. Then I heard screaming and yelling, followed by footsteps and running.

(I felt like Clint Eastwood in *Hang 'Em High*.)

"Are you all right, can you move? Steven, talk to us," I hear the invisible people around me say.

I take a deep breath and tell them, "yea, I think so. Now get this hood off my head so I can see if I'm hurt."

They take the hood off and untie the rope. I stand up and someone removes the shackles from my hands. I realize that the cable was faulty and it had snapped. I see Mike Long run over to me showing worry and disbelief.

"I can't believe you are okay Steven, that would have killed an ordinary man." Mike says.

I smile warmly at him as Special Effects comes over. They tell me it was a faulty cable and wanted to try it again.

"Okay," I said. "Just as long as it doesn't falter around my neck." Well luckily it worked the next time and I hung there swinging back and forth. Back and forth. Back and forth. Getting sleepy? Me too. Time for a nap. When I get up I'll tell you a story you'll be fascinated by. Let's just say you can bet on it. You've got no idea what in store. So hurry up and open volume four!

CHAPTER 83
(Follow The Leader. Casino. The Royal Flush In Order.)

You're back! And so am I. Sin City. Las Vegas, Nevada. A movie called *Casino*. I am doubling Jimmy again, no delay involved this time. I arrive in Vegas and head to the Production Office. What a group of great crazy men I see. Directed by Martin Scorsese. Starring Robert De Niro, Joe Pesci, James Woods and Sharon Stone. Wow, what a cast. Now, Sharon Stone?! I laugh to myself, remembering the words Jimmy said about ever working with her again. I believe he said, "I'll never work with that 'blankety blank' again. That bitch of a witch." I had to ask him about this situation. I couldn't wait until I heard his excuse. I go to his room after I get settled and we say our hellos. I start laughing and he looks at me. He asks what I was laughing about. I say, "Sharon Stone is in this movie, I thought Jimmy boy wasn't going to work with her anymore."

Jimmy just shook his head and quoted the Godfather. "Just when I thought I was out, they pull me back in!"

I laughed. I asked if he had seen her yet and he said he had. "Did you give her hugs and kisses?" I inquired.

"Hey, yarmulke boy. Shut up before I put a matzah ball in your mouth," Woods said in his Godfather impression.

We both laughed. Now as I have commented once or twice throughout the book, I am a people watcher. I love to watch what goes on. This film was no different and I quickly noticed something that took my interest like never before. Every day on set, it was amazing. I would notice a pecking order with Scorsese, De Niro, Pesci and Woods. I'll say it again. Scorsese, De Niro, Pesci and Woods. That was the order. Of what? Everything. I found it fascinating to watch. My eyes were glued to every move. They would walk in that order, talk in that order, get food in that order. When they sat down, it would be in that order. It reminded me of the Marx Brothers. Groucho, Harpo, Chico and Zeppo. That is the order they would always do anything. Here, Scorsese was Groucho and Woods was Zeppo, always waiting at the end in the wings. This formation and order didn't happen for one day or two days, it was the whole show. It seemed like a silent agreement between the four of them. Perhaps the same mysterious status quo that made Lucas give Spielberg space when he was on the set, was at work here as well. It was so wonderful and spellbinding to watch, I thought I should take a picture of it. You know what they say, a picture is worth a thousand words.

So one day on set I saw them sitting in their chairs and once again it was in order. Scorsese, De Niro, Pesci, Woods and Stone. I walked over to the side and very casually picked up my camera. Scorsese's eyes turned towards me. De Niro's eyes locked onto me. Right on cue, Pesci's eyes fell upon me. De Niro's hand goes up to the sky.

"No pictures!" He shouts at me.

I already have the camera up to my eye and through the lens I see James Woods shaking his head, "no." Nobody sees him because he is Zeppo, the last guy in line, but I do.

I lower the camera as Scorsese says, "Steven, I'm sorry but we don't take pictures around here."

Then I hear Pesci, "get the fuck outta' here."

Then I hear Woods say to Pesci, "that's my stuntman."

Then Pesci says, "fucking stuntmen. They don't have no brains."

I yell out to Pesci, "be careful. I'm from Brooklyn."

He jumps up and runs towards me with his fists laughing. Gives me a hug.

I look at him and ask, "can I take a picture now?"

He says," get the fuck outta' here."

Everyone laughs. I was so close to getting that picture, but it seemed they preferred the Anthony Quinn way when it came to photos. Just my luck. The most memorable moment on this project happened the third day on set. Woods calls me over and introduces me to Pesci, De Niro and Scorsese. He tells them I'm a wonderful stuntman and a black belt. That was Jimmy, always talking me up. That's one of the meanings of a true friendship and why at times I was always by his side defending him on and off the set. And he, I. In one way or another. Brothers in arms. He then tells them that I can kick a cigar out of someone's mouth.

Pesci takes out his cigar and says, "he ain't kicking this out. This cost a box of ziti."

Woods smiles and calls over a stagehand and asks for a cigarette. He gets one and turns to De Niro. "Here, Bob. Put this in your mouth and he will kick it out," Jimmy explains.

If looks could kill, Woods would have been dead. "You are crazy Jimmy. No way am I putting that in my mouth." De Niro looked at me and then at Jimmy who put a hand on his back.

"Come on Bob, Steven won't hit you. He's a professional at this."

De Niro wouldn't put it in his mouth, so Jimmy looks at Pesci.

"Get out of here, not me," he says.

Woods laughs. "Come on, you cigar smoking elf. What, you got no guts? Put it in your mouth." Everybody is laughing. I step back as Pesci pushes his way forward.

"No guts, no guts!? Give it to me," Pesci urges.

Jimmy hands him the cigarette.

Pesci looks at me and says, "kid, I'm going to put the damn cigarette in my mouth and if you hit me. You're a dead man."

I look at both of them and say, "I'm not kicking the cigarette out of his mouth."

Woods wouldn't have it. "Come on Steven, he is all ready for you, you won't miss. Use your Kung Fu magic."

I finally relent and tell Joe Pesci I was going to do a whip kick. "I might miss the first time just to get the distance down."

He gets impatient and tells me to hurry it up.

I get into position and throw my first kick. I miss by two inches. I have my distance and timing down and now I am ready to do it for real. Woosh! Target hit. The cigarette goes flying.

Pesci spits and looks at me. "Damn, you are lucky. You would have had a war on your hands if you would have hit me."

De Niro and Scorsese are laughing and Woods is having a good time watching all of it. Who else can say they kicked a cigarette out of Joe Pesci's mouth? I was relieved I didn't miss and it's funny, even doing a big stunt, I wasn't as nervous as I was here. Then, guess what I asked. Can I take a picture?

I hear Pesci, "no, you fucking guido."

CHAPTER 84
(Freezing My Matzah Balls Off For Actor Kurt Russell.)

Now imagine this. Working for the science fiction guru, Mister John Carpenter. *Escape From LA.* I was very ardent to work for him. Ardent, look it up. I get to set and go to Wardrobe. They have all these clothes laid out and tell me, "go pick what you want to wear."

Well, I thought, that's all you have to tell me. I was surprised because in most cases, Wardrobe is very insistent with what you are going to wear. So guess what I did? I find some high waisted baggy pants. I pick out a belt and boots. I bring it over and am ready to go. Then they ask me where my shirt is.

I say, "well, I'm skinny and very muscular, I think it would look good if I had my shirt off. Would you mind?"

They seem to accept that and ask me where my pads were. I told them I had heard the fight I was supposed to do was going to be in an arena with dirt so, "I don't think they are necessary." I was fine if they were fine and they said they were. When I'm being featured, I always try to look different and I think this is another opportunity to be noticed. For noticed is what you want to achieve. I patted myself on the back. This was a genius move since there was going to be four, five dozen stuntmen there. I always wondered why they didn't have any warrior stunt woman. I would have. It would have been cool, but let's move on. Production calls and they tell me to be on set at ten o'clock.

"Ten in the morning?" I ask.

"No, ten at night," they reply.

I think to myself, ten at night!? It's the middle of winter, I'm going to be freezing my little hiney off. They are filming at the Rose Bowl, the UCLA football stadium. They have turned it into a primitive looking fighting arena for the film. I go get my wardrobe and put it on. They begin filming the first part of my fight on the first night. Little did I know they only wanted the beginning and they were going to move on to Snake's action. Kurt Russell. Everyone else has clothes but me. I'm shirtless and freezing my ass off. It felt like my great plan backfired but I'm procrastinating, thinking to myself as the hours and days went by that they will get back to me, they will get back to me. But I was making myself suffer every day, stuck in my false hope. Should I get a shirt? Something warm?

"NO STEVEN, IT'S TOO LATE. THEY WILL GET BACK TO YOU! THEY HAVE YOUR LEAD UPS ALREADY. ANY MOMENT YOU WILL FINISH THE FIGHT WITH YOUR SKINNY MUSCLES AND IT WILL LOOK

GREAT," the voice in my head screamed out. So I waited and waited, freezing. I'm standing around for most of the time during the week of shooting, no heating lamps. No warmth. I waited a week to be featured and come to find out I was more or less background. They didn't finish the fight with me until five days later. That's why I didn't want to put on a shirt because I figured they would get back to me sooner or later. It just happened to be much later. Freezing and being everyone's entertainment for a week, boy did I punish myself good. At this time that we were shooting, the Super Bowl between the Cowboys and Steelers was going on. I mean literally at the time we were filming. How did I know this? I couldn't care less, but John Carpenter was a big fan. Guess what? In the Rose Bowl stadium, they had a giant screen for replays as you know. It also could show television and that is what it was doing, per John Carpenter's request. To my astonishment, every twenty minutes we would stop filming so he could watch fifteen minutes of football. On top of that, he would purposely move cameras so that he could keep the game muted, but out of camera view. It was a sight to see and a funny experience to go through as this went on all night long.

Now John Carpenter was a quiet man, small in stature. But when he spoke, people listened and things were done. Fast. Kurt Russell was just like you would see him in a movie He seemed like he was one of the normal ones. Actors, that is. Cool as a cucumber. Never took anything too seriously. It seemed like he enjoyed every moment. At that moment, I had enough guts to ask him what it was like to work with Elvis.

He sang to me, "Steven, a little less conversation and a little more action. How's that?"

What made it special, is that he sounded like Elvis. I thought that was pretty neat.

CHAPTER 85
(Actress Fran Drescher And Her Bingo Wings.)

Moving on, but not onto Fran Drescher starring in *The Beautician And the Beast*. Did a little fight on the show. She watched. She got excited. She asked me out. I said, "no." She had bingo wings. (Look it up in the urban dictionary. Don't laugh too hard when you do).

END OF STORY.

CHAPTER 86
(The Quest. Fight Choreographing The World. The Ultimate.)

The Quest, starring Jean Claude Van Damme. This movie was a journey into sanity. These guys that I was teaching I must say, the ability to think clearly and have sound judgement, really was a quest for me to bring them back to reality. I got called to work on this film as a Fight Coordinator, not realizing I was going to be talked into being a nanny. This movie was starring Jean Claude Van Damme. Directed by Jean Claude Van Damme, but not really. Let me explain. I'm on my way, it's my first time. Thailand. Come to find out, it was a country where the majority of the people were five foot six, five foot seven at the most. I mean, I was a giant at five foot nine. Going through the script I got very excited. In the story, some scenes are competitions, where multiple fighters from different countries with different styles fight each other to win the tournament. I start thinking about the different styles of fighting from different countries I would have to put together, thinking about what an extraordinary opportunity I had received. I arrive in beautiful Thailand and the next morning meet with Jean Claude and the Producer, Moshe Diamant. I called him Mushy for short. He didn't like it very much, but for some reason, I couldn't pronounce his real name so it stuck. We started talking about the fights and I speak up with an interesting and curious question.

"I noticed in the script, it doesn't say who fights who or who you fight, Jean Claude." Jean Claude tells me he doesn't know yet who fights who yet and it doesn't matter right now.

"Steven, at this moment I want you to interview everyone, put together and film their fights. You decide the match ups for each country. Then I will decide watching the video which country fights which country and who I fight," Jean Claude tells me.

Well, I say to him, "Jean Claude, that's a lot of wasted time and energy. Matchups that you might change after you watch them and where I spent all that time putting them together?" I explained to him if I took two guys and have them fight each other, they get used to the fight and their movements. If he decides to switch them, it would kill the momentum they had going. I repeated myself, "that's so much time wasted."

Van Damme didn't seem to care and he told me to film all of them in the matchups that I choose and he said that he'll make the changes. I asked if Jean Claude would be there every day watching the fights I put together and he said he wouldn't be. He wanted his fight double to do his parts. I told him that would be me.

I agreed to work out each one and get to know their styles and personality better. I start the procedure. I call in these actors, all chosen from different countries by Van Damme himself. In the film, they represent fighters from Germany, the Soviet Union, Scotland, Spain, Turkey, Brasil, Korea, Siam, Greece, France, China, Japan, Okinawa, Africa and Mongolia. And man, I must tell you they were all wonderfully talented, but guess what, the majority didn't know anything about action acting. Never worked in a movie before.

I found a place to work out with them and looked forward to the monumental task before me. I called each one of these guys up and wanted to save Abel Qissi for my last session as he was playing Khan, the lead bad guy. The Mongolian. He was very nice and wanted to meet me right away, but when I told him I was saving the best for last, he laughed. I was excited to start putting all these fights together and film them to show Jean Claude Van Damme. Little did I know, that this was going to be the hardest pissing contest that I was ever involved in. They provided me with a workout area where the ground was dirt. In fact, it was a tennis court. Two of them. All I had to do was take down a net. It became my own private gladiator arena. I got a hold of some mats and on this first day, went through a couple of hours working out and training with each one of them. The guy from China, Peter Wong, was extremely talented. A favorite of mine. He happened to be one of Jet Li's guys.

Little did I know, later on in my future, we would run across each other and work together again. After working with him for a couple of days, I knew I had something special. He is what I call perfection in style and grace. He and I hit it right off the bat and became good friends. He was one that didn't need me as a nanny. A true professional, did as he was told. I moved onto each one of them with each having special talents and moves I found that could contribute to the fights. The Sumo wrestler from Japan never worked a movie before. I found him stifling. His moves were straight forward and simplistic. I knew I had to do something simple, visual and creative to end his fights quick. The guy from Africa, I had to work with in action acting and rely more on his costume and basic broad style fighting to put together his battle since he was chosen not to move on. He needed a nanny. But a very nice guy. The guy from Brasil was very flamboyant. He was demanding in the simple sense that he thought he knew better. It was a constant war between us.

Get this, if I set him up taking a hit, he would take a stand and simply say, "nobody can ever hit me like this."

I would laugh at that comment and say, "this is a movie, it's not real."

He just couldn't understand that, just like some of the others. The guy from Germany I found to be very talented. Raw and Basic. These are the moves I chose for him. Fire and great meaning in his movements. Evil, great pick for a Nazi. But then again if I may say, a delightful guy to work with in real life. But he needed a nanny too. Now the guy from France, he was a big pain in the baguette. I called him Mister Know It All. He knew nothing. Very Insecure. His attitude? Well, let me say that he was very overwhelmed by all the talent around him and couldn't act his way out of a paper bag. Everything seemed difficult and instead of listening and understanding, he would be in constant denial. Yes, he was nanny material too. He was too difficult to communicate with, so I chose to take him out early. The guy from Greece was very unique and special because he had all ground moves, Judo and Ju-jitsu. A very mysterious Jesus like guy, this was his normal behavior. I liked him a lot, but unfortunately, he also became nanny material. My juices were flowing with him.

This is something we don't usually see too much on film, complete ground work. And he was strong. I decided to put him in the running to fight Van Dame. I worked out with Scotland. A nice guy and found him to be humorous. His last name was Lambert. No relation. His acting was flat. His fighting was simple and besides, I thought no way Van Damme was going to fight anybody in a dress. We got along great. His techniques were very light and lacked fire and I couldn't get what I wanted out of him. For sure, he was no Mel Gibson in *Braveheart*. Van Damme's only bad pick, I thought. So he was another one I thought to take out right away. He needed a nanny. Turkey was an animal. Heavy handed. Kept on hitting people. It hurt. He had a lot of animation in his body, too much. I couldn't tone him down. He was like a Tasmanian Devil. Became great friends, a very loyal man. He always called me, "Mister Director."

(My friend Azdine wanted to tear Jean Claude's head off.)

Nanny. Siam was an actor I had worked with before. Jen Sung was his real name. We knew each other, it's funny how things work. Very nice guy. I was excited for his fight with Kahn. it was a joy to work with him. He listened, he understood. It was a joy to kill him. Simplicity in his body language and most importantly, didn't really have any facial expressions. He wasn't very scary. More of a baby face and since he was fighting with Khan, I knew his death had to be very elaborate. Nanny. Korea, he was a good guy. I felt bad, but he was boring. Took him out quick. Nanny. Soviet Union. As Joel Grey would say, "he moves like a pregnant yak." A gentleman he was. Awkward. Delayed reactions. Might I say, a terrible actor. Another bad pick by Van Damme. Getting rid of him quick. Nanny.

Last but not least, was the man. The Mongolian. Our first meeting not only consisted of working out, but he decided to take me out to see the sights in Thailand. It wasn't long before I felt I had a gold mine with him. First off, he had starred in many films in the past. Second, he had worked with Jean Claude before and third, his body language and knowledge of acting was superb. We became very close friends and as far as all the men, he became my second in command. Always keep people close by you that are well respected, a very important lesson to learn. About two weeks go by and everything is going well. I've more or less matched everybody up in my secret and secure notebook that I call my fight bible. I always have one of those. Who is fighting who and who is fighting Van Damme.

I bring everyone down to the tennis court at the same time. I want to go over a few things and want everyone to hear and see what I am doing. I have noticed in the background, two guys sitting there. One is Mushy, the Producer and one guy I was not familiar with, haven't met. I explained to them everything I teach one person, it will be a learning experience for all. I began teaching each country the first five moves of their fight. As the days progressed, I found each one asking me when they would fight Jean Claude. I'm looking at them, trying to avoid the subject, ultimately going, "well that decision hasn't been made yet." Yet, as the days and weeks go by throughout the training, each of one of them individually starts putting on more pressure and are insisting that they were promised a fight with Jean Claude. I'm trying to put everything together in my mind to make it a tournament that actually works, to make everyone happy. Giving them great stuff but knowing they all can't fight Jean Claude. By now I know they know that, but they were promised and they are starting to make demands. These conversations and problems were visually seen but never really heard by Mushy at the workouts. Just about every day he would sit down and watch in the background. That guy that was with him, I finally met him. His name was Peter Molata. A Martial Artist and a good friend of Jean

Claude. He brought him down just to hang out with. Now let me explain something that should be obvious. Not everyone can fight Van Damme if they are eliminated in the first or second round.

As the days went by, the strategic order I set up in my mind on paper and on video, began to fall apart. The little chess pieces I had placed began to talk to me in my head during dreams at night. I remember them clearly. Germany would hear France say that he was promised a fight with Jean Claude before speaking up and saying Germany was promised a fight with him as well. Now China, Japan and Greece hear that Germany is also wanting to fight Jean Claude and they speak up saying it was them who were promised. This agitates Scotland a few feet away and now Scotland is getting upset. I turn my attention at Scotland but only for a moment as Brasil and Siam push forward and tell me it was they who were promised. I could see fire in each of their eyes as they closed upon me, demanding I fix this massive injustice. I awoke in a cold sweat, my mind afire. I recounted the dream. Countries ready to war over one thing. No, not a thing, a man. A man named Jean Claude Van Damme who knowingly led them to believe the impossible. In other words, he lied to them.

As the dawn broke the horizon, I set out to find Jean Claude. He and I had things to discuss. A problem he created and that I needed to correct. I went to the Production Office and made it known I needed a meeting with Jean Claude and Mushy. The next day we sat down and first off, I showed them the videos of the fights I was putting together. Greece and Germany. Brasil and China. Right off the bat, Jean Claude agreed with me on Kung Fu versus Capoeira. But with Germany and Greece, which I thought was one of my best fight pieces, he said no. Putting together boxing and grappling I thought was a magnificent fight. We went back and forth and I tried my best to change his mind but to no avail. Now let me tell you that when you deal with somebody like Van Damme, you get to understand what makes them tick. At least he agreed with one. But I was disturbed that all that work with Greece and Germany was for nothing. A setback in wasted time. I also showed him a short quickie with Turkey and Scotland where Scotland lost. He agreed with that. I then told them we, you, guys had a problem going on.

"I need one of you to come over with me and let these guys know who is fighting you, Jean Claude. Every one of these guys has told me that you told them they were going to get to fight you. You and I both know that is impossible to happen in a tournament setting. It has gotten to the point where they do not want to work until I give them an answer, you gotta understand they are pissed off. There's going to be a mutiny if you don't fix this. So I need one of you to explain that to them since it is ultimately your decision and again, you gave each and every one of them a promise that they were going to fight you." The two of them didn't seem to care.

"Let me ask you, did you do it on purpose? And why? Just to get 'em here?" I couldn't get an answer. They both looked at me and were understanding, but not wanting to understand the seriousness of what was happening. They told me they still didn't know who was fighting Jean Claude.

Again I said, "then you have to explain that to them because they are not understanding it when I say it. They need to hear it from the man, you Van Damme."

They told me to continue filming and working out with the countries and the next meeting they would decide who fights who. I was shocked. These guys were expecting an answer from me at our next workout and here, the star and the Producer are telling me just to ignore the question for now. To go against my code that I always like to follow which is do the right thing. It's all the same, they want answers. I left the meeting shaking my head, very uncomfortable with the task set before me. I returned to the tennis court the next day and was met by the many faces of the countries I was training. Some were mad, some were curious and some just didn't give a damn because they knew they were fighting Jean Claude already. Nevertheless, I started the workout and called Germany and Greece up to the front. I broke the news to them that Jean Claude didn't want them to fight each other anymore and that got them upset as they knew as well as I, they had a great fight put together.

Then Greece spoke up. "What about Jean Claude, am I going to fight him?"

I tried to avoid answering directly. "As it is now, everything is up in the air," I replied.

He took a step forward, I could see he wasn't going to relent. "Jean Claude promised me," he spat. "I don't care about anyone else, but I am planning to fight him and until I get confirmation, I'm not making a goddamn move."

Then Germany stepped forward. "He promised me I was going to fight him and I'm not doing anything unless I get an answer."

I raised my hands up in the air and spoke. "Now listen. You guys better calm down. Most of you have never worked on films before and don't know how things are done. These problems can happen and you will only make it more difficult for me and for yourselves if you continue to act this way." All of a sudden, arguments flew from all sides like a hail of arrows. No matter what I said to calm them down they kept arguing. Explaining that this was one of the reasons why they were there. Not to fight each other, but to fight Jean Claude as he had promised. This continued throughout the week, some people were sitting and wouldn't work. I thought I would let these few men cool off for a few days, hoping they would get back to work. They always made it clear it was nothing personal. When in the middle of all this, they invited me out for a night on the town so to speak. I knew I had a lot of work to do, but I finally relented. I would go with them. Boy, was that a big mistake.

We were going to a bar in Phuket, so I was told. We arrive at ten at night to a fortress, a wall that must be sixteen feet high with shards of glass protruding from the top. It was more or less an open parking lot. We walk up to these huge set of doors with a half a dozen Gigantor security guards and Azdine, country - Turkey, walks up to security and says, "open sesame, the stars from the quest are here."

I can't believe he said that. All I can hear from inside is this music and erratic screaming and shouting. I ask the guys, "what the hell is this place?"

They smile and say, "you'll see and you'll enjoy."

So we head inside. And guess what? My jaw drops to the floor. I see rows and rows with different tables. Not four or five, but fifty to sixty of them. Guess what was on the tables? It wasn't food, it was females of all ages. From young to old. Scantily clad and dancing, if that's what you want to call it. Right in the middle of this was a huge open bar. I was horrified, scared shitless and upset that these guys took me here. Just in the fact that this might lead to some kind of weirdness or physical confrontation. These guys at the bar look like maniacs and wouldn't it just be my luck if they got upset. Not at me, but all the guys I am with. They are mostly all ego maniacs. I said to the guys, "let's get out of here, I'm outta here. This place is the Devil's lair. I'm history." I tried to convince them all they should get the hell out of here with me. I was serious. In an instant, they all looked at me like I was crazy. I tried to explain this was no place to be, but they just laughed in my face. I got a cab and went back to the hotel, warning all of them to stay out of any trouble in this kind of environment. The next day at our workout they all told me what a grand time they had. I just shook my head and said, "you guys are all nuts."

We proceeded to workout which to my surprise consisted of talking about what went on last night. When they weren't talking about the scantily clad girls, some of which they brought back, they went back to the same old thing which was asking what the deal was with Jean Claude. I continued to deflect the question, which upset people even more. They refused to workout as the days went by and even Abdel came to my side as he had many times before, trying to calm everyone down. He was a good friend to me and he understood what I was dealing with, especially with Jean Claude. He knew his M.O. In fact, he already told me he had a discussion with Van Damme and explained to him it wasn't fair what he was doing. The arguments continued and the countries were getting unruly. Jean Claude was quickly going to learn he was about to have a mutiny on the bounty. It was time for a second meeting. I knew that I had to choose my words carefully.

Either demand they come down and explain to these guys what was going on, or let them know that there wasn't going to be any working out if they were continued to be left in the dark. A few hours later I was in the office and began to tell them what was on my mind.

"Please understand, most of these guys are very upset. They want to know who is fighting you, Jean Claude and will not workout until they do. I can schedule workouts but I'm telling you nothing will get done until this question is answered. I have been trying my best to motivate them but this question has been asked too many times, they have had it," I explained.

Jean Claude nodded and sat back in his chair. "Yes, I am aware Germany, Greece and Turkey are giving you a hard time." Jean Claude could see the surprise in my eyes.

"How do you know?" I asked him. In my mind, I am thinking he is spot on, but who would tell him this? Could it be Abdel? He was on my side, it couldn't be him. Then who? I didn't know, but I made it clear that he needed to tell them who they were going to fight if they were going to train anymore.

Jean Claude looked at me and said, "Steven, you tell them that only a select few are going to fight me and if they don't like that then they will be replaced. They are to listen and obey everything you say and tell them because it is coming directly from me. Do you understand?"

Now that I knew what he wanted me to say I had no problem telling these guys and I told Jean Claude that. Then with renewed confidence, we continued to the videos of each country fighting. Jean Claude then decided on who would fight who in the first rounds. He picked Brasil and France, with Brasil winning. Then as we were moving onto the next one, he stopped.

"By the way, I want a fight put together with my friend, Peter Malota," Jean Claude said.

"Who is that?" I asked. I quickly am reminded he is the guy who is there in the stands practically every day watching from a distance with Mushy. Jean Claude's friend.

"I want you to give him a country and give him two fights," he says.

I shake my head in disbelief. "Jean Claude, there aren't any countries left," I replied.

Jean Claude was adamant. "Find a country or make up a country for him. I want him to have two fights. One against Soviet Union and the other against me."

I agreed, thinking where I could put him, but let Jean Claude continue on. "I want Japan to fight Okinawa with Japan winning. China versus Korea with China winning. Turkey fights Scotland with Turkey winning. Siam fights Africa with Siam the victor. Mongolia versus Greece, Mongolia wins."

I quickly write down these notes in my notebook and look up at Jean Claude. "Wonderful. Now we have the first round done. I will get to work right away." I left the meeting and started thinking about how I was going to break the news to the countries about who was fighting Van Damme. This is going to be a problem. I think I'm getting a headache. I thought about it and decided to tell them one by one starting with Turkey. A Thai restaurant in town was the location. A nice conversation was my plan. We sat down and started talking and then we ordered our meal. A few minutes went by and we finally came to the topic at hand. I told Turkey very straight forward that although we have some great fights planned out for him, he ultimately would be eliminated before fighting Van Damme. As the last word left my lips, I could see the time bomb I had just set off. The fire in Turkey's eyes grew and grew and grew.

"He promised me!" Turkey bellowed.

I tried to calm him down but the door had been blown open.

"No! I was promised!" Turkey raised his hand like the mighty Thor raising his hammer and BAM! Brought it down onto the wooden table. I jumped back. Not because I was scared, but because the wooden table I had been leaning on exploded! Yes, exploded. The table shattered like glass, pieces hitting me all over the place as Turkey stood up enraged.

The owner, a small Thai man, came running over shouting in his language. "You leave now! Leave now! Get out, out!"

I quickly had to think of damage control and reached into my wallet. I found a crisp one hundred dollar American bill and gave it to him. He took it and his eyes lit up. Then he went back to yelling, telling a worker to call the police. I quickly ushered Turkey out the door and brought him to a place where I could calm him down. Another restaurant, where he promised not to break anything else. I finally made him understand and it was the beginning of a beautiful friendship. At that moment, I decided it would be best to break the news to all of them at once, to avoid any more tables being broken. Haha. So the next time we met at the tennis court, I brought all of them together and told them what they didn't want to hear.

"I have met with Jean Claude, and he has decided who will be fighting who in the first round and who will be moving onto the second round. If you don't like it, you will be replaced. As in on a plane tonight. Again, I say to you, this is no joke.

It is not coming from me, this is from Van Damme. You're forgetting. I'm a worker just like you. Some people are my bosses too. All of you will have great fights that will look wonderful on your reel and Jean Claude is impressed by all the footage he has seen. Whatever you do in this movie, it will greatly help you in the future, but this is the decision that has been made. If anyone has a problem with that, walk behind me now. Otherwise, I look forward to working with all of you even more." I finished my speech and waited. Not one person moved from their spot. Relief swept through me as I smiled back at the countries before me. "Okay," I said. "Let's begin."

Peter Malota was there too and we talked for a while so I could get a feeling for him and fit him into a country. Little did I know, I should have chosen Siberia. After having him throw a few kicks and punches, he sat down and I continued to think about finding him a country. I began putting the first round fights together. First was Japan and Okinawa. I knew Van Damme had said he wanted this fight short and quick. I put together five, six moves and they got to work practicing. Next, I called China and Korea up. China was going to go through this match and fight Jean Claude and that was something I wanted very badly. I had to be careful Jean Claude didn't realize that, since it seemed a lot of things I wanted and liked, he threw aside. Why? Your guess is as good as mine. But I think he simply wanted to butt heads. I knew I had to be smart. He wasn't fond of doing different things. He wanted to stay with the status quo. Things from other movies that he knew, went over well. But I wasn't having any of that. I had many discussions with him about doing different moves. Some of them even went into arguments.

Yes, once or twice, I almost argued myself out of a job. If you are going to say something you always must be careful how you say it. I needed to break him from this thought process. And I did. As you see in this action, there are no moves from his past. I had planned for China to use multiple styles. In this first fight, he was using snake and may I say, he slithered so beautifully. It was a joy to watch. Turkey and Scotland were next. Jean Claude had made it clear he wanted Scotland to lose in one or two moves, and he would get no argument from me. I brought them up and gave Scotland three moves. "Turkey, you see my fist? I want you to give a sun fist right in the crotch. Scotland goes down."

Scotland looked at me and said, "that's it?"

I told him that was it. "You'll be remembered. A one shot Scottish pony. Make sure you make a good face for your fans," I commented.

He was, to say the least, upset. He looked at me and said, "I don't need to practice that."

I raised my hands and said, "one move can get you a lot of work. I suggest you practice."

Scotland turned and walked away.

Turkey smiled and said, "I win."

I laughed. "Yes. you do and I'm glad there are no tables around. Now go find him and practice." He smiled and went after Scotland.

I bring up France and Brasil and tell them this fight was going to be very memorable. "France, you are going to lose this fight but you're going to look like the Eiffel tower," I told him.

France was still upset that he wasn't fighting Van Damme. I reiterated what I had said earlier. He could stay and do the fight or he was free to go. He chose to stay. I moved on to Siam and Africa and told them it would be a short fight with Africa losing. Africa was okay with losing which surprised me and made me want to work harder with him to look good. Then I went to my good friend Abdel, Mongolia. Called him up along with Greece. "Greece man, come up here," I said. "This fight is going to be a beautiful thing. I am going to make you shine, but Greece, you are going to take second place and Mongolia will move on."

Greece didn't take too kindly to that.

I said, "Greece, you were chosen to fight Mongolia. He is the lead bad guy. It's the next best thing to fighting Jean Claude. In some cases, it's going to be even more recognizable fighting the lead bad guy and we will put together a magnificent piece, so don't resist."

Unfortunately, he did. He started vocalizing his concerns loud enough that Mushy who was in the stands, heard it and came down.

In his direct Israeli way, he said, "did you forget what Mister Lambert said? We can have you out on a flight tonight."

Greece shook his head and told Mushy that he remembered.

"Do you want me to go into the office and book you a flight home?" Mushy continued.

Before Greece could answer, I spoke up. "Back off Mushy." I turned to Greece. "This is going to an impressive fight, Greece. Something the audience will remember for a long time. So I suggest you go to your corner and start working on it."

He looked at me, then back at Mushy, before he nodded. As I was going through pairing up all the countries, it suddenly dawned on me where I could put Peter Malota. A bright light went off. I looked at his hair, his posture. He is THE MATADOR. Spain. I started thinking, the wheels are turning, I got it. A smile came to my face. I called Peter over. "Spain, that's your country." I explained to him he would fight like a matador, every move would be like he was fighting a bull in a ring. He didn't quite understand. I snapped into a rigid position, my right hand across my chest, my left in a fist in the air. I raised my chin up and walked like a matador with his sword raised up and threw a few kicks going right back into the matador stance.

Peter had a big smile on his face and he loved it.

"Every move, you start looking like a matador and every move you end looking like a matador," I told him. He loved the idea and thanked me profusely for it. Even though you will find it hard to understand my thinking, this turned out to be my favorite fight. There weren't any fancy moves, it wasn't the man, it was simply the look of it. The body language. He portrayed it well. Sometimes, visual can be the best thing for a fight and a matador fight like this hasn't really been done before. I called Soviet Union over and wanted them to start working on the fight. This was going to be a short fight. Russia had the fight ability of a novice. I always wondered how much they paid him. Who knows, maybe he paid them. I began setting it up and Spain was to come out on top. I made it a point that night to show Van Damme his friend, the matador and the moves he learned. Guess what. He called me a genius. It wasn't but a day ago that he called me an asshole. Lastly, I put together the fight between USA (Van Damme) and Germany. Germany, Nazi. This guy played it well. He had feeling, emotional contact. His facial expressions were vicious. He had determination, a sense of cruelty in every move. He was a very good practitioner and wonderful with his body language, which is a very important thing to have in your arsenal. Most Stuntmen, Martial Artists and Actors do not understand this, and the teachers who do really understand are very few out there. Remember this word, analyze. Examine methodically and in detail, the constitution or structure. The movement. Typically for purposes of explanation and interpretation. Another teaching moment to think about. I played Jean Claude, filmed it over the course of three days and showed it to him and Mushy.

We watched it and when it was over, he looked at me and said, "you're no me."

I thought for a few seconds then replied back, "well Jean Claude, you are no me, either. We are both individuals. God made us all different in many ways, so our talents are different. Isn't that right 'ole wise one? Oh excuse me, I am the older wise one."

We all laughed as Jean Claude told me he didn't want to do a number of moves I had put together for him. We spent forty five minutes arguing. Here we go again. Why didn't he want to do these moves? As I said before, simply because he had never done them before. He was scared. I told him, "Jean Claude, these moves I am giving you will be of interest to all of the audience because they will notice these new moves you are performing. They will be totally impressed."

We went back and forth until I think I finally tired him out. He agreed and I left the place mentally exhausted. The next day on the tennis court, I started putting together the second round. Turkey and Japan. Turkey loses to Japan with a belly shot. Japan loved the idea. I love this guy, he never gave me a problem. Turkey, what do you think by now? He wasn't happy, to say the least. I'll never forget when I showed him the first move. I turned around to Japan and I did the impression of the Hulk, flexing. I ran towards that big belly in front of me. Smack right into it and flew backwards onto the ground. I rolled over and looked at Turkey.

"That's it," I said.

What did he do? He spit on the ground.

I said, "don't improv. The audience is going to love it. It happens so fast and it's such a shock, they are going to laugh their asses off in a good way." I sent him to his corner to practice being the Hulk and bouncing off bellies. Boy, I gotta tell you. It's hard working with people who have never worked in the motion picture business before. Spitting on the ground, can you believe it? They just don't understand. Brasil and China, here we go. My third favorite. It was such a contrast between Capoeira and Kung Fu that this was going to be a long fun fight. I call this one my pride and joy. Expression of the body, that was my purpose with this fight. Next up, Mongolia and Siam. This was an important fight. A fight that had a three way meaning. Mongolia hated USA and USA was friends with Siam in this story. I needed to show many important things in this match. A series of emotions from all three. And especially a grand death at the end. I wanted Mongolia to pick up Siam and break his back. Both of them were very hesitant to do this move, so guess what? I had to step in for Siam and do it half a dozen times to show him how it would go. I told Kahn, "you don't have to worry about breaking my back. If you do, they can just fly in another Fight Coordinator."

By now, he had total confidence in my ability as did the others, since I stepped in many times to rehearse any moves which they didn't understand. Then came USA versus Spain. I wanted this fight to confuse USA, so I put little moments in where that would occur. My quest was very difficult, I needed to make sure that each one of these fights were different from the other. I needed to give each one its own character. Having filmed all these fights, I once again returned to Van Damme and showed him the footage. First was Turkey and Japan, the old belly shot. Jean Claude thought it was funny and he laughed. The second one I showed him was China and Brasil.

Halfway through it, he looked away from the footage and said to me, "too long."

I shook my head and said, "watch the whole thing. I want to make it a good fight so no one knows who wins. It will enhance everything else that we are doing if you give these guys good stuff to do. I want to show these other fighters are strong and hard to take down so the audience starts thinking, who will Jean Claude fight and how will he beat them. And the most important thing, Jean Claude, is it makes the movie better. You gotta give these guys some good stuff and some screen time." You see, I had a hard time convincing Van Damme to let these guys show off. "It will enrich this whole battle. If you let these guys perform, it will make you look stronger. It will make the movie better. If you're the only guy that's doing all the cool moves, everything else is going to be boring. I shortened up some of the other fights so we can have these longer dramatic pieces with the better guys."

Again, we went back and forth and once again my persistence won out. I then showed him Siam and Mongolia and was ready for another fight.

To my surprise, he just stared at me and said, "I like it. Let's move on."

Finally, I showed him America and Spain with me playing him. He loved it. I thought maybe he loved it because Malota was his pal. I thanked him and got the hell out of there. He always exhausts me mentally whenever I talk to him. There's always an issue. You Stunt Coordinators that have worked for him in the past, you know what I am talking about. Time went by, here comes the third round, when I got a message to come to the office. I met with Van Damme and Mushy Mushy, who to my bewilderment, told me they were not sure if the fights I put together were going to be final. Meaning they wanted to change them!

I asked why and he said, "Germany, France and Greece were making remarks that they were not happy about not fighting Van Damme and saying bad things about the movie."

I shook my head. "Who is telling you this?" I asked. "Mushy, I don't have time to worry about things like this. I have a job to do and if it's you who is spreading these rumors, with all due respect, it needs to stop. These guys are only letting out steam. They are working hard, putting in a lot of hours and besides, they are just saying words. How can you blame them, they were lied to. On top of that, if we keep changing these fights around, nothing will get done. It took me three weeks to put this together and to start from the beginning is a nightmare."

I asked both of them if they liked what they saw so far on film and they said they did with a nod of their head.

So I say, "well take out the personality and the conflict and what the snitch tells you. Words are just meaningless. You are happy with the performance, let's keep it. Please. We have worked too hard." They understood, but they were still thinking about changes. I left the room devoid of energy. Worried that I was going to have to start from the beginning. Now, I was on set and overheard some of the things being said. He wasn't. So how he knew what those comments were only left me scratching my head. As I walked out, I saw Mark Stefanich, the Stunt Coordinator. He invited me to breakfast and that is where he asked me how things were going. I told him what was going on in detail, exactly like you all just read. I told him, "look, Mark. I need some help here. If Van Damme changes things it will make everything more complicated. I'm starting over. What I have now should be set in stone. Can you talk to him and settle him down?"

He smiled at me and said, "No. That's why I brought you, Steven. I've worked with Van Damme, I know to stay out of it. I don't want to deal with that maniac." He laughed and I found myself laughing as well, but inside I felt like a beaten man, worried. If he changes things it would only create more problems with these guys and I told Mark that. Mark finally agreed to set a meeting with Jean Claude so we could all talk. Long story short, I got my way, we are all set. Moving onto the third round, we had Japan against Mongolia. When we shot this and Mongolia punched Japan in the stomach, I wanted his belly to shake in slow motion. It was great. Seventy two frames a second. Then we had America versus China. China performed Tiger. It took me three days to put this beautiful fight together. When I took it to Jean Claude, again he didn't want to do the moves I put together. Some Martial Arts movie stars get a bad habit of just doing their punches and kicks they are used to. Again, I was disgusted. "Listen, Jean Claude, we have had this discussion before. We need to show the audience things they have never seen you do before.

Not the same tired thing. Every fight you do is supposed to be better and different. That is what the audience expects. You can't fight China and Mongolia the exact same way. I could get every one of your movies and show you that every punch and every kick is the same."

Boy, did those comments make him mad. It was a verbal battle going back and forth with Mushy sitting there like a statue. By the way, he is another sunglasses boy. He always wore sunglasses, even inside. In fact, there were a few times when I would turn to him and say, "take off those God damn sunglasses and say something."

His reaction was no reaction. Van Damme finally decided he would decide the day of, if there were any changes to the fight that I had put together and that was fine with me because I knew I would win in most cases.

You're not going to change what is good on the day of. Why you ask? Because it's on the day. No time to really change anything. Again, why you ask? Well, let me tell you here and now.

On the credits, it says Director: Jean Claude Van Damme. But as far as I am concerned, it was the Director Of Photography who directed the acting in this movie. It was Mark Stefanich who directed all the stunt and it was me who directed all the fights.

What I am saying to you readers, is Jean Claude every morning, would more or less sit in his chair or not be there. Once he was gone for just about a whole week.

When it came to the actors and the dialogue, the D.P. directed. When it came to the fights, it was me and the D.P. who directed. When it came to the stunts, you guessed it. It was Mark Stefanich and the D.P. who were directing. Jean Claude, whenever he was there, he would simply move an actor, move a piece of furniture, or say those famous words he loved to repeat. "Action, roll cameras and don't do that."

That was his directorial expertise.

(The credits say he directed, but we know different.)

Within the next week and a half ,everyone was working on the first round and the second round as I was teaching Jean Claude all the moves that I put together for him. That was no easy task. Every new move he wasn't comfortable with, he would give lip service on. It took me a week to complete something he should have been able to do in a matter of days because he was so hard headed. Towards the end of preproduction, I would continue to hear from Van Damme that he was unhappy about what some of the countries were saying about him. In the back of my mind, I was always expecting to be fired simply because I cared. I was a fighter in my beliefs. This particular day, I was fed up with it and asked him who was telling him this. He wouldn't tell me and at the day's end I met up with Mark Stefanich again who had a news flash for me.

"I found out who is snitching to Van Damme. Guess who it is?"

I shook my head. I had been thinking about this for weeks and still couldn't decide.

"Who is a great friend of Jean Claude?" he asks me.

I think for a second and say, "it can't be Abdel. He has backed me up a number of times."

Mark shakes his head and tells me to guess again. "It is a fight with a country you think that is so wonderful," he tells me.

I didn't know. "Who?!" I asked.

"Spain," Mark finished.

My mouth dropped. I thought, "Malota."

Mark nodded and laughed. "He wants your job. He is trying to convince Jean Claude to fire you. He is also trying to make everyone look worse than he is by getting Jean Claude upset at them," Mark explained.

I couldn't believe Peter would do that! What a crapweasel. Yes, look it up. I said crapweasel. I'm impatient, I'll tell you now. It means a sneaky untrustworthy or insincere person. The next day, I brought everyone together, all twelve countries. Malota is trying to get me fired? Okay, let me let the whole world know, at least these twelve countries. Let's see what they think about him bad mouthing them to Jean Claude. Peter Malota, the snitch. I said, "listen guys, there is somebody here that is telling Jean Claude all the derogatory statements that you guys have been making. The snide remarks, the threats, the unhappiness that you have been expressing through no fault of your own since you were lied to. A snitch is amongst us."

This was my *Stalag 17* moment. A film with William Holden. It was about a group of POWs in a camp and one of them was giving information to the Germans. A snitch. Peter Malota.

(The Matador, Peter Malota. Talented troublemaker that tried to steal my job.)

This was the moment he was going to be caught. Rent and watch this movie and you'll know exactly what I'm talking about. At the end of this movie, they kill the snitch. In our movie, it came close. As I am talking, I am looking at their faces for a hint. China, France, Siam are all confused or a straight face. "Who is this country you may ask? It just so happens I am very good at geography. What is the country next to Portugal?" I ask. I pace back and forth and stop, and turn, right in front of Spain. "Get up, I want to talk to you," I tell the snitch.

He gets up and we walk across the room. I look back and see all the other countries whispering behind me. I take Spain across the tennis court and tell him, "Peter, I took you under my wing. I found a country for you. Spain, the matador. It was meant to be. I made a beautiful routine for you. I eat with you, I laugh with you. I open up that door of trust, became your friend and you are the guy who is talking to Jean Claude."

Peter looked away and said, "Jean Claude is my friend, he should know what is being said."

I could not believe what I was hearing. "You know there is probably nothing I can do about this. Your fight is all put together already and I know you are a good friend of Jean Claude, so you will be staying. But let me tell you this. I don't like what you did. I don't like what you are and your behavior is sickening to me. You even told Jean Claude things I said in humor, just to settle these guys down. I had to be a psychiatrist and agree sometimes to make things work. You don't have the brains to understand that. The door is closed to you, Peter. I will work with you, but we are no longer friends."

I waited for fists to fly but he just shrugged his shoulders. I must say I really was ready for a fist fight. But he casually said, "who cares."

Now it takes a lot for me to get upset and to be honest, I wanted to be a bull for a few seconds and pretend like my hand was a horn, stick it right in his face. He was the Matador after all. But I turned around and walked away.

The only time I really talked to Malota from then on out was when I had to work with him on his fights and it took a lot of verbal discussion to prevent the other eleven countries from beating him up. They too, never talked to him again. He was a lonely man. One quiet night, sound asleep and having pleasant dreams, a phone call comes. A ring a ding ding. I pick it up, half asleep. It's the manager of the hotel!

He explains, "some of the actors in the show are in a big argument with some women downstairs and they are making so much noise they are beginning to wake people up."

I ask him, "what do you expect me to do. You're calling the wrong person."

The Manager and I were very friendly with each other. After all, he saw me almost every day on the tennis court and thought I was some big time guy. When no one else picked up, he called me. "We can't get ahold of anybody else," the Manager replied.

I agree to check out what is going on. I get dressed and head downstairs to find half a dozen girls outside in a courtyard and on a balcony screaming, are our lead fighters. Spain, Germany, Siam, Soviet Union, Scotland, Brazil, Turkey. The wild bunch.

"Give us our money," the girls yelled.

"Go away you half rate prostitutes," Germany yelled back.

I got in the middle of it and told everyone to calm down.

"They owe us money," the girls shouted.

I looked up at the balcony of drunk men.

"They didn't put out enough, they are no fun. We ain't giving them a penny more," Turkey shouted back as I shake my head in disbelief, laughter and disgust.

This goes back and forth for a period of time until finally, the Thai cops came and I'm trying to calm the police down who want to arrest the guys. I am explaining to the fighters to shut up and to not make this any worse. We go up to the room and it is a pig pen. The bathroom was a mess, they missed the bowl. Broken bottles everywhere and worst of all, two of them were in their underwear with their "bangkoks" half hanging out. Yes, they were wearing tighty whities.

How do I know? Because Turkey came over to me and did the Hulk flex. I just shook my head in disgust, but I laughed. I'm apologizing to the police, trying to explain to the Manager I can take care of this, while the room reeks of alcohol and sweat. I finally get the Manager to tell the cops to leave and to my amazement, they do.

I told the Manager the company would pay for any damages and wanted to put these guys to bed. He agreed and I took each fighter and got them into their room and to sleep.

Well, I finally got to sleep at four in the morning, waking up and hoping this incident hasn't gone to the powers. Guess what? At breakfast, everyone knew what happened and they were pissed. Then I hear a voice.

"Steven Lambert, Moshe wants to meet with you."

I go over to the office and see Moshe, I mean Mushy and the Production Manager, Nikolas Korda. They tell me they managed to calm the hotel management down. This is good, I thought to myself.

"We also think you are very good at taking care of these guys, they listen to you, Steven. So guess what? We are promoting you to a second position. We are making you the official babysitter of each country," Moshe says.

This is not good. I start laughing, unsure if he was serious or joking. I reply, "I'll tell you what. Stick your promotion where the sunshine doesn't go, I don't want it. What do you mean babysitter?" I laughed.

"You are their nanny, Steven. Whatever happens in regards to them, it is your responsibility. We are serious."

My laugh died away and I nodded. "Okay, I need to make a phone call to the Screen Actors Guild."

Nikolas looked at Moshe and Moshe looked at me, his eyes hidden behind his sunglasses. "Why do you want to call them?" Nikolas inquired.

"I want to get my contract and show you guys that nowhere in there does it say I am a babysitter in my contract. Fight Coordinator, yes. Babysitter, hell no," I told them flatly. "You can't pay me enough." Jean Claude came in and told us he heard what happened and Moshe quickly told him that they appointed me babysitter of the world to deal with future problems.

"That is a great idea!" boomed Jean Claude.

"No, that is NOT a great idea," I boomed back. "That is not my job and I'm not going to take it. I am the Fight Coordinator, not the babysitting Coordinator. That's your problem, not mine." I stood up, amazed that everyone in the room thinks that I am actually going to be the resident babysitter. "Is there anything else we need to discuss?"

Nikolas shrugged. "No, you can go. That is all." I turned and walked towards the door.

As I touched the knob, I heard Jean Claude behind me say, "do a good job taking care of your children."

I turned back and shook my head. "Not this guy."

I left quickly, still in a state of shock. The funny part is, a babysitter I did become. You can call it the nurturing, caring and teaching side of me that couldn't stay away from it. I became the Babysitting Fight Coordinator, the first one (and probably last) of all time.

As Moses once said, "so let it be written, so let it be told." Alas, my quest ended with the most taxing movie I ever worked on.

(My children.)

CHAPTER 87
(Actress Julia Roberts. The Electrocution And The Kiss.)

A few weeks later, I get a call from Mister, in my past life I could have been a jester, Conrad Palmisano. Full of humor, great with practical jokes, he is. A number one guy. He was asking me to double Patrick Stewart in a film called *Conspiracy Theory*. I was very excited, as I always had a taste to double him but never got the opportunity until now. The scene is when Patrick Stewart tries to drown Mel Gibson in a jacuzzi. I would be doubling Patrick Stewart while Mel Gibson would be doing the action himself, which I thought was interesting. I arrive on set at Warner Brothers and see this big jacuzzi. About eight feet wide and ten feet deep. Much bigger than a normal jacuzzi. We work out the scene with me, Conrad, Patrick Stewart, Julia Roberts and Mel Gibson. Mind you, there is no water in the jacuzzi yet. Great, everything is set. The next morning, I come on set and the first thing I do is find effects. Why? LOL. I want to make sure my matzah balls aren't going to be too cold. I had to double check they weren't putting cold water in the jacuzzi.

You readers should know by now my extreme dislike for getting into cold water. The freezing Steven was not a move I wanted to repeat. I wait until sets starts filling the jacuzzi and asked if he was going to warm the water up. He said it would be nice and warm and laughed himself. Okay, great. I'm a happy guy. One important thing taken care of. The day goes by, lunch comes and then we get ready to rehearse the scene. All the powers gather. I see the jacuzzi steaming, nice and hot (oh yeah) as Conrad discusses with the powers where in the scene they are going to start.

The beginning middle or the end. They decide to start in the middle of the confrontation. That means they are in the water. Conrad turns to me and casually tells me to go into the jacuzzi. As I start walking over, the D.P. suddenly calls out. "Hey Steven, because we are in the middle of the fight, we need water splashed around the sides for effect."

So Conrad tells me to jump in and that will splash the water around.

I look at him, "cannonball?"

"Knock yourself out, Steven," he smiles.

It's eight feet deep, I thought. No problem. I tell everybody I am going to do a cannonball. I start from three feet away and everyone is backing up to avoid getting wet. I start running and everyone has a smile on their face, waiting to see this cannonball. I jump up five feet into the air and when I reach the maximum height, I bring my legs up and in. Cannonball here we go. I hit that water and like a rock, I started to go down. From the second my legs hit this beautiful steaming water, my mind and body went into shock. It wasn't because the water was too warm! Not only did I go into shock, I WAS shocked. A thousand needle pricks all over my body at once! I screamed bubbles and my mind told me to get the hell out of there. I never knew I could jump that high. I hit bottom and popped up. I was like a jack in a box and like a torpedo, not touching anything. I popped out like a cork in a bottle.

I landed on the concrete still screaming. "Ahhhhhhh! The jacuzzi electrocuted me, the freaking thing electrocuted me!"

Everyone, including Mel Gibson and Patrick Stewart, came over to see what was going on. All of a sudden, the effects guy speaks up.

"That's impossible. You can't be electrocuted in there," he states.

I'm still shaking, I can remember the volts pulsating through my body. It literally knocked the wind out of me, I'm trying to catch my breath.

"Oh, yea? Touch it. Touch the water," I shot back.

Conrad turns to me with a puzzled look. "Are you sure you got electrocuted?" Connie asks.

Am I sure? AM I SURE!? "Go ahead, touch it. Touch the water," I tell him. "Touch it, somebody touch it, already!"

No one is moving a muscle. Fifty people around this jacuzzi and no one wants to touch the water. They are acting like I'm nuts and I can't believe it. I yell out, "chickens. Touch the water!"

Everybody has got a look on their face. A no way, not me kind of look. Then to my surprise, the prop guy comes over and he leans down. He makes a knife hand and slowly lowers it to the surface of the water. Everybody is as as a mouse. Five seconds go by, ten seconds by. I finally shout, "TOUCH THE WATER. I DID. MY WHOLE BODY DID."

Three seconds later, he put his hand into the water. Like a rocket, his hand goes flying into the sky. He goes, "yep, that water is electrified all right. There might be a loose wire in the lightbulb."

I nodded. "Yeah, maybe there is."

All of a sudden, out of the crowd comes Julia Roberts and guess what I got? A big hug, asking me if I was all right. Followed by a kiss on the cheek.

I say, "yeah, I will be if I can get another hug."

She laughs as everybody else does.

I got that second one. They take the time they need to drain it and fix it and I go to my trailer until it was time to get dressed again for the scene. The time comes. Take two, for this Jew. Everybody walks over to the jacuzzi and Conrad tells me to do my cannonball and jump in. I turn and lock eyes with him and laugh in an endearing way.

"I ain't going in," I say as everyone laughs. I ask someone to touch the water first.

The FX guy smiles and slowly sticks his hand towards the water and stops. Everyone is quiet except me. I laugh, bringing everyone else to join me.

"It's good Steven," Conrad tells me. "We checked it out earlier and the water is warm and safe."

I nod and say, "I want to see it."

Finally, the FX guy gets enough guts to stick the tips of his fingers in, ready to jump back. The water is fine now.

I laughed as I waive back to Connie, jumping in the air yelling, "here I go, CANNONBALL!!"

CHAPTER 88
(Stuntmen's Association. The Straw That Broke The Camel's Back.)

My final realization of the group I belonged to. It was shortly after this picture that I happened to be home and got a letter in the mail from the Stuntmen's Association. It was about our monthly meeting. Woohoo, this is never fun. In the letter, it went through the discussions they were going to have in the meeting. Finance, job prospects (yeah right), upcoming events, etc. What caught my eye, is that they had written they would also be discussing a serious matter involving another member, Carl Ciarfalio. Carl was the real deal, a good friend of mine and I thought highly of his moral character and his talent. The letter went on to say he had broken a rule in the organization in regards to working extra. I was confused about this and so I called the Stuntmen's Association to inquire. The secretary explained to me what supposedly happened. Carl worked extra driving a car on a SAG film. That didn't sound like something Carl would do on purpose, there must be some good reason. Usually, I say I am too busy to go to these meetings. Meetings where nothing ever gets done and arguing and conniving are more or less all that happens. Yes, you can tell at this point in time, I was tired. Meetings where they never have a discussion about how to bring more work into this joint, but Carl was different. I needed to be there to see and hear. I know him to be a good man. I decided to go and see what exactly was going on. I called the secretary and told her to mark me as coming, as protocol requires. When the night came, I saw about thirty five to forty five guys there and the membership was about a hundred and twenty eight. Those meetings were never full. Nobody cared. I saw Carl and noticed nobody was hanging with him.

Unfortunately, this was typical. When there is a problem with somebody, nobody wants to be your friend. You can't be seen with the person who is thought to be in trouble. It might be seen. Some may get mad and you think you could lose a job. That's a pretty sad way of thinking. NOT I. You see there were always cliques downstairs before we went up. I thought this was typical and so to show my support, I walked over to him and let everybody see. I stuck out my hand and shook his and turned and waved at everybody saying, "hello."

I asked what had happened. He simply explained to me that he wasn't working, he was desperate and needed a job, so he took a special ability extra gig. It would seem to me that this group should hire the members of the stunt organization that need it and deserve it. But they don't. If he or someone spoke up, saying they needed work, it always seemed like the powers of the group would put down that

645

person for complaining. It gave the impression that the more that someone needed work, the more somebody hurt, the more they wouldn't help them. I could never figure out this way of thinking, but this train of thought was a common occurrence. I could see the compassion in Carl's eyes and I knew he would never break rules unless he had to. He explained to me that he had to. At once I understood and agreed. He had a family and a child. He needed the money. He said he had to buy food, rent and clothes for his kid and I again understood. I felt empathy. Soon I would find out that very few did. I had just finished a show and told him that if I had known that he was hurting, I would have worked him in an instant. I felt a sadness that I wasn't aware of his situation.

You see, it sounds funny but the guy who is hurting doesn't mean that he has lost his sense of being proud. And like Carl, when you are proud, you don't talk about your problems. It's hard. You try your best to give little hints that you need a job, but most people just don't see it let alone sorry to say, care. But again, I understood the embarrassment about admitting to someone who is working, that you need money and a job. The time for the meeting came and we all went up. I sat next to Carl to give him a feeling of strength and support and that seemed to shock a lot of members there. It was like he had leprosy. Nobody wanted to sit next to him. They were afraid. It was a sight to see.

Charlie Picerni would have said, "f you blanking cowards."

He's the best. Charlie is like Superman. He stands up to truth, justice and the American way. The gavel hit the desk and the meeting was started. First, the President started talking about the daily topics. Then when he got to Carl, he asked Carl to leave the room. To my shock and surprise, he did without a word. The President began to read the rule which Carl broke, to the entire gathering before him. Listen, I understood that rules were rules and if they were broken a price had to be paid, but this one was far too steep and unjust in my view. There were plenty of others who broke rules and they were berated, suspended or simply nothing happened to them. They weren't kicked out! It seemed to me that Carl had the short straw and was being given treatment he in no way shape or form deserved. Why? It's simple. Carl wasn't one for running shows, unfortunately. He was a working stuntman, an action actor. So there was a different thought process on him which was, he simply couldn't help them, he didn't have anything to offer. It was sad, but true as far as they were concerned. Me? My thoughts? He was more valuable than most for this organization. He had a talent that very few had in this organization. He was a real stuntman and a gifted actor. And most importantly, a real person.

Then a stuntman stood up, a stuntman that I had once taken a three hour road trip with. He was there along with stuntman Bob Jaregi. Bob and I were on a movie with this person singing with the radio. Oldies but goodies to this stuntman who stood up in his chair. This stuntman also told me that he has never had a day off work in his life. Those are two hints you can use to figure out who it is, you readers out there. If not, that's life. He started explaining in a hostile way, that it IS permissible to take a job outside of the film industry, but to do what Carl did was completely wrong. It was breaking the rules.

"This is not allowed and if we allow this, I am telling you now, I will not hire anybody in this room. On top of that, I will quit this organization," he said.

That put everyone in a panic and silence suffocated the room. Just about everyone except Tom Morga and me. Tom Morga was another great friend of Carl. We would not be silenced. A few people stood up and voiced their opinions. Most in agreement with this stuntman that is threatening his fellow members. I'm thinking to myself while this is going on, where is everybody's understanding? WHERE THE HELL IS THE EMPATHY? Why isn't anybody asking why he did this? When Tom Morga brought up the word, "why," the Board of Directors and everyone else seemed to avoid this word.

It didn't matter to them. It seemed like understanding wasn't in the equation for these royals, as most think of themselves. They finally brought Carl back into the room. As I watched him, I got a feeling like he felt he was walking to the gallows. It was like watching a funeral, so distressing. He stepped up to the podium, eyes locked onto him, daring to speak. They asked him if he wanted to speak and explain his side before they began their voting to decide if he would stay or be kicked out. I thought this was a cowardly move. Keeping him out of the room, only to bring him back to hear his plea was disgraceful and heartbreaking and a good amount of suffering. I was. Needless to say, poor Carl. I didn't see or hear any compassion in the many other voices there. He spoke about his situation and the hardships he was enduring and spoke the words I had heard outside and more. This time, it was more of a plea for forgiveness. He was broke and not getting work. No rent money so he took this job to make some. He apologized profusely over and over to everyone and that it was the wrong thing to do, but it was desperate times. It was heartbreaking. Then this same stuntman stood up again and viciously denounced Carl's story right in front of him and all of us.

"You could have gotten a job out of the movie business," he spat.

Carl reacted right away with love in his heart and said, "yes, I could have and I did. But it hurt too much to be out of the industry and it wasn't enough. I was wrong, I'm sorry."

After he spoke, there were literally five minutes of debate. I thought to myself, here is a man that loves what he does and loves this organization. The Stuntmen's Association. And this group can't and won't see that because of the barren barrel of empty feelings that the majority of this group has. It was ridiculous to me what was going on. Shameful. He was asked to leave again so they could do a secret vote. You would write "Yes" or No" on a piece of paper and put it in a hat. "Yes" he stays or "No" he does not. Can you believe it? I guessed that they are so ashamed that they didn't want anybody to know how they voted. Again, I thought that was a chicken shit thing to do. Hide what you really feel. Brotherhood. In their heads, where did it go wrong? The anxiety in the room was crushing. We all voted. I voted that he should stay of course and stood up and said so right then and there. So did Tom Morga and Roy Clark. Others that should have been there to support him, to my surprise, weren't. I wondered if they just didn't want to get involved. Tom Morga and Brian Williams would go out of the room to visit Carl so he wouldn't be lonely. I went out to the hall to see Carl as well, who had a look of defeat and pain on his face. When Carl was called back in, again that long walk to the podium took place. Only this time, unfortunately, it would be for the last time. They told him the decision. He was out of the group. Now listen to this, he is just standing there. Seconds go by. His face starts to visually turn. He starts crying. Yes, he physically starts crying. A broken man.

He doesn't say anything but, "I'm sorry. Thank you." He hurries out of the room and as soon as he closes the door, there is silence. That is when the fist of fury arose in me. I stood up like I was in a war and at the same time, hurt, ashamed and feeling betrayed.

I spoke. "What is life all about? Where is your compassion? Where is your empathy? Why don't you understand? You guys should be ashamed. This man loved this group. This man would have done anything for this group and everyone in here. He is one of the best stuntmen around. His acting ability, far better than you all. One of the best action actors in the business. Not just with his talent but with his compassion and personality. And you kick him out because he needed to pay his bills, needed to take care of his family with a child?! You are supposed to be a group of blood brothers, but it seems all you want is blood. You guys are heartless!"

The gavel bangs down on the table. "You are out of order, Lambert," a voice booms back.

"Good," I reply. "I want to make it clear that what you just did was a despicable act. You could have suspended him or forgave him."

The gavel bangs but I ignore. it.

"You suspend or forgive many guys for breaking rules far worse than this. Because it's your time of the month to go on a power trip against this guy, you kick him out of this group!? You all should be ashamed!"

He raises the gavel in the air.

"This is not the way you should conduct business and life and if you bang that thing one more time, I am going to stick it where the sun don't shine." I waited a moment. Everybody seemed afraid to move a muscle. They were shocked at what I just said but they knew I meant every word. They were smart not to speak up. They knew me and knew I meant it. I was on fire and I didn't want to burn anybody if you know what I mean.

"Lambert, that is enough!"

I reach up to my head and take off my hat. It flies like a shuriken across the room and lands on the ground in front of the Board. I say," I've had enough of this." I turn around and walk out, still smoking inside. I don't close the door, I SLAM it!

It quickly became apparent that night, that this generation of the Stuntmen's Association was not the group I always thought it was when I joined. You think about this and maybe someday you can tell me who is wrong and who is right. What I thought the Stuntmen's Association did to Carl was a mistake. In fact, you could call it a massive one in character in my outlook.

CHAPTER 89
(Our Hero Stuntman Troy Gilbert Takes On Director James Cameron.)

A titanic one. Like the boat. That's where I found myself, working for one of the smartest and well known Directors of our time, James Cameron. On the flight alone there were about fifteen stuntmen. When I got to the hotel there were massive amounts more from all over the world. Canada, Australia, Mexico and England. It was a magnificent happening, one I had never experienced before. All these fantastic stunt people. A foreshadowing of the times that were blowing towards us, to me. Never have so many stuntmen gathered in one place on a film. Think of it this way, it was like all the munchkins in the *Wizard Of Oz*. Hundreds of us in one spot. And guess what? Just like the munchkins, some people got in trouble too. There were incidents all over the place and people getting scolded and being sent home. People drunk, some fighting. Theft, if you can believe it. There were even a couple of guys that simply just disappeared. Who knows, they might have gone down with the titanic. Never have the events that I am about to recall happened in such a way. It was a momentous time. A momentous place. Am I sounding too much like Orson Welles? Okay, I'll move along. We arrive on set, on the boat. The big boat. They built a huge section of the ship, a tremendous exterior set that is also interior with railings and giant smokestacks. That is where I met Stunt Coordinator Simon Crane. He was an Englishman who I had discovered got two phone calls. One from Vic Armstrong and one from Andy Armstrong, asking him to bring me aboard. That he did and I felt like that was a great honor for them to have done that.

You see, this is what you should do, give credit to those who have helped you. (See *Indiana Jones And The Last Crusade*, motorcycle sequence, now you understand? Means a lot to me.) He explained he would assign all of us different pieces of actions to do. Falling, sliding, rolling, crashing and hanging as the boat starts to tilt and break apart. My first assignment is running, falling and sliding as the ship begins to tilt and people are running and falling all over the place. No problem, I thought. Running, falling and sliding is easy and fun, I can do that. So the first day was an easy one. The boat was pretty flat and the angle was around fifteen degrees at this time. Simon told us the next day would be a bit more difficult as the deck would be tilted a few degrees more and the wildness would be greater. As he had said, the next day I came in and saw the boat was now at a thirty degree angle.

People were given stunts, falling backwards over railings, ten foot drops. People hitting chairs and tables, hitting other people and smokestacks, as well as trying to avoid all the above. Some successful, some not. All kinds of rigging and technical setups had to be done for this. Mind you, this was hundreds of people doing these stunts at once. After hours of setting this all up, and after the first take, Cameron came out and started to complain that he wasn't happy. We had to make major changes which took hours to reset, but we also needed to explain to him that in some cases we couldn't go the direction he wanted us to go. There were some things and some people that needed to be avoided, so there wouldn't be any accidents.

Cameron seemed to be upset at that statement saying, "I want people to crash into each other."

We explained that yes, we had that for him in cuts, but we can't take somebody going sixty feet and crash them into something or somebody. They would kill each other. We told him we had some handheld shots, similar to what he needed, but in different spots. Finally, we were ready to shoot this escapade. With literally countless things going on at the same time, it was needless to say things didn't work out as planned.

People were getting hurt, tangled amongst multiple cables and misdirected. Imagine this, take two fists full of jelly beans. Bring your hands back and throw them on the ground towards each other. Watch them hit each other, bounce off each other. Watch the misdirection of some going into others. Flying in the air. Think of those visuals. It was a mess. When Cameron cut the cameras, he stepped out and this was the beginning of a bad attitude.

Yet, as the hours and days went by, it would get worse and worse. The more the boat titled, the more dangerous things became, the harsher Cameron would become. Again, the Stunt Coordinator and others explained to him that we were now at a thirty plus angle and now have multiple actions in the shot. Everything was a free fall for all. Having to turn one's body to avoid obstacles and people planned and unplanned was extremely difficult and sporadic.

A chair or stuntman that wasn't there in rehearsal would appear because of the hundreds of other stuntmen doing their actions. It was a butterfly effect throughout the sequence. One wrong move creates another. Cameron didn't care, nor did he understand. Case in point. A stuntman from Mexico broke his shin in half, the bottom of his legs turned the other way. He was screaming in pain and I will never forget the words Cameron spoke.

"Get him off the deck and bring me someone else."

No compassion, no caring. As cold as ice. This happened consistently. People breaking arms. People breaking ribs. People getting knocked out. People cutting themselves wide open. People breaking noses. I remember my good friend Vince

Deadrick Jr., hit a smokestack and broke his ribs. It took three guys to carry him off and that's what Cameron said.

"Get him off the boat," he yelled. "Just bring me another guy. We don't have time for this."

Everyone just took it, as they thought working with Cameron was a great honor and that he was kind to stuntmen. Or so we were led to believe. We endured this day after day. Always abuse. This was a big weight on Simon Crane's shoulders. Not only did he have to appease James Cameron, but he had to make his stuntmen happy as well. That didn't always happen.

There was one stunt woman who was going to do a hundred foot plus high fall. A very complex fall, hitting certain things and missing others off the boat. She didn't rig it fast enough for Simon Crane, who quickly got upset at her in a rude way, I thought. He told her to get out of the costume and he replaced her with one of his guys.

She tried to explain she needed to rig it a certain way so she would purposely avoid certain objects. Guess what the guy he replaced her did? Took even more time to rig it! I thought that was a very self centered decision. Not understanding your people. I thought he would realize after all this time, that they were trying to get the best for you too, Simon Crane. They are pushing themselves to the limit for you.

To this day I have not seen any acknowledgment or appreciation for the men and women that were working so hard for you on this boat. Of course we understand the pressure you are under as a Stunt Coordinator. But as we realize what you are going through, you should understand what we were going through and acknowledge us in some way.

Unfortunately, that never happened. He should have worked it out with respect and understanding with the Director and his stuntmen and that just wasn't happening. I was there for about three weeks and after the second, all the stunt people were physically and mentally tired. Banged up and exhausted from the abuse that they were given.

(Always make sure you are remembered in a scene. I'm the one hanging in the middle.)

To repeatedly come down on your stuntmen who were literally breaking bones for you, enough is enough. We were at a point where the ship was at about an eighty five percent angle and everyone was hanging on for dear life. All of a sudden, Simon Crane went up to the bridge and tells all of us that Cameron wants to talk to us. Mind you, we are all rigged up, ready to do these very dangerous stunts. After what seemed like an eternity, James Cameron comes out.

He grabs the megaphone from Simon and says, "let me tell you all something. My three year old daughter could do better than you guys." We are all shocked by this statement. I can't believe what I had just heard as he proceeded to continue to insult us. "I am not happy with the performances you are giving me. You are all taking too much time. You look like a bunch of extras afraid to let go. You are all a bunch of monkeys that can be replaced. There is no acting or excitement and you are all boring me to tears," he continues undaunted.

All of a sudden, it was like the sky opened up and the sky turned into a porthole and a grenade popped out with the pin pulled. It was a stuntman. He roared like a lion back at Cameron. All the stunt eyes came upon him. Then he spoke.

"Let me tell you something, Cameron. I came on this show very proud. Thinking I was working with one of the best Directors to have ever worked in motion pictures. The things I have heard about you including how exceptional and creative you are, how well you work with your cast and your crew excited me. But what I have experienced here, what I have experienced with you, I am embarrassed by your attitude. The way you treat people, the disrespect you give us, it's downright despicable."

I'm watching this man and by now he is standing up straight like a statue. I'll never forget his last words he shouted like a General defending his men. I was so proud watching this man.

"You should be ashamed of yourself. Mister James Cameron! I don't know about anyone else here, but me? I quit! I'm through! I don't want to work for you, goodbye!" He yells. He gets out of the porthole and jumps down like a lion and turns his head, giving Cameron one last look before he makes his way off the ship.

It was unbelievable.

Everything is quiet, everybody is watching at first. Then I see movement. Then I hear cheers. Then I hear roars. Everybody is cheering this stuntman. Then I see one, I see two, I see five, I see ten, I see twenty, I see forty, I see sixty, including me, following this individual off the ship. More and more follow. Everybody leaves. It was like the pied piper and we were the mighty mice following his lead. Who is this brazen man who spoke up, you ask? His name is TROY GILBERT. Troy leads and we follow off of the boat. I honor this man, I respect him. One of my unsung heroes.

We were told later on, that after we left Cameron looked at Simon Crane and said, "your stunt people can't do this."

Simon turned around and said, "well, they did."

Cameron then fired Simon Crane! However, one of the Producers told Cameron that if he didn't want this getting out to the public, he had better apologize to Simon Crane and find a way to get these men back to work. So Cameron rehired Simon and talked to him. He apologized to Crane and it wasn't long before Crane met with us.

"I know you are all going back to the hotel and that is all well and fine. But tomorrow, I would like you all to come back here as Cameron has something important that he wants to say to us. He wants to apologize," Simon Crane imparted.

We talked amongst ourselves and agreed to hear what he had to say. That is exactly what we did. The next day we all packed our clothes ready to go home, not knowing what to expect. We arrived on set and got out waiting for Cameron. When he arrived everyone was quiet again, all you heard were mumbles. We watched as he came to the front of the room and stood on a table.

"Listen," he said. "I want to apologize to one and all of you. But the first one I want to apologize to is Troy Gilbert. Where is Troy?"

Troy raises his hand within the crowd.

Cameron continues. "Troy, you were right. I was wrong. To all you stunt people, I was wrong. There was no excuse or reason for my behavior. Please come back to work. I am sorry. I will leave the room for you to reconsider and discuss it with Simon."

Cameron left and Crane asked for us to give him one last chance and that's exactly what we did. He came back into the room and we all cheered. He said thanks. Everything was fine from then on out.

Little do you know, all you readers out there, that this went on. It surprises me to this day, two thousand nineteen, that no tabloids or television shows or any of the mainstream news media picked this up.

Or on the other hand, maybe they did and Cameron simply stopped it. It was a huge mess, on this one night stand that could have been the rise and fall of *The Titanic*.

(Titanic. One of my dearest friends. John "Bad" Meier.)

CHAPTER 90
(The Great Gene Lebell Leaves. The Unraveling Begins.)

It wasn't long after that when things in the Stuntmen's Association got wild once again. I got a call from a member who spilled the beans on what a large portion of the young political stunt boys on the Board of Directors of the Stuntmen's Association were planning. Over the years, anytime a member tried to get approval to do something, it would have to be voted on by all the members. The stunt guys knew they could convince themselves, but it was the majority of old timers that were giving them difficulty. It seemed that process had bothered some of the younger members and they were concocting a plan to put a stop to it. How you might ask? Easy. Get the older members to drop out. Each person in the Stuntmen's Association had to pay dues each year. When they turned sixty five, those dues were no longer required. This was a very old by-law that no one dared try to change. Until now. The younger stuntmen proposed a scheme. A vote to oust this rule and make the old timers pay.

They knew that the older stuntman wouldn't pay because they had others bring it up every now and then in a casual passing so to speak. They knew there would be a war and this is what they wanted. When they wouldn't pay, they would quit and the power would go to these individuals. Everyone thought I would join them on this fantastic idea which they would discuss in detail over a cigar smoking get together. Well, they were dead wrong. I refused the invitation and told them how insane that way of thinking was. Trying to get these guys, these great guys who worked hard their whole lives for the Association and other members, out of the group by cheating them from this right, was wrong. They have supplied tens of thousands of jobs since the start, 1961. I was very disappointed inside. I had to do something. So the next meeting that came up, I went to. The other members were surprised to see me as I was a rarity at these meetings but always very memorable in one way or another. I guess I was a memorable Kung Fu stunt Ju. That's what happens when you speak the truth. All the young guys there knew I was probably going to say something, so they kept their eyes on me. Memorable. We sit down and multiple people on the Board Of Directors, including the President, begin talking about old news and matters of the past. When they get to speaking about new business, they tell everyone in the room that they are going to take a vote on removing the by-law that states anyone over sixty five does not have to pay membership dues. Before they even finished talking, Roy Clark jumps out of his seat!

"Who do you think you are? I have been in the organization for fifty years. I have worked many people from this group over the years, both young and old. This by-law was made in nineteen sixty one at the beginning of the group's foundation. Not you or anybody else is going to change that. And if you vote on this, I am sure I and every old timer here will pack up and quit. That's what you want, isn't it?" he said.

All the old guys stand up. Some explain it like John Moio, in an educational way, why this is a bad idea. Some explain in an outrage. At the end, I stand up.

"Look guys, there are other ways to make money and pay our monthly nut. Having not to pay is like an award when you reach sixty five in this group. It may not mean much to you, but to these guys it means the world. It isn't about the money, it is about the principal. It is the years they put in. Now you are telling them to forget about their achievements and what they have done? I told you this on the phone when you tried to sneak around these guys! Why don't you tell everyone you called up people on the phone before this meeting to try and persuade them. All you guys want to do is make these older members leave so you can take control and make all the decisions. That is not what a brotherhood does. It will be all over if this goes through, that you care about money more than your brothers." I finished and sat down.

I got a big applause. One of the few young punks that stood up out of their chair. That made some of the Board Of Directors and others furious. You see, they weren't used to being spoken to like that. That was the right thing to communicate to everyone. And then the legend rose to his feet. Gene Lebell was the last one to stand up. I have never seen Gene so mad.

He simply told them, "I don't know about any of you other guys, but I am finished with this organization. I quit."

Everybody's mouth dropped. He walked out and this seemed to affect everyone in some way. I know this because we did take a vote and come to find out to my surprise, the vote was for keeping the by-law. The next day, I called Gene Lebell to let him know he didn't have to pay and there was no reason to quit.

"I'm finished with that group," Gene told me. "I am tired of it. It's dishonest and it's corrupt and this organization isn't what it was. I'm finished!"

Well the very next day, this is all over the stunt industry that Gene Lebell quit. I also found out this same day, that Stunts Unlimited called Gene up to join. Guess what? Here is the genius of Stunts Unlimited. They thought the world of him. That is exactly what Gene did. He is now a member of the great organization called Stunts Unlimited. I was happy for Gene for many reasons. One being that sorry to say, Stunts Unlimited as a whole is a far better group to be in. They have always been team players and always took care of their own. Young, old, disabled, retired, everyone. Their members always come first. Unfortunately, I can't say that for the Stuntmen's Association and believe me that bothers me. I ask myself sometimes, why is that? I just simply come up with, it's the choices this group makes. They seem to have the wrong outlook on which road to take. The selfish one or the compassionate road. I once loved the Stuntmen's Association and the one word I thought it stood for. Brotherhood. But it seemed to be a fantasy. Maybe it was just a hope. Don't get me wrong, there were some wonderful things that happened to me and friendships I still have in my forty two years or so I had with this group. Not only that, but a month later I went up to the office of Stunts Unlimited and to my astonishment, let me tell you what I saw. It was great. A big smile came upon my face. Stunts Unlimited has the standard Director's chairs for their members. They are all the same. I looked at Gene's chair but it wasn't a chair. It was a throne. A king's throne. The only guy in there with a throne.

Again, that was the genius of Stunt's Unlimited. They know who legends are and so respected this man to the point where he deserved a chair like this. It felt magical and for the Stuntmen's Association, they deserved that big punch in the gut. Now if you are interested in the names of the people that were on the Board during the time of Carl Ciarfalio's ouster and Gene Lebell's quitting, you just simply have to ask these two wonderful men the year it happened. Look up the roster of the year and you can see who was the President and who was on the Board Of Directors. And that's how this stunt monkey floated. What does that mean? If you ever see me, just ask me.

CHAPTER 91
(Director John Carpenter And James Woods's Wonderful Surprise.)

Now listen to this. If you were doing a film and needed an actor to portray an action hero, which person would you choose of the three pictured here? Maybe Arnold, maybe Stallone. Sorry to say, you might not choose not James Woods. Right!?

(I picked James Woods. Can you blame me? Sorry, Arnold, sorry Sly. I'm sure you understand.)

Well, John Carpenter chose the one in the middle to be his action star. YES, Woods. It was on a movie, a scary movie. *Vampires* was its name. I get a company call from Dracula. Yes, believe it or not, the person on the other end told me that it was mandatory that they talked like Bella Lugosi. He asked me if I was available to come on and double Woods.

I say in a Renfield voice and laugh, "yes, master yes. I do. Hehahehaheh." I hung up and I called Woods immediately after. He picked up.

I said, "thank you."

He asked, "who is this?"

I said, "your favorite Jewish stuntman."

He said, "oh, oh, did you get a call from vampires?"

I told him I did.

Right away he started explaining. "I am an action star in this one. Move over Arnold and Stallone."

I started laughing while he continued telling me about the movie. I hear and feel an excitement and joy in his voice that I never heard before as he explains to me how excited he is to play this macho man. To you readers, watch the film, it is good and hilarious. Woods's co-star was Sheryl Lee. She was a great actress. Not. Only for silent films, which John Carpenter had decided. She was so bad, Carpenter cut out just about all her lines which worked because she had got bitten by a vampire. So that was Carpenter's excuse for her not talking. It was hilarious. Every time she was on screen, she would be like a silent muppet. The genius of James Woods used that to his advantage. Woods was on full throttle this picture. Improv city. He was absolutely fantastic to watch. If you ever see this movie again, remember what I'm telling you and listen and watch closely. The dialogue that Jimmy gives us is priceless. Now let's get to the meat and potatoes.

The party scene, remember that? The vampire hunters decide to have a party in town and invite some ladies of the night. The lady's acting was superb. True professionals. That was because they weren't acting at all. Listen to this fact. The majority of them were real "call girls" from the local town! The real deal. This is one for the pages of time. Somebody should write this in a book. Good thinking, Steven. For three days we worked on this scene and you gotta understand besides Woods, Baldwin, Lee and Guinee, all the rest of those guys were action actors (stuntmen). All friends of mine, so don't let their wives know. Just about everyone excluding a couple of stunt girls, behind the camera, cast themselves into the scene after wrap. Get it? Did I you ask? Well, like I explained when I was in that fortress with all the guys in *The Quest,* this Jew boy is too smart to partake in that party. And it was a hardy party for, some. Now let's make like a bat and fly on.

Danny Baldwin was a nice guy but quite the nervous character. Didn't quite understand how to simply perform in a scene. His experience as an actor wasn't really evident in this picture. It seemed to me and others that he was flying like a kite, high in the sky. If you wanted him to do something, you had to pull his strings to get him down to earth by giving him massive cups of coffee and a lot of sugar for confidence. Figure that one out. He had trouble hitting his marks too. For some reason, he had a wobble in his walk, but he was happy. Just like a moon shine. A very wasted talent who couldn't get his lines out a lot of times and who didn't seem happy playing second fiddle to James Woods. They did have a friendship going on before this film started, which allowed Jimmy to always get what he wanted out of Baldwin by giving him the confidence he required as an actor.

Now I must mention something that surprised me and overwhelmed me with emotion on this show, something I will always remember. On the phone with James Woods at the beginning of this story, he had asked me how I was doing with my problem. Remember my wife? I went to a big town called Splitsville. Population one.

As Humphrey Bogart said, "this is the end of a beautiful friendship."

In other words, if we are talking about a team of horses, I got unhitched. Okay, I'll say it. Divorced. As you can understand, I was in no condition to work. I was a wreck. A mental one. I also told Jimmy I hadn't seen my two kids in a while. By the way, Woods being Woods convinced me that I will feel a lot better working, and that is how I got onto this picture. He explained why I should come, being the big brother he was. After a week of filming went by, I got a strange call time as I looked at my next day schedule one night. That was abnormal because I always come in when Jimmy came in for obvious reasons. I called the Production Office who insisted they had talked to Jimmy and got the okay. I didn't understand but agreed to be picked up at three in the afternoon. Three came and my driver arrived. I got in, still wondering what a strange thing to be coming to set at a different time than Jimmy. A few blocks away from basecamp, my driver gets on his phone.

"I have Steven Lambert, we are a couple blocks away now," he says.

When we arrive on set, I look out to see a huge crowd. What is going on? I get out of the car and this barricade of people in front of me are just looking at me. I spot Woods and Carpenter in the front smiling. I wonder to myself, "what the hell are they greeting me for?" This is a first. There must be a practical joke coming. That's when Carpenter spoke up and said, "I have a big surprise for you."

I see the back of the crowd open up and the silhouettes of two children walking forward. I look closer and realize that these two children are my children! My daughter Natasha and my son Kristian.

My mouth dropped open. They run over to me and I give them a big hug as everyone around me is smiling and watching. I'm just in shock as tears are going down my face. I stand up with my son in my arms and my daughter hugging my waist right beside me.

"This is a gift from me, Woods and company," John Carpenter says. "We called their mother up and convinced her to let the kids come."

I was again in shock, how the hell did they do that? I didn't know, but I didn't care.

He introduces me to this woman who he says will be my children's nanny. "They will have two babysitters and I am moving you all to the top floor suite. They will take them to the movies, to dinner, anywhere they want to go," Carpenter told me. "On the company's dime. I understand how upset you were and I can't imagine how difficult this was for you."

I wiped the tears from my eyes and hugged Woods and Carpenter. For two weeks they treated my kids like a prince and princess. They would bring them to set and make them up like vampires. They even had their own Director's chairs with their names on them. Carpenter would ask them if they liked the scene before he would call print. Most of the time they said yes, but once we heard "no" to a James Woods scene.

The cast and crew erupted in laughter while James Woods said, "not only do I have a Director, but I have a critic alongside," as he walked over to my daughter and asked her how he could correct the mistakes.

She would reply, "don't be so mean and don't shoot them so much." A big smile was on her face when she said that. How happy she was to assist me here.

Much laughter in the background. They would feed them whatever they wanted and make sure they were entertained while I was working. It truly was a touching and heartfelt two weeks we had together.

(Two wonderful and talented men. John Carpenter and James Woods with my daughter.)

You may think of John Carpenter as the master of horror, but let me tell you he is a master of heart. You may think of James Woods as many of the characters he plays, a cunning master of deceit, but he really is a master of compassion. My good pal.

(I'll always be grateful to John Carpenter and James Woods.)

I had a quick discussion with James Woods about how surprised I was that their mom let them come to see me.

Woods's reply was, "what do you think? With me around you never have to worry."

I erupted in laughter from this classic Jimmy Woods.

CHAPTER 92
(Boy, Those Enchiladas.)

Did you ever get a call for work, a one day gig, you have no idea what you're doing on it? You don't ask, you just take it. You show up, arrive on the set. You ask the Second Assistant what's up, what am I doing, what's the name of this show.

"Scary Movie 2," he replies.

I think to myself, oh, a scary movie huh. I ask him what I am doing. My mind is in thought. Would I be murdering somebody or disemboweling someone, maybe hanging somebody by their balls?

"Probably sitting on a toilet," he says.

I looked at him. "Sitting on a toilet? Doing what?"

He smiles and says, "you're going to be shitting. Yea, you might be doubling James Woods."

I am thinking, oh surprise, I wonder what's going on? Is this what my career has come to? Sitting on a crapper? My pal James Woods.

As he said to me before we shot, "I am going to give this film a possessed voodoo doo doo. Just watch, Steven."

I couldn't do anything but laugh, watch and wonder what was going to happen. Let me explain. I am doubling my good friend, James Woods. I get a wardrobe fitting and it is a father's outfit, the priestly kind. When I got to set and got the sides, all I could find Jimmy doing was being in the bathroom and getting possessed. It doesn't read any action! But I don't know, maybe he will fall in the bathtub and almost drowns. When I see him, I ask, "what are you doing and what am I doing?"

He says, "I don't know yet. But I got an idea and I'm not going to say anything until they role camera."

I ask him what I was going to do and he said, "well, I thought I would bring you along just in case, get you a job."

He would always relish the enjoyment we both got out of it when he let me know about the many times I worked for him and did nothing. I always thought that was cool. Like a big brother, in his mind, he always made it a point to look after me. I thanked him and was very appreciative.

We set cameras for rehearsal and Jimmy leans over and whispers to me, "watch this."

Let me tell you now, my understanding was that this movie was serious. I never saw the first one. I had no idea what I was going to visually experience until they roll cameras. The Director asked Jimmy what he was going to do and he just replied, "watch."

He walks in and tells everyone no rehearsal, he is ready to film. Jimmy pulls down his pants and sits on the toilet as he kisses the bible. I am looking and watching this thinking, wow this is going to be a weird scene. I'm oblivious. They roll cameras. I am watching very carefully for when the stunt comes. Then Woods begins. His face gets one color of red and then it becomes a vibrant red. He starts shaking his body, looking up to the sky with his mouth open. Making all kinds of weird, intense faces. I am thinking what, is he going to have a heart attack? It is the weirdest thing I ever saw him do. I thought to myself again, wow what great acting. They cut for a moment and put flies on his face. It's absurdly weird and very uncomfortable to the eye at first. I gotta tell you, I almost have to look away, it's so strange. But then as he continues getting worse, all of a sudden, I hear a playback from the sound department. It's some kind of noisy air. It's a fart. Then I hear another sound. This sound was like throwing rocks in a puddle of water. One, two, three times I hear it. Consecutively. I realize then, he is taking a dump! Boy, was I confused! I have to continue watching.

Then I hear him say, "boy, those enchiladas."

After a minute or so they cut and everyone around me bursts out with laughter. I am in the dark, wondering why they are laughing. Jimmy gets his accolades and walks over to me.

With a big smile, I asked, "what the hell did I just witness?"

Jimmy says, "They loved it. They thought it was genius."

I told him, "it wasn't only genius, but that scene was going to live forever. Jimmy, I thought this was a horror movie."

He looked at me, "weren't you horrified? This is a comedy."

I replied, "I had no idea."

Woods smiled. "I hope they put it in the film, if not they are stupid for multiple reasons. First, it is a classic piece of film for that movie and second, I got paid a lot of money for free."

We both broke out laughing and that is how I got a free day of work and a memory of one of the funniest, wild, serious, dramatic and craziest actors I have ever seen. James Woods. You must take time to watch, it's hilarious and I thought it was serious. https://www.youtube.com/watch?v=4vcNnS9k884

CHAPTER 93
(Actor Sven Thorsen And His Sveetheart. Here We go Again.)

Bells are ringing and they are not church bells, they are synagogue bells. I pick up my nineteen forties black phone. Remember those old dial rotary phones? They weigh a ton. I once saw a stuntman whose name was Chongo, pick one of these up and hit his daughter upside her head. Knocked her out cold. But that is a story that is never supposed to be told, lol. I carefully pick mine up so I wouldn't knock myself out, and hear a familiar voice on the line. It is Sam Firstenberg. The Shmulik himself! It has been about fifteen years since we last worked together and I am always surprised and may I say, delighted when we talk. Most of the time it is for lunch or to ask me how I am doing. We would always call each other now and then. We spoke for a while about old times, how his children and Itzy were. Just in case you forgot, that is Sam's wife. She's the best. When he suddenly mentioned he wanted to have lunch together and give me a surprise.

I asked, "what is it? A free coupon for a Bar-Mitzvah?"

He laughed. I told him that I wasn't going to have lunch unless we went to the special deli he would always take me to. A little place on Pico Blvd.

"I am going to have my usual. A pastrami sandwich and an order of potato pancakes with applesauce. No sour cream, please."

He laughed and gave in, saying tomorrow would be fine to go.

"Tomorrow is the Sabbath, you are not supposed to be carrying any money," I said.

He said, "okay, you pay for it." He always had a great sense of humor, that Shmulik. The next day we meet and he plops down a script in front of me.

"What's this?" I ask.

He says, "I am doing a new film and want you to be my Stunt Coordinator."

I wipe my mouth and look at him, before responding. "You mean it took you fifteen years to finally come to your senses and you want another hit? So you are bringing me back?"

Shmulik nearly spits up his Stewart's cream soda. Indeed he was and you can bet I was on board. "It is a film called The Alternate, starring Eric Roberts," Shmulik explained.

I had never worked with Eric, but I knew he was the brother of Julia Roberts. (Prreeeeeetty woman walking down the street.) A few days later, I sign my contract and give my budget to the Producer and Production Manager. The Producer on this film was MISTER VILLIAN. He sat me down with the budget I gave him, saying he disagreed with a couple of things on it, even though I told him why we needed such things.

I told him, "listen, I am calling in a lot of favors to make the budget as cheap as I can again."

Again, what do you mean again?" the Producer asks.

"This is a Shmulik film," I stated.

He looked at me with confusion. He didn't know what a Sam Firstenberg picture is like when it came to money. Firstenberg always looked at the big picture. I explained my relationship with Sam and how I knew what would work and what wouldn't. It kind of went in one ear and out the other and this Producer still wanted to cut some things to save money. I told him that before I set and call the day or days of action, I would let him know a few days before and he agreed with that and we moved on. I also explained that once I called the action in, he cannot change his mind.

In other words, "if you change your mind it has to be within 24 hours of the day of action. Let me make one other thing clear. I don't even like doing that. So if you say yes and then change your mind and make me cancel the stunt people, then they lose this job and the job they could have been working. So it is not a very smart thing to do."

(Sam Firstenberg, The Shmulik. Brainstorming. We are waiting for an answer. Anytime now.)

Again, he agreed. Most of the movie was shot at the Ambassador Hotel in Los Angeles. It was abandoned ever since Kennedy's assassination. For me, it kinda felt the same way as being in the graveyard for *Ninja: The Domination*. I was treading over sacred ground. Portraying violence over a sanctified hotel. There I met Eric Roberts. During our long conversation, he mentioned that Sam told him I was James Woods's stunt double. I told him yes for many, many years. To my surprise, he knew James Woods and we discussed him for a bit. I started training him and he did pretty well, but I had no intentions of making him a superhero. Even though I was doubling him, you never want to put action in sequences that make YOU look good. You can't put together moves for yourself. You must fit the action to the story, scene and character. And if the actor's performance and scene are good, that's where you will get your accolades. I had a week and a half prep on this show, one of the shortest prep times I have been given on a movie. Sam introduced me to one of the Producers named Bryan Genesse. A nice guy, I thought. During this first day of prep, location scouting in the Ambassador hotel.

Another unknown fact, secret passageways all over the place that the caretaker introduced us to. This is where ninety nine percent of our work takes place in or right outside this hotel shrine of Robert Kennedy. Here, I had the freedom to look around. I went into the kitchen where he was shot. Such an eerie feeling. Everything was still here. Stainless steel sinks, ovens, and counters. By the way, Shmulik is with me and I turn to him. I can't imagine being one of the people here seeing Sirhan Sirhan shoot Kennedy. What a sad day in history.

Shmulik says, "can you imagine if it didn't happen? He would have become President."

I said "yes, there is a big gap of history missing now. How sad."

We turned and made our way back to the set to talk action. This freedom I had was due to Sam Firstenberg's confidence in me, knowing that what I came up with, he would more or less insert his dialogue and acting in and amongst the action that I presented to him. When we started talking about some of the action we were going to do, I started explaining my ideas. Now if the D.P. had any comments or changes he wanted to make, I would always listen to him as he was coming from a visual standpoint. But the person I found interrupting my thoughts the most was the Producer, Bryan Genesse. He had some good thoughts, but the more I talked, the more he would comment and try to take control. I turned and looked at him and said, "what's up Mister Producer? This is my job. It sounds like you have some experience doing fights."

He smiled and said, "yeah. I am a ranked Black Belt in Canada in Kung Fu and Tae Kwan Do."

I said, "you and every Producer. Sam didn't tell me that. That's great. It is always good to have another professional on set, but why doncha' keep it to yourself and I'll call you when I need ya. Thank you though for your ideas."

He blinked a few times in shock as I smiled. He spoke, "why are you joking like that Steven?"

I explained with a smile. "You are the Producer and I appreciate your suggestions, but you hired me to do this job. So let me do it first, let me put it together and then if you have some ideas you can play them off what you hired me for. Nothing personal, Bryan. That is just the Brooklyn in me, let me put it together and then I will show it to you and your actors. Let me do my job and you do yours at this moment."

Bryan looked at me and said, "I can see how excited you are, I can't wait until we get to the fight scenes with me and Eric Roberts."

I glanced at him funny, not understanding what he meant. "You and Eric?" I repeated as a question.

Shmulik slaps me across the chest and says, "Steven. Bryan is not only the Producer, he is the lead bad guy."

(Bryan Genesse. Producer, actor and he insisted on doing his own stunts. He was good.)

I had no idea he was the co-star! I said, "whaaaaaat?" Realizing that I put my foot in my mouth a little bit, I turned and said, "now I understand why you are giving me your two cents."

He looked at me oddly. "Two cents," he said.

I laughed. "Yea they are good two cents, don't worry, we'll use them. Well in that case, let's follow the same guidelines I told you as a Producer. Keep it to yourself."

Needless to say, we became good friends at the end of the day and he did come up with some good things that I was more than happy to put in. I've always believed if somebody has a good idea, let's use it. Not lose it. Like I lost my head. Guess who else I saw? It was the head thief, Ice-T. Sam was there, Bryan was there, everyone. As soon as he saw me, he came right over.

"Steven!" he said.

"T!" I shouted back.

We said our greetings and Ice-T couldn't wait to get out the story about my head and for ten minutes that is what he did. Of course, in between his story, I told my story which made it better. A little Lambonade with that Iced-T. It was a very funny, memorable and Ice-T moment. We had everybody laughing. Eric Roberts and his wife were on the floor. Little unknown fact. His wife in the movie was his actual wife in real life. Double the money, double the pleasure. You get it? All in the family. Another merry merriment memory (tongue twister) was when lunchtime came. I had half a dozen stunt guys working on this show. From John Meier to Sven Thorsen and Terry Leonard. I am sitting with Shmulik, Eric Roberts, Ice-T and the Producer when Leonard starts channeling his inner Hans Christian Anderson. It was time to tell stunt stories. We had half an hour for lunch and when the time was up, the Second Assistant blew the whistle. But nobody was paying an ounce of attention to him, they were all focused on listening to Terry Leonard. The Producer, Director, everyone. The whistle is blown two, three, four times more.

Ice-T tells him to, "shut up or I'll unplug you and put that whistle up your a-hole."

Everyone laughed. Forty five minutes go by, an hour goes by and everyone is still listening to the stories, everyone is laughing hysterically. After another forty five minutes, we end story time. It was a classic. Days and weeks go by and we are filming, having a fun time. We get to a piece of action where I am doubling Eric Roberts on the roof of The Ambassador Hotel. I get knocked off the roof by the bad guy. I grab the American flag and with all fifty states, I fall three stories. Losing my balance, I fall again, six, holding onto Old Glory and stopping about seven feet from the ground. Releasing a handful, I drop down and pose all in one shot. NINJA.

For this, I would be using a decelerator. I have to now depend on my guy to stop me before I hit the ground. I've never liked depending on someone else assisting me. But here I had no choice. I did it twice and it went wonderful, everyone enjoyed it. My equipment specialist was Kurt Lott and his assistant Jane Austin. Husband and wife, how about that. I thought I was being a nice guy. I even gave them both parts in the film. I picked them both for their talent, friendship and besides, Kurt belonged to my stunt organization and I wanted to show loyalty. They packed everything up afterwards.

I told them, "you guys did a wonderful job." I start walking down the hall and here comes guess who? THE VILLAIN.

He stops me and says, "Steven. I just want you to know, that I am not paying for the decelerator, the guys who brought it out or your adjustment."

I looked at him confused and said, "we already shot it. It is a print! I told you what you had to do if you didn't like something and you gave the okay to do this."

Well, it didn't matter because he reiterated the company was not going to pay for it. He stuck to his guns and wouldn't move an inch. I was already in a heated mood that day. Unfortunately, par for the course, my children's mother wouldn't let me see them and I was not in the mood to deal with THE VILLAIN. I simply went ballistic as I let him know how I felt, my voice echoing through the halls of The Ambassador Hotel. He tried to walk away but I wasn't going to let him. I followed him like a shadow and yelling my displeasure, when Eric Roberts came to find out what the hell was going on. I told him what was going on and he tried to get me to calm down. But he would need a bigger bucket of water to douse the fire that was ignited within me. I proceeded with my verbal attack at The Villain, until Shmulik came to see what in God's name was going on. I told him what The Villain had said and he told me in his usual way not to worry. I continued on unabated for another ten minutes until the Villain ran away. Tail between his legs. Let me say to you people out there, losing your temper is not the thing to do. But sometimes I was just a pissed off Jew. I went downstairs to talk to Kurt Lott and told him what my Producer had said.

"I'm going to deal with this and you are going to get paid, but in case you don't, here is three hundred dollars apiece." I reached into my pocket and took out a wad of hundred dollar bills and counted out six big ones and handed it to them. "Now if you get paid, great everything is fine and well. But if you don't, I will take it to the Guild. In the meantime, I want you to have this money and if you get paid, call me and let me know and you can just give it back to me. Cool?"

I gave them cash. I didn't have to do that, but I felt bad and wanted to show them that I appreciated their work and took their professionalism and friendship seriously. They agreed to let me know if they got paid and packed up and left. Shortly after, I had a meeting with Shmulik and Bryan Genesse. In the middle of the meeting, Mister Villain walks in. Wait a minute, let's take a five minute break. I bet you are wondering the name of this Villain. I'll tell ya what, why don't you get a drink? How about a DeMartini. Have some food with that, a hot dog. We'll call it a Frank. Now that you have digested this information and you know his name, let's move on. By the way, Mister Villain in two thousand eighteen ran for Los Angeles city council. He lost. I wonder why. I explained to the Producer that we had three days of rehearsal, and filmed the decelerator and printed it twice. He had no answer other than he didn't have enough in the budget. Nevertheless, the Production Manager assured me that they would get paid and that was that.

Two weeks went by and I hadn't heard anything in regards to if Kurt Lott and his wife did get paid or not. I was surprised and so I called Kurt up and asked him if he got paid. He said he did and I inquired when he received the check. He told me it came a few days ago.

"Well, I asked you to call me," I said. "You know how heated I was and if you got paid a few days ago I would have liked to know." I'm waiting for him to mention the six hundred I gave him, that now he should give me back, but he never did. So I brought it up and asked him if he could return it the next time he saw me.

"Sure thing," he agreed.

Well dear readers, weeks went by and I finally did see him. I waited for him to come over and give me my money, but it never happened. Now years have gone by and I am still waiting for my six hundred dollars back. He is very successful financially and it just surprises me how strange some people can be. I thought I did a very nice thing and was never reciprocated for it. And believe me, it's not the money, it's the principal. I can say that is just the way humanity is, but it makes me wonder whose grandmother raised him. Again, I say thank you, Grandma Rita. It is all about principal.

Now here is another fine, funny mess of a situation. Bryan Genesse versus guess who? The Viking, Sven Thorsen. The moron, I say that with love and respect. Laughter. Too funny. I am working on the set, busy getting action together, while in the hotel Sven is enjoying himself smoking a cigar next to a big open window right off the set. Bryan Genesse walks by and he doesn't know who Sven is, all he sees is this giant Viking smoking a cigar in the hallway.

"Hey, you need to put that out. There is no smoking in here," Bryan warns Sven.

As many of you now know, that is the last thing you want to say to Sven. Looking at Bryan and then at his cigar, Sven speaks up. "If I put out the cigar now, it is going to lose its taste."

Bryan looks at Sven in confusion and disbelief on his face. "Listen, I am a Producer on this show and I am telling you to put it out," Bryan responds.

Sven looks at his cigar and then back to Brian. "Okay, but let me have five more minutes with my sveetheart. I am not done making love to her yet, allow me few more kisses on my cigar, Mister Producer," Sven tells Bryan.

Needless to say, Bryan Genesse is not happy. He tells him to put out the cigar at once.

"Excuse me, Mister Producer," Sven replies. "What is your name?"

A bright red anger spread across Bryan's face. "It doesn't matter," he snapped back.

Taking a puff on his cigar and exhaling, Sven shrugs his massive shoulders. "It is just I would like to know who I am talking to. From one Gentleman to another. Mine is Sven Thorsen, I am a stuntman on this show working for Steven Lambert. Now it is your turn, you idiot."

Instead of answering, Bryan furiously turns around and goes to find me on set. I am in the middle of filming and as soon as Shmulik cuts, he goes right to me and explains his confrontation with Sven and he is not a happy camper. As soon as he finishes, I start laughing. Bryan asks me what was so funny. I told him it's a joke.

"You have to understand Sven. This is how he is. He is a practical joker," I explained. "That's his huma'."

Bryan didn't find it as funny and demanded I come with him to tell Sven never to smoke inside again. I tell Shmulik that I would be right back and head through the hotel. I am walking in front of Bryan and when I turn the corner, I am the first one that Sven sees. I can't help but have a smile on my face, as I see one appear on his too. I wonder what is coming now. I take a deep breath and put on my serious face as Bryan joins us in the hallway.

"Listen," I told Sven, "the Producer doesn't want you to smoke inside anymore. You gotta listen to him on this. It makes me look bad, it makes you look bad. Do you understand? You need to apologize to Bryan."

Sven looks at me and then at Bryan and I knew what was coming next.

"Come here baby," Sven tells Bryan.

I just put my hand to my head saying, "oh no, here it comes."

Sven takes out another cigar and offers it to Bryan. "I am sorry for not listening to you Mister Producer. Here is a cigar, have one from me. I come from another country and I sometimes forget Americans can be so sensitive."

Bryan is just dumbfounded and yells, "I am not American, I am Canadian!"

Sven replies with a simple, "oh! That's worse."

Bryan takes the cigar and shakes hands with Sven.

"You two lovebirds good now? Everything lovie dovie?" I ask.

As I step back to turn the corner, I see Sven pull out his cutter.

"Let me cut the tip of your cigar for you," he tells Bryan.

As I head out, I see Bryan put the cigar in his mouth and Sven light it. I pop my head around the corner and say, "NO SMOKING IN THE HALLWAY!"

Bryan and Sven look at me before Bryan says, "you Americans are always so sensitive."

Sven laughs and says, "you learn fast Bryan."

As I turn the corner I say, "I hope you two foreigners have a good time," just shaking my head smiling.

CHAPTER 94
(The One. Jet Li. Jason Statham.)

Now I am proud to say I have worked with many movie Martial Artists. From Segal to Chuck Norris, Brendan Lee to now Jet Li. I get a call from Gary Hines. A great stunt man and dirt bike rider.

They called him Skyshot. Can you guess why? He was first class on a motorcycle. He flew in the air like a butterfly. A class act. He asked me if I wanted to double Jason Statham in a movie called *The One,* starring Jet Li. I said, "hell yeah."

I get about two weeks on the set doing some gags. The first day I get introduced to Jason Statham. We got along great. I start rehearsing a fight with Jet Li, doubling Statham where I get kicked and go over a three story railing where I do a back half twist and grab onto the railing three stories down, saving myself. We rehearse it a couple times, I am cabled off as it was three stories high. The first day of shooting, Jet Li comes onto set with all his men speaking in Mandarin. Or is it Cantonese? Take your choice.

All of a sudden, he stops, looks at Gary Hines and says, "who stunt guy?"

Gary points at me and I introduce myself and stick out my hand to shakes Jet Li's. He takes it and shakes it with a serious glare.

Still clasping hands, he says, "youknowMartialArts? Youknowhowkick? Youknowhowkick?"

As you can see, Jet Li talks very fast, so I had to take a few seconds to absorb what he was saying.

"Show me kick," Jet says.

I get into a stance facing him.

He says, "no, not me. Him, him."

I see he is pointing to one of his guys. I smile and ask, "why not you?"

He gives a look of surprise, as his merry men gave me the same look. He smiled and says," okay, okay, kick at me, kick at me. What kick you do?"

I nodded and said, "I will do a whip kick."

Well as soon as I did my whip kick about six inches away from him, he jumped back into his stance. As I came down, I threw a roundhouse with the other leg at one of his Chinese stuntmen about three inches away from his face. He jumped back in surprise. As I come down from that, I jump up and do an axe kick at another Stuntman to his right. As I come down, they all have jumped back into stances with big smiles.

Jet Li looks at me and says, "yes, yes, yes, good, good, good."

And just like that I gained his confidence and it became comfortable, they all warmed up to me. I always enjoyed watching and talking to Jet Li and his guys. I would always have wonderful conversations with him in his trailer.

One time he invited me in to have some Dim Sum and to my surprise, he reached into a cabinet and took out some Hong Kong cigarettes. Yeah, he smokes.

He saw the look on my face and he said, "bad for you."

I told him I understood. "Can I have one too?"

So we sat there smoking and we continued eating Dim Sum in his trailer. The cigarette tasted funny and I kind of felt funny and always wondered if there was any pakalolo in it. Besides, we found ourselves laughing at stupid stuff. It was a rare moment with the one and only, Jet Li.

(I always love surprising the talent when I work. And Jet Li was surprised.)

(Jason Statham, his first movie. He promised me I'd be with him always. He lied.)

CHAPTER 95

(Oceans Eleven, Twelve, And Thirteen. Actors Clooney, Pitt And Cheadle.)

Oceans Eleven, starring George Clooney, Brad Pitt and Directed by Steven Soderbergh. Oh and *Oceans Twelve*. Oh, and *Oceans Thirteen*. How about that, I did them all.

I am proud to say I am the only action actor that worked on all three. How about that, every time they picked me. A great pal of mine, John Robotham (his father's name was George. He worked with the Duke, John Wayne on quite a few of his movies) gives me a call and asks me if I wanted to play a part.

"Deal me in," I said. I was dealt my hand thrice as all three movies I got a character part in. This was thanks to Soderbergh who took a liking to me and told me, "we'll see you on the next one, Steven."

(Making sure I'm noticed. A trick you should always remember.)

On *Oceans Twelve,* I played the casino roulette dealer. On *Oceans Eleven*, I was never introduced to George Clooney or Brad Pitt, only Don Cheadle. At the end of the first day, Cheadle and I started having conversations. You know, the usual stuff. Where we were born: I said Brooklyn, New York.

He said, "I can tell."

As soon as I mentioned that I was a Martial Artist, his eyes went big. He asked me to tell him about what I had done which caused him to open up to me, that he himself practiced Kung Fu. This was exciting news to me and Don wanted to know if we could work out together. I agreed in a heartbeat and told him we would find a good time in the next few days to do just that. That time came most unexpectedly. We were shooting the scene where Cheadle and our gang break into a vault when I feel a tap on my shoulder. I turn around and see Don Cheadle. He asks me if I wanted to play. I was about to ask him how we were going to do that when we were right in the middle of the set. Then he brought up his hands. Sticky hands. That is what he wanted to play. I was shocked and he asked me if I knew this and I said, "yeah, man." I brought up my hands and we started slow, rotating back and forth. In and out, over and under. He was testing me and I had a smile on my face the whole time. His touch was soft and fluent, the way it should be. I could tell he was a very experienced man in this. As he started to go faster, I looked away. I wasn't watching. I was feeling, emotional contact, which he commented he was very impressed with. All of a sudden, his hand shot out like a piston right to my face. Using my upper and middle gait, I turn. His fist barely missed me. He rotated his other hand, this time trying to get under me. I quickly blocked his belly shot with my other hand and came up right to his neck. He jumped back all excited. "Yea, I got a partner!" he exclaimed.

We continued doing sticky hands as Soderbergh, Pitt and Clooney came over to watch. By the end, we were pouring sweat. That's how hard and respectful we were going. He told me he was going to ask for me on the next film he did so that we could continue to work out more, can you believe that!? He asked for my card. I thanked him. I always think about how good Don Cheadle was and why he has never done any Martial Art movies. He would be great.

On *Oceans Twelve,* I was playing a roulette dealer. I was caught cheating and they called security on me. During rehearsal, I simply let them walk me out. But when they rolled cameras, I resisted. Cameras are rolling and it took three guys two and a half minutes of struggling to get me out. For all you out there, that is the way to do it. Don't let them know what you are going to do. After, Soderbergh called me over to his Director's chair. He was sitting there along with Brad Pitt and George Clooney.

"That was excellent Steven, we don't have to do that again. That's the reason I brought you back," he said.

Brad Pitt stuck out his hand and simply said, "great job."

George Clooney, to my surprise, didn't say anything. He snubbed me. I guess he felt I was doing too good of a job. The snob. Just kidding. This is great. They brought me back for *Oceans Thirteen*. I play a bad guy running from security after I rob a casino. I get to the lobby when a big security guy comes out. Bob Minor, a great action actor. Six foot three, two hundred and forty pounds. He gives me a stiff arm and I crash into it, flying up and landing on my back. Soderbergh loves it.

"I'll see you on fourteen," he says.

I'm still waiting.

CHAPTER 96
(Actor Al Pacino And The Relentless Paparazzi.)

For this next gig, I'm playing a paparazzi. It's an acting gig on a movie with Al Pacino called *Simone*. I arrive on set and the Stunt Coordinator, Webster Whinery greets me. He takes me over to a motorcycle and explains to me that I am riding double on the back, taking pictures of Al Pacino on the move, in a limousine. I say, "is that all?"

He says, "yeah."

I say, "okay." So I get dressed and put on my wardrobe. A couple hours later, they want to rehearse. I meet up with Stuntman Paul Lane who is the driver of the bike. Hop on, back to back and we're on the move and we arrive on the set. Props comes over and they hand me a camera, one of those old fashioned cameras where you have to take out the bulb and put in another one. They hand me about a dozen bulbs and I put them in my jacket.

The Director explains to us, "I want you to ride alongside the limousine. When Al Pacino rolls down the window a bit, Steven you start taking pictures and we are going to let this run a full city block. You take as many pictures as you can. Got it?"

I said, "yeah."

He goes, "okay, let's rehearse it. Just pretend to take the pictures, Steven"

We go to our marks and the Director calls action. Camera truck follows. Pacino rolls down the window a bit and I start taking pictures. Snap. I take out the bulb, put another one. Snap. I take out the bub and put another one in. I managed to take about seven to eight pictures before we reached the end of the block.

The Director said, "that looks nice, let's shoot it."

But as I am going back to number one, I am thinking, this is kind of boring. What can I do to make it more interesting? Better think quick Steven. Ah, I got it, I say to myself. We arrive and get ready to do it again. Director calls, "action" and we take off.

I see Pacino roll down the window a bit. Maybe three inches. I snap. I take out the bulb and instead of just dropping it, I decide to play ninja and throw it right through the opening about an inch away from his head. He jumps back, surprised. He looks at me again. I have another bulb in. I snap!

I pull it out and I throw another shuriken, I mean bulb. It hits the window on purpose. Pacino starts yelling at me through the window. I put another bulb in and snap it real quick. I take it out. I have two in my hand now. I throw them, one right after the other. Right through the window. They miss him by inches. He improvs some more. The dialogue is obscene. I reach in my pocket and take three out and just throw it at him. One hits him in the head. Oh, shit. I hope he's not mad. He jumps back.

I hear the Director yell, "cut."

Paul Lane stops. Webster Whinery comes running over to me. He's angry. He's yelling. I'm smiling.

"Why were you throwing the bulbs at Pacino? Nobody told you to do that."

I said, "Webster, listen. I'm an actor on this movie. I'm allowed to act. I decided I would try to improv a little."

Webster says, "no, you don't understand. This Director only wants you to do what he tells you to do. Nobody told you to do that, Steven."

I explain to him again, "Webster. You hired me as an actor so I am allowed to take certain liberties as an actor. I understand you hired me and you are the Stunt Coordinator and I thank you for that, but I am doing an acting part, not a stunt." Just then, the limo comes by and the window opens.

It's Al Pacino. He looks at me and says, "that was great. I loved it! I didn't know you were going to do that."

I asked, "were you surprised?" He nods.

"Oh yeah, yeah. We kept it going and it was great." He looks at the limo driver and waives him on. Before he leaves, I say, "sorry I hit you."

He replies, "I saw it coming."

"Okay," as I'm laughing. I look at Webster, his mouth is open. He's surprised, to say the least. I smile and say to him, "you want to thank me now or later?"

He chose now. Threw me a big compliment. Made me feel great. Yet, he is still a little worried what the Director will say. We walk on over to him. He says nine words to me.

Webster says, "loved it, Steven. It was a work of art." "Only you can get away with that Steve, only you."

My part is finished. Lunch comes, then it goes. I'm hanging around all day. Then they wrap. My boss comes over. Webster tells me I am finished and to go sign out. That's what I do. As I'm writing my John Hancock, the First Assistant Director comes over to me.

He says, "Steven, you aren't finished. You are coming back tomorrow."

I said, "coming back tomorrow? Are we going to do another camera angle of what we did?"

He said, "No. Al Pacino liked you so much, he put you in another scene."

I said, "oh, okay."

(The Godfather, Serpico, Scarface, acting with the Ninja, Remo, and Franco. Would you believe?)

I take a short walk and find Webster and say, "hey. Guess what? The First Assistant said I'm coming back tomorrow."

Webster says, "no you're not. You're finished. I just talked to him and he said you're done."

I said, "no. I just talked to him. He said Pacino liked me so much he gave me another scene."

Webster says, "nah, can't be. Let me go find out."

And he does and I'm back. I asked what I was doing tomorrow.

"You are playing the same character at his beach house. You are looking in the window taking pictures."

I say, "that's it?"

Webster says, "yeah."

Tomorrow comes and I arrive on the beach house set.

The Director says to me, "okay, I want you to jump on the deck and take pictures of him through the window. He sees you and comes out. He grabs the camera away from you and runs to the water and throws the camera in the ocean, destroying all the pictures."

I say, "okay."

He tells me they are shooting this in about an hour. Guess what? I say to myself this is boring. What can I do to make it interesting? I notice above the window there is an iron rod extending from the roof. So I climb up and check out the railing. It's solid. I hang upside down like a bat. Only my feet holding on to the rod. Perfect. I am about five feet from the floor.

Come time to shoot it, I walk over to the Director and say, "I got an idea. Instead of me just jumping on the deck and looking into the window, why don't I go on the roof and hang down like a bat off this rod. Then Pacino can run out and pull the camera from my arms and I'll fall off upside down."

He looks at me and says, "but you'll fall right on your head."

I laugh and reply, "no I won't. I'll tuck and roll and make it look like a crash."

He goes, "you can do that?"

I said, "yes sir."

He calls over Pacino and tells him what I was going to do.

"Oooooooh. terrific," he says. "Marvelous."

Take one. Cut, print. Now the lessons of this story are INVENT! TAKE LIBERTIES! EXPLORE YOUR OPTIONS! TEST THE WATER! Do that and you get another scene with Al Pacino. It works.

CHAPTER 97
(Actress Jodi Foster, Mr. Nutcase Dwight Yoakam And Director David Fincher.)

My next job was indeed a reason to panic. Not because it was starring the very talented Jodi Foster, but because of what I am going to explain to you. That's right. *Panic Room* was the name of this gig. Let's start with Jodi Foster. What a calm and intelligent dame. Her ways were magical as she orchestrated controlling the set. Conducting the cameras where she wanted them and directing the scenes with her smile and her grace. She did this in such a way that it didn't hurt anybody's feelings. A very multi-talented woman. Boy, does she take control. The actor I was doubling had a physical scene that directly brought us close together. You may ask why.

The simple reason was she couldn't control the actor I was doubling, so she decided to keep the pullover mask on the actor's face to punish him all through the show. Since he had a pullover face mask in the scene, she decided to use me as the actor. I thought that was genius since the actor I was doubling was mentally way out of control. Jodi really knew how to utilize her body language to enhance the scene. That was cool and I was excited for multiple reasons. One, she was an Academy Award winner. Two, I was impressed with her being so physical. Three, her improv instincts were spectacular along with her body language. And four, the most important, she smelled so good and looked so cute. One hell of a package, prime stock. That's when the clueless cowboy walked in. I mean, if you wanna call him a cowboy.

Maybe I shouldn't, that's an insult to those guys. I noticed he was behaving very erratic, walking in circles on the set. Bumping into people, not even excusing himself, nor saying hello to anybody. Then he came over to me and told me his name. Dwight Yoakam. This is the actor I am doubling. I could smell his breath was in good spirits. GET IT? That's when Jodi Foster turned her back and went to get ready for camera.

That is when she said, "Dwight, your stunt double is playing you."

He stood there dumbfounded. He asked who I was and the Stunt Coordinator told him I was doubling him on the show. We explained to him what we were doing and Yoakam insisted he could do it himself. Director David Fincher agreed with a sadistic smile, much to Jodi Foster's dismay. As the scene went on, Yoakam began going all over the place. He wasn't able to get anything done. Manhandling Jodi as she was trying to go through the action we put together. She would go the right way and he would go the wrong way.

Take after take. It got so bad that Jodi reiterated that his stuntman, me, should do this scene. She was almost insisting this to David Fincher. I was a happy camper because she simply got her way. The power of a strong woman, it is amazing. So I put on the mask and did the scene. Jodi was incredible. It worked the first take. Forrest Whittaker was also there. A very quiet and introverted man who always stood back and kept to himself. A listener he was. It seemed like he ignored everything, but I had a feeling he was just taking everything in.

Now the man I was doubling, Mister Dwight Yoakam was a whoooooole 'nother story. Loco in the cabeza, he was. Big time. He was always late and very confrontational. He never understood and didn't really care what the Director or Jodi Foster wanted him to do. He was always very irrational. An actor he was not.

He didn't care about hitting marks. He would be on Jodi's mark or Forrest's mark instead of his own. He would always look like he was talking to a God damn door. We get to scene a few days in where Dwight's character goes crazy and gets a guy to the floor and starts beating and stomping on him. He is late as usual, so Jodi Foster recommended that I should do the whole scene and just get close ups of Yoakam. I remember her words.

"Quick extreme close up," she said as everybody on the set giggled.

It is nothing but a stomp fest with the guy on the floor. David Fincher wanted about two dozen kicks, so I was going to improv and just go crazy. I assure the stunt guy that was getting stomped on, that I wouldn't hit him.

"Just try to keep an eye on me so you know what I am doing. I will exaggerate them so you have ample time to see." He knew they would just be light taps.

"It's okay Steven, I know your reputation," he replied.

As they rolled camera, I went through about two dozen kicks. Crescent kicks, axe kicks, every kind of kick in the book. I was making them look sloppy. In the middle of rehearsal, guess who walks in? Yes, he was late again. He saw what I was doing and told the Director that he wanted to do it. David Fincher and the Stunt Coordinator agree to let Dwight Yoakam do what he wants. I walk over to the Coordinator and say, "aren't you going to work out some kicks with him?"

He shakes his head and says, "no, we are going to do what you suggested and let him improv."

I told him, "wait a minute. That idea was for me, not for him." I looked at Dwight who was pacing around the set and then back at the Coordinator before saying, "look, I am a Martial Artist. I can control my kicks. I don't know how good it will look, how real it will be if he just starts going wild without any rehearsal or direction."

Nevertheless, they decide to proceed anyway and I go behind camera as they call, "action." The fight starts and the stuntman falls down and here comes Dwight Yoakam in his shit kicking boots. He starts leaning on the wall, because he can't even lift his leg, and starts throwing kicks. Full blast, like a baseball bat. Missing a couple of times, putting a couple of holes right in the wall. Imagine what that guy felt like, taking this. He starts stomping on the stunt guy like he is about to put out a fire, never stopping, never not touching. I am watching the look of pain on the stuntman's face as he is screaming in agony. Not fake screaming, real screaming. I can't believe what I am seeing as he is screaming after every kick. Ten kicks into it, I look at the Coordinator and ask if he is going to stop it.

He shakes his head "no."

"But he is really hitting him. He's hurting him," I point out.

He raises a finger, but it is not to call "cut." Instead, it goes right to his lips and annoyingly shushes me. That's right, he shushed me! I instantly got upset. Not because he shushed me, although I wanted to break his finger off, but because he is letting this happen.

I look back at Yoakam and now he is hitting the stuntmen in the rib and stomach area, swinging his leg like a bat while holding onto the wall. I then glance at David Fincher and saw of all things, that he was smiling! I didn't know if it was because it looked so real or if it was because he was sadistic and enjoyed the stuntman getting beaten up. That's the way I saw it. Something inside me just Brooklynized and I just snapped and ran right into the middle of the shot, tiger clawing Dwight, and pulling him off camera. Everybody's mouth went wide. The Coordinator asked why I did that and David Fincher wasn't too happy. I look at the helpless stuntman as angry words poured down on me. I could see he was in pain, not moving with tears in his eyes and no one was helping him.

"You see this man getting kicked for real and you don't lift a finger to help him!?" I erupted. I help him up and watch as he goes over to the garbage can. What do you think happens? He starts throwing up his guts, dropping down to his knees and holding his ribs and other places in pain.

I ask if he was all right and he looks at everyone before saying in a raspy voice, "I'm all right." This poor guy is worried about losing future jobs. We all knew he wasn't okay, but of course he was going to say he was to protect his hopes for future work. I never saw him again after that and had no idea if he went to the hospital or what happened to him. I knew I did right though, who is to say how much worse it would have gotten if I stayed quiet.

I thought I would be fired on the spot, but to my surprise, the Stunt Coordinator wanted me to do the stomping again. I thought about why before deciding that they liked the look of my kicks better. On camera, a real kick doesn't look real. A real punch doesn't look like a real punch. I knew why they wanted me to do this. Body language. I walked the stuntman over and helped him lay on the floor. He was very much in pain from before. I did it and I went through about thirty different kicks, banging on the wall and stomping on the wall. At the end, I was exhausted. After they cut, there was silence for about four seconds before everyone applauded. Everyone loved it.

David Fincher walked over and said with a big shit eating grin, "great Steven. Between your kicks and the real kicks, I am going to have plenty."

I wondered if he really enjoyed the pain he saw, but from what I have heard, HE DOESN'T TREAT STUNTMEN TOO NICELY. Please go to the link - https://www.youtube.com/watch?v=eGtVthP1b2Q. This sums up David Fincher. Strange man, I rest my case. Here comes my next challenge. In the next couple of days, I had to do a piece of action where Jodi Foster causes me to fall two stories from a staircase and land on a statue with a spear on the banister, impaling me. Bye, bye Dwight Yoakam. By the way, I saw Mister Yoakam on the set and asked him if he was interested in doing this.

He simply looked at me and said, "F, no. I am a lover, not a faller."

I looked at him and repeated, "lover? Where did you get that?"

Needless to say, he didn't enjoy Brooklyn humor as he walked away telling me to "F off."

I smiled and gave a wave. "See ya later." We were going to use a decelerator for this fall, so I wouldn't end up as a Steven Shishkabob. I went over to the Stunt Coordinator and asked him if I could offer up my own guy. For you readers out there, let me explain. When you are doing something with this amount of danger, meaning you are on a cable and are relying on an individual stopping you a moment or two before you penetrate this spearhead on the staircase, you want somebody that you know and trust and have confidence in working the controls to stop you on the decelerator.

The Coordinator simply said, "no, I am bringing in the guy."

I looked at him and said, "with all due respect, after what happened the other day, I would like to bring my own guy."

Again, he said, "no."

I looked at him and said, "well then, I gotta go. I quit." It wasn't a quick decision. I thought about this and after seeing the inexperience I saw from this man and the risk of me getting hurt after I had an argument with him, was too great. He seemed more interested in keeping his job than making sure stuntmen were safe. So quitting was exactly what I did. I never worked or this guy again. Hoorah! As far as I was concerned, the panic I witnessed was real and there was no room for people like me who cared to put a stop to it. Why give these people a second chance to injure you.

CHAPTER 98
(El Guapo! Director Alfonso Arau And My Field Of Dreams.)

Holy Mariachi Batman, listen to who is calling now. It wasn't the Production Manager or the First Assistant, which is routine, but the Director himself! I hear his booming, galvanizing, joyful voice and I recognize this handsome, charming, intelligent, handsome, very handsome man. "EL GUAPO!" I replied. "Let me say, you are the son of a motherless goat. And wherever there is injustice you will find us, wherever there is suffering, we'll be there."

Alfonso Arau laughed on the other end. "You are better than the three amigos, they were all big chickens. You are not. You are a stuntman! They could not even ride horses."

We laughed. I asked him how he was. "I am fine, Steven."

That brought a smile to my face. There were very few people who called me "Steven."

I asked him what was up and he replied, "I am doing a movie called *The Painted House*, a period piece, and I want you to do it with me." Alfonso had a way about him and he reminded me of a General conducting his army.

"Of course, I will," I told him warmly. When I came into the office to get the script, he explained to me that it was a family film with some action in it. Some fights, a minor foot chase and a murder. I told him I would read the script and get back to him.

I asked him how long he wanted me on the film and he told me, "the whole time. I enjoy your company."

I thanked him and took a hike, went home. After I read it, I realized there wasn't much action in it. I did notice that there was a baseball game on the farm. I wondered who was going to put together the game. Were they going to leave that up to me or someone else? If they were going to have me do it, that would be a first and fun. It reminded me of *Field Of Dreams* with Kevin Costner. Well, maybe that's a bit much. At the next meeting, I was told that I would indeed be the one putting together the game.

"Okay Alfonso," I said. "I will have to go over with you the story points you want and you need, inning by inning. If you have any specific situations, who you want to feature who you want to get out, who is at bat, who's on first, what's on second, and I don't know is on third."

Alfonso looked at me confused for a few moments before a smile broke out as he got the joke. Good ole' Abbott and Costello. I told Alfonso that once I saw the location, I could start mapping out the baseball game. Who would have thought I would be doing a baseball game. That is why I loved this film because it was endearing and had a story to it.

No big fights, car chases or explosions, just a beautiful tale. In fact, the guy who wrote the book for this movie, Mister John Grisham was there. Imagine that. Big time. Our first introduction was in a huge lunch tent. There weren't many people there so I walked over. He was reading a book called The Painted House. I thought that was unusual and wondered if he was brushing up on his own work for the movie. I walked over and said, "hello, I'm your Stunt Coordinator, Steven Lambert."

"John's my name," he says.

I ask, "I have a question about some of the action. I would like to know what your thoughts are. There is a confrontation between two of the actors, as you know.

There is somewhat of a fight involved. Because of the period of the film, I am planning wild punches and wrestling in an amateur way. Is that the way you see it?"

Grisham casually closed his book and said, "that is a good way to turn the page on this chapter. That is a good idea, Steven," as he got up and walked away.

I thought to myself, wow, he sure knows how to make a guy feel at home. Well, you have heard me talk about meeting actors from the past, and how excited I get. Well, in this case, it was completely reversed.

I am about to work with a kid actor and guess who it is? Logan Lerman, Young Forrest in *Forrest Gump*. It's been nine years. He kinda looks the same, but he's not. To work with an actor who gave such a high quality performance with Tom Hanks, on a show like this was very rare. Let alone that he was a kid. In the middle of our first conversation, Martial Arts were brought up. He said that he was taking Tae Kwan Do. I told him my main style was Kung Fu.

"Hey, let's have fun. You do a kata for me and I do one for you. But wait a minute, let me go to my trailer," I told him. I went to my trailer and retrieved a staff. I went back to Logan and said, "okay, let's put on a show. You do a kata first Logan and I will do one with the staff."

With everyone watching, including the Director and John Grisham, Logan proceeded with his kata. At the end, everybody applauded. I walked over and said, "not bad for a white belt."

Everyone laughed. Walking into the center of the conversation, I asked them to give me room. Lifting the staff and pointing it towards them, I proceeded to make a full circle. "This is how much room I need," I say. As soon as I completed the circle, I flipped the staff fifteen feet up into the air.

It rotated twice, coming down right into my hands and I never stopped until you saw the BANG of the end of the staff hitting the ground. There was cheering in the air. It was a wonderful set to be on. *Apocalypse Now, The Hunt For The Red October* and *The Silence Of The Lambs.*

Actor Scott Glenn. One of the leads, a physically fit guy. Now he was an actor I was looking forward to possibly doubling. Not so much on this show, but for the future. I must get him to like me. That's the key.

Unfortunately, that moment never turned on its light bulb. You get it, or are you still in the dark? Every time he worked, he came and went. Didn't get the chance. The cast and crew were great, we all got along and had a wonderful time. Laughing, playing and learning together like a family on set.

I have to say out of all the films I have done, THIS is my favorite. You think I'm joking? NOT.

The reason being it was a story from a beautiful time, a real story. It had family. It was an era from another time. It dealt with love, old fashioned values and had an open charm to it when life was a lot simpler.

No ridiculous action that has to do with a good guy or bad guy. No ninjas, no cops, no big adventures. Just a simple movie that I so enjoyed.

(Doing a fight and putting together a baseball game on the most beautiful picture I ever worked on.)

CHAPTER 99
(Holes. Improvisation Is The Key.)

One thing you gotta remember, as I segue to the next film, is that if you want to win, be prepared to lose. That way you fight harder. An example of this would be me playing a cowboy in a Western film. That is a challenge since cowboys don't like us city boys to work in them there Western movies. Yet, I was asked to do just that on a film called *Holes*. The Stunt Coordinator called me up and offered me a character part as a cowboy. I said, "yipee ki-yay mother F --er. Do I get to horseback?"

He laughed, "you betcha."

Back in the Big Apple, New York City, when I was just a young buck, we all wanted to be cowboys and now I got my chance. Being a stuntman, I have been able to take on a variety of action without much difficulty. As a city boy that never grew up in the Western world, cowboys are the one thing that gives us city boys pause. Normally, you have to either be born into a western family with horses, wagons and rodeos. You see, "cowboying" is an art, just like Martial Arts is an art. A horse is more dangerous than a vehicle. You control the vehicle, but a horse has a brain and controls itself. The horse must know that you know what you are doing. If you show any uncertainty in the techniques that you are trying to elicit, forget about it.

You are simply not going to be able to control your mount. You have to understand a horse's behavior and temperament. I learned this from a great family called the Lilley's. Training with them for years, I grew to the understanding that horses are complex animals and learned about the when, where and how of controlling the horse. Yet, even though I have had a lot of experience horse backing, I would never call myself a cowboy out of respect for that profession and the privileges that are given to me as a punk kid from Brooklyn. The only horse I ever had were little plastic figures along with my cowboys and Indians. At the same time, I knew through my Kung Fu training, I would perform just as needed or as the wranglers wanted me to. It is important to listen to those guys.

If they see you make one mistake, you're outta there. Even more so as a wannabe cowboy. The Stunt Coordinator told me I would be in a gang on horseback coming off of a boat. I looked forward to it and when the day came, I went to Wardrobe to get my clothes. To my surprise and joy, guess what?

The Wardrobe lady said, "go knock yourself out. Pick your own clothes."

I love when that happens. Not often. Wardrobe usually makes it a big deal, you see they have this dream for an Academy Award for best wardrobe. But I understand, it is just as important to them as it is to any other department. When I had finished getting dressed, BAM! I looked like I came out of a scene from *Red River*. A Montgomery Cliff want to be. I looked like I could play with John Wayne in *Rio Bravo* or Steve McQueen in *Mr. Horn* or Tom Selleck in *Monte Walsh*. I am back in time and playing it to the hilt.

Okay, am I overdoing it? If anyone asked me what era I would have like to been born in, this is it, you betcha. The shit kicking, cow busting, pistol shooting, saddle stomping wild west.

(WANTED DEAD OR ALIVE: PUNK KID FROM BROOKLYN.)

Who knows, I could have been part of the O.K. Corral standing beside Wyatt Earp and Doc Holliday. Or maybe roaming the plains with wild Bill Hickok. Maybe I could have stopped Jack McCall from killing my partner. Dreams, aren't they wonderful? The day came for my big scene, getting off the boat with my cowboy gang. Our direction was to walk through the town square and that's what I did, making sure I put myself right next to the lead bad guy, played by Scott Plank. Off camera, a real neat guy. A few years later, I am sorry to say, he died of a heart attack.

In rehearsal, I am looking around me because I realize that quite frankly, this whole walk is boring! At least for me, it is. I need some "me" in this. So when we do our rehearsal, I see a man selling vegetables on a cart. This sparks my interest. When they call, "action" and we roll, they would get my improv surprise. As always, I think to myself, "thank you, James Woods for tipping me off to this little gimmick that I have used throughout my career." Sure enough, they call, "action."

I grab my reigns and I break off from the bunch. I walk backwards a few feet as everyone continues forward. Stuntman Brian Williams gives me the "what the hell you doing" glance. I smirk and walk up to the lead actor in front of me and give him a backhand across the chest. He looks at me in shock as I laugh. Then he breaks out laughing too. A few seconds later, I break out of this boring walk, separate myself from my gang and head over to the vegetable cart. The gang wonders where I am going, but continues the walk of boring. The salesman looks up at me as if to say, "this wasn't in the script."

He has a pile of vegetables including carrots in front of him, so I reach over and pick up a bunch of carrots with both hands, which by the way, are the most visible vegetable there. Believe me, if I was a decent juggler, I would have picked up the tomatoes. I take the biggest carrot in the bunch and throw the rest down right in his face. I look at his agape mouth and take a bite of my carrot and give him a scowl. He does nothing which was exactly what I wanted. I walk back to my gang and see Brian Williams and offer him the carrot. He declines it so I feed it to my horse. This is how you get noticed, how you make the scene better. Of course, you gotta have guts and smarts.

At the end of our walk, they "cut."

I hear the Director in the background as everyone grows quiet. "Hey, that cowboy with the carrot. That was some real good improv there," he says.

All eyes were upon me and I made sure not to show a smile on the outside. I didn't want to steal all the limelight, I just tipped my hat like a real cowboy. The Director printed it and we moved on. The rest of the day I kinda hung out, when my boss came over to me and asks me to come with him.

As we are heading off, he says, "remember a few days ago when you, me and Jack Liley were teaching you how to rear a horse?"

I told him, "yea."

He said, "well we have a night shot and I want you to ride through town with a Molotov cocktail and rear a horse by a school. And throw the Molotov into the school window."

Like a little schoolboy, I looked at him and said, "you're kidding. Is that what that was for?"

Alex Daniels the Stunt Coordinator told me that Jack was happy with how I reared the horse and they were going to talk to the head wrangler and try to convince him to let me do the scene. With rearing a horse, you gotta know exactly what you are doing and can perform and say you've done it a thousand times. In my case, I had only done it a dozen times. But as I mentioned, here comes the Brooklyn Kung Fu Cowboy, partners.

We meet up with the head wrangler who looked at me very condescending and asked, "have you ever reared a horse before?"

In a split second, I thought about the question very carefully. That's what I call street sense. He wasn't asking how many times I have reared one, just IF I had before. I told him yes, I had. So he went and got the horse. Little did he know I had practiced on that horse and we both knew each other l. But I am still risking a situation here. But you see, I never asked to do this so I am pretty much in the clear. Just mounting the horse correctly, his eyes were upon me and judging every move. I proceeded to mount as both our rear ends were towards the head wrangler. I walked the horse once in a three sixty, then forward and then back. I stopped for two seconds, looked at the wrangler, and reared. I went up, straight up.

(A city boy playing a cowboy. A dream come true. Thank you, Jack Liley.)

I thought I was going over but managed to lean forward just in time and we came down. I kicked the horse and cantered and stopped in front of them. I asked, "so what do you think? I got the job?"

The Head Wrangler stepped back and said, "move 'em on, head 'em up."

I asked, "what does that mean?"

He spit tobacco and said, "you ain't bad. Go on."

Thank you, Jack Liley.

(There's a story here. Ask Phil Colada. Let's just say rest in peace, Mr. horse.)

CHAPTER 100

(No Americans On This Film. Not Allowed.)

Heading south of the border once again, to the land of enchiladas. (James Wood's on the toilet.) I am working with the handsome man once again. Alfonso Arau. El Guapo! A flick called *Zapata*. A Mexican film with Mexican stuntmen. And me. After the film had wrapped, I expected to see my name credited. Guess what? It wasn't!

When I asked, I was told, "sorry Steven. You did a great job, but we can't list an American stuntman on a Mexican picture."

Are you kidding!? I was just floored by this, but I guess understood. It meant a lot that Alfonso had chosen me to work on this film, a punk kid from Brooklyn, America. Just shows you how highly he thought of me.

(I'm a gringo. They wouldn't give me credit. Ole, oy vey. The swines.)

Okay, my next movie I am going to become a movie reviewer. It's called *Along Came Polly*. Jennifer Aniston was sweet, very personable and she was a beaut. Now Ben Stiller was a whole new ball game. I found him to be rude, very self centered and arrogant. Friendly? Not in the least. Why you ask? I just told you. Or just ask the crew, they may tell you. I give him one and a half pickles, and they are not kosher. Movie review out.

Then came *Dodgeball* starring Vince Vaughn and Ben.....oh boy. Here we go again. Starring that wonderful actor we just discussed, Ben Stiller. I was action acting in a scene where I was supposed to get hit by a dodgeball. I say supposed to because at first, it didn't go as they had planned. Let me explain the scene, you've all seen it (I hope). I am in the stands with a couple of hotdogs and cokes going to my seat when a ball hits me right upside the head and I go flying back onto the people in the stands.

(So you think Ben Stiller is funny? Only in the movies.)

Now they had a machine on the court, that was as big as a ship's cannon and it looked like one too. The balls were spit out at certain speeds, zero to thirty five miles an hour. At first, they started at fifteen in rehearsal and eventually the dial went up to thirty five. Yes, I am going to get a ball launched at me upside my head at thirty five miles per hour. That should knock some sense into me. Now let me say. I felt like a carnival game at Coney Island. You know, one of those where the animals go back and forth as the kid tries to knock it over. I was the pin and the kid was the machine. The kid kept missing. It got so frustrating because the machine had no accuracy. Let me remind you I was a moving target. Those balls would go above me, in back of me, in front of me and everywhere but me, hitting everyone else in the stands. There were extras in them there stands and smart ones at that. The next day they called SAG and demanded stunt pay and they got it. Haha. This was a three hour scene that went on just to hit me in the head, can you believe it? Eventually, they scrapped the machine and decided to try to do it the old fashioned way, hit me by hand! Here is a list of people who tried and failed: THE WHOLE CAST CREW. That includes Vince Vaughn who made everybody laugh because he got so frustrated that he ran up to the stands and put himself two feet in front of me, threw the ball and hit me in the head. It bounced off my head but I didn't fall.

So he pushed me over before raising his hands and yelling, "I got him!"

Everybody laughed. Oh by the way, Ben Stiller just sat in his chair being Ben Stiller. He seemed like a fun guy only in the movies.

CHAPTER 102
(It's Hobo Time. Gone With The Wind.)

He wasn't on team fun, but I sure was. Working on *Jaws,* well, maybe a smaller version. A television show called *Shark,* starring a guy I can always depend on, Mister James Woods. Hold on a minute, what year is it now? Two thousand and six!? Okay, you know what time it is. It's howdy hobo time! The year of the hobo, me. I decided to go hobo. Three years gone rogue. Divorced and now the judge says I can only see my kids once a month. Lawyers took half my bankroll and my wife took the other. So I bought a conversion van all decked out with a radio, television, bed, couch and last but not least, a fridge. I was what you call a high class hobo. I was ready to leave my world and explore everything around it. The whole word. Okay, maybe just the United States. Okay, maybe just California. For two years I rambled around, going from campsite to campsite. City to city, boy there is a lot of them. Fishing, camping and hunting I did. I was Huckleberry Finn with a rolling house. On the last Friday of the month I would pick up my kids, three days was all we were allowed to be together. It was heartbreaking. They so loved me and I loved them. In any case, we would travel someplace, a day it took, stopping to have fun here and there. Second day was our destination.

We laughed, we learned, we bonded. They were special moments. The third day was the trip home. Boy, the last day always was the hardest, the most difficult for all of us because it always went so quick. Yet, they loved it and every moment was a party exploring the wonders of the land. But one of these moments got me in trouble. We were underneath the blue skies and white clouds, a mild wind was flowing through the trees, slicing through the leaves. (Think I can be a poet?) Anyway, enough of this beatnik talk. Let's talk guns, bb guns. I bought one for myself and the kids. We decided to blow some holes in some milk containers. My son fired first. Bam, bam, bam, the milk container sprung a leak. I took the gun away from him, ran over, went to my knees, opened my mouth and like a faucet flowing into my mouth, started downing it.

I turned to my children and said, "come on, your turn. This is the hobo way to drink milk." To this day, they remember those moments. That's when a cop dropped in. He just happened to be strolling through the park this day, wouldn't ya know it? Why me? He took out a badge showing he was with the Party Poopers Association. I mean the Forest Rangers. We had a discussion, I was busted. I explained to him it was just a kid's gun, a bb gun. I thought he understood, at least that's the impression he gave me. He wrote me up a ticket and confiscated the toy gun. He asked me for my information. Name, telephone number, and he asked me where I lived. He said it was just routine.

I laughed and pointed to my hobo van and said, "you're looking at it."

He said, "that's where you live?"

I said, "that's right, what of it? I'm living in my van down by the river, just like Chris Farley." He didn't find that funny, but I sure did. I also gave him my P.O. box. I thought that was the end of that. No big deal. I looked at the ticket and noticed it didn't say anything about the gun being a bb gun or a toy. I scratched my head and didn't think anything of it. A few weeks later, I got a letter stating I was to appear in court for having an illegal and unregistered gun! And it read if I didn't show up, there would be a warrant out for my arrest. I was shell shocked. I called my lawyer up and he said he would make a phone call. He did and told me that I have to go in and give myself up, before or on this date.

I erupt, "it was a toy gun, a bb gun, what are they talking about?" I hang up, ready to proclaim my innocence. I went in and as soon as they found out who I was, they handcuffed me! I asked them why they were doing this and they kept silent until the judge arrived. When the judge came, he looked through my file and asked me what I was doing with a real gun.

"It wasn't a real gun your honor. It was a toy bb gun. You have it, the cop took it," I told him.

He replied, "I didn't see anything about a bb gun on the report."

I told him to find the gun and he will see for himself. Well, into the slammer I went for a couple hours until they brought me back into the courtroom and there was the judge and the gun. The bb gun. He apologized and I thanked the Lord. This "no big deal" got me arrested and put behind bars for a few hours and that was something I wasn't expecting nor would want to do again. Not my kind of living. Man, I don't know how these guys in prison survive it. This is me being melodramatic. Two hours I stood in there, it felt like maximum security. A caged animal I was. It felt like a lifetime, all alone. No windows, just bars. I thought I'd never see the sun again. Lol. After that ordeal, I went back to the hobo way of life.

CHAPTER 103
(Catching A Criminal.)

This last hobo story is something I never expected. I call it the tale of the Hobo Hero. That is my next story. Like I said before, my van was down by the river. But in this case, the ocean. My son and I were together, the sun was shining. We were going surfing. We took our boards and wetsuits and spent two to three hours in the water having a blast when lunchtime came around. We packed up and headed back to the vehicle.

As we approached the parking lot and turned the corner, about thirty feet away, I squint into the rows of cars trying to find my ride. I spot it in the distance and as I do, a picture comes into my mind. I'm thinking, I see someone in my vehicle. I start telling myself that it has to be someone in the next car over and my mind is playing tricks on me. A few feet closer, this picture starts getting clearer. My eyes dart here, there, everywhere, trying to get a sense of what I am seeing. A few moments later, the picture comes into complete focus and I see the truth. There IS someone in my vehicle! Imagine this. I've got both boards in my hands, I drop them and take out my phone and call 911. I scoop up my son in my arms and I start running towards my vehicle. When we get ten feet away, I put my son down. Telling my son to run with me wherever I go, I head straight for the guy. He sees me, jumps out and starts running. I look inside and see all my things are all over the place. The guy robbed me! The robber looks back at me and that is when I take off, phone in my hand. I can't run too fast because my son is behind me, but I have to keep the guy in my sights. The thief heads onto the sand and I follow. I turn to my son and tell him again to run with me. I take off like a gazelle running across the beach, trying to tell 911 where I am at. Passing lifeguard station number 26, I tell 911 that's where I am. I continue running, look back and wait for my son to catch up.

I start running again and pass lifeguard station 25. I yell into the phone, "now I am at station 25." I hang back and wait for my son before I see the robber getting away, so I continue after him.

"Lifeguard station 24, 24!" I scream into the phone. I continue run- no, I have to wait for my son! Waiting…..waiting….hey what do you want from me he is a little kid…..okay, I continue running after him, shouting at people I pass.

"Hey, that guy robbed my car and he is robbing other people's as well. Call the police!" I yelled. Did they? I have no idea as my concern was catching this crook. I looked back and saw my son barely managing to keep up with me. I saw the thief emptying out his pockets as he ran, throwing things onto the sand. I saw my wallet among other things and made a mental note of where it fell or made a choice to run and pick it up. I finally caught up with him and told him not to move until the police came. He didn't want to stick around for that so he started to take off again. Now I didn't want to hit him because I had heard on the news that some people had done something similar and the bad guy sued them and won. Figure that one out. I didn't want to get sued. So every time he ran, I would just grab him around his neck and throw him onto his back on the sand. He would get up again and I would grab around his neck and throw him onto the sand. This repeated itself four, five times before he realized he wasn't going anywhere. That's when he saw a thirty foot embankment leading off of the sand. He starts running up this embankment and I follow behind him. Quickly realizing if he gets to the road, I might lose him in traffic while I'm waiting for my son. I think on my feet. I see he is running at an angle up this embankment, so I decide to run straight up. My geometric calculation worked and I got to the top before he did. As he came to the top of the embankment, there I was, running straight at him. I did a body block right at his face and bam! We both start rolling down the thirty foot embankment full of rocks and hard dirt. I was a Johnny Cool roller and him? He fell like a drunk seal. At the same time, I see two cops running down the sandy beach. Did I say running? I meant walking. Cops, most of them are out of shape. Too many donuts. They arrive just as we hit the bottom of the embankment.

I get up and tell the cops, "here is your bad guy. Take him away."
The cops look at me, not sure who the bad guy is yet when my son speaks up and saves the day.

"That's my pa," he says.

The cops take a better look at us and decide with apprehension, that I was the good guy. We walk back to my vehicle and the police have this guy handcuffed a few feet away. After taking my information, two or three other cops in suits come walking over. They ask me to sit and wait, so I do. Thirty minutes go by when more cops show up. This time in vans and other unmarked police cars. I am sitting there with my son realizing there are about thirty cops there now. What the hell is going on, I am thinking. A couple of suit men come over to me and ask me if I knew who this guy was. Besides being a thief, I had no idea.

"You see that van up there?" one of the suited cops asks.

I look up at this two tiered parking lot, up to the high side of the lot and saw an old van up above. I nodded, curious as to why it was there.

"That is his van," the cop told me. "Guess what? You just caught one of the top ten most wanted child molesters. You see those curtains in his van, covering all his windows?"

I reply, "yeah."

"Behind those curtains in the van he has three video cameras. We just looked at the tapes. You know who he was doing?" I shake my head no, trying to put the puzzle pieces together. "All the mom and dads who change their kids by the car, or all the women who put on or take off their bathing suits to go to the beach, he zooms in and films them naked. We've been looking for this guy for a long time and you caught him."

I was shocked, stunned.

"We will call you to testify. You can either come in to court or do it over the phone," they told me.

I chose the latter. That is exactly what happened a few weeks later. I didn't want to go to court since I didn't want him to see my face again. He was locked up and that was how the hobo became a hero. Catching a top ten wanted man. A punk kid from Brooklyn, who would have thought. It's all true, just ask my son. Or the city. How do ya like that diddy?

CHAPTER 104
(God Bless Michael Woods. We Cried Like Babies.)

At this time, I would get tons of calls from my friends, from work, from James Woods, asking me where I was and what was going on. I ignored them all. I did this for a few years until two thousand and eight when Jimmy left me a voice message, one of many.

This one said, "hey Steven, I talked to Alan Haft and he said you are shipwrecked on a desert island, your own mind! If you don't call me, I'm going to kick your rabbi ass."

I finally broke down and decided to call him back as I felt kind of lonely and we spent hours on the phone as Jimmy explained to me what divorce is all about and how women are and how life is. Boy, you should have been in one that conversation. Talking about women with James Woods? It was earth shatteringly funny. We'll skip explaining it to you. I laughed until I cried, as he tried to bring me back to reality. That's when he mentioned the television show *Shark* and that he wanted me to double him and coordinate it.

"It's a television show, so don't worry Steven. We'll be together for a long time. You'll have a shoulder to cry on," Jimmy said.

I finally saw the light and decided to put out my campfire. Steven Lambert was coming back! No more hobo. It really was an experience. You should try it sometime. As Jimmy had said, a short time later, I got a call from the Producer who wanted me to double Woods and be the Stunt Coordinator. I told him I would gladly do that. He told me to come in two days later and sign my contract. We hung up and it wasn't long before I got another call, this time from the Executive Producer. He told me he wanted me to stunt double Woods, but not stunt coordinate, that he had already chosen someone in that position. I ask him if he minded telling me who that was. He told me that Ron Stein was going to run it. For you stunt beginners out there, the reason why I asked was that I could understand the situation a lot better and have more of an understanding how to deal with it. I say to him that the Woods would like me to be the Stunt Coordinator. The Executive Producer told me flatly, that no, it would be Ron Stein.

So I say to him, "may I take one more moment of your time and explain to you how valuable I can be to you and your production. Not only can I run your show and double James Woods, I would also be useful for nondescript pieces of action. So you'll be getting three for the price of one. And one other thing which is the most important. I've been with Jimmy a long time. He trusts me as I trust him and I understand him as he does me. I could be very helpful to you, believe me, I can. Especially if there happened to be any good, bad or indifferent situations. Believe me, I have been useful in that way before." Guess what? It went right over the Executive Producer's head and I hung up very confused and a bit perplexed. This wasn't my first rodeo dealing with situations like this. I decided to call Woods and discuss the matter with him. He wasn't there, so I left a message. I told him the situation and wanted to know if he could figure out what was what and talk to the Producers. The next day, a different Producer calls me back and says he spoke to Jimmy and that I would be coordinating. I told him the Executive Producer said otherwise and he told me not to worry, that I had the job and he would transfer me over to the Executive Producer. A few seconds later, I heard his voice on the other end. I told him that Jimmy being the star, wanted me as Stunt Coordinator and that the Producer told me I had the job. Shark, a person who pursues something aggressively. That was the name of this show and of this Executive Producer who AGAIN told me that Ron Stein would be coordinating the show, not me.

I asked, "have you talked to Jimmy?"

He replies, "no."

Well somebody is talking to him. I'm getting these phone calls. I ask, "don't you think you should?"

He replies, "don't tell me what to do."

I say, "oh no, I'm not telling you what to do, I just asked."

He replies, "from my understanding, the buck stops here and I don't have to ask."

I reply, "That's true."

He thanked me and hung up. Neither side wanted to budge. Producers, what can I say? I went into heavy contemplation about this situation. I broke out the Brooklyn Street smarts and decided to call Ron Stein and ask him to meet with me. I knew Ron and he was a very nice guy from Stunts Unlimited. Always treated me well. In fact, I worked with him a couple of times in the past. Those guys always pay well. He knew of the problem we were having and he was gracious enough to meet with me.

I couldn't understand why some high powered people from the Stuntmen's Association had told me he was snake like. But it's funny, you learn or you should learn to take what people say with a grain of salt and always decide for yourself. I have worked with Ron Stein before. The last time I did, I took a bullet hit and went flying six feet in the air. Came down flat on my back. He paid me a hundred dollars a foot, that's six hun. If I was working for the Stuntmen's Association, I would have got a hundred, or maybe nothing. I always wondered why Stunts Unlimited knew how to pay a person. In comparison to Stunts Unlimited, you were a scrooge.

Maybe after you read this, you'll put a little more cash on the table for the guys who take risks. I met with Ron and told him, "look, I will relinquish the job as Stunt Coordinator, but I have to say that Jimmy is very particular when it comes to action. Having somebody there that he is comfortable with, believe me, will make everything better. I have been there and done that. I am letting you know this Ron because I respect you and we are friends. I know him very well and if you do something without me being there, he can become very unhappy for whatever reason, and believe me with him that is easy to do. Don't say I didn't warn you. I'm letting you know this now."

Ron nodded, smiled and said, "I will do you one better because I also respect you very much and know you are one hell of a stuntman."

That caught my attention. "Well thank you," I said. I guess it never hurts to charm a guy.

Ron says, "any big stunt, any big piece of action we have with or without Woods, any non-descript part or stunt, I will give you first pick at. Every episode."

That made me smile and I thanked him graciously. This lesson taught me that it is always best to confront problems head on and find the middle ground. I couldn't and wouldn't just sit back. I had to find a solution and that I did. Teamwork. That's what I call it. There's no snake in Ron Stein. But the people who mouthed it might just have a forked tongue themselves. When I arrived on the first day for *Shark* at Warner Brothers, it was a beautiful day, the sun was shining. I couldn't wait and I was excited to blow this Executive Producer's mind, you know the one. Whatever stunt I was going to do, I was going to make sure he was watching and if he wasn't, I'd pull him over by his tie and say, "watch this." I couldn't wait to make him stand up and take notice. You want to know the reason? That phone call. I couldn't get it out of my mind. It was like a drum beating. The buck stops here he said. So arrogant he was. I turned the corner of the stage and about twenty feet away from the door, Jimmy happens to come out. Our eyes locked onto each other.

I took a deep breath and said, "Jimmy."

He didn't say a word back, just stared into my eyes and walked over, face to face. He had a look of, I don't know how else to say it, but despair. That word, it instantly broke my heart, tore at my emotions.

"Michael. Did you know Michael, my brother, passed away?" Streaming tears came down his cheeks as he opened up his arms and embraced me in a bear hug. I was taken aback because it showed, I guess how close we were and he was opening up in a way he never did before. I hear him say, "my brother died, Steven."

I instantly hugged him back and said, "I know Jimmy, I am so sorry. He loved you so much. You were his everything, his big brother." Tears rolling down my face, I could hardly speak. We continued embracing each other, it seemed like eternity. I could feel his pain, his sorrow and anguish as he stood there and hugged me as we cried, I couldn't stop. I was honored at that moment that he trusted me enough to show his emotions like that. James Woods just broke down in my arms, I thought. I felt so sad for him yet so lucky to be one of the ones chosen to share his grief with, this very good and private man. My dear friend. Let me end this story by giving a small eulogy about Michael Woods.

Yes, I did know that he had passed away from a heart attack while waiting to see an ER Doctor about vomiting and sore throat. James so cared and loved Michael and his wife and children being that his family are few. Michael always had a job in just about every movie that Jimmy ever did. I know this and got to know Michael very well and watching these two brothers on the set was such an enlightening thing to see. They laughed together, made fun of each other and when they got a chance, they both ganged up and made fun of me. And by the way, I so enjoyed those moments. Let's say I was a big target, always. The way I wore my clothes to the way I blew my nose (like a freight train). They even surprised me once by gifting me a yarmulke right on the set. And yes, he tried to get me to dance the Hora and succeeded just a little bit. Michael was very smart and had the same genius wit as Jimmy did. They were so much alike and boy did they care for each other. Jimmy always watched over him and Michael so looked up to his big brother. I know this because Jimmy talked about him all the time when we were together and always brought him everywhere and always made sure that his family was doing well. Jimmy adored him, his little brother.

CHAPTER 105
(Fire! Explosions! They Are Hunting Me Down.)

This last fire burner on *Shark* is a very memorable and a very unexpected moment for me. And proves people really do have a sixth sense. Let's explain. True to his word, my boss called me up with a non-descript part that had nothing to do with doubling Woods. I was playing a SWAT along with stuntman Chad Randall and one of the lead actors, Henry Simmons. He was being doubled by Stuntman Henry Kingi Jr. So the moment comes and I get into my SWAT gear and the boss gathers us up and takes us to the warehouse. He explains we would be exiting a vehicle, getting out and running into the warehouse, barging into the big double doors and finding the ticker. Realizing it is about to detonate, we turn tail and rush back through the same way we came. He makes a point that we must all stay abreast of each other. The reason forthcoming. As time goes by, I glance around noticing six to seven windows in this warehouse and they all have huge pots in them, filled with gasoline and other flammable substances. I spot about four pots in a semi circle right in front of us. I look at the doorway and see double, triple stacked pots ready to be ignited on each side of the doorway.

The smell of the gasoline hits me and all I could think about was, "this is going to be some fourth of July." The boss makes it clear that he needs us to hit the street at the same time because the FX guy is going to blow the warehouse as soon as he sees the first foot that steps off the sidewalk and into the street. So there can't be no laggers. I go to my honey wagon and an hour later, the boss man calls us to go over the scene with the Director. We do just that and the FX guy is telling us when he is going to blow the pots and I can tell he seems a bit nervous and unsure in his body language. Fidgety he was. Nevertheless, we break for forty five minutes before we shoot and that little birdie starts to speak to me. You know that one we have in our head sometimes?

The birdie is telling me, "tweet, tweet, something is not right, Steven. You need more safety then what has been provided. No fire gel. No mention of Nomax." (Fire proof underwear.) I kept going back to my perceived uncertainty of the FX guy. Well, I couldn't say anything. At most, it would make me come across as if I didn't trust my boss and at the least, make me seem like I was scared of the stunt. Or crazy. Like when I got hit with the car by Aaron Norris. If you mention it to the powers, they would simply look at you like you're a whack job. You either have to don't do it or just do the best you can. As always, I decided to try to do the best I could and rely on my ability in case something happens. The time comes and they roll cameras, all six or seven of them. Action! We burst through the double doors, run in and stop. We go through the motions of looking around the warehouse. We spot the ticker and we get our cue to get the hell out. We turn around. The doorway is twelve feet away, the gutter is about twenty feet away. Now what happens after this will always be freeze framed in my head. We take the first step. We take the second step. And then the Devil's Hell arrives. A fire-wall erupts behind us and in front of us. Fifteen feet high and eighteen feet wide. BOOM! BOOM! The pots start going off. Through my goggles, all I see is red, yellow and orange. The heat engulfs me and it feels like time has stopped, but my legs hadn't.

Something inside said, "RUN!"

This possessed my body and made me go faster. I couldn't see anybody around me. I hit the doors and flew outside and wondered when I was going to get out of this erupting volcano. I look to my right, to my left, engulfed in flames. I am running like a Banshee into the street.

(Escaping the bowels of Hell. Thank God for water.)

The heat is just intense, as the rest of the explosions behind me, in front of me, and above me throw me to the ground. I get up, still confused. Not really realizing what had happened. I am gasping for breath. That is when I noticed the other SWAT guys on fire! I turn and see Henry Kingi Jr. He is running around like a bull that just got his nuts cut off. Screaming. His bald head is on fire, his back is on fire. His legs are on fire. He had nothing on but a t-shirt and pants and he was doubling Henry Simmons who was bald. I look the other way and saw Chad Randall on fire. I look down and notice that I am smoldering and I am hot. It took me a few seconds to take off my vest as it was so hot. I pulled off my helmet and my half melted goggles. My gloves are smoking and hot. My boots are steaming. I look at our two fire safety people. Yes, two for three Stunt people. I notice one is running in after Kingi Jr. who is on fire. The other is running out, yes running away. I wanted to disprove my lying eyes, but it was the truth! So we now have one safety person with one fire extinguisher. The other is still running, I mean she could have just left the fire extinguisher, you think?

Now I am dealing with two people on fire on opposite ends of each other. I decide to bulldog Randall and hand and body put him out. They are both burned but Kingi is real bad and the ambulances come. Moments go by as everyone is just is in hysterics. Fingers are pointed, faces of confusion, people start leaving and conversations start happening and I get unusual looks.

Questions start flying at me. "Steven, how come you didn't get burned?"

I look at them and now here is where the sixth sense comes in. "You want to know the truth?" I say. "Fifteen minutes before the shot, something inside of me said I needed to do something to make me safer. Call it intuition or call it blind luck. I went to craft services and asked if I could have one of those five gallon bottles of water. They said I could and I also found a pail and filled it with water and soaked my SWAT uniform and Nomax in it and then put it on soaking wet."

First came the perplexed looks, then the questions, then came the comments that I was lucky and then that I was smart and the big statement was, why didn't the other people do it. I shrugged my shoulders, what could I say? I'm only the boss of me, not them. After about forty five minutes there were comments about OSHA coming down to talk to everybody. Heads of departments were turning tail the minute they uttered "OSHA."

Me being not hurt, and just an ND stunt guy on this show, was told I could leave, so I packed up and headed home. Why would they want to talk to me anyway? I'll tell you why, because I was part of it. A few days go by when I start getting phone calls from OSHA. I had a hunch they were going to hunt me down. The first one comes in the morning, the second one comes in the afternoon and third one comes in the evening. I listen to all of them. The old style way on the big ole' answering machine. Remember those? Each one explaining they want to talk to me about the incident that occurred. Many questions were left on my answering machine such as, who set this piece of action up? Who were the safety people and how come you didn't get burned? And the big question. We heard you put something special on your body and clothes. We want to know what that was. I hadn't heard from the boss yet so another few days go by and the phone calls aren't stopping. Higher ups from OSHA are calling me now, I ignore them all. Then one day, I get a call from a stuntman named Joe Ordaz. I pick it up and say hello, not remembering that his specialty is fire and he is connected to OSHA. He explains that it is a matter of importance that I talk to OSHA, that they need to talk to me.

I say, "why me? I wasn't the boss. Haven't they talked to him yet? Whatever he says, goes. Why do they need to talk to me?"

He tells me that I seem to be the chosen one.

"Why am I the chosen one?" I ask.

Joe told me it was because I was the only one that didn't get burned! I laughed and explained to Joe about my sixth sense and that compound called H20. He couldn't believe it either.

"They aren't going to stop until they talk to you Steven," Joe warned me.

I told him I would think about it and hung up. A few days later, I was at the Association when the secretary told me that someone from OSHA had stopped by and asked for my address. To my relief, she refused to give it but had said she would pass along they wanted to speak to me. She wasn't the only one. Stuntman after stuntman told me OSHA was moving Heaven and Earth to find me. I decide it is finally time to talk to them before they try to shimmy down my fireplace. One morning the bells chime, so I pick up the line. Putting the receiver to my ear, I hear the word "OSHA."

I say hello and they introduce themselves, surprised I finally answered. I told them I would speak with them but not over the phone.

They say, "how about our office?"

I said, "no, Jerry's Deli. That's the only place I'll meet ya. Take it or leave it."

Guess what, they took it. Fools. Little did they know what my plan was. Jerry's Deli on Ventura Blvd. You take the 405 to the 101 East and exit on Coldwater Canyon. Now if you exit on Woodman Avenue, you've gone too far. You want to loop around and….oh, sorry about that. It really is worth a visit. (They should sponsor this book). Anyway, they arrive and the host brings them to my table.

They introduce themselves and I tell them, "sit down, park yourselves." Moments go by in casual conversation as the waitress comes and asks, "would you gentlemen like to order now?"

As the two OSHA boys look at the menu, I say, "yes. I am ready. Steak sandwich with grilled onions, a side of potato pancakes with extra applesauce. A side of matzah brei, not so eggy please and a bowl of matzah ball soup. A piece of chocolate cake and a vanilla milkshake."

I happened to see the two OSHA boys and their four eyes looking at me in bewilderment.

"What are you guys having?" I ask.

They say, "a cup of coffee."

With a big smile, "is that all? Because you're buying or I'm leaving."

They look at each other and nod. "Yes, we'll pay. We have it in the budget."

I laughed and told them, "Good. We understand each other. Let's rock and roll." Jerry's is quite the upscale place and if they wanted answers from me, I was going to make sure I got a good meal from them. That is the Brooklyn street smarts and my stomach talking. We start our talk and they pull out a tape recorder. Now I realize I really have to be careful what I say, I don't want to get anyone in trouble that shouldn't be in trouble. They start the interrogation and I tell them what you readers already know. They are amazed.

One of the many questions was, "what the special substance was you put on your clothes and why were you the only one that had it?"

I smile, giggle, then laugh. They watch as I raise my glass of H20. I say, "his is the special substance. Behold, water!"

They look, mesmerized as I explain to them what I did. They look like two monkeys scratching their heads. An hour and a half later, we finished talking. They exited stage left and I went stage right. The next day I get a call from the show's Executive Producer. Remember he's the one that said the "buck stops here." He had listened to the recorder and was amazed himself. That is when he made a statement that surprised me.

"We would like you to take over the show, Steven," he said.

I thought for a moment and said, "with all due respect, the only person that should be fired is the FX guy. He knew what the direction was and he wasn't supposed to push the button until the first foot hit the gutter. His visual was about ten feet and he could see us from a mile away when we stepped into the gutter. He blew it before we even stepped outside."

I quickly learned that he had been fired and they had a brand new FX guy for me if I took the show. Again to be clear, me taking the show would mean they would fire Ron Stein and I didn't want any part of that. I told him flatly that Ron Stein should not be fired and proceeded to explain that it wasn't anybody else's fault, but FX. The direction was clear and if it was simply followed, no one would have gotten hurt. Ron Stein had nothing to do with it, it could have happened to any Coordinator.

"So in short, no, I am not going to take the job as Stunt Coordinator. I thank you for the offer."

He replies, "well if you don't take it, we are going to have to get somebody else."

I took a deep breath and said, "I think you should keep Ron Stein and I will have a discussion with Jimmy Woods about it."

A moment went by. "I don't take kindly to threats, Steven," the voice on the line replied back.

"Oh, no, no. You're misunderstanding me. It is not a threat. It is simply an individual who knows how to play as a team with loyalty and common sense. If it is not his fault, why is he being replaced?" Fade out. Dialing, one, three, one, zero, four, seven, zero.

"Hi, Jimmy." Woods for you readers out there. I take an hour on the phone with Mister Woods explaining everything you just read and the reasons why Ron Stein shouldn't be fired. One of the many reasons is doing what's right. Friendship, loyalty, team player, and honesty.

"But most important and you know I very rarely ask you for favors. If you can help this situation, please do." And he did. My next day back, I had a big smile on my face when I walked over to Ron Stein and shook his hand.

"Thanks," we both say to each other. Everything's great. Oh by the way, the next time I worked, I saw James Woods and said, "thank you."

His reply, "you owe me a big Jewish dinner."

I could see in his face that he was so proud he had helped. It was a wonderful moment in time. Let's roll on through time.

CHAPTER 106
(The Chipmunks And John Moio Trying To Crack My Nuts.)

Remember when you were a little fellow?? Five, six, years old? For me, it was the fifties. Some of my favorite cartoons were *Yogi Bear, Felix the Cat, and Woody Woodpecker.* One of my chosen diddies was, well, I'll put it like this.

"Simon! Theodore! Alvin.....Alvin?!" Still don't have it? How about listening to my favorite Christmas song. "We've been good but we can't last. Hurry Christmas, hurry fast. Want a plane that loops the loop. Me, I want a hula hoop." Yep, 2009 I get a call from Doctor Jekyll, he's the good side. Mister Hyde must have been asleep for the moment, but I'm sure he'll show up. He always does. Now if you have been reading this book, you know who I am talking about. Yep, I love this guy but sometimes he is a pain in the tuchus. Mister Moio. John Moio that is. He has helped so many and oh how they forget. That's the problem with civilization. People get what they want and then they leave and forget where they came from. Some of these become a success and forget about you. That's the wrong way to go through life. John Moio has helped more people than I have hair on my head, well at least when I had hair on my head. He asks me if I'm available.

I say, "for who? You?"

He says, "just answer me, God Damn it!"

I laugh, we are always biting at each other. "Yea," I say.

He asks me if I want to work with Alvin and the other chipmunks. A chance to work with my favorite cartoon!? How the world turns. Some days go by and Moio tells me I am doubling David Cross, the lead bad guy. I am trying to capture the rogue rodent on his mini bike on a high speed chase down the street in my limo. At the end of the scene, the limo goes up on the curve and I go flying out of the sunroof, diving forward roll onto the hood of the car and onto the ground. We do it and if I may say, it went beautiful. Cut, print. The next scene we shot in Chinatown. It's dim sum time. A dozen pork baos. I took all the stunt guys to the Mayflower to have lunch. One of the best restaurants in the community. You should have seen stuntman Larry Holt's face. He didn't know what he was eating. One of the nicest guys I ever met in my life. If you ask me, too nice. Example. If you stab somebody in front of him and asked him if he saw it, he wouldn't answer you. Why? Because he's afraid he might hurt the guy's feelings. Back to the scene. I rehearse this. I am chasing him when I fall to the ground and Alvin turns his mini bike right at me and heads right for me. Right for where the sun don't shine. You know, your Mexican maracas, your kosher matzah balls, your Chinese dumplings.

Moio asked me if I had brought my cup and I told him, "you're damn right I did. Three. Medium, large and extra large." He laughed. I was told stuntman Larry Holt was going to take the mini bike, run with it and let it go ten feet before me and hopefully it goes into my crotch.

"So you're telling me on this hundred million dollar movie, you didn't make a track for it!?" I ask surprised.

Moio shrugs. "No, that's why I have Larry."

I looked at him dumbfounded.

Moio looks at me and says, "just put on your triple layer, lay down, put a zip tie on your lips and don't look."

I look at him and say, "I'll zip tie you and use you as my punching bag."

Larry speaks out. "Calm down guys."

We both turn around. "Shut up Larry," Moio says.

Then I say, "we are having fun what's the matter with you?" For all those who know Larry, you will understand how funny this is. I go to my trailer and get dressed with all my cups and hip pads to top it off. I walked out of my room looking like there was an inflated balloon between my legs. I go to set and lie down ready to go. Moio wanted to rehearse it.

I sat up and said, "rehearse it!? Just shoot it, we don't need no rehearsal. How many times you want that bike to hit my stones? They can only take so much."

Moio gave me the evil eye as the powers agreed.

As soon as they roll cameras, I hear Larry Holt say, "I'm running Steven!" He releases the bike and it starts doing figure S's. It misses my crotch completely and instead rolls over my shin! They cut as I try to compose myself from the pain.

Before I can say anything, Moio says, "let's do it again."

Larry is apologizing up and down and Moio is trying to get the crew to reset the scene. I tell Larry to just please try to be more accurate and do the best he can. I told Moio to lock off the front wheel of the bike and it won't go where it isn't supposed to. As usual, Moio didn't like my two cents but did it anyway. Lol. They roll cameras, Larry starts running with the bike and there it goes over my thigh this time. We did it again and it went around me, came back and rolled over my freaking face! Larry Holt, don't give him a job as a sharpshooter. We did manage to eventually get a couple of good whacks in the old sacks and boy when it hit my crotch, it sent vibrations throughout my body. I did what you would call a natural reaction. Even with the cup, I still felt it everywhere. It was like a guy taking a baseball bat and swinging it like a golf club. I let out a howl but it quickly turned into a screech! They cut. The screech continued.

I took a breath, shot up and simply said, "I don't give a rat's ass about sound. That's a print. You got it camera?"

They said, "yes."

I looked at Moio. "We moving on?"

He replied with laughter, "moving on."

(Working with John Moio. I repeat, it's always the hard way.)

With all my scrapes and bruises, what did I get? Just like I said in the past. If it was Stunts Unlimited I would have gotten a thousand plus, easy. Instead, I got a hundred. Doing it about fifteen times So break it down, that's just over six dollars each time. Oh, boy. Stuntmen's Association doing what they do. It's funny. Every time I work for somebody in the Stuntmen's Association, I always dreamed that the adjustments were coming from Stunts Unlimited. No doubt everybody else in that group did too.

CHAPTER 107
(Politics, Lies, And Where Is The Friendship?)

Now let me ask you again, do you remember those classic shows you used to watch as a kid? We discussed cartoons, now I want to talk about live action shows. For me, it was *The Man From U.N.C.L.E., The Riflemen, Get Smart, Wanted Dead Or Alive.*

There are some shows you just remember forever. Imagine being called to work on one of these shows. It happened to me with a movie called *The Green Hornet.* One of my favorites Kato, Bruce Lee. I thought, what a great honor to be working on a picture like this. Of course, he wouldn't be in this but it still felt connected to his legacy. I said yes and when I said thank you, it was coming from a different part of me. A great moment in time that I get an opportunity like this to work on such a title. The day arrived and I was anxious to learn what the story was like, who was playing Kato, who was playing the Green Hornet. When I got to set, I said my hellos and went to my trailer where I saw a call sheet on the wall. I look at it, searching for my name. Find it. ND bad guy, Steven Lambert. I go up to the top and see the Green Hornet, my eyes dart to the side, eager to see the actor. Maybe it will be Josh Brolin, maybe Brad Pitt. Maybe Tom Cruise. Seth Rogan, it says. My heart felt like it went up to my throat. Seth Rogan?! What? Isn't he a comedian? What the hell is this about? I say to myself that maybe he is going to play it serious. Then I look at Kato and see that Jay Chou is playing him. Who the hell is he? I've never heard of him. Hope he is good. I go to set and begin to watch.

Days went by and I found myself sick go my stomach. I have watched hours upon hours of this, three days in whole. Seth Rogan is playing it in the most ridiculous, sarcastic, insincere and shameful stupid way that you could portray a character. Watching the guy who played Kato, he was horrible. Bruce had a confident aura around him, a sense of control and liberation. A confident attitude that was in control. I mean that's why they called it the Kato show in the orient. This guy had none. The story and action was subpar. They did action for the sake of doing action, which you should never do. To me, they destroyed a work of art and there is a long list of sequels, some of which I mentioned above that befell the same fate. All my excitement went out the window and you could say I was embarrassed inside. Rest assured that it will happen again to another great classic. That's showbiz.

I want to end this film with a story that left me confused, angry, shocked, and has affected my soul (meaning - emotional or intellectual energy or intensity) deeply to this day. I felt defeated in the belief of the word friendship. Meaning a state of mutual trust and support between pals. Here we go. I was running late to get to the set on this particular day. I pull up to the gatehouse at Warner Brothers and am met by a young, anxious security guard.

"Sorry, we are all full in here. You need to turn around and find street parking," he told me.

I looked at the time, shook my head and explained. "I'm supposed to have an assigned parking spot inside. I'm in a rush, I am late. Please. I have to park and get to set. I need to check in, my boss is waiting for me. I am working on the Green Hornet. Is there any way I could park inside, check in and then come back and park on the street? I just want to let my boss know I am here. Please."

The young guard shook his head. "No. Everyone has to find street parking."

I looked back at the line of cars behind me, knowing full well there wasn't going to be any spots on the street for at least five blocks and beyond. I was five minutes late and it would take me another forty five minutes to find a spot and walk back. I pleaded with him again, but he wouldn't budge.

That is when an older security guard came by and asked what the hold up was. I explained to him I was running late and if I look for a parking spot outside it will make me forty five minutes late.

"Please," I ask him. "I only wanted to park for a moment to check in and then I'll park outside." The guard saw how distraught I was about being late, which I rarely ever am, and told the young guard he would get me a spot. I thanked both of them profusely and pulled forward. The old guard stepped out to show me where to park. As the gate raised and I passed by the guard house, the young guard gave me a look of resentment.

"You're going to get a big surprise today," he spat with a smirk.

I looked at him bewildered, not understanding, and It just went over my head. Off to set I went. I checked in with my boss, Andy Armstrong and apologized that I was late. He told me that it was no big deal and we went to work. Halfway through the day, I am sitting in a room amongst many people. I was reading a book I found on set. A biography of the film actress Betty Hutton. I had just gotten finished introducing myself to a man I highly respected from Hong Kong. A Martial Artist and stuntman. Andy Cheng. We talked and amongst our conversation I told him I admired his work. I mentioned to him that he was very artistic and that I liked the way he puts his work on screen. I say my goodbyes and I go off and continue reading my book. Roughly twenty minutes go by. Then Andy Armstrong comes in. I am thinking he just wants to say hello. Shoot the breeze. Then I realize he has a concerned look on his face. "What is the matter?" I asked him.

"I just spoke to the Producers and they told me one of our stuntmen was very rude to the guard at the gate. Cursing him out and shouting vulgarities. They want that person off the show, after today."

It quickly dawned on me that this stuntman he was referring to, was ME. "What are you talking about?" I ask. "Is this about the incident I had at the gate with the guard?"

He replied, "yes."

I shook my head. "I never cursed at him, or said bad language. He told you that? He's lying," I pled my case. "Andy, you know me. I don't curse. I would never talk to somebody like that. No matter what the circumstances were." I explained to Andy exactly what occurred at the gate. I told him I never once got angry, nor did I use profanity. "That would be stupidity on my part and you should know I'm not that kind of a person. I was nice, I was pleasant and I was thankful. Did you ever see me do anything like that? ANDY, YOU'RE MY FRIEND. YOU SHOULD BELIEVE ME."

Now I could understand if Andy said that he believed me but had no choice but to let me go because it came from the Producers. Instead, he looked at me, shook his head and muttered, "I don't believe that, Steven."

I looked at him, unsure of what to say. "Andy, we have known each other for many years. We have had a lot of laughs together. You know I wouldn't do something like that or lie about it. Who you talking to? Other jealous stuntmen?"

He nodded his head yes.

I looked into his eyes for some form of understanding but was met with none.

"Sorry, Steven," Andy said. "This will be your last day."

I was shocked. I was actually hurt by his words and coldness.

Again and again, I told him, "I will not lie to you." I was stunned by his disbelief. I thought about having the Producers call the young guard, but I knew he wasn't going to tell them the truth and the old guard wasn't there at the moment that I needed him to be a witness. I just couldn't believe he didn't trust I was telling the truth. What can I do? Then it dawned on me what the young guard meant as I passed by.

"You're in for a big surprise today," he had told me.

Now I understood what he meant. How horrible that is to lie about someone. And how sad it is for a friend to believe those lies. At the end of the day, I went home. It was also the last time I spoke to Andy or Vic Armstrong. To this day, I would like to know why. I may never know. What I do know is the hurt and the betrayal that I feel to this day. How sad. There is so much manipulating the truth and lying in this business that after a while, the people you think would realize true loyalty and honesty, turn out to be no more than dubious friends. Personally me, myself, I remember when Mister Andy Armstrong unfortunately twice, got fired off of shows. Each time I found myself in a Stuntmen's Association meeting defending my friend Andy Armstrong from pretty much the whole membership. The members were saying everything from, "he has no talent" to "kick him out of America." Believe me, he was like the plague. Most hid from him back then, but I didn't. I defended him each time. That is the meaning of true friendship. I rest my case, your honor. The moral of the story is never be late. And if you are late, pick the guard booth with the older looking security guard.

CHAPTER 108
(Hey You! Do You Want To Be Noticed?)

In this parable, which means a simple story used to illustrate a moral or spiritual lesson, I want to play a professor. Not the professor on *Gilligan's Island*, but a professor of the arts. The art of knowing what you have in front of you, and knowing when and how to use it. It takes strength, courage and confidence. Let's talk about opportunities that you have when you work on A movies or B movies, and it's even easier on C's. This first piece of work was called *The Horde*. The Coordinator was familiar with me and my work and he explained to me that he needed stunt guys that could act and he didn't have much dough to pay me. He knew me well enough to know that I cared about the opportunity and the work much more than the cash. On top of that, I knew myself well enough to know that this could turn out to be interesting or fun. Another chance to make something out of nothing, I thought. I always enjoyed that, but most guys don't. They want the cash. So I accepted. I was paired with 9 actors, all henchmen of the lead bad guy. It was a one day shoot for me, I was told. The film was kind of like that movie, *The Hills Have Eyes*. About a group of campers who get captured by inbred mutants who live in the woods, so we had a lot of special effects makeup slapped on our faces. I always hated that makeup muck. The Director is all over the place going over the action and is telling everybody what to do. In my view, that's pretty hard when he didn't know what he was doing himself. That left five or six including me, in the background to fend for ourselves. The others had some dialogue. On the first rehearsal, I notice everyone doing nothing. Everyone is standing around not doing anything special. The second rehearsal it happens again. The whole scene is boring, they looked like gnomes. They didn't realize and understand that they had something they were failing to utilize. Character, improv, acting. Nobody was doing nothing. They had, like Mel Gibson in *Braveheart* said, "freedoooooom!"

That's what we all had and they weren't applying it. But I was going to. So when we rolled camera, I decided I was going to show them the freedom they had. I was going to show them all. So guess what? I went from boring gnome, to guess who? GOLLUM from *The Lord Of The Rings*! All eyes watched as this little skinny Kung Fu Jew from Brooklyn turned into Gollum. I made my way to the front of the pack. I could feel the eyes on me as I gave myself some dialogue.

What did I say? "Okokwe'lldothat. I'lldothat!" That's exactly what I said and how I said it, bobbing and moving around erratically throughout the scene with a weird obscure voice repeating my dialogue. "I'lldothat, okokwe'lldothat!" Guess what else I put in there? The infamous Bruce Lee scream. It was hysterical in a weird way. My version of Gollum.

When they yelled, "cut. Print," that is when I turned back into myself as the Director came over.

A big smile on his face, he turned to the other actors. "That was great, did you see what he did? Don't copy him but do something unusual like that."

Come the second take, I did my thing even more and what did they do? I couldn't believe it, they did the same thing they did before. Stand around like zombies, not understanding the opportunity, the freedom before them. What numb nuts. No guts no glory. We moved on to other scenes and got to one with a big rock mountain in it. When we rolled, noticed I said rolled and not rehearsal because again I wanted it to be a surprise, I got up onto that boulder swinging my arms and acting like Gollum. When they stopped rolling, I jumped off that boulder, about a seven foot drop and as I landed everyone jumped back. Guess who was the center of attention? The punk kid from Brooklyn. All you actors out there, when you read a script, yes it tells you what to do. But you also have the FREEDOM to embellish, to make something out of nothing. You want to give everyone there the best work you can give them. I have always done that my whole career, from the very beginning. A big budget film or a low budget film, it doesn't matter. Remember this. Did you hear me? Remember. Because remember is what you want them to do and you will stand out amongst the chosen. Okay, it's wrap time on this movie they call *The Horde*. My one and only day is over. I get the junk off my face and go to sign out. There, I am met by the Stunt Coordinator who tells me the Director wants to know if I was available for the next seven days of shooting! He said he loved my character so much he wanted to add me to the cast. I was surprised and asked if he was going to double my pay and put my name up in lights. He laughed.

I said, "tell your Director, the Spider will continue." That was my character's name. Gollum wasn't done, in fact he had one of his best performances still to come. In this scene I was to play a guard, a simple guard watching over a girl the lead bad guy had tied up in bed. At rehearsal, I just stand there like Gollum hunched over but not talking, not moving. As usual, the Director continued on, not knowing what the hell he was doing. When they rolled cameras, the magic opportunity came to life. I had about seventeen seconds before the bad guy comes in, so what do I do? I go over to her jumping like a monkey and get up on the bed. My body envelopes her as I sniff and smell. Like a spider, I crawl and consume her, taking whiffs of her body, a crazed grin plastered on my face. Every now and then I make eye contact with the actress tied up. I could tell she is thinking, "what the hell is this guy is doing?"

She was scared to death. I could hear here think, "this wasn't done in the rehearsal!" I jump down with perfect timing, just as the bad guy enters and I hop over to my position as he swats me across the head. I thought to myself, "it's about time an actor gets a correct thought and adds to their acting." The Director cuts and the girl sits up in shock.

"Holy hell, I didn't know you were going to do that. It scared the crap out of me," she said.

(She smelled good.)

The Director clasps his hands, "yes and it looked wonderful! We had a camera right on your face." He turns to me in exuberance and literally tries to embrace me and to kiss me. I am pushing him back, telling him that Gollum doesn't play that game, back off Jack.

"Okay, I get it, you're happy," I say.

He nods excitedly. "You were wonderful Steven, you made that scene look great," he said.

I tell you readers this because it works. You just have to have IN CAPITAL LETTERS….CHUTZPAH! Believe me, it works. I did it with Soderberg, I did it with Spielberg and I did I with Firstenberg. Three great Directors and one that is a hero of mine.

CHAPTER 109
(Movie: White House Down. Cowards and Unprofessionalism.)

Here is a potboiler that never ceases to amaze me. James Woods calling on the phone. Calling me personally. There is always a special moment when I think to myself, pure fun. Nothing but fun. He tells me we are going to Canada for a show called *White House Down*, starring Channing Tatum and Jamie Foxx. What a cast. Jamie had just won an award for playing Ray Charles which I saw and thought was a fabulous performance. Jimmy asks me if I'm on board and I start singing to him. The song? I'll sing it to you. "I will follow yoooouuu, follow you wherever you may go."

He abruptly stopped me and told me, "shut up you idiot," while we were both laughing. He says he'll call me in a week and we hang up. A week goes by and no phone call.

I call Jimmy and asked him, "what's up? I haven't gotten any word yet from anybody. Just checking in."

He tells me he will look into it and call me back in an hour. Sixty minutes later, right on cue, Jimmy is on the other end of the line. He tells me he spoke with the Stunt Coordinator and Producer and found out because they are filming in Canada, they can't bring anyone from America. The wheels are turning in my head and I say, "thank you, Jimmy. I know we will work with each other again, but you need to know something. The Producer and your Stunt Coordinator, they are misleading you. They are not telling you the truth."

Jimmy continued to explain that in Canada, they are not allowed to bring in people out of country. It's their Guild's rules.

I clear my throat and I say, "Jimmy, I don't mind not going if it's going to be a hassle. But let's think for a moment. Please, listen to what I know is fact. A fact that I want you to know. He has two American stuntmen there as we speak, from California. I know that for a fact. Second of all, they don't want anybody there that they don't have control over in the hiring process. Let me remind you it stems from ego, insecurity and jealousy which are in play right now. You're going to need a stuntman aren't you? You are asking me to come aboard Jimmy, not them and that scares them. They don't realize I would listen to them as much as I would watch over and protect you and the action that was presented pertaining to you, Jimmy. This is strictly a power trip. You know we've been there before and the Stunt Coordinator wants to give the job to his friend. And let me say, there's probably about a hundred plus stunts in the movie. That means he's got a hundred friends to give out a job to. You have one. You want to give the job to your one stunt friend Jimmy, your bubbeleh. So all I am saying is that what they told you isn't the truth."

After a few minutes of talking, Jimmy begins to understand and tells me he will call me back in half an hour.

I reply sincerely, "Jimmy it is okay, you don't have to if you think it's going to be a problem. Believe me, I understand. I just want you to know what's going down."

He replies, "let me get to the bottom of this."

Well a half an hour later, I get a call. Not from Jimmy, but from one of the Producers. BANG! He tells me there was a misunderstanding and I would be coming up tomorrow, continuing to apologize. I tell him enough already with the suck up. "Yes, I am available," I tell him. "Boy, Jimmy must have reamed you a new asshole," I laugh.

He replied, "yes he did."

We both start laughing. I say, "I'm glad you have a sense of humor about it." Tomorrow comes and I arrive in Canada and check into my hotel. I call Jimmy up and he invites me over to his hotel. I go over and what a hotel it is. Every room was a luxurious sweet, about five thousand dollars a night.

"Steven, I tried to get you into this hotel but the Producers wouldn't let me," Jimmy tells me.

I start laughing and tell him, "who the hell would book a stuntman into a hotel like this?" Yet, Jimmy has attempted to book me in his hotels many times. Something I found quite bemusing and evidence of our strong friendship but I always knew that wasn't happening.

(The three amigos. Two Jews and a Goyim. James Woods, me and Alan Haft.)

He decides he wants to check out a camera shop and we head out of the hotel. We happened to run into a few Producers of the show, and the one who called me up on the phone. I'm introduced to him. I say to him, "it's nice to meet the one who got reamed by Mister Woods," and I bring a little smile with it. Jimmy starts in on the PR spiel about me. Telling them what I have done and how great I am. I smile and nod at the praise he is doling out before me and for me. I should be used to it, but never am. My friend. I always get so embarrassed. He means well. We then hoofed it to the camera shop and I head over to the part of the store with the four to five hundred dollar cameras and he starts looking at the forty to fifty thousand dollar cameras! Haha. I'm listening to him ask the salesman if they would throw this case in or that lens in. The salesman tells him those things aren't included. Here is where I come in. I rub my hands together, butt in and take over.

"Listen here. For that kind of dough, they should be! I'm not going to let my friend buy this unless you throw something in." Before he could make the choice, I say, "the lens, we want the lens."

The salesman shakes his head. "Sorry, that's a seven, eight hundred dollar lens, I can't do that."

I grab Jimmy's hand and start hauling him out the door and say to the salesman, "see ya. Wouldn't want to be ya. You just lost a deal."

A second goes by. "Wait," I hear the salesman say. "You got a deal."

Jimmy narrowed his selection down to three cameras that he would consider and ultimately decided on one. As we left and shut the door, he gives me a big smile.

He pushes me in fun and says, "you kike, you Jew. That is why I bring you along."

I laugh. "I know that's why," I say. "Lunch is on you, right?"

After he bought the camera, I became the model of the year. That's right, wherever we were, Jimmy had to get me to pose for a picture. I'll give you an example. We walked by a store with mannequins in it and Jimmy had me stand by the window and he manipulated me into different positions and stand there for five to ten minutes as he took different angles. This happened not once or twice but around a dozen times. Every now and then he sends me a picture to remind me of my modeling career. It was hilarious you had to be there. We moved on as I continued to model throughout the days and we got into talks like, "how's your Director, Roland Emmerich?"

Jimmy looked at me and smiled saying, "he's a nice guy, but he's a bit of a Muscle Mary."

"What's that mean?" I asked.

Jimmy smiled. "You know, Steven. A sausage boy."

I look at him still perplexed. I say, "Jimmy, I don't get it."

He starts laughing and then explains to me, "he's a sailor boy."

We both start falling to the floor in tears. Then I ask, "what about Channing Tatum? The only thing I ever saw him in was some weird dance movie, *Magic Mike*. He looks more like a flamingo to me than a tough guy."

Jimmy asks, "what the hell is a flamingo?"

I say to him, "touché."

He says, "Channing Tatum is a cool guy."

I ask about Jamie Foxx.

"A very nice guy, but he doesn't talk much," he tells me. "He's got a freaking entourage a mile long. Me? All I got is you."

I laugh. Then I ask about the set.

"It is an unbelievable set but they are keeping it under wraps," I am told by Jimmy.

I scratch my head. "Under wraps? Why is that?"

Jimmy gives a half smile and leans in close. "The word is there is another movie, Olympus Has Fallen, that is very similar to this one."

I shake my head and say, "you're telling me that they are doing the same exact movie as this one and they both know it? Who is the Academy Award genius who did this? What's gotten into Hollywood these days? If I had the money they have on this picture, I could make twenty original films that are better than this one."

We both laughed and moved on. We spent the whole day together. After all who gets to shop with James Woods. We looked at clothes, antique shops and oh yeah, still modeling. Just walking the streets watching everybody recognize and wanting to shake my friend's hand. James Woods enjoys people. Loves to have conversations about everything. A lot of times with humor and boy I must tell you, Jimmy's wit is like none other. Hilarious and shocking. Then he brings me to this one deli. A fantastic deli it was. Home cooking. It wound up being our go to place and once a day we would eat there. They knew Jimmy Woods and they treated us like Kings. A day in a life of palling around with Jimmy Woods. Oh, let's not forget politics. There is always a little of that. And boy, a lot of that is off the wall funny but true, coming out of my friend. It's the delivery. A week went by and I was getting bored. No call sheet under my door, no phone call to tell me when I was needed. Just more or less hanging around the hotel. Boring. So that night Jimmy called me, dinner time. We talked about his day on the set and other things, with a mention that I was bored. He was surprised to hear that I hadn't even been on set yet, so he invited me for the next day.

"Pop on over to my hotel," he says. "Eight AM. Seven thirty and I'll have a cup of coffee for ya." I called the Production Office to let them know I was invited by Jimmy Woods to the set.

"Just calling you to let you know where I am going if you need me," I told them. The next day, I met him at his hotel and we took his limo down to the set.

When we got there, he said, "follow me. I want to introduce you to Jamie Foxx."

We go over to the corner of the stage which was blocked off. Three to four bodyguards are standing around and Jimmy explains to them who I am.

"My stuntman," he says.

They let us in with a lot of funny looks on the way. I thought to myself, the strange rolling of the eyes and the shit eating smirks that they gave us weren't only for Mr. Woods, but his little skinny stunt guy also. The insides of my mind were laughing. I see a row of ten to fifteen Director chairs, all for Foxx's entourage I deducted. We go down the line. Wow, this is a lot of baggage, possibly "hanger oners" you can call them. Fifteen to twenty by my count. Wow. Finally, we turn the corner and see Jamie Foxx.

He nods to Woods as if to say, "it's okay, come here." Right away, Woods introduces me to Jamie and here we go with the PR spiel. I only bring it up because it's always the icebreaker with Jimmy, but it's nice.

He starts, "Steven was the only stuntman allowed to perform on the Statue Of Liberty to this day," Jimmy tells Jamie. "Ninja. Thirty seven stories high, two hundred feet across. He did a slide for life from one window to the next. Can you believe that? And he's a black belt in Martial Arts."

Okay, let's stop for a second. The minute my friend mentioned that I was a black belt in Martial Arts, all of a sudden, the circle of bodyguards got closer. I felt their eyes upon me looking me up and down. I thought to myself, "oh Jimmy, why did you have to say that." With my funny bone going off, I stuck out my hand and said, "Mister Jamie Foxx. Steven Lambert here," as Woods continued with my accolades. Blah, blah, blah. I said, "I gotta tell ya, your performance portraying Ray Charles in the movie was some of the best work I've seen. It was a fantastic piece. I really mean it. You're one hell of an actor." That must have struck a piano string, as he smiled back at me, raised his hand, put it on my shoulder and looked into my eyes.

"That means a lot to me. Thanks. Cool," he says.

I reply back, "I say it because I mean it."

He then asked where I came from. "New York, I bet," he said.

"Brooklyn," I replied.

"Texas for me," he shot back.

"Do you Cowboy?" I asked.

He shook his head. "Far from it."

We laughed when Jimmy said, "the only horsepower he's been on is a vehicle in the hood."

I looked back at Foxx who was laughing at his co-star and friend.

Then Jamie mentioned what he heard from Jimmy about me and asked, "you're a Martial Artist, a black belt, huh?"

I said, "yes, but I believe a black belt symbolizes how much you know, not how well you know it." A moment of silence passes.

Then Jamie spurts out, "who are you? Bruce Lee?"

I said with a smile, "ahhh, emotional contact. Never take your eyes off your opponent or you miss all the heavenly glory."

He says, "that's pretty good you should be an actor."

I reply back, "no thanks, that's too boring. I'll stick with stunts."

He laughed with the rest of his gang. I gotta tell you, Jimmy Woods looked at me like I was nuts but I think that is one of the reasons why he loves me. (This did happen.) Jamie Foxx clasped his hands together.

"Let me see you do something. Throw some punches," he says.

I face him and he shakes his head, "no, not with me. With one of these guys."

He points to one of his bodyguards and I look and saw a chest and I look up even more into the guy's face. He's a big one. My mind spoke to me, "Steven, what did Jimmy get you into now?" I looked at Jamie and made sure I had the right guy. Jamie confirmed I did and the bodyguard gave a little smile like if to say, look at this little toothpick. I think to myself, boy I hope I don't embarrass myself. I took a deep breath and said to the guy, "you want to play?"

He shrugged and said, "come on."

I think he thinks, what harm could this skinny little dude do? "All right," I said. "Throw a punch, make it a good one."

He smiled and said, "what do you want me to throw?"

I opened my mouth and said, "make it anything you want." That's what surprised him, Jamie, Jimmy and to an extent, even me. I see Jimmy in the corner with a shit eating smirk, his eyebrows raised in wonder and worry about what was going to happen. My mind speaks to me, "make sure you stay more than arms distance, Steven. Use that little trick so you can see what's coming." He asked if I was ready and I said I was, bringing my hands up to chest level, taking a deep breath, then exhaling relaxed. Immediately going on my toes. A second went by and he threw a right at lighting speed as my arm moved up to block it. But then it stopped! I realized it was a fake! All of a sudden, his left came at me and with a reflexive response, my left shot up. Open handed Wing Chun mantis block with a tiny left side shuffle. It stopped it but it rocked me back about three or so inches. My left hooked to his ribs, stopping before contact, then shooting up to his jaw. Stopping just before contact. I opened up my fist, brought it in back of his neck, hooked him and with all my might threw him about four feet forward. He turned, just as I did, but with my turn I threw a front left snap kick right to his face, stopping before contact.

I must say it was a thing of beauty and was I lucky. He was shocked and I was shocked. Thank God I didn't embarrass myself. Jamie Foxx applauded, Jimmy Woods is jumping up and down like little Teddy Shields, remember that guy at the beginning of the book? Everyone else was all smiling and patting me on the back.

"Look at this hundred and fifty five pound stick getting the best of you," they say to the biggun.' It was another moment in time that is embedded into my brain. Boy, was I fortunate it turned out that way. Later that day, Jimmy introduced me to Director Roland Emmerich. He was a busy rude dude and our greetings were brief. Tatum was sitting next to him so we talked after Jimmy introduced us. We had a brief discussion. It felt like cardboard, like his acting. Nothing personal, he was a nice guy but his work doesn't do anything for me. His acting seems the same, all the time. But he's a good dancer. He mentioned some of the action he was doing by himself and I told him that was great as an actor, the more you can do the better it will look. Just be safe and don't let your ego make you think you can do something that you can't. That's the key. He gave me a strange look like he never quite heard anybody say that before. We moved on throughout the day on set, when Jimmy goes to hair and makeup. I hang around watching everything when the Stunt Coordinator, John Stoneham Jr.'s assistant came up to me. (I forgot his name, but let's call him Mister He Knows It.) He asked me what I was doing on set and I asked him what he meant by that.

"You're not supposed to be here unless you are called," he told me in an arrogant way.

Very calmly and cool, I put up my hands and said, "this is no way to treat anybody. I didn't think it was a big deal, I'm not in anybody's way. Since you're so insistent about it, I was invited by James Woods. If it's that big of a deal, bring it up to Woods. I'm sure you guys will have a lovely conversation. In fact, if you'd like, I'll bring you over to him right now and you can tell him."

Mr. Assistant froze and looked like he did a Mr. Hankey in his pants. South Park. I must tell you he was shocked by my comment. I don't why. I was just telling the truth. That's what he should do. He quickly told me that it would be best if I went back to the hotel and John would call me when I was needed. He told me they were going to do rehearsals in a couple of days and would need me then. Shaking my head in confusion and not wanting to make this a big deal, which obviously for him it was, I agreed and went to tell Jimmy. I decided to simply tell him there was nothing for me to do here and I'm bored. I'm going back to the hotel. That was fine with him and as I got my ride back, I thought how strange this situation was. A few days go by when finally I get a call that they were going to pick me up at ten in the morning to rehearse. It's about damn time, I thought. I've done enough sight seeing in this city. And modeling. Yes, it continued. They pick me up and I arrive on the stage. There, I'm shocked. After weeks, I finally meet the man. Mister John Stoneham Jr. in person. He is short and very to the point which when you are a punk kid from Brooklyn, you pick up on. Normally when you first meet, you would think you would have a nice conversation, make friends a bit. Make you feel at home. There was none of that. As quick as our meeting was, it ended. Being there for five weeks and only seeing each other for fifteen seconds was very strange. He disappeared forever. Nevermore. A few minutes go by and I look and notice they are laying down three six inch thick pads, three abreast followed by four length wise. I walk over to about ten to fifteen stunt guys with Stoneham Jr.'s assistant (sorry, I forgot his name again but he knows who he is) being in the mix and introduce myself.

Then I ask Mr. Assistant, "may I ask what those pads are for. Because you see, I really don't know what is going on here. I never got a script and I wasn't told anything about Jimmy Wood's action. It seems like everybody is trying to hide something from me. See, this is a strange way of going about things. It's different. I feel like you are trying to hide something."

He nods and says, "we aren't allowed to discuss what we are doing."

I look up at him in bewilderment wondering why these conversations on this set are so strange. "Okay," I tell him, still wondering what was going on here. Mister Assistant came over and told me that Stoneham had to leave, but he wanted me to rehearse an air ram.

"Have you done an air ram before?" he asks

"Yes, I have," I smile.

He looks me up and down and says, "how good are you?"

I tell him, "well since you're so to the point. I'm excellent. I could be a gazelle or I could be an elephant and fall on my ass. Whatever you need. Does that answer your question, with all due respect?"

I give a smile. He don't. He just nods and says they were going to film a rehearsal and show it to the powers. He tells me I was going to take an explosion and be blown back with the air ram. No problem, I thought. Mister Gazelle is ready. As they start putting down the air ram, I noticed they had three of them. Why are there three of them if it's just me? I walk over and ask one of the guys setting them up.

"We are filming three guys being blown back," he tells me. I scratch my head and say, "why three? It was my impression that I was the only one."

He confirms that is true but adds, "there is only one doing it but we are filming three guys in rehearsal. I guess they are doing a test on you guys."

I said, "a test on the guys? In the script, it reads James Woods is being blown back. Well, I'm James Wood's double. That's what I'm here for. Why do we need three guys? There's no competition here.

I'm the guy."

He shrugs and tells me, "I don't know, I was just told to set this up."

That's when two guys came out. One went to the left air ram, the other went to the right air ram and the middle one was meant for me. I was the Hebrew National salami between two goyim. I walk over and I look at the guy to the left of me, I look at the guy to the right of me. They look pretty young. I ask the guy to the right, "hey, how old are you?"

He replies he is twenty five. I ask the guy to the left, he tells me he is twenty seven. I smile, both of them staring at me.

"Fifty nine and proud of it," I told them. You want to know why I said that to them? I realized what the hell was going on here. This is a goddamn test and the plan is that this is going to determine who is going to double James Woods and they are too chicken shit to tell me! It's gotta be. A thousand times I have been on sets, it's my Brooklyn street sense. I know when I'm being conned. I'm trying to figure out what is going on. Why the competition, why are they telling me that after flying me all the way to Canada I have to compete for the job to double Jimmy? It was weird, man.

Now let me say. I could have handled this two ways. I could have told Jimmy and let him handle it and said screw you guys, I'm not competing against anybody. Or I could just follow along, do it. I think the latter is going to be more interesting and fun. You think I'm worried about not smelling the roses? Not this guy. I'm going to fly high and burst their bubble. Let's rock.

The two young punks smiled and said, "you're fifty nine? You don't look it."

I shrugged and said, "we'll see who will book it."

They tell us we are all going at the same time as we get on the air rams. We get ready as a thought comes into my mind.

I call out, "wait a minute, do we all have the same pressure in each machine?"

They say we do, so I walk over to my gage, look at the pressure. I walk over to the gage to my left and check the pressure. I walk over to the gage to my right and check the pressure. Everyone is watching me with a very intrigued look. I guess they are not used to individuality. Okay, they are all set the same. That's the professional in me. Trust and verify when games are being played. I smiled back with confidence as we all get on backwards onto the air ram. I set myself. Cameras are rolling. We get a countdown. Mister Assistant calls it out. THREE, TWO, ONE.

I say to myself, "KUNG FU!"

Everybody goes on one, three of us go flying back. The guy to the left of me hits the ground hard on his back. The guy to the right of me falls down on his side. How do I know this? Because I am still traveling high in the sky going back. Probably about nine feet further. Not only that, but approximately four feet higher. When I came down, I didn't splatter. I back roll not once, not twice, but three times. When I came up, I struck the pose. Ninja like. For you non-Martial Artists, let's say spidey-like. The two young whippersnappers were shocked. I look up and smile, bowing to them graciously as they are still on the floor. Everyone else in the room is shocked as well. In the pose, I ask, "anything else you need?" I looked at Stoneham Jr.'s assistant as I noticed two or three of the Producers watching and applauding.

"No," he said. "Let's move on."

That night I met Jimmy for dinner at the deli. I told him what happened and he was amazed, shocked and even laughed. He told me not to worry, I was his one and only stunt double. He raised his camera for a picture, instructing me to open my mouth bigger, BIGGER, and put the pastrami sandwich up to it like I was about to take a bite. That's the life of a stunt model. A few days went by when Jimmy called and asked if I had time to go out to lunch. I told him I had plenty of time and we met at his hotel. When we started talking, I felt something wasn't right here. Something was out of place with him. We went to eat and as we sat down, I saw he had an angst about him.

I asked, "Jimmy, what's up? What's the matter?"

He looked at me and said, "I don't want you to get upset."

My heart dropped to my stomach as I prepared for bad news.

"You know that stunt flying back you are supposed to do for me?

" I said, "yeah."

He said, "they did it already."

I asked him where he heard that. "I found out through wardrobe," he said. The wardrobe lady mentioned to me she saw the stunt you were supposed to do, Steven. I said oh, that is my double Steven Lambert. She said no, it wasn't Steven Lambert, it was somebody else. The next day I went in, Steven and gave them a piece of my mind how rotten that was," he said.

I just sat back in disbelief. They couldn't have. They can't. They did! I was furious and he saw that and tried to calm me down, promising there would be other shows that I could do. It took me the whole day to cool down but only after I decided to call the Stunt Coordinator.

But I quickly realized I didn't have his telephone number, I never got it.

But I did have Mr. Assistant's number. So I called him and explained to him, "listen I know this isn't any of your concern, but you know what is going on. I don't know the next time I am going to see your boss, but give him a message from me. Tell him I said he is a coward. Nowhere near a professional. I would have had more respect for him if he told me what he was going to do to my face. But no, he chose to be a yellow bellied chicken. An insecure one, a jealous one. There is no other reason why. And just so you'll know it, if I do meet up with him, I'll repeat that to his face and more if needed." There was silence on the other end. "You got it?" I asked.

He replied, "yes."

I told him, "thank you. Have a wonderful day. Let me say one other thing. Mister Woods isn't too happy either, but I don't think you guys really care." I hung up right after. The betrayal of confusion was put away. For now.

A few days later I was surprised that I got a call to come down to the set for the final battle in the film between James Woods and Channing Tatum. The scene is in the Oval Office and Jimmy hasn't arrived on set yet. But the Producers are there, Mister Assistant is there as well as a whole lot of other people. I walk over to all the Producers and I spurt out, "good morning. Where is your coward of a Stunt Coordinator? I WANT TO PERSONALLY GIVE HIM A PIECE OF MY MIND."

One Producer turned to me and asked me to calm down.

I looked at him and said, "calm down? You know what he did to me and you guys are a bunch of cheaters. You played along with the whole thing."

They were silent as they turned white as a sheet. I had made my point. I turned and walked away. They have Channing Tatum taking a military Humvee with an M134 mini-gun, a huge six barrel machine gun that is on top and he is going to be firing at Woods. They have the mantle with trophies in the background that are to be destroyed by this gun. They have this gun about fifteen feet away from where Jimmy and now me would be standing. They are still setting up so I leave and an hour later they are ready to rehearse with me standing in for Jimmy. I come back and notice the M134 giant machine gun is pointing right at my face, meaning they just might rehearse with the gun. I walk over to the First Assistant and say, "I've been around big guns before and have seen this same type used on The Hulk and I know they have big concussion blasts coming out of its muzzle that could rip somebody's face off. So I wanted to ask if are they going to be firing the gun directly at him."

He said "yeah."

So I went to find the FX guy and he confirmed the gun would be placed fifteen feet away. I asked him if I could see the gun firing in rehearsal. He told me they were not prepared for that as the First Assistant came back over to me.

"John Stoneham Jr. said it was perfectly safe where it is," the First Assistant said to me.

Well, I explained to him that we need to do a test.

"You are not the Stunt Coordinator," he told me flatly.

I nodded. "I know, but I am telling you that unless I see a rehearsal, James Woods nor I aren't getting in front of that gun."

We went back and forth, me giving him a number of reasons why doing it this way is very dangerous.

Finally, he walked away. Twenty minutes later he came over to me, very bitterly saying that they were going to do a rehearsal and if I wanted to see it then I should follow him.

They set up a false wall with tables stacked up on each other to symbolize the mantel with trophies and ornaments on top with a dummy to boot. And it wasn't this guy. They set it up and have the M134 fifteen feet away. I am watching behind the gun. They call, "action." BAMBAMBAMBAMBAMBAMBAMBAMBAMBAM!!

Guess what happened?

Those trophies and marble never stood a chance. The plastic of the trophies and the marble were embedded in the wall and all over the floor. Shrapnel went all over the place and the dummy? The skin, I mean the material on its face, neck, shoulder and chest were ripped off.

I look at the First Assistant raised my eyebrows and say, "do you really want your actor to be in the middle of that? I don't think so. I don't. I have another way we can do it where it will work without the possibility of anyone getting hurt and right now the way you have it, I have to tell you that possibility is very high. So high it is a fact. It is called common sense. You see, someone once told me I am a genius at common sense."

He shook his head and said, "no, we are doing it this way."

I told him very bluntly, "that no, Jimmy and I aren't doing this and I think he will listen to me because you see, he's got common sense too. Not like others on this show. Let me give you an example. You hoodwinked me. You took away my air ram. That was gutless and you knew about it."

He got upset and walked away in a fury.

I was pissed. The next thing I know, here come the Director, Producers and the First Assistant, all walking towards me.

If looks could kill, I'd be a dead man. My anger quickly turned to worry and concern. I almost did what Mister Assistant did. A Mister Hankey in my pants, but I stood strong and kept Mister Hankey in. I wasn't about to be scared shitless in my pants.

Truth.

Justice.

The American way.

(When it comes to safety, sometimes you stand alone.)

The Director asks, "is there a problem?"

I said, "yes sir. There is a big problem. A safety problem." I explained with concern, passion and fear what I had just seen and how unsafe it was.

Roland Emmerich looks at me and simply says, "who the hell are you? My Stunt Coordinator says we can do it, so we are doing it."

Now readers, notice he did not say he "trusts" his Stunt Coordinator. If he had said that, he would then be liable for any accidents that took place. I could tell they were choosing their words very carefully.

I take a deep breath and say, "have you seen my body of work? And I have been with Jimmy for over three decades now and know him very well. I know when things are unsafe and this tops the list." Minutes go by as I try to argue my case, telling them why it is a very bad idea to proceed in this way, while they try to tell me that I have no business saying otherwise. I stood firm, not budging knowing I am going against extremely powerful people that could crush me in a second. One thing led to another when all of a sudden, a Producer points behind me.

"John Stoneham Jr. is right behind you. Why don't you ask him?" he says.

Without moving a muscle or looking in back of me, I say, "I don't care who is in back of me. What I say is correct and I'll deal with him later. I have a way that we can do this but you have to hear me out. I don't understand why your Coordinator hasn't thought of this. I can think of two reasons. He's gutless and he doesn't want to stand up to you or he is lacking in knowledge."

The Director asked me to continue with clenched teeth. I explained that if you angle the vehicle and the weapon to the side and the foreground of Jimmy and you angle the cameras to the side, low, then you can make it look like the gun is directly upon him. Then you go for close ups, singles and two shots at the beginning middle and end of the shot. Then you can put squibs on me or Jimmy and blow us away in the side shot. The Director was fuming and surprisingly the head FX guy stuck his head in and said I was right. But guess what? Stoneham Jr. never said a word during this fifteen minute conversation. I finished talking and as people parted ways, I felt like I had become like the black plague. Then knowing Stoneham Jr. was behind me, I turned but he was gone. I think he ran away. Chickens do run fast. I'm sorry readers. He did something that was horrible to me that a professional should never do. Then I notice things are being moved, cameras are going to the side, how do ya like that? They are listening to me! Twenty minutes go by and I still feel like a man in a bubble. No one wants to talk to me. Half an hour goes by when a P.A. comes over and tells me Jimmy wants me to come to his trailer. I exit the set thinking I might be in a bit of trouble, but wait! I was just protecting my actor, my friend. I didn't do anything wrong. I knock on his door and tell him it was me and he says to come in.

"Steven, I heard what happened," he says.

"Let me tell you what happened Jimmy," were the first words out of my mouth.

"I know what happened," he replies. "And it means the world to me. You were right and they were wrong. The head FX guy told me everything you explained."

I nodded saying, "I am sure he left out certain details, let ME explain." So I did and when I finished I thanked Jimmy for taking my side.

"But Steven," he smiles. "Do me a favor. For God sake, don't go back on the set. They hate you because you were right." He started laughing and I joined in.

I told him I would stay in the background.

"Here is another thing," Jimmy said. "I called my agent and he is sending over a contract that states from now on you will be on every show, every stunt that I am working on. I was talking to someone and they mentioned that Mel Gibson and Clint Eastwood had clauses like that in their contract for their stunt guys."

I told him, "Jimmy, you call me all the time. You don't need to do that."

He smiled again. "Too late, the contract will be here tomorrow and you're signing."

I gave in and smiled saying, "better late than never. What took you so long?"

He replied, "always know, Steven that contract or not, you will always be with me when there is action." It warmed my heart. "Thanks, pal," I said. "I can't tell you how much that means."

What a beautiful moment. What a day. A week goes by when I get a phone call that I was working the following day. We are on the set. The scene is where Woods and Jamie Foxx are struggling with each other in the Oval Office. Channing Tatum's character has set curtains on fire causing the sprinklers on the ceiling to go off. Nobody is happy. Why? Because the fricking water was freezing. They get ready to rehearse and Stoneham Jr. isn't there, just Mr. Assistant.

(From right to left. The good, the bad and the ugly.)

Now doing a struggle in a fight like this, it's more of a dance. Like Gene Kelly and Jerry Mouse. Fred Astaire and Ginger Rodgers. Jamie Foxx is an athletic guy. Jimmy, unfortunately, is not. It seemed to me that Jamie Fox was getting annoyed and Mr. Assistant kept making it worse every time he tried to fix the problem. You gotta understand that Jimmy doesn't like to do much physical activities. Jimmy God bless him, isn't much for action and will try to make a movement simple and less physical as possible. It just doesn't look real and natural that way. Soaking wet in dim lighting, Jimmy keeps bringing up my name.

"Let Steven, my stunt double do it," he says.

This is in rehearsal. The Director decides no, they were going to shoot it and get what they could get. They tried it once, twice, three times. You could see Jamie Foxx is getting impatient. It's obvious to everybody. That is when I see the writing on the wall. I say to myself, this is never going to happen the way it should. I walk over to Mr. Assistant. I asked Mr. Assistant if I could do it for Jimmy. "Give me a chance. We don't have to practice moves," I told him. "Let me just improv so it will look more real and since I know how to move with a person, you will get the best action that way." It went in one ear and out the other. I asked, "why?"

He had no answer. Fifth take, sixth take still was not any better. I went over to the Director and practically begged for him to let me do it. He was adamant. In fact, he was so adamant, what came out of his mouth next made me realize what the hell was going on.

"The Stunt Coordinator doesn't want you to do anything," he said.

I said, "whaaaaat?" That is when it hit me. I realized that this was being done on purpose. They don't want me to double Jimmy, they don't want me on film. Why? It's beyond me. I'm sorry but nobody is going to do it better than me. That's a fact, Jack. They have me here, they are paying me, so why not use me? After another half a dozen takes and Jamie Foxx expressing his unhappiness, I spoke out. "Guys, what the hell is going on. Give me a shot here."

Jamie Foxx looked at me and said, "yeah, why don't we try it with Steven?"

Jimmy nodded in agreement.

Right then, Mr. Assistant opened his mouth and removed all of my doubts by saying, "because John Stoneham Jr. doesn't want Steven doubling Jimmy." There was shock and silence on the set.

Woods looks at the Assistant and asks, "what do you mean he doesn't want him doubling me?" Mr. Assistant shrugged his shoulders. "I don't know why. He just doesn't."

I quickly said, "it's beyond me why and I am just as confused as you are Jimmy. They tricked me before with a stunt I was supposed to do and they did it with someone else."

Jamie Foxx looked up at the Director and said "I want to use Steven. Do you understand?" I hear this from Jamie Foxx and I look at him. He is not a happy guy. Jimmy motions to me to come over. He smiles and says, "it's your turn. Show them what they can't do, Steven."

Jimmy steps aside and I walk in there.

I hear from the Director, "let's rehearse this to make sure I don't see his face."

I look up to Roland and say, "I do this for a living. I guarantee you, you'll never see that it's not Jimmy. You're telling me if you use another stunt double that you won't see his face? That's an insult. Nobody hides better than me."

The Director says, "let's rehearse it and see."

I said, "I have a better idea. Let's roll cameras and shoot it." I explained out loud that, "this is a struggle, a wrestling match. It is supposed to look spontaneous and real. It's not a choreographed fight with punches and kicks. Let's just improv."

I look at Jamie Foxx and asked him what he thought and if I was making sense. He nodded and told me I was. He speaks up, "yeah it will look more real that way."

The Director complies. They roll cameras. He agrees and I get into position and I look at him and we grab each other.

I say, "are you ready to dance? You take me wherever you want to take me, do whatever you want to do and I'll go with you and you try to do the same thing with me. If we fall or lose our balance, it don't matter. Let's just keep on going. Throw the shit out of me Jamie. You do your thing and I'll do mine."

He smiles and says, "I like that."

This is going to be great, I thought. They called action and we moved. It was like two lightning bolts coming together as the rain poured down. We were at war and it was a beautiful dance. We finished the storm. We cut to a big applause. I turn around like a banshee and scream, "DID ANYBODY SEE MY UGLY MUG!?" There was silence. "Well!? Did anybody see my face?"

James Woods yells out, "hell, no."

Jamie looks up at Mr. Assistant and says, "what the hell was wrong with that? I couldn't even tell it wasn't James Woods."

Indeed, the first take was wonderful. We did another one for safety which was even better than the first. They printed them both.

I call out, "make sure you tell your Stunt Coordinator. By the way how come he is not here whenever I am here? I'll tell you why. He is a big chicken. He knows he is wrong."

Mister Woods calls out, "okay, Steven. They got the picture."

I call out, "I'm pissed and I am ashamed of what's going on. Are you guys finished with me for this scene?"

Roland Emmerich says, "let's move on."

I walk off the set and go to my trailer. Taking off my wet clothes and trying to calm down, I hear a knock on the door. I ask "who is it?"

I hear Jimmy's voice so I open the door and see Jimmy standing there. Guess who else is with him? Jamie Foxx.

I said, "come in." I am thinking in my head I am in trouble. They both explain to me that they just finished speaking to the Director, the First Assistant and one of the Producers. They explained to me that they now know what was going on.

"It was all a plan from the beginning to simply not use you," Jimmy says.

"To try and embarrass you," Jamie Foxx says. "You sure showed them."

I say, "yeah, but look what went on. This has been going on for the whole time guys and it's not fair." I look at Jamie and say, "you know how underhanded that is? It's a sick sad game of insecurity and jealousy that your Stunt Coordinator played. I have my pride. It's not fair. That is why I am upset." They both agreed.

Jamie Foxx looks at me and says, "I'll never use that fool, Stoneham Jr. again."

That night, Jimmy and I went out to eat and the whole night we discussed what happened. It was hilarious. During our conversation, Jimmy again told me what he had talked about briefly in the past with me always laughing it off. He brought up the "Q" word. Quit. He wanted to retire from the world of cinema. Each time he said that I would laugh and say, "yeah right." I tell him I could never see him getting out. He loved acting too much. Well we did this show in two thousand thirteen and it is two thousand nineteen and he is still retired. But I still think he isn't going to quit. He'll never quit. I know it. It's in his blood and he'll be back. I'm waiting for that phone call. You hear me, Jimmy? I'm waiting. Take care, my friend. I love you man.

CHAPTER 110
(New Orleans. A Waste Of Time.)

I'm out of the city of the maple leaf mounties and back in the USA. I get a call from a stunt girl and guy named HB and Leigh Hennessy. They come up with a proposal to go three way partners to open a stunt gym in New Orleans. Well, I thought to myself, I'm kind of tired of L.A. and my business in this town. It might be fun, Steven. I always enjoy teaching and helping others. I've done about everything and for sure more than once. I really was never happy being in a situation going on interviews to coordinate show as most of it just came to me. The powers don't really do the research on who they hire. Most of the time, it's simply politics. Who smiles better.

Okay, I say to myself. Let's try the pelican state, New Orleans. After a few days of thought, I agree. They found a place and send me pictures and boy, what a beautiful place it was. Reminded me of a fort. I drove down and looked at it and we all decided to make it a stunt gym and a place where Stunt Coordinators and Producers can train their actors. It was great. I knew we needed equipment and I had plenty, but we needed more. All three of us had a meeting and I laid out by laws, including me, explaining that I would not be there often. I would spend six months of my complete time putting the gym together and then they would continue to run it with me coming in when needed. They agreed.

When I returned to Los Angeles, I packed up my stuff and getting the okay from my partners, I spent another three thousand dollars for other pieces of gym equipment with the expectation to be reimbursed when I returned. I then went to a great friend and legend, Bob Yerkes. He was a stunt circus performer, he was. I asked if I could borrow an airbag and he agreed. He gave me one that was worth ten thousand dollars plus and other various pieces of equipment I would be able to use that totaled in the thousands. I thought to myself, how wonderful this man is to trust me with this equipment. That's friendship. He trusted me with all of it. It broke my heart.

I was leaving my kids in Los Angeles and I made it clear to my so called partners that I wouldn't be at the gym all the time after the period I stated. I arrived back to New Orleans with everything and Leigh paid me back but guess what? HB didn't have the money. In fact, he let me know he didn't have any money at all, contrary to the previous conversation. We all came to an understanding that he would work for the money, fixing the place up. Painting, flooring electrical and so forth, alongside me. It was perfect. Except for one thing. He didn't work!

He made excuses and never showed up and when he did show up, he worked for twenty minutes and then had another excuse that he had to leave. This happened constantly. Four, five months went by without any help from him. The fourth month came and the place looked beautiful, we open our doors to the public. I decided to have a big shindig and invite all the stunt people of New Orleans at the house I was renting. It was very cool.

So many nice people showed up. Ashley Hudson, Kevin Beard. Two very cool cats as well as many other outstanding people. What a nice surprise, even Chuck Percini Jr. showed up and brought some guy named Jeff Galpin with him. Along the way during these four months I have heard much scuttlebutt from the stunt players here about this guy, Jeff Galpin. Always unsavory. I won't go into detail, simply a very mean man. Doesn't know how to treat people correctly and from what I understand, he thinks he is the king of stunt swamps around here.

I bring this up because in the middle of this swinging party I was having, I was inside with some people laughing and playing. When all of a sudden, a girl in tears comes running in. Since I was the host, I asked why. She explained to me that Jeff Galpin was outside in my backyard harassing all the stunt people with threats of loss of work unless they listen to him. I got up and went to the problem, cool and collective. With Percini following me, knowing me and curious about what I was about to do, we set out around a corner. To my surprise, right in the middle of it, I observed everyone cowering with fear. There is Jeff Galpin yelling at everyone. I stop Jeff Galpin by saying, "put a plug in it. Why are you yelling at these people? You are at my gathering and everyone should have respect. Shame on you." I ask a couple of the stunt people, "was he threatening you?"

They say, "yes."

I look at Mister Galpin and ask him to apologize to everyone.

He smiles and says, "not a chance."

I look at him and smile back and say, "let me show you something, Jeff," asking him to follow me. He does and Percini follows with a couple of other people. We head inside with everybody wondering what is going to happen. I hand him his coat, look up to him and smile at him.

"Now get out and don't let the door hit you in the arse. And if you got anything else to say, do it," I tell him. I raise my hands, palms up and shrugging my shoulders. Little does he know that is a fighting position, just in case. He looks at me for a second.

I say, "you better not say or do anything if you know what's good for ya and leave."

That's just what he did, took off. I went outside and I took it upon myself to apologize for his actions to everybody. I told every one of them if they run into any trouble with Mister Galpin, to just let me know. I also told that to Mister Galpin. To leave these people alone. I never saw the alligator man again. It was also around this time that HB still hadn't put in work and hadn't changed or gotten money or paid the rent with us.

So we all had a meeting and Leigh and I came to a conclusion to terminate his partnership. We have been open for four months already and many stunt people have joined the place. A lot of the Stunt Coordinators here feel I am there to run shows since I had more credits than them! I try to explain to them that no, I was here to simply provide a gym for them and their actors to train. It didn't seem to matter regardless of how much I tried to persuade them. I wasn't interested in running shows. Sometimes people are so insecure, trust just goes out the window and that old thing comes a knocking. Insecurity. Let's not forget his brother, jealousy.

One Stunt Coordinator I want to mention in New Orleans is Kevin Beard. A great guy, nothing but class. A friendship I'll never forget. He even hired me. He is the man that should be running all the shows here. A lot of integrity and talent and I have a lot of respect for him. He used my facility and brought his guys there to train. One day, Stunt Coordinator J.J. Perry called me up and said he was doing a Stallone picture and wanted to know if he could use my facility.

I was overjoyed. This man, Mister Perry. You talk about talented, he's got it all. Mentally and physically. A good guy. I charged them five hundred a day and they have been working out there for two, three weeks. We are making money. When J.J. Perry would bring Stallone and his boys to train, I would close the doors so they could have their privacy. First, second, third day goes by. I would always be outside working on a piece of equipment for the gym. Never meeting Stallone and really didn't care or think about it, when he walks out one day. He comes right over to me and says hello.

We start talking, shooting the breeze. He says he remembers working with me from the past. I look at him and nervously swallowing and I say, "do you remember the incidents on Rambo?" I get that one word that Rocky always said.

"Yea."

I wouldn't dare mention Mark DeAlessandro and the pantsing.

But with a smile and a laugh he says, "I understand what happened Steven. I've heard nothing but good things about you."

I look at him and utter, "well good. Now I don't have to be nervous."

He makes a couple of fists and throws them at me, you know, in a way a friend would do. They hit me in the chest. We both laugh. I often think about that moment and say to myself, "aw, man I wish I would have blocked him. That was Rocky, man."

We stood and talked about Brooklyn, about New York. About my talents. About his talents. I expressed the deep seeded feelings I had about his physical and fighting experience. I told him that there was not a better actor in fights, ever. In fact, there weren't too many stunt people that could keep up with his fight ability. He said he was very appreciative of my thoughts and thanked me. It was a forty five minute conversation that I'll never forget. Just him and I. He was just a regular good guy.

(A wasted year but a beautiful place.)

Time goes by and then wouldn't you know it, the unexpected happens. Leigh Hennessey now tells me she doesn't have money to pay the rent. She ran out of money and only could pay half, I was told. I felt betrayed. I reminded her of the deal we had, but she didn't and couldn't change her answer. She also wanted to be full partners keep in mind. I tried to be nice and understanding and said okay. I agreed to pay rent for two months and then she could pay me back. Guess what? A month later she tells me her husband lost "half of his job," whatever that means and now she can't pay anything! I told her she needed to get money, take a loan or borrow it. It's not my responsibility. We made an agreement. Then she makes up a story, an excuse. She starts telling me how unfair it is since she has to pay rent and I was living there in the extra room we had. I invited her to live there in the other empty room, but she declined because she had a house. That shouldn't have anything to do with her paying rent for our facilities. She demands that she isn't paying until we start making money. Four days go by and I have a conversation with her on the phone. It's still the same and in fact, she tells me she isn't coming in or doing anything until I agree to her demands.

A day and a half go by and I make my move. I decide to say goodbye. Out of business sign goes up. I had enough. I pack up my van with my personal equipment that I had brought, plus the stuff I had borrowed from my friend Bob Yerkes. I left a good seven to ten thousand dollars worth of equipment there, never asking for half of that, just letting her have it. I was disgusted with the whole thing. I thought that was big of me. Halfway home I get a phone call from a stunt friend named Leslie Hoffman. She tells me that Leigh Hennessey is spreading a rumor. She made multiple phone calls to Los Angeles including the stunt groups, saying I ran out on her and that I stole equipment, including Bob Yerkes's airbag.

In fact, she even claimed that I stole her horse saddle. That saddle was mine, I brought it from L.A. In fact, thank God for stuntman Phil Collada. He knew my saddle from cowboying with him many years before. He told the truth, he knew it was my saddle. And the airbag? I had the airbag in my car to bring back! I told Leslie I was bringing it back to Yerkes at that very moment. It was my responsibility. He leant it to me. It's not her airbag, it's my obligation to return it. And that's exactly what I did, explaining to Bob what she had said. Bob told me not to worry about it and he was kind enough to write a letter saying that, "what Leigh Hennessey is claiming is a bold faced lie. Steven Lambert did exactly what he was supposed to do, which was the right thing. Return it. And I thank him for that."

I posted the letter on Facebook. It was all part of a plan by Leigh Hennessey because she knew she was the villain and she didn't want people to know the truth of what really happened. She wanted to get revenge for me leaving, yet she was the one that bailed on our partnership first. She forced the issue. I begged her many times to come into work. She simply refused, so I had no choice. It's sad that someone would take the path of lies. I sometimes sit back and wonder why people make the mistake of simply not doing the right thing. They try to hide the mistakes they make and blame it on others, not realizing the shame they bring to themselves. When I get back, I get a call from Stuntmen's Association. They want me to come in and explain myself.

"Explain what?" They have an attitude. I have a discussion with them briefly on the phone, I'm unhappy with the tone of the conversation. I have been a triple A plus member for that organization and always hired members and never did anything wrong for the thirty seven years I have been with this group. In fact, I can honestly say, I have lost work being so loyal. And now? They are questioning my morals and are making me feel like I am the bad guy. You know, let me say something. There really is no brotherhood unless you are running a show. Then everyone wants to be your brother. They'll kiss your hiney. Then they will look at the truth. It's an unfortunate way of thinking, but it is the reality of life. At the end of your reign, you're very lucky and blessed if you have an equal amount of friends as you do digits on one hand. I don't want you to think I made that up, it comes from a great stuntman named Terry Leonard. He also once said, "at the end of your career, all you have is memories, a few friends and eight by tens." Pictures, that is. I say okay, I'll come in.

CHAPTER 111
(Stuntmen's Association Get Your Act Together. I'm Out.)

Days go by before that happens and I get multiple phone calls explaining the mischief of three men. Let's have fun, make it interesting. After all, I'm saying this for reasons, a purpose. A learning experience. The three men they mentioned and I'll give you their initials were JW, who reminds me of Chuck Schumer, HO who reminds me of Adam Schiff and EB who reminds me of Nancy Pelosi. They are all in the organization. Unfortunately, I found them to be liars, cheaters. In other cases, thieves. You may ask why I am so harsh. Well, I can tell you it isn't so much what they did to me, it's what they have done to other people in a preciously valued Stunt organization and its members. I value the organization, Stuntmen's Association and its history. Some of the greatest stuntmen were from its past and its future. There are many men I respect in it. And many I don't. Some might say there are some that feel the same way about me but not for the reasons I have just stated. It took a punk kid from Brooklyn in and made him a member. That meant so much to me.

A great organization that takes a man in who has nothing. An organization that more or less started the stunt world. The tremendous respect I had for it. Only the members at this time knew what these three and others have done to this organization. Example: JW fibbed. He deceived. What did he do? Let's just say he wasn't a brother.

Again, the organization knows. He got kicked out of the organization for these deeds and then he wrote a letter to the membership basically saying that there isn't a talented person in the group. And that is putting it mildly, my friends. I always wonder if that letter still exists. Then there is HO. When you try to deliberately keep other members off the Board Of Directors by bad mouthing the people who are trying to get on, just because they disturb your own agenda and then get caught red handed, that's not brotherhood. Then EB. When you blame people for your mistakes, say things that you aren't and never think about other people's feelings. That's not brotherhood. Just ask Peter Stater and Conrad Palmisano. They know the truth. Hey, some people still won't knock these guys even if they do wrong constantly. Why? Because they still have power. Most won't knock power, would ya? Me? I'd rather feel good about myself and what I do to others. Unfortunately, there are too many people that think that way and put their evil self interest before their morals and integrity. Not with a team of their peers, meaning members. Instead, they go down the wrong road and damage and hurt others in order to get to their goals. It's unfortunate, but that is the movie business.

People will do anything to succeed. My suggestion? Take the right path. Help others, never harm. Do the right and honest thing and you will succeed. Always stand up for the truth. It may hurt you, but it is the right thing to do. It's funny. Money? I never paid much attention to it. It was about doing something that people noticed. Doing what was right. That's what the good book says. That's all they ask. And when they looked, they were amazed. They saw something they had never seen before. That was always my desire. It wasn't money nor politics. You can call me a dummy. Enough of this, let's move on. I went in that evening and walked into the office. As I thought, most of the guys there treated me like a stranger. I was next in line. Sitting at the desk was JW, in the big chair with his feet on the desk and a cigar in his mouth. I wanted to kick it out, but I resisted. A big shit eating smile was plastered on his face. I found it very uncomfortable. I went in and we started our discussion. Accusations starting flying. I went to my defense, which was the truth and I explained, but I have to say I let my temper get the best of me. A couple of people there got a little scared. Some people rubbed me the wrong way, like OK. This man sticks his nose so far up people's backsides, it causes indigestion. It's almost comical. Ask people like Diamond Farnsworth. He's had to put his hand behind him and pull him out sometimes.

Sorry OK, you should pay attention to this and learn what not to do. I felt like I wasn't getting anywhere. The negativity was all over the room. There was no brotherhood. There was no friendship. There was no intent to listen to my side of the story. Déjà vu. Some things never change. It got heated in the room and my blood started boiling. I went into my pocket and took out something that I had for about forty two years. Something that I cherished, something that I was honored to have when I first came in. Something that meant the world to me. It was a buckle I was given when I first joined the Stuntmen's Association.

I looked at everybody in disgust and looked at the buckle before saying, "it's not the buckle that makes the man, it's the man that makes the buckle. And what is in his soul and in his heart. I know what is in mine. I can see the difference from yours. I'm finished, I quit."

Like James Stewart throwing down his Sheriff's badge in the O.K. Corral, I tossed my buckle on the desk, turned around and walked away. I was a beaten man. I didn't feel good, but I was free, You see, you ask yourself is it the right thing to do to stand up for common sense commandments, maybe the ten or more, that grandmas and mothers, grandfathers and fathers, have taught since the beginning of time. Just do the right thing. That's my number one commandment, always. And my friends, that's exactly what I tried to do.

Word quickly spread of my departure and doors that were once open to me began to shut. It didn't matter to me. I had done the unthinkable, attained the unattainable. This punk kid from Brooklyn who had no direction suddenly became the Director when it came to action. The people, the places and experiences were enough to fill lifetimes. I have done things that mere mortals dream about. They couldn't take away my past and they can't take away my future. They only took a moment in time from me. The people who respect me and understand me will always be my friends. And I loved and respected so many people from the organization called the Stuntmen's Association of motion pictures. I will always have much gratitude for what that place did for me.

Years go by. I'm having fun doing nothing. Watching the new and the old stunt people. Some good stuff, some bad stuff as it was, is and always will be. This morning I got my coffee, turned on the news and sat down to work on this book with my writer. You see, the things that were my priorities in the past have changed. Now there are only three things I am really focused on these days. My movie script, which I am in the process of making and which I hope you will all one day see. The title: *Ninja, The Resurrection*. I found a wonderful Director for it. Mister Alon Newman. So gifted. Second, is this book which I have told to you now of my life's endeavors. It is the truth, nothing but the truth. With a little icing here and there of course. This is Hollywood after all. And one more, which is the most important. Here I am at the end of my journey. Or is it? I glance at the shadow behind me. I know it well. It belongs to one of my own. This brings me to my third priority, my son. Through him, I can instill my knowledge, with him I can teach him my ways and because of him, I can live on in his footsteps.

(I love you, son. Live long and prosper.)

To come full circle and begin again. And that's exactly what this is, isn't it? With every ending, there is a start. A new journey. So my dear readers, let's end and start anew. Remember my lessons, my stories and explanations so that they may better you as they bettered me. Take this to heart and live every day to the fullest. Be humble and know where you come from, be thankful for where you go and be happy where you end up. Each life is a journey with bumps, ditches and peaks. I've told you mine. Now go live yours. The blank pages await your action. The journey continues. For it will always continue in one way or another, through one person or another. Through time, through generations and through humanity. I thank you, dear readers, for coming along on this crazy, funny, touching and exhilarating ride, may it leave you better off than when you started. There are only these words left to say.

The Beginning. God bless.

(Thank you for the etching Mark Covell. Meant so much.)

(Sometimes people aren't what they seem to be.)

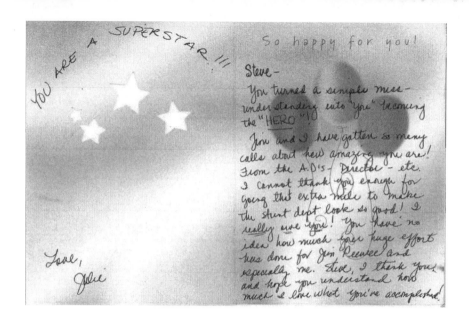

I have always so enjoyed helping friends. Oh, but how soon they forget.

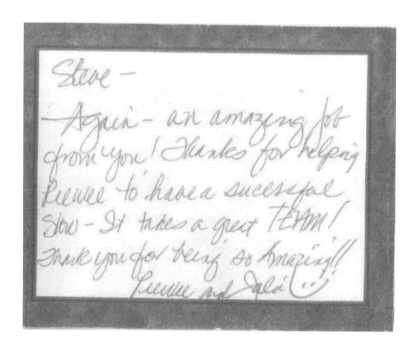

L'ERMITAGE
hôtel de grande classe

11/87

Steve —
Once again, you made me look
like a pro — THANK you!
You were great on the show, my friend —
and we got some good laughs from the audience, too!
Hope to see you real soon, Steve + thanks
again for your help!

Joe Piscopo

PS: Best to "the mrs!"

9291 Burton Way, Beverly Hills, California 90210 · (213) 278-3344
VisualSlideshow.com

(Joe Piscopo. One of the nicest men I have ever met, in and out of our crazy business.)

ZP
Zephyr Productions
1801 AVENUE OF THE STARS / LOS ANGELES, CALIFORNIA 90067 / (213) 277-4866

September 11, 1984

Mr. Steven Lambert
P.O.Box 224
Toluca Lake, California 91602

Dear Steve:

Just a note to thank you for the outstanding job you did
as Stunt Coordinator on "Playing With Fire."

The picture came in on time and on budget.

Much of the success of our film is because of the
quality work done by the crew.

Many thanks for being a part of this project.

Best wishes,

Jim Begg
Producer
"Playing With Fire"

JB/b

VisualSlideshow.com

(He passed away too soon. He was a good man.)

Johnny Martin
600 Spring Rd. #69
Moorpark, CA 93021
(805) 531-0210

Mr. Steve Lambert
4810 Whitsett Ave.
N. Hollywood CA 91607

Hello Steve,

I just wanted to say thanks for speaking nice about me the other day. This business is so hard to get into, but having a guy like you in my corner really helps me out. Thanks again for being a friend.

Sincerely,

Johnny Martin
Stuntman

(Always cherished this one.)

I met Johnny Martin when he first was trying to be a stuntman. He had a wonderful outlook on life and extremely talented were my thoughts. Honest, good communicator and a get out and go attitude. I believed in him back then and now look at you Johnny, you're an established Director. Well done. Take care of you and your family. Always, Steven Lambert.

(You should have listened to James Woods in the first place.)

With Gratitude and Affection

Jason Alexander

(A down to earth good Joe.)

(A going away gift from the mayor and the crew of Liberty Island. 18 karat painted gold.)

PHILLIP R. NOYCE
c/o WRITERS & ARTISTS AGENCY
11726 SAN VINCENTE BOULEVARD, SUITE 300
LOS ANGELES, CALIFORNIA 90049
(213) 820-2240

October 14, 1988

Steve Lambert
P.O. Box 2224
Toluca Lake, CA   90066

Dear Steve,
    I never took the time to tell you what a terrific
job you did as Stunt Coordinator and in training Rutger
with the sword.
    After two very successful test screenings of the
Directors cut, the audiences reaction to Rutger in the
film was 93% excellent. This could never have been
achieved without his excellent training. His handling
of and movements with the sword gave him the ability
to look highly skilled and truly believable. And the
audiences screams and oohs & aahs during the action
scenes proved this.
    Once again, thanks for all your hard work and
devotion. I look forward to working with you again.

Sincerely,

Phillip Noyce

(The Australian kangaroo. All over the place with joy. Smart, good crazy and full
of fun.)

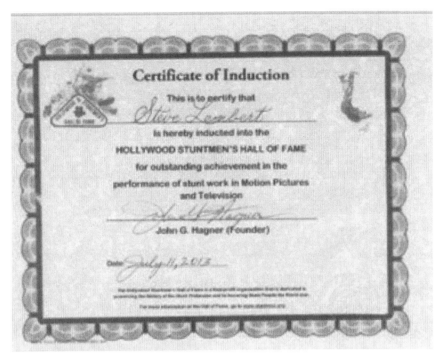

(Many thanks to a stuntman who has seen them all, before I came along. Mister John Hagner.

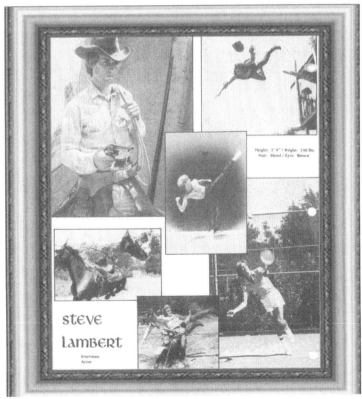

(My first composite. Twenty two years old. Trying to imitate Steve McQueen.

(Here's to you, the greatest. Mister Douglas Lim Wong. My friend.)

Printed in Great Britain
by Amazon

62789083R00429